STREET ATLAS

Berkshire

First published in 1990 by

Philip's, a division of
Octopus Publishing Group Ltd
2-4 Heron Quays, London E14 4JP

Third colour edition 2004
Second impression with revisions 2006
BERCB

ISBN-10   0-540-08494-8 (pocket)
ISBN-13   978-0-540-08494-4 (pocket)

© Philip's 2006

oS Ordnance Survey®

This product includes mapping data licensed from
Ordnance Survey® with the permission of the
Controller of Her Majesty's Stationery Office.
© Crown copyright 2006. All rights reserved.
Licence number 100011710.

Printed by Toppan, China

Contents

III   **Key to map symbols**

IV   **Key to map pages**

VI   **Route planning**

VIII   **Administrative and Postcode boundaries**

1   **Street maps** at 2⅔ inches to 1 mile

154   **Index** of towns and villages

156   **Index** of streets, hospitals, industrial estates, railway stations, schools, shopping centres, universities and places of interest

Digital Data

The exceptionally high-quality mapping found in this atlas is available as digital data in TIFF format, which is easily convertible to other bitmapped (raster) image formats.

The index is also available in digital form as a standard database table. It contains all the details found in the printed index together with the National Grid reference for the map square in which each entry is named.

For further information and to discuss your requirements, please contact Philip's on 020 7644 6932 or james.mann@philips-maps.co.uk

Key to map symbols

Motorway with junction number	
Primary route – dual/single carriageway	
A road – dual/single carriageway	
B road – dual/single carriageway	
Minor road – dual/single carriageway	
Other minor road – dual/single carriageway	
Road under construction	
Tunnel, covered road	
Rural track, private road or narrow road in urban area	
Gate or obstruction to traffic (restrictions may not apply at all times or to all vehicles)	
Path, bridleway, byway open to all traffic, road used as a public path	
Pedestrianised area	
DY7 Postcode boundaries	
County and unitary authority boundaries	
Railway, tunnel, railway under construction	
Tramway, tramway under construction	
Miniature railway	
Walsall Railway station	
Private railway station	
London Underground station	
Tram stop, tram stop under construction	
Bus, coach station	

Ambulance station	
Coastguard station	
Fire station	
Police station	
Accident and Emergency entrance to hospital	
H Hospital	
+ Place of worship	
i Information Centre (open all year)	
P Parking	
P&R Park and Ride	
PO Post Office	
Camping site	
Caravan site	
Golf course	
Picnic site	
Prim Sch Important buildings, schools, colleges, universities and hospitals	
River Medway Water name	
River, weir, stream	
Canal, lock, tunnel	
Water	
Tidal water	
Woods	
Built up area	
Church Non-Roman antiquity	
ROMAN FORT Roman antiquity	
87 / 58 Adjoining page indicators	

Acad	Academy	Inst	Institute	Recn Gd	Recreation
Allot Gdns	Allotments	Ct	Law Court		Ground
Cemy	Cemetery	L Ctr	Leisure Centre	Resr	Reservoir
C Ctr	Civic Centre	LC	Level Crossing	Ret Pk	Retail Park
CH	Club House	Liby	Library	Sch	School
Coll	College	Mkt	Market	Sh Ctr	Shopping Centre
Crem	Crematorium	Meml	Memorial	TH	Town Hall/House
Ent	Enterprise	Mon	Monument	Trad Est	Trading Estate
Ex H	Exhibition Hall	Mus	Museum	Univ	University
Ind Est	Industrial Estate	Obsy	Observatory	W Twr	Water Tower
IRB Sta	Inshore Rescue	Pal	Royal Palace	Wks	Works
	Boat Station	PH	Public House	YH	Youth Hostel

■ The small numbers around the edges of the maps identify the 1 kilometre National Grid lines

■ The dark grey border on the inside edge of some pages indicates that the mapping does not continue onto the adjacent page

The scale of the maps on the pages numbered in blue is 4.2 cm to 1 km • 2⅔ inches to 1 mile • 1: 23810

0 ¼ ½ ¾ 1 mile
0 250m 500m 750m 1 kilometre

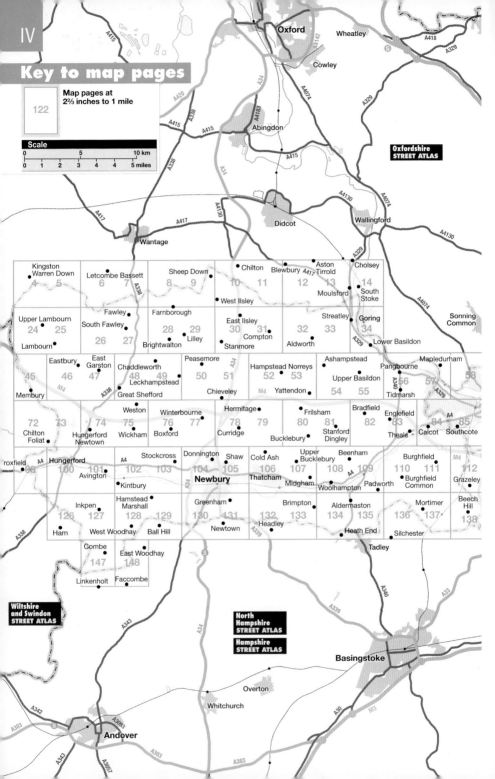

IV

Key to map pages

**Map pages at
2⅔ inches to 1 mile**

122

Scale
0   5   10 km
0   1   2   3   4   4   5 miles

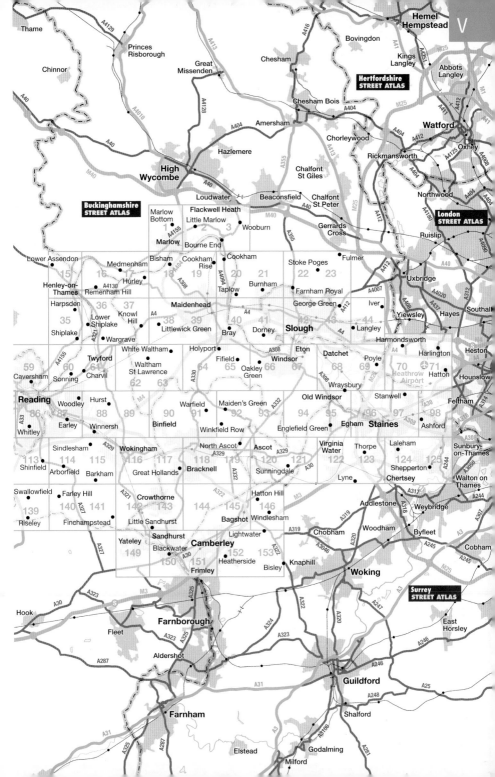

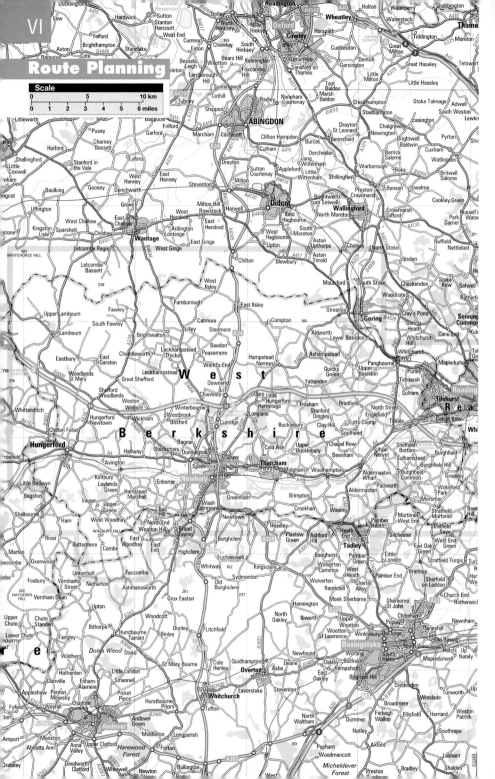

Route Planning

Scale

0				5			10 km
0	1	2	3	4	5		6 miles

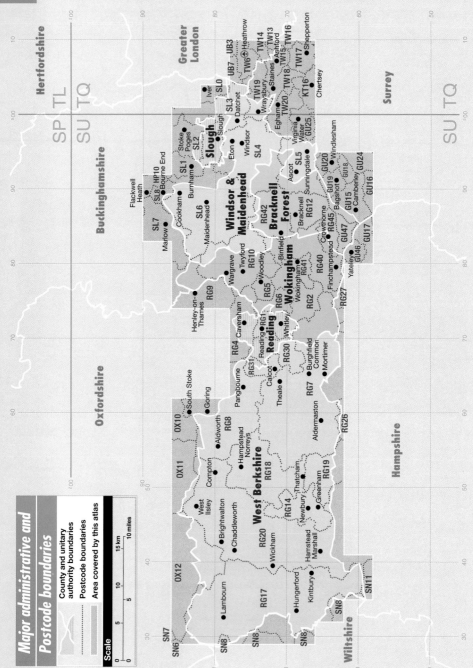

Major administrative and Postcode boundaries

	County and unitary authority boundaries
	Postcode boundaries
	Area covered by this atlas

Scale

0 5 10 15 km
0 5 10 miles

Hertfordshire

Greater London

Buckinghamshire

Oxfordshire

Surrey

Hampshire

Wiltshire

SP TL
SU TQ
SU TQ

Slough

Windsor & Maidenhead

Bracknell Forest

Wokingham

Reading

West Berkshire

UB7 UB3
TW6 Heathrow
TW14 TW13
TW15 Ashford
TW17
TW19 Staines
Wraysbury TW18 TW16
Egham TW20 KT16
Virginia Water GU25
Chertsey

Iver SL0
SL3 Slough
Datchet
Eton Windsor SL4
SL2
Stoke Poges SL1
Burnham
SL6 Maidenhead
Cookham
SL7 Marlow
SL8 HP10
Bourne End
Flackwell Heath

Ascot SL5
GU20
GU19 GU18
Sunningdale Windlesham
Bagshot GU24
GU15 Camberley GU16
RG45 Crowthorne
Bracknell RG12
RG42
RG10
Binfield
RG40 Finchampstead GU47
Woodley GU17
Twyford Yateley GU46
Wargrave RG5
RG9 Woosehill RG6 Wokingham
Henley-on-Thames RG2 RG27
RG4 Caversham RG1
RG31 Reading Whitley RG30
Calcot Burghfield Common
Theale RG7 Mortimer
Pangbourne RG26
South Stoke OX10
Goring
RG8 Aldermaston
Aldworth
Compton Hampstead Norreys
OX11 RG18
West Ilsley
Brightwalton RG14 Thatcham RG19
Chaddleworth Newbury Greenham
RG20 Wickham Hamstead Marshall
Hungerford Kintbury
OX12 Lambourn
RG17
SN7 SN8 SN8 SN8 SN8 SN11
SN6

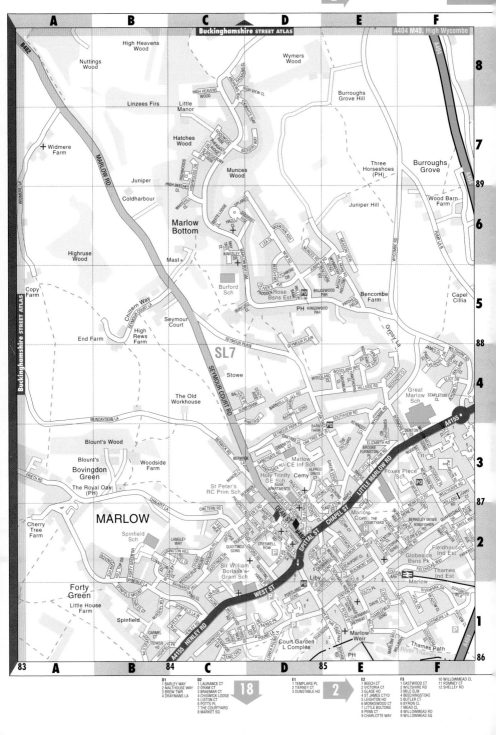

Buckinghamshire STREET ATLAS

A B C D E F

8

7

89

6

5

88

4

3

87

2

1

86

83 84 85

D1
1 BARLEY WAY
2 MALTHOUSE WAY
3 BREW TWR
4 DRAYMANS LA

D2
1 LAURANCE CT
2 ORAM CT
3 BRAEMAR CT
4 CHISWICK LODGE
5 LISTON CT
6 POTTS PL
7 THE COURTYARD
8 MARKET SQ

E1
1 TEMPLARS PL
2 TIERNEY CT
3 DUNSTABLE HO

E2
1 BEECH CT
2 VICTORIA CT
3 GLADE HO
4 ST JAMES CTYD
5 LEIGHTON HO
6 MONKSWOOD CT
7 LITTLE BOLTONS
8 PENN CT
9 CHARLOTTE WAY

F3
1 EASTWOOD CT
2 WILTSHIRE RD
3 MILE CL
4 BEECHINGSTOKE
5 BUTLER CT
6 BYRON CL
7 MEAD CL
8 WILLOWMEAD RD
9 WILLOWMEAD SQ

10 WILLOWMEAD CL
11 ROMNEY CT
12 SHELLEY RD

Buckinghamshire STREET ATLAS

HP10

HP10

Chiltern Way

Horton Wood

Bloom Wood

Chiltern Way

New Farm

PH

Sheepridge

Chiltern Way

Bloom Farm

Merton's Hole Cottage

SL7

Pigeon House Farm

Fern House

Cemy

Fern

Wilton Farm

MARLOW RD

Well End

Coronach

Little Marlow CE Sch

ABBEY CHAPMAN MEAD

Pump Farm

The King's Head (PH)

Little Marlow

SL8

Manor House

The Spade Oak (PH)

The Abbey

MILE ELM

1 BUTLER CT
2 BRISTOW CT
3 GRATTON CT
4 DOUGLAS CT
5 RAVENSCOURT

Abbotsbrook

SPADE OAK FARM

LC

LC

WESTHORPE PARK CVN SITE

Westhorpe House

Sewage Works

The Moor

River Thames

6 HOBART CT
7 MARCHANT CT
8 WASHINGTON CT
9 SWALLOW HO
10 SWIFT HO

Westhorpe Farm

Cock Marsh

Noah's House

Thames Path

Patches

FIELDHOUSE LA

Hotel

Stone House

Coney Copse

SL6

Winter Hill

GIBRALTAR LA

WINTER HILL

Harvest Moon

Greythatch

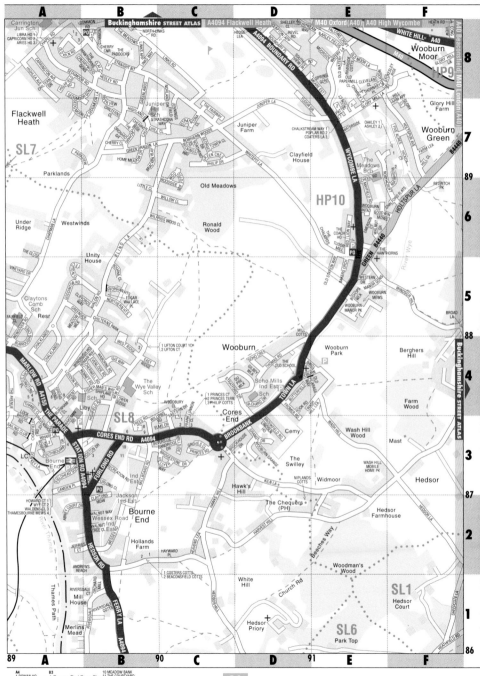

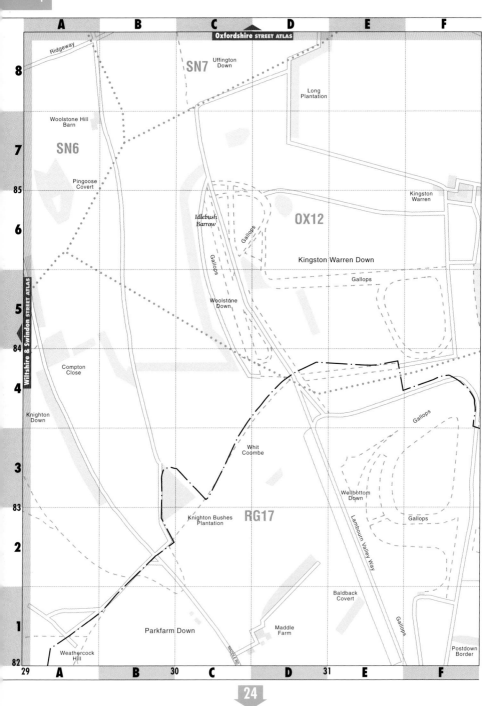

Wiltshire & Swindon STREET ATLAS

Ridgeway

SN7

Uffington Down

Long Plantation

Woolstone Hill Barn

SN6

Pingoose Covert

Idlebush Barrow

Gallops

OX12

Kingston Warren

Kingston Warren Down

Gallops

Gallops

Woolstone Down

Compton Close

Knighton Down

Gallops

Whit Coombe

Wellbottom Down

Gallops

Knighton Bushes Plantation

RG17

Lambourn Valley Way

Baldback Covert

Gallops

Parkfarm Down

Maddle Farm

Postdown Border

Weathercock Hill

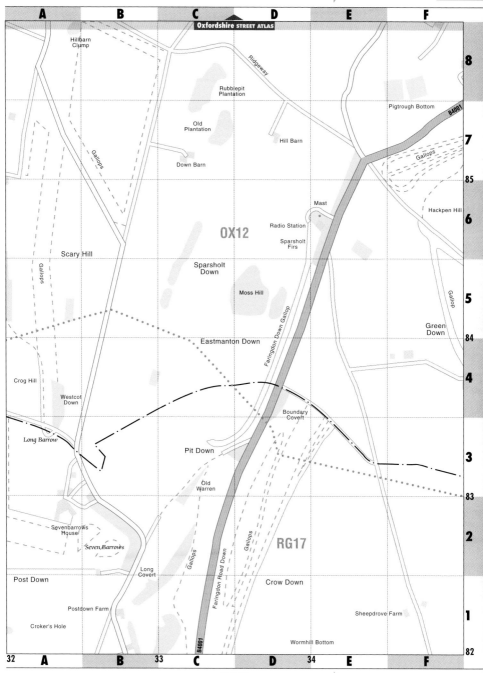

Oxfordshire STREET ATLAS

Map labels:

Hillbarn Clump
Ridgeway
Rubblepit Plantation
Pigtrough Bottom
B4001
Old Plantation
Hill Barn
Gallops
Down Barn
85
Mast
Hackpen Hill
Radio Station
OX12
Sparsholt Firs
6
Scary Hill
Sparsholt Down
Gallops
Moss Hill
Gallop
5
Green Down
84
Eastmanton Down
Faringdon Down Gallop
Crog Hill
4
Westcot Down
Boundary Covert
Long Barrow
Pit Down
3
Old Warren
83
Sevenbarrows House
Gallops
Gallops
2
Seven Barrows
RG17
Post Down
Long Covert
Crow Down
Faringdon Road Down
B4001
Postdown Farm
Sheepdrove Farm
1
Croker's Hole
Wormhill Bottom
82

32   A   B   33   C   D   34   E   F

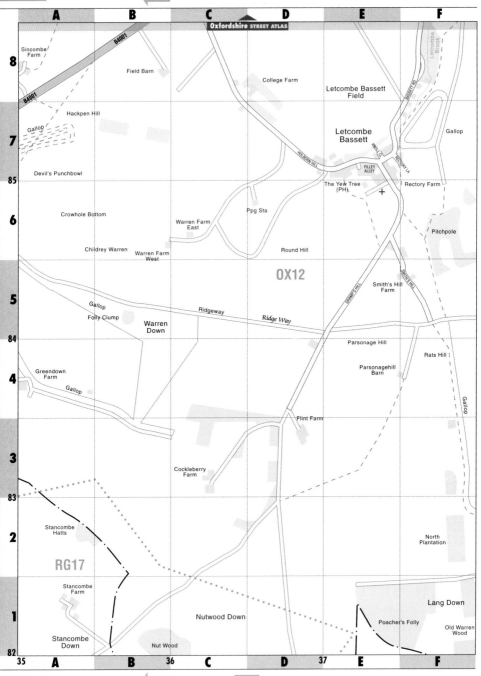

Oxfordshire STREET ATLAS

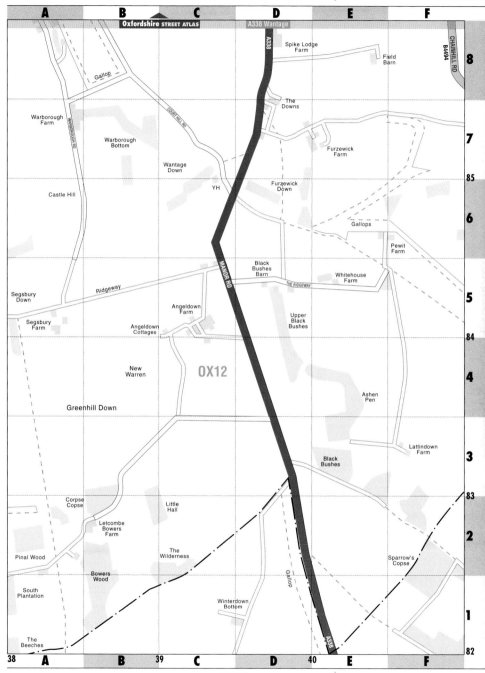

Oxfordshire STREET ATLAS

A338 Wantage

A338

CHAIN HILL RD
B4494

Spike Lodge Farm

Field Barn

The Downs

Gallop

Warborough Farm

WARBOROUGH RD

COURT HILL RD

Warborough Bottom

Wantage Down

Furzewick Farm

YH

Furzewick Down

Castle Hill

Gallops

Pewit Farm

Black Bushes Barn

MANOR RD

THE RIDGEWAY

Whitehouse Farm

Segsbury Down

Ridgeway

Angeldown Farm

Upper Black Bushes

Segsbury Farm

Angeldown Cottages

New Warren

OX12

Ashen Pen

Greenhill Down

Lattindown Farm

Black Bushes

Corpse Copse

Little Hall

Letcombe Bowers Farm

Pinal Wood

The Wilderness

Gallop

Sparrow's Copse

Bowers Wood

South Plantation

Winterdown Bottom

The Beeches

A338

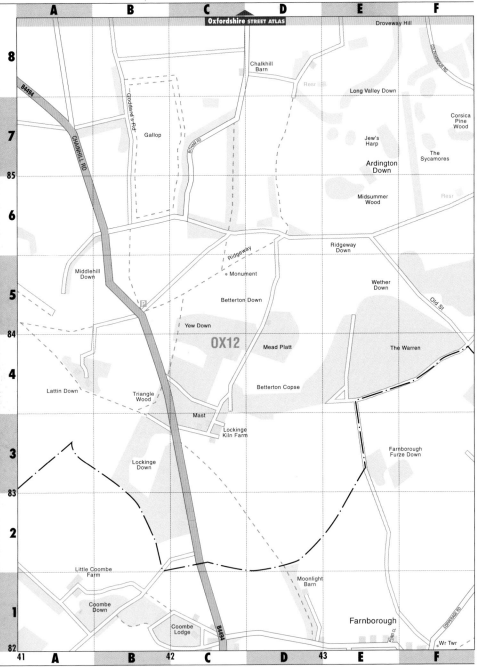

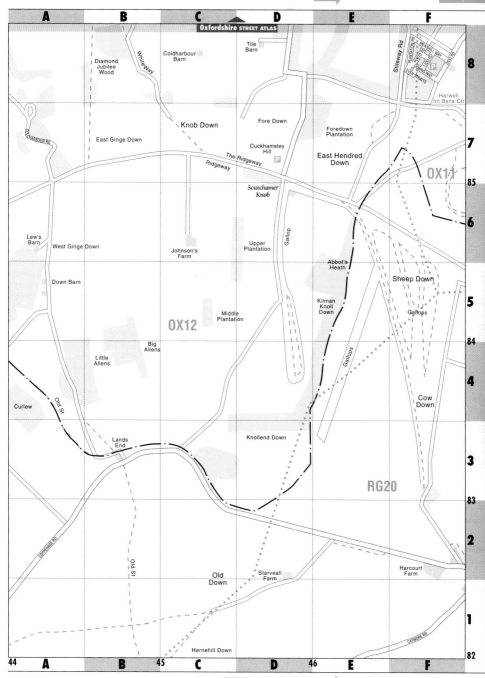

Oxfordshire STREET ATLAS

| A | B | C | D | E | F |

Tile Barn

Diamond Jubilee Wood

Coldharbour Barn

White Way

Stileway Rd

PLANTATION RD MEADHILL WAY

P

DOWNS WAY

OVER SPRINTS

Harwell Int Bsns Ctr

Knob Down

Fore Down

Foredown Plantation

COLDHARBOUR RD

East Ginge Down

Cuckhamsley Hill

East Hendred Down

The Ridgeway
P

Ridgeway

OX11

Scutchamer Knob

Lew's Barn

West Ginge Down

Johnson's Farm

Upper Plantation

Gallop

Abbot's Heath

Sheep Down

Down Barn

OX12

Middle Plantation

Kilman Knoll Down

Gallops

Gallops

Big Allens

Little Allens

Cow Down

Curlew

Old St

Knollend Down

Lands End

RG20

COPPERAGE RD

Old St

Old Down

Starveall Farm

Harcourt Farm

CATMORE RD

Hernehill Down

| 44 | A | B | 45 | C | D | 46 | E | F |

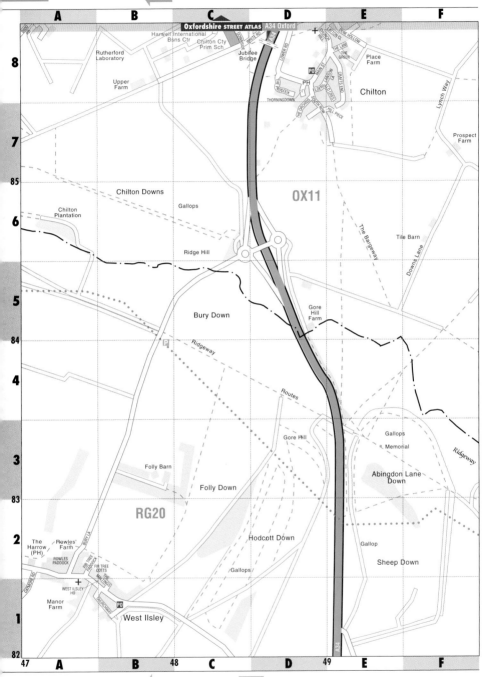

Oxfordshire STREET ATLAS A34 Oxford

Rutherford Laboratory

Harwell International Bsns Ctr

Chilton Cty Prim Sch

Upper Farm

Jubilee Bridge

PH

PO

THORNINGDOWN

Place Farm

The Green

Chilton

Prospect Farm

Lynch Way

OX11

Chilton Downs

Gallops

Chilton Plantation

Ridge Hill

The Bargeway

Tile Barn

Downs Lane

Bury Down

Gore Hill Farm

Ridgeway

P

Routes

Gore Hill

Gallops

Memorial

Ridgeway

Folly Barn

Folly Down

Abingdon Lane Down

RG20

Hodcott Down

Gallop

Gallops

Sheep Down

The Harrow (PH)

Rowles' Farm

ROWLES PADDOCK

WEST ILSLEY HO

Manor Farm

PO

West Ilsley

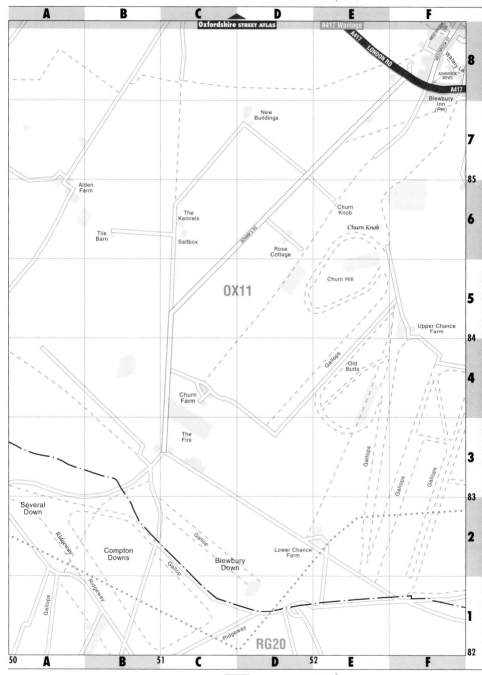

Oxfordshire STREET ATLAS

A417 Wantage

A417

LONDON RD

A417

WESTBROOK ST

Watery La

ASHBROOK MEWS

Blewbury Inn (PH)

8

New Buildings

7

85

Alden Farm

The Kennels

Churn Knob

6

Tile Barn

Saltbox

ROHAMS RD

Churn Knob

Rose Cottage

Churn Hill

OX11

5

84

Upper Chance Farm

Gallops

Old Butts

4

Churn Farm

The Firs

Gallops

3

Several Down

Gallops

83

Ridgeway

Compton Downs

Gallop

Blewbury Down

Lower Chance Farm

Gallops

2

Ridgeway

Gallop

Gallops

Ridgeway

RG20

1

82

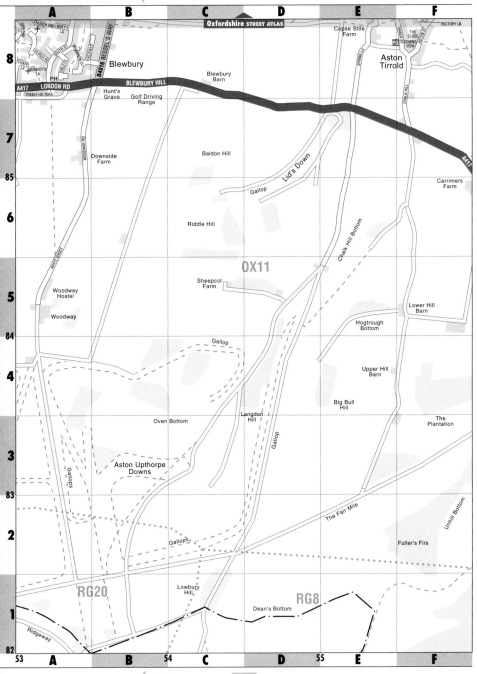

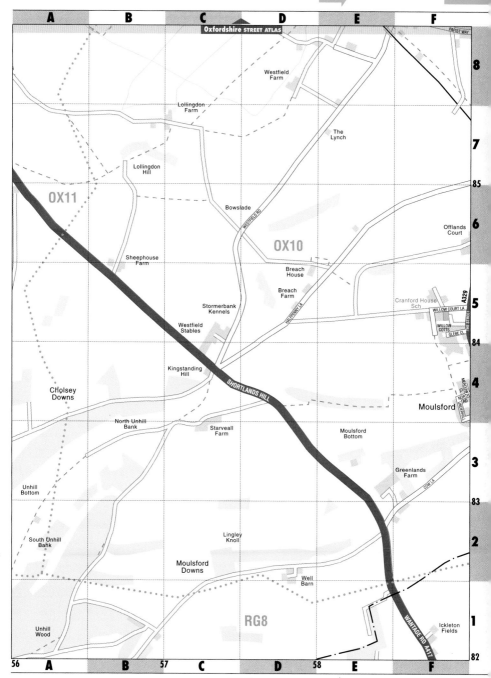

Oxfordshire STREET ATLAS

PAPIST WAY

8

Westfield Farm

Lollingdon Farm

The Lynch

7

Lollingdon Hill

85

OX11

Bowslade

WESTFIELD RD

6

OX10

Offlands Court

Sheephouse Farm

Breach House

Breach Farm

Cranford House Sch

A329

5

Stormerbank Kennels

HALFPENNY LA.

WILLOW COURT LA.

THE STREET

WILLOW COTTS

Westfield Stables

GLEBE CL.

84

Kingstanding Hill

SHORTLANDS HILL

MEADOW CL.

NORTH CL.

BIRCH HILL

4

Cholsey Downs

Moulsford

North Unhill Bank

Starveall Farm

Moulsford Bottom

3

Greenlands Farm

Unhill Bottom

COW LA.

83

South Unhill Bank

Lingley Knoll

2

Moulsford Downs

Well Barn

WANTAGE RD A417

Ickleton Fields

1

RG8

Unhill Wood

82

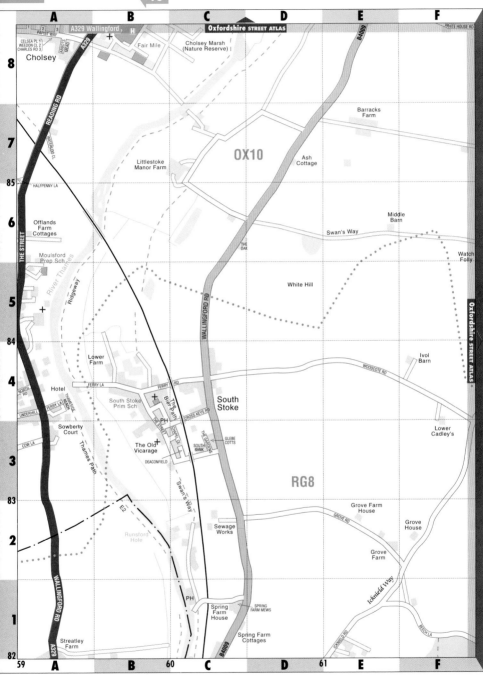

Oxfordshire STREET ATLAS

WHITE HOUSE RD

A B C D E F

A329 Wallingford

PAPIST WAY

CELSEA PL 1
WEEDON CL 2
CHARLES RD 3

Fair Mile

Cholsey Marsh
(Nature Reserve)

Cholsey

8

READING RD

Barracks
Farm

OX10

7

Ash
Cottage

Littlestoke
Manor Farm

85

HALFPENNY LA

Middle
Barn

6

Offlands
Farm
Cottages

Swan's Way

THE STREET

Moulsford
Prep Sch

River Thames

THE OAK

Watch
Folly

Ridgeway

White Hill

5

84

WALLINGFORD RD

Lower
Farm

WOODCOTE RD

Ivol
Barn

Hotel

FERRY LA

FERRY RD

NORTH RD

South Stoke
Prim Sch

THE BIER PATH

South
Stoke

Lower
Cadley's

UNDERHILL

FERRY LA

THAMESIDE

CROSS KEYS RD

4

THE STREET

PH

CHAPEL CL

THE ELVENDONS

GLEBE
COTTS

Sowberry
Court

COW LA

Thames Path

The Old
Vicarage

SOUTH
BANK

RG8

3

DEACONFIELD

Swan's Way

Grove Farm
House

GROVE RD

Grove
House

83

E2

Runsford
Hole

Sewage
Works

Grove
Farm

2

Icknield Way

PH

Spring
Farm
House

SPRING
FARM MEWS

WALLINGFORD RD

A329

1

BEECH LA

Streatley
Farm

Spring Farm
Cottages

CONFIELD RD

B4009

82

59 A B 60 C D 61 E F

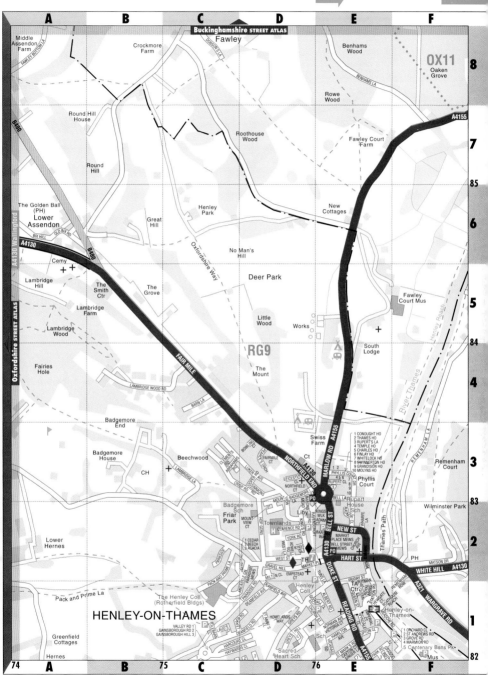

Buckinghamshire STREET ATLAS

HENLEY-ON-THAMES

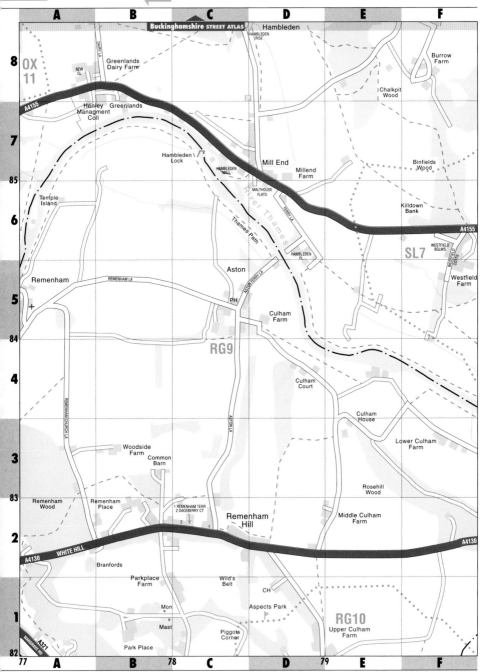

OX
11

Hambleden

HAMBLEDEN RISE

Greenlands
Dairy Farm

NEW
CL

DAIRY LA

Burrow
Farm

Chalkpit
Wood

A4155

Henley
Managment
Coll

Greenlands

Hambleden
Lock

Mill End

HAMBLEDEN
MILL

Millend
Farm

Binfields
Wood

MALTHOUSE
FLATS

River Thames

FERRY LA

Killdown
Bank

A4155

Temple
Island

Thames Path

HAMBLEDEN
PL

SL7

WESTFIELD
BGLWS

WESTFIELD COTTS

Westfield
Farm

Remenham

REMENHAM LA

Aston

ASTON FERRY LA

PH

Culham
Farm

RG9

REMENHAM CHURCH LA

ASTON LA

Culham
Court

Culham
House

Lower Culham
Farm

Woodside
Farm

Common
Barn

Rosehill
Wood

Remenham
Wood

Remenham
Place

1 REMENHAM TERR
2 DACEBERRY CT

Remenham
Hill

Middle Culham
Farm

A4130

WHITE HILL

A4130

Branfords

Parkplace
Farm

Wild's
Belt

CH

WARGRAVE RD

A321

Mon

Mast

Park Place

Piggots
Corner

Aspects Park

RG10

Upper Culham
Farm

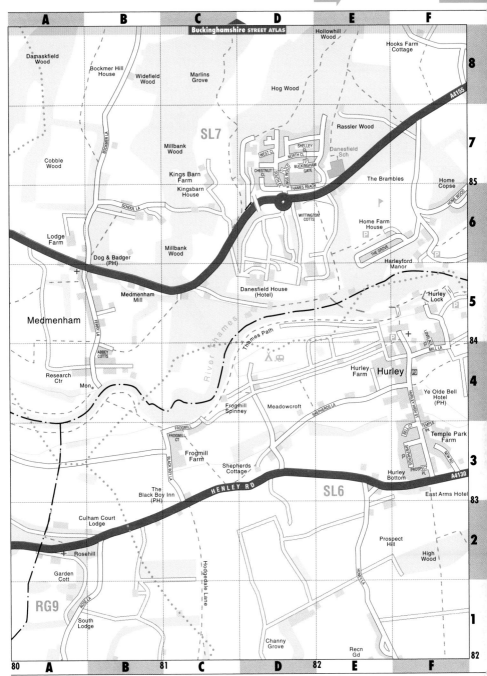

Buckinghamshire STREET ATLAS

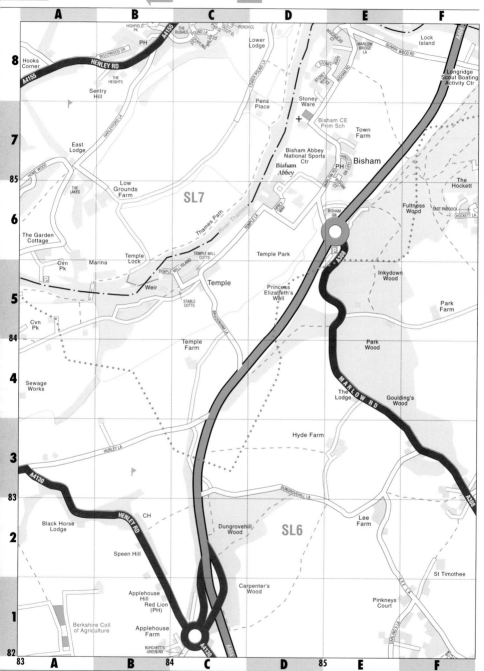

Map labels

Hooks Corner
HENLEY RD
A4155
BEECHWOOD DR
HIGHFIELD PK
THE RUSHES
POUND LA
PH
PERCH CL
Lower Lodge
Lock Island

THE HEIGHTS
Sentry Hill
Pens Place
Stoney Ware
Bisham CE Prim Sch
Town Farm
Longridge Scout Boating Activity Ctr

East Lodge
Bisham Abbey National Sports Ctr
Bisham
The Hockett

HOME WOOD
THE LAKES
Low Grounds Farm
SL7
Bisham Abbey
PH
BISHAM GN
EAST PADDOCK
HOCKETT LA
Fultness Wood

The Garden Cottage
Thames Path
River Thames
TEMPLE LA
Inkydown Wood

Cvn Pk
Marina
Temple Lock
TEMPLE MILL COTTS
Temple Park
Park Farm

Weir
STABLE COTTS
TEMPLE MILL ISLAND
Temple
Princess Elizabeth's Well
Park Wood

Cvn Pk
BRADENHAM LA
Temple Farm
A308

Sewage Works
MARLOW RD
The Lodge
Goulding's Wood

HURLEY LA
Hyde Farm

A4130
HENLEY RD
CH
DUNGROVEHILL LA
Lee Farm
A308

Black Horse Lodge
Speen Hill
Dungrovehill Wood
SL6

Applehouse Hill
Red Lion (PH)
Carpenter's Wood
Pinkneys Court
St Timothee

Berkshire Coll of Agriculture
Applehouse Farm
BURCHETT'S GREEN RD
A4130
A308
LEE LA

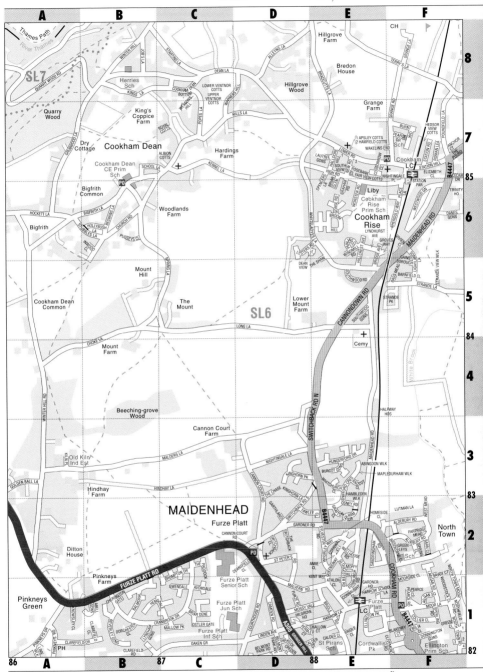

F1
1 NORTH TOWN CL
2 ALYSON CT
3 NORTH GN
4 NORTH TOWN MEAD
5 NORTHDEAN

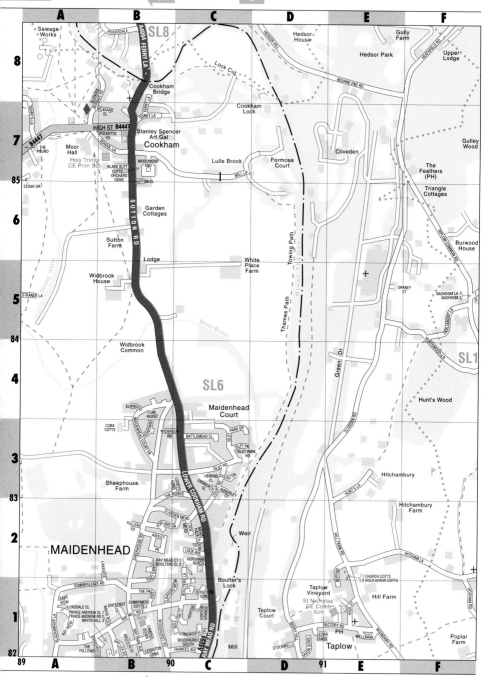

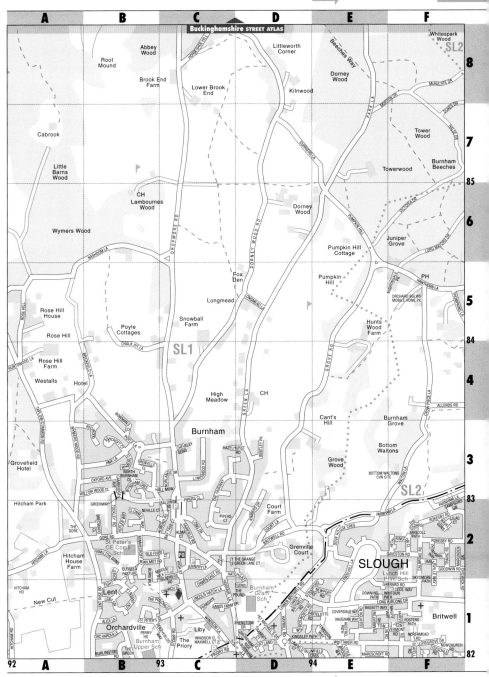

Buckinghamshire STREET ATLAS

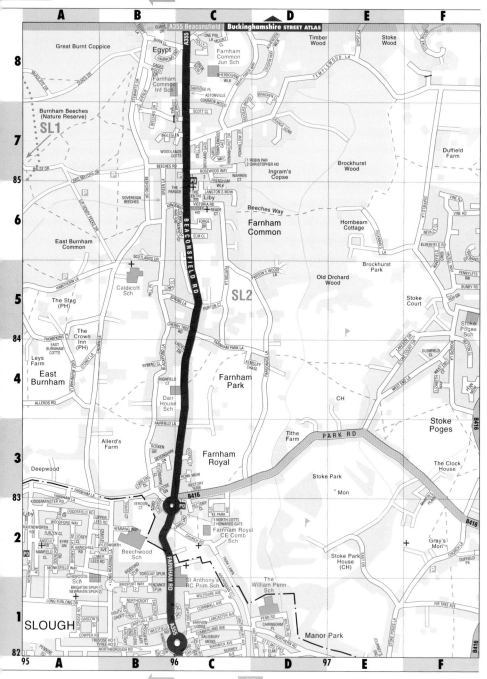

M40 High Wycombe

M40 London (A40)

SL9

8

Fulmer

The Pickeridge

FULMER CHASE

Fulmer Hall

The Black Horse (PH)

Fox & Pheasant (PH)

JARDINE COTTS

TEMPLEWOOD LA

STOKE COMMON RD

HAY LA

BRADBURY GDNS

CHURCH ROW

NORTH ROW

SOUTH ROW

Fulmer Inf Sch

ALLHUSEN GDNS

Fulmer House Farm

Furzeney Wood

ALDERBOURNE LA

Church Farm

Beeches Way

Alder Bourne

Watersplash Farm

7

Stoke Common

Fernacres Farm

Penn Wood

Fulmer Rise Estate

85

SL2

Frame Wood

Mill House Farm

FRAMEWOOD MANOR

Fulmer Common

WEXHAM PL

FULMER COMMON RD

HAWKSWOOD GR

LANGLEY CNR

6

Hollybush Hill

Fairfield Lodge

CHAPEL COTTS

Teikyo Sch (UK)

Upton Wood

Upton Lake

Upton Farm

5

Stoke Poges Sch

The Stag (PH)

Sefton Park

SEFTON PARK COTTS

HOME FARM WAY

HARTS LA

Twin Trees Farm

The Thames Valley Nuffield

Rowley Wood

SL3

84

Iver Heath

4

PH

Wexham Street

Sports Ctr

THURLEY COTTS

CH

Galleons La

Rowley Wood

Black Park Country Park

Blackpark Lake

V Ctr

3

Berry Farm

BUCKLAND GATE

Gallions Wood

Spring Wood

Rowley Farm

SAWMILL COTTS

83

Bell Farm

Rowley Lake

2

Red Lion (PH)

RED LION COTTS

Wexham Park

STOKE GN

Stoke Place

Stoke Green

William Hartley 'Yd

OPAL CT

WEXHAM PARK LA

UXBRIDGE RD

A412

1

82

A   B   C   D   E   F

98   99   00

GERARDS CROSS RD

BELLS HILL

GRAYS PARK RD

PARK RD

STOKE RD

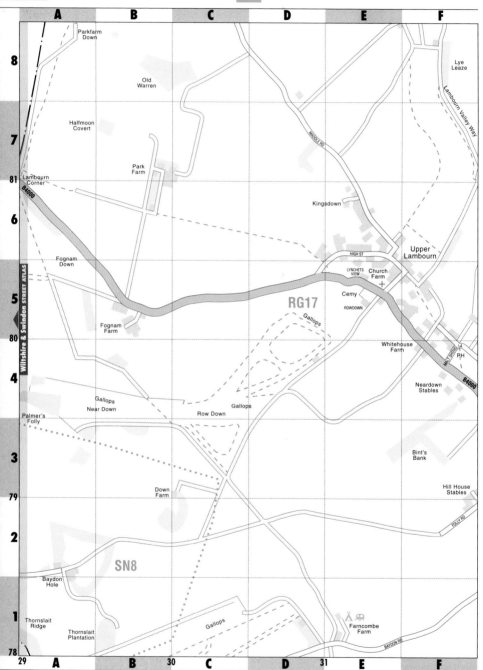

A   B   C   D   E   F

8

Parkfarm
Down

Old
Warren

Lye
Leaze

Halfmoon
Covert

7

Lambourn Valley Way

Park
Farm

MIDDLE RD

81

Lambourn
Corner

B4000

6

Kingsdown

Upper
Lambourn

Fognam
Down

HIGH ST

LYNCHETS
VIEW

Church
Farm

Wiltshire & Swindon STREET ATLAS

5

RG17

Cemy

ROWDOWN

Gallops

Fognam
Farm

80

Whitehouse
Farm

MILL BROOK LA

PH

B4000

4

Neardown
Stables

Gallops
Near Down

Gallops

Row Down

Palmer's
Folly

Bint's
Bank

3

Hill House
Stables

Down
Farm

79

FOLLY RD

2

SN8

Baydon
Hole

1

Thornslait
Ridge

Gallops

Farncombe
Farm

Thornslait
Plantation

BAYDON RD

78

29   A   B   30   C   D   31   E   F

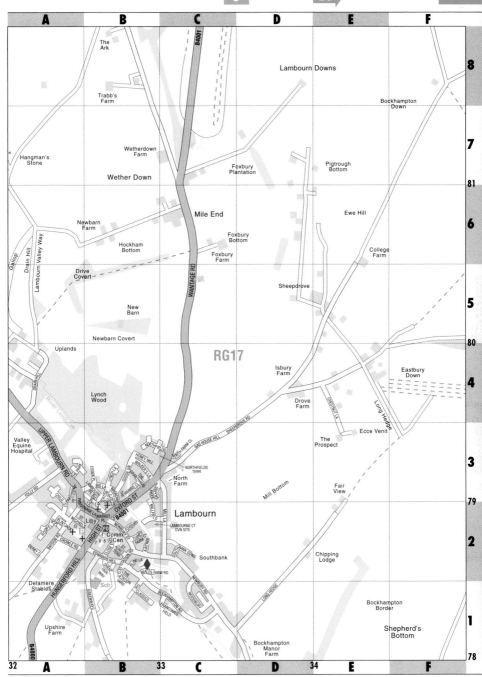

| A | B | C | D | E | F |

The Ark

Trabb's Farm

Lambourn Downs

Bockhampton Down

8

Hangman's Stone

Wetherdown Farm

Foxbury Plantation

Pigtrough Bottom

7

Wether Down

81

Newbarn Farm

Mile End

Ewe Hill

6

Hockham Bottom

Foxbury Bottom

Foxbury Farm

College Farm

Drive Covert

Sheepdrove

Gallop
Drain Hill
Lambourn Valley Way

New Barn

5

Newbarn Covert

80

Uplands

RG17

Isbury Farm

Eastbury Down

4

Lynch Wood

Drove Farm

River Lambourn

Valley Equine Hospital

Ecce Venit

The Prospect

3

UPPER LAMBOURN RD

Northfields

GAS HOUSE HILL

NORTH FARM CL

SHEEPDROVE RD

CHESTNUT LA

Long Hedge

North Farm

NORTHFIELDS TERR

Mill Bottom

Fair View

79

Lambourn

OXFORD ST
B4001
MARKET
Liby Pl
HIGH ST

LAMBOURNE CT CVN SITE

CLARK GDNS

Comm Cen

Southbank

Chipping Lodge

2

HUNGERFORD HILL

Delamere Stables

Sch

BEALES FARM RD

NEWBURY RD

LONG HEDGE

Bockhampton Border

1

Upshire Farm

Bockhampton Manor Farm

Shepherd's Bottom

B4000

78

| A | B | C | D | E | F |

33

B2
1 THREE POST LA
2 PEGASUS CT
3 LION MEWS
4 THE OLD SCHOOL YD
5 COLLEGE HO
6 BAYDON HO
7 HIND'S HEAD

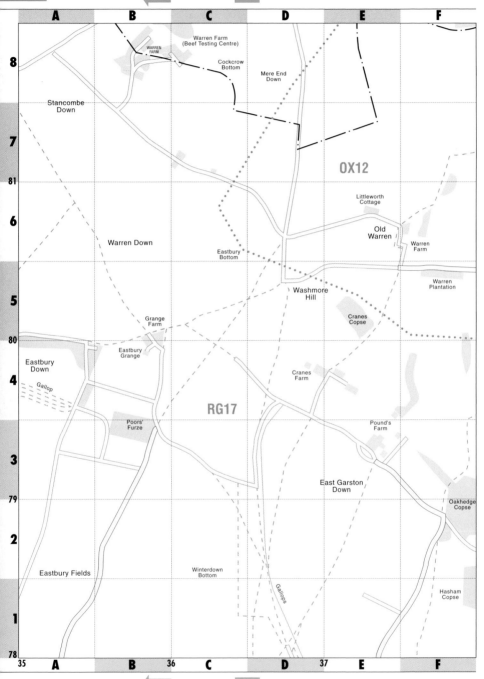

A **B** **C** **D** **E** **F**

8

Warren Farm
(Beef Testing Centre)

WARREN
FARM

Cockcrow
Bottom

Mere End
Down

Stancombe
Down

7

OX12

81

Littleworth
Cottage

6

Old
Warren

Warren Down

Warren
Farm

Eastbury
Bottom

Warren
Plantation

5

Washmore
Hill

Cranes
Copse

Grange
Farm

80

Eastbury
Grange

Eastbury
Down

Cranes
Farm

4

Gallop

Pound's
Farm

RG17

Poors'
Furze

3

East Garston
Down

79

Oakhedge
Copse

2

Eastbury Fields

Winterdown
Bottom

Gallops

Hasham
Copse

1

78
35 **A** **B** **36** **C** **D** **37** **E** **F**

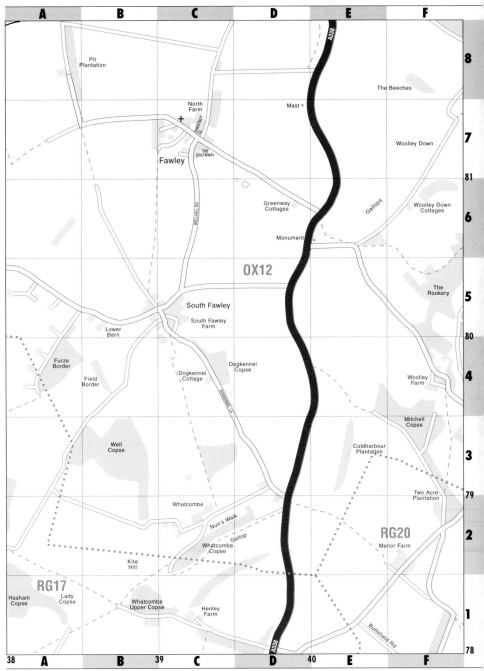

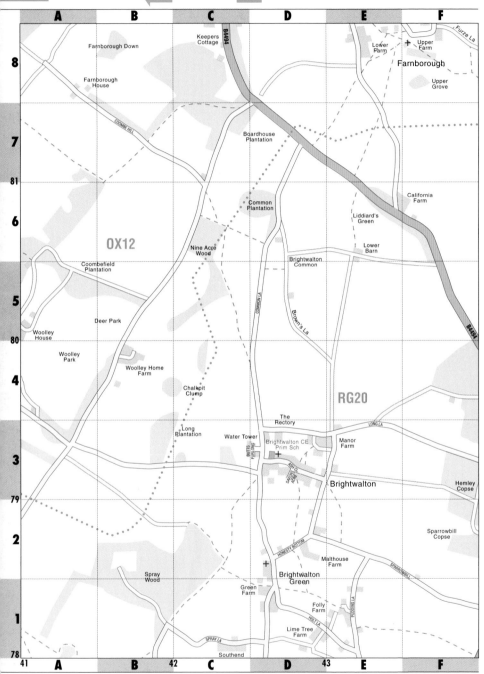

A   B   C   D   E   F

8

7

81

6

5

80

4

3

79

2

1

78

41   A   B   42   C   D   43   E   F

Farnborough Down

Keepers
Cottage

Lower
Farm

Upper
Farm

Farnborough

Farnborough
House

Upper
Grove

COOMBE HILL

B4494

Boardhouse
Plantation

California
Farm

Common
Plantation

Liddiard's
Green

OX12

Nine Acre
Wood

Brightwalton
Common

Lower
Barn

Coombefield
Plantation

COMMON LA

Brown's La

B4494

Deer Park

Woolley
House

Woolley
Park

Woolley Home
Farm

Chalkpit
Clump

RG20

Long
Plantation

The
Rectory

LONG LA

Water Tower

Brightwalton CE
Prim Sch

Manor
Farm

BUTTS
FURLONG

Hemley
Copse

Brightwalton

Sparrowbill
Copse

Spray
Wood

HONESTY BOTTOM

Malthouse
Farm

SPARROWBILL

Green
Farm

Brightwalton
Green

Folly
Farm

PUDDING LA

HOLT LA

SPRAY LA

Lime Tree
Farm

Southend

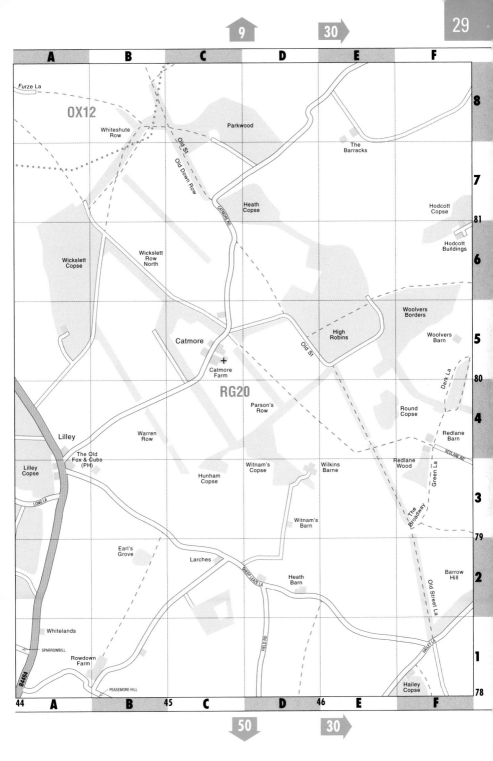

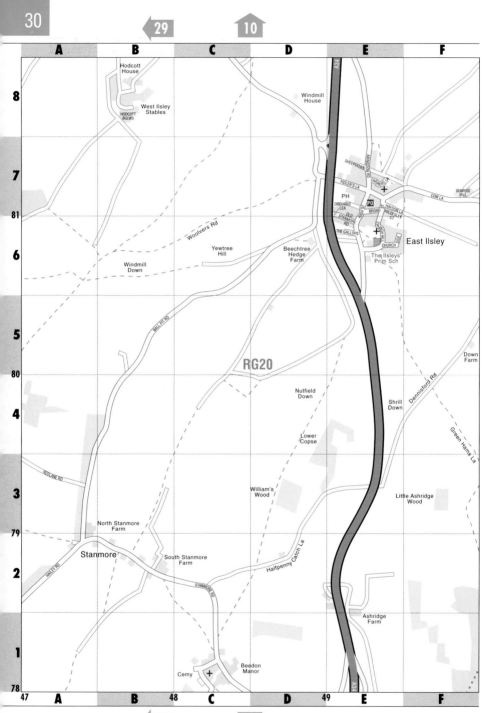

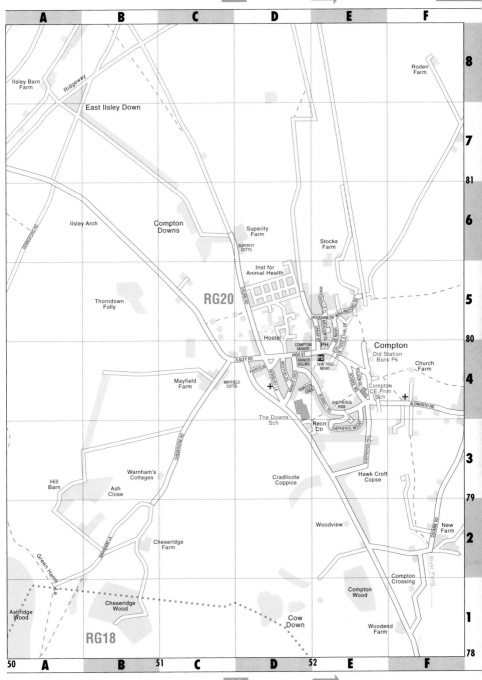

Map Labels

A B C D E F

8 Roden Farm

Ilsley Barn Farm
Ridgeway
East Ilsley Down

7

81

6 Compton Downs
Ilsley Arch
Superity Farm
SUPERITY COTTS
Stocks Farm

Inst for Animal Health

RG20

5 Thorndown Folly
WHITEHILLS CL
HOCKHAM MEADOW
CHEAP ST
WALLINGFORD RD

Hostel
Compton
Old Station Bsns Pk

80 COMPTON MANOR
HIGH ST
PH
PO
YEW TREE MEWS
Church Farm

Ilsley Rd
MANOR BGLWS
FAIRFIELD
WESTFIELDS
MANOR CRES
Compton CE Prim Sch

4 Mayfield Farm
MAYFIELD COTTS
COMPTON CRES
BURRELL RD
SHEPHERDS RISE
SCHOOL RD
WILSON CL
ALDWORTH RD

The Downs Sch
Recn Ctr
SHEPHERDS MOUNT

3 Hill Barn
Warnham's Cottages
CHESERIDGE RD
Cradlicote Coppice
SHEPHERDS HILL
Hawk Croft Copse

Ash Close

79

2 Cheseridge Farm
WORDELL LA
Woodview
New Farm
COOMBE RD
River Pang
Compton Crossing

Green Hams La

1 Ashridge Wood
Cheseridge Wood
Cow Down
Compton Wood
Woodend Farm

RG18

50 A B 51 C D 52 E F 78

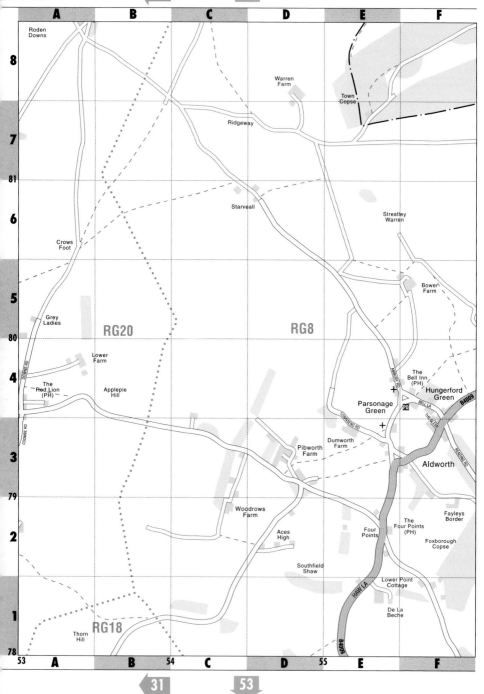

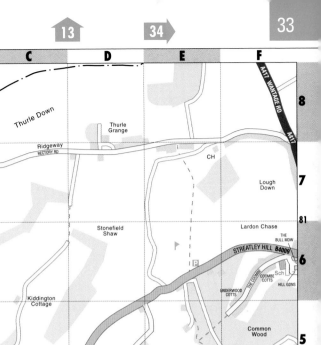

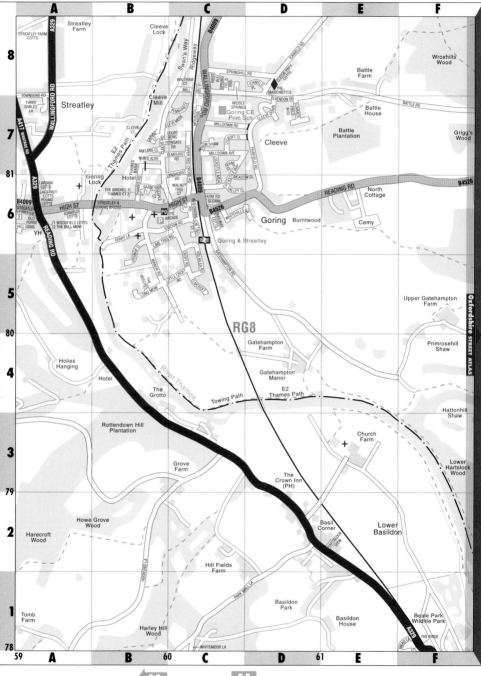

RG8

Streatley

Goring

Cleeve

Lower
Basildon

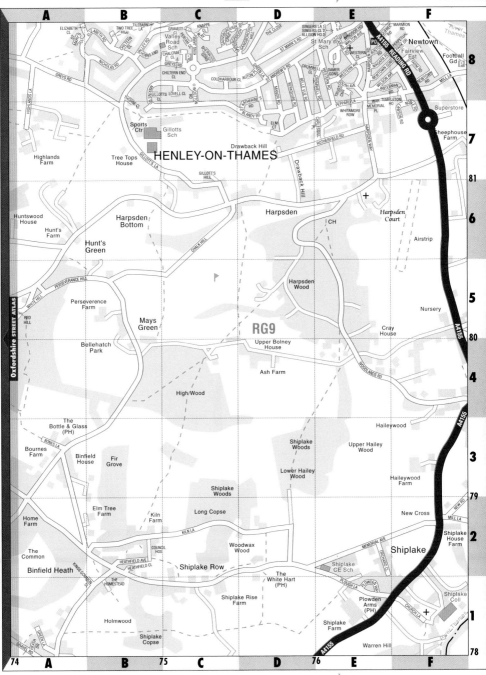

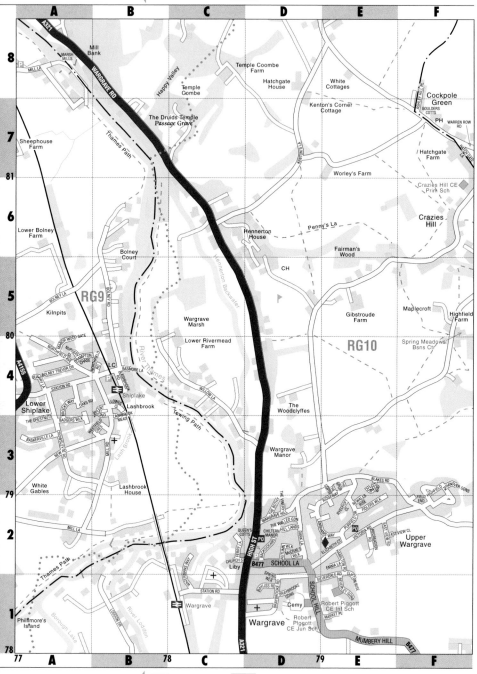

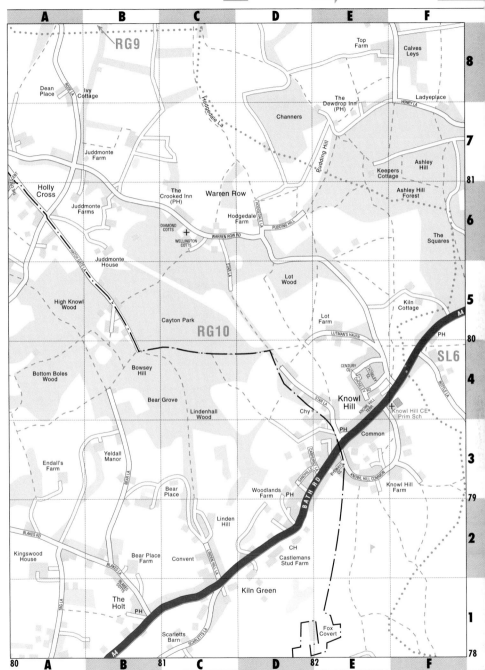

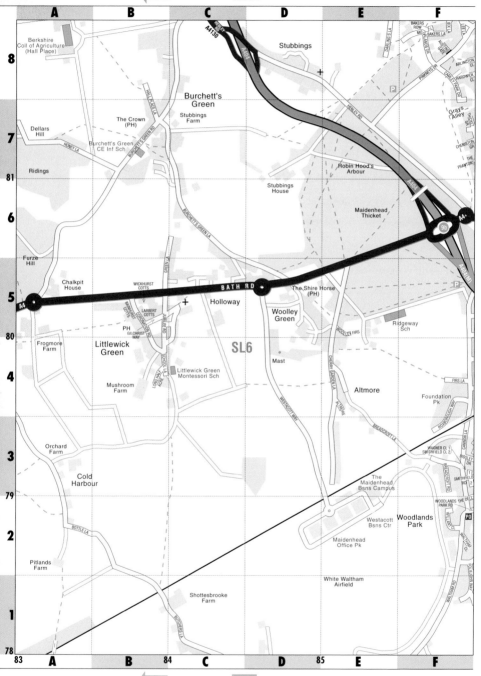

A　B　C　D　E　F

8

7

81

6

5

80

4

3

79

2

1

78

Berkshire
Coll of Agriculture
(Hall Place)

Stubbings

BAKERS
ROW

BAKERS LA

Grays
Alley

Burchett's
Green

Stubbings
Farm

The Crown
(PH)

Dellars
Hill

Burchett's Green
CE Inf Sch

Robin Hood's
Arbour

Ridings

Stubbings
House

Maidenhead
Thicket

9b

A4

Furze
Hill

Chalkpit
House

WICKHURST
COTTS

BATH RD

The Shire Horse
(PH)

Holloway

A4

Woolley
Green

Ridgeway
Sch

PH

Larbert
Cotts

Littlewick
Green

SL6

Frogmore
Farm

Mast

Mushroom
Farm

Littlewick Green
Montessori Sch

FIRS LA

Altmore

Foundation
Pk

Orchard
Farm

Cold
Harbour

The
Maidenhead
Bsns Campus

Westacott
Bsns Ctr

Woodlands
Park

BOTTLE LA

Maidenhead
Office Pk

Pitlands
Farm

White Waltham
Airfield

PO

Shottesbrooke
Farm

83　A　B　84　C　D　85　E　F

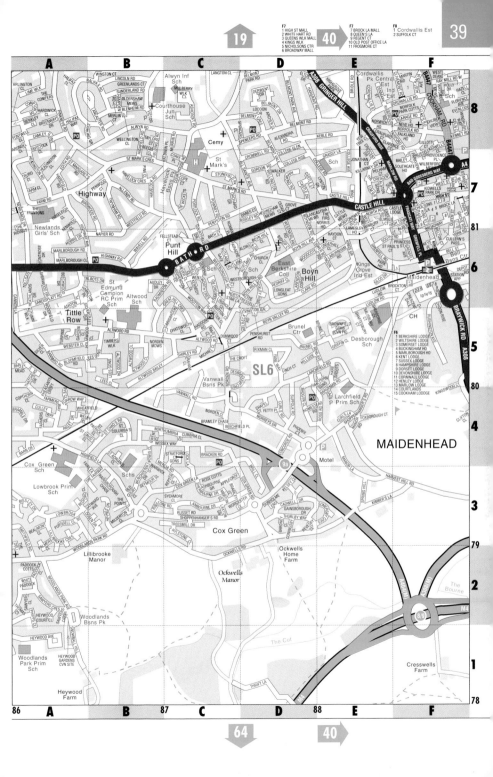

SL1

MAIDENHEAD

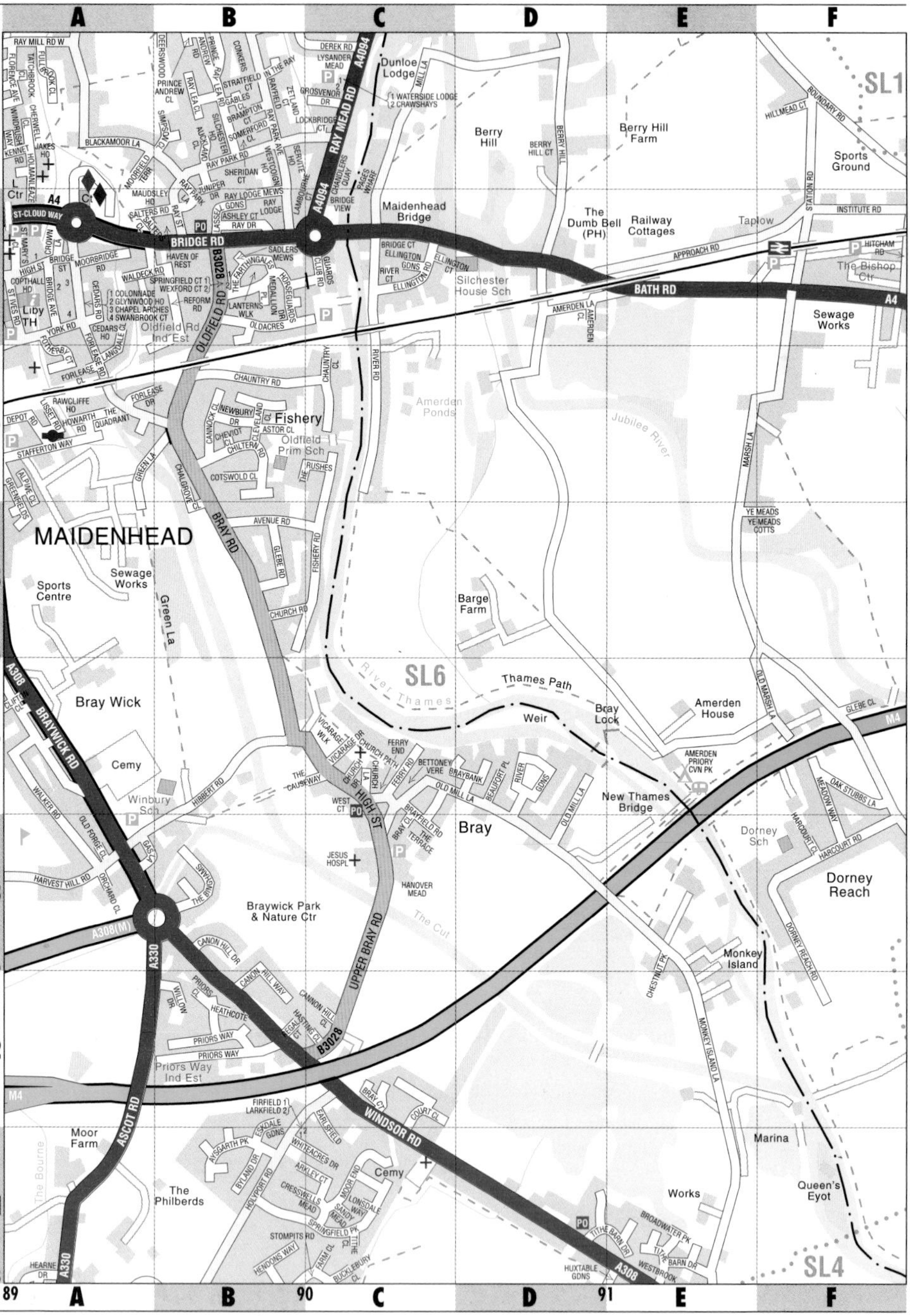

SL6

SL4

Grid references (top): A B C D E F

Rows: 8, 7, 81, 6, 5, 80, 4, 79, 3, 2, 1, 78

Selected labels:

RAY MILL RD W
Dunloe Lodge
LYSANDER MEAD
1 WATERSIDE LODGE
2 CRAWSHAYS
Berry Hill
Berry Hill Farm
Berry Hill CT
RAY MEAD RD
DEREK RD
GROSVENOR DR
LOCKBRIDGE
PRINCE ANDREW CL
HAVEN OF REST
BLACKAMOOR LA
Maidenhead Bridge
The Dumb Bell (PH)
Railway Cottages
Taplow
HILLMEAD RD
ROUNDHAY RD
Sports Ground
INSTITUTE RD
ST-CLOUD WAY
BRIDGE RD
A4
A404
BATH RD
A4
HITCHAM RD
The Bishop Ctr
BRIDGE CT
ELLINGTON
RIVER CT
Silchester House Sch
Sewage Works
AMERDEN LA
MARSH LA
Amerden Ponds
Jubilee River
RAWCLIFFE
HOWARTH
The QUADRANT
Fishery
ASTOR CL
Oldfield Prim Sch
CHAUNTRY RD
CHAUNTRY
RUSHES
YE MEADS
YE MEADS COTTS
STAFFERTON WAY
DEPOT
GREEN LA
BRAY RD
AVENUE RD
GLEBE RD
FISHERY RD
CHURCH RD
Amerden House
OLD MARSH LA
GLEBE CL
MAIDENHEAD
Sports Centre
Sewage Works
Barge Farm
Thames Path
Weir
Bray Lock
Amerden Priory Cvn Pk
M4
River Thames
BRAYWICK RD
Bray Wick
Cemy
Winbury Sch
HIBBERT RD
Ferry
HIGH ST
Bettoney Vere
BRAYBANK
OLD MILL LA
Bray
New Thames Bridge
Dorney Sch
OAK STUBBS LA
MCGROW WAY
HARCOURT RD
A330
A308(M)
BRAYWICK
A330
Braywick Park & Nature Ctr
JESUS HOSPL
HANOVER MEAD
The Cut
UPPER BRAY RD
Dorney Reach
Monkey Island
CHESTNUT PK
DORNEY REACH RD
Moor Farm
ASCOT RD
HEARNE DR
The Philberds
CANON HILL DR
CANON HILL WAY
CANON LA
HASTINGS
B902
PRIORS WAY
Priors Way Ind Est
WINDSOR RD
B902
A308
Cemy
STOMPITS RD
HENDONS
FIRFIELD 1
LARKFIELD 2
Marina
Queen's Eyot
Works
BROADWATER PK
TITHE BARN DR
WESTBROOK
HUXTABLE GDNS

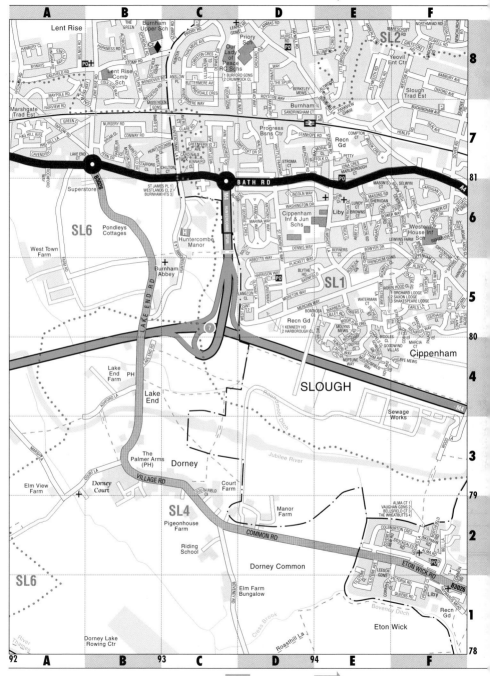

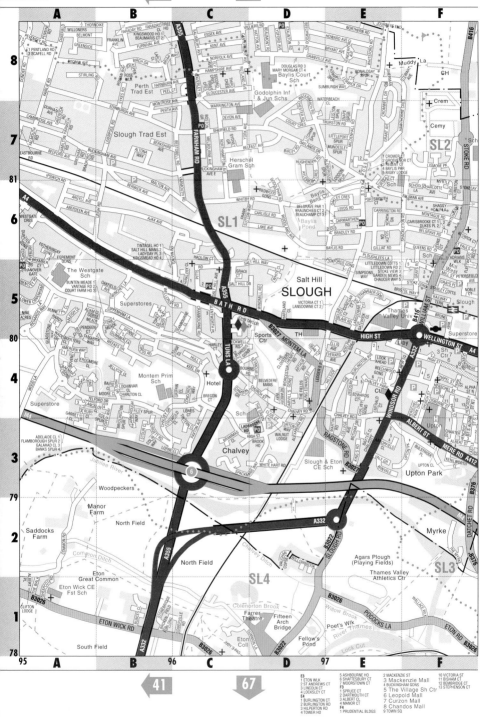

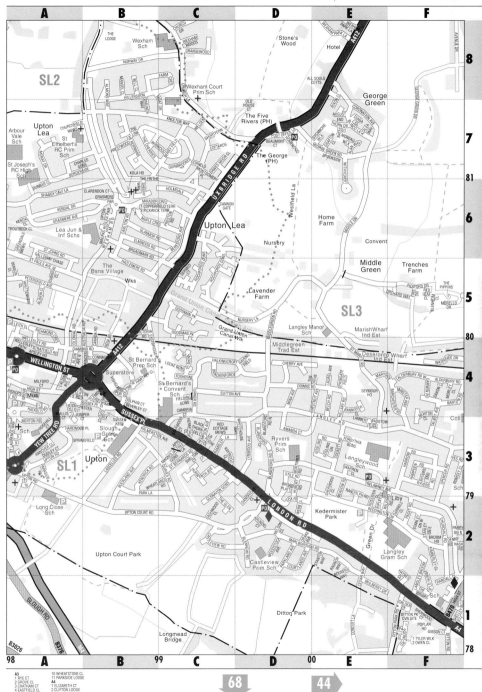

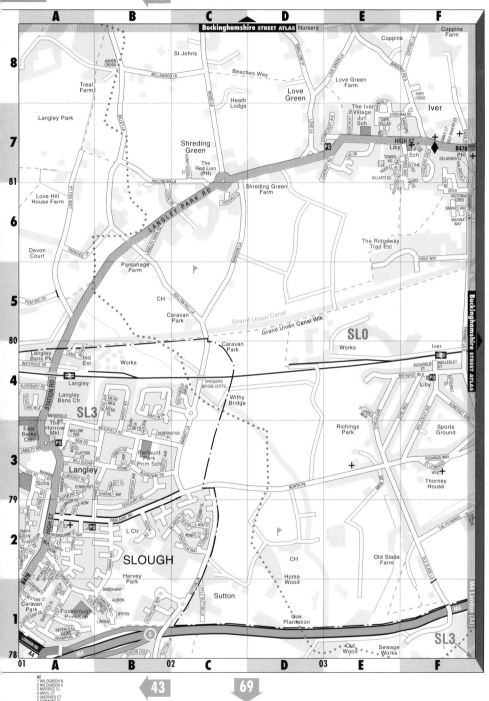

Buckinghamshire STREET ATLAS

Buckinghamshire STREET ATLAS

A2
1 WILDGREEN N
2 WILDGREEN S
3 MORRICE CL
4 ANVIL CT
5 SKERRIES CT
6 SIMMONS CL
7 KNIGHTSBRIDGE CT

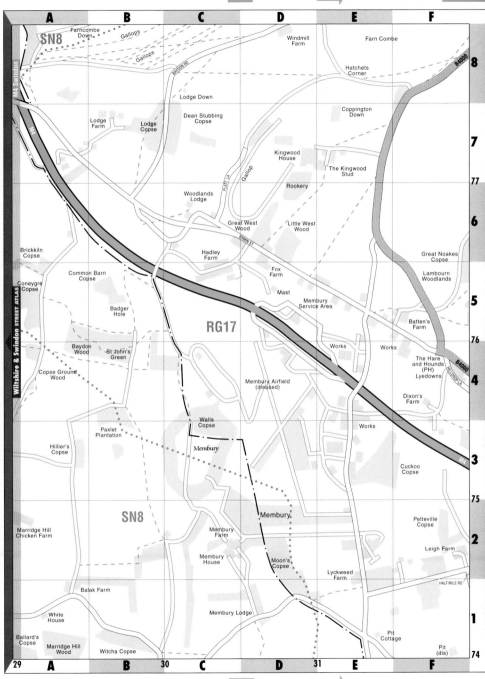

A B C D E F

SN8

Farncombe Down
Gallops
Gallops
Windmill Farm
Farn Combe

8

B4000

M4 Swindon

Hatchets Corner

Lodge Down

Coppington Down

BAYDON RD

Lodge Farm
Lodge Copse
Dean Stubbing Copse

M4

7

Kingwood House

The Kingwood Stud

77

PLATT LA
Gallop

Woodlands Lodge

Rookery

6

Great West Wood
Little West Wood

ERMIN ST

Brickkiln Copse

Hadley Farm

Fox Farm

Great Noakes Copse

Common Barn Copse

Mast

Membury Service Area

Lambourn Woodlands

5

Coneygre Copse

Badger Hole

Works

Works

Batten's Farm

76

Baydon Wood
St John's Green

RG17

The Hare and Hounds (PH)
Lyedowns

HILLDROP LA

B4000

Copse Ground Wood

Membury Airfield (disused)

Dixon's Farm

4

Hillier's Copse

Paxlet Plantation

Walls Copse

Works

Cuckoo Copse

3

Membury

SN8

Membury

Petteville Copse

75

Marridge Hill Chicken Farm

Membury Farm

Membury

Leigh Farm

2

Membury House

Moon's Copse

Lyckweed Farm

HALF MILE RD

Balak Farm

White House

Membury Lodge

Pit Cottage

1

Ballard's Copse

Marridge Hill Wood

Witcha Copse

Pit (dis)

74

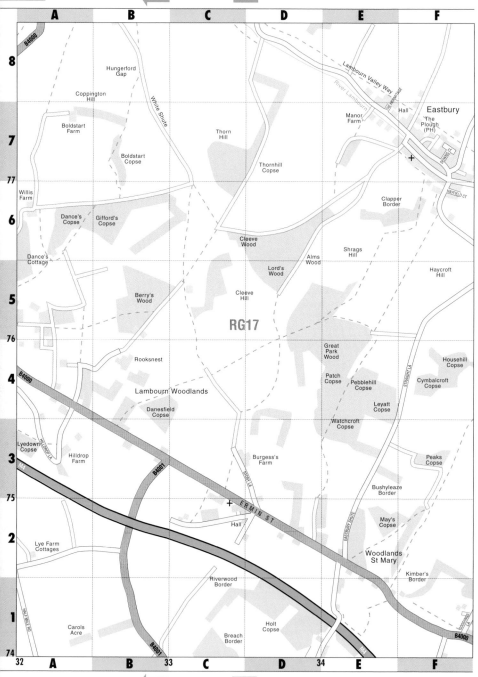

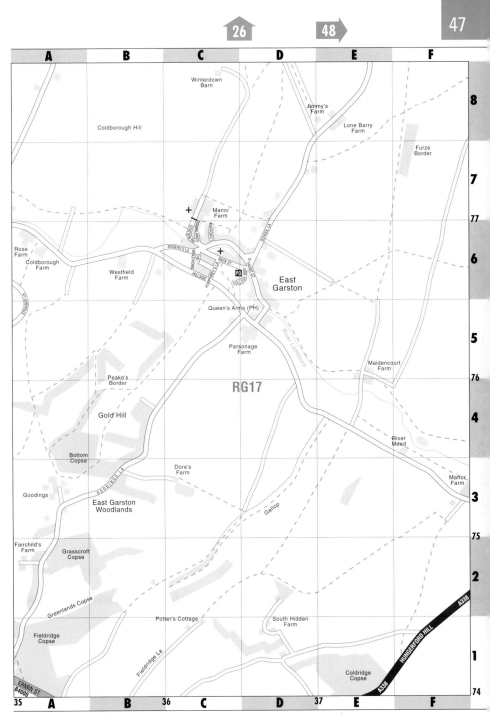

A   B   C   D   E   F

8

7

77

6

5

76

4

75

3

2

1

74

35   A   B   36   C   D   37   E   F

Winterdown Barn

Coldborough Hill

Jimmy's Farm

Lone Barry Farm

Furze Border

Manor Farm

Rose Farm

Coldborough Farm

Westfield Farm

ROGERS'S LA

DOWN LANG

STATION RD

BURFORDS

THE MALTINGS

HILLSIDE

BACK ST

PINFOLD

COLLEGE

NEWBURY RD

PO

SCHOOL LA

East Garston

Queen's Arms (PH)

Parsonage Farm

River Lambourn

Maidencourt Farm

RG17

Peake's Border

Gold Hill

Bottom Copse

River Mead

Manor Farm

GOODINGS LA

Dore's Farm

Goodings

East Garston Woodlands

Gallop

Fairchild's Farm

Grasscroft Copse

Greenlands Copse

Potter's Cottage

South Hidden Farm

Fieldridge La

HUNGERFORD HILL

A338

A338

Fieldridge Copse

Coldridge Copse

ERMIN ST
B4000

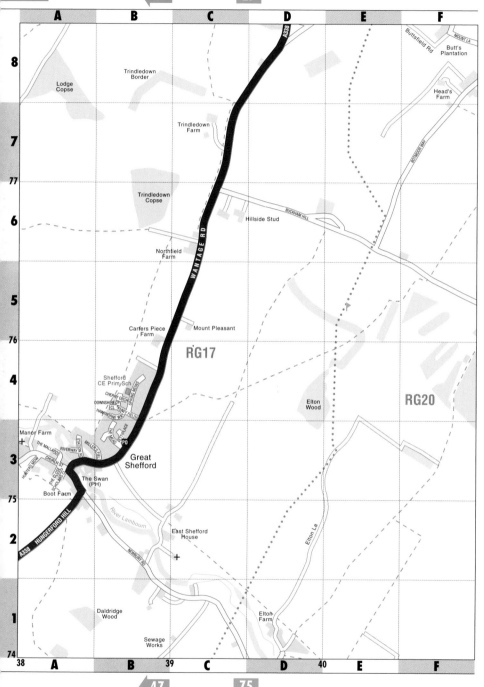

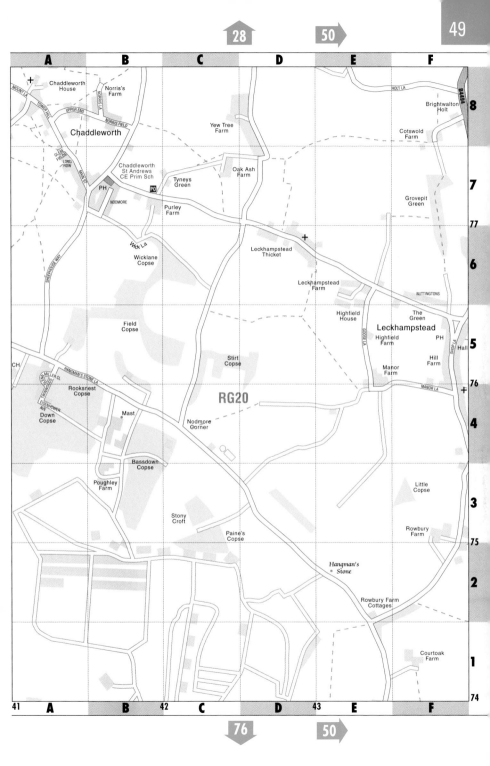

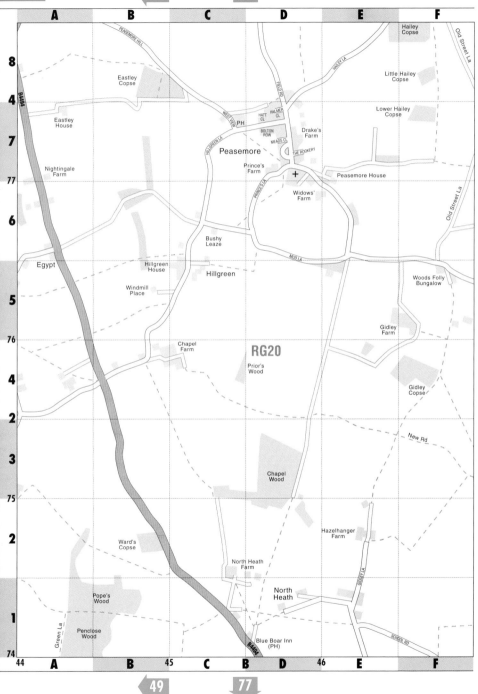

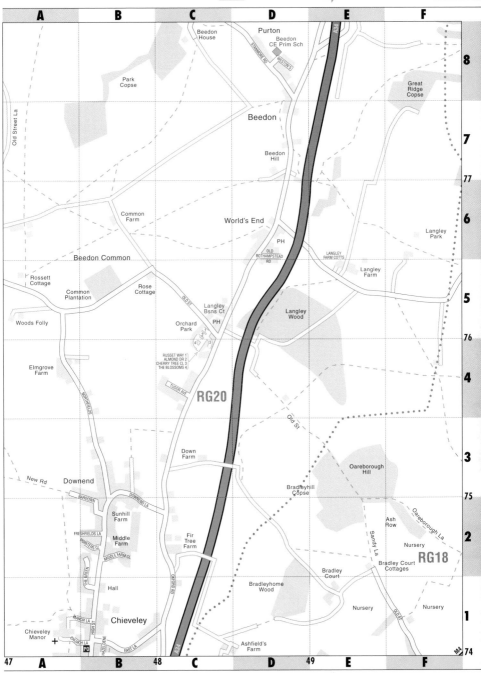

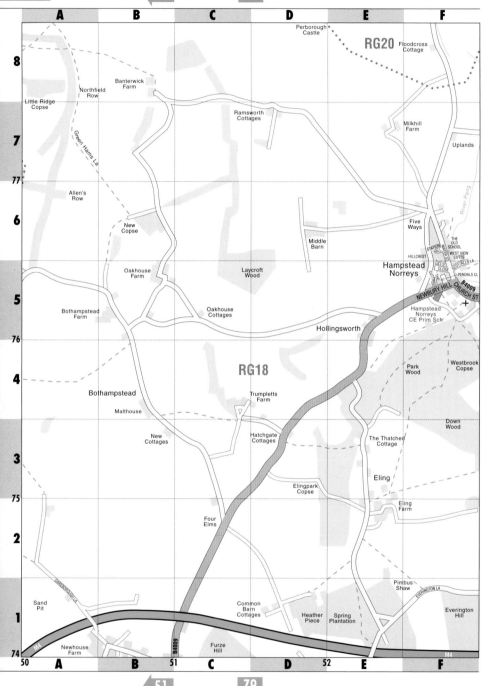

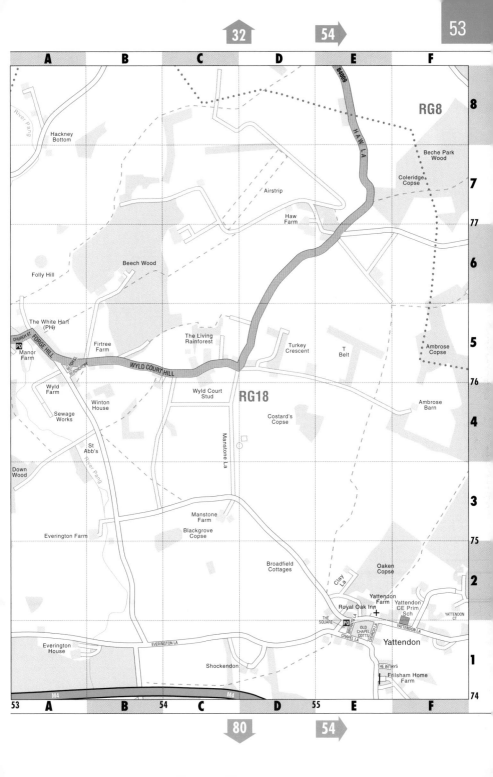

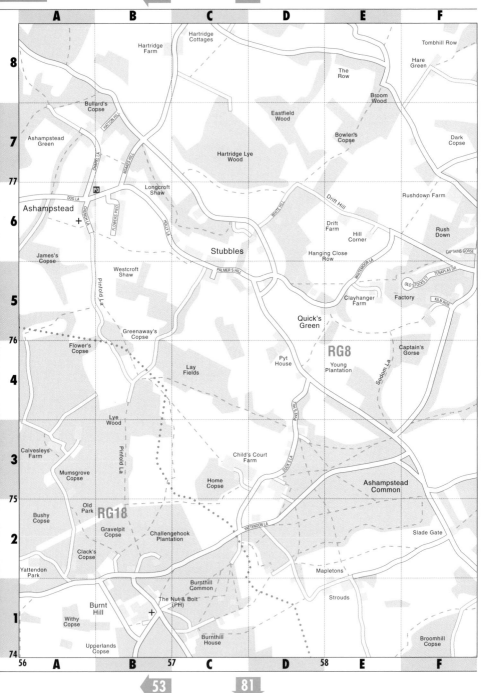

8

Tombhill Row

Hartridge
Cottages

Hartridge
Farm

The
Row

Hare
Green

Broom
Wood

Bullard's
Copse

Eastfield
Wood

Bowler's
Copse

Dark
Copse

7

Ashampstead
Green

Hartridge Lye
Wood

77

Longcroft
Shaw

Rushdown Farm

Drift Hill

DOG LA

P.O.

Ashampstead

6

Drift
Farm

Hill
Corner

Rush
Down

James's
Copse

Stubbles

Hanging Close
Row

CAPTAINS GORSE

Westcroft
Shaw

PALMER'S HILL

Clayhanger
Farm

Factory

OLD STOCKS CT

TENAPLAS DR

5

Quick's
Green

KILN RIDE

Greenaway's
Copse

76

RG8

Captain's
Gorse

Flower's
Copse

Lay
Fields

Pyt
House

Young
Plantation

4

Lye
Wood

Calvesleys
Farm

PAYS HILL

Child's Court
Farm

Mumsgrove
Copse

3

Pinfold La

Ashampstead
Common

Home
Copse

Old
Park

75

Bushy
Copse

RG18

YATTENDON LA

Slade Gate

Gravelpit
Copse

Challengehook
Plantation

2

Clack's
Copse

Mapletons

Yattendon
Park

Strouds

Burnthill
Common

Broomhill
Copse

Withy
Copse

The Nut & Bolt
(PH)

Burnt
Hill

1

Upperlands
Copse

Burnthill
House

74

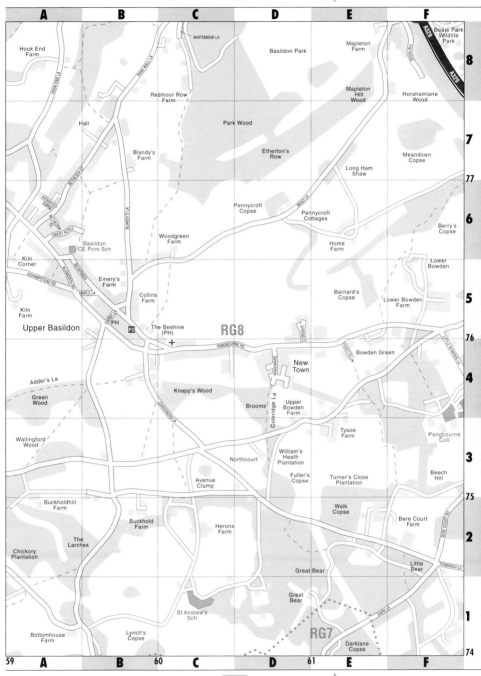

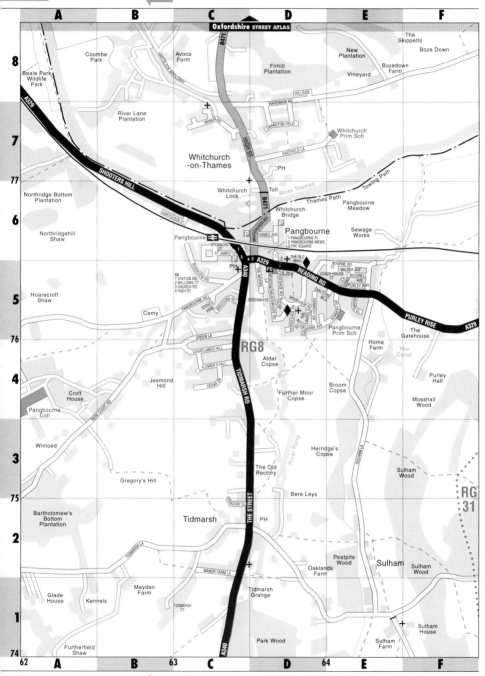
8

7

77

6

5

76

4

3

75

2

1

74

A B C D E F

The Skippetts
Boze Down

Coombe
Park

Avoca
Farm

New
Plantation

Bozedown
Farm

Firhill
Plantation

Vineyard

River Lane
Plantation

HILLSIDE
HARDWICK RD

Whitchurch
Prim Sch

SWINSTON FIELD

EASTFIELD LA

Whitchurch
-on-Thames

PH

River Thames

Northridge Bottom
Plantation

Whitchurch
Lock

Toll

Thames Path

Towing Path

Pangbourne
Meadow

Whitchurch
Bridge

SHOOTERS HILL

HARTSLOCK CT

Northridgehill
Shaw

Pangbourne

THAMES AVE

Pangbourne
1 PANGBOURNE PL
2 PANGBOURNE MEWS
3 THE SQUARE

Sewage
Works

SYCAMORE
CT
ST JAMES

THE OLD
MILL

BOURNE RD
WILDER AVE
BUCKNELL
AVE

Hoarecroft
Shaw

RIVERSIDE RD

A329

Liby

PO

READING RD

COACH HOUSE
CT

PURLEY WAY

C6
1 STATION RD
2 WILLOWS CT
3 CHURCH RD
4 HIGH ST

THE MOORS

MEADOWSIDE RD

CHILTERN
WLK

Cemy

PANGBOURNE HILL

STOKES
VIEW

BRECCON HILL

GREENWAYS

WOODVIEW CL

Pangbourne
Prim Sch

KENNET PL

PURLEY RISE

A329

RG8

GREEN LA

COURTLANDS HILL

FLOWER'S HILL

Home
Farm

The
Gatehouse

The
Canal

Jesmond
Hill

CEDAR LA

Alder
Copse

Further Moor
Copse

Broom
Copse

Mosshall
Wood

Purley
Hall

Croft
House

Pangbourne
Coll

BERE COURT RD

TIDMARSH RD

Winloed

River Pang

Herridge's
Copse

SULHAM LA

Sulham
Wood

**RG
31**

Gregory's
Hill

The Old
Rectory

Bere Leys

STORCHAY CL

Bartholomew's
Bottom
Plantation

THE STREET

PH

Tidmarsh

Peatpits
Wood

Sulham

Sulham
Wood

TIDMARSH LA

MANOR FARM LA

Oaklands
Farm

Glade
House

Kennels

Mayden
Farm

TIDMARSH
CT

Tidmarsh
Grange

Sulham
House

Furtherfield
Shaw

A340

Park Wood

Sulham
Farm

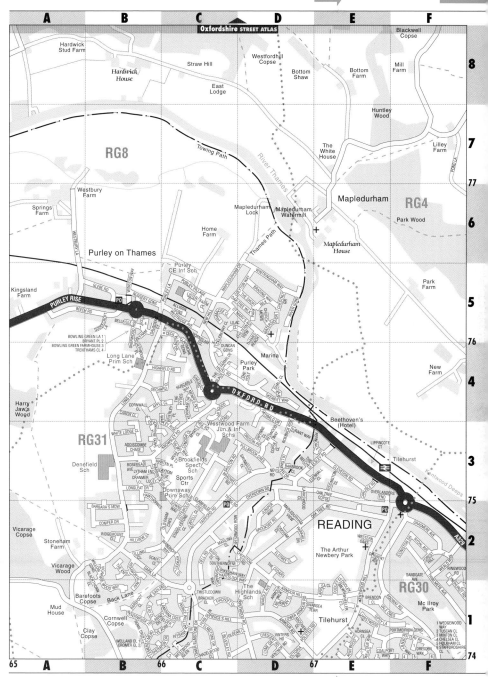

Oxfordshire STREET ATLAS

8

Hardwick Stud Farm
Straw Hill
Westfordhill Copse
Bottom Shaw
Bottom Farm
Mill Farm
Blackwell Copse

Hardwick House
East Lodge

7

Huntley Wood

Lilley Farm

RG8
Towing Path
River Thames
The White House

77

Westbury Farm
Mapledurham
RG4

Springs Farm
Mapledurham Lock
Mapledurham Watermill
Park Wood

6

Kingsland Farm
Home Farm
Mapledurham House
Park Farm

Purley on Thames

Purley CE Inf Sch

WESTBURY LA
GLEBE RD
NURSERY GDNS
WINSTON WAY
MAPLEDURHAM DR
WINTRINGHAM WAY
BRADING WAY
OAK TREE ROAD
THE SHORE

5

PURLEY RISE
BEECH RD
P.O.
SHERWOOD RD
LYTHAM AVE
LUSTER CL
ALLISON
FARM VILLAGE
CL
LILAC

Purley Village

Park Farm

76

BOWLING GREEN LA 1
BRYANT PL 2
BOWLING GREEN FARMHOUSE 3
TRENTHAMS CL 4
Long Lane Prim Sch

CECIL AYE
DUNCAN GDNS
Marina

4

HIGHFIELD RD
ORCHARD
OXFORD RD
Purley Park

New Farm

Harry Jaw's Wood

CORNWALL CL
CAREW CL
APPLE CL
THE HYDES

Westwood Farm Jun. & Inf Schs
Beethoven's (Hotel)

3

RG31
WHITE LODGE CL
ADDISCOMBE CHASE
Brookfields Spect Sch
LIPPINCOTE CT
Tilehurst

Denefield Sch
ROSEMEAD AVE
LYTHAM END
MARTEN PL
CRANMER CL
LONGLEAT DR
Sports Ctr
Downsway Prim Sch
NEVIS CL
BARBROOK CL
OVERLANDERS END

75

BARBARA'S MDW
CONIFER CL
RIDGEMOUNT CL
HILLVIEW CL
OVERDOWN RD
P.O.
MAPLEDURHAM VIEW
OAK TREE RD
READING
GRASMERE AVE
A329

2

Vicarage Copse
The Arthur Newbery Park
WESTERN OAKS
RG30

Stoneham Farm
Vicarage Wood
SOUTHERNCROFT
PIKESHAW WAY
The Highlands Sch
ARMOUR HILL
SANDGATE AVE
Mc Ilroy Park

RIDGEWAY
BACK LANE
THISTLEDOWN
BRACKEN RD
SWANSEA TERR
PORTMEIRION GDNS

1

Barefoots Copse
Cornwell Copse
PIERCE'S HILL
HORNSEA CL
BRENDON CL
WESTERN
COALPORT WAY
POTTERY RD
DRESDEN WAY

Mud House

Clay Copse
WELLAND CL 1
CROMER CL 2
IVY BANK
HAZELWOOD
WINTERS HD
Tilehurst
1 WEDGEWOOD WAY
2 TUSCAN CL
3 MINTON CL
4 CHELSEA CL
5 HOLKHAM CL
6 STAFFORDSHIRE

74

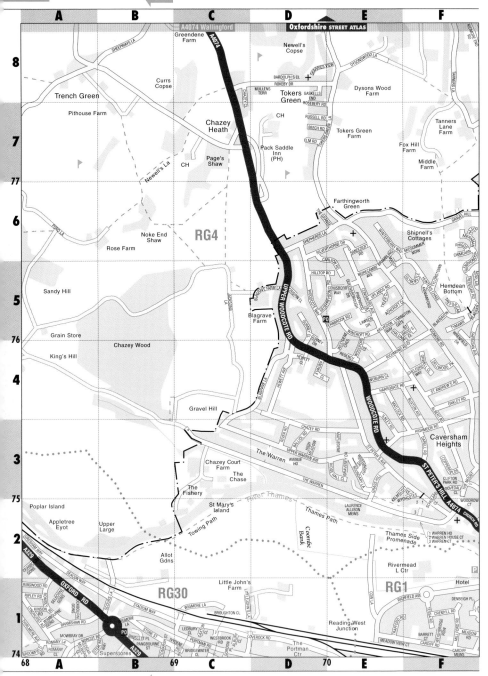

8

7

77

6

5

76

4

3

75

2

1

74

Greendene
Farm

Newell's
Copse

Trench Green

Currs
Copse

Dysons Wood
Farm

Pithouse Farm

STARRIES VIEW

DYSERSWOOD LA

BARDOLPH'S CL
ROKEBY DR

Tokers
Green

GASKELLS
END
ROSEBERY RD

Chazey
Heath

MULLENS
TERR

CH

RUSSELL RD

Tokers Green
Farm

Tanners
Lane
Farm

CHAZEY LA

BEECH RD

Pack Saddle
Inn
(PH)

ELM RD

Fox Hill
Farm

Page's
Shaw

Middle
Farm

CH

Newell's La

Farthingworth
Green

GRAVEL HILL

RG4

Noke End
Shaw

Shepherds La

Shipnell's
Cottages

SILVERTHORNE RD

WINTERBERRY WY

Rose Farm

SANDCROFT
RD

CARLTON RD

SUMMIT
MEW

Sandy Hill

HILLTOP RD

Hemdean
Bottom

BLAGRAVE FARM LA

UPPER WOODCOTE RD

MORECAMBE
AVE

UPLANDS RD

JACKSONS
LA

CONISBORO
WAY

Blagrave
Farm

ASHCROFT CL

Grain Store

PO

PINBROOK RD

King's Hill

Chazey Wood

HEWETT
CL

LAWSON RD

RICHMOND RD

HARROGATE RD

WOODBURN CL

Gravel Hill

St ANDREW'S RD

OAKLEY RD

HIGHMOOR RD

Chazey Court
Farm

CHAZEY RD

Caversham
Heights

The Chase

The Warren

AVENUE HO

ST PETER'S AVE

The Warren

CLIFTON
PARK RD

The
Fishery

ST PETER'S HILL A4074

WOODROW
CT

River Thames

LAURENCE
ALLISON
MEWS

St Mary's
Island

Thames Path

CHURCH RD

Poplar Island

Towing Path

Coombe
Bank

Thames Side
Promenade

1 WARREN HO
2 WARREN HOUSE CT
3 WARREN CT

Appletree
Eyot

Upper
Large

Allot
Gdns

Rivermead
L Ctr

RG1

Hotel

RG30

Little John's
Farm

Reading West
Junction

Oxford Rd

A329

Superstores

PO

A329

The
Portman
Ctr

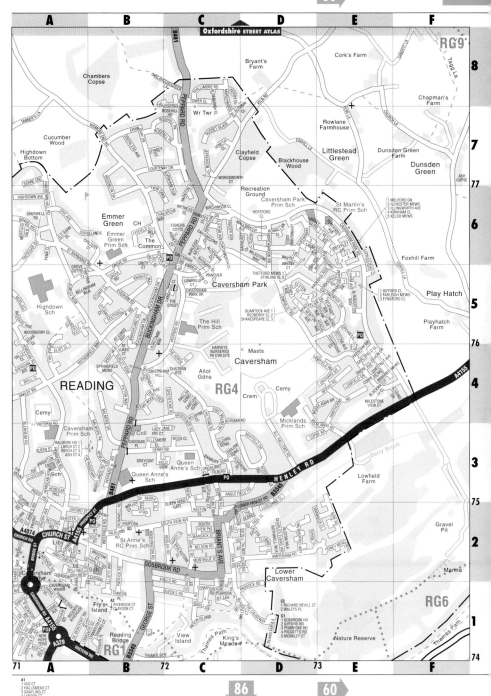

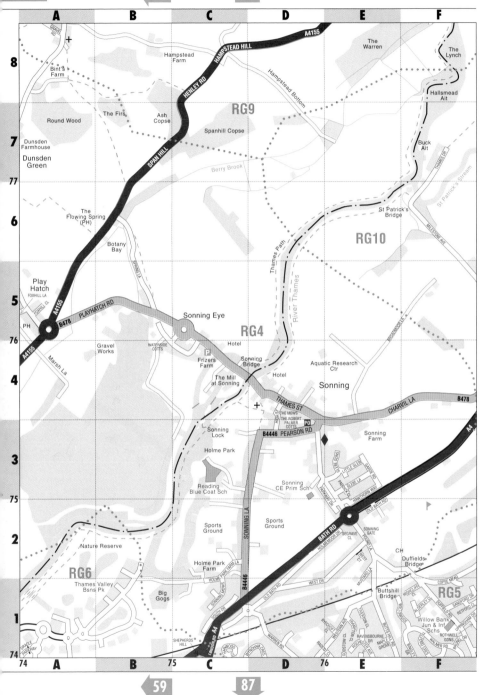

A B C D E F

8

7

77

6

5

76

4

3

75

2

1

74

A4155
The Warren
The Lynch
Hampstead Hill
HENLEY RD
Hampstead Farm
The Lynch
Bint's Farm
Hallsmead Ait
RG9
Hampstead Bottom
Round Wood
The Firs
Ash Copse
Spanhill Copse
Dunsden Farmhouse
Dunsden Green
SPAN HILL
Berry Brook
Buck Ait
St Patrick's Bridge
St Patrick's Stream
RG10
The Flowing Spring (PH)
Botany Bay
Thames Path
MILESTONE AVE
Play Hatch
FOXHILL LA
A4155
B478
PLAYHATCH RD
Sonning Eye
River Thames
RG4
Marsh La
Gravel Works
WATERSIDE COTTS
Hotel
Sonning Bridge
Aquatic Research Ctr
PH
Frizers Farm
The Mill at Sonning
Hotel
Sonning
CHARVIL LA
B478
Sonning Lock
Thames St
THE MEWS
THE ROBERT PALMER COTTS
PO
B4446 PEARSON RD
Sonning Farm
A4
Holme Park
LITTLE GLEBE
GLEBE LA
HAWTHORN WAY
Reading Blue Coat Sch
Sonning CE Prim Sch
SONNING LA
Sports Ground
Sports Ground
BATH RD
SEGRAVE CL
SONNING GATE
CH
Duffields Bridge
RG6
Nature Reserve
Holme Park Farm
HOLME PARK FARM LA
SONNING LA
B4446
OLD BATH RD
WEST DR
Buttshill Bridge
COPSE MEAD
RG5
Thames Valley Bsns Pk
Big Gogs
SOUTH DR
LONDON RD A4
SHEPHERDS HILL
WYNDHAM CRES
WOOD
WARREN RD
Willow Bank Jun & Inf Schs
RETFORD CL
ROTHWELL GDNS
WILMER RD
ORACLE PARKWAY

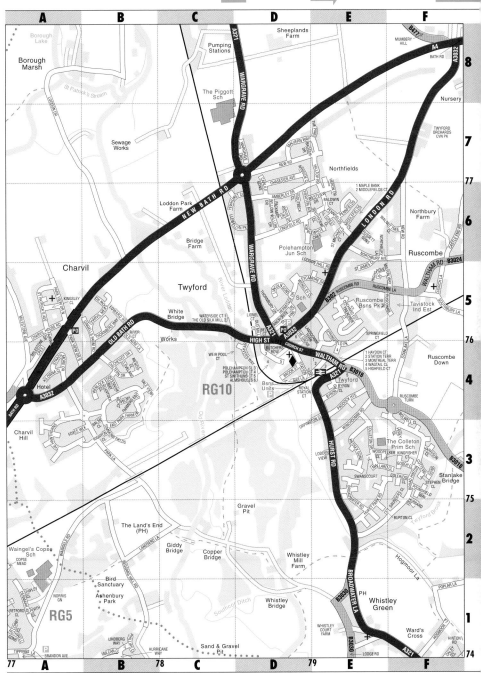

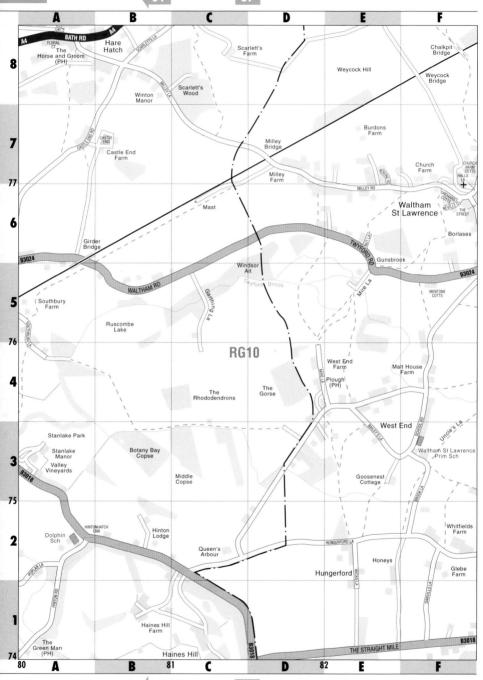

RG10

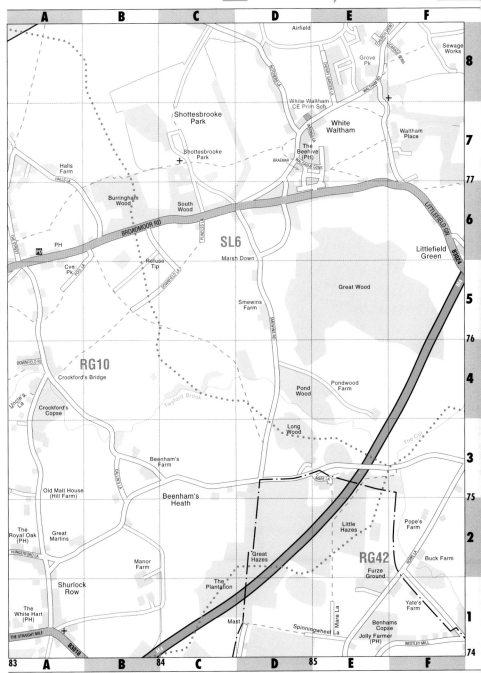

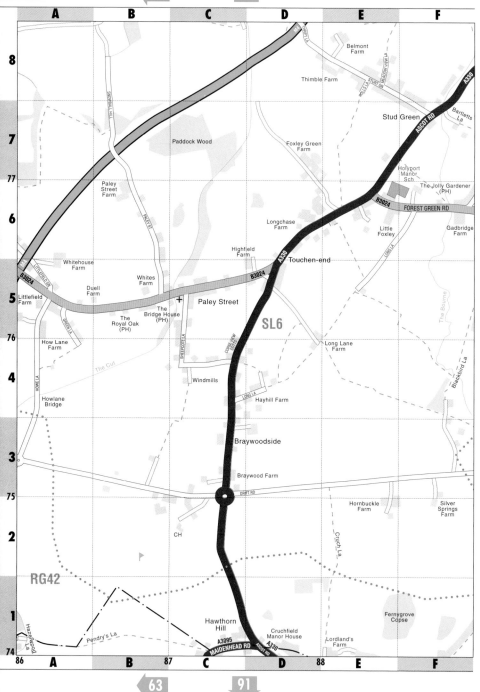

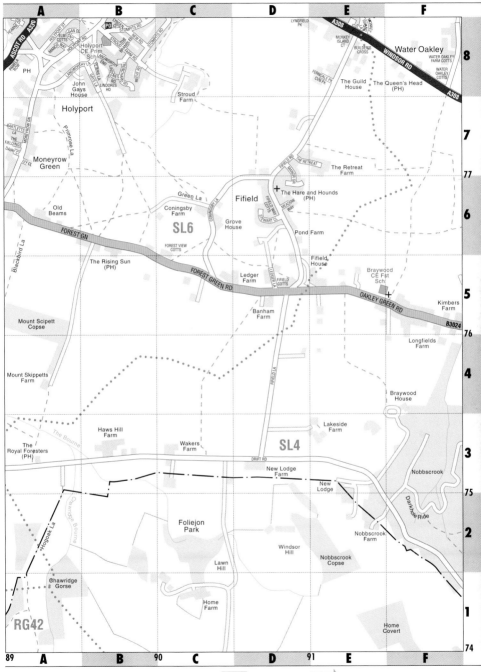

Water Oakley

WATER OAKLEY
FARM COTTS

WATER
OAKLEY
COTTS

The Guild
House

The Queen's Head
(PH)

Stroud
Farm

Holyport

Holyport
CE Prim
Sch

John Gays
House

Moneyrow
Green

Old
Beams

Green La

Coningsby
Farm

Fifield

Grove
House

The Retreat

The Retreat
Farm

The Hare and Hounds
(PH)

FOREST GN

SL6

FOREST VIEW
COTTS

The Rising Sun
(PH)

Pond Farm

Fifield
House

Braywood
CE Fst
Sch

Kimbers
Farm

FOREST GREEN RD

Ledger
Farm

FIFIELD
COTTS

OAKLEY GREEN RD

B3024

Longfields
Farm

Mount Scipett
Copse

Banham
Farm

Mount Skippetts
Farm

Braywood
House

The Bourne

Haws Hill
Farm

Wakers
Farm

SL4

Lakeside
Farm

The
Royal Foresters
(PH)

DRIFT RD

Nobbscrook

New Lodge
Farm

New
Lodge

Darkhole Ride

Foliejon
Park

Windsor
Hill

Nobbscrook
Copse

Nobbscrook
Farm

Chawridge
Gorse

Lawn
Hill

Home
Farm

RG42

Home
Covert

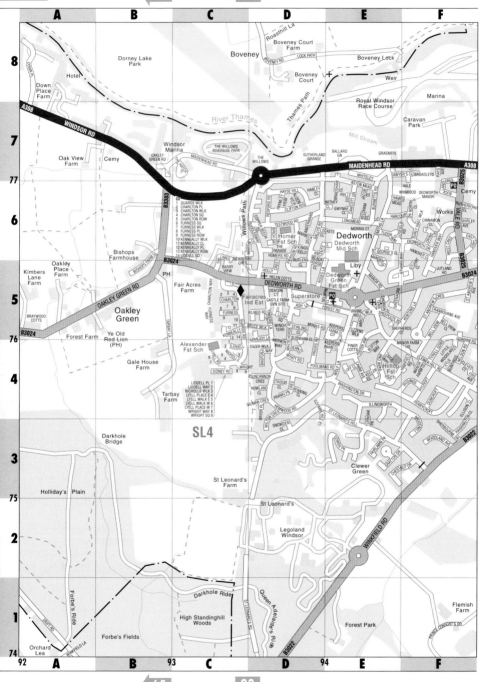

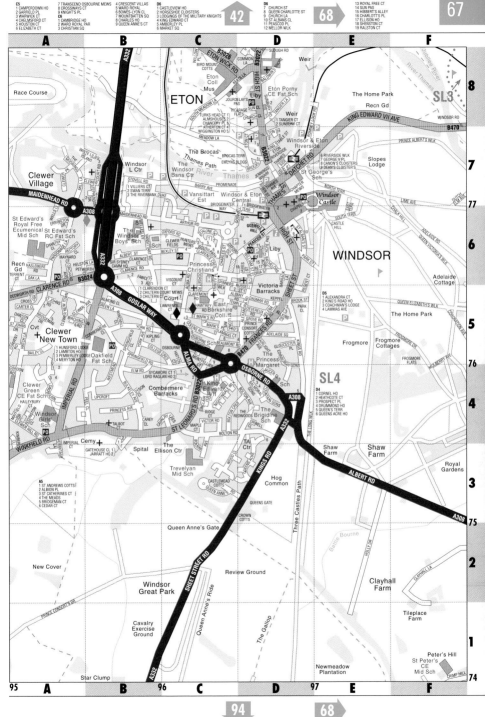

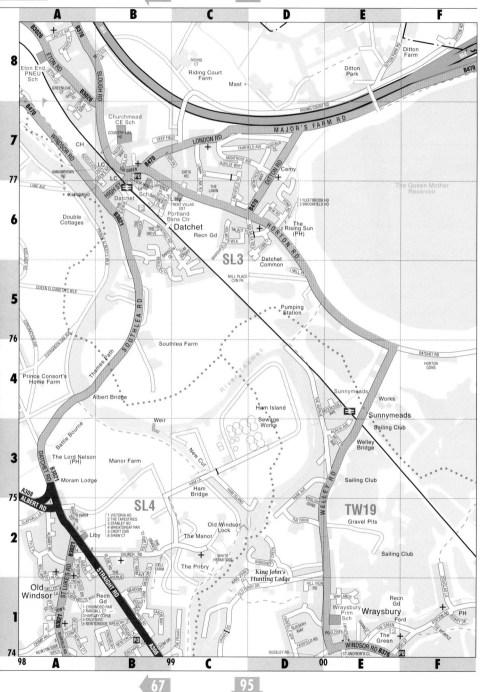

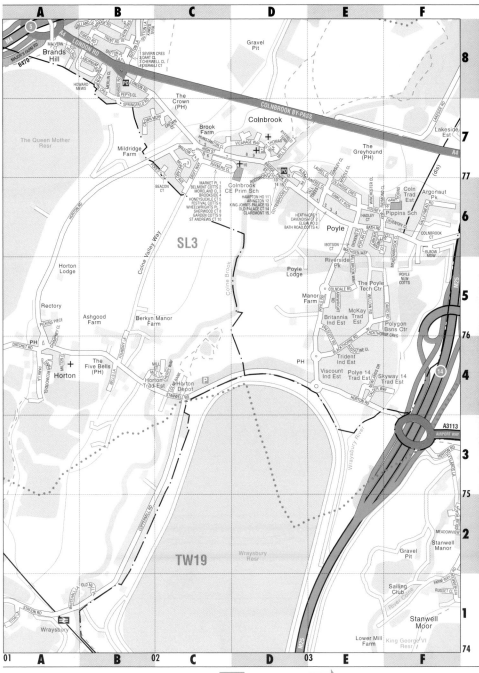

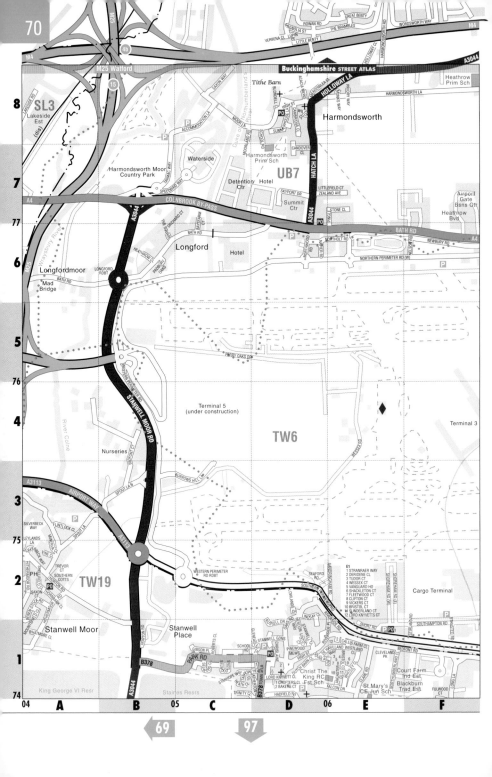

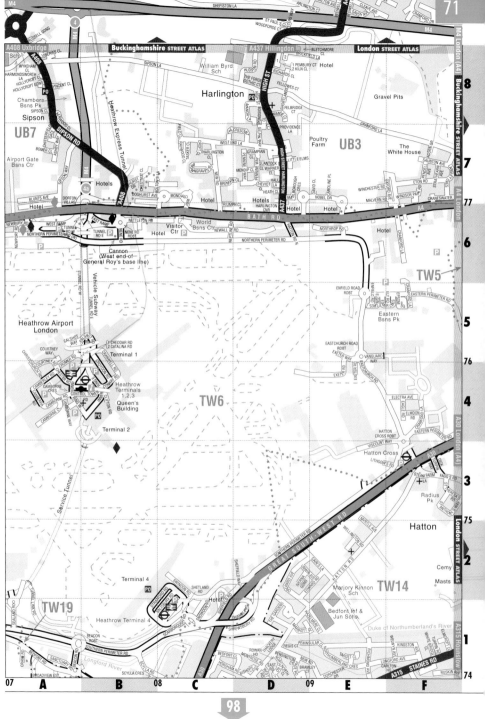

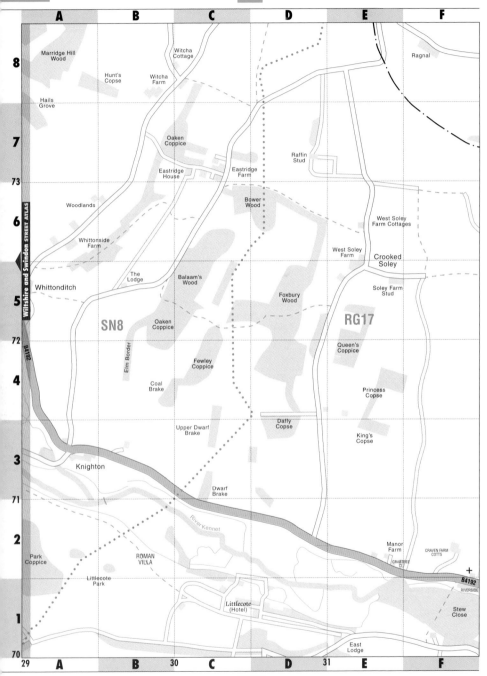

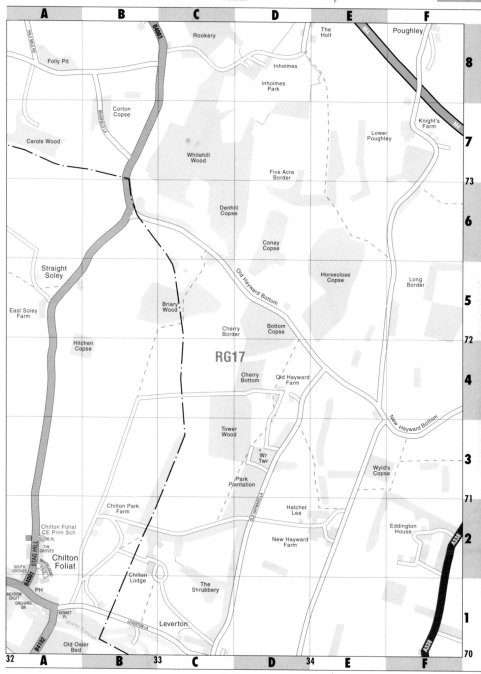

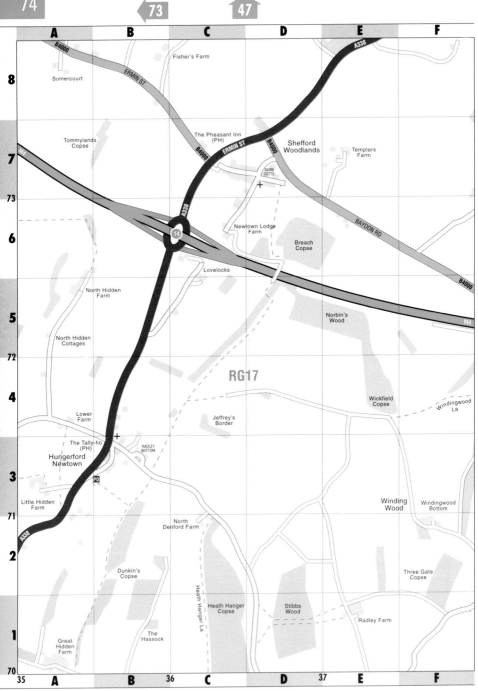

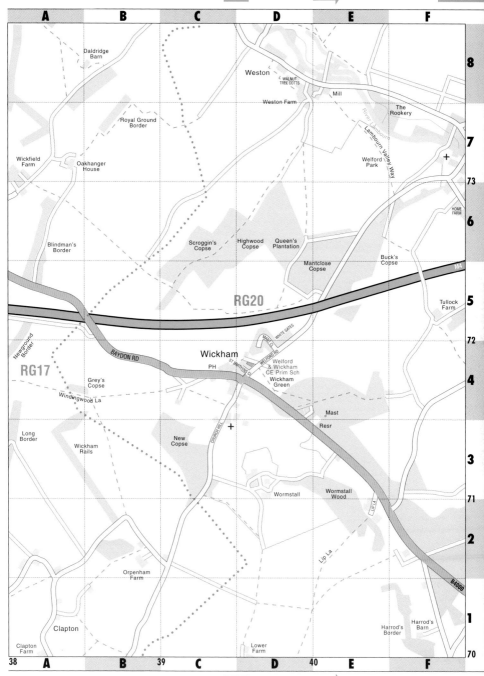

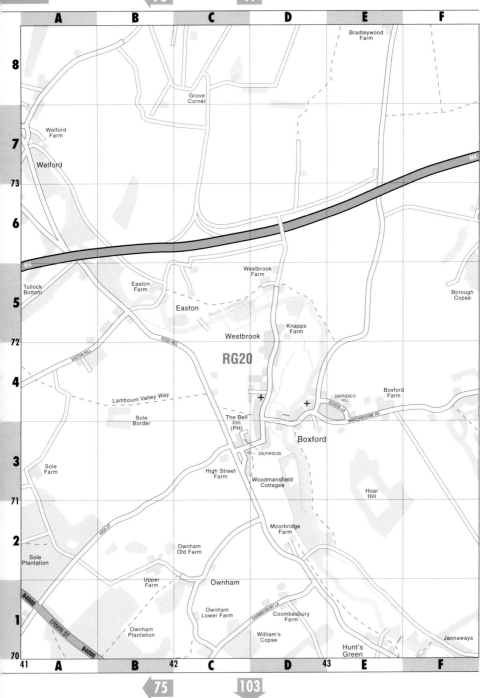

50 78

A	B	C	D	E	F

8

Green La

Hop Castle

Penclose Farm

Penclose Cottage

Fir Tree Cottage

B4494

SCHOOL RD

Ogdown House

7

73

M4

Wyfield Manor Farm

New Found Out Cottages

Pound Cottage

Winterbourne Stream

6

Phillip's Hill

Bussock Wood

Bussock Mayne

Borough Hill

Lower Farm

Winterbourne Arms (PH)

Winterbourne Farm

Pebble La

Vauxhall Copse

5

Wyfield Copse

Winterbourne

COUNCIL HOS

Beans Hill

72

Mud Hall Cottage

Winterbourne Manor

+

Winterbourne Wood

RG20

Mapleash Copse

Bussock Hill House

RG14

4

WINTERBOURNE RD

Leonard's Plantation

Winterbourne Holt

Holly Copse

Home Farm

ARLINGTON LA

Mary Hare Gram Sch

3

Boxford Common

Pit King Farm

Snelsmore Common Country Park

P

71

Broomclose Border

Withy Copse

Barrett's Wood

2

Sheppard's Copse

Mount Hill

Honeybottom

Swilly Copse

A34

Bagnor Wood

Copse Barn

Bagnor Marsh

Ashpiece Copse

Hill's Pightle

B4494

A34

Snelsmore House

CH

1

70

44 A	B 45	C	D 46	E	F

104 78

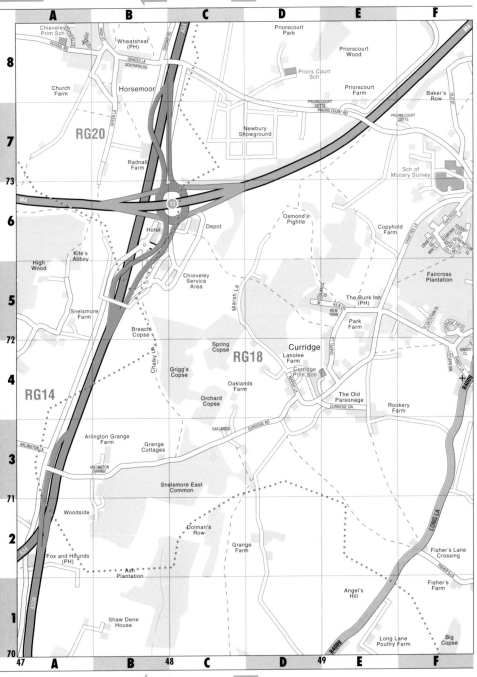

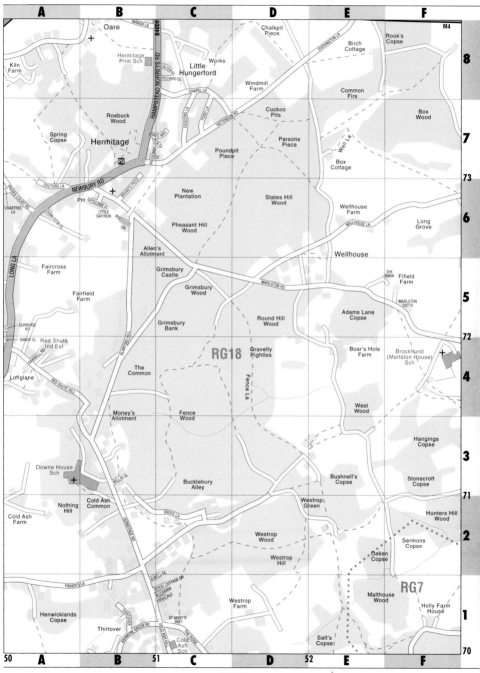

M4

8

7

73

6

5

72

4

3

71

2

1

70

A   B   C   D   E   F

Oare

Kiln Farm

Hermitage Prim Sch

Little Hungerford

Works

Chalkpit Piece

Birch Cottage

Rook's Copse

Windmill Farm

Roebuck Wood

Spring Copse

Hermitage

Cuckoo Pits

Common Firs

Box Wood

PO

Poundpit Piece

Parsons Piece

Well La

Box Cottage

DOCTORS LA   NEWBURY RD

PH

New Plantation

States Hill Wood

Wellhouse Farm

Long Grove

LITTLE SAFFRON

WOODSIDE DR

Pheasant Hill Wood

WELLHOUSE LA

Allen's Allotment

Wellhouse

LONG LA

Faircross Farm

Grimsbury Castle

MARLSTON RD

THE BARN

Fifield Farm

Fairfield Farm

Grimsbury Wood

MARLSTON COTTS

CURRIDGE RD

SANDY CL

Red Shute Ind Est

Grimsbury Bank

Round Hill Wood

Adams Lane Copse

72

SAWMILL RD

Longlane

RED SHUTE HILL

The Common

RG18

Gravelly Rightles

Boar's Hole Farm

Brockhurst (Marlston House) Sch

SLAPTING HILL

Fence La

Money's Allotment

Fence Wood

West Wood

Hangings Copse

Downe House Sch

WELL'S CL

Bucklebury Alley

Bushnell's Copse

Stonecroft Copse

71

Cold Ash Farm

Nothing Hill

Cold Ash Common

HERMITAGE RD

DRIVE LA

Westrop Green

Hunters Hill Wood

Sermons Copse

FISHER'S LA

Westrop Wood

Oaken Copse

RG7

Henwicklands Copse

SEWELL CL

GORSE COTTAGE DR

WOODSIDE

ANNACALE

Westrop Hill

Malthouse Wood

Holly Farm House

Thirtover

ASHMORE GREEN RD

THE RISE

ST MARY'S HO

COLD ASH RD

Westrop Farm

Salt's Copse

Cold Ash Sch

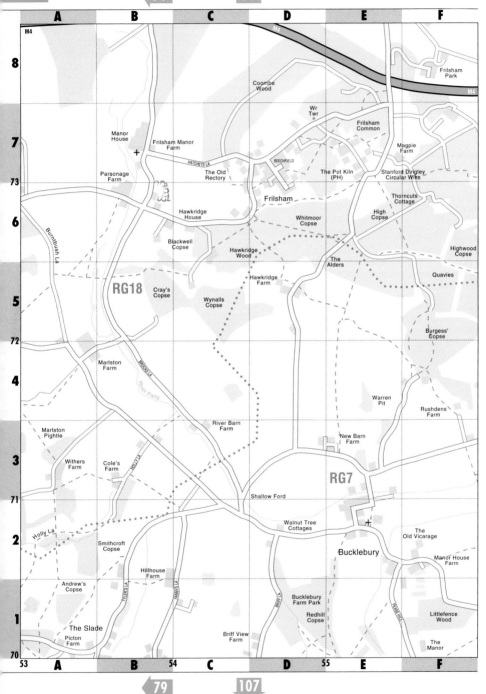

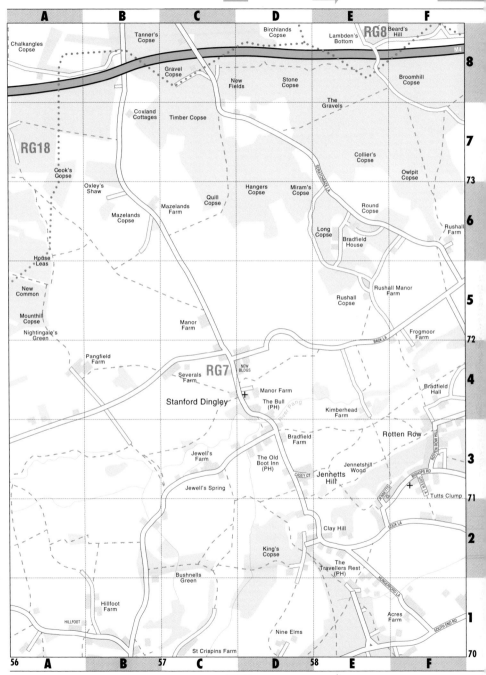

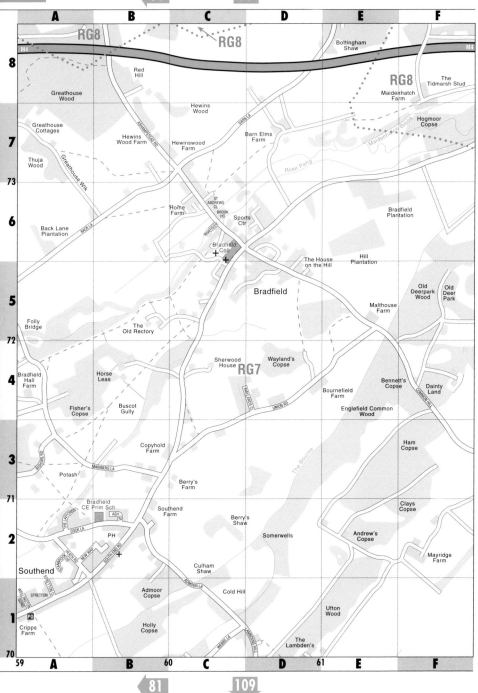

A **B** **C** **D** **E** **F**

RG8

RG8

M4

Bottingham
Shaw

8

Red
Hill

RG8

The
Tidmarsh Stud

Greathouse
Wood

Hewins
Wood

Maidenhatch
Farm

Hogmoor
Copse

Greathouse
Cottages

7

Hewins
Wood Farm

Hewinswood
Farm

Dark La

Barn Elms
Farm

Maidenhatch Brook

Thuja
Wood

Greathouse Wlk

73

River Pang

Bradfield
Plantation

6

Back La

Home
Farm

ST
ST
ANDREWS
CL

BROOK
HO

Sports
Ctr

Back Lane
Plantation

Riverside

Bradfield
Coll

The House
on the Hill

Hill
Plantation

Old
Deerpark
Wood

Old
Deer
Park

5

Bradfield

Malthouse
Farm

Folly
Bridge

The
Old Rectory

72

Sherwood
House

Wayland's
Copse

RG7

Bennett's
Copse

Dainty
Land

4

Bradfield
Hall
Farm

Horse
Leas

Bournefield
Farm

Common Hill

Fisher's
Copse

Buscot
Gully

Pang Fields Ct

Union Rd

Englefield Common
Wood

Ham
Copse

3

Bishops Rd

Potash

Mariners La

Copyhold
Farm

Berry's
Farm

The Bourne

Clays
Copse

71

Bradfield
CE Prim Sch

The Lickfolds

ASH
ST

Southend
Farm

Berry's
Shaw

Andrew's
Copse

Cook La

2

Southend

PH

New Way

South End Rd

Somerwells

Mayridge
Farm

Stretton

Admoor La

Culham
Shaw

Admoor
Copse

Cold Hill

Ufton
Wood

1

Wellington Gdns

Stretton

PO

Cripps
Farm

Holly
Copse

Webbs La

Lambden Hill

The
Lambden's

70

59 **A** **B** **60** **C** **D** **61** **E** **F**

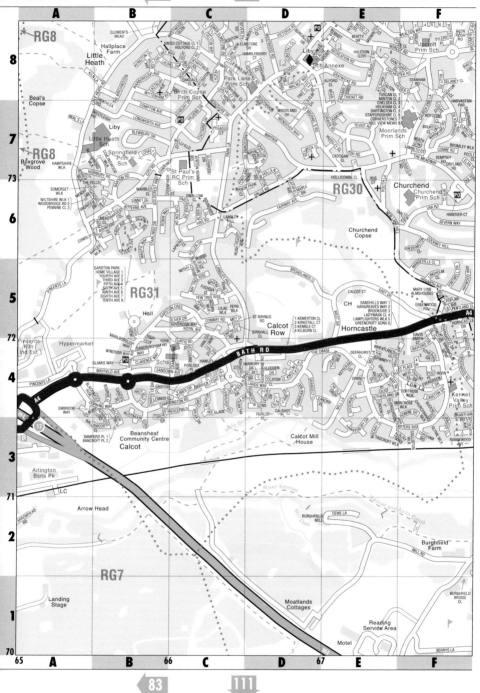

83

57

D8
1 APPLESHAW CT
2 ELIZABETH CT
3 SOVEREIGN PK

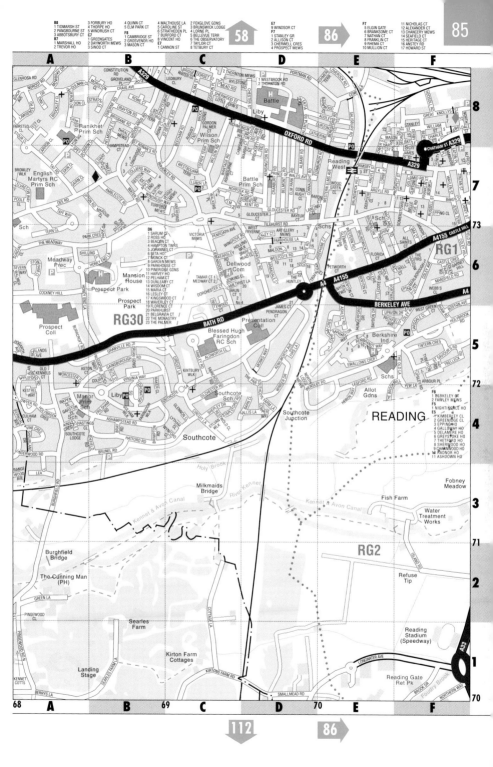

88
1 TIDMARSH ST
2 PANGBOURNE ST
3 ABBOTSBURY CT
87
1 MARSHALL HO
2 TREVOR HO

3 FORBURY HO
4 THORPE HO
5 WINDRUSH CT
C7
1 GREENGATES
2 DAYWORTH MEWS
3 SINOD CT

4 QUINN CT
5 ELM PARK CT
F8
1 CAMBRIDGE ST
2 GROSVENOR HO
3 MASON CT

4 MALTHOUSE LA
5 CAROLINE ST
6 STRATHEDEN PL
7 BURFORD CT
8 VINCENT HO
9 CANNON ST

2 FOXGLOVE GDNS
3 BRUNSWICK LODGE
4 LORNE PL
5 BELLEVUE TERR
6 THE OBSERVATORY
7 TAYLOR CT
8 TETBURY CT

E7
9 WINDSOR CT
F7
1 STANLEY GR
2 ALLISON CT
3 CHERWELL CRES
4 PROSPECT MEWS

F7
5 ELGIN GATE
6 BRANKSOME CT
7 NATHAN CT
8 FRANKLIN CT
9 RHEMA CT
10 MULLION CT

11 NICHOLAS CT
12 ALEXANDER CT
13 CHANCERY MEWS
14 SEAFIELD CT
15 HERITAGE CT
16 ANSTEY RD
17 HOWARD ST

58

86 ▶

85

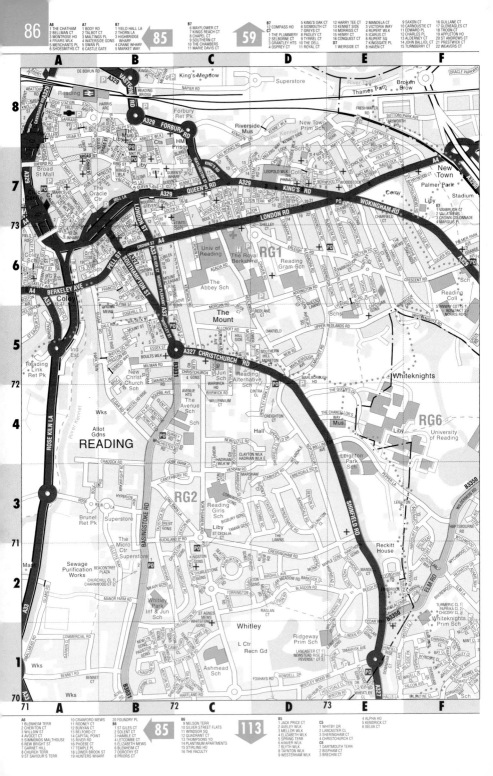

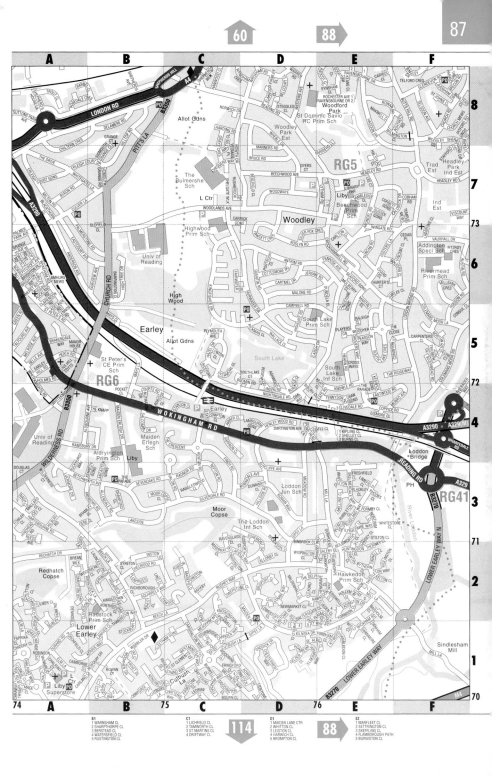

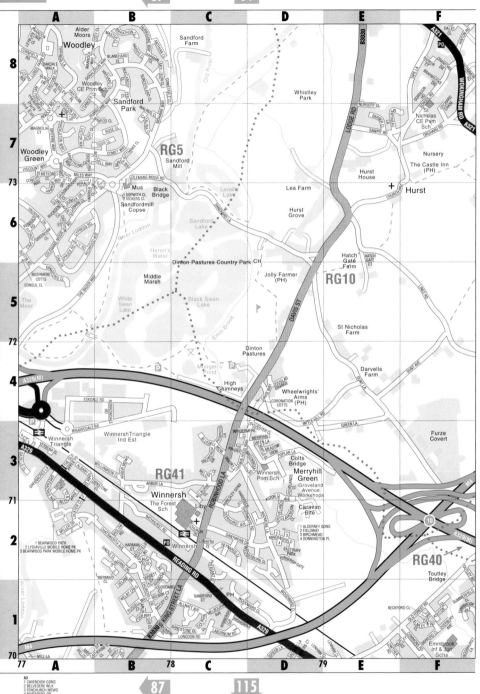

A B C D E F

8

7

73

6

5

72

4

3

71

2

1

70

Woodley
Alder Moors
Sandford Farm
Whistley Park
St Nicholas CE Prim Sch
Nursery
Woodley CE Prim Sch
Sandford Park
Magnolia CT
Woodley Green
RG5
Sandford Mill
The Castle Inn (PH)
Colemans Moor Rd
Mus
1 SOPWITH CL
2 VICKERS CL
Black Bridge
Sandfordmill Copse
Lavell Lake
Lea Farm
Hurst House
Hurst
Sandford Lake
Hurst Grove
River Loddon
Heron's Water
Sandford Lake
Rushmere Cotts
Consul Cl
Middle Marsh
White Swan Lake
Black Swan Lake
Dinton Pastures Country Park CH
Jolly Farmer (PH)
Hatch Gate Farm
Hatch Gate CT
RG10
The Moor
Emm Brook
St Nicholas Farm
Dinton Pastures
Davis St
Darvells Farm
A329(M)
Eskdale Rd
Mungell's Pond
High Chimneys
Wheelwrights' Arms (PH)
Coronation Cotts
Green La
Furze Covert
Wharfedale Rd
Winnersh Triangle
Winnersh Triangle Ind Est
Windermere
Sylvester Cl
Merryhill Green La
Colts Bridge
Merryhill Green
Groveland Workshops
RG41
Winnersh
Winnersh Prim Sch
Caravan Site
1 ALDERNEY GDNS
2 FIELDWAY
3 BIRCHMEAD
4 DONNINGTON PL
RG40
The Forest Sch
Library
Eastbury Park
A329
A329(M)
1 BEARWOOD PATH
2 LYDIAVILLE MOBILE HOME PK
3 BEARWOOD PARK MOBILE HOME PK
Winnersh
Reading Rd
Toutley Bridge
Mermaid Cl
Sandford La
PH
Beckford Cl
River Loddon
M4
Mill La
Longdon Rd
Laburnum Rd
King Street La
Emmbrook Inf & Jun Schs

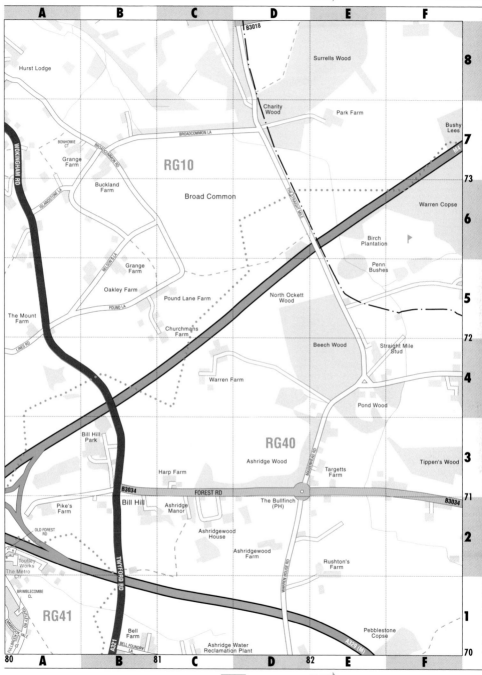

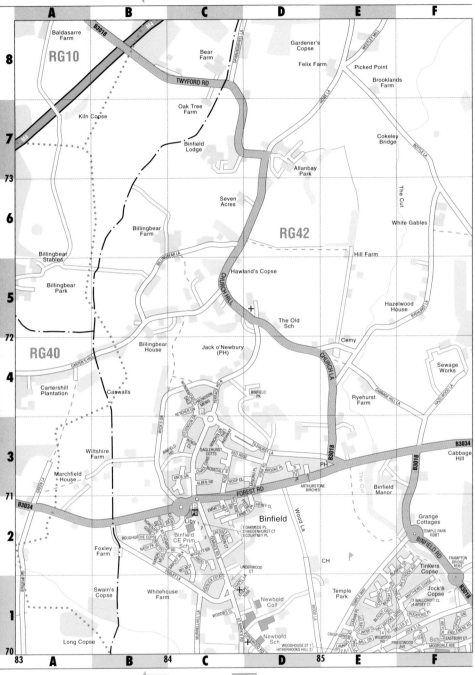

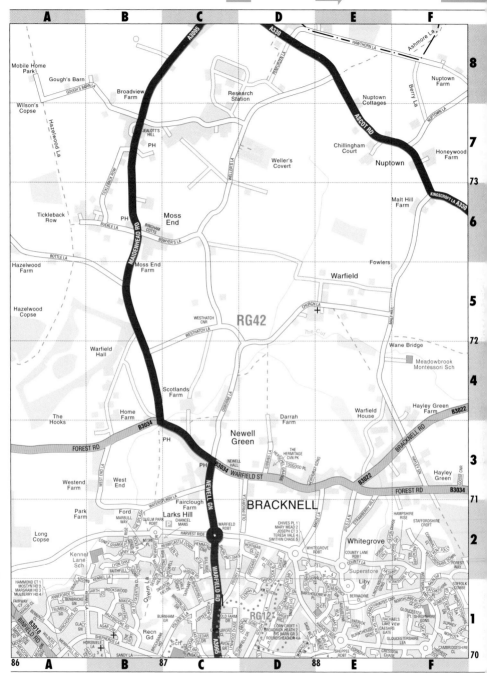

A **B** **C** **D** **E** **F**

Mobile Home Park

Gough's Barn

GOUGH'S BARN LA

Broadview Farm

Wilson's Copse

Hazelwood La

JEALOTT'S HILL

PH

TICKLEBACK ROW

Research Station

Weller's Covert

Nuptown Cottages

HAWTHORN LA

Ashmore La

Nuptown Farm

Berry La

NUPTOWN LA

8

Chillingham Court

Nuptown

ASCOT RD

Honeywood Farm

7

73

Tickleback Row

PH

BUCKLE LA

MAIDENHEAD RD

Moss End

BINGHAM COTTS

BOWYER'S LA

WELLER'S LA

Malt Hill Farm

KINGSCROFT LA A330

6

BOTTLE LA

Hazelwood Farm

Moss End Farm

Fowlers

Warfield

Hazelwood Copse

WESTHATCH CNR

WESTHATCH LA

RG42

CHURCH LA

MALT HILL

5

Wane Bridge

The Cut

72

Warfield Hall

Meadowbrook Montessori Sch

Scotlands Farm

OSBORNE LA

Warfield House

Hayley Green Farm

BRACKNELL RD

B3022

4

The Hooks

Home Farm

B3034

Darrah Farm

Newell Green

THE HERMITAGE CVN PK

TOOGOOD PL

OSBORNE LA

BINFIELD GDNS

Hayley Green

HAYLEY GR

HAYLEY GREEN LA CNR

3

FOREST RD

WEST END LA

West End

PH

PH

B3034 WARFIELD ST

NEWELL HALL

B3022

FOREST RD

B3034

71

Westend Farm

WATERSPLASH LA

Fairclough Farm

OLD PRIORY LA

BRACKNELL

HAMPSHIRE RISE

STAFFORDSHIRE CROFT

Park Farm

Ford

MARBULL WAY

THE SPA LA

Larks Hill

CHANCEL MANS

HARVEST RIDE

WARFIELD RDBT

Whitegrove

Superstore

Whitegrove

FOREST WAY

2

Long Copse

Kennel Lane Sch

CONEY GRANGE

NEWELL GN

WARFIELD GN

HEMMBRIDGE

CHIVES PL 1
MARY MEAD 2
JOSEPH CT 3
TERESA VALE 4
SWITHIN CHASE 5

COUNTY LANE RDBT

Liby

BERNADINE

1

HAMMOND CT 1
MOSTYN HO 2
MARSHAM HO 3
MULBERRY HO 4

FAIRWAY CT

B3018 BINFIELD RD

WARFIELD RD

A3095

RECN GD

CORN CROFT 1
BROADRICK HEATH 2
BIG BARN GR 3
ROUNDSHEAD DR 4

RG12

GLOUCESTERSHIRE LEA

70

86 **A** **B** **87** **C** **D** **88** **E** **F**

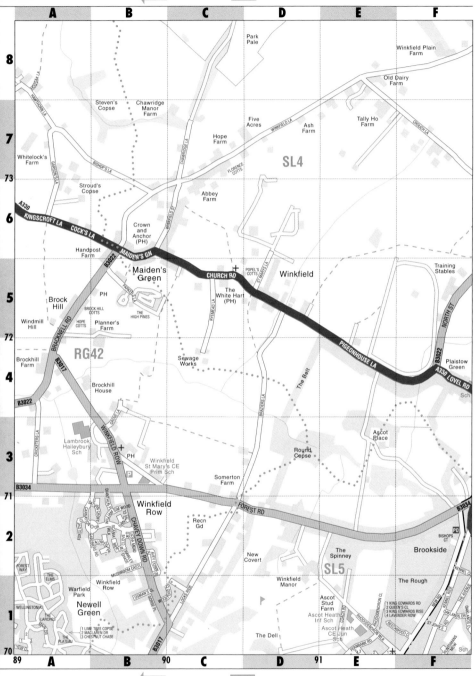

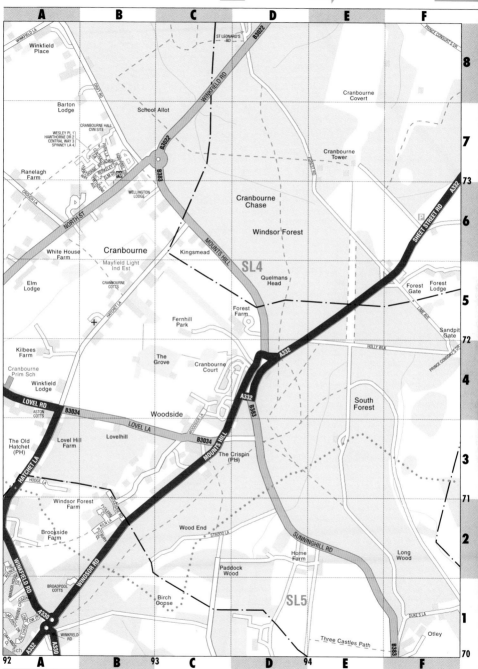

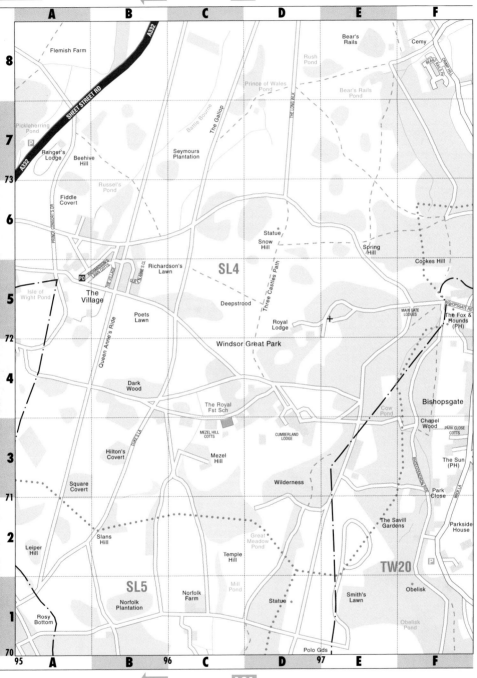

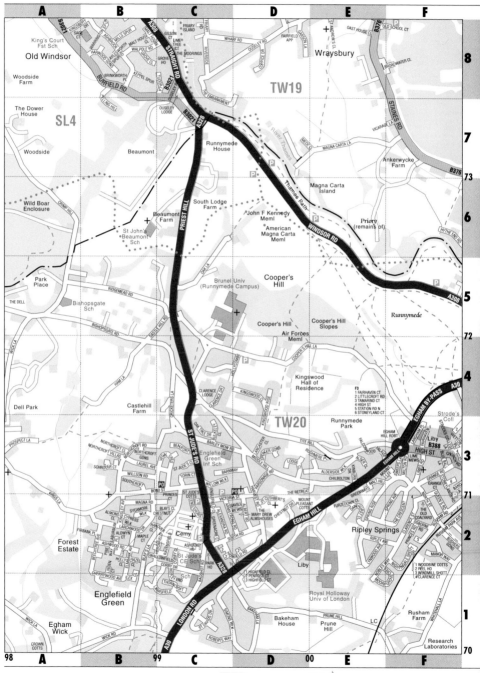

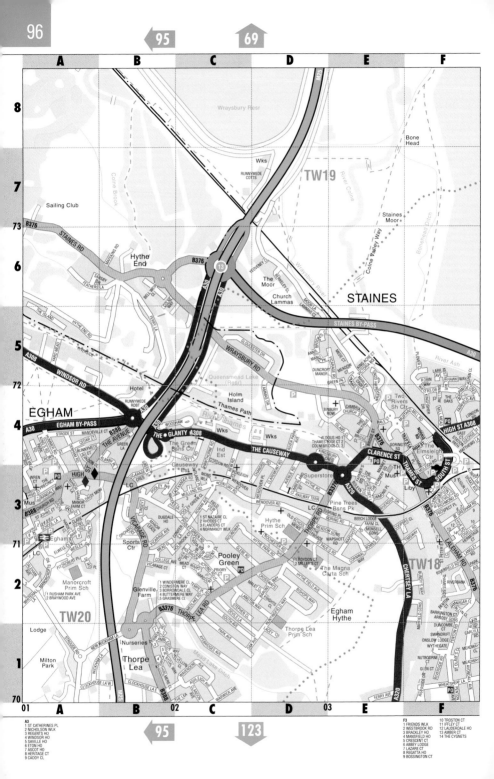

A3
1 ST CATHERINES PL
2 NICHOLSON WLK
3 REGENTS HO
4 WINDSOR HO
5 SAVILLE HO
6 ETON HO
7 ASCOT HO
8 HERITAGE CT
9 CADDY CL

F3
1 FRIENDS WLK
2 WESTBROOK RD
3 BRACKLEY WAY
4 MANSFIELD HO
5 CRESCENT CT
6 ABBEY LODGE
7 LAZARE CT
8 REGATTA HO
9 BOSSINGTON CT

10 TROSTON CT
11 IFFLEY CT
12 LAUDERDALE HO
13 AMBER CT
14 THE CYGNETS

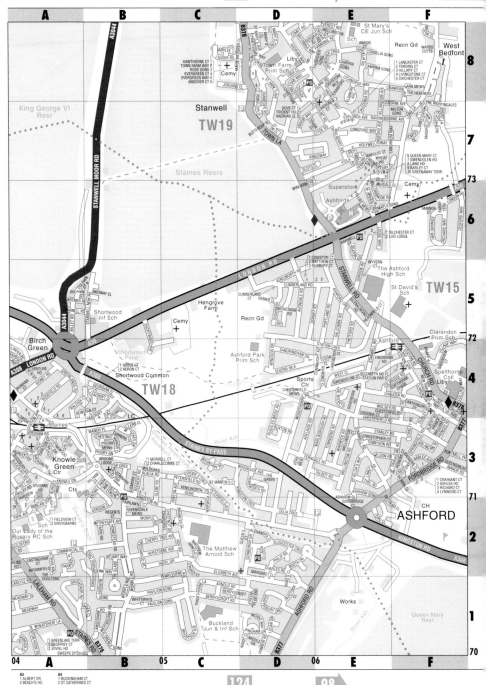

A3
1 ALBERT DR
2 BEACH'S HO
3 GRESHAM CT
4 FRIENDSHIP HO
5 PHOENIX PL
6 PULLMANS PL
7 GRANGE CT
8 THE BEECHES

A4
1 BUCKINGHAM CT
2 ST CATHERINES CT
3 DAVID CT
4 NORMAN CT
5 CLAYDON CT
6 MAYNARD CT
7 GREENLANDS CT
8 DORCHESTER CT
9 JUBILEE CT

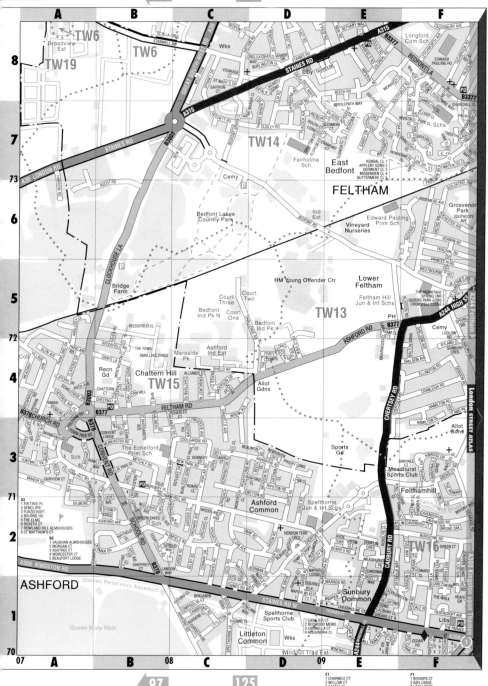

E1
1 CHARMILE CT
2 WILLOW CT
3 CASTLE CL
4 KILLIGREW HO
5 GRANTHAM HO
6 PRINCE ALBERT CT

F1
1 BISHOPS CT
2 ASH LODGE
3 LIME LODGE
4 OAK LODGE
5 ELM CT
6 WILLOW LODGE
7 SYCAMORE LODGE
8 PRISCILLA HO
9 Sunbury Cross Ctr

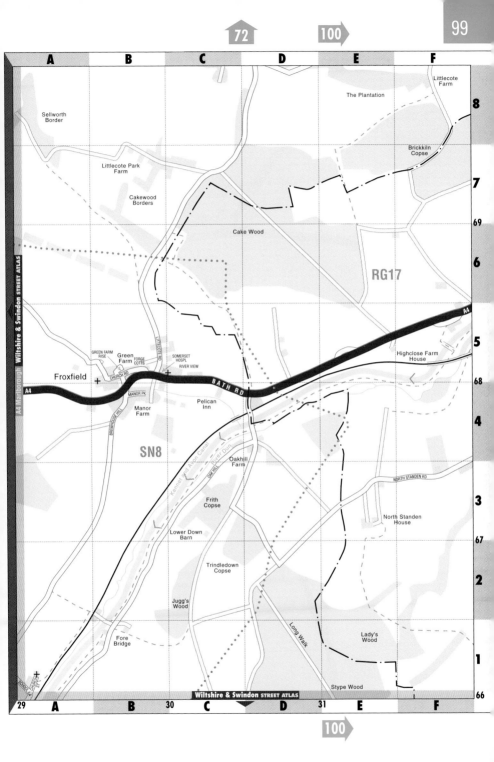

A B C D E F

8
Littlecote Farm
The Plantation
Sellworth Border
Brickkiln Copse
7
Littlecote Park Farm
Cakewood Borders
69
Cake Wood
6
RG17
A4
5
Green Farm Rise
Green Farm
Forge Cotts
Somerset Hospl
River View
Littlecote Rd
Highclose Farm House
Froxfield
68
Bath Rd
A4 Marlborough
A4
Manor Px
Pelican Inn
4
Manor Farm
Brewhouse Hill
SN8
North Standen Rd
Oakhill Farm
Kennet and Avon Canal
River Dun
Oakhill Rd
North Standen House
3
Frith Copse
67
Lower Down Barn
Trindledown Copse
2
Jugg's Wood
Long Walk
Lady's Wood
Fore Bridge
1
School Path
Church Path
Stype Wood
66
29
A B 30 C D 31 E F

Wiltshire & Swindon STREET ATLAS

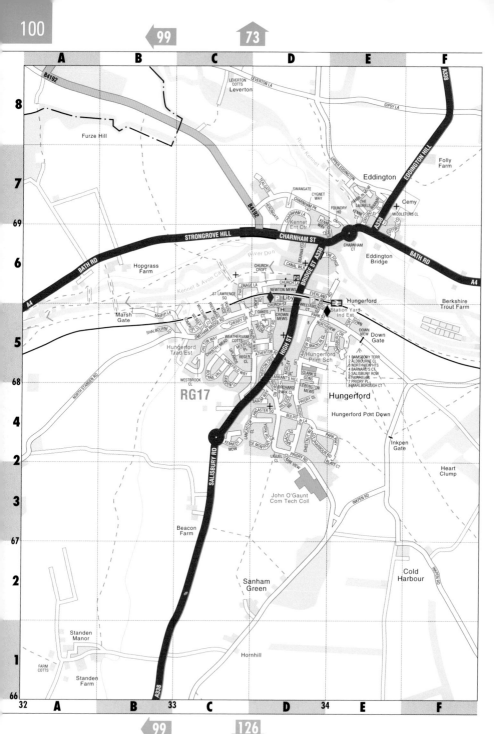

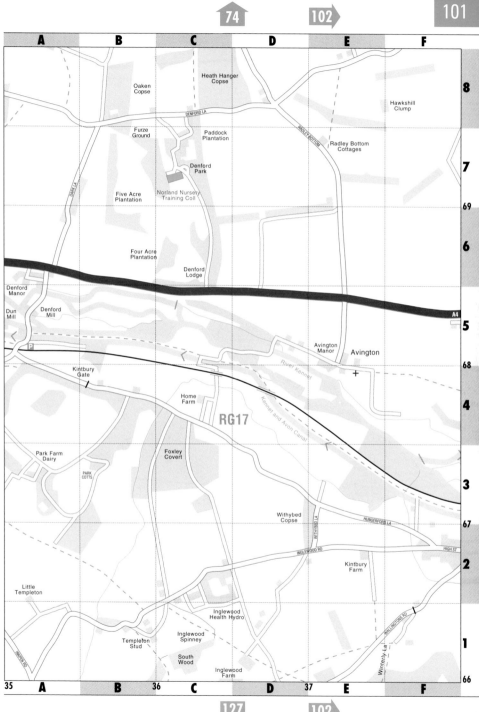

Oaken Copse

Heath Hanger Copse

Hawkshill Clump

DENFORD LA.

Furze Ground

Paddock Plantation

RADLEY BOTTOM

Radley Bottom Cottages

Denford Park

Norland Nursery Training Coll

Five Acre Plantation

PARK LA.

Four Acre Plantation

Denford Lodge

Denford Manor

Dun Mill

Denford Mill

P

A4

Avington Manor

Avington

Kintbury Gate

River Kennet

Home Farm

RG17

Kennet and Avon Canal

Park Farm Dairy

PARK COTTS

Foxley Covert

Withybed Copse

WITHYBED LA.

HUNGERFORD LA.

INGLEWOOD RD.

HIGH ST

Kintbury Farm

Little Templeton

Inglewood Health Hydro

Templeton Stud

Inglewood Spinney

South Wood

Inglewood Farm

Winterly La.

BALLINGTONE RD.

INKPEN RD.

8
7
69
6
5
68
4
3
67
2
1
66

A B 36 C D 37 E F
35

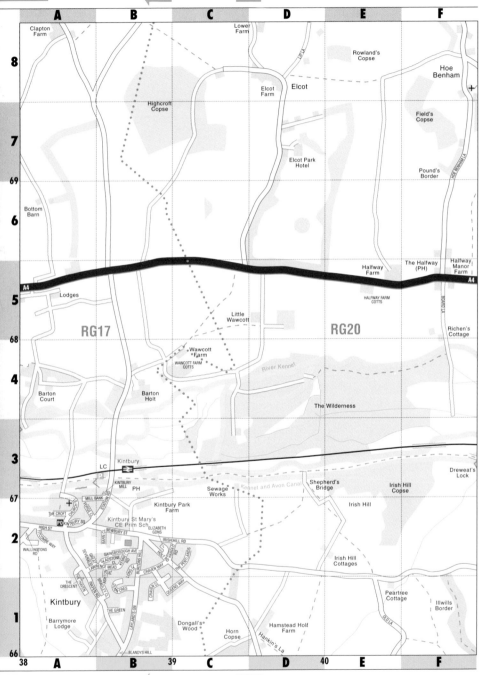

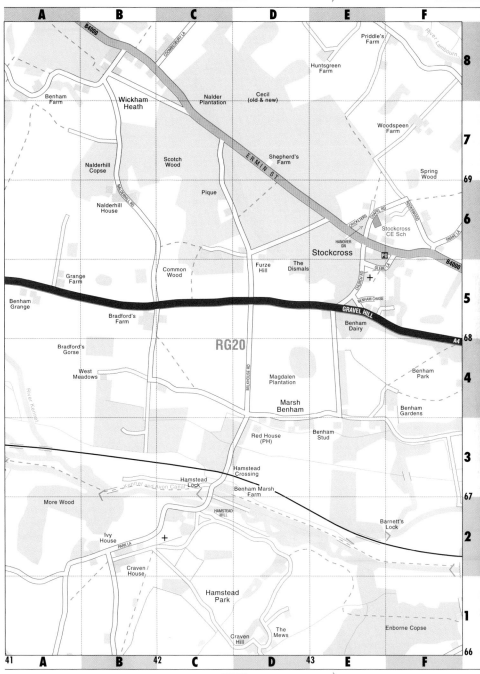

8

7

69

6

5

68

4

3

67

2

1

66

A B C D E F

Priddle's Farm

Huntsgreen Farm

River Lambourn

B4000

COOMBESBURY LA

Benham Farm

Wickham Heath

Nalder Plantation

Cecil (old & new)

Woodspeen Farm

Nalderhill Copse

Scotch Wood

Shepherd's Farm

ERMIN ST

Spring Wood

Nalderhill House

NALDERHILL RD

Pique

CAPEL RD

CRICKETERS

Stockcross CE Sch

BROCKSMEAD

SNAKE LA

Common Wood

Furze Hill

The Dismals

HANOVER GN

Stockcross

PO

B4000

CHURCH RD

GLEBE LA

BENHAM CHASE

Grange Farm

Benham Grange

Bradford's Farm

GRAVEL HILL

Benham Dairy

A4

Bradford's Gorse

RG20

West Meadows

Magdalen Plantation

Benham Park

Marsh Benham

Benham Gardens

Red House (PH)

Benham Stud

River Kennet

Hamstead Crossing

Kennet and Avon Canal

Hamstead Lock

Benham Marsh Farm

Barnett's Lock

More Wood

HAMSTEAD MILL

Ivy House

PARK LA

Craven / House

Hamstead Park

Enborne Copse

Craven Hill

The Mews

41 A B 42 C D 43 E F

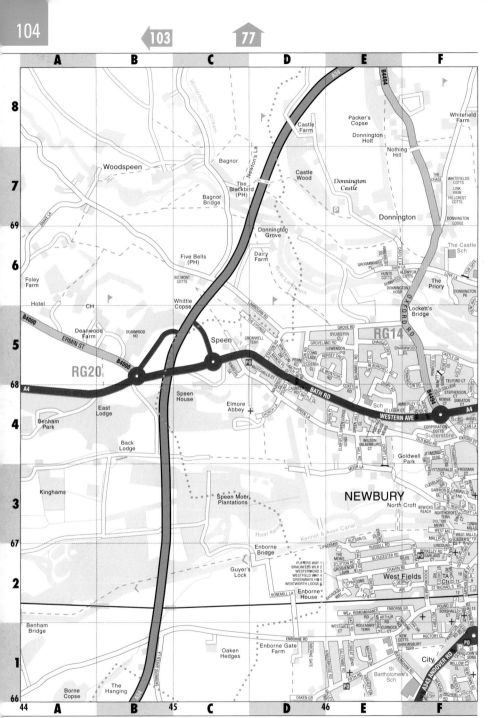

8

7

69

6

5

68

4

3

67

2

1

66

44 A B 45 C D 46 E F

Woodspeen

Bagnor

The Blackbird (PH)

Bagnor Bridge

Five Bells (PH)

BELMONT COTTS

Whittle Copse

Foley Farm

Hotel

CH

Deanwood Farm

DEANWOOD HO

Speen

Cromwell Terr

RG20

B4000

ERMIN ST

B4000

A4

East Lodge

Benham Park

Back Lodge

Kinghams

Speen House

Elmore Abbey

Speen Moor Plantations

North Croft

Enborne Bridge

Guyer's Lock

Enborne House

Benham Bridge

Enborne Gate Farm

Oaken Hedges

Borne Copse

The Hanging

Castle Farm

Packer's Copse

Donnington Holt

Nothing Hill

Whitefield Farm

Castle Wood

Donnington Castle

THE CHASE

WHITEFIELDS COTTS

LINK VIEW

HILLCREST COTTS

Donnington

DONNINGTON LODGE

Donnington Grove

Dairy Farm

River Lambourn

The Castle Sch

GROOMBRIDGE PL

HUNTS COTTS

DONNINGTON HOSP

ALDWYCH COTTS

LOVE LA

The Priory

DONNINGTON PK

RG14

Lockett's Bridge

OXFORD RD

NEWBURY

RG14

GROVE RD

SYLVESTER RD

LEWENDON RD

GROVELAND RD

CHAUC...

CHARMWOOD

BATH RD

WESTERN AVE

A4

Goldwell Park

B4494

Superstore

Kennet & Avon Canal

River Kennet

West Fields

City...

A343 ANDOVER RD

St Bartholomew's Sch

ENBORNE RD

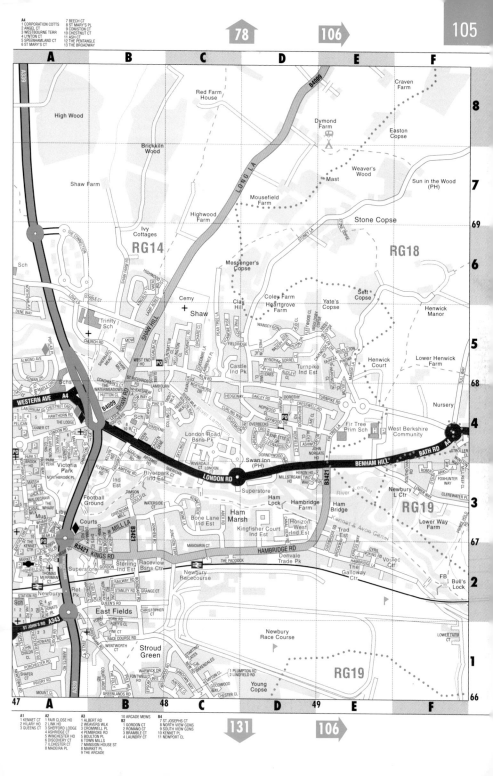

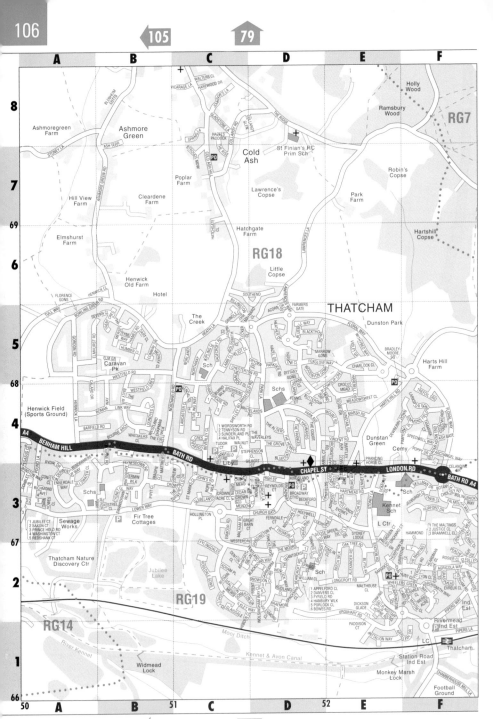

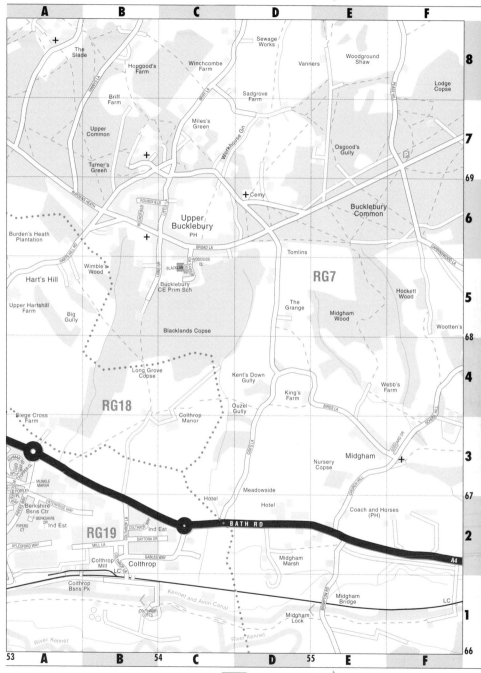

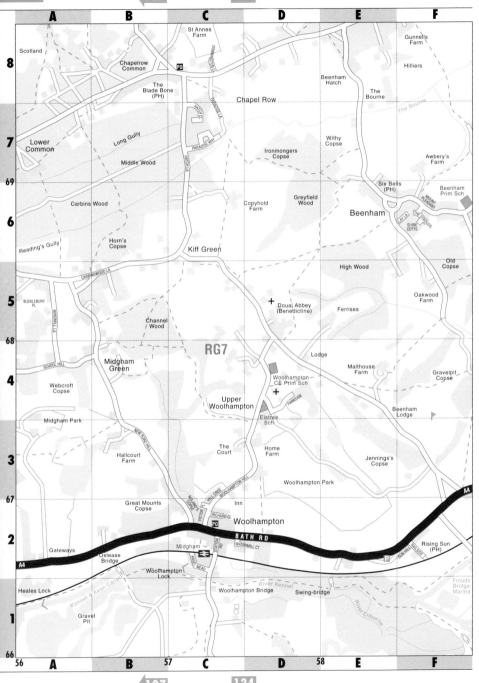

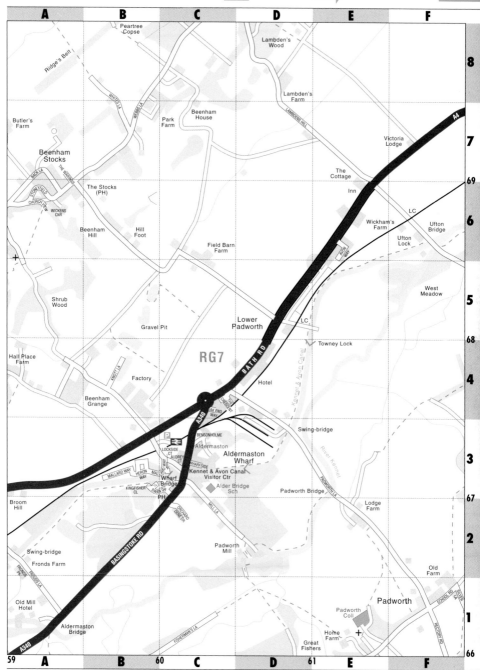

82
110
135
110

A B C D E F

8
7
69
6
5
68
4
3
67
2
1
66

Peartree Copse
Lambden's Wood
Lambden's Farm
LAMBDENS HILL
Victoria Lodge
A4
Ridge's Belt
WHITE LA
WEBB LA
Park Farm
Beenham House
The Cottage
Inn
LC
Butler's Farm
Beenham Stocks
BACK LA
THE WILDERNESS
The Stocks (PH)
Wickham's Farm
Ufton Bridge
STOKE HILL
CHURCH LA
WICKENS CNR
Beenham Hill
Hill Foot
Field Barn Farm
Ufton Lock
West Meadow
Shrub Wood
Gravel Pit
Lower Padworth
LC
RG7
Towney Lock
Kennet & Avon Canal
Hall Place Farm
KNOTT LA
Factory
BATH RD
Hotel
Swing-bridge
River Kennet
Beenham Grange
OAK END WAY
CRESCENT
A340
Benson Holme
Aldermaston
Aldermaston Wharf
PONDS LA
Lodge Farm
P
LOCKSIDE CT
AUDREY
WHARF
WAY
MALLARD WAY
HERON WAY
SWAN DR
MALL
WHARFSIDE
Kennet & Avon Canal Visitor Ctr
Padworth Bridge
Broom Hill
KINGFISHER CL
Wharf Bridge
PH
Alder Bridge Sch
Old Farm
ORCHARD DENE DR
MILL LA
Padworth
Swing-bridge
Fronds Farm
Padworth Mill
Padworth Coll
SCHOOL RD
Old Mill Hotel
BASINGSTOKE RD
FISHERMAN'S LA
Home Farm
RECTORY RD
A340
Aldermaston Bridge
Great Fishers

59 60 C 60 D 61 E 61 F

A340

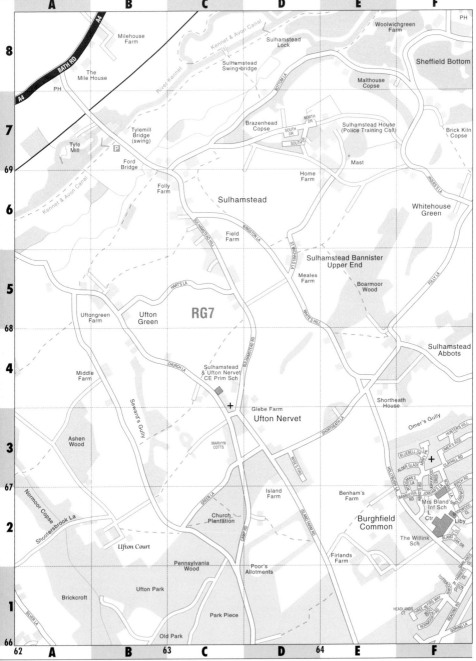

109
83

A **B** **C** **D** **E** **F**

8

Milehouse Farm

Woolwichgreen Farm

PH

Sulhamstead Lock

Kennet & Avon Canal

Sheffield Bottom

BATH RD

A4

The Mile House

PH

River Kennet

Sulhamstead Swing-bridge

WITHEM LA

Malthouse Copse

7

Tylemill Bridge (swing)

Brazenhead Copse

NORTH DR

SOUTH DR

Sulhamstead House (Police Training Coll)

Brick Kiln Copse

Tyle Mill

P

SOUTH

MOSS LA

69

Ford Bridge

Mast

Folly Farm

Kennet & Avon Canal

Home Farm

Whitehouse Green

6

Sulhamstead

SULHAMSTEAD HILL

KINGSTON LA

Field Farm

ST MICHAEL'S LA

Sulhamstead Bannister Upper End

Meales Farm

Boarmoor Wood

FOLLY LA

5

HART'S LA

WHITE'S HILL

Uttongreen Farm

Ufton Green

RG7

SULHAMSTEAD HILL

Sulhamstead Abbots

68

4

CHURCH LA

Middle Farm

Sulhamstead & Ufton Nervet CE Prim Sch

Shortheath House

Seward's Gully

Glebe Farm

+

Ufton Nervet

Ashen Wood

SHORTHEATH LA

Omer's Gully

HUNTER'S HILL

3

MARVYN COTTS

OMER'S RISE

BLUEBELL CL

ALDER GLADE

CLAYHILL RD

+

BEACH LA

67

Normoor Copse

WISS'S HILL

GREEN LA

Benham's Farm

HOLLYBUSH LA

MAN'S LA

BANNISTER RD

JOHNSON'S

BIRCH RD

Mrs Bland's Inf Sch

Shootersbrook La

Island Farm

CAMP RD

Burghfield Common

L Ctr

Liby

2

Ufton Court

Church Plantation

ISLAND FARM RD

The Willink Sch

BLAND'S

OAK DR

Pennsylvania Wood

Poor's Allotments

Firlands Farm

Brickcroft

Ufton Park

HEADLANDS CT

THREE FIRS WAY

RECHAMPTON

REDHATCH DR

BEECHES RD

1

BURGH LA

Park Piece

GORING LA

TOTTERS LA

Old Park

66

62

A **B** 63 **C** **D** 64 **E** **F**

109
136

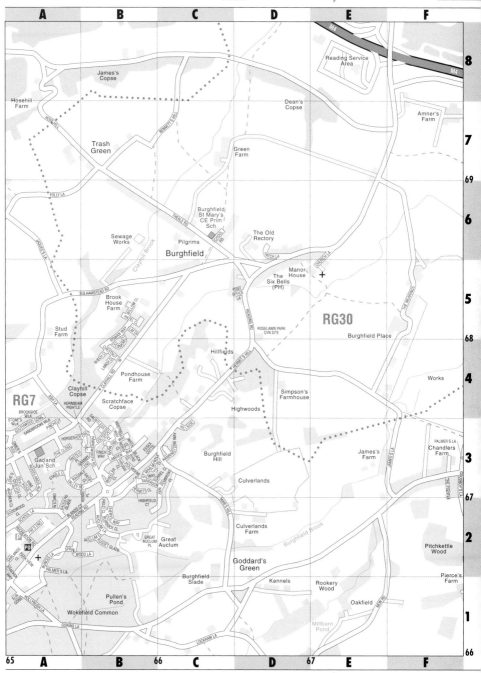

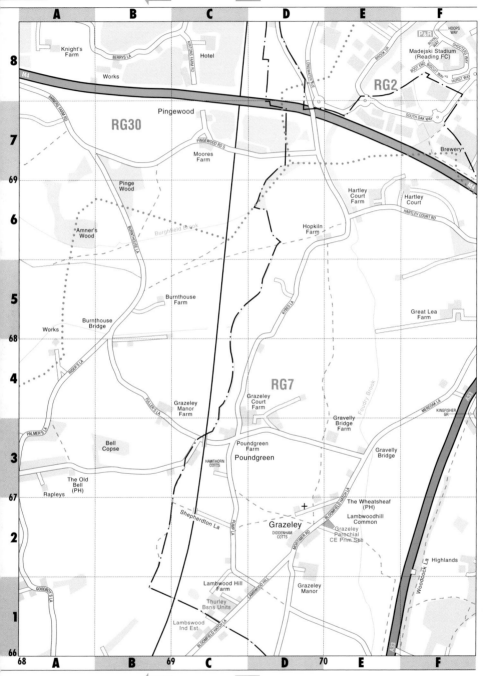

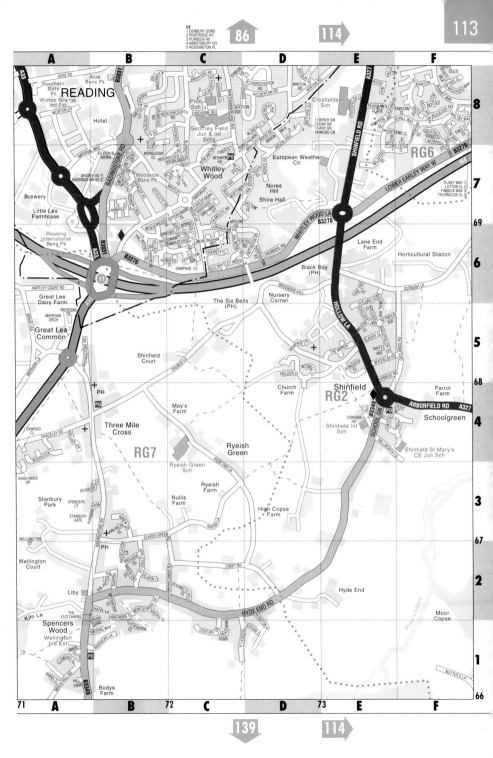

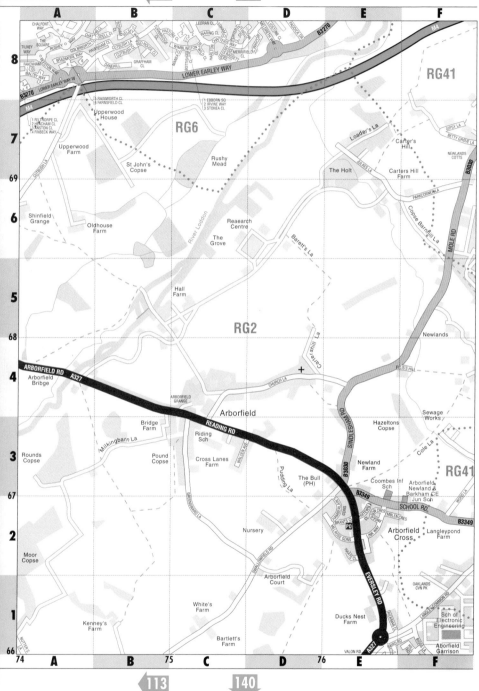

A B C D E F

8

7

69

6

5

68

4

3

67

2

1

66

RG41

RG6

RG2

RG41

M4

LOWER EARLEY WAY

B3270

B3030

MOLE RD

B3270

M4

1 FELTHORPE CL
2 HENCHAM CL
3 ANSTON CL
4 FINBECK WAY

1 RAINWORTH CL
2 FARNSFIELD CL

1 EBBORN SQ
2 IRVINE WAY
3 STONEA CL

Chalfont Way
The Square
Tilney Way
Fakenham Way
Maltby Way

Bradmore Way

Rushey Cl
Oldmarth

Chatteris

Odell Cl

Selcroft

Pamfram Cl

Cutbush La

Red House Cl

Grafham Cl

Damehill

Ledran Cl

Waring Av

Whimlington

Haslett

Embers

Paddock Rd

Hasting Cl

Merrifield

Hartlon

Markenfield

Upperwood House

Upperwood Farm

St John's Copse

Rushy Mead

Shinfield Grange

Oldhouse Farm

River Loddon

Reaearch Centre

The Grove

Barett's La

Loader's La

Carter's Hill

The Holt

Sulke's La

Carters Hill Farm

Newlands Cotts

Gipsy La

Betty Grove La

B3030

Parkcorner La

Copse Barn Hill La

Hall Farm

Carter's Hill La

Newlands

Ellis's Hill

ARBORFIELD RD
A327

Arborfield Bribge

Arborfield Grange

Arborfield

READING RD

Sindlesham Rd

Church La

Sewage Works

Hazeltons Copse

Cole La

Bridge Farm

Milkingbarn La

Riding Sch

Pound Copse

Cross Lanes Farm

Pudding La

Greenwaard La

Walter's Av

The Bull (PH)

B3030

Newland Farm

Coombes Inf Sch

Arborfield Newland & Barkham CE Jun Sch

RG41

Rounds Copse

Nursery

B3349

School Rd

B3349

Langleypond Farm

Moor Copse

Small Shield Rd

Arborfield Court

White's Farm

Arborfield Cross

Eversley Rd

PO

Oaklands Cvn Pk

Kenney's Farm

Bartlett's Farm

Ducks Nest Farm

Valon Rd

A327

Langley Common Rd

Baird Rd

Sch of Electronic Engineering

Aborfield Garrison

Nutters

74 75 76

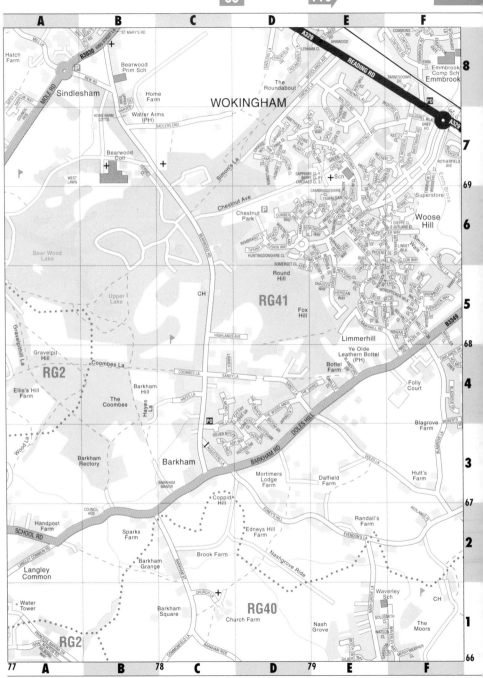

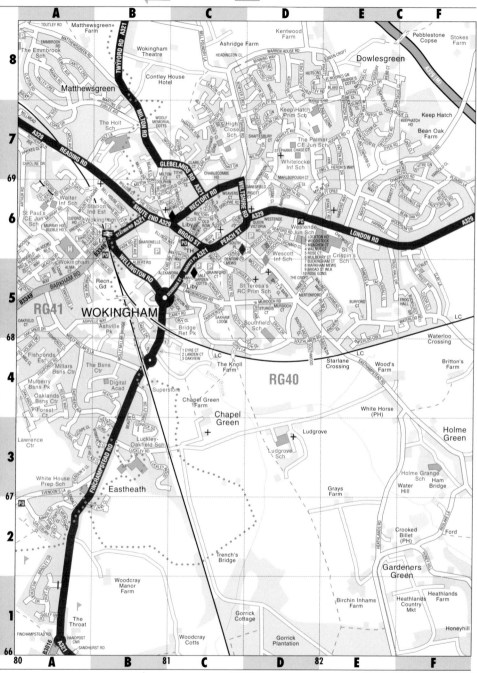

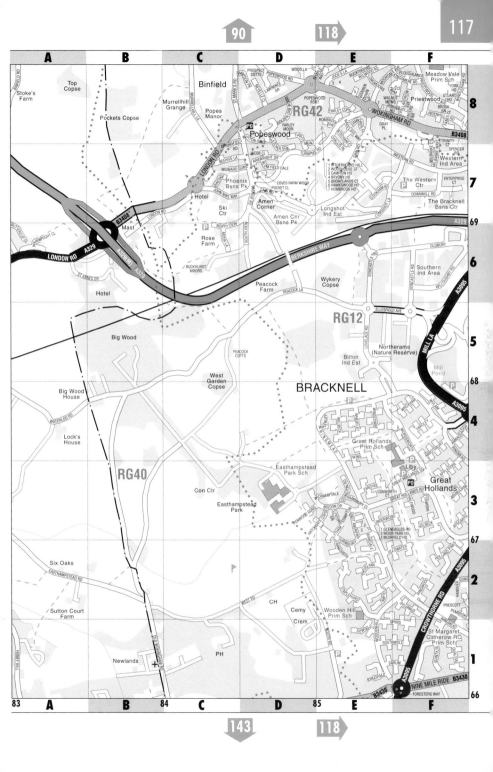

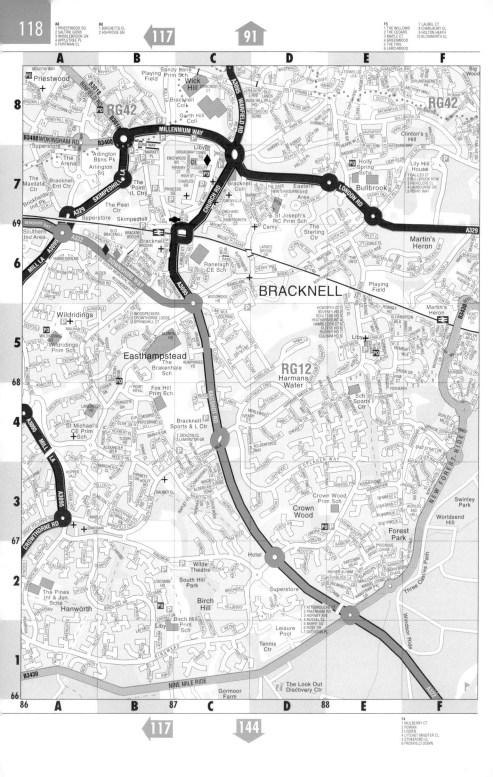

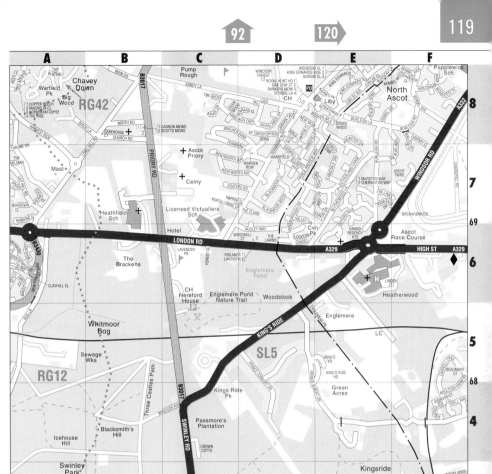

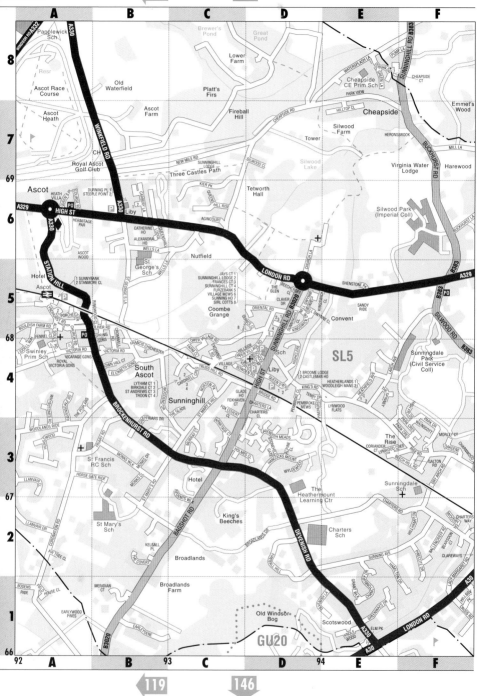

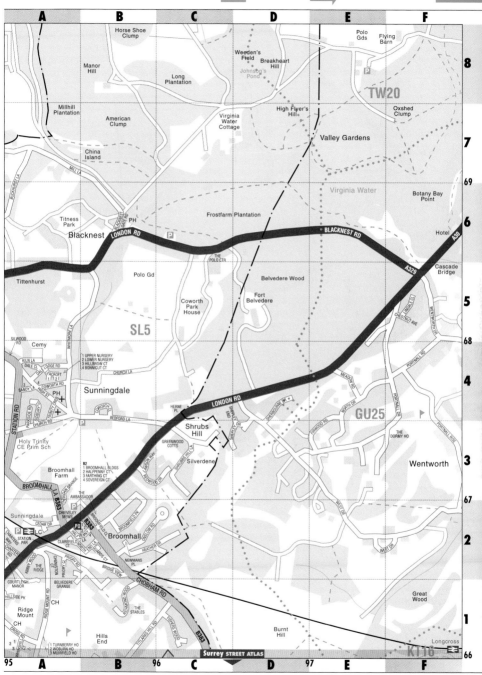

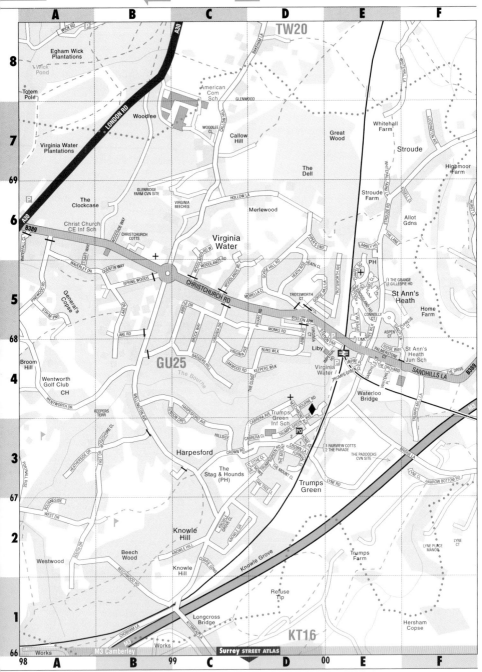

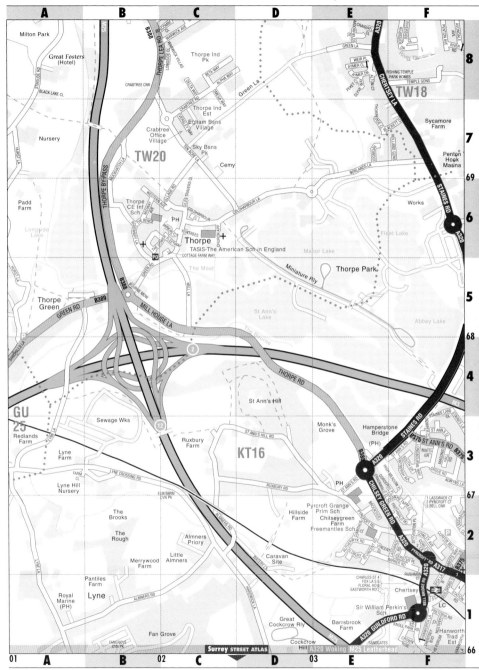

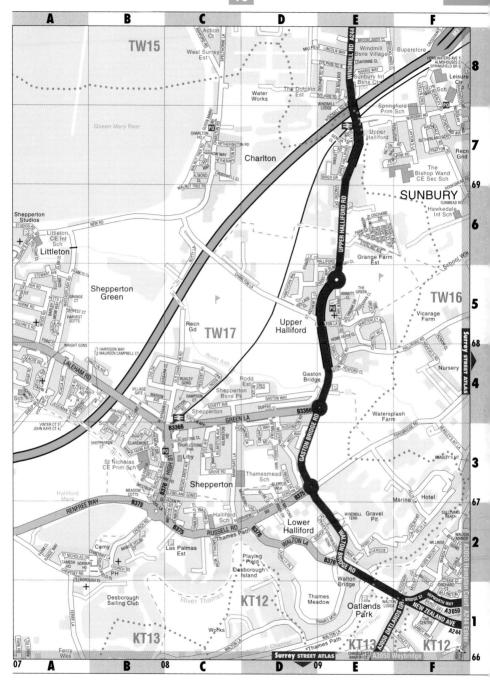

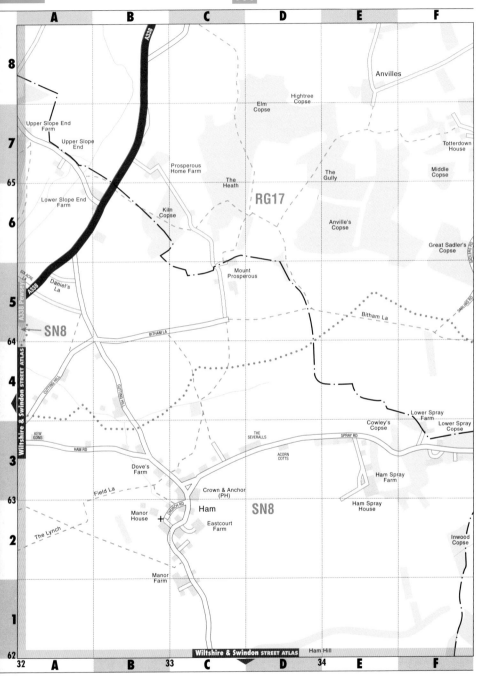

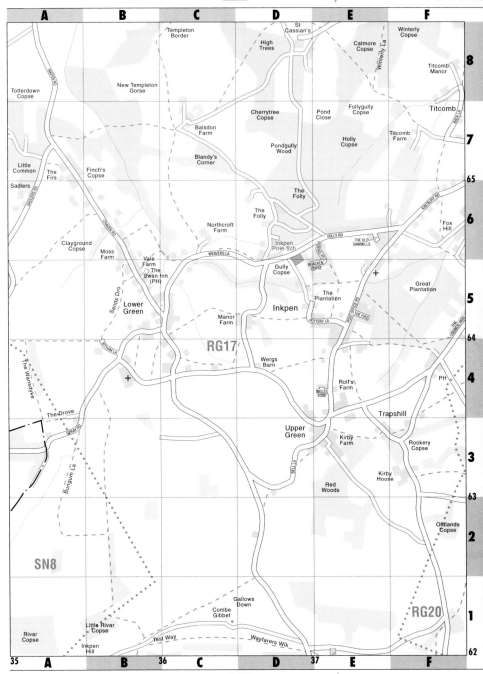

101
128

A B C D E F

Titcomb
Manor

Winterly
Copse

St
Cassian's

Templeton
Border

8

High
Trees

Catmore
Copse

Winterly La

New Templeton
Gorse

Titcomb

Totterdown
Copse

Cherrytree
Copse

Pond
Close

Follygully
Copse

Titcomb
Farm

7

Balsdon
Farm

Pondgully
Wood

Holly
Copse

BACK LA

Little
Common

Blandy's
Corner

65

The Firs

Finch's
Copse

The
Folly

Fox
Hill

Sadlers

CRAVEN RD

KINTBURY RD

6

Clayground
Copse

Northcroft
Farm

The
Folly

The Folly

Inkpen
Prim Sch

FOLLY RD

THE OLD
SAWMILLS

Moss
Farm

WEAVERS LA

ROBINS HILL

BRACKEN
COPSE

Vale
Farm
The
Swan Inn
(PH)

Gully
Copse

+

Great
Plantation

5

Sands Dro

Lower
Green

The
Plantation

Inkpen

POST OFFICE RD

THE FIRS

THE COMMON KIDS

Manor
Farm

Wergs
Barn

POTTERY LA

RG17

64

BITHAM LA

+

4

The Wansdyke

INGLES
EDGE

Rolf's
Farm

PH

Trapshill

The Drove

SPRAY RD

Upper
Green

Kirby
Farm

Rookery
Copse

3

Bungum La

BELL LA

Kirby
House

63

Red
Woods

Oldlands
Copse

2

SN8

RG20

Gallows
Down

Combe
Gibbet

1

Rivar
Copse

Little Rivar
Copse

Test Way

Wayfarers Wlk

Inkpen
Hill

P

62

35 A 36 B C 37 D E F

147
128

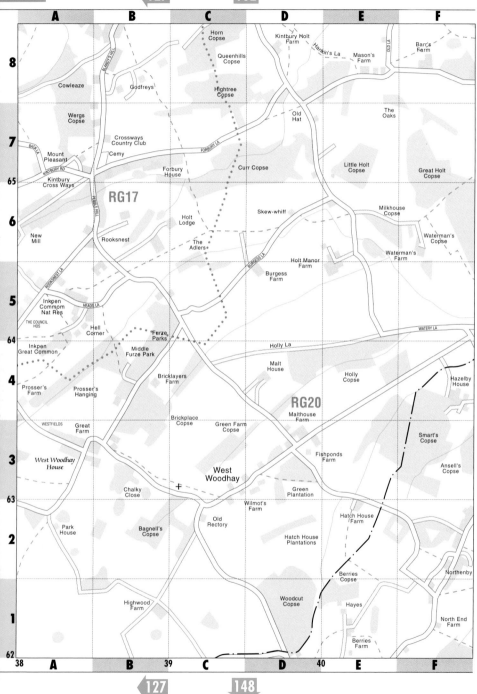

127
102

A   B   C   D   E   F

8

Cowleaze

Godfreys

Horn Copse

Queenhills Copse

Hightree Copse

Kintbury Holt Farm

Hankin's La

Mason's Farm

Barr's Farm

OLD LA

7

Wergs Copse

Crossways Country Club

Cemy

FORBURY LA

Old Hat

The Oaks

Mount Pleasant

KINTBURY RD

Forbury House

Curr Copse

Little Holt Copse

Great Holt Copse

65

Kintbury Cross Ways

BACK LA

FROXIL HILL

RG17

6

New Mill

Rooksnest

Holt Lodge

The Adlers

Skew-whiff

Milkhouse Copse

Waterman's Copse

Holt Manor Farm

Waterman's Farm

BURGESS LA

5

Inkpen Commom Nat Res

ROOKSNEST LA

HEADS LA

THE COUNCIL HOS

Hell Corner

Ferze Parks

Burgess Farm

WATERY LA

64

Inkpen Great Common

Middle Furze Park

Holly La

Malt House

Holly Copse

Hazelby House

4

Prosser's Farm

Prosser's Hanging

Bricklayers Farm

RG20

Malthouse Farm

Smart's Copse

WESTFIELDS

Great Farm

Brickplace Copse

Green Farm Copse

Ansell's Copse

3

West Woodhay House

West Woodhay

Fishponds Farm

63

Chalky Close

Green Plantation

Hatch House Farm

2

Park House

Bagnell's Copse

Old Rectory

Wilmot's Farm

Hatch House Plantations

Berries Copse

Northenby

1

Highwood Farm

Woodcut Copse

Hayes

North End Farm

Berries Farm

62

38   A   B   39   C   D   40   E   F

127
148

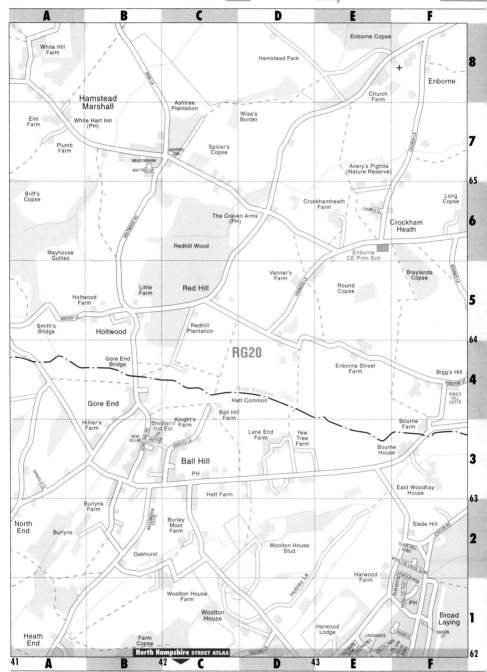

A **B** **C** **D** **E** **F**

RG20

8

Skinners
Green
Farm

Skinners
Green

NEWBURY

John Rankin
Jun & Inf
Schs

BARTLEMY CT
BARTLEMY D
MONTGOMERY
THE GATES

MEADOW RD
CROFT RD

ROEBUTS CL
THREE ACRE RD
CULVER RD
CHANDOS RD

WEST
CEDAR
MOUNT

7

Round Hill

COPE HALL LA

Oaken
Copse

FAIRVIEW

HIGHLANDS

WASHBURY
HO
ORLANDS

TYDEHAMS

WEATHER GDNS

MONK'S LA

ROBINS CL
BYRON CL
RUPERT RD

CHARTER
RD

Crook's
Copse

65

Foxgrove

Wash
Common
Farm

WILMOT WLK 1
GOODWIN WLK 2
VILLIERS WLK 3
NORTON CL 4

Wr Twr

ESSEX ST

CARY CL

PO

STUART RD

Falkland Meml

RG14

Newbury
RUFC

Slockett's
Copse

6

Wheatlands
Farm

WHEATLANDS LA

STUART CL
THOMPSON
JOHN
BOYS
HO

MELDON
BATTERY END
Falkland
Prim Sch

SPENCER RD

ANDOVER RD

Park House
Sch &
Sports Coll

Redding's
Copse

Redding's
Copse

ENBORNE LODGE LA
KINGS
MEAD

GILROY
BELL
GROVE

CLARE AVE
MANDELL
DRAPERS
HILL
PHOENIX
WLK

ST GABRIELS

ORLANDS

ROUND END
HENDRICK RD

WARREN RD

Warren
Lodge

Wash
Common

Gorse Covert

5

Boame's
Farm

BOAME'S LA

GRANGE
GDNS

NORMAY RISE
WILLOWMEAD CL
THE GRANGE

CHILTERN
CRESC

THE HOLLIES

COWELL

BADSWORTH
GDNS

64

ENBORNE ST

BELL HILL

CONIFER CREST
BADGERS RIDGE
SMALLRIDGE

SANDPIT HILL

River Enborne

Oakleaze
Farm

4

Bunker's Hill

ANDOVER DRO

Enborne
Row

Wash Water
House

The
Woodpecker
(PH)

SPRING GDNS

Wash Water

WASH WATER

Wash Water

3

STATION RD

Common
Farm

Riding
Centre

PICKWOOD RD

Falkland
Farm

Horris Hill
Sch

B4640

63

Poultry
Farm

RG20

Woodedge
Farm

Horris Hill

2

The Chase
(National Trust)

Sewage
Works

Wheatlands
Farm

SHEEPWASH LA

WOODBINE

BEENHAM LA

WOODBINE RD

1

A343

Great Pen Wood

P

Brown Hill
Plantation

Deadman's
Bottom

Tot Hill
Tot Hill
Farm

Woodbine
Farm

62

A343 Andover

North Hampshire STREET ATLAS

A34 Winchester

B4640

44 **A** **B** 45 **C** **D** 46 **E** **F**

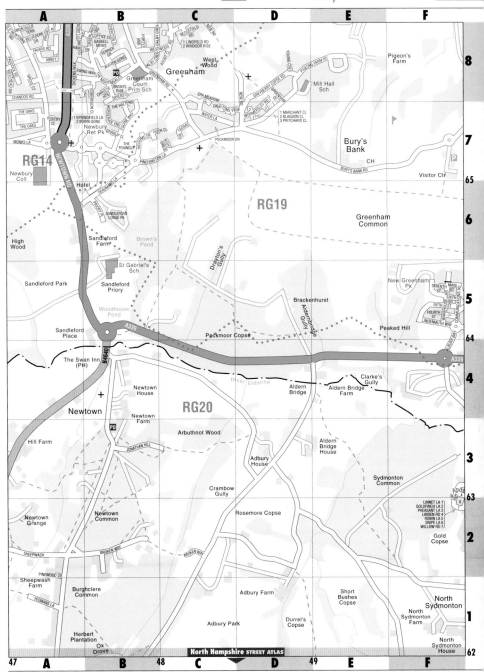

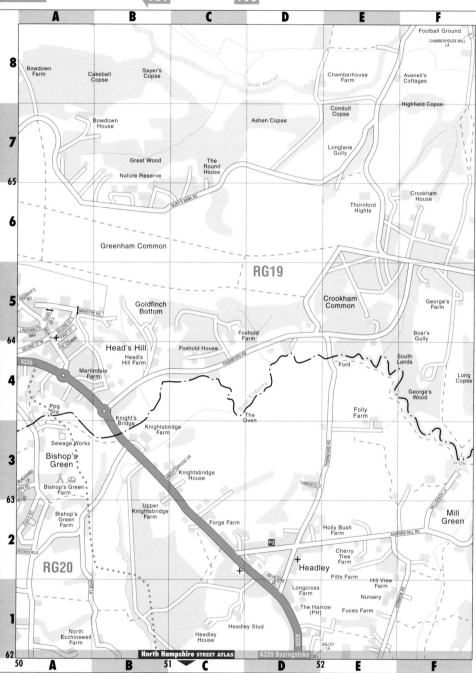

North Hampshire STREET ATLAS

A339 Basingstoke

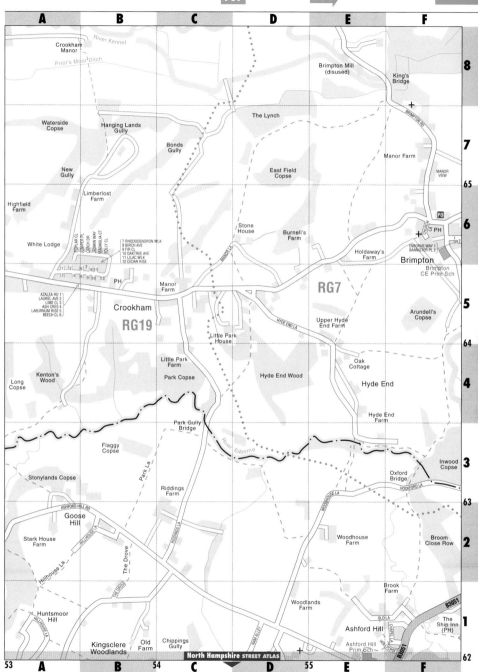

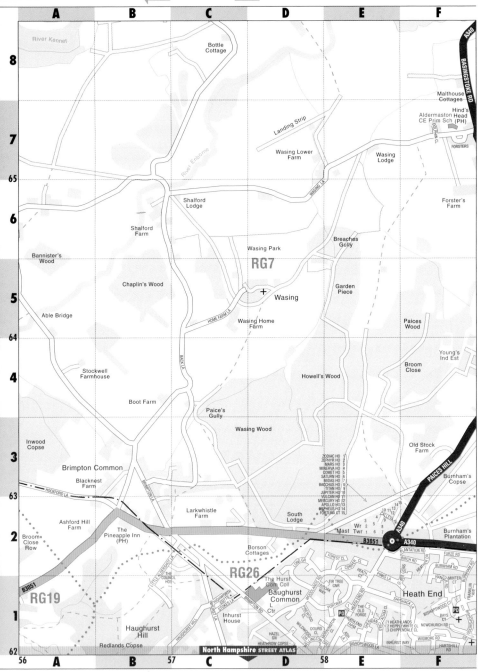

River Kennet

Bottle Cottage

Landing Strip

Malthouse Cottages

Hind's Aldermaston Head CE Prim Sch (PH)

POLPHIN CL

FORSTERS

Wasing Lower Farm

Wasing Lodge

River Enborne

Shalford Lodge

Forster's Farm

Shalford Farm

Wasing Park

Breaches Gully

RG7

Chaplin's Wood

Wasing

Garden Piece

Bannister's Wood

Able Bridge

HOME FARM LA

Wasing Home Farm

Paices Wood

Stockwell Farmhouse

BACK LA

Howell's Wood

Broom Close

Young's Ind Est

Boot Farm

Paice's Gully

Wasing Wood

Inwood Copse

Old Stock Farm

PAICES HILL

Brimpton Common

Blacknest Farm

Burnham's Copse

HOCKFORD LA

BRIMPTON LA

Larkwhistle Farm

South Lodge

ZODIAC HO 1
ZEPHYR HO 2
MARS HO 3
MINERVA HO 4
COMET HO 5
SATURN HO 6
MIDAS HO 7
BACCHUS HO 8
TITAN HO 9
JUPITER HO 10
MERCURY HO 11
APOLLO HO 13
ORPHEUS HO 14
FORTUNA CT 15

Ashford Hill Farm

The Pineapple Inn (PH)

Broom Close Row

Mast Twr

B3051

A340

Burnham's Plantation

B3051

RG19

LITTLE LIVERPOOL LA

THE COUNCIL HOS

Borson Cottages

RG26

The Hurst Com Coll

Baughurst Common L Ctr

FOREST CL

PLANTATION RD

BIRCH CL

MEMBERS CT

FURZE RD

BURNHAM RD

Heath End

HIGHWORTH COT
STORES LA

HAUGHURST HILL

BRIMPTON RD

INHURST LA

Inhurst House

FIR TREE CNR

FORTUNE

WOLVERTON RD

HEATH CL

PINKS LA

CONDOR CL

THE OLD FORGE

RHYSHACK LA

BISHOPSWOOD CT

BAYS CT

PO

NEWCHURCH RD

Haughurst Hill

DOURO CL

HAZEL GN

WELDON RD

HEATHROW COPSE

BISHOPS WOOD LA

WIGMORE CT

INHURST WAY

HARTSHILL CT

1 HEATHLANDS
2 HEPPLEWHITE CL
3 CHIPPENDALE CL

Redlands Copse

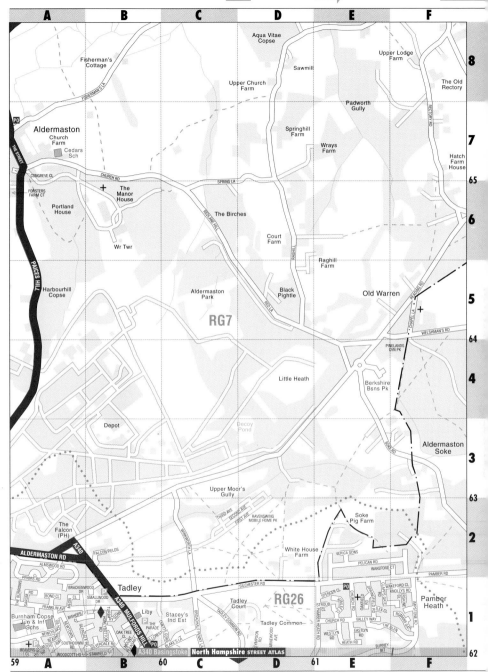

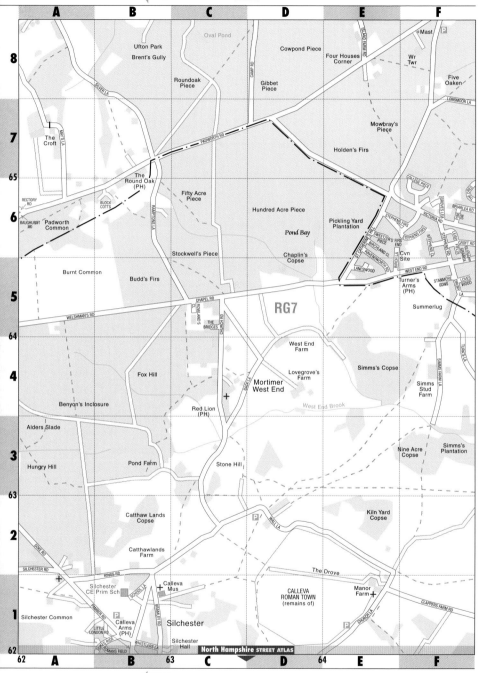

A B C D E F

8

Ufton Park
Brent's Gully

Oval Pond

Cowpond Piece

Four Houses
Corner

Mast

Wr
Twr

Five
Oaken

Roundoak
Piece

Gibbet
Piece

Mowbray's
Piece

LONGMOOR LA

7

The
Croft

PADWORTH RD

Holden's Firs

COLLEGE PIECE

65

The
Round Oak
(PH)

Fifty Acre
Piece

BRIARLEA RD

6

RECTORY
RD

BLOCK
COTTS

Hundred Acre Piece

Pickling Yard
Plantation

STEPHENS FIRS

VICTORIA RD

CROFT RD

BAUGHURST
RD

Padworth
Common

RAMPTONS LA

Pond Bay

SWELTER'S
PIECE

BIRCHLAND CL

STEPHENS FIRS

ST CATHERINE'S

Chaplin's
Copse

RAVENSWORTH LA

Cvn
Site

5

Burnt Common

Budd's Firs

CHAPEL RD

LANESWOOD

WEST END RD

Turner's
Arms
(PH)

STANMORE
GDNS

LOVES
WOOD

WELSHMAN'S RD

ROWLAND'S
CL

THE
BRIDGES

CHURCH RD

RG7

Summerlug

64

West End
Farm

SIMMS FARM LA

4

Fox Hill

BACK LA

Lovegrove's
Farm

Mortimer
West End

West End Brook

Simms's Copse

TURK'S LA

Simms
Stud
Farm

Benyon's Inclosure

Red Lion
(PH)

Alders Slade

Nine Acre
Copse

Simms's
Plantation

3

Hungry Hill

Pond Farm

Stone Hill

63

Catthaw Lands
Copse

WALL LA

Kiln Yard
Copse

2

Catthawlands
Farm

The Drove

SOKE RD

SILCHESTER RD

KINGS RD

SCHOOL LA

Calleva
Mus

CALLEVA
ROMAN TOWN
(remains of)

Manor
Farm

CLAPPERS FARM RD

1

Silchester Common

PAMBER RD

LITTLE
LONDON RD

Calleva
Arms (PH)

BRAMLEY RD

Silchester

CHURCH LA

Silchester
CE Prim Sch

62

SOKE RIDE

ROMANS FIELD

WHISTLERS LA

Silchester
Hall

62 A B 63 C D 64 E F

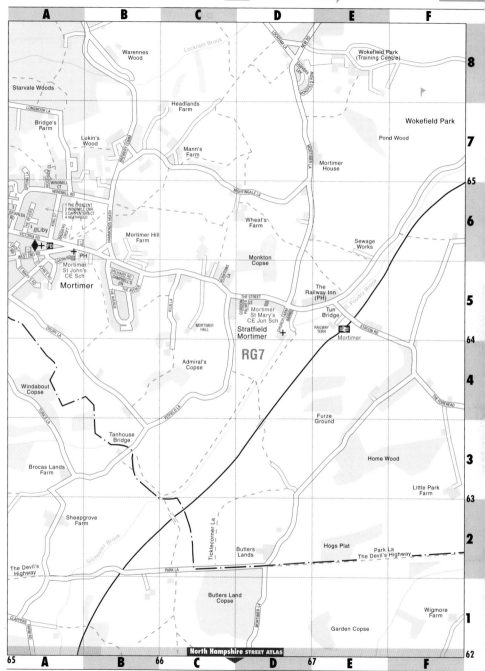

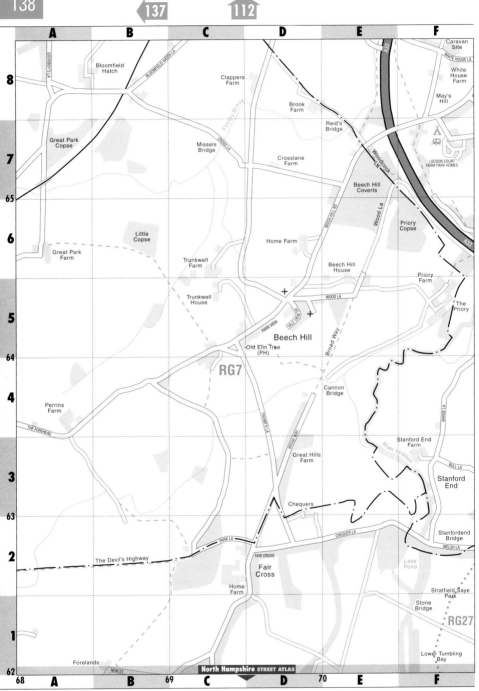

A B C D E F

8

Caravan Site
WHITE HOUSE LA
White House Farm
May's Hill

Bloomfield Hatch
BLOOMFIELD HATCH LA

Clappers Farm

Brook Farm

Reid's Bridge

Great Park Copse

Missels Bridge

Crosslane Farm

Beech Hill Coverts

LODDON COURT FARM PARK HOMES

Woodcock LB

7

65

Little Copse

Home Farm

Priory Copse

A 33

6

Great Park Farm

Trunkwell Farm

Beech Hill House

Priory Farm

Wood La

The Priory

Trunkwell House

WOOD LA

5

64

PARK VIEW

Beech Hill

Old Elm Tree (PH)

Broad Way

RG7

Cannon Bridge

Perrins Farm

THE FOREHEAD

Stanford End Farm

BARGE LA

4

BRILL LA

Stanford End

River Loddon

THORPE LA

BIGG WAY

Great Hills Farm

3

63

Chequers

Stanfordend Bridge

CHEQUER LA

WELSH LA

PARK LA

FAIR CROSS

Lake Pond

2

The Devil's Highway

Fair Cross

Home Farm

Stratfield Saye Park

Stone Bridge

RG27

1

Forelands

Lower Tumbling Bay

62

NEW ST

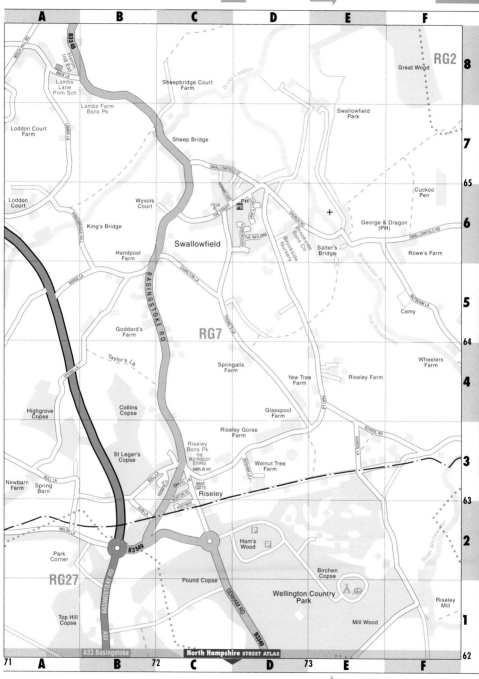

A B C D E F

8
7
65
6
5
64
4
3
63
2
1
62

RG2

Great Wood

Swallowfield
Park

Loddon Court
Farm

BELCHER RD

B3349

Heron
Ind Est
BACK LA
Lambs
Lane
Prim Sch

Lambs Farm
Bsns Pk

LAMBS LA

Sheepbridge Court
Farm

River Loddon

Sheep Bridge

Loddon
Court

KINGSBRIDGE HILL

Wyvols
Court

King's Bridge

BARGE LA

Handpost
Farm

BASINGSTOKE RD

Swallowfield

SWALLOWFIELD ST

NORMANS LA

VILLA
PL
PH
THE STREET
PO

CURL'S WAY

SCHOOLHOUSE LA

THE NAYLORS

CHURCH RD

Brookside
Bsns Ctr

Brookside
Nursery

Salter's
Bridge

Cuckoo
Pen

George & Dragon
(PH)

SWALLOWFIELD RD

Rowe's Farm

Blackwater River

BUTBEAM LA

Cemy

The Broadwater

Wheelers
Farm

CHARLTON LA

THORN'S LA

RG7

Taylor's La

SPRING LA

Goddard's
Farm

Springalls
Farm

Yew Tree
Farm

Riseley Farm

PARK LA

SCHOOL RD

SCHOOL LA

Highgrove
Copse

Collins
Copse

Glasspool
Farm

Riseley Gorse
Farm

Walnut Tree
Farm

BENHAM LA

St Leger's
Copse

Riseley
Bsns Pk
THE
OLD RISELEY
STORES
HAPLIN HO

Riseley

BULL LA

BELL LA

FROGFIELD

CHAPEL LA

NORTON RD

KENT
COTTS

Newbarn
Farm

BULL LA

Spring
Barn

SUN LA

PORTWAY

WELSH LA

RG27

B3349

Park
Corner

BASINGSTOKE RD

Pound Copse

ODIHAM RD

B3349

P
Ham's
Wood
P

Birchen
Copse

Wellington Country
Park

River Whitewater

Riseley
Mill

Mill Wood

Top Hill
Copse

A33

71 A 72 C 73 E F
B D

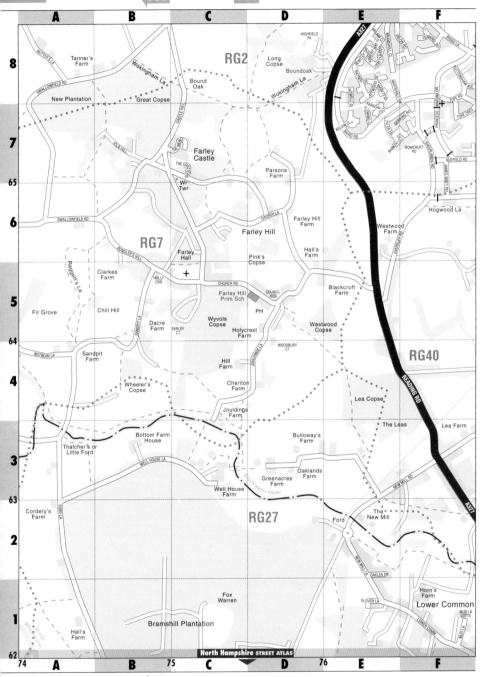

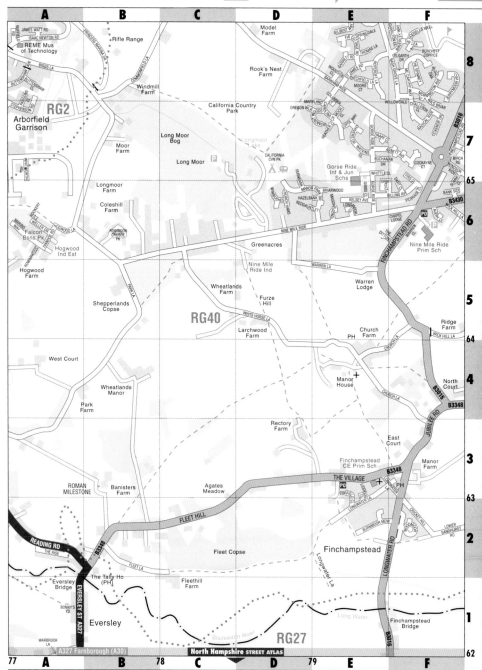

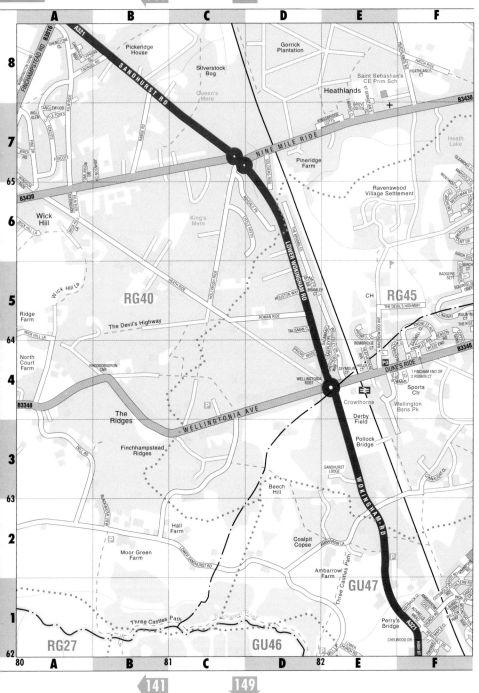

8

7

65

6

5

64

4

3

63

2

1

62

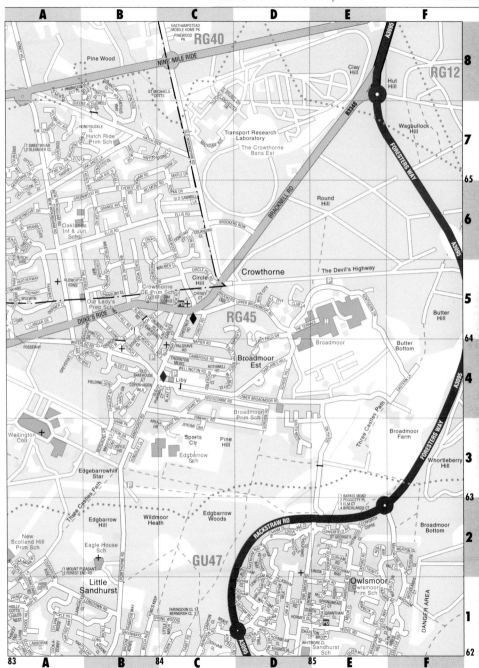

A B C D E F

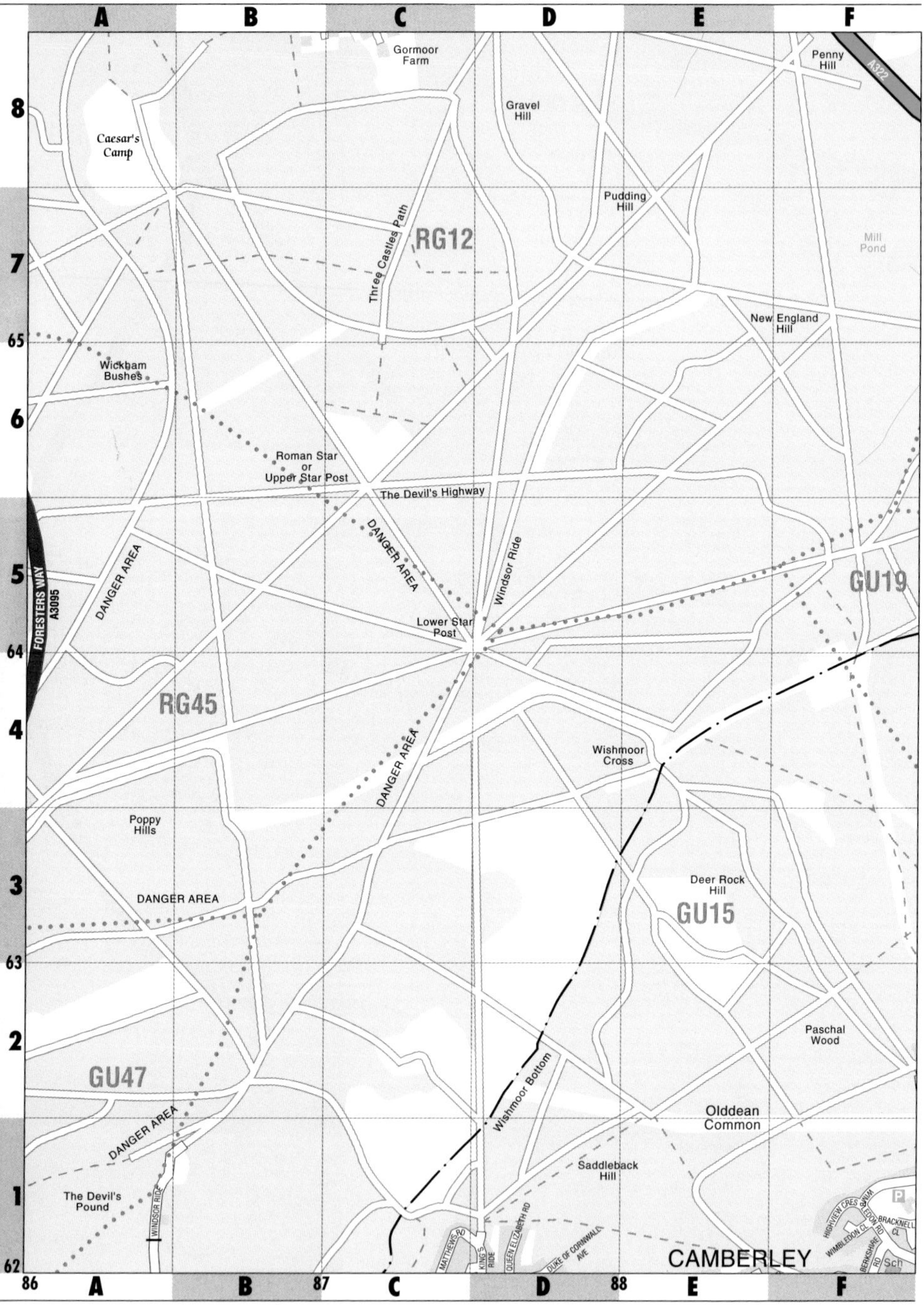

Gormoor Farm

Penny Hill

A322

Gravel Hill

Caesar's Camp

8

Pudding Hill

RG12

Mill Pond

7

Three Castles Path

New England Hill

65

Wickham Bushes

6

Roman Star or Upper Star Post

The Devil's Highway

DANGER AREA

Windsor Ride

GU19

5

FORESTERS WAY

A3095

DANGER AREA

Lower Star Post

64

RG45

4

DANGER AREA

Wishmoor Cross

Poppy Hills

Deer Rock Hill

3

DANGER AREA

GU15

63

Wishmoor Bottom

Paschal Wood

2

GU47

Olddean Common

Saddleback Hill

1

DANGER AREA

The Devil's Pound

WINDSOR RIDE

P

HINDHEAD CRES

BRACKNELL

WIMBLEDON

CL

MATTHEW RD

KING'S RIDE

QUEEN ELIZABETH RD

DUKE OF CORNWALL'S AVE

BERKSHIRE RD

Sch

CAMBERLEY

62

86 A B 87 C D 88 E F

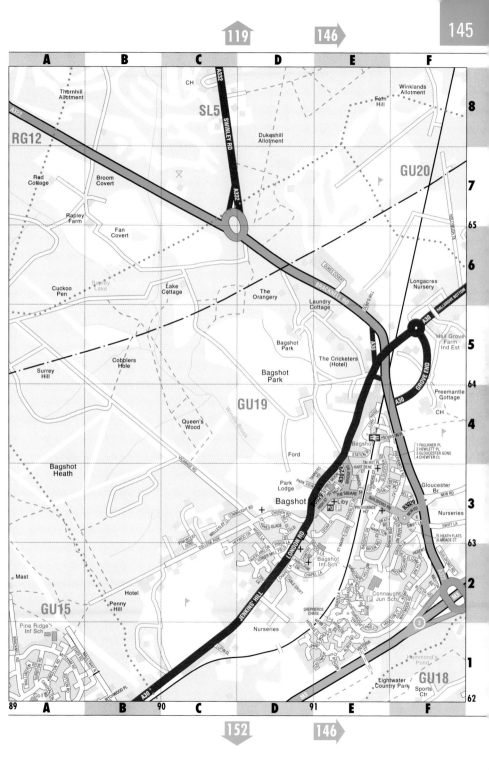

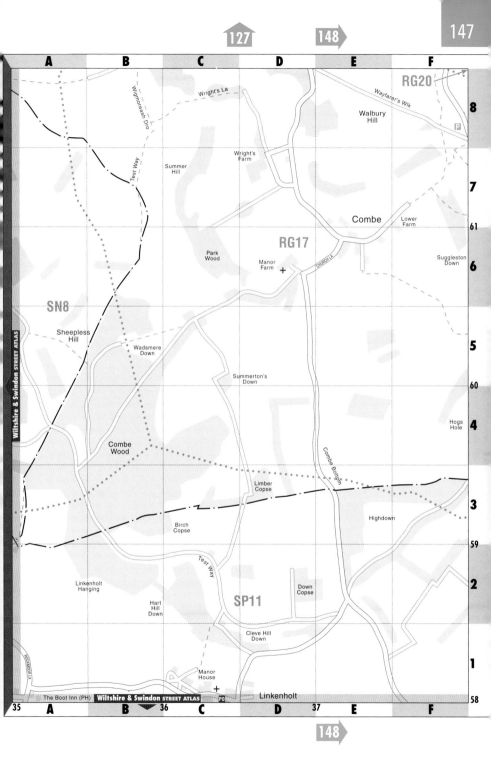

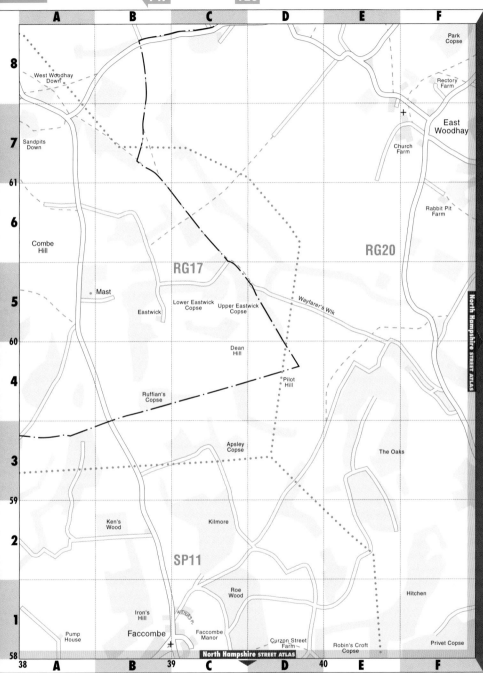

A   **B**   **C**   **D**   **E**   **F**

8

Park
Copse

West Woodhay
Down

Rectory
Farm

East
Woodhay

7

Sandpits
Down

Church
Farm

61

Rabbit Pit
Farm

6

Combe
Hill

RG20

RG17

5

Mast

Lower Eastwick
Copse

Upper Eastwick
Copse

Wayfarer's Wlk

Eastwick

60

Dean
Hill

4

Pilot
Hill

Ruffian's
Copse

The Oaks

3

Apsley
Copse

59

Ken's
Wood

Kilmore

2

SP11

Roe
Wood

Hitchen

1

Iron's
Hill

ARTHUR'S ?

Pump
House

Faccombe

Faccombe
Manor

Curzon Street
Farm

Robin's Croft
Copse

Privet Copse

58

38   **A**   **B**   39   **C**   **D**   40   **E**   **F**

North Hampshire STREET ATLAS

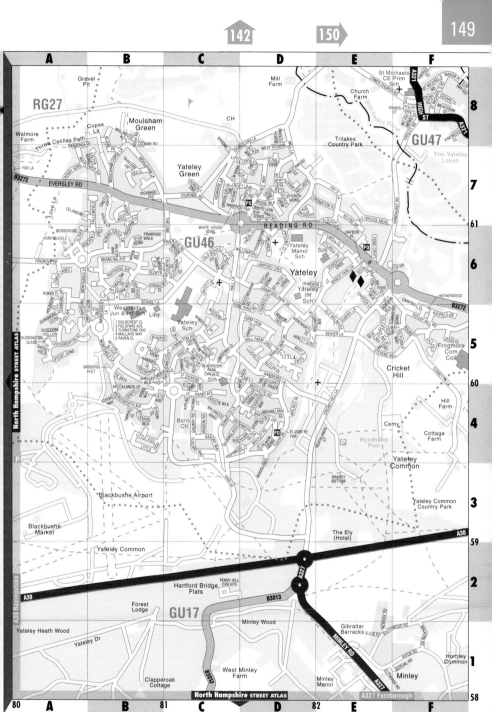

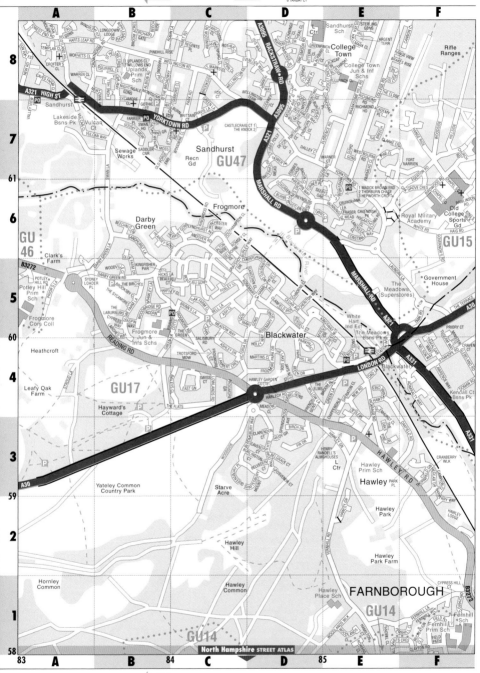

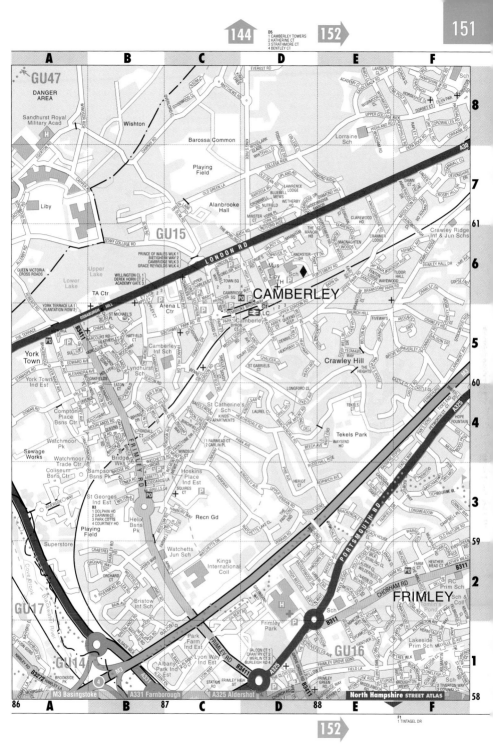

152

A8
1 HARTVALE CT
2 CAESARS CT
3 CAESARS CL

151

145

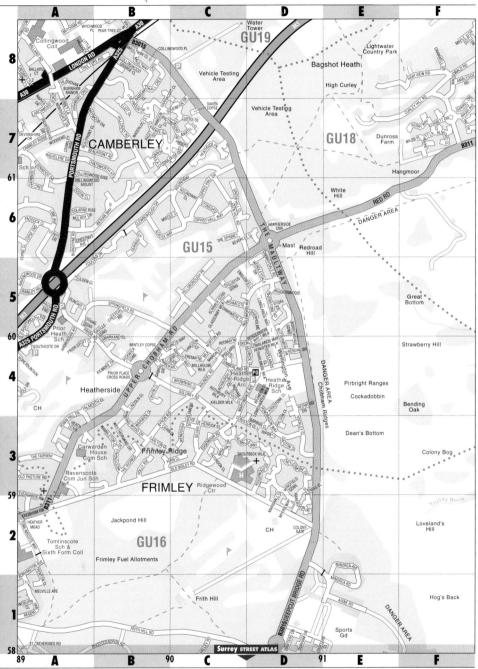

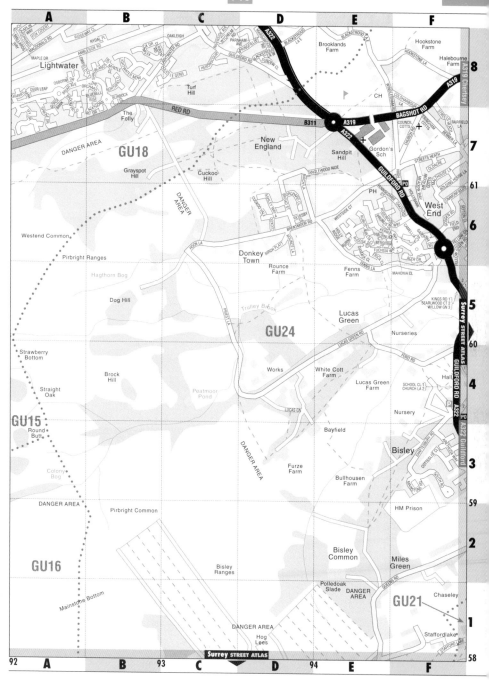

Index

Church Rd **6** Beckenham BR2......... **53** C6

Place name	**Location number**	**Locality, town or village**	**Postcode district**	**Page and grid square**
May be abbreviated on the map	Present when a number indicates the place's position in a crowded area of mapping	Shown when more than one place has the same name	District for the indexed place	Page number and grid reference for the standard mapping

Public and commercial buildings are highlighted in magenta. **Places of interest** are highlighted in blue with a star ☆

Abbreviations used in the index

Acad	**Academy**	Comm	**Common**	Gd	**Ground**	L	**Leisure**	Prom	**Promenade**
App	**Approach**	Cott	**Cottage**	Gdn	**Garden**	La	**Lane**	Rd	**Road**
Arc	**Arcade**	Cres	**Crescent**	Gn	**Green**	Liby	**Library**	Recn	**Recreation**
Ave	**Avenue**	Cswy	**Causeway**	Gr	**Grove**	Mdw	**Meadow**	Ret	**Retail**
Bglw	**Bungalow**	Ct	**Court**	H	**Hall**	Meml	**Memorial**	Sh	**Shopping**
Bldg	**Building**	Ctr	**Centre**	Ho	**House**	Mkt	**Market**	Sq	**Square**
Bsns, Bus	**Business**	Ctry	**Country**	Hospl	**Hospital**	Mus	**Museum**	St	**Street**
Bvd	**Boulevard**	Cty	**County**	HQ	**Headquarters**	Orch	**Orchard**	Sta	**Station**
Cath	**Cathedral**	Dr	**Drive**	Hts	**Heights**	Pal	**Palace**	Terr	**Terrace**
Cir	**Circus**	Dro	**Drove**	Ind	**Industrial**	Par	**Parade**	TH	**Town Hall**
Cl	**Close**	Ed	**Education**	Inst	**Institute**	Pas	**Passage**	Univ	**University**
Cnr	**Corner**	Emb	**Embankment**	Int	**International**	Pk	**Park**	Wk, Wlk	**Walk**
Coll	**College**	Est	**Estate**	Intc	**Interchange**	Pl	**Place**	Wr	**Water**
Com	**Community**	Ex	**Exhibition**	Junc	**Junction**	Prec	**Precinct**	Yd	**Yard**

Index of localities, towns and villages

A

Abbotsbrook 2 F3
Aldermaston 135 A7
Aldermaston Wharf ...109 C3
Aldworth 32 F3
Altmore 38 E4
Arborfield 114 C4
Arborfield Cross 114 F2
Arborfield Garrison ...141 A7
Ascot 120 A6
Ashampstead 54 A6
Ashford 97 F2
Ashford Common 98 D2
Ashford Hill 133 E1
Ashmore Green 106 B8
Aston 16 C5
Aston Tirrold 12 E8
Avington 101 E5

B

Bagnor 104 C7
Bagshot 145 D3
Ball Hill 129 C3
Barkham 115 C2
Beech Hill 138 D5

Beedon 51 D7
Beenham 108 E6
Beenham Stocks ...109 A7
Binfield 117 C8
Binfield 90 D2
Birch Hill 118 C2
Bisham 18 E7
Bishopsgate 94 F4
Bishops Green 132 A3
Bisley 153 F3
Blacknest 121 A6
Blackwater 150 D5
Blewbury 12 B8
Borough Marsh 61 A8
Bourne End 3 B2
Boveney 66 C8
Boxford 104 C6
Boxford 76 D3
Boyn Hill 39 D6
Bracknell 118 D6
Bradfield 82 D5
Brands Hill 69 A8
Bray 40 D3
Bray Wick 40 A4
Braywoodside 64 C3
Brightwalton 28 E3
Brightwalton Green ...28 D2
Brimpton 133 F6
Broadmoor Estate ...143 D4

Brookside 92 F2
Broomhall 121 B2
Bucklebury 80 E2
Bullbrook 118 E7
Burchett's Green 38 C8
Burghfield 111 C6
Burghfield Common ...110 E2
Burnham 21 C3
Burnt Hill 54 B1
Burroughs Grove 1 F7
Bury's Bank 131 E7

C

Calcot 84 B3
Calcot Row 84 D5
Camberley 151 D6
Catmore 29 C5
Caversham 59 D4
Caversham Heights ...58 F3
Caversham Park 59 C5
Chaddleworth 49 B8
Chalvey 42 C3
Chapel Row 108 C8
Charlton 125 D7
Charvil 61 A5
Chattern Hill 98 B4
Chavey Down 119 A8

Chazey Heath 58 C7
Cheapside 120 E7
Chertsey 124 B2
Chieveley 51 D1
Chilton 10 E8
Chilton Foliat 73 A2
Cholsey 14 A8
Churchend 84 F6
Cippenham 41 F4
Cleeve 34 D7
Clewer New Town ...67 A5
Clewer Village 67 A7
Cockpole Green 36 F8
Cold Ash 106 D7
Cold Harbour 38 A3
College Town 150 E8
Colnbrook 69 D7
Colthrop 107 B2
Combe 147 E7
Compton 31 E4
Cookham 20 B7
Cookham Dean 19 B7
Cookham Rise 19 E6
Cores End 3 C4
Cox Green 39 C3
Cranbourne 93 B6
Crawley Hill 151 E5
Crazies Hill 36 F6
Cricket Hill 149 F5

Crockham Heath ...129 F6
Crooked Soley 72 E6
Crookham 133 B5
Crown Wood 118 D3
Crowthorne 143 D5
Curridge 78 D4

D

Darby Green 150 B6
Datchet 68 C6
Dedworth 66 E6
Donkey Town 153 D6
Donnington 104 E7
Dorney 41 C3
Dorney Reach 40 F3
Dowlesgreen 116 E8
Downend 51 B3
Dunsden Green 59 F7

E

Earley 87 B5
East Bedfont 98 E7
East Burnham 22 A4
Eastbury 46 F7
East Fields 105 B2

East Garston 47 D6
Easthampstead 118 B5
Eastheath 116 B3
East Ilsley 30 F6
Easton 76 C5
East Woodhay 148 F7
Eddington 100 E7
Egham 96 A4
Egham Hythe 96 E2
Egham Wick 95 A1
Egypt 22 B8
Egypt 50 A5
Elcot 102 D8
Eling 52 E3
Emmbrook 115 F8
Emmer Green 59 B6
Enborne Row 130 B4
Englefield 83 B5
Englefield Green ...95 B1
Eton 67 C8
Eversley 141 B1

F

Faccombe 148 B1
Farley Castle 140 C7
Farley Hill 140 D6
Farnborough 150 E1
Farnborough 28 F8
Farnham Common ..22 D6
Farnham Park 22 C4
Farnham Royal 22 C3
Fawley Berkshire ...27 C7
Fawley Buckinghamshire ..15 C8
Feltham 98 E6
Felthamhill 98 F3
Fern 2 E5
Fifield 65 D6
Finchampstead ...141 E2
Fishery 40 B6
Flackwell Heath 3 A7
Forest Estate 95 A2
Forest Park 118 E3
Forty Green 1 A1
Frilsham 80 D6
Frimley 151 F2
Frimley Ridge 152 B3
Frogmore 150 C6
Froxfield 99 A5
Fulmer 23 C8
Furze Platt 19 C2

G

Gardeners Green ..116 E2
George Green 43 E7
Goddard's Green ..111 D2
Gore End 129 B4
Goring 34 D6
Grazeley 112 D2
Great Hollands ...117 F3
Great Lea Common ..113 A5
Great Shefford 48 B3
Greenham 131 C8

H

Ham 126 C2
Hambleden 16 D8
Ham Marsh 105 C3
Hampstead Norreys ..52 F5
Hampstead Marshall ..129 B7
Hanworth 118 A2
Hare Hatch 62 B8
Harlington 71 C8
Harmans Water ..118 D5
Harmondsworth ...70 E8
Harpesford 122 C3
Harpsden 35 D6
Hart's Hill 107 A5
Hatton 71 F2
Hatton Hill 146 C5
Hawley 150 E3
Headley 132 D2
Head's Hill 132 B4
Heath End 134 F1
Heatherside 152 B4
Heathlands 142 E8
Hedsor 3 F3
Henley-on-Thames ..15 C1
Hermitage 79 B7
Highway 39 B7
Hillgreen 50 C5
Hoe Benham 102 F8
Hollingsworth 52 E5
Holloway 38 C5
Holly Cross 37 A6
Holme Green 116 F3

Holtwood 129 B5
Holyport 65 A7
Horncastle 84 E5
Horton 69 A4
Hungerford 100 E4
Hungerford Twyford ..62 E2
Hungerford Newtown ..74 A3
Hurley 17 F4
Hurst 88 F6
Hythe End 96 B6

I

Inkpen 127 D5
Iver 44 F7

K

Kiff Green 108 C6
Kiln Green 37 D1
Kintbury 102 A1
Knowle Green 97 A3
Knowle Hill 122 C2
Knowl Hill 37 E4

L

Lake End 41 B4
Laleham 124 C6
Lambourn 25 C2
Langley 44 A3
Larks Hill 91 C2
Leckhampstead 49 F5
Lent Rise 41 A8
Letcombe Bassett ...6 E7
Lightwater 153 A8
Lilley 29 A4
Limmerhill 115 E5
Linkenholt 147 D1
Little Heath 84 A8
Little Hungerford ..79 C8
Little Marlow 2 D5
Little Sandhurst ..143 B1
Littlestead Green ..59 E7
Littleton 125 A6
Littleton Common ..98 D1
Littlewick Green ...38 B4
Longford 70 C6
Longfordmoor 70 A6
Love Green 44 D8
Lower Assendon ...15 A6
Lower Basildon 34 E2
Lower Caversham ..59 D2
Lower Common ...140 F1
Lower Earley 87 A1
Lower Feltham 98 E5
Lower Green 127 B5
Lower Halliford ..125 D2
Lower Padworth ..109 D5
Lower Shiplake 36 A4
Lucas Green 153 E5
Lyne 123 B1

M

Maidenhead 39 F4
Maidenhead Court ..20 C4
Maiden's Green 92 B5
Malpas 83 E6
Mapledurham 57 E6
Marlow 1 B2
Marlow Bottom 1 C6
Marsh Benham ...103 D4
Martin's Heron ...118 F6
Matthewsgreen ..116 A8
Mays Green 35 B4
Medmenham 17 A5
Merryhill Green ...88 D3
Middle Green 43 E5
Midgham 107 E3
Mile End 25 C6
Mill End 16 D7
Minley 149 F1
Moneyrow Green ...65 A7
Mortimer 137 A5
Mortimer West End ..136 D4
Moss End 91 C6
Moulsford 13 F4
Moulsham Green ..149 B8

N

Newbury 104 B3
Newell Green 92 A1
Newtown Henley-on-Thames ..35 F8
Newtown Newbury ..131 B4

New Town Pangbourne 55 D4
New Town Reading ..86 F7
North Ascot 119 F8
North Street 83 D5
North Sydmonton ..131 F1
North Town 19 F2
Nuptown 91 E7

O

Oakley Green 66 B5
Oare 79 B8
Oatlands Park 125 E1
Old Warren 135 E5
Old Windsor 95 A8
Orchardville 21 B1
Owlsmoor 143 E1

P

Padworth 109 F1
Paley Street 64 C5
Pamber Heath ...135 F1
Pangbourne 56 D6
Parsonage Green ..32 E4
Peasemore 50 C7
Pingewood 112 C7
Pinkneys Green 19 A1
Play Hatch 60 A5
Pooley Green 96 C2
Popeswood 117 D8
Poughley 73 F8
Poundgreen 112 C3
Poyle 69 E6
Priestwood 118 A8
Punt Hill 39 C6
Purley on Thames ..57 B6
Purton 51 D8

Q

Quick's Green 54 D5

R

Reading 86 B4
Remenham 16 A5
Remenham Hill 16 C2
Ripley Springs 95 E2
Riseley 139 C3
Rotten Row 81 F3
Ruscombe 61 F6
Ryeish Green 113 C4

S

St Ann's Heath ...122 E5
Sandford Park 88 B8
Sandhurst 150 C7
Sanham Green ...100 D2
Schoolgreen 113 F4
Shaw 105 C5
Sheepridge 2 E7
Shefford Woodlands ..74 D7
Shepperton 125 C3
Shepperton Green ..125 B5
Shinfield 113 E4
Shiplake 35 F2
Shiplake Row 35 C2
Shreding Green 44 C7
Shrubs Hill 121 C3
Silchester 136 C1
Sindlesham 115 A8
Skinners Green ...130 B8
Slough 42 D5
Sonning 60 E4
Sonning Eye 60 C5
South Ascot 120 B4
Southcote 85 C4
Southend 82 A2
South Fawley 27 C5
South Stoke 14 C4
Speen 104 C5
Spencers Wood ..113 A1
Staines 96 E6
Stanford Dingley ..81 C4
Stanford End 138 F3
Stanmore 30 A4
Stanwell 97 C7
Stanwell Moor 70 A1
Stanwell Place 70 C1
Stockcross 103 E6
Stoke Poges 22 F3
Straight Soley 73 A5
Stratfield Mortimer ..137 D5
Streatley 34 A7

Stroude 122 F7
Stroud Green 105 B1
Stubbles 54 C6
Stud Green 64 E7
Sulham 56 E2
Sulhamstead 110 C6
Sulhamstead Abbots ..110 F4
Sulhamstead Bannister
    Upper End 110 D5
Sunbury 125 F6
Sunbury Common ..98 E1
Sunningdale 121 B4
Sunninghill 120 C4
Sunnymeads 68 E4
Sutton 44 C1
Swallowfield 139 C6

T

Tadley 135 B1
Taplow 20 E1
Temple 18 C5
Thatcham 106 E5
Theale 83 D4
The Holt 37 B1
The Mount 86 C5
The Village 94 A5
Thorpe 123 C6
Thorpe Green 123 A5
Thorpe Lea 96 B1
Three Mile Cross ..113 B4
Tidmarsh 56 C2
Tilehurst 57 E1
Titcomb 127 F7
Tittle Row 39 A5
Tokers Green 58 D8
Touchen-end 64 D6
Trapshill 127 E4
Trash Green 111 B7
Trumps Green ...122 D3
Twyford 61 C5

U

Ufton Green 110 B5
Ufton Nervet 110 D3
Upper Basildon 55 A5
Upper Bucklebury ..107 C6
Upper Green 127 D3
Upper Halliford ..125 D5
Upper Lambourn ..24 F6
Upper Wargrove ...36 F2
Upper Woolhampton ..108 C4
Upton 43 B3
Upton Lea 43 C6

V

Virginia Water ...122 C6

W

Waltham St Lawrence ..62 F6
Warfield 91 E5
Wargrave 36 D1
Warren Row 37 C6
Wash Water 130 D3
Wasing 134 D5
Water Oakley 65 F8
Welford 76 A7
Well End 2 F5
Wellhouse 79 E6
Wentworth 121 F3
West Bedfont 97 F8
West End Chobham ..153 F6
West End Twyford ..62 E3
West Fields 104 E2
West Ilsley 10 B1
Weston 75 D8
Westridge Green ...33 B4
West Woodhay ...128 C3
Wexham Street 23 C4
Whistley Green 61 E1
Whitchurch-on-Thames ..56 C7
Whitegrove 91 E2
Whitehouse Green ..110 F6
Whiteknights 86 E5
White Waltham 63 E7
Whitley 86 C1
Whitley Wood 113 C7
Wickham 75 C4
Wickham Heath ..103 B8
Wick Hill Bracknell ..118 C8
Wick Hill Wokingham ..142 A6
Wildridings 118 A5
Windlesham 146 C4
Windsor 67 E6

Winkfield 92 D5
Winkfield Row 92 B2
Winnersh 88 B3
Winterbourne 77 C5
Wokingham 116 B5
Wooburn 3 D4
Wooburn Green 3 F7
Wooburn Moor 3 F8
Woodlands Park ...38 F2
Woodlands St Mary ..46 E2
Woodley 87 D7
Woodley Green 88 A7
Woodside 93 C4
Wooley Green 38 D5
Woolhampton 108 D2
Woose Hill 115 F6
World's End 51 D6
Wraysbury 68 E1

Y

Yateley 149 D6
Yateley Green 149 C7
Yattendon 53 F1
York Town 151 A5

A

Abattoirs Rd RG1 86 A8
Abberbury Cl RG14 104 E6
Abbetts La GU15 151 B3
Abbey Cl Bracknell RG12 118 D4
Newbury RG14 131 A8
Slough SL1 41 E6
Wokingham RG40 116 C7
Abbey Cotts SL7 17 B4
Abbey Ct
Camberley GU15 151 D5
Chertsey KT16 124 B2
Laleham TW18 124 C5
Abbey Dr TW18 124 C5
Abbey Gdns KT16 124 A3
Abbey Gn KT16 124 A3
Abbey Jun Sch RG1 86 C5
Abbey Lodge 6 TW18 96 F3
Abbey Mead SL8 2 F5
Abbey Mews TW18 124 C5
Abbey Pk RG7 110 F3
Abbey Rd Bourne End SL8 2 F5
Chertsey KT16 124 B2
Lower Halliford TW17 125 A1
Virginia Water GU25 122 D5
Abbey River Cotts KT16 124 C3
Abbey Sq RG1 86 B7
Abbey St RG1 86 B7
Abbey Way SL7 18 D6
Abbey Wood SL5 121 A2
Abbeyfields Pk KT16 124 C2
Abbot Cl TW18 97 D1
Abbot's Wlk Reading RG1 86 B8
Windsor SL4 66 E5
Abbots Dr GU25 122 C5
Abbots Mead OX10 14 A8
Abbots Rd
Burghfield Common RG7 110 F2
Newbury RG14 105 A1
Abbots Way KT16 123 F2
Abbotsbury RG12 117 F4
Abbotsbury Ct 3 RG30 85 B8
Abbotsbury Ho 4 RG2 113 C8
Abbotsmead Pl RG4 59 A2
Abbotts Way SL1 41 D6
Abelia Cl GU24 153 E6
Abell Gdns SL6 19 B1
Aberaman RG4 58 F6
Aberdeen Ave SL1 42 A6
Aberford Cl RG30 85 C7
Abex Rd RG14 105 C3
Abingdon Cl RG12 118 E4
Abingdon Dr RG4 59 C6
Abingdon Rd
East Ilsley RG20 30 E7
Sandhurst GU47 143 C1
Abingdon Wlk SL6 19 E3
Abington SL3 69 D7
Abney Court Dr SL8 3 A2
Abrahams Rd RG9 15 C3
Acacia RG9 15 D2
Acacia Ave
Littleton TW17 125 A4
Sandhurst GU47 143 D1
Wraysbury TW19 68 E3
Acacia Ct RG12 118 B6
Acacia Mews UB7 70 D8
Acacia Rd Reading RG1 86 C6
Staines TW18 97 B3
Academy Cl GU15 151 E8
Academy Gate GU15 151 B6
Academy Pl GU47 150 E7
Accommodation La UB7 70 C8
Acer Cl RG42 119 A8
Acer Dr GU24 153 F6
Ackrells Mead GU47 142 F1
Acorn Cotts SN8 126 D3
Acorn Dr Thatcham RG18 106 D5
Wokingham RG40 116 C7
Acorn Gr UB3 71 F7
Acorn Rd GU17 150 B5
Acorn Wlk RG31 84 C5
Acre Bsns Pk RG2 113 B8
Acre Pas SL4 67 D6
Acre Rd RG2 113 A8
Acre The SL7 1 F2
Action Ct TW15 125 C8
Adam Cl Slough SL1 42 A5
Tadley RG26 134 E1
Adam Ct RG9 15 E2
Adams Way RG6 86 F2
Addington Cl SL4 67 A4
Addington Rd RG1 86 D6
Addington Specl Sch
RG5 87 F6
Addiscombe Chase RG31 57 B3
Addiscombe Rd RG45 143 C4
Addison Cl SL0 44 E6
Addison Ct SL6 20 B1
Addison Rd RG1 59 A1
Adelaide Cl SL1 42 A4
Adelaide Rd Reading RG6 87 A6
Staines TW15 97 D3
Windsor SL4 67 F6
Adelaide Sq SL4 67 D5
Adelphi Gdns SL1 42 E4
Adey's Cl RG14 105 B1
Adkins Rd RG10 62 E7
Admirals Ct RG2 86 A5
Admiralty Way GU15 150 F4
Admoor La RG7 82 C1
Adrians Wlk SL2 42 F5
Adwell Dr RG6 87 D1
Adwell Sq RG9 15 D2
Adwood Ct RG19 106 E3
Agar Cres RG42 91 B1
Agars Pl SL3 68 A8
Agate Cl RG41 115 E7
Aggisters La RG41 115 C3
Agincourt SL5 120 C6
Agincourt Cl RG41 115 E6
Agricola Way RG19 106 F2
Ainsdale Cres RG30 85 A4
Aintree RG17 25 B2
Aintree Cl Newbury RG14 105 C1
Poyle SL3 69 E6
Air Forces Meml* TW20 95 D4
Airport Gate Bsns Ctr
UB7 71 A7
Airport Way TW19 70 A3
Aisne Rd GU16 152 E1
Ajax Ave SL1 42 B6
Alan Pl RG30 85 A5
Alan Way SL3 43 E7
Alandale Cl RG2 113 D8
Albain Cres TW15 97 E6
Albany Ct GU16 151 C1
Albany Park Dr RG41 88 A3
Albany Park Ind Est
GU15 151 C1
Albany Pk Frimley GU15 151 C1
Poyle SL3 69 D7
Albany Pl TW20 96 B4
Albany Rd
Old Windsor SL4 68 A2
Reading RG30 85 D7
Windsor SL4 67 D5
Alben Rd RG42 90 C3
Albert Ave KT16 124 A6
Albert Cl 3 SL1 42 F3
Albert Dr 1 TW18 97 A3
Albert Pl SL4 42 A1
Albert Rd Ashford TW15 97 F3
Bagshot GU19 145 E1
Bracknell RG42 118 B8
Camberley GU15 151 C5
Caversham RG4 58 F4
Crowthorne RG45 143 B5
Englefield Green TW20 95 D2
Henley-On-T RG9 15 E1
1 Newbury RG14 105 A3
Windsor SL4 67 E3
Wokingham RG40 116 B5
Albert St Maidenhead SL6 39 F7
Slough SL1 42 F3
Windsor SL4 67 B6
Albert Wlk RG45 143 B5
Albion SL3 44 B1
Albion Cl SL2 43 A5
Albion Cotts SL6 19 C7
Albion Pl 2 SL4 67 A5
Albion Rd GU47 150 B8
Albury Cl RG30 58 C1
Albury Ct TW15 98 D2
Albury Gdns RG31 84 E3
Albury Way RG19 131 F4
Alcot Cl RG45 143 B4
Aldborough Spur SL1 42 E7
Aldbourne Ave RG6 87 A4
Aldbourne Cl RG17 100 D5
Aldbourne Rd SL1 41 B8
Aldeburgh Cl RG4 59 C8
Aldebury Rd SL6 19 F2
Alden View SL4 66 D6
Aldenham Cl RG4 59 C6
Aldenham Terr RG12 118 C3
Alder Bridge Sch RG7 109 C3
Alder Cl
Englefield Green TW20 95 E3
Lower Earley RG6 87 D1
Newbury RG14 105 D4
Slough SL1 41 F5
Alder Ct RG12 118 B6
Alder Dr RG31 84 C6
Alder Field Cl RG7 83 F4
Alder Glade RG7 110 F3
Alder Gr GU46 149 C5
Alderbourne La SL3 23 E8
Alderbrook Cl RG45 142 E4
Alderbury Rd SL3 43 F4
Alderbury Rd W SL3 43 F4
Alderley Cl RG5 60 F1
Alderman Willey Cl
RG41 116 B6
Aldermaston CE Prim Sch
RG7 134 F7
Aldermaston Rd RG26 135 A2
Aldermaston Sta RG7 109 C3
Alderney Ct 13 RG1 86 D7
Alderney Gdns RG41 88 D2
Alders The RG18 106 D4
Alderside Wlk TW20 95 E3
Aldin Ave N SL1 43 A4
Aldin Ave S SL1 43 A4
Aldous Ho TW18 96 E4
Aldridge Pk RG42 92 B2
Aldridge Rd SL2 22 A1
Aldryington Prim Sch
RG6 87 B4
Aldwick Dr SL6 39 D6
Aldworth Cl
Bracknell RG12 118 A5
Reading RG30 85 C5
Aldworth Gdns RG45 143 A5
Aldworth Rd
Compton RG20 31 F4
Upper Basildon RG8 55 A5
Aldwych Cotts RG14 104 F6
Aldwyn Ct TW20 95 B2
Alexander Ct 12 RG1 85 F7
Alexander Fst Sch SL4 66 C4
Alexander Rd
Egham TW20 96 C3
Thatcham RG19 106 E2
Alexander Wlk RG12 118 B4
Alexandra Ave GU15 151 A5
Alexandra Cl
Ashford TW15 98 D1
Staines TW18 97 D2
Alexandra Ct
Ashford TW15 98 D2
1 Windsor SL4 67 D5
Wokingham RG40 116 C5
Alexandra Ho SL5 120 B6
Alexandra Rd
Ashford TW15 98 E2
Englefield Green TW20 95 C2
Maidenhead SL6 39 D8
Reading RG1 86 D6
Slough SL1 42 D3
Windsor SL4 67 D5
Alford Cl RG30 84 D8
Alfred Ct 3 SL8 3 B3
Alfred Davis Ct SL7 1 D3
Alfred Sutton Prim Sch
RG1 86 F6
Alice Gough Meml Homes
RG12 118 B6
Alice Ho TW18 97 A2
Alice La SL1 21 B1
Alison Cl RG7 110 F1
Alison Dr GU15 151 F5
All Hallows Rd RG4 59 D3
All Saints Ave SL6 39 D7
All Saints CE Inf Sch RG1 85 E7
All Saints CE Jun Sch
SL6 39 C6
All Saints Cl RG40 116 C7
All Saints Cres GU14 150 E1
All Saints Ct RG1 85 E6
All Saints Rd GU18 146 C1
All Saints Rise RG42 91 E1
All Souls Cotts SL3 43 E8
All Souls' Rd SL5 120 A5
Allanson Rd SL7 1 F3
Allcot Cl TW14 98 F7
Allcroft Rd RG1 86 C5
Allenby Rd
Maidenhead SL6 39 B7
Sandhurst GU15 151 A6
Allendale Cl GU47 143 A2
Allendale Rd RG6 87 B3
Allerds Rd SL2 22 A4
Alleyns La SL6 19 D8
Allhusen Gdns SL3 23 E8
Alliance Ct TW15 98 C4
Allington Ave TW17 125 E6
Allington Ct SL2 42 F6
Allison Ct 2 RG1 85 F7
Allison Gdns RG8 57 C5
Allison Ho RG9 35 E8
Allkins Ct SL4 67 D5
Allnatt Ave RG41 88 C1
Allonby Cl RG6 87 D2
Allsmoor La RG12 118 F6
Allyn Cl TW18 96 F2
Alma Ct Burnham SL1 21 C2
Eton SL4 41 F2
Wokingham RG41 116 A5
Alma Rd Eton SL4 41 F2
Windsor SL4 67 C5
Alma St RG30 85 C8
Almners Rd
Chertsey KT16 123 C2
Lyne KT16 123 B1
Almond Ave RG14 105 A5
Almond Cl
Charlton TW17 125 C7
Englefield Green TW20 95 B2
Windsor SL4 67 B5
Wokingham RG41 115 C4
Almond Dr Caversham RG4 59 F4
Chieveley RG20 51 C5
Thatcham RG18 106 D4
Almond Rd SL1 21 C2
Almons Way SL2 43 B8
Almshouses Eton SL4 67 D7
Reading RG1 86 A7
Sunbury TW16 125 F8
Twyford RG10 61 D5
Almswood Rd RG26 135 A2
Alpha Ho 4 RG1 86 C6
Alpha St N 6 SL1 43 A4
Alpha St S SL1 42 F3
Alpha Way TW20 123 C8
Alphington Ave GU16 151 F1
Alphington Gn GU16 151 F1
Alphington Rd RG2 113 B8
Alpine Cl Ascot SL5 120 D3
Maidenhead SL6 40 A6
Alpine St RG1 86 B6
Alsace Wlk GU15 151 B1
Alsford Cl GU18 152 F7
Alston Gdns SL6 39 E7
Alston Mews RG19 106 C2
Alston Wlk RG4 59 D2
Altmore SL6 38 E4
Alton Ct TW18 123 E8
Alton Ride GU17 150 C6
Altona Way SL1 42 B7
Altwood Bailey SL6 39 B5
Altwood Cl
Maidenhead SL6 39 B5
Slough SL1 41 E8
Altwood Dr SL6 39 B5
Altwood Rd SL6 39 B5
Altwood Sch SL6 39 B5
Alvista Ave SL6 41 B7
Alwyn Inf Sch SL6 39 C8
Alwyn Rd SL6 39 B8
Alwyns Cl KT16 124 A3
Alwyns La KT16 124 A3
Alyson Ct 2 SL6 19 F1
Amanda Ct Ashford TW15 97 F6
Slough SL3 43 D3
Ambarrow Cres GU47 142 F1
Ambarrow La GU47 142 E2
Ambassador RG12 117 F4
Ambassador The SL5 121 B2
Amber Cl RG6 87 C4
Amber Ct 13 TW18 96 F3
Amber Hill GU15 152 B4
Amberley Cl RG14 104 F4
Amberley Ct SL6 20 C3
Amberley Dr RG10 61 D6
Amberley Pl 5 SL4 67 D6
Amberley Rd SL2 41 E8
Amberwood Dr GU15 151 F7
Amblecote Rd RG30 85 B7
Ambleside Cl RG5 87 E7
Ambleside Dr TW14 98 F7
Ambleside Rd GU18 153 B8
Ambleside Way TW20 96 B1
Ambrook Rd RG2 113 B8
Ambrose Pl RG1 85 F7
Ambury Rd RG8 32 E4
Amen Corner Bsns Pk
RG12 117 D7
Amerden Cl SL6 40 D7
Amerden La SL6 40 D7
Amerden Priory Cvn Pk
SL6 40 E4
Amerden Way SL1 42 A4
American Com Sch
TW20 122 C7
American Magna Carta
Meml* TW20 95 D6
Amersham Rd RG4 59 D2
Amethyst Cl RG41 115 D7
Amethyst La RG30 85 C6
Amherst Rd RG6 87 A6
Amhurst Mews RG6 87 A6
Amity Rd RG1 86 E7
Amity St RG1 86 E8
Ammanford RG4 58 F5
Amners Farm Rd RG30 112 A7
Ampere Rd RG14 105 B3
Anarth Ct KT13 125 E1
Ancaster Dr SL5 119 E8
Ancastle Gn RG9 15 D2
Anchor Ct SL6 19 F7
Anchorite Cl RG10 61 D5
Andermans SL4 66 D6
Anders Cnr RG42 117 F8
Anderson Ave RG6 87 A6
Anderson Cres RG2 114 E2
Anderson Dr TW15 98 C4
Anderson Pl GU19 145 E4
Andover Cl
East Bedfont TW14 98 F7
Reading RG31 57 D1
Andover Ct TW19 97 D8
Andover Dro RG20 130 B4
Andover Rd
Blackwater GU17 150 C6
Newbury RG14 130 D6
Andrew Cl RG40 116 E5
Andrews Cl RG7 83 E3
Andrews Rd RG6 87 B3
Andrews Reach SL8 3 A2
Andrews Way SL7 1 D8
Angel Ct RG14 104 F4
Angel Mead RG7 108 C2
Angel Pl RG42 90 C2
Angers Cl GU15 152 C7
Angle Field Rd RG4 59 C3
Anglers Way RG1 86 D7
Anglesey Cl TW15 98 A5
Angus Cl RG31 84 E4
Annadale RG18 79 C1
Anne Cl SL6 19 E2
Anneforde Pl RG42 91 A1
Anners Cl TW20 123 C6
Annesley Gdns RG41 88 C2
Annett Cl TW17 125 E5
Annie Brookes Cl TW18 96 D5
Ansculf Rd SL2 22 A2
Anslow Pl SL1 41 C8
Anson Cres RG2 113 D8
Anson Ct TW19 97 E8
Anson Wlk RG2 113 D8
Anstey Pl RG7 111 A3
Anstey Rd 16 RG1 85 F7
Anston Cl RG6 114 A8
Antares Cl RG41 115 F6
Anthian Cl RG5 88 B8
Anthony Wall RG42 118 F8
Anthony Way SL1 41 D6
Antrim Rd RG5 87 D6
Anvil Cl RG7 113 A1
Anvil Ct 4 Slough SL3 44 A2
Thatcham RG18 106 D3
Wokingham RG40 116 C5
Apex Dr GU16 151 D1
Aplin Way GU18 146 A1
Apollo Ho RG7 134 E2
Appelford Cl RG19 106 E2
Apple Cl Purley On T RG31 57 B4
Wokingham RG41 115 F5
Apple Tree Cl RG14 130 E7
Apple Tree Way GU47 143 D1
Appleby End RG30 85 B7
Appleby Gdns TW14 98 F7
Applecroft SL6 39 C3
Appledore RG12 117 F3
Appleford Cl RG19 106 D2
Appleford Rd RG30 85 A5
Appleshaw Ct 1 RG31 84 D8
Appleton Ho 19 RG1 86 D7
Appletree La
Shinfield RG7 113 B2
Slough SL3 43 C3
Appletree Pl 4 RG42 118 A8
Appley Ct GU15 151 B6
Appley Dr GU15 151 B6
Approach Rd
Ashford TW15 98 C2
Taplow SL6 40 E7
April Cl GU15 151 C2
Apsey Ct RG42 90 E1
Apsley Cotts SL6 19 E7
Apsley Ho SL1 43 A4
Aquila Cl RG41 115 E6
Aragon Cl TW16 98 F1
Aragon Ct RG12 118 C5
Aragon Rd GU46 149 C4
Arbery Way RG2 140 E8
Arbor La RG41 88 B3
Arbor Mdws RG41 88 B3
Arborfield Cl SL1 42 E3
Arborfield Grange RG2 114 C4
Arborfield Rd RG2 113 F4
Arborfield, Newland &
Barkham CE Jun Sch
RG2 114 F2
Arbour Cl RG1 85 F5
Arbour Vale Sch SL2 43 A7
Arc The RG1 86 B7
Arcade Mews 10 RG14 105 A3
Arcade The Goring RG8 34 C6
9 Newbury RG14 105 A3
Archangel Way RG18 106 F4
Archer Cl SL6 39 D8
Archway Rd RG4 59 A2
Arden Cl RG12 119 A7
Ardingly RG12 118 A4
Ardler Rd RG4 59 C2
Ardrossan Ave GU15 152 A5
Ardrossan Cl SL2 22 C1
Ardwell Cl RG45 142 E5
Arena The RG12 118 A7
Arenal Dr RG45 143 C3
Arethusa Way GU24 153 F3
Argent Cl TW20 96 C2
Argent Terr GU47 150 E8
Argonaut Pk SL3 69 F6
Argosy Gdns TW18 96 F2
Argosy La TW19 97 D8
Argyle Rd Newbury RG14 104 F2
Reading RG1 85 E7
Argyle St RG1 85 E7
Argyll Ave SL1 42 A6
Aries Ho HP10 3 A8
Arkle Ave RG19 105 F3
Arkley Ct SL6 40 C1
Arkwright Dr RG42 117 D7
Arkwright Rd Poyle SL3 69 E5
Reading RG2 86 B3
Arlington Bsns Pk
Bracknell RG12 118 B7
Theale RG7 83 F3
Arlington Cl
Bracknell RG42 118 A8
Maidenhead SL6 39 A8
Arlington Grange RG18 78 B3
Arlington La RG14 77 F3
Arlington Rd TW15 97 F3
Arlington Sq RG12 118 A7
Armadale Ct RG30 85 D6
Armitage Ct SL5 120 C3
Armitage Dr GU16 151 F1
Armour Hill RG31 57 D1
Armour Rd RG31 57 D1
Armour Wlk RG31 57 D1
Armstrong Rd TW20 95 C2
Armstrong Way RG5 88 A7
Arncliffe RG12 118 A4
Arndale Way TW20 96 A3
Arne Cl RG41 88 A3
Arnett Ave RG40 141 F7
Arnewood Ave RG26 135 D1
Arnhem Rd RG14 105 B3
Arnold Rd TW18 97 C1
Arnside Cl RG10 61 D7
Arnwood RG41 115 E8
Arrowhead Rd RG7 83 F2
Arrowsmith Way RG19 106 E1
Artemis Ho RG14 105 B4
Arthur Cl GU19 145 E1
Arthur Pl RG1 86 D7
Arthur Rd Newbury RG14 104 E2
Slough SL1 42 D4
Windsor SL4 67 C6
Wokingham RG41 116 A6
Arthur's Pl SP11 148 C1
Arthurstone Birches
RG42 90 D3
Artillery Dr RG19 106 E1
Artillery Mews RG30 85 D6
Arun Cl RG41 88 B1
Arun Ct RG30 85 C6
Arundel Cl SL6 39 A8
Arundel Ct SL3 43 D2
Arundel Rd Frimley GU15 152 C4
Woodley RG5 87 E7
Ascot Cl RG14 131 C8
Ascot Heath CE Jun Sch
SL5 92 E1
Ascot Heath Inf Sch SL5 92 E1
Ascot Ho 7 TW20 96 A3
Ascot Race Course SL5 119 F6
Ascot Rd
East Bedfont TW14 98 B6
Holyport SL6 65 A8

Ascot Rd *continued*
Newell Green RG42 ... 91 E8
Ascot Sta SL5 ... 120 A5
Ascot Twrs SL5 ... 119 F7
Ascot Wood SL5 ... 120 A6
Ascott Way RG14 ... 105 D4
Ash Cl Blackwater GU17 ... 150 C5
Brightwalton RG20 ... 28 D3
Slough SL3 ... 44 B3
Ash Copse RG4 ... 59 F7
Ash Cres RG19 ... 133 A5
Ash Ct Ashford TW15 ... 98 C3
Caversham RG4 ... 59 B3
11 Newbury RG14 ... 105 A4
Ash Gate RG18 ... 106 F4
Ash Gn RG2 ... 113 D8
Ash Gr Bradfield RG7 ... 82 B2
East Bedfont TW14 ... 98 E7
Staines TW18 ... 97 C2
Stoke Poges SL2 ... 22 F5
Ash La
Burghfield Common RG7 ... 111 A4
Tadley RG26 ... 134 E1
Windsor SL4 ... 66 D5
Ash Lodge 2 TW16 ... 98 F1
Ash Rd Littleton TW17 ... 125 A5
Reading RG30 ... 84 E7
Ash Terr RG18 ... 106 B8
Ash Tree Gr RG20 ... 129 B7
Ash Way RG41 ... 115 D3
Ashampstead Rd
Bradfield RG7 ... 82 B7
Reading RG30 ... 85 B4
Upper Basildon RG8 ... 55 A5
Ashbourne RG12 ... 117 F3
Ashbourne Ct RG30 ... 85 C7
Ashbourne Gr SL6 ... 39 C3
Ashbourne Ho 5 SL1 ... 42 E4
Ashbourne Way RG19 ... 106 B3
Ashbrook Mews OX11 ... 11 F8
Ashbrook Rd SL4 ... 95 B8
Ashburton Rd RG2 ... 86 C2
Ashbury Dr
Farnborough GU17 ... 151 A1
Reading RG31 ... 84 C7
Ashby Ct RG2 ... 113 B7
Ashby Way UB7 ... 71 A7
Ashcroft Cl RG4 ... 58 E5
Ashcroft Ct SL1 ... 21 B3
Ashcroft Rd SL6 ... 39 C8
Ashdale Pk RG40 ... 142 D6
Ashdene Cl TW15 ... 98 C1
Ashdene Ho TW20 ... 95 C2
Ashdown SL6 ... 20 B3
Ashdown Cl RG12 ... 119 A7
Ashdown Ho 11 RG1 ... 85 E5
Ashen Cross SL0 ... 44 B8
Ashenden Wlk SL2 ... 22 D8
Asher Dr SL5 ... 119 C8
Ashes The RG7 ... 113 B2
Ashfield Gn GU46 ... 149 F5
Ashford Ave TW15 ... 98 B2
Ashford CE Prim Sch
TW15 ... 98 B2
Ashford Cl TW15 ... 97 E4
Ashford Cres TW15 ... 97 E5
Ashford High Sch The
TW15 ... 97 E5
Ashford Hill Prim Sch
RG19 ... 133 E1
Ashford Hill Rd RG19 ... 132 F2
Ashford Hospl TW15 ... 97 E6
Ashford Ind Est TW15 ... 98 C4
Ashford La SL4 ... 41 B4
Ashford Park Prim Sch
TW15 ... 97 D4
Ashford Rd
Feltham TW13,TW15 ... 98 E4
Littleton TW15 ... 98 C1
Staines TW18 ... 124 D8
Ashford Sta TW15 ... 97 F4
Ashgrove Rd TW15 ... 98 D3
Ashlea Ho TW15 ... 97 F3
Ashleigh Ave TW20 ... 96 C1
Ashley HP10 ... 3 E7
Ashley Cl Earley RG6 ... 87 B2
Oatlands Park KT12,KT13 ... 125 F1
Ashley Ct SL6 ... 40 B7
Ashley Dr GU17 ... 150 C4
Ashley Hill Pl RG10 ... 36 F7
Ashley Park Ave KT12 ... 125 F1
Ashley Pk SL6 ... 20 B2
Ashley Rd RG1 ... 85 E5
Ashley Way GU24 ... 153 D6
Ashman Rd RG19 ... 107 A3
Ashmead Prim Sch RG2 ... 86 C1
Ashmere Cl RG31 ... 84 C4
Ashmere Terr RG30 ... 85 E8
Ashmore Green Rd
RG18 ... 106 B7
Ashmore Rd RG2 ... 86 C1
Ashridge Ct 4 RG14 ... 105 A2
Ashridge Gn 2 RG42 ... 118 B8
Ashridge Rd RG40 ... 116 D8
Ashton Cl RG31 ... 84 C8
Ashton Pl Kintbury RG17 ... 102 B2
Maidenhead SL6 ... 39 A6
Ashton Rd Newbury RG14 ... 105 B2
Wokingham RG41 ... 88 F1
Ashtree Cnr RG20 ... 129 C7
Ashtree Ct 3 TW15 ... 98 B3
Ashtrees Rd RG5 ... 87 F8
Ashurst Dr TW17 ... 124 E5
Ashview Cl TW15 ... 97 E3
Ashview Gdns TW15 ... 97 E3
Ashville Pk RG41 ... 116 B5
Ashville Way RG41 ... 116 A5
Ashwell Ave GU15 ... 151 F6
Ashwell Ct TW15 ... 97 E6
Ashwood RG5 ... 87 D4
Ashwood Cl RG31 ... 84 B6
Ashwood Dr RG14 ... 105 D4
Ashwood Rd TW20 ... 95 B2
Ashworth Dr RG19 ... 106 C2
Askew Dr RG7 ... 113 B3
Aspen Cl Slough SL2 ... 42 B8
Staines TW18 ... 96 F5
Aspen Ct GU25 ... 122 E5
Aspen Gdns TW15 ... 98 C3
Aspin Way GU17 ... 150 B5
Astleham Rd TW17 ... 124 E6
Astley Cl RG41 ... 115 F7
Aston Ave RG31 ... 84 B8
Aston Cl RG8 ... 56 D5
Aston Cotts SL4 ... 93 A4
Aston Ct RG30 ... 85 B5
Aston Ferry La RG9 ... 16 D5
Aston La RG9 ... 16 C3
Aston Mead SL4 ... 66 E6
Aston St OX11 ... 12 F8
Astonville SL2 ... 22 C8
Astor Cl Maidenhead SL6 ... 40 B6
Winnersh RG41 ... 88 D3
Astra Mead RG42 ... 92 B2
Atfield Gr GU20 ... 146 D4
Atherton Cl Reading RG30 ... 84 F8
Stanwell TW19 ... 70 D1
Atherton Cres RG17 ... 100 D5
Atherton Ct SL4 ... 67 D7
Atherton Pl RG17 ... 25 B3
Atherton Rd RG17 ... 100 D5
Athlone Cl SL6 ... 19 E1
Athlone Sq SL4 ... 67 C6
Atrebatti Rd GU47 ... 143 C1
Atte La RG42 ... 91 C2
Attebrouche Ct RG12 ... 118 D2
Attwood Dr RG2 ... 140 E8
Auburn Ct RG4 ... 59 A2
Auckland Cl SL6 ... 40 B8
Auckland Rd RG6 ... 87 A6
Auclum Cl RG7 ... 111 B2
Auclum La RG7 ... 111 B2
Audley Cl RG14 ... 105 D5
Audley Dr SL6 ... 39 B6
Audley St RG30 ... 85 E8
Audley Way SL5 ... 119 D6
Audrey Ct RG7 ... 109 C3
Augur Cl TW18 ... 96 F3
August End Reading RG30 ... 85 C8
Slough SL3 ... 43 E7
Augustine Cl SL3 ... 69 E4
Augustine Wlk RG42 ... 91 E1
Augustus Gdns GU15 ... 152 C5
Austen Gdns RG14 ... 131 B8
Austin Rd RG5 ... 87 F6
Austinsgate SL6 ... 39 F8
Australia Ave SL6 ... 39 F8
Australia Rd SL1 ... 43 B4
Auton Pl RG9 ... 35 D8
Autumn Cl Caversham RG4 ... 59 C7
Slough SL1 ... 41 F5
Autumn Wlk
Maidenhead SL6 ... 39 A5
Wargrave RG10 ... 36 D2
Avalon Rd Bourne End SL8 ... 3 B5
Earley RG6 ... 87 C3
Avebury Bracknell RG12 ... 118 A3
Slough SL1 ... 42 A6
Avebury Sq RG1 ... 86 D5
Aveley Wlk 2 RG1 ... 86 B5
Avenue Dr SL3 ... 23 F1
Avenue Ho RG4 ... 58 D3
Avenue Hts RG2 ... 86 C4
Avenue Rd Egham TW18 ... 96 D3
Feltham TW13 ... 98 F5
Maidenhead SL6 ... 40 B5
Avenue Sch The RG2 ... 86 C4
Avenue Sucy GU15 ... 151 B4
Avenue The Bourne End SL8 ... 2 F4
Camberley GU15 ... 151 B5
Crowthorne RG45 ... 143 B5
Datchet SL3 ... 68 B6
Egham TW20 ... 96 B4
Farnham Common SL2 ... 22 B8
Lightwater GU18 ... 146 A1
Maidenhead SL6 ... 20 C3
Mortimer RG7 ... 137 B5
North Ascot SL5 ... 92 F1
Old Windsor SL4 ... 68 B2
Staines TW18 ... 124 B8
Wraysbury TW19 ... 68 D4
Averil Ct SL6 ... 41 C7
Avery Cl RG40 ... 141 F6
Avington Cl RG31 ... 84 B8
Avocet Cres GU47 ... 150 E8
Avocet Ct 4 RG1 ... 86 A6
Avon Cl Reading RG31 ... 84 F5
Slough SL1 ... 41 E6
Avon Ct RG42 ... 90 C2
Avon Gr RG12 ... 91 C1
Avon Pl RG1 ... 86 D8
Avon Rd TW16 ... 98 F1
Avon Way RG7 ... 109 E6
Avondale SL6 ... 19 C1
Avondale Ave TW18 ... 96 F1
Avondale Rd TW15 ... 97 D5
Avonway RG14 ... 105 D4
Axbridge RG12 ... 118 E4
Axbridge Rd RG2 ... 86 C2
Ayebridges Ave TW20 ... 96 C1
Aylesbury Cres SL1 ... 42 D7
Aylesford Way RG19 ... 107 A2
Aylesham Way GU46 ... 149 B6
Aylesworth Ave SL2 ... 22 B2
Aylesworth Spur SL4 ... 95 B8
Aylsham Cl RG30 ... 84 E8
Aymer Cl TW18 ... 123 E8
Aymer Dr TW18 ... 123 E8
Ayrton Senna Rd RG31 ... 84 C7
Aysgarth RG12 ... 118 A3
Aysgarth Pk SL6 ... 40 B1
Azalea Cl RG41 ... 88 B2
Azalea Rd RG19 ... 133 A5
Azalea Way Frimley GU15 ... 152 B6
Slough SL3 ... 43 E7

B

Babbage Way RG12 ... 118 A3
Babbington Rd RG2 ... 113 D6
Bacchus Ho RG7 ... 134 E2
Bachelors Acre SL4 ... 67 D6
Back La Beenham RG7 ... 109 A7
Brimpton RG7 ... 134 C4
Kintbury RG17 ... 127 F7
Shinfield RG7 ... 139 A8
Silchester RG7 ... 136 D4
Stanford Dingley RG7 ... 81 E4
Back St RG17 ... 47 C6
Backsideans RG10 ... 36 D2
Bacon Cl GU47 ... 150 D6
Bad Godesberg Way SL6 ... 39 F7
Baden Cl TW18 ... 97 B1
Bader Gdns SL1 ... 42 A4
Bader Way The RG5 ... 88 A5
Badgebury Rise SL7 ... 1 C7
Badgemore La RG9 ... 15 D3
Badgemore Sch RG9 ... 15 D2
Badger Cl SL6 ... 39 D4
Badger Dr
Lightwater GU18 ... 146 A1
Twyford RG10 ... 61 D7
Badgers Cl TW15 ... 97 F3
Badgers Copse GU15 ... 151 E4
Badgers Croft RG7 ... 137 A6
Badgers Glade RG7 ... 111 A2
Badgers Hill GU25 ... 122 C4
Badgers Holt GU46 ... 149 B5
Badgers Ridge RG20 ... 130 D4
Badgers Rise RG4 ... 59 A5
Badgers Sett RG45 ... 142 F5
Badgers Way
Bracknell RG12 ... 118 F7
Marlow Bottom SL7 ... 1 D7
Badgers Wlk RG9 ... 36 A3
Badgers Wood SL2 ... 22 C7
Badgerwood Dr GU16 ... 151 D2
Badminton Rd SL6 ... 39 B6
Badsworth Gdns RG14 ... 130 D4
Bagnols Way RG14 ... 104 E2
Bagshot Gn GU19 ... 145 E3
Bagshot Inf Sch GU19 ... 145 E2
Bagshot Rd Ascot SL5 ... 120 C2
Bracknell RG12 ... 118 C4
Englefield Green TW20 ... 95 C2
Bagshot Sta GU19 ... 145 E4
Baigents La RG20 ... 146 D4
Bailey Cl Maidenhead SL6 ... 39 F7
Windsor SL4 ... 67 A5
Bailey Ho 9 SL8 ... 3 A4
Bailey's La RG10 ... 62 E3
Baileys Cl GU17 ... 150 C4
Baily Ave RG18 ... 106 B4
Bain Ave GU15 ... 151 B2
Bainbridge Rd RG31 ... 84 B4
Bainhurst Cotts SL6 ... 38 B5
Baird Cl SL1 ... 42 B4
Baird Rd Arborfield RG2 ... 140 E7
Arborfield Cross RG2 ... 114 E1
Bakeham La TW20 ... 95 D1
Bakehouse Ct SL5 ... 119 B8
Baker St
Aston Tirrold OX11 ... 12 F8
Reading RG1 ... 85 F7
Bakers Ct TW19 ... 70 D1
Bakers La SL6 ... 38 F8
Bakers Orch HP10 ... 3 E5
Bakers Row SL6 ... 38 F8
Baldwin Ct RG10 ... 61 E6
Baldwin Pl SL6 ... 39 C7
Baldwin Rd SL1 ... 21 C2
Baldwin's Shore SL4 ... 67 D8
Balfour Cres
Bracknell RG12 ... 118 B4
Newbury RG14 ... 130 C6
Balfour Dr RG31 ... 84 B4
Balfour Pl SL7 ... 1 C4
Balintore Ct 8 GU47 ... 150 D8
Ball Pit Rd RG20 ... 30 B5
Ballamoor Cl RG31 ... 84 B3
Ballard Ct GU15 ... 152 A8
Ballard Gn SL4 ... 66 E7
Ballard Rd GU15 ... 152 A8
Ballencrieff Rd SL5 ... 120 F2
Balliol Rd RG4 ... 58 D3
Balliol Way GU47 ... 143 E1
Balme Cl RG10 ... 61 B4
Balmoral SL6 ... 19 B1
Balmoral Cl SL1 ... 41 E7
Balmoral Gdns SL4 ... 67 D4
Balmoral Grange TW18 ... 124 B7
Balmore Dr RG4 ... 59 B4
Balmore Ho RG4 ... 59 B3
Balmore Pk RG4 ... 59 B3
Bamburgh Cl RG2 ... 86 C3
Bamford Pl RG31 ... 84 B4
Banbury RG12 ... 118 E2
Banbury Ave SL1 ... 41 F8
Banbury Cl RG41 ... 116 A6
Banbury Gdns RG4 ... 59 C3
Bancroft Cl TW15 ... 98 A3
Bancroft Pl RG31 ... 84 B3
Bangors Cl SL0 ... 44 F7
Bangors Rd S SL0 ... 44 E8
Bank Apartments SL7 ... 1 D3
Bank Side RG40 ... 141 F6
Banks Spur SL1 ... 42 B4
Bankside Cl RG2 ... 86 D2
Bannard Rd SL6 ... 39 A5
Bannister Cl SL3 ... 43 E4
Bannister Gdns GU46 ... 149 F5
Bannister Pl RG7 ... 133 F6
Bannister Rd RG7 ... 110 F2
Barbara Cl TW17 ... 125 B4
Barbara's Mdw RG31 ... 57 B2
Barbel Cl RG6 ... 87 B8
Barber Cl RG10 ... 88 E7
Barberry Way GU17 ... 150 F2
Barbon Cl GU15 ... 152 D3
Barbrook Cl RG31 ... 57 D3
Barchester Rd SL3 ... 43 F4
Barclay Rd RG31 ... 84 D4
Barclose Ave RG4 ... 59 C3
Bardney Cl SL6 ... 39 D3
Bardolph's Cl RG4 ... 58 D8
Bardown RG20 ... 51 B2
Barefoot Cl RG31 ... 57 B1
Barfield Rd RG18 ... 106 A4
Barge La RG7 ... 139 A5
Bargeman Rd SL6 ... 39 E5
Barholm Cl RG6 ... 87 E2
Barkby RG6 ... 87 C2
Barker Cl RG2 ... 140 E7
Barker Ct RG10 ... 88 F8
Barker Gn RG12 ... 118 B4
Barker Rd KT16 ... 123 F2
Barkers Mdw SL5 ... 119 D8
Barkham Manor RG41 ... 115 C3
Barkham Rd
Wokingham RG41 ... 115 D3
Wokingham RG41 ... 116 A5
Barkham Ride RG40 ... 141 E8
Barkham St RG40 ... 115 C2
Barkhart Dr RG40 ... 116 C7
Barkhart Gdns RG40 ... 116 C7
Barkis Mead GU47 ... 143 E2
Barkwith Cl RG6 ... 87 E2
Barley Cl RG19 ... 106 F2
Barley Ct TW19 ... 97 E7
Barley Fields HP10 ... 3 E8
Barley Mead
Bracknell RG42 ... 91 E1
Maidenhead SL6 ... 39 A5
Barley Mow Rd TW20 ... 95 C3
Barley Mow Way TW17 ... 125 A5
Barley Way 1 SL7 ... 1 D1
Barley Wlk RG31 ... 84 A5
Barn Cl Ashford TW15 ... 98 B3
Bracknell RG12 ... 118 D7
Camberley GU15 ... 151 E6
Farnham Common SL2 ... 22 B8
Kintbury RG17 ... 102 B2
Maidenhead SL6 ... 19 F2
Reading RG30 ... 85 D4
Barn Cotts RG17 ... 74 D7
Barn Cres RG14 ... 130 D7
Barn Dr SL6 ... 39 A4
Barn Farm SL7 ... 1 D3
Barn La RG9 ... 15 C4
Barn Owl Way RG7 ... 111 B3
Barn The RG18 ... 79 F5
Barnard Cl RG4 ... 59 C6
Barnard's Ct RG17 ... 100 D5
Barnards Hill SL7 ... 1 C2
Barnes Terr 12 RG14 ... 104 F2
Barnes Way SL0 ... 44 F6
Barnett Ct RG12 ... 118 C7
Barnett Gn RG12 ... 118 B3
Barnett La GU18 ... 152 F7
Barnfield Iver SL0 ... 44 E7
Slough SL1 ... 41 D5
3 Yateley GU46 ... 149 D5
Barnfield Cl SL6 ... 19 F5
Barnhill Cl SL7 ... 1 D4
Barnhill Gdns SL7 ... 1 D4
Barnhill Rd SL7 ... 1 D4
Barnsdale Rd RG2 ... 86 D3
Barnway TW20 ... 95 C3
Barnwood Cl RG30 ... 85 E8
Baroma Way RG9 ... 15 E2
Baron Ct RG30 ... 85 E7
Barons Way TW20 ... 96 D2
Baronsmead RG9 ... 15 D2
Barossa Rd GU15 ... 151 D7
Barr's Rd SL6 ... 41 B7
Barracane Dr RG45 ... 143 B5
Barrack La SL4 ... 67 D6
Barracks La RG7 ... 113 B1
Barrett Cres RG40 ... 116 E6
Barrett Ct RG1 ... 58 F1
Barrett's La RG2 ... 114 D6
Barrington Cl RG6 ... 87 B6
Barrington Ct TW18 ... 96 F2
Barrington Ho RG2 ... 113 B7
Barrington Way RG1 ... 85 E5
Barrow Lodge SL2 ... 22 C1
Barry Ave SL4 ... 67 C7
Barry Pl RG1 ... 86 A8
Barry Sq RG12 ... 118 D2
Barry Terr TW15 ... 97 F6
Barry View SL4 ... 66 C5
Bartelotts Rd SL2 ... 21 E1
Bartholomew Ct 9
RG14 ... 104 F2
Bartholomew Pl RG42 ... 91 E1
Bartlemy Cl RG14 ... 130 E8
Bartlemy Rd RG14 ... 130 E8
Bartletts La SL6 ... 65 A7
Barton Cl TW17 ... 125 B3
Barton Rd Reading RG31 ... 84 B7
Slough SL3 ... 43 F4
Barton's Dr GU46 ... 149 D4
Barwell Cl RG45 ... 142 F4
Basemoors RG12 ... 118 E7
Basford Way SL4 ... 66 D4
Basil Cl RG6 ... 86 F1
Basildon CE Prim Sch
RG8 ... 55 A6
Basildon Pk* RG8 ... 34 D1
Basingstoke Rd
Aldermaston RG7 ... 109 B2
Reading RG2 ... 86 B3
Riseley RG7 ... 139 B1
Shinfield RG7 ... 113 B3
Swallowfield RG7 ... 139 B5
Three Mile Cross RG7 ... 113 A5
Baskerville La RG9 ... 36 A3
Baslow Rd RG41 ... 88 B2
Basmore La RG9 ... 36 B4
Bass Mead SL6 ... 19 F5
Bassett Cl RG6 ... 114 C8
Bassett Rd OX12 ... 6 F8
Bassett Way SL2 ... 21 E1
Batcombe Mead RG12 ... 118 E2
Bates Cl SL3 ... 43 E7
Bath Ct SL6 ... 39 C6
Bath Rd Camberley GU15 ... 151 D6
Colthrop RG7,RG19 ... 107 D2
Froxfield SN8,RG17 ... 99 C4
Harlington TW6,UB7,TW5 ... 71 D6
Harmondsworth TW6,UB7 ... 70 E6
Hungerford RG17 ... 100 F6
Knowl Hill RG10,SL6 ... 37 D2
Littlewick Green SL6 ... 38 C5
Maidenhead SL6 ... 39 C6
Maidenhead SL6 ... 40 E7
Newbury RG20 ... 104 D4
Padworth RG7 ... 109 D4
Poyle SL3,UB7,TW6 ... 69 E6
Reading RG30,RG31,RG1 ... 85 C5
Slough SL1 ... 42 C5
Slough,Cippenham SL1,SL6 ... 41 D6
Sonning RG4 ... 60 E2
Thatcham RG18 ... 105 F4
Thatcham RG18 ... 106 C4
Woolhampton RG7 ... 108 D2
Bath Road Cotts SL3 ... 69 E6
Bathurst Cl SL0 ... 44 F4
Bathurst Rd RG41 ... 88 B2
Bathurst Wlk SL0 ... 44 F4
Battalion Way RG19 ... 106 E1
Battery End RG14 ... 130 D6
Battle Cl RG14 ... 104 D4
Battle Hospl RG30 ... 85 D8
Battle Prim Sch RG30 ... 85 D7
Battle Rd Goring RG8 ... 34 F7
Newbury RG14 ... 130 D6
Battle St RG1 ... 85 F8
Battlemead Cl SL6 ... 20 C3
Batty's Barn Cl RG40 ... 116 D5
Baughurst Rd RG7 ... 136 A6
Baxendales The RG14 ... 105 C1
Baxter Cl SL1 ... 42 E3
Bay Cl RG6 ... 86 F1
Bay Dr RG12 ... 118 E7
Bay Rd RG12 ... 118 E8
Bay Tree Ct SL1 ... 21 C2
Bay Tree Rise RG31 ... 84 C5
Baydon Dr RG1 ... 85 E5
Baydon Ho 6 RG17 ... 25 B2
Baydon Rd Lambourn RG17 ... 24 E1
Shefford Woodlands RG17 ... 74 E7
Wickham RG20 ... 75 B4
Bayeux Ct RG30 ... 85 D7
Bayfield Ave GU16 ... 151 E2
Bayford Cl GU17 ... 151 A1
Bayford Dr RG31 ... 84 F4
Bayley Cres SL1 ... 41 A8
Bayley Ct RG41 ... 88 B1
Baylis Bsns Ctr SL1 ... 42 D6
Baylis Court Sch SL1,SL2 ... 42 D8
Baylis Par SL1 ... 42 E7
Baylis Rd SL1 ... 42 E6
Bayliss Rd RG10 ... 36 D1
Bays Ct RG26 ... 134 F1
Baysfarm Ct UB7 ... 70 C6
Beach's Ho 2 TW18 ... 97 A3
Beacon Ct Colnbrook SL3 ... 69 C7
3 Reading RG30 ... 85 D6
Beacon Rd TW6 ... 71 A1
Beacon Rdbt TW6 ... 71 A1
Beaconsfield Cotts SL8 ... 3 B2
Beaconsfield Rd SL2 ... 22 C6
Beaconsfield Way RG6 ... 87 A2
Beacontree Plaza RG2 ... 86 B2
Beal's La RG31 ... 84 A7
Beale Cl RG40 ... 116 B7
Beale Park Wildlife Pk*
RG8 ... 55 F8
Beales Farm Rd RG17 ... 25 B2
Bean Oak Rd RG40 ... 116 F6
Beancroft Rd RG19 ... 106 D2
Bear La Newbury RG14 ... 105 A3
Wargrave RG10 ... 37 B3
Bear Wharf RG1 ... 86 A6
Beard's Rd TW15 ... 98 E2
Bearfield La RG17 ... 73 B7
Bears Rail Pk SL4 ... 94 F8
Bearsdon Ct SL5 ... 120 F2
Bearwater RG17 ... 100 D6
Bearwood Coll RG41 ... 115 B7
Bearwood Park Mobile Home
Pk RG41 ... 88 A2
Bearwood Path 5 RG41 ... 88 A3
Bearwood Prim Sch
RG41 ... 115 B8

Bearwood Rd RG41 ....115 C6
Beasley's Ait La TW16,
TW17 ....125 F3
Beattie Cl TW14 ....98 F7
Beatty Dr RG30 ....84 E8
Beauchamp Ct Sl4 ....42 E6
Beauchief Cl RG6 ....113 F8
Beaufield Cl RG5 ....87 D7
Beaufort Cl Sl7 ....1 E2
Beaufort Gdns Marlow Sl7 .1 E2
  North Ascot Sl5 ....119 E8
Beaufort Lodge **5** TW15 .98 B3
Beaufort Pl Sl6 ....40 D4
Beauforts TW20 ....95 C3
Beaufront Cl Gu15 ......152 A7
Beaufront Rd Gu15 ......152 B7
Beaulieu Cl
  Bracknell RG12 ....119 A6
  Datchet Sl3 ....68 B5
Beaulieu Ct Gu17 ....150 B5
Beaulieu Gdns Gu17 ....150 C5
Beaumaris Cl Sl1 ....42 C8
Beaumont Cl Sl6 ....39 A3
Beaumont Cotts Sl4 .....67 C6
Beaumont Ascot Sl5 ....119 F5
  Slough Sl3 ....43 D7
Beaumont Dr TW15 ......98 D3
Beaumont Gdns RG12 ...118 E4
Beaumont Rd Slough Sl2 .42 D8
  Windsor Sl4 ....67 C5
Beaumont Rise Sl7 ....1 E2
Beaver Cl RG41 ....116 B3
Beaver La Gu46 ....149 E5
Beaver Way RG5 ....88 B7
Beavers Cl RG26 ....135 A1
Beck Ct RG1 ....86 C6
Becket Ho **4** RG41 ....118 F2
Beckett Cl RG40 ....116 E6
Beckford Ave RG12 ....148 B3
Beckford Cl RG41 ....88 F1
Beckford Ct RG19 ......106 D3
Beckfords RG8 ....55 A5
Beckings Way HP10 ......3 C7
Beckwell Rd Sl1 ....42 C4
Bede Wlk RG2 ....86 C3
Bedfont Cl TW14 ....71 C1
Bedfont Ct TW19 ....70 B4
Bedfont Green Cl TW14 ..98 C7
Bedfont Ind Pk TW15 ....98 D5
Bedfont Ind Pk N TW15 ..98 C5
Bedfont Inf Sch TW14 ....71 E1
Bedfont Jun Sch TW14 ...71 E1
Bedfont La TW14 ....98 F8
Bedfont Lakes Cntry Pk*
  TW14 ....98 C6
Bedfont Rd
  Feltham TW14,TW13 .....98 D6
  Stanwell TW19 ....70 F1
Bedford Ave Sl1 ....42 A7
Bedford Cl
  Maidenhead Sl6 ....39 A3
  Newbury RG14 ....130 C5
Bedford Dr Sl2 ....22 B6
Bedford Gdns RG41 ....115 F7
Bedford La Sl5 ....121 B4
Bedford Rd RG1 ....85 F8
Bedfordshire Down RG42 .91 F2
Bedfordshire Way RG41 .115 E6
Bedwins La Sl6 ....19 B6
Beech RG9 ....15 D2
Beech Ave Sl4 ....151 D4
Beech Cl Ashford TW15 ..98 D3
  Brimpton RG19 ....133 B5
  Burghfield Common RG30 .111 A3
  Hampstead Norreys RG18 ..53 A5
  Maidenhead Sl6 ....39 B8
  Stanwell TW19 ....70 F1
Beech Ct Caversham RG4 .59 B3
  1 Marlow Sl7 ....1 E2
  7 Newbury RG14 ....105 A4
Beech Dr Gu17 ....150 D4
Beech Glen RG12 ......118 B5
Beech Hill Rd
  Beech Hill RG7 ....138 E6
  Spencers Wood RG7 ....113 A1
  Sunningdale Sl5 ....120 F3
Beech La Earley RG6 .....87 B2
  South Stoke RG8 ....14 F1
Beech Lodge TW18 ......96 E3
Beech Rd
  East Bedfont TW14 ....98 E8
  Mapledurham RG4 ......58 D7
  Newtown RG20 ....132 A7
  Purley On T RG8 ....57 B5
  Reading RG2 ....86 E2
  Slough Sl3 ....43 E4
Beech Ride Gu47 ......143 B1
Beech Tree La TW18 ...124 B7
Beech Tree La TW18 ...124 B7
Beech Wlk RG19 ....106 E2
Beecham Rd RG30 ......85 C8
Beechbrook Ave Gu46 .149 D5
Beechcroft RG18 ....53 A5
Beechcroft Cl Sl5 ......120 D5
Beechcroft Ct RG12 ....118 B6
Beeches Dr Sl2 ....22 B7
Beeches Rd Sl2 ....22 B7
Beeches The Goring RG8 ..34 B5
  Reading RG31 ....57 D3
  8 Staines TW18 ....96 F3
Beechfield Pl Sl6 ....39 C4
Beechingstoke **4** Sl7 ....1 F3
Beechmont Ave Gu25 ..122 D4
Beechnut Cl RG41 ......115 F5

Beechnut Dr Gu17 ......150 B6
Beechtree Ave
  Englefield Green TW20 ...95 B2
  Marlow Bottom Sl7 ....1 D5
Beechwood Ave
  Reading RG31 ....84 D8
  Staines TW18 ....97 B2
  Woodley RG5 ....87 D7
Beechwood Cl Sl5 ....92 F1
Beechwood Dr
  Maidenhead Sl6 ....39 A6
  Marlow Sl7 ....18 B8
Beechwood Gdns Sl1 ....42 E4
Beechwood Prim Sch
  RG5 ....87 E7
Beechwood Rd
  Slough Sl2 ....42 D8
  Wentworth Gu25 ....122 B1
Beechwood Sch Sl2 .....22 B2
Beedon CE Prim Sch
  RG20 ....51 D8
Beedon Dr RG12 ....117 E3
Beehive La RG12 ....117 C7
Beehive Rd
  Bracknell RG12,RG42 ..117 D7
  Staines TW18 ....96 F3
Beenham Prim Sch RG7 .108 F6
Beeston Way RG6 ......114 A8
Beggars Hill Rd RG10 ...61 B1
Beighton Cl RG6 ....113 F8
Belfast Ave Sl1 ....42 D7
Belfry **1** RG1 ....86 A6
Belfry Mews Gu47 .....149 F8
Belgrave Ct Gu17 ......150 D3
Belgrave Par Sl1 ....42 E6
Belgrave Rd Sl1 ....42 F6
Belgravia Ct **2** RG30 ...85 D6
Bell Bridge Rd KT16 ...123 F1
Bell Bsns Ctr Sl6 ....39 F6
Bell Cl Sl2 ....43 B8
Bell Cnr KT16 ....123 F2
Bell Ct Caversham RG4 ..59 B6
  Hurley Sl6 ....17 F3
  Twyford RG10 ....61 D5
Bell Foundry La RG40 ..116 C8
Bell Hill RG14,RG20 ...130 B4
Bell Holt RG14 ....130 C5
Bell House Gdns RG41 .116 B6
Bell La Aldworth RG8 ....32 F4
  Blackwater Gu17 ....150 C5
  Eton Sl4 ....41 F2
  Henley-On-T Rg9 ....15 E3
  Inkpen RG17 ....127 D3
Bell Pl Gu19 ....145 F3
Bell St Henley-On-T Rg9 .15 E2
  Maidenhead Sl6 ....39 F6
Bell Street Mews RG9 ...15 E2
Bell View Sl4 ....66 F5
Bell View Cl Sl4 ....66 F5
Bell Weir Cl TW19 ....96 B6
Belle Ave RG6 ....87 A5
Belle Vue Cl TW18 ....124 A8
Belle Vue Rd
  Henley-On-T Rg9 ....35 D8
  Reading RG1 ....85 F7
Belleisle RG8 ....57 B5
Bellever Hill Gu15 ......151 E5
Bellevue Terr **5** RG1 ...85 E7
Bellingham Cl Gu15 ...152 C4
Bellingham Wlk RG4 ....59 A5
Bellman Ct **2** RG1 ......86 A8
Bells Hill Sl2 ....23 A4
Bells Hill Gn Sl2 ....23 A5
Bells La Sl3 ....69 B4
Bellsfield Ct Sl4 ....41 F2
Bellswood La Sl0 ....44 B8
Belmont Sl2 ....42 A8
Belmont Cotts
  Colnbrook Sl3 ....69 C7
  Speen RG20 ....104 C6
Belmont Cres Sl6 ....39 D8
Belmont Dr Sl6 ....39 D8
Belmont Mews Gu15 ...151 C3
Belmont Park Ave Sl6 ...39 D8
Belmont Park Rd Sl6 ....39 D8
Belmont Rd
  Camberley Gu15 ....151 C4
  Crowthorne RG45 ......143 B6
  Maidenhead Sl6 ....39 D8
  Reading RG30 ....85 D7
Belmont Vale Sl6 ....39 D8
Belton Rd Gu15 ....151 E5
Belvedere Ct Gu17 .....150 D3
Belvedere Dr RG14 ....130 C4
Belvedere Grange Sl5 .121 A1
Belvedere Mans Sl1 .....42 C4
Belvedere Wlk **2** RG41 ..88 A3
Belvoir Cl Gu16 ....151 F1
Bembridge Ct
  Crowthorne RG45 ......142 E4
  12 Slough Sl1 ....42 F4
Bembridge Pl RG1 ......86 C7
Bembricke Gn RG42 .....91 A1
Bence The TW20 ....123 B6
Bencombe Rd Sl7 ....1 E5
Benedict Dr TW14 ....98 D8
Benedict Gn RG41 ......91 E1
Benen-Stock Rd TW19 ...70 A2
Benetfeld Rd RG42 ......90 B2
Benett Cl RG14 ....104 F5
Benett Gdns RG14 .....104 F5
Benham Chase RG20 ...103 E5
Benham Hill
  Newbury RG18 ....105 F4
  Thatcham RG18 ....106 A4
Benham La RG7 ....139 D3
Benhams La RG9 ....15 E8

Benjamin Ct TW15 ......98 C1
Bennet Ct RG42 ....86 A1
Bennet Rd RG2 ....86 A1
Bennett Ct Gu15 ....151 C5
Bennett's Hill RG7,RG30 .111 C7
Bennetts Cl Sl1 ....42 A5
Benning Cl Sl4 ....66 D4
Benning Way RG40 ....116 D8
Bennings Cl RG42 ....91 A1
Bensington Ct TW14 ....71 D1
Benson Cl Reading RG2 ..86 D3
  Slough Sl2 ....43 A5
Benson Rd RG45 ....142 F5
Bensonholme RG7 ......109 C3
Bentley Copse Gu15 ...152 B4
Bentley Ct **1** Gu15 ....151 D5
Bentley Dr RG12 ....140 E8
Bentley Pk Sl2 ....21 D3
Benyon Ct RG1 ....85 E6
Benyon Mews RG1 ......85 E6
Beomonds KT16 ....124 A2
Beomonds Row KT16 ..124 A2
Bere Court Rd RG8 ......56 B4
Bere Rd RG12 ....118 E3
Beresford Ave Sl2 ....43 C6
Beresford Rd RG30 .....85 E8
Bergenia Gdns Gu24 ...153 E6
Berkeley Ave RG1 ....85 F7
Berkeley Ct TW19 ....96 D6
Berkeley Ct **1** RG1 .....85 F6
Berkeley Dr Sl4 ....93 B7
Berkeley Gdns KT12 ...125 F2
Berkeley Mews Marlow Sl7 .1 F2
  Slough Sl1 ....41 E7
Berkeley Rd RG14 ......104 F2
Berkley Cl Sl6 ....39 A8
Berkshire Ave Sl1 ....42 B8
Berkshire Bsns Ctr
  RG19 ....107 A2
Berkshire Bsns Pk RG7 .135 E4
Berkshire Coll of Agriculture
  Sl6 ....18 A1
Berkshire Coll of Agriculture
  (Hall Place) Sl6 ....38 A8
Berkshire Dr
  Reading RG31 ....84 C7
  Thatcham RG19 ....107 A2
Berkshire Ind Hospl RG1 .85 E5
Berkshire Lodge **1** Sl6 .39 F6
Berkshire Rd
  Camberley Gu15 ....151 F8
  Henley-On-T RG9 ....35 F8
Berkshire Way RG12 ...117 D6
Bernadine Cl RG42 ......91 E1
Bernard Ct Gu15 ....151 B4
Berners Cl Sl1 ....41 E6
Bernersh Cl Gu47 ......143 C1
Berries Rd Sl6 ....20 A8
Berry Field Sl2 ....43 C7
Berry Hill Sl6 ....40 D7
Berry Hill Ct Sl6 ....40 D8
Berrybank Gu47 ....150 E6
Berrycroft RG12 ....118 D8
Berryscroft Ct TW18 ....97 C1
Berryscroft Rd TW18 ....97 C1
Berstead Cl **5** RG6 .....87 B1
Berwick Ave Sl1 ....42 A6
Berwick Cl Sl7 ....1 D3
Berwick La Sl7 ....1 C3
Berwick Rd Sl7 ....1 C3
Berwyn Ho RG2 ....113 C7
Beryl Cl RG41 ....115 E7
Bessel's Way OX11 .....12 A8
Bestobell Rd Sl1 ....42 C7
Beswick Gdns RG12 ...118 F8
Beta Ho **8** RG30 ....85 D6
Beta Way TW20 ....123 C8
Betam Rd RG1 ....86 D7
Betchworth Ave RG6 ....87 A3
Bethany Waye TW14 ....98 E8
Bethesda Cl RG8 ....55 A6
Bethesda St RG8 ....55 A5
Betjeman Wlk Gu46 ....149 B4
Betteridge Rd RG19 ...106 F2
Bettoney Vere Sl6 ....40 C4
Betty Grove La RG41 ...114 F7
Bevan Gdns RG42 ......118 A8
Beverley Cl
  Frimley Gu15 ....152 D6
  Marlow Sl7 ....1 B2
  Thatcham RG18 ....106 C4
Beverley Ct Sl1 ....43 B4
Beverley Gdns
  Maidenhead Sl6 ....19 B1
  Wargrave RG10 ....36 E3
Beverley Rd Reading RG31 .57 C1
  Sunbury TW16 ....125 F8
Bevers The RG7 ....137 A6
Bewicks Reach RG14 ..104 F3
Bexley Ct RG30 ....85 D6
Bexley St Sl4 ....67 C6
Bibury Cl RG5 ....87 D4
Bicknell Rd Gu16 ......151 E2
Biddles Cl Sl1 ....41 E5
Bideford Cl RG5 ....87 F5
Bideford Spur Sl2 ....22 E8
Biggleswade Way Gu15 .152 C4
Big Barn Gr RG42 ....91 D1
Big La RG17 ....125 B3
Bigbury Gdns RG2 ....86 D3
Bigfrith La Sl6 ....19 B6
Bigg's Hill Cotts RG20 .129 F4
Biggs La
  Arborfield Cross RG2 ..114 F1

Biggs La continued
  Barkham RG2,RG40 ....141 A8
Billet La Sl0,Sl3 ....44 B7
Billet Rd TW18,TW19 ...97 A5
Billing Ave RG40 ....141 F6
Billingbear La RG42 .....90 B5
Billington Way RG18 ...106 C5
Bilton Ind Est RG12 ....117 E5
Binbrook Cl RG6 ....87 D2
Binbury Row TW18 ......96 E4
Binfield CE Prim Sch
  RG42 ....90 C2
Binfield Ho RG42 ....90 C3
Binfield Pk RG42 ....90 D4
Binfield Rd
  Bracknell,Priestwood
  RG42 ....118 A8
  Wokingham RG40 ......116 F7
Bingham Cotts RG42 ....91 B6
Bingham Dr TW18 ....97 D1
Bingham Rd Sl1 ....41 A8
Binghams The Sl6 ....40 B3
Bingley Gr RG5 ....88 A7
Binsted Dr Gu17 ....150 D5
Birch Ave Brimpton RG19 .133 B5
  Reading RG30 ....85 A8
Birch Cl Gu15 ....151 E8
Birch Copse Prim Sch
  RG31 ....84 C8
Birch Ct RG45 ....142 F6
Birch Dr Gu17 ....150 D3
Birch Gn RG2 ....86 E3
Birch Gr Bracknell RG12 .118 C5
  Slough Sl2 ....42 E3
  Upper Halliford TW17 ..125 E7
  Windsor Sl4 ....66 D6
Birch Hill Prim Sch
  RG12 ....118 B1
Birch La Mortimer RG7 .136 E5
  West End Gu24 ....153 D7
  Winkfield RG12,Sl5 ....119 B8
Birch Platt Gu24 ....153 D6
Birch Rd
  Burghfield Common RG7 .111 A3
  Tadley RG26 ....135 A1
  Wokingham RG40 ......146 E4
  Windlesham Gu20 .....146 C1
Birch Side RG45 ....143 A6
Birch Tree View Gu18 .146 A1
Birches The
  Blackwater Gu17 ....38 B6
  Goring RG8 ....34 B6
Birchetts Cl **1** RG42 ..118 B8
Birchfields Gu15 ....151 C4
Birchington Rd Sl4 ......67 A5
Birchland Cl RG7 ......136 E6
Birchlands Ct Gu47 ....143 E2
Birchmead RG41 ....88 D2
Birchview Cl Gu46 .....149 D4
Birchwood Cl RG4 ......59 C6
Birchwood Dr Gu18 ...146 C1
Birchwood Rd RG14 ...105 D4
Birchwoods The RG31 ...84 B8
Bird Mews RG40 ....116 B6
Bird Mount Cotts Sl4 ....67 C8
Birdhill Ave RG2 ....86 D2
Birds La RG7 ....107 E4
Birdwood Rd
  Maidenhead Sl6 ....39 B7
  Sandhurst Gu47 ....150 F6
Birkbeck Pl Gu47 ......143 E1
Birkdale Gu12 ....117 E2
Birkdale Ct Sl5 ....120 C4
Birkhall Cl RG31 ....84 C5
Birley Rd Sl1 ....42 D7
Biscuit Way RG2 ....112 F8
Bisham Abbey National
  Sports Ctr Sl7 ....18 D7
Bisham CE Prim Sch Sl7 .18 E6
Bisham Ct Bisham Sl7 ..18 E6
  11 Slough Sl1 ....42 F4
Bisham Gn Sl7 ....18 E6
Bisham Rd Sl7 ....18 E6
Bishop Ct Sl6 ....39 D6
Bishop Ctr The Sl6 ......40 F7
Bishop Duppas Pk
  TW17 ....125 E2
Bishop Wand CE Sec Sch The
  TW16 ....125 F7
Bishop's La Sl4 ....92 B7
Bishop's Rd RG6 ....87 A6
Bishopdale RG12 ......118 A5
Bishops Ct
  1 Bracknell RG12 ......118 F1
  North Ascot Sl5 ....92 F2
Bishops Dr
  East Bedfont TW14 .....71 D1
  Wokingham RG40 ......116 C6
Bishops Farm Cl Sl4 ....66 C4
Bishops Gate Sl4 ....92 E6
Bishops Orch Sl2 ....22 B2
Bishops Rd Slough Sl1 ..43 A4
  Stanford Dingley RG7 ...81 F3
Bishops Way TW20 ....96 D2
Bishops Wlk HP10 ....3 E3
Bishopsgate Sch TW20 .95 B5
Bishopsgate Sch TW20 .95 B5
Bishopswood Ct RG26 .134 F1
Bishopswood La RG26 .134 E1
Bishopswood Rd RG26 .134 F2
Bispham Ct **2** RG1 .....86 C6
Bissley Dr Sl6 ....39 A2
Bitham La Ham RG17 ..126 B5
  Inkpen RG17 ....127 A5
Bitham Rd OX12 ....8 C7
Bittern Cl GU47 ....150 D8

Bitterne Ave RG31 ......84 B6
Bix Hill RG9 ....15 A6
Bix La Sl6 ....38 F8
Black Boy La Sl6 ....17 C3
Black Horse Cl Sl4 ......66 D5
Black Lake Cl TW20 ...123 A8
Black Park Cntry Pk & Visitor
  Ctr* Sl3 ....23 F3
Black Park Rd Sl3 ....23 E4
Blackamoor La Sl6 ......40 A8
Blackberry Cl TW17 ...125 E5
Blackbird Cl
  Burghfield Common RG7 .111 B3
  Sandhurst Gu47 ....150 D8
Blackbird La East RG12 .132 A3
Blackbush Bsns Ctr
  Gu46 ....149 C4
Blackbush Park Cvn Site
  Gu46 ....149 C5
Blackcap Pl Gu47 ......150 E8
Blackdown Way RG19 .106 D2
Blackett Cl TW18 ....123 F7
Blacklands Rd RG7 ....107 C5
Blackley Cl RG6 ....87 E3
Blackmeadows RG12 ..118 C3
Blackmoor Cl Sl5 ......119 D7
Blackmoor Wood Sl5 ..119 D7
Blacknest Gate Rd Sl5 .120 A6
Blacknest Rd Gu25,Sl5 .121 E6
Blackpond La Sl2 ....22 B4
Blacksmith Row Sl3 ....44 A2
Blacksmith's La TW18 .124 C6
Blacksmiths La KT16 ..124 A2
Blackstroud La E Gu18,
  Gu24 ....153 E8
Blackstroud La W Gu18 .153 D8
Blackthorn Cl Earley RG6 .87 A7
  Purley On T RG31 ....57 B1
Blackthorn Dell Sl3 .....43 C3
Blackthorn Dr
  Lightwater Gu18 ....153 B7
  Thatcham RG18 ....106 D5
Blackthorne Cres Sl3 ...69 E5
Blackthorne La RG12 ...69 E4
Blackwater Ctr
  Caversham RG4 ....59 E4
  Shinfield RG7 ....113 B1
Blackwater Rise RG31 ...84 B4
Blackwater Sta Gu17 ..150 E4
Blackwater View RG40 .142 B2
Blaenant RG40 ....58 F5
Blaenavon RG40 ....58 F5
Blagdon Cl RG10 ....131 D7
Blagdon Rd RG2 ....86 D2
Blagrave Farm La RG4 ..58 D5
Blagrave La RG4 ....58 D4
Blagrave Rise RG31 .....84 C6
Blagrave St RG1 ....86 B8
Blagrave Way RG1 ......85 F8
Blair Rd Sl1 ....42 E5
Blaire Pk Gu46 ....149 B8
Blake Cl
  Crowthorne RG45 ......143 C4
  Wokingham RG40 ......116 E8
Blake's La RG26 ....135 C1
Blakeney Cl Sl6 ....19 F1
Blakeney Fields RG17 ...48 B4
Blakes Cotts Reading RG1 .86 C7
  Wargrave RG10 ....37 B1
Blakes Rd RG10 ....36 F3
Blakes Ride Gu46 ......149 B6
Blamire Dr RG42 ....90 F2
Blanchard Cl RG5 ....88 B8
Bland's Cl RG7 ....110 F2
Blandford Cl Sl3 ....43 D3
Blandford Rd RG41 ....115 E4
Blandford Rd N Sl3 .....43 D3
Blandford Rd S Sl3 ......43 D3
Blands Ct RG7 ....111 A2
Blandy Rd RG9 ....35 D7
Blandys Hill RG17 ......128 B8
Blane's La Sl5 ....119 C3
Blatch's Cl RG7 ....83 D3
Blay's La TW20 ....95 B2
Blays Cl TW20 ....95 C2
Bledlow Cl RG14 ....130 C5
Blenheim Cl
  Slough Sl3 ....43 F5
  Wokingham RG40 ......115 E6
Blenheim Cotts RG18 .106 B8
Blenheim Ct **6** RG1 ....86 B6
Blenheim Gdns RG1 ....86 C6
Blenheim Ho
  Caversham RG4 ....59 A3
  Maidenhead Sl6 ....19 D8
  Newbury RG14 ....104 F2
  Reading RG1 ....86 C6
  Slough Sl3 ....43 D2
Blenheim Terr **1** RG1 ..86 A6
Blessed Hugh Faringdon RC
  Sch RG30 ....85 C5
Bletchmore Cl UB3 ......71 D8
Blewbury Dr RG12 .....118 E5
Blewbury Dr RG31 ......84 B7
Blewbury Hill OX11 .....12 B8
Blinco La Sl3 ....43 E7
Blind La
  Bourne End HP10,Sl8 ...3 B6
  Lambourn RG17 ....25 B2
Block Cotts RG7 ....136 B6
Blom Field Dale RG42 .117 D2
Blondell Cl UB7 ....70 D8

Bloomfield Dr RG12 ......91 C1
Bloomfield Hatch La RG7 ......138 B8
Bloomfield Rd SL6 ......39 A5
Bloomsbury Way GU17 ...150 D3
Blossom Ave RG7 ......83 E4
Blossom La RG7 ......83 E4
Blossoms The RG20 ......51 C4
Blount Cres RG42 ......90 E1
Bloxworth Cl 10 RG12 ...118 F5
Blue Ball La TW20 ......95 F3
Blue Coat Wlk RG12 ....118 D4
Bluebell Dr RG7 ......110 F3
Bluebell Hill RG12 ......118 E8
Bluebell Mdw RG41 ......88 C3
Bluebell Mews GU15 ....151 D7
Bluebell Rise GU18 ....153 B8
Bluebell Way RG18 ....106 D5
Bluecoats RG18 ......106 D4
Bluethroat Cl GU47 ....150 E8
Blumfield Cres SL1 ......41 E8
Blumfield Ct SL1 ......21 D1
Blundell's Rd RG30 ......84 E8
Blunden Dr SL3 ......44 C2
Blunts Ave UB7 ......71 A7
Blyth Ave RG19 ......106 E2
Blyth Wlk 7 RG1 ......86 B5
Blythe Cl SL0 ......44 F7
Blythe Ho SL1 ......41 D5
Blythewood La SL5 ....119 E7
Blythwood Dr GU16 ....151 D2
Boadicea Cl SL1 ......41 E5
Boames La RG20 ......129 F5
Board La RG20 ......102 F5
Boarlands Cl SL1 ......41 F6
Boathouse Reach RG9 ....15 E1
Bobgreen Ct RG2 ......113 C6
Bobmore La SL7 ......1 F3
Bockhampton Rd RG17 ...25 C1
Bockmer La SL7 ......17 B7
Bodens Ride SL5 ......119 F1
Bodin Gdns RG14 ......131 B8
Bodmin Ave SL2 ......42 A8
Bodmin Cl RG19 ......106 C2
Bodmin Rd RG5 ......87 C5
Body Rd 1 RG1 ......86 A7
Bog La RG12 ......119 A5
Boham's Rd OX11 ......11 D6
Bold's Ct SL2 ......23 A5
Bolding House La GU24 .153 F7
Boldrewood RG7 ......110 F2
Boleyn Cl TW18 ......96 E3
Bolingbroke Way RG19 .106 F3
Bolney La RG9 ......36 A5
Bolney Rd RG9 ......36 B5
Bolney Trevor Dr RG9 ....36 A4
Bolton Ave SL4 ......67 D4
Bolton Cres SL4 ......67 C4
Bolton Rd SL4 ......67 C4
Bolton Row RG20 ......50 D7
Bolton's La TW6,UB7 ......71 B7
Boltons La RG42 ......90 F1
Bolwell Cl RG10 ......61 F4
Bomer Cl UB7 ......71 A7
Bomford Cl RG18 ......78 F6
Bond Cl RG26 ......135 A1
Bond St TW20 ......95 C3
Bond Way RG12 ......118 B8
Bone La RG14 ......105 C3
Bone Lane Ind Est RG14 .105 C3
Bonemill La RG20 ......104 D2
Bones La RG9 ......35 A3
Bonhomie Ct RG10 ......89 A7
Bonnicut Ct SL5 ......121 A4
Bonny's Yd RG27 ......141 A1
Boole Hts RG12 ......118 A4
Boot End RG2 ......112 F8
Booth Dr Staines TW18 ....97 D2
Wokingham RG40 ......115 E1
Borderside Slough SL2 ....43 A7
Yateley GU46 ......149 A6
Borrowdale Cl TW20 ......96 B1
Borrowdale Gdns GU15 .152 D4
Borrowdale Rd RG41 ......88 B4
Boscawen Way RG19 ....107 A3
Boscombe Cl TW20 ......123 C8
Bosham Cl RG6 ......114 B8
Boshers Gdns TW20 ......95 F2
Bosman Dr GU20 ......146 B6
Bossington Ct 9 TW18 ...96 F3
Bostock La RG7 ......83 A2
Boston Ave RG1 ......85 F6
Boston Dr SL8 ......3 B3
Boston Gr SL1 ......42 C7
Boston Rd RG9 ......35 E8
Bosworth Gdns RG5 ......87 E4
Botany Cl RG19 ......106 F3
Botham Dr SL1 ......42 E3
Bothy The RG10 ......36 D2
Botmoor Way RG20 ......48 F7
Bottisham Cl RG6 ......114 C8
Bottle La Knowl Hill SL6 ...38 A2
Newell Green RG42 ......91 A6
Bottom La RG7 ......110 D8
Bottom Waltons Cvn Site SL2 ......21 F3
Bouldish Farm Rd SL5 ..120 A5
Boult St RG1 ......86 C7
Boulters Cl
Maidenhead SL6 ......20 C1
Slough SL1 ......42 A4
Woodley RG5 ......87 F8
Boulters Ct SL6 ......20 C1
Boulters Gdns SL6 ......20 C1
Boulters Ho RG12 ......118 E5
Boulters La SL6 ......20 C1
Boulton Pl 5 RG14 ......105 A3
Boulton Rd RG2 ......86 A3
Boults Wlk RG2 ......86 B5
Boundary Cl RG31 ......84 C6
Boundary La RG4 ......58 E3
Boundary Pl HP10 ......3 D8
Boundary Rd
Newbury RG14 ......105 B2
Staines TW15 ......97 C3
Taplow SL1,SL6 ......40 F8
Wooburn Green HP10 ......3 D8
Boundoak RG2 ......140 D8
Bourn Cl RG6 ......87 C1
Bourne Arch RG18 ......106 B4
Bourne Ave
Chertsey KT16 ......124 A6
Reading RG2 ......86 B4
Windsor SL4 ......67 C3
Bourne Cl Bourne End SL8 ...3 B5
Reading RG31 ......84 B4
Bourne End Bsns Ctr 1 SL8 ......3 B3
Bourne End Rd SL6,SL8 ...20 E8
Bourne End Sta SL8 ......3 A3
Bourne Ho 4 TW15 ......98 A3
Bourne Mdw TW20 ......123 B5
Bourne Rd
Pangbourne RG8 ......56 E5
Slough SL1 ......42 D4
Thatcham RG18,RG19 ......106 B4
Wentworth GU25 ......122 D4
Bourne Vale RG17 ......100 C5
Bourne-Stevens Cl RG1 ..86 B7
Bourneside GU25 ......122 A2
Bourton Cl RG30 ......84 F7
Bouverie Way SL3 ......43 E2
Boveney Cl SL1 ......42 A4
Boveney Ho RG12 ......118 E5
Boveney New Rd SL4 ......41 E2
Boveney Rd SL4 ......41 C1
Bovingdon Hts SL7 ......1 B2
Bowden Cl TW14 ......98 E7
Bowden Rd SL5 ......120 D4
Bowdown Ct 10 RG14 ....104 F2
Bower Ct SL1 ......41 F6
Bower Way SL1 ......41 E6
Bowes Rd Egham TW18 ....96 E2
Thatcham RG19 ......106 D2
Bowes-Lyon Cl 6 SL4 ....67 C6
Bowfell Cl RG31 ......57 C2
Bowland Dr RG12 ......118 E2
Bowling Ct RG9 ......15 D3
Bowling Green Farmhouse RG8 ......57 B5
Bowling Green La RG8 ...57 B5
Bowling Green Rd RG18 .106 B6
Bowlings The GU15 ......151 C6
Bowman Ct RG45 ......142 F4
Bowmans Cl SL1 ......21 B3
Bowry Dr TW19 ......68 F1
Bowyer Cres RG40 ......116 C8
Bowyer Dr SL1 ......41 E6
Bowyer Wlk SL5 ......119 E8
Bowyer's La RG42 ......91 C6
Boxford Ridge RG12 ......118 B6
Boxshall Ct RG14 ......104 F2
Boyd Ct RG42 ......118 A8
Boyn Hill Ave SL6 ......39 D6
Boyn Hill Cl SL6 ......39 D6
Boyn Hill Rd SL6 ......39 D6
Boyn Valley Rd SL6 ......39 D5
Boyndon Rd SL6 ......39 D7
Boyne Hill CE Inf Sch SL6 ......39 D6
Bracebridge GU15 ......151 A5
Bracken Bank SL5 ......119 C8
Bracken Cl Ashford TW16 ..98 F2
Farnham Common SL2 ......22 D8
Purley On T RG31 ......57 C1
Bracken Copse RG17 ......127 E5
Bracken La GU46 ......149 B6
Bracken Rd SL6 ......39 C4
Bracken Way
Burghfield Common RG7 ..111 A2
Flackwell Heath HP10 ......3 B7
Brackendale Cl GU15 ....151 E3
Brackendale Rd GU15 ....151 D4
Brackendale Way RG6 ......87 A5
Brackenforde SL3 ......43 C4
Brackens The RG45 ......143 A7
Brackenwood GU15 ......152 D5
Brackenwood Dr RG26 ..135 A1
Brackley Ho 8 TW18 ......96 F3
Bracknell & Wokingham Coll RG40 ......116 C6
Bracknell Beeches RG12 ......118 B6
Bracknell Bsns Ctr The RG12 ......117 F7
Bracknell Cl GU15 ......144 F1
Bracknell Coll
Bracknell RG12 ......118 C7
Bracknell,Wick Hill RG12 ..118 C8
Bracknell Enterprise Ctr RG12 ......118 A7
Bracknell Rd
Bagshot GU19 ......145 E6
Camberley GU15 ......145 A1
Crowthorne RG45 ......143 D6
Winkfield RG42 ......92 A5
Bracknell Sta RG12 ......118 B6
Brackstone Cl RG4 ......59 C2
Bradbury Gdns SL3 ......23 D8
Bradcutts La SL6 ......19 E8
Bradenham La SL7 ......18 C5
Bradfield CE Prim Sch RG7 ......82 B2
Bradfield Coll RG7 ......82 C6
Bradfields RG12 ......118 D4
Bradford Rd SL1 ......42 A7
Brading Way RG8 ......57 D5
Bradley Cl RG17 ......102 B1
Bradley Dr RG40 ......116 A2
Bradley Rd SL1 ......42 E6
Bradley-Moore Sq RG18 ......106 E5
Bradmore Way RG6 ......114 A8
Bradshaw Cl SL4 ......66 E6
Bradwell Rd RG31 ......57 C3
Braemar SL6 ......63 D7
Braemar Ct 3 SL7 ......1 D2
Braemar Gdns SL1 ......42 A4
Braemore Cl RG19 ......106 D2
Braeside RG12 ......117 C7
Brakenhale Sch The RG12 ......118 B5
Brakes Rise GU47 ......150 E8
Bramber Ct SL1 ......42 A5
Bramber Mews RG4 ......59 E4
Bramble Cl TW17 ......125 D6
Bramble Cres RG30 ......84 E8
Bramble Ct 3 RG14 ......105 B2
Bramble Dr SL6 ......39 A4
Brambledown TW18 ......124 B8
Bramblegate RG45 ......143 A6
Brambles The
Crowthorne RG45 ......142 D6
Holyport SL6 ......65 B8
Newbury RG14 ......130 E8
Bramblings RG4 ......58 E6
Bramcote GU15 ......152 C5
Bramley Ave TW17 ......125 E6
Bramley Chase SL6 ......39 C4
Bramley Cl
Chertsey KT16 ......124 B1
Earley RG6 ......87 B3
Maidenhead SL6 ......39 C3
Staines TW18 ......97 C2
Bramley Ct
Crowthorne RG45 ......142 D5
East Bedfont TW14 ......71 D1
Bramley Gr RG45 ......142 D5
Bramley La GU17 ......150 B5
Bramley Rd
Camberley GU15 ......151 B2
Silchester RG7 ......136 B1
Bramling Ave GU46 ......149 B6
Brammas Cl SL1 ......42 C3
Brampton Chase RG9 ......36 A4
Brampton Ct SL6 ......40 B8
Bramshaw Rd RG30 ......58 A1
Bramshill Cl RG2 ......140 E8
Bramwell Cl RG19 ......106 F2
Bran Cl RG30 ......84 E8
Brandon Ave RG5 ......88 A8
Brandon Cl GU15 ......152 D4
Brands Rd SL3 ......69 B8
Brandy Bottom GU46 ......149 E3
Branksome Cl GU15 ......151 E6
Branksome Ct 6 RG1 ......85 F7
Branksome Hill Rd GU47 ......150 E8
Branksome Park Rd GU15 ......151 E6
Brants Bridge RG12 ......118 E7
Brants Cl RG2 ......114 E2
Brattain Ct RG12 ......118 D6
Braunfels Wlk RG14 ......104 E2
Bravington Cl TW17 ......124 F4
Bray Cl SL6 ......40 C4
Bray Ct SL6 ......40 C2
Bray Rd Maidenhead SL6 ...40 B5
Reading RG30 ......85 B4
Braybank SL6 ......40 C4
Braybrooke Dr RG10 ......88 F8
Braybrooke Gdns RG10 ...36 D1
Braybrooke Rd
Bracknell RG42 ......91 B1
Wargrave RG10 ......36 D1
Braye Cl GU47 ......143 C1
Brayfield Rd SL6 ......40 C4
Brayford Rd RG2 ......113 C8
Braywick Park & Nature Ctr* SL6 ......40 B3
Braywick Rd SL6 ......40 A4
Braywood Ave TW20 ......96 A2
Braywood CE Fst Sch SL4 ......65 E5
Braywood Cotts SL4 ......66 A5
Braziers La RG42,SL4 ......92 D4
Breach Sq RG17 ......100 D4
Breadcroft La SL6 ......38 E3
Breadcroft Rd SL6 ......38 F3
Bream Cl SL7 ......18 C8
Brean Wlk RG6 ......87 A2
Brechin Ct 3 RG1 ......86 C6
Brecon Ct SL1 ......42 C4
Brecon Rd RG5 ......87 F8
Bredon Rd RG41 ......88 F1
Bredward Cl SL1 ......21 B2
Breech The GU47 ......150 E7
Breedons Hill RG8 ......56 C5
Bremer Rd TW18 ......97 A5
Brendon Cl
Harlington UB7 ......71 C7
Reading RG30 ......57 E1
Brent Cl RG19 ......106 D2
Brent Gdns RG2 ......86 B3
Brent Rd SL8 ......3 A4
Brentmoor Rd GU24 ......153 D6
Brerewood RG6 ......86 F2
Bret Harte Rd GU16 ......151 E1
Brew Twr 3 SL7 ......1 D1
Brewery Comm RG7 ......137 B7
Brewery Ct RG7 ......83 E3
Brewhouse Hill SN8 ......99 B4
Briant's Ave RG4 ......59 C2
Briants Piece RG18 ......79 B6
Briar Ave GU18 ......153 A8
Briar Cl Burnham SL6 ......41 B7
Caversham RG4 ......59 A5
Briar Dene SL6 ......19 C1
Briar Glen SL6 ......19 E6
Briar Rd TW17 ......125 A4
Briar Way SL2 ......42 B8
Briarlea Rd RG7 ......136 F6
Briars Cl RG8 ......56 E5
Briars The SL3 ......43 F1
Briarwood RG40 ......141 E6
Briarwood Cl TW13 ......98 E5
Brickfield La Burnham SL1 .21 B4
Harlington UB3 ......71 D8
Brickfields Ind Pk RG12 .118 A7
Bridge Ave
Cookham Rise SL6 ......19 E6
Maidenhead SL6 ......40 A7
Bridge Cl
Lower Halliford KT12 ......125 F1
Slough SL1 ......41 F6
Staines TW18 ......96 E4
Bridge Ct Chertsey KT16 ..124 C2
Taplow SL6 ......40 C7
Bridge End GU15 ......151 B4
Bridge Gdns TW15 ......98 C1
Bridge La GU25 ......122 F3
Bridge Rd Ascot SL5 ......120 D4
Bagshot GU19 ......145 E3
Camberley GU15 ......151 B3
Chertsey KT16 ......124 B2
Maidenhead SL6 ......40 B7
Bridge Ret Pk RG40 ......116 B5
Bridge St Caversham RG4 ..59 A2
Colnbrook SL3 ......69 D7
Hungerford RG17 ......100 D6
Maidenhead SL6 ......40 A7
Newbury RG14 ......105 A3
Oatlands Park KT12 ......125 F2
Reading RG1 ......86 A7
Staines TW18 ......96 E4
Bridge View
Maidenhead SL6 ......40 C7
Sunningdale SL5 ......121 B2
Bridge Wlk GU46 ......149 D7
Bridge Works GU15 ......151 B3
Bridgeman Ct 5 SL4 ......67 A5
Bridgeman Dr SL4 ......67 A5
Bridges Cl RG41 ......115 F7
Bridges The RG7 ......136 C5
Bridgestone Dr SL8 ......3 C3
Bridgewater Cl RG30 ......58 C1
Bridgewater Ct SL3 ......44 A2
Bridgewater Terr SL4 ......67 D6
Bridgewater Way SL4 ......67 D6
Bridle Cl SL6 ......19 E1
Bridle Rd SL6 ......19 E1
Bridlepath Way TW14 ......98 E7
Bridlington Spur SL1 ......42 B4
Bridport Cl RG6 ......87 D2
Bridport Way SL2 ......22 B1
Brierley Pl RG31 ......57 C4
Briff La RG7 ......107 C7
Brigham Rd RG1 ......59 A1
Brighton Pl RG6 ......87 A6
Brighton Rd RG6 ......87 A6
Brighton Spur SL2 ......22 B1
Brightside Ave TW18 ......97 C1
Brightwalton CE Prim Sch RG20 ......28 D3
Brightwalton Gn RG20 ......28 D2
Brigidine Sch The SL4 ......67 D4
Brill Cl Caversham RG4 ......59 A4
Maidenhead SL6 ......39 D3
Marlow SL7 ......1 C2
Brimblecombe Cl RG41 ......89 A1
Brimpton CE Prim Sch RG7 ......133 F6
Brimpton La RG7 ......134 B3
Brimpton Rd
Brimpton RG7 ......133 F7
Reading RG30 ......85 B4
Tadley RG26 ......134 D1
Brinkworth Pl SL4 ......95 B8
Brinn's La GU17 ......150 C5
Brinns Cotts GU17 ......150 C5
Briony Ho RG2 ......113 B7
Brisbane Rd RG30 ......85 B8
Bristol Cl TW19 ......70 E1
Bristol Ct 10 TW19 ......70 E1
Bristol Way SL1 ......42 F5
Bristow Ct Caversham RG4 .59 B2
Marlow SL7 ......2 A3
Bristow Inf Sch GU15 ......151 B2
Bristow Rd GU15 ......151 B3
Britannia Ind Est SL3 ......69 E5
Britannia Way TW19 ......97 D8
Brittain Ct GU47 ......150 C7
Britten Rd RG2 ......86 B5
Britwell Rd SL1 ......21 D2
Brixham Rd RG2 ......86 B2
Broad Hinton RG10 ......61 F3
Broad La Bracknell RG12 .118 D6
Bucklebury RG7 ......107 C6
Wooburn Green HP10 ......3 F5
Broad Oak Ashford TW16 ..98 F2
Slough SL2 ......22 C1
Broad Oak Ct SL2 ......22 C1
Broad Platts SL3 ......43 D3
Broad St East Ilsley RG20 ..30 E7
Reading RG1 ......86 A7
West End GU24 ......153 D6
Wokingham RG40 ......116 C6
Broad St Wlk RG40 ......116 C6
Broad Street Mall RG1 ......86 A7
Broad Way RG7 ......138 D3
Broad Wlk GU16 ......151 E2
Broadacre TW18 ......97 A3
Broadcommon La RG10 ..89 C7
Broadcommon Rd RG10 ..89 B7
Broadhalfpenny La RG26 ......135 C1
Broadlands Ave TW17 ...125 C3
Broadlands Cl RG31 ......84 D5
Broadlands Ct RG42 ......117 E8
Broadlands Dr SL5 ......120 D2
Broadley Gn GU20 ......146 D4
Broadleys SL4 ......66 F7
Broadmark Rd SL2 ......43 B6
Broadmeadow End RG18 ......106 F4
Broadmoor Hospl RG45 .143 E5
Broadmoor La RG4,RG10 ..60 E5
Broadmoor Prim Sch RG45 ......143 D4
Broadmoor Rd RG10, SL6 ..63 B6
Broadpool Cotts SL5 ......93 A1
Broadrick Heath RG42 ......91 E1
Broadview Est TW19 ......98 A8
Broadwater Cl TW19 ......95 E8
Broadwater La RG10 ......61 E1
Broadwater Pk SL6 ......40 E1
Broadwater Rd RG10 ......61 E2
Broadway Bracknell RG12 .118 C7
Maidenhead SL6 ......39 F7
Staines TW18 ......97 B3
Thatcham RG19 ......106 D3
Winkfield SL4 ......93 B7
Broadway Ctyd RG19 ......106 D3
Broadway Green Farm Ind Est GU18 ......146 D2
Broadway Mall 6 SL6 ......39 F7
Broadway Rd GU18, GU20 ......146 C2
Broadway The
Laleham TW18 ......124 C7
Lambourn RG17 ......25 B3
13 Newbury RG14 ......105 A4
Sandhurst GU47 ......150 B8
Brocas Rd RG7 ......110 F1
Brocas St SL4 ......67 D7
Brocas Terr SL4 ......67 D7
Brock Gdns RG30 ......85 C8
Brock Hill Cotts RG42 ......92 A5
Brock La SL6 ......39 F7
Brock Lane Mall 7 SL6 ...39 F7
Brock Way GU25 ......122 C5
Brockbank Ho RG42 ......91 B1
Brockenhurst Dr 5 GU46 ......149 D5
Brockenhurst Rd
Ascot SL5 ......120 B3
Bracknell RG12 ......119 A6
Brockhurst (Marlston House) Sch RG18 ......79 F4
Brocklands GU46 ......149 B4
Brockley Cl RG30 ......85 A8
Brocks La RG7,RG18 ......80 B4
Brocks Way RG9 ......36 A4
Brocksett Cl RG30 ......85 D7
Brockton Ct SL6 ......39 F6
Brockway SL3 ......44 B1
Broken Furlong SL4 ......42 B1
Broken Way RG20 ......131 B2
Bromley Wlk RG30 ......84 F7
Brompton Cl 5 RG6 ......87 D1
Brompton Dr SL6 ......19 C2
Bromycroft Rd SL2 ......22 A2
Bronte Rise RG14 ......131 B8
Brook Cl Sandhurst GU47 .143 E1
Stanwell TW19 ......97 F8
Wokingham RG41 ......116 A8
Brook Cotts GU46 ......149 C6
Brook Cres SL1 ......41 E7
Brook Dr Bracknell RG12 ..118 E5
Reading RG30 ......112 E8
Brook Gn RG42 ......117 F8
Brook Ho Bradfield RG7 ...82 C7
Newbury RG14 ......105 A3
Slough SL1 ......42 D3
Brook La RG10 ......62 F3
Brook Lea RG4 ......59 C1
Brook Path SL1 ......41 F6
Brook Rd Bagshot GU19 ..145 E2
Camberley GU15 ......151 B4
Brook St Twyford RG10 ......61 D4
Windsor SL4 ......67 D5
Brook St W RG1 ......86 A6
Brookbank HP10 ......3 D3
Brookdene Cl SL6 ......19 F2
Brooke Furmston Pl SL7 ...1 E3
Brooke Pl RG42 ......90 D3
Brooker's Hill RG2 ......113 D6
Brookers Cnr RG45 ......143 A5
Brookers Row RG45 ......143 C6
Brookfield Ct GU18 ......146 C1
Brookfield Ho SL3 ......68 D6
Brookfield Rd HP10 ......3 D3
Brookfields Specl Sch RG31 ......57 C3
Brookhouse Dr SL8 ......3 C3
Brooklands Cl TW16 ......125 E8
Brooklyn Dr RG4 ......59 B6
Brookmill The RG1 ......85 F5
Brooks Rd RG18 ......106 E4
Brooksby Cl GU17 ......150 B5
Brooksby Rd RG31 ......57 D2
Brookside Chertsey KT16 .123 E2
Colnbrook SL3 ......69 C7
Reading RG31 ......84 F4
Sandhurst GU47 ......150 C8
Slough SL3 ......43 E7
Wokingham RG41 ......115 F7

Brookside Ave
  Staines TW15 .....97 D3
  Wraysbury TW19 .....68 E4
Brookside Bsns Ctr RG7 .....139 D6
Brookside Cl RG6 .....87 D2
Brookside Nursery RG7 .139 D6
Brookside Pk GU14 .....151 A1
Brookside Wlk RG7 .....111 A4
Brookway RG14 .....105 E2
Brookway Trad Est RG14 .....105 E3
Broom Acres GU47 .....143 B1
Broom Cl RG31 .....84 C5
Broom Field GU18 .....153 A7
Broom Gr RG42 .....115 D4
Broom Hill
  Cookham Rise SL6 .....19 E6
  Stoke Poges SL2 .....23 A5
Broom Ho SL3 .....43 F2
Broom Way GU17 .....150 E4
Broome Cl GU46 .....149 C7
Broome Ct RG12 .....118 B6
Broome Lodge
  Ascot SL5 .....120 D4
  Staines TW18 .....97 B3
Broomfield TW18 .....97 A2
Broomfield Cl SL5 .....121 B2
Broomfield Gate SL2 .....22 B1
Broomfield Pk SL5 .....121 B2
Broomfield Rd RG30 .....84 F8
Broomhall Bldgs ⑪ SL5 .121 B2
Broomhall La SL5 .....121 A3
Broomsquires Rd GU19 .145 F2
Broughton Cl RG30 .....58 C1
Broughton Mews GU16 .151 F1
Brownfield Gdns (Cvn Pk) SL6 .....39 E5
Browngraves Rd UB7 ....71 C7
Browning Cl
  Frimley GU15 .....152 C4
  Thatcham RG18 .....106 C4
Brownlow Dr RG42 .....91 C1
Brownlow Rd RG1 .....85 E7
Brownrigg Cres RG12 .....118 E8
Brownrigg Rd TW15 .....98 A4
Browns Ct SL1 .....43 E6
Brownsfield Rd RG18 .106 C4
Bruan Rd RG14 .....130 F8
Bruce Ave TW17 .....125 C3
Bruce Cl SL1 .....42 A5
Bruce Rd RG5 .....87 D7
Bruce Wlk SL4 .....66 D5
Brucewood Par SL7 .....1 F5
Brudenell SL4 .....66 F3
Brummell Rd RG14 .....104 E5
Brunel Cl SL6 .....39 E5
Brunel Ctr SL6 .....39 D5
Brunel Dr
  Crowthorne RG45 .....143 C8
  Woodley RG5 .....60 F1
Brunel Rd Maidenhead SL6 .39 D5
  Theale RG7 .....83 F2
Brunel Ret Pk RG2 .....86 A3
Brunel Univ (Runnymede Campus) TW20 .....95 C5
Brunel Way SL1 .....42 F5
Brunswick RG12 .....118 A2
Brunswick Hill RG1 .....85 E7
Brunswick Lodge ❸ RG1 .85 E7
Brunswick St SL0 .....85 E6
Bruton Way RG12 .....118 E2
Bryant Ave SL2 .....42 E8
Bryant Pl RG8 .....57 B5
Bryants La RG18 .....53 E1
Brybur Cl RG2 .....113 D8
Bryer Pl SL4 .....66 D4
Bryony Ho RG42 .....117 E8
Bryony Way TW16 .....98 F2
Bsns Ctr The RG41 .....116 B4
Bsns Village The SL2 .....43 B5
Buccaneer Cl RG5 .....88 B8
Buccleuch Rd SL3 .....68 A7
Buchan The GU15 .....152 A8
Buchanan Dr RG40 .....141 E7
Buckden Cl RG5 .....88 A6
Buckfield Ct SL0 .....44 A4
Buckham Hill RG17,RG20 ..48 D6
Buckhurst Gr RG40 .....116 F5
Buckhurst La SL5 .....121 A6
Buckhurst Moors RG12 .117 C6
Buckhurst Rd SL5 .....120 F7
Buckhurst Way RG6 .....87 A3
Buckingham Ave SL1 .....42 B7
Buckingham Ave E SL1 ...42 C7
Buckingham Ct
  ❶ Staines TW18 .....97 A4
  Wokingham RG40 .....116 C6
Buckingham Dr ❹ SL1 ..42 F4
Buckingham Gate SL1 .....17 D7
Buckingham Gdns ❸ SL1 .42 F4
Buckingham Ho SL6 .....39 F6
Buckingham Rd RG14 ...104 F1
Buckingham Way GU16 .151 F1
Buckland Ave SL3 .....43 B3
Buckland Cres SL4 .....66 F6
Buckland Gate SL3 .....23 B2
Buckland Jun & Inf Sch TW18 .....97 C1
Buckland Rd RG2 .....86 B3
Buckle La RG42 .....91 B6
Bucklebury RG12 .....118 A2

Bucklebury CE Prim Sch RG7 .....107 C5
Bucklebury Cl SL6 .....40 C1
Bucklebury Farm Pk* RG7 .....80 D1
Buckleberry Pl RG7 .....108 A5
Bucknell Ave RG8 .....56 E5
Bucknell Cl RG31 .....84 F4
Buckside RG4 .....59 A2
Buckthorn Cl RG40 .....116 E7
Buckthorns RG42 .....117 E8
Budebury Ct TW18 .....97 A3
Budebury Rd TW18 .....97 A3
Budge's Cotts RG40 .....116 E8
Budge's Gdns RG40 .....116 E7
Budge's Rd RG40 .....116 D7
Budham Way RG12 .....118 B3
Buffins SL6 .....20 E2
Builder's Cross SL6 .....65 E8
Bulkeley Ave SL4 .....67 B4
Bulkeley Cl TW20 .....95 C3
Bull La Bracknell RG42 ....118 B8
  Riseley RG7 .....139 A3
Bull Mdw The RG8 .....33 F6
Bullbrook Dr RG12 .....118 F8
Bullbrook Row RG12 .....118 E7
Bullmarsh Cl RG7 .....150 E8
Bulmershe Sch The RG5 ..87 C7
Bulmershe Way RG1 .....86 F6
Bulpit La RG17 .....100 D4
Bulstrode Pl SL1 .....42 F3
Bunby Rd SL2 .....22 F5
Bunces Cl SL0 .....121 B2
Bunces La RG7 .....111 A2
Bundy's Way TW18 .....96 F2
Bungalow Dr RG31 .....84 D8
Bungler's Hill RG7 .....140 B6
Bunkers Hill RG14 .....130 C5
Bunten Meade SL1 .....42 B5
Bunyan Ct ❷ RG1 .....86 A6
Burbage Gn RG12 .....118 F4
Burbidge Cl RG31 .....84 F3
Burbidge Rd TW17 .....125 A5
Burbury Woods GU15 ...151 E6
Burchell Rd RG14 .....104 E5
Burchett Coppice RG40 .141 F8
Burchett's Green CE Inf Sch SL6 .....38 B7
Burchett's Green Rd SL6 .38 B7
Burchetts Green La SL6 ..38 C6
Burchetts Way TW17 .....125 B3
Burcombe Way RG4 .....59 B4
Burcot Gdns SL6 .....19 E3
Burdens Heath RG7 .....107 A6
Burdett Cl RG7 .....86 D3
Burdock Cl
  Burghfield Common RG7 ..111 B2
  Lightwater GU18 .....153 B8
Burfield Rd SL4 .....95 B8
Burford Cl SL7 .....1 C5
Burford Ct ❼ Reading RG1 .85 F8
  Wokingham RG40 .....116 E5
Burford Gdns SL1 .....41 C8
Burford Rd GU15 .....151 B4
Burford Sch SL7 .....1 C5
Burford's RG17 .....47 C6
Burges Way TW18 .....97 A3
Burgess Cl RG5 .....87 D4
Burgess La RG17,RG20 ...128 D6
Burgett Rd SL1 .....42 B3
Burghead Cl GU47 .....150 D7
Burghfield Bridge Cl RG30 .....84 F1
Burghfield Mill RG30 .....84 D2
Burghfield Rd RG30 .....84 F2
Burghfield St Mary's CE Prim Sch RG30 .....111 C6
Burgoyne Rd
  Ashford TW16 .....98 F2
  Camberley GU15 .....152 A6
Burleigh Gdns TW15 .....98 C2
Burleigh La SL5 .....119 E8
Burleigh Mews SL5 .....119 C6
Burleigh Rd
  Frimley GU16 .....151 D1
  North Ascot SL5 .....119 E7
Burley Orch KT16 .....124 A3
Burley Way GU17 .....150 D6
Burlingham Cl RG2 .....113 C6
Burlings The SL5 .....119 F7
Burlington Cl SL1 .....42 E4
Burlington Cl TW14 .....98 D8
Burlington Ct
  Blackwater GU17 .....150 D3
  ❶ Slough SL1 .....42 E4
Burlington Rd
  Burnham SL1 .....21 B1
  Reading RG30 .....84 D7
  ❷ Slough SL1 .....42 E4
Burlsdon Way RG12 .....118 E8
Burn Wlk SL1 .....21 B2
Burne-Jones Dr GU47 ...150 D6
Burnet Cl GU24 .....153 E6
Burnetts Rd SL4 .....66 E6
Burney Bit RG26 .....135 E1
Burnham Beeches (Nature Reserve)* SL2 .....22 A7
Burnham Cl Bourne End SL8 .3 A4
  Windsor SL4 .....66 D5
Burnham Copse Inf Sch RG26 .....135 A1
Burnham Copse Jun Sch RG26 .....135 A1
Burnham Gr RG42 .....91 C1
Burnham Gram Sch SL1 ..21 D1
Burnham Hts* SL1 .....41 C7
Burnham La SL1 .....41 E7

Burnham Manor GU15 ...152 A8
Burnham Rd RG26 .....134 F2
Burnham Rise RG4 .....59 C7
Burnham Sta SL1 .....41 D7
Burnham Upper Sch SL1 .41 B8
Burniston Cl ❺ RG6 .....87 E2
Burnmoor Mdw RG27 ...141 E2
Burns Cl RG5 .....87 E4
Burns Wlk RG18 .....106 C4
Burnt Oak
  Cookham Rise SL6 .....19 F7
  Wokingham RG40 .....141 F8
Burnt Pollard La GU24 ..146 E1
Burnthouse Gdns RG42 ...91 E1
Burnthouse La RG7, ...112 B6
Burrcroft Rd RG30 .....85 A5
Burrell Rd RG20 .....31 E4
Burrells The KT16 .....124 B1
Burroughs Cres SL3 .....3 A4
Burroway Rd SL3 .....44 B3
Burrows Hill La TW6, TW19 .....70 C3
Burrows The RG26 .....135 A1
Burton Cl Twyford RG10 ..61 E2
  Windlesham GU20 .....146 D4
Burton Way SL4 .....66 E4
Burtons Hill RG17 .....102 B2
Burway Cres RG16 .....124 A5
Burwell Cl RG6 .....87 C1
Burwood Par KT16 .....124 A2
Bury La RG20 .....10 A2
Bury's Bank Rd RG19 ...132 C6
Bush Rd TW17 .....124 F4
Bush Wlk RG40 .....116 C6
Bushell Way RG2 .....140 E8
Butchers La SL6 .....63 D8
Butchers Row RG10 .....61 D4
Bute St RG30 .....85 B5
Butler Ct ❼ SL7 .....1 F3
Butler Rd Bagshot GU19 .145 F2
  Crowthorne RG45 .....143 B6
Butlers Cl SL4 .....66 D6
Butson Cl RG14 .....104 E3
Buttenshaw Ave RG2 ...141 A8
Buttenshaw Cl RG2 .....141 A8
Butter Market RG1 .....86 B7
Buttercup Cl RG40 .....117 A6
Buttercup Pl RG18 .....106 D4
Buttercup Sq TW19 .....97 D7
Butterfield
  Camberley GU15 .....151 B4
  Wooburn HP10 .....3 D4
Buttermere Ave SL1 .....41 C8
Buttermere Cl TW14 .....98 F7
Buttermere Dr GU15 .....152 D4
Buttermere Gdns RG12 .118 C6
Buttermere Way TW20 ...96 B1
Buttersteep Rise GU20, SL5 .....119 C1
Butts Furlong RG20 .....28 D3
Butts Hill Rd RG5 .....87 F8
Buxton Ave RG4 .....59 B2
Buxton Rd TW15 .....97 D3
Bybend Cl SL2 .....22 B4
Byefield Rd RG30 .....85 B4
Byeways Cl RG10 .....37 E3
Byland Dr SL6 .....40 B1
Byreton Cl RG6 .....87 B2
Byron Cl SL3 .....44 A2
Byron Gr GU15 .....152 B3
Byron Ct ❽ Marlow SL7 ...1 F3
  Newbury RG14 .....130 F7
  Twyford RG10 .....61 E4
  Yateley GU46 .....149 C4
Byron Ct GU15 .....151 C5
Byron Dr RG45 .....143 B3
Byron Rd Earley RG6 .....87 A7
  Twyford RG10 .....61 E4
Bythorn Cl RG6 .....87 E2
Byways RG14 .....41 A8
Byways Yateley GU46 .....149 B5
Bywood RG12 .....118 A2
Byworth Cl RG2 .....113 B7

C

Cabbage Hill La RG42 .....90 E4
Cabin Moss RG12 .....118 C2
Cabrera Ave GU25 .....122 D3
Cabrera Cl GU25 .....122 D3
Cadbury Cl TW16 .....98 E1
Cadbury Rd TW16 .....98 E1
Caddy Cl ❾ TW20 .....96 A3
Cadogan Cl RG6 .....87 A3
Cadogan Ct Camberley GU15 .151 E3
  Reading RG30 .....84 E7
Cadogan Pl SL3 .....68 B7
Cadogan Pl RG4 .....59 B3
Cadwell Dr SL6 .....39 D3
Caesar's Camp Rd GU15 .152 B3
Caesar's Cl ❸ GU15 .....152 B3
Caesar's Way TW17 .....125 D3
Caesars Gate RG42 .....91 E1
Cages Wood Dr SL2 .....22 B8
Cain Rd RG12 .....117 E6
Cain's La TW14 .....98 D8
Cairn Cl GU15 .....152 B3
Cairngorm Pl SL2 .....22 D2
Cairngorm Rd RG19 .....106 F2
Caistor Cl RG31 .....84 B5
Calard Dr RG18 .....106 A5
Calbourne Dr RG31 .....84 B4
Calbroke Rd SL2 .....21 F2
Calcot Jun Sch RG31 .....84 C4

Calcot Place Dr RG31 .....84 F4
Calcott Pk GU46 .....149 C6
Caldbeck Dr RG5 .....87 F7
Calder Cl Maidenhead SL6 .19 E1
  Reading RG30 .....84 F8
Calder Ct Maidenhead SL6 .19 D1
  Slough SL3 .....43 F1
Calder Way SL3 .....69 E4
Caldicott Sch SL2 .....22 B5
Caldwell Rd GU20 .....146 D5
Caledonia Rd TW19 .....97 E2
Caleta Cl RG4 .....59 D2
Calfridus Way RG12 .....118 F6
California Cntry Pk* RG40 .141 C7
California Cvn Pk RG40 .141 D7
Calleva Mus* RG7 .....136 B1
Calleva Roman Town* RG7 .....136 D1
Callin's La RG10 .....63 B3
Callington Rd RG2 .....86 C1
Callis Farm Cl TW19 .....70 E1
Callow Hill GU25 .....122 C7
Calshot Pl RG31 .....84 D4
Calshot Rd TW6 .....71 B5
Calshot Way Frimley GU16 .151 F1
  Harmondsworth TW6 .....71 A4
Calvin Cl GU15 .....152 B4
Camberley Inf Sch GU15 .....151 C5
Camberley Sta GU15 .....151 D5
Camberley Twrs ❶ GU15 .....151 C5
Camborne Cl Earley RG6 ..87 A1
  Harmondsworth TW6 .....71 A4
Camborne Cres TW6 .....71 A4
Camborne Rd S TW6 .....71 A4
Camborne Way TW6 .....71 A4
Cambria Ct Slough SL3 ....43 C4
  Staines TW18 .....96 F4
Cambria Gdns TW19 .....97 E8
Cambrian Cl GU15 .....151 B5
Cambrian Way
  Reading RG31 .....84 D4
  Wokingham RG40 .....142 A8
Cambridge Ave
  Burnham SL1 .....21 B3
  Slough SL1 .....42 A7
Cambridge Cl SL3 .....69 E3
Cambridge Ho ❶ SL4 ...67 C6
Cambridge Rd
  Crowthorne RG45 .....143 C4
  Littleton TW15 .....98 C1
  Marlow SL7 .....1 D2
  Sandhurst GU47 .....143 E1
Cambridge Sq GU15 .....151 C6
Cambridge St ❶ RG1 .....85 F8
Cambridgeshire Cl
  Bracknell RG42 .....91 F1
  Wokingham RG41 .....115 E6
Camden Pl Bourne End SL8 .3 B3
  Reading RG30 .....84 B4
Camden Rd SL6 .....39 C6
Camelford Cl GU16 .....151 F3
Camellia Ct GU24 .....153 F6
Camellia Way RG41 .....115 D7
Camilla Cl TW16 .....98 F2
Camley Gdns SL6 .....39 A8
Camley Park Dr SL6 .....38 F8
Camm Ave RG4 .....66 E4
Camp Rd RG7 .....110 D2
Campbell Cl GU46 .....149 F6
Campbell Pl GU16 .....151 F3
Campbell Rd RG45 .....143 B3
Campbell's Gn RG2 .....117 C8
Camperdown SL6 .....20 B1
Camperdown Ho ❶ SL4 ...67 C6
Campion Cl GU47 .....150 D7
Campion Ho
  Bracknell RG42 .....117 E8
  ❺ Newbury RG14 .....104 F2
Campion Way RG40 .....116 D7
Canada Rd SL1 .....43 B4
Canal View Rd RG14 .....105 B2
Canal Way RG1 .....86 D7
Canal Wharf
  Hungerford RG17 .....100 D6
  Newbury RG14 .....105 A3
Canberra Cl GU46 .....149 A7
Canberra Rd TW6 .....71 A5
Candleford Cl RG12 .....91 C1
Candover Cl UB7 .....70 D7
Canford Ct RG30 .....85 D8
Canhurst La RG10 .....36 F2
Cannock Cl SL6 .....40 B8
Cannock Way RG6 .....87 C1
Cannon (West end of General Roy's base line)* TW6 .71 B6
Cannon Cl GU47 .....150 D8
Cannon Court Rd SL6 .....39 C6
Cannon Gate SL2 .....43 C6
Cannon Hill Cl SL6 .....40 C2
Cannon Hill La SL6 .....40 C2
Cannon La SL6 .....40 C2
Cannon Mews SL5 .....119 B8
Cannon St RG1 .....85 F7
Cannondown Rd SL6 .....19 F3
Canon Hill Dr SL6 .....40 B3
Canon's Cloisters SL4 ...67 D7
Canopus Way TW19 .....97 E8
Cansfield End RG14 .....104 F3
Canterbury Ave SL2 .....22 B1
Canterbury Ct TW15 .....97 F4
Canterbury Rd RG2 .....86 C3

Cantley Cres RG41 .....116 A6
Cape Villas SL0 .....44 E7
Capital Point ❶ RG1 .....86 A6
Capper Rd GU15 .....151 A7
Capricorn Ho HP10 .....3 A4
Captains Gorse RG8 .....54 F6
Caraway Rd RG6 .....87 C3
Carbery La SL5 .....120 B6
Carbinswood La RG12 ...108 B5
Cardiff Mews RG4 .....58 F1
Cardiff Rd RG1 .....58 F1
Cardigan Cl SL1 .....41 F6
Cardigan Gdns RG1 .....86 E5
Cardigan Rd RG1 .....86 E6
Cardinal Cl RG4 .....59 B2
Cardinal's Wlk TW16 .....98 E2
Cardinals Wlk SL5 .....41 C7
Cardwell Cres SL5 .....120 C4
Carew Cl RG31 .....57 B4
Carew Rd TW15 .....98 C2
Carey Cl SL4 .....67 B4
Carey Rd RG40 .....116 C5
Carey St RG1 .....85 F7
Caribou Cl RG5 .....87 E8
Carisbrooke Cl
  Caversham RG4 .....59 C6
  Maidenhead SL6 .....39 C6
Carisbrooke Ct SL1 .....42 F6
Carland Cl RG6 .....113 F8
Carlinwark Dr GU15 .....151 F7
Carlisle Rd Reading RG31 .57 E3
  Slough SL1 .....42 D6
Carlton Cl Frimley GU15 .152 B3
  Woodley RG5 .....87 E6
Carlton Ct TW18 .....97 F1
Carlton Ho TW14 .....71 F1
Carlton Rd Ashford TW16 .98 F1
  Caversham RG4 .....58 E5
Carlyle Ct RG45 .....143 C5
Carlyle Rd TW18 .....97 A1
Carmarthen Rd SL1 .....42 E6
Carnarvon Rd RG1 .....86 E6
Carnation Cl RG45 .....143 B8
Carnation Dr RG42 .....92 B2
Carnegie Rd RG14 .....105 A2
Carnoustie RG12 .....117 E2
Carnoustie Ct ❶ RG41 ..86 D7
Carolina Pl RG40 .....142 E1
Caroline Dr RG41 .....116 A7
Caroline Pl UB3 .....71 E7
Caroline St ❺ RG1 .....85 F7
Carpenters Cl GU16 .....151 F1
Carpenters Ct RG7 .....137 A4
Carrick Gdns RG5 .....87 D7
Carrington Ave HP10 .....3 A4
Carrington Jun Sch HP10 ..3 A4
Carrington Rd SL1 .....42 E6
Carroll Cres SL5 .....119 F5
Carsdale Cl RG1 .....85 E5
Carshalton Rd GU15 .....145 A1
Carshalton Way RG6 .....87 D1
Carston Gr RG31 .....84 C4
Carter Cl SL4 .....67 A5
Carter's Hill RG40,RG42 ..90 A4
Carters Rise RG7 .....111 B3
Carthew Dr RG5 .....87 F7
Carwarden House Com Sch GU15 .....152 A3
Cary Cl RG14 .....130 D6
Casey Ct RG7 .....81 D3
Cassia Dr RG41 .....115 C3
Cassiobury Ave TW14 .....98 F8
Cassocks Sq TW17 .....125 D2
Castle Ave SL3 .....68 A8
Castle Cl
  ❶ Charlton TW16 .....98 E1
  Frimley GU15 .....151 F4
Castle Cres Reading RG1 ...85 F6
Castle Ct SL6 .....39 C5
Castle Dr SL6 .....39 D7
Castle End Rd RG10 .....62 B7
Castle Farm Cvn Site SL4 .....66 C5
Castle Gate ❻ SL4 .....67 C6
Castle Gr RG1 .....104 F5
Castle Hill Maidenhead SL6 .39 D7
  Reading RG1 .....85 F6
  Swallowfield RG2,RG7 ..140 C7
  Windsor SL4 .....67 D6
Castle Hill Rd TW20 .....95 D6
Castle Hill Terr SL6 .....39 D7
Castle Ind Pk RG14 .....105 C5
Castle La GU15 .....104 E6
Castle Lodge SL4 .....67 A5
Castle Mews SL6 .....39 D7
Castle Rd GU15 .....151 F4
Castle St Reading RG1 .....86 A5
  Slough SL3 .....42 F3
Castlecraig Ct GU47 .....150 D7
Castleman Ho SL1 .....120 D4
Castlemead Cotts SL4 ....67 C3
Castleton Ct SL7 .....1 B1
Castleview Ho ❶ SL4 .....67 D6
Castleview Prim Sch SL3 .43 D2
Castleview Rd SL3 .....43 C2
Castor Ct GU46 .....149 B7

Caswall Cl RG42 ....90 C2
Caswall Ride GU46 .....149 F5
Catalina Cl RG5 ....88 B7
Catalina Rd TW6 ....71 B5
Catcliffe Way RG6 ....113 F8
Catena Rise GU18 .....146 B1
Catesby Gdns GU46 ...149 A5
Catherine Dr TW16 ....98 F2
Catherine Ho SL5 .....120 B6
Catherine Rd RG14 ...105 A2
Catherine St RG30 ....85 E8
Catlin Cres TW17 .....125 D4
Catmore Rd RG20 .....29 C7
Caunter Rd RG14 .....104 D4
Causeway Est TW20 ...96 F6
Causeway The
  Caversham RG4 ....59 D1
  Egham TW18,TW20 .....96 D4
  Maidenhead SL6 ......40 C4
  Marlow SL7 ....1 E1
Causmans Way RG31 ...57 C2
Cavalier Cl
  Newbury RG14 ....105 C5
  Theale RG7 ....83 D2
Cavalier Ct TW15 .....98 D1
Cavalry Cres SL4 .....67 C4
Cavendish Cl
  Ashford TW16 ....98 F2
  Burnham SL6 ....41 A7
Cavendish Ct
  Ashford TW16 ....98 F2
  Blackwater GU17 ....150 D3
  Newbury RG14 ....105 E5
  Poyle SL3 ....69 A6
Cavendish Gdns 1 RG41 .88 A3
Cavendish Meads SL5 .120 D3
Cavendish Pk GU47 ...150 E6
Cavendish Rd
  Ashford TW16 ....98 F2
  Caversham RG4 ....59 C6
Caversham Hill RG4 ...59 C1
Caversham Park Dr RG4 .59 C5
Caversham Park Prim Sch
  RG4 ....59 D6
Caversham Park Rd RG4 .59 E6
Caversham Prim Sch
  RG4 ....59 A3
Caversham Rd RG1 ....59 A1
Caversham Wharf RG1 .59 A1
Caves Farm Cl GU47 ..150 A8
Cawcott Dr SL4 ......66 E6
Cawsam Gdns RG4 ....59 C4
Caxton Cl RG30 ......58 C1
Caxton Ct RG9 ....21 C1
Cecil Aldin Dr RG31 .57 C5
Cecil Cl TW15 ....98 C1
Cecil Rd Ashford TW15 .98 C2
  Iver SL0 ....44 E7
Cecil Way SL1 ....21 F1
Cedar RG9 ....15 D2
Cedar Ave GU17 .....150 D5
Cedar Chase SL6 .....40 C3
Cedar Cl Bagshot GU19 .145 E3
  Laleham TW18 ....124 C6
  Wokingham RG40 ....116 C6
Cedar Ct Egham TW20 .96 A4
  Maidenhead SL6 .....39 D7
  Marlow SL7 ....1 E2
  6 Windsor SL4 ......67 A5
Cedar Dr Bracknell RG42 .91 C1
  Maidenhead SL6 .....40 A7
  Marlow Bottom SL7 ...1 C7
  Pangbourne RG8 .....56 C4
  Sunningdale SL5 ....121 A2
Cedar Gr RG19 ......106 C3
Cedar Ho TW16 ......98 F1
Cedar Mount RG14 ...130 F8
Cedar Rd RG5 ....87 F6
Cedar Rd
  East Bedfont TW14 ..98 D7
  Reading RG2 ....86 E1
Cedar Rise RG19 ....133 B5
Cedar Way Charlton TW16 .98 E1
  Slough SL3 ....43 E2
Cedar Wood Cres RG4 .59 B4
Cedars Cl GU47 .....149 F8
Cedars Ho SL6 ......40 A7
Cedars Rd SL6 ......40 A7
Cedars Sch RG7 ....135 A7
Cedars The
  2 Bracknell RG12 ..118 F5
  Greenham RG19 .....131 C7
  Reading RG31 ....57 D2
  Slough SL2 ....21 F2
Celandine Cl RG45 ..143 C6
Celandine Ct GU46 ..149 B7
Celandine Gr RG18 .106 F3
Celia Cres TW15 ....97 D2
Cell Farm SL4 ......68 B2
Cell Farm Ave SL4 ..68 B2
Celsea Pl OX10 .....14 A8
Cemetery La TW17 ..125 B2
Centenary Bsns Pk RG9 .15 E1
Central Dr SL4 .....41 F6
Central Est SL6 ....39 E8
Central La SL4 .....93 B7
Central Wlk RG40 ..116 C6
Centre The
  Farnham Common SL2 .22 C6
  Oatlands Park KT12 .125 F1
  4 Sandhurst GU47 ..150 D8
Century Cl RG10 ....37 E4
Century Dr RG7 ....113 C1
Cerotus Pl KT16 ...123 F2
Chackfield Dr RG41 .115 D8

Chaddleworth St Andrews CE
  Prim Sch RG20 .....49 B7
Chaffinch Cl
  Reading RG1 ....84 B7
  5 Sandhurst GU47 ..150 D8
Chafford Cl RG41 ..115 E5
Chagford Rd RG2 ...86 B1
Chain St RG1 ....86 A7
Chainhill Rd Ox12 ...8 A7
Chalcott SL1 ....42 E3
Chalcraft Cl RG9 ...35 C8
Chalfont Cl RG6 ....87 A1
Chalfont Ct RG6 ....87 A1
Chalfont Way RG6 ..87 A1
Chalford Flats HP10 .3 F6
Chalford Rd RG14 ..104 E2
Chalgrove Cl SL6 ...40 B6
Chalgrove Way RG4 .59 B6
Chalk Hill
  Aston Tirrold OX11 .12 F8
  Shiplake RG9 ....35 C6
Chalk Pit La SL1 ...21 B4
Chalkhousegreen La
  RG4 ....59 C8
Chalklands SL8 .....3 A4
Chalkpit Cotts RG7 .83 C6
Chalkpit La SL7 ....1 B2
Chalkpits The HP10 .3 E6
Chalkstream Way HP10 .3 E7
Challenge Rd TW15 ..98 D5
Challenor Cl RG40 .141 F7
Challis Pl RG42 ...117 E8
Challow Ct SL6 .....19 D1
Chalmers Rd TW15 ..98 B3
Chalmers Rd E TW15 .98 C3
Chalvey Gdns SL1 ..42 E4
Chalvey Gr SL1 ....42 B4
Chalvey Pk SL1 ....42 E4
Chalvey Rd E SL1 ..42 E4
Chalvey Rd W SL1 .42 D4
Chamberhouse Mill La
  RG19 ....130 F1
Chamberlain's Gdns
  RG2 ....114 E2
Chambers Bsns Pk UB7 .71 A8
Chambers The 10 RG6 .86 B7
Champion Rd RG4 ..59 C1
Champney Cl SL3 ...69 A4
Chancel Mans RG42 .91 C2
Chancellor's Way The
  RG2,RG6 ....86 E4
Chancery Mews 16 RG1 .85 F7
Chancery Pl SL4 ...67 D7
Chanctonbury Dr SL5 .120 E1
Chandlers Cl TW14 .98 F8
Chandlers La RG46 .149 D8
Chandlers Quay SL6 .40 C8
Chandos Mall 8 SL1 .42 F4
Chandos Rd Egham TW18 .96 D3
  Newbury RG14 .....131 A8
Chantry Cl SL4 ....67 A6
Chantry Cl GU16 ..151 D1
Chantry Mead RG17 .100 C5
Chantry Rd
  Bagshot GU19 ......145 D2
  Chertsey KT16 .....124 C2
Chapel Arches SL6 .40 F7
Chapel Cl Bracknell RG12 .118 D6
  South Stoke RG8 ...14 C3
Chapel Cotts SL2 ..23 B5
Chapel Ct
  Hungerford RG17 ..100 D6
  Maidenhead SL6 ....39 D4
  8 Reading RG1 .....86 B7
  Thatcham RG18 ....106 C3
Chapel Hill Reading RG31 .84 C8
  8 Windsor SL4 .....67 D6
Chapel La
  Ashampstead RG8 ...54 B7
  Bagshot GU19 .....145 D2
  Binfield RG42 ......91 C8
  Blewbury OX11 .....12 A8
  Curridge RG18 .....78 E4
  Farnborough GU14 .151 A1
  Headley RG19 ......133 F1
  Hermitage RG18 ....79 C8
  Lambourn RG17 .....25 B3
  Riseley RG7 ....139 C3
  Shinfield RG7 .....113 B2
  Silchester RG7 ....135 F5
  Stoke Poges SL2 ...23 B5
  Yattendon RG18 ....53 B5
Chapel Lodge RG40 .141 F6
Chapel Rd
  Camberley GU15 ...151 B5
  Flackwell Heath HP10 .3 A8
  Silchester RG7 ....136 C5
  Stockcross RG20 ..103 E6
Chapel Sq
  Sandhurst GU15 ...150 F6
  Thorpe GU25 ......122 E5
Chapel St Marlow SL7 .1 E2
  Slough SL1 ....42 F4
  Thatcham RG18,RG19 .106 D3
Chapel Terr RG42 ...90 C1
Chapels Cl SL1 ....44 E5
Chaplain's Hill RG45 .143 D4
Chaplin Cres TW16 .98 E2
Chapman La HP10,SL8 .3 A6
Chapman Wlk RG18 .106 B4
Chapter Mews SL4 ..67 D7
Chard Cl RG5 ......87 E6
Charfield Cl RG4 ..59 A5
Charlbury Cl 8 RG12 .118 F5
Charlecombe Cl TW18 .97 B3
Charlecombe Ho RG40 .116 C6
Charles Ct TW15 ...98 C4

Charles Evans Way RG4 .59 D2
Charles Gdns SL2 ..43 A7
Charles Ho
  Henley-On-T RG9 ...15 E3
  8 Windsor SL4 .....67 C6
Charles Rd Cholsey OX10 .14 A8
  Staines TW18 ......97 D2
Charles Sq RG12 ..118 C7
Charles St Chertsey KT16 .123 F1
  Newbury RG14 .....130 D6
  Reading RG1 ....85 F8
  Windsor SL4 ....67 C6
Charlotte Cl RG18 .106 E5
Charlott's Pl 2 SL4 .67 D6
Charlotte Ave SL2 .42 F6
Charlotte Ct RG18 .79 A6
Charlotte Way 9 SL7 .1 E2
Charlton SL4 ......66 C5
Charlton Cl Slough SL1 .42 B4
  Wokingham RG40 ..141 F8
Charlton Ct RG42 .143 D1
Charlton Ho TW17 .125 C7
Charlton La
  Swallowfield RG7 .139 C5
  Upper Halliford TW17 .125 D5
Charlton Pl
  Newbury RG14 .....105 A4
  2 Windsor SL4 .....66 C5
Charlton Rd TW15 .125 C7
Charlton Row 8 SL4 .66 C5
Charlton Sq 4 SL4 .66 C5
Charlton St 4 SL4 .66 C5
Charlton Wlk 3 SL4 .66 C5
Charville Dr RG31 .84 B4
Charmile Ct 1 TW16 .98 F2
Charmwood Cl RG14 .104 F5
Charndon Ct RG2 ..86 B5
Charnham Ct RG17 .100 E6
Charnham La RG17 .100 D6
Charnham Pk RG17 .100 D6
Charnwood SL5 ....120 F3
Charnwood Ct RG2 .86 B2
Charnwood Ho 9 RG1 .85 E5
Charrington Rd RG31 .84 C4
Charta Rd W TW20 .96 C2
Charter Cl SL1 ....42 F3
Charter Pl TW18 ...97 A2
Charter Rd
  Newbury RG14 .....130 F7
  Slough SL1 ....42 F3
Charterhouse Cl RG12 .118 E4
Charteris Rd RG9 ..15 D2
Charters La SL5 ...120 D4
Charters Rd SL5 ..120 D4
Charters Sch SL5 .120 D2
Charvil House Rd RG10 .61 A5
Charvil La RG4 ....60 F4
Charvil Meadow Rd RG10 .61 B5
Chase Gdns RG42 .116 F7
Chase The Ascot SL5 .93 A1
  Crowthorne RG45 .143 A6
  Maidenhead SL6 ...19 E8
  Marlow SL7 ....2 A3
  Newbury RG14 .....104 F7
  Reading RG31 ....84 D4
  Staines KT13 .....125 E1
Chaseside Ave RG10 .61 D7
Chaseside Gdns KT16 .124 B2
Chatfield SL2 .....42 A8
Chatham Ct
  Bracknell RG12 ...118 B3
  3 Slough SL1 ......43 A3
Chatham St RG1 ...86 A8
Chatham The 1 RG1 .86 A8
Chatsworth Ave RG41 .88 B2
Chatsworth Cl
  Caversham RG4 ....59 C6
  Maidenhead SL6 ...40 B3
Chatsworth Hts GU15 .152 B7
Chatteris Way RG6 .114 C8
Chattern Ct TW15 .98 B4
Chattern Hill TW15 .98 B4
Chattern Rd TW15 .98 C4
Chatters The RG7 .140 C7
Chatton Cl RG6 ...114 A8
Chaucer Cl
  Caversham RG4 ....59 A5
  Windsor SL4 ....67 D4
  Wokingham RG40 .116 F6
Chaucer Cres RG14 .104 E5
Chaucer Gr GU15 .151 D5
Chaucer Rd Ashford TW15 .97 F4
  Crowthorne RG45 .143 B4
  Wokingham RG40 .116 F6
Chaucer Way Slough SL1 .42 F7
Chauncy Cl SL6 ...40 C6
Chauntry Cl SL6 ...40 C6
Chauntry Rd SL6 ..40 B6
Chavey Down Rd RG42 .92 B2
Chawridge La SL4 .92 C5
Chazey Cl RG4 ....58 C8
Chazey Rd RG4 ....58 B8
Cheam Cl RG12 ...118 D4
Cheap St Compton RG20 .31 E5
  Newbury RG14 .....105 A2
Cheapside Ct SL5 .120 B8
Cheapside CE Prim Sch
  SL5 ....120 B8
Cheapside Rd SL5 .120 D7
Cheddar Rd TW6 ...71 B5
Cheddington Rd RG30 .84 E7
Cheeseman Cl RG40 .116 B7
Cheffrey Ct TW15 .98 B2
Chelford Way RG4 .58 F2

Chelmsford Ct 4 SL4 .67 C5
Chelsea Cl RG30 ...84 F8
Chelwood Dr GU47 .142 F1
Chelwood Rd RG6 ..87 B2
Cheney Cl RG42 ...90 C2
Cheney Ct RG45 ..143 C5
Cheniston Cl SL5 .121 A2
Cheniston Gr SL6 .38 C7
Chepstow Rd RG1 .57 D2
Chequer La RG7 ..138 E2
Chequers Bridge Cotts
  SL0 ....44 C4
Chequers Orch SL0 .44 F7
Chequers Way RG5 .87 C7
Cherbury Cl RG12 .118 E5
Cherington Gate SL6 .19 B1
Cherington Way SL5 .119 E7
Cheriton Cl RG14 .131 B8
Cheriton Ct 2 RG1 .86 A6
Cheriton Way RG17 .150 D5
Cherries The SL2 .42 A6
Cherry Ave SL3 ...43 D4
Cherry Cl Caversham RG4 .59 C8
  Flackwell Heath HP10 .3 B7
  Newbury RG14 .....104 F4
Cherry Cnr HP10 ..3 B8
Cherry Garden La
  Littlewick Green SL6 .38 E4
  White Waltham SL6 .63 E8
Cherry Gr
  Hungerford RG17 ..100 C5
  Reading RG2 ....86 E2
Cherry Orch
  Great Shefford RG17 .48 B4
  Staines TW18 ......97 A3
  Stoke Poges SL2 ...23 A5
Cherry Tree Ave TW18 .97 B2
Cherry Tree Cl
  Chieveley RG20 ....51 C4
  Sandhurst GU47 ...143 D1
Cherry Tree Dr RG12 .118 D6
Cherry Tree Gr RG41 .115 D4
Cherry Tree Rd SL2 .23 F6
Cherrydale Rd GU15 .152 D5
Cherrywood Ave TW20 .95 B1
Cherrywood Gdns HP10 .3 A8
Chertsey Bridge Rd
  KT16,TW18 ....124 D2
Chertsey Bvd KT16 .123 F1
Chertsey La TW18 .96 F2
Chertsey Mus* KT15 .124 A3
Chertsey Rd
  Ashford TW15 ,TW16 .98 D2
  Feltham TW13,TW16 .98 E4
  Lower Halliford TW17 .125 A4
  Shepperton TW17 ..124 F2
  Sunningdale SL5 ..121 A4
  Staines TW18 ......97 B1
Chertsey Sta KT16 .123 F1
Chertsey Wlk KT16 .124 A2
Chervil Way RG7 ..111 B2
Cherwell Cl
  Brands Hill SL3 ...69 B8
  Maidenhead SL6 ...40 A8
Cherwell Cres 8 RG1 .85 F7
Cherwell Rd
  Bourne End SL8 ....3 B4
  Caversham RG4 ....59 A6
Cheseridge Rd RG20 .31 C4
Cheshire Ct SL1 ..43 B4
Cheshire Pk RG42 .91 E2
Chessholme Ct TW16 .98 E1
Chessholme Rd TW15 .98 C2
Chester Cl Ashford TW15 .98 D3
  Newbury RG14 .....105 C1
Chester Rd
  Harlington TW6 ...71 A4
  Slough SL1 ....42 C6
Chester St Caversham RG4 .59 A2
  Reading RG30 ......85 D8
Chesterblade La RG12 .118 E2
Chesterfield Mews TW15 .97 F4
Chesterfield Rd
  Ashford TW15 ......97 F3
  Newbury RG14 .....105 A1
Chesterman St RG1 .86 B6
Chesterment Way RG6 .87 D1
Chesters Rd GU15 .152 B5
Chesterton Dr TW19 .97 F7
Chesterton Rd RG18 .106 C5
Chestnut Ave
  Camberley GU15 ..152 A6
  Caversham RG4 ....59 E4
  Slough SL3 ....43 D4
  Wentworth GU25 ..121 F5
  Wokingham RG41 ..115 C7
Chestnut Cl
  Ashford,Chattern Hill TW15 .98 B4
  Ashford,Felthamhill TW16 .98 F2
  Blackwater GU17 ..150 D4
  Englefield Green TW20 .95 C2
  Fawley OX12 ....27 C7
  Harlington UB7 ....71 C7
  Maidenhead SL6 ...20 D1
  Medmenham SL7 .....17 D7
  Theale RG7 ....83 D3
Chestnut Cotts RG8 .34 A6
Chestnut Cres
  Newbury RG14 .....105 A4
  Shinfield RG2 .....113 F4
Chestnut 10 RG14 .105 A4

Chestnut Dr
  Burghfield Common RG30 .111 B4
  Englefield Green TW20 .95 D2
  Windsor SL4 ....66 F3
Chestnut Gr
  Purley On T RG8 ...57 D5
  Staines TW18 ......97 C2
Chestnut Ho RG45 .143 C5
Chestnut La RG17 .25 C4
Chestnut Manor Cl TW18 .97 B3
Chestnut Pk SL6 ..40 E3
Chestnut Rd TW15 .98 B4
Chestnut Wlk
  Hungerford RG17 ..100 D4
  Upper Halliford TW17 .125 E5
Chestnuts The RG9 .36 A3
Chetwode Cl RG40 .116 C6
Cheveley Gdns SL1 .21 C3
Cheviot Cl Frimley GU15 .152 C4
  Harlington UB3 ...71 D7
  Maidenhead SL6 ...40 B6
  Newbury RG14 .....130 C5
Cheviot Dr RG10 ..61 B4
Cheviot Rd
  Sandhurst GU47 ...142 F2
  Slough SL3 ....44 A1
Chewter Cl GU19 ..146 B6
Chewter La GU20 ..146 B6
Cheylesmore Dr GU16 .152 D3
Cheyne Rd TW15 ..98 D2
Chichester Ct Slough SL1 .43 B4
  Stanwell TW19 .....97 F7
Chichester Rd RG30 .84 E8
Chicory Cl RG6 ...86 F1
Chieveley Cl RG31 .84 C8
Chieveley Mews SL5 .121 A2
Chieveley Prim Sch
  RG20 ....78 A8
Chilbolton TW20 ..95 E3
Chilcombe Way RG6 .87 D2
Child Cl RG40 ....116 D8
Child St RG17 ....25 A3
Childrey Way RG31 .84 B8
Chillingham Way GU15 .151 C4
Chilsey Green Rd KT16 .123 E2
Chiltern Cl
  Henley-On-T RG9 ..35 B8
  Newbury RG14 .....130 C5
  Staines TW18 ......97 A3
Chiltern Coll The RG4 .59 B3
Chiltern Court Mews SL4 .67 B6
Chiltern Cres RG4 .87 A8
Chiltern Ct
  Caversham RG4 ....59 B6
  Windsor SL4 ....67 B6
Chiltern Dr RG10 .61 B4
Chiltern End Cl RG9 .35 C8
Chiltern Gn HP10 ..3 A8
Chiltern Hts RG4 .59 C6
Chiltern Manor RG10 .36 D2
Chiltern Rd Burnham SL1 .41 B8
  Caversham RG4 ....59 C4
  Marlow SL7 ....1 C2
  Sandhurst GU47 ...142 F1
Chiltern View RG8 .57 D5
Chiltern Wlk RG8 .56 D5
Chilterns Cl HP10 .3 B7
Chilterns Pk SL8 .3 B5
Chilton Ct SL6 ...41 C7
Chilton Cty Prim Sch
  OX11 ....10 C8
Chilton Ent Ctr RG7 .83 E3
Chilton Foliat CE Prim Sch
  RG17 ....73 F2
Chilton Way RG17 .100 C5
Chilwick Rd SL2 ..21 F1
Chimney La HP10 ..3 E8
Chippendale Cl
  Blackwater GU17 ..150 A4
  Tadley RG26 ......134 E1
Chippenham Cl RG30 .113 F8
Chisbury Cl RG12 .118 E3
Chiswick Lodge 8 SL7 .1 D2
Chitterfield Gate UB7 .71 A7
Chittering Cl RG6 .87 C1
Chive Rd RG6 .....87 A1
Chivers Dr RG40 .141 E7
Chives Pl RG42 ..91 D1
Chobham Rd GU16 .152 A2
Cholmeley Pl RG1 .86 E6
Cholmeley Rd RG1 .86 E6
Cholmeley Terr RG1 .86 E7
Cholsey Rd RG19 .106 C3
Choseley Cl RG40 .37 E4
Choseley Rd RG10 .37 E4
Chrislaine Cl TW19 .70 D1
Christ Church CE Inf Sch
  GU25 ....122 B6
Christ The King RC Fst Sch
  TW19 ....70 E1
Christ the King RC Prim Sch
  RG2 ....113 C8
Christchurch Cotts
  GU25 ....122 B6
Christchurch Ct 4 RG45 .67 C5
Christchurch Dr GU47 .150 D6
Christchurch Gdns RG45 .67 C5
Christchurch Rd
  Harlington TW6 ...71 A4
  Reading RG2 ....86 C5
  Virginia Water GU25 .122 C5
Christian Sq 5 SL4 .67 C6
Christie Cl GU18 ..146 C1

Christie Hts RG14 ....131 B8
Christie Wlk GU46 ......149 C4
Christopher Ct
Ashford TW15 ....97 E3
Newbury RG14 ....105 B2
Christopher Ho SL2 ......22 C7
Chudleigh Gdns RG2 ....86 C2
Chuff Cnr RG42 ....91 D2
Church App TW20 ......123 C6
Church Ave RG9 ....15 E2
Church Cl Eton SL4 ....67 D8
Hamstead Marshall RG20 ..124 B8
Laleham TW18 ....124 C6
Lambourn RG17 ....25 B2
Maidenhead SL6 ....39 D6
Winnersh RG41 ....88 C2
Church Cotts SL6 ....20 E2
Church Croft RG17 ....100 D6
Church Dr SL6 ....40 C4
Church End La RG30 ......84 F7
Church Farm Barns
RG7 ....137 D5
Church Farm Cotts 62 F7
Church Gate RG19 ......106 D3
Church Gr SL3 ....43 C8
Church Hams RG40 .....141 D6
Church Hill Binfield RG42 ..90 C5
Camberley GU15 ....151 E5
Chilton OX11 ....10 D8
East Ilsley RG20 ....30 E6
Hurst RG10 ....88 E6
Wickham RG20 ....75 C3
Woolhampton RG7 ......107 E3
Church La Arborfield RG2 ..114 D4
Ascot SL5 ....120 E4
Ashampstead RG8 ....54 A6
Barkham RG40 ....115 C1
Binfield RG42 ....90 E4
Bisley GU24 ....153 F4
Brimpton RG7 ....133 F6
Burghfield Common RG30 ..111 E6
Caversham RG4 ....59 E7
Chieveley RG20 ....51 B1
Combe RG17 ....147 E6
Finchampstead RG40 ..141 E4
Hamstead Marshall RG20 ..129 F7
Hungerford RG17 ....100 D6
Maidenhead SL6 ....40 C4
Newbury RG14 ....104 D4
Newell Green RG42 ....91 D5
Shinfield RG2 ....113 C5
Shiplake RG9 ....35 F1
Silchester RG7 ....136 E1
Slough SL2,SL3 ....43 C8
Stoke Poges SL2 ....22 F2
Sunningdale SL5 ....121 B4
Swallowfield RG7 ....140 D6
Thatcham RG19 ....106 D3
Twyford RG10 ....61 F5
Ufton Nervet RG7 ....110 C4
3 Windsor SL4 ....67 D6
Yattendon RG18 ....53 E1
Church Mews
Purley On T RG8 ....57 D5
Woodley RG5 ....87 F8
Yateley GU46 ....149 D7
Church Par TW15 ....97 F4
Church Path SL6 ....40 C4
Church Rd
Aldermaston RG7 ....135 B7
Arborfield RG7 ....140 C5
Ascot SL5 ....120 A5
Ashford TW15 ....97 F4
Bagshot GU19 ....145 D3
Blewbury OX11 ....12 A8
Bracknell RG12 ....119 C7
Caversham RG4 ....59 A2
Cookham Dean SL6 ....19 B6
Egham TW20 ....96 A3
Farnham Royal SL2 ....22 C2
Frimley GU16 ....151 D1
Froxfield SN8 ....99 B5
Ham SN8 ....124 A8
Little Marlow SL7 ....2 C5
Lower Halliford TW17 ...125 B2
Maidenhead SL6 ....40 B5
Newbury RG14 ....105 B5
Old Windsor SL4 ....68 B2
3 Pangbourne RG8 .....56 C6
Sandhurst GU15 ....150 F7
Sandhurst, Little Sandhurst
GU47 ....142 F1
Sandhurst,Owlsmoor
GU47 ....143 E1
Silchester RG7 ....136 C5
Silchester,Pamber Heath
RG26 ....135 E1
Stockcross RG20 ....103 E5
Sunningdale SL5 ....121 A4
Swallowfield RG7 ....139 D6
West End GU24 ....153 F7
Windlesham GU20 ....146 C4
Winkfield SL4 ....92 C5
Winkfield,Chavey Down
SL5 ....119 B8
Church Rd E RG45 ......143 B5
Church Rd W RG45 .....143 B4
Church Row SL3 ....23 D8
Church Side SL6 ....30 E6
Church Sq TW17 ....125 B2
Church St Burnham SL1 ..21 C1
Caversham RG4 ....59 A2
Crowthorne RG45 ......143 B4
Froxfield SN8 ....99 A1
Great Shefford RG17 .....48 A3

Church St continued
Hampstead Norreys RG18 ..52 F5
Henley-On-T RG9 ....15 D1
Hungerford RG17 ....100 D6
Kintbury RG17 ....102 A2
Reading RG1 ....86 B6
Slough SL1 ....42 D4
Slough, Upton Park SL1 ...42 F4
Staines TW18 ....96 E4
Theale RG7 ....83 D3
Twyford RG10 ....61 D4
Wargrave RG10 ....36 C2
7 Windsor SL4 ....67 D6
Church Terr
8 Reading RG1 ....86 A6
Windsor SL4 ....66 E5
Church View
Beenham RG7 ....109 A6
8 Slough SL1 ....43 A3
White Waltham SL6 ....63 E8
Yateley GU46 ....149 D7
Church Views SL6 ....39 F8
Church Way RG17 ......100 D5
Church Wlk KT16 ....124 A3
Churchend Prim Sch
RG30 ....84 F6
Churchfield Mews SL2 ...43 B7
Churchfield Pl TW17 ....125 B2
Churchill Cl
East Bedfont TW14 ....98 F7
Flackwell Heath HP10 .....3 B7
Reading RG2 ....86 B2
Churchill Ct TW18 ....97 C2
Churchill Dr Marlow SL7 ...1 F4
Winnersh RG41 ....88 B1
Churchill Rd
North Ascot SL5 ....119 F7
Slough SL3 ....43 F2
Churchmead CE Sch SL3 ..68 B7
Churchward Wlk RG31 ...84 F4
Churchway RG20 ....10 B1
Churn Rd RG20 ....31 D5
Cinnamon Cl Earley RG6 ..86 F1
Windsor SL4 ....66 F6
Cintra Ave RG2 ....86 C5
Cintra Cl RG1 ....86 D5
Cippenham CI SL1 ....41 F6
Cippenham Inf & Jun Schs
SL1 ....41 D6
Cippenham La SL1 ....42 B5
Circle Hill Rd RG45 .....143 C5
Circuit La RG30 ....85 C5
City Rd RG31 ....84 B7
Clacy Gn RG42 ....91 A1
Claires Court Sch
Maidenhead SL6 ....20 B1
Maidenhead SL6 ....39 E7
Clairmore Gdns RG31 ...57 C4
Clandon Ave TW20 ....96 C1
Clanfield Cres RG31 ......57 C2
Clanfield Ride RG17 ....150 D5
Clappers Farm Rd RG7 ..136 F1
Clappers Mdw SL6 ....20 C1
Clapps Gate Rd RG26 ..135 E1
Clapton App HP10 ....3 D8
Clare Ave RG40 ....116 C7
Clare Ct RG40 ....116 C7
Clare Dr SL2 ....22 B8
Clare Gdns TW20 ....96 A3
Clare Rd Maidenhead SL6 ..39 D6
Slough SL6 ....41 C7
Stanwell TW19 ....97 E8
Clare Wlk RG14 ....130 C5
Clarefield Cl SL6 ....19 B1
Clarefield Ct SL5 ....121 A2
Clarefield Dr SL6 ....19 A1
Clarefield Rd SL6 ....19 B1
Claremont Poyle SL3 .....69 D6
Shepperton TW17 ......125 B3
Claremont Ave GU15 ..151 F5
Claremont Cres RG14 ..105 D4
Claremont Dr TW17 ....125 B3
Claremont Gdns SL7 ......1 E2
Claremont Rd
Egham TW18 ....96 D3
Marlow SL7 ....1 E2
Windsor SL4 ....67 C5
Clarence Cres SL4 ....67 C6
Clarence Ct Egham TW20 ..95 F2
Maidenhead SL6 ....39 E8
Windsor SL4 ....67 B6
Clarence Dr
Camberley GU15 ....152 B7
Englefield Green TW20 ...95 C4
Clarence Lodge TW20 ...95 C4
Clarence Rd
Henley-On-T RG9 ....15 D2
Windsor SL4 ....67 B6
Clarence St Egham TW20 ..95 F2
Staines TW18 ....96 E4
Clarence Way RG31 ....84 B4
Clarendon Cl RG41 ....88 D2
Clarendon Copse SL6 ....39 D6
Clarendon Ct
Blackwater GU17 ....150 D3
Slough SL3 ....43 B6
Windsor SL4 ....67 B6
Clarendon Gdns RG14 ..105 A4
Clarendon Prim Sch
TW15 ....97 F4
Clarendon Rd
Ashford TW15 ....97 F4
Reading RG30 ....87 A6
Clares Green Rd RG7 ..113 B3
Clareways SL5 ....120 F2
Clarewood Dr GU15 ....151 E6
Clarewood Ho GU15 ...151 E7
Clark's Gdns RG17 ......100 D5

Clarke Cres GU15 ....150 E7
Classics The RG17 ....25 B1
Claver Dr SL5 ....120 D5
Claverdon RG12 ....118 A2
Clay Cl Flackwell Heath HP10 ..3 B8
Purley On T RG31 ....57 B1
Clay Cnr KT15 ....124 B1
Clay Hill Cres RG14 ....105 D5
Clay La Beenham RG7 ...108 F6
Wokingham RG40 ....116 F5
Claycots Sch SL2 ....22 A1
Claydon Ct
2 Caversham RG4 ....59 A2
8 Staines TW18 ....97 A4
Claydon Gdns GU17 ...151 A1
Clayhall La SL4 ....67 F2
Clayhill Cl RG12 ....119 A6
Clayhill Rd RG7,RG30 ..111 A8
Clayton Cl SL3 ....44 A3
Clayton Gr RG12 ....118 E8
Clayton Rd GU14 ....150 F1
Claytons Comb Sch SL8 ...3 A5
Claytons Mdw SL8 ....3 B3
Cleares Pasture SL1 ......21 B2
Clearsprings GU18 .....153 A8
Cleeve Ct TW14 ....98 D7
Cleeve Down RG8 ....34 D7
Cleeve Ho RG12 ....118 E5
Cleeve Park Cotts RG8 ..34 D8
Cleeve Rd RG8 ....34 B7
Clements Cl Slough SL1 ..43 B8
Spencers Wood RG7 ....113 A1
Clements Mead RG31 ....57 B1
Clements Rd RG9 ....15 C3
Clent Rd RG2 ....86 B4
Cleopatra Pl RG42 ....91 E1
Clerewater Pl RG19 ....105 F3
Clerics Wlk TW17 ....125 D3
Cleve Ct RG8 ....34 B7
Clevedon Dr RG6 ....87 A2
Clevedon Rd RG31 ....57 E3
Clevehurst Cl SL2 ....23 A6
Cleveland RG10 ....61 B4
Cleveland Cl
Maidenhead SL6 ....40 B6
Wooburn Green HP10 ....3 E8
Cleveland Dr TW18 ....124 B8
Cleveland Gr RG14 .....104 F3
Cleveland Pk TW19 ......70 E1
Clevemede RG8 ....34 C7
Cleves Ct SL4 ....66 F4
Cleves Way TW16 ....98 F2
Clewborough Dr GU15 ..152 B6
Clewborough House Sch
GU16 ....151 F1
Clewer Ave SL4 ....67 B5
Clewer Court Rd SL4 .....67 B7
Clewer Fields SL4 ....67 C6
Clewer Green CE Fst Sch
SL4 ....67 A4
Clewer Hill Rd SL4 ....66 F4
Clewer New Town SL4 ...67 A5
Clewer Pk SL4 ....67 A7
Clifford Gr TW15 ....98 A4
Cliffords Way SL8 ....3 B5
Clifton Cl SL6 ....40 A4
Clifton Ct **3** TW19 ....70 E1
Clifton Lodge Eton SL4 ...43 A4
Clifton Park Rd RG4 ......59 A2
Clifton Rd Harlington TW6 ..71 B4
Newbury RG14 ....104 E2
Slough SL1 ....43 B4
Wokingham RG41 ....116 A8
Clifton Rise
Wargrave RG10 ....36 E1
Windsor SL4 ....66 D6
Clifton St RG1 ....85 F7
Clintons Gn RG42 ....118 A8
Clitheroe Rd GU17 .....149 E1
Clive Ct SL1 ....42 D4
Clive Gn RG12 ....118 B4
Clivedale Rd RG5 ....87 E4
Cliveden* SL6 ....20 E7
Cliveden Mead SL6 ......20 C2
Cliveden Pl TW17 ......125 C3
Cliveden Rd SL6 ....20 E4
Clivemont Rd SL6 ....39 E8
Clockhouse La
Ashford TW14,TW15 .....98 B5
East Bedfont TW14,TW15 ...98 B5
Clockhouse La E TW20 ...96 B1
Clockhouse La W TW20 ..96 A1
Cloister Mews RG7 ....83 E2
Cloisters The
Caversham RG4 ....59 A3
Frimley GU16 ....151 D1
Slough SL1 ....42 D4
Clonmel Cl RG4 ....59 D2
Clonmel Way SL1 ....21 B2
Close The
Aston Tirrold OX11 ....12 F8
Bourne End SL8 ....3 A6
Bracknell RG12 ....118 C5
Burghfield Common RG7 ..111 A3
Burnham SL1 ....41 D6
Great Shefford RG17 .....48 A3
Hampstead Norreys RG18 ..52 F5
Henley-On-T RG9 ....35 D8
Lightwater GU18 ....146 A1
North Ascot SL5 ....119 D7
Sandhurst GU47 ....150 E8
Thatcham RG18 ....106 A4
Virginia Water GU25 ...122 D4
Woodley RG5 ....87 E5
Clough Dr RG18 ....78 F6

Clove Cl RG6 ....86 F1
Clover Cl RG40 ....116 E7
Clover La GU46 ....149 A6
Club La RG45 ....143 D5
Clumps The TW15 ....98 A4
Clyde Rd TW15 ....97 E7
Clyve Way TW18 ....123 E8
Coach Ho The HP10 ....3 E6
Coach House Cl GU16 ..151 E3
Coach House Ct RG8 .....56 E5
Coach Rd SL5 ....92 E1
Coach Ride SL7 ....1 D4
Coachman's Ct RG14 ..105 A3
Coachman's Lodge **3**
SL4 ....67 D5
Coachmans Dr GU47 ..130 B7
Coalmans Way SL1,SL6 ..41 A8
Coalport Way RG30 ......57 B2
Coaters La HP10 ....3 E7
Cobb Cl SL3 ....68 D6
Cobbett's La GU46 .....149 F5
Cobblers Cl SL2 ....22 B3
Cobham Cl SL1 ....41 F5
Cobham Ho RG2 ....113 E4
Cobham Rd RG5 ....87 F7
Cochrane Cl RG19 ......106 E3
Cochrane Pl GU20 .....146 D5
Cock La RG7 ....82 A2
Cock-A-Dobby GU47 ..143 A1
Cockayne Ct RG40 .....141 F7
Cockett Rd SL3 ....43 E3
Cockney Hill RG30 ....84 F6
Cody Cl RG5 ....88 B8
Coe Spur SL1 ....42 B3
Coftards SL2 ....43 C7
Cokers Ct **3** SL8 ....3 A4
Cold Ash Hill RG18 .....106 C7
Cold Ash St Mark's CE Prim
Sch RG18 ....79 C1
Cold Harbour La RG20 ...20 E2
Coldharbour Cl
Henley-On-T RG9 ....35 C8
Thorpe TW20 ....123 C6
Coldharbour La
Thorpe TW20 ....123 D6
West End GU24 ....153 F8
Coldharbour Rd
Chilton OX12 ....9 A7
Hungerford RG17 ....100 D4
Coldicutt St RG4 ....59 C1
Coldmoorholme La SL8 ...3 E4
Colemans Moor La RG5 ..87 F5
Colemans Moor Rd RG5 ..88 A6
Colemorton Cres SL4 ...41 C2
Coleridge Ave GU46 ..149 E5
Coleridge Cl
Crowthorne RG45 ......143 C4
Twyford RG10 ....61 F3
Coleridge Cres SL3 ....69 E6
Coleridge Rd TW15 ......97 F4
Coley Ave RG1 ....85 F6
Coley Hill RG1 ....85 F6
Coley Park Prim Sch
RG1 ....85 E5
Coley Pl RG1 ....86 A6
Coley Prim Sch RG1 .....86 A6
Colin Way SL1 ....42 B3
Coliseum Bsns Ctr
GU15 ....151 A3
Collaroy Glen RG18 ....106 C7
Collaroy Rd RG18 ....106 C8
College Ave Egham TW20 ..96 B2
Maidenhead SL6 ....39 E7
Slough SL1 ....42 E3
College Cl GU15 ....151 D7
College Cres
Sandhurst GU47 ....150 E8
Windsor SL4 ....67 C5
College Glen SL6 ....39 D7
College Ho **5** RG7 ....25 B2
College Piece RG7 ......136 F6
College Rd
Bracknell RG12 ....118 D5
Maidenhead SL6 ....39 E7
Reading RG6 ....86 F6
Sandhurst GU47 ....150 E8
Slough SL1 ....41 F5
College Ride
Bagshot GU19 ....145 C2
Camberley GU15 ....151 D7
College Rise SL6 ....39 D7
College Town Inf Sch
GU47 ....150 E8
College Town Jun Sch
GU47 ....150 E8
College Way
Ashford TW15 ....97 F4
East Garston RG17 ....47 D6
Colleton Dr RG10 ....61 E3
Colleton Prim Sch The
RG10 ....61 E3
Collier Cl SL6 ....19 F1
Colliers Way RG30 ....85 B7
Collingwood Coll GU15 ..152 A8
Collingwood Ct KT16 ..124 A1
Collingwood Grange Cl
GU15 ....152 A7
Collingwood Mount
GU15 ....152 A7
Collingwood Pl GU15 ..152 A8
Collingwood Rise GU15 ..152 A7
Collingwood Wlk RG31 ..84 B7
Collins Cl RG14 ....105 C4
Collins Dr SL6 ....78 F6
Collis St RG2 ....86 B5
Colliston Wlk RG31 ......84 F3

Collum Green Rd SL2 ....23 A8
Colmworth Cl RG6 ......114 A8
Coln Cl SL6 ....39 F8
Coln Trad Est SL3 ....69 F6
Colnbrook By-Pass
Colnbrook SL3,UB7 ....69 D7
Harmondsworth UB7 ......70 C7
Colnbrook CE Prim Sch
SL3 ....69 D7
Colnbrook Ct SL3 ....69 E6
Coindale Rd SL3 ....69 F6
Colne Bank SL3,TW19 ...69 C4
Colne Orch SL0 ....44 F6
Colne Reach TW19 ....69 C4
Colne Way TW19 ....96 B6
Colnebridge Cl TW18 ....96 E4
Colonel's La KT16 ......124 A3
Colonial Rd
East Bedfont TW14 ....98 E8
Slough SL1 ....43 A4
Colonnade SL6 ....40 A7
Colony Gate GU16 .....152 D2
Colston Cl RG31 ....84 C8
Colthrop Bsns Pk RG19 ..107 A1
Colthrop Cotts RG19 ...107 B1
Colthrop La RG19 ......107 B2
Colthrop Way RG19 ...107 B2
Coltsfoot Cl RG7 ....111 B3
Columbia Ct RG40 .....141 E8
Colville Gdns GU18 ....153 C6
Colyer Cl RG18 ....79 C8
Colyton Way RG8 ....57 D5
Combe Rd RG30 ....84 F7
Combe View RG17 ......100 D4
Combermere Cl SL4 ......67 B5
Comet Rd RG7 ....134 E2
Comet Way SL7 ....87 D8
Comet Way RG5 ....88 B7
Comfrey Cl RG40 ....116 E8
Commerce Pk RG2 ....83 E3
Commercial Rd
Reading RG1 ....86 A1
Staines TW18 ....97 A2
Common Hill RG2 ....82 F4
Common La
Brightwalton RG20 ....28 D5
Eton SL4 ....42 D1
Common Rd Dorney SL4 ..41 D2
Headley RG19 ....132 F1
Slough SL3 ....44 A1
Common The HP10 ....3 B8
Common Wood SL2 ......22 C8
Commonfield La RG40 ..141 B8
Commonfields GU24 ..153 F6
Commons Rd RG41 ....88 F1
Communications Rd
RG19 ....131 F5
Compass Cl TW15 ....98 C1
Compass Ho **7** RG1 ...86 B7
Compton Ave RG31 ......84 B7
Compton CE Prim Sch
RG20 ....31 A4
Compton Cl
Bracknell RG12 ....117 E3
Earley RG6 ....87 C4
Sandhurst GU47 ....141 E7
Compton Ct SL1 ....41 E7
Compton Dr SL6 ....39 A8
Compton Manor RG20 ...31 D4
Compton Place Bsns Ctr
GU15 ....151 A4
Comsaye Wlk RG12 ....118 C4
Concorde Rd SL6 ....39 D4
Concorde Way Slough SL1 ..42 C4
Woodley RG5 ....87 F5
Condor Cl RG31 ....57 C3
Condor Rd TW18 ....124 C6
Conduit La SL3 ....43 E1
Conegar Ct SL1 ....42 E5
Coney Grange RG42 .....91 B2
Congreve Cl RG7 ....135 A7
Conifer Cl RG26 ....134 E2
Conifer Crest RG14 ....130 C4
Conifer Dr
Camberley GU15 ....152 A6
Purley On T RG31 ....57 B2
Conifer La TW20 ....96 C3
Conifers The
Crowthorne RG45 ......143 A7
Maidenhead SL6 ....39 A8
Coningham Rd RG2 ....113 C6
Coningsby RG12 ....118 C5
Coningsby Cl SL6 ....39 D3
Coningsby La SL6 ....65 C6
Conisboro Ave RG4 ......58 E5
Conisboro Way RG4 .....58 E5
Coniston Cl
Frimley GU15 ....152 C3
Marlow SL7 ....106 A3
Reading RG30 ....85 F5
Woodley RG5 ....87 F5
Coniston Cres SL1 ....41 C8
Coniston Ct Ashford TW15 ..97 D5
Lightwater GU18 ....146 B1
3 Newbury RG14 ......105 A4
Coniston Dr RG30 ....57 F2
Coniston Way TW20 .....96 B1
Conkers La RG18 ....40 B8
Connaught Ave TW15 ...97 E4
Connaught Cl
Crowthorne RG45 ......142 F3
Maidenhead SL6 ....19 E1
Reading RG30 ....85 D7
Yateley GU46 ....149 B6
Connaught Jun Sch
GU19 ....145 E2

Connaught Rd
Bagshot GU19 ....145 C3
Camberley GU15 ......151 F5
Newbury RG14 ....105 B3
Reading RG30 ....85 D7
Slough SL1 ....43 B4
Connection The RG4 ..105 A6
Conniston Cl SL7 ....1 B2
Connolly Ct GU25 ....122 E5
Connop Way GU16 ....151 F3
Conought Ho RG9 ......15 E3
Conquest Ct 16 RG1 ...86 C7
Consort Dr GU15 ......152 C7
Constable Cl SL6 ......88 B8
Constable Way GU47 ..108 E6
Constitution Rd RG30 ..85 B8
Consul Cl RG5 ....88 A6
Control Tower Rd TW6 ..71 B4
Convent Lodge TW15 ..98 B3
Convent Rd Ashford TW15 ..98 B3
Windsor SL4 ....67 A5
Conway Cl GU16 ......151 F1
Conway Dr Ashford TW15 ..98 C2
Thatcham RG18 ......106 B5
Conway Rd Burnham SL6 ..41 B7
Harlington TW6 ....71 B4
Reading RG31 ....84 C5
Conygree Cl RG6 ......87 B1
Cooke Rise RG42 ......91 B2
Cookham Cl GU47 ....143 C1
Cookham Dean Bottom
SL6 ....19 C8
Cookham Dean CE Prim Sch
SL6 ....19 B7
Cookham Lodge 15 SL6 ..39 F6
Cookham Montessori Sch
SL6 ....19 F7
Cookham Rd
Bracknell RG12 ......117 E7
Maidenhead SL6 ......19 F1
Cookham Rise Prim Sch
SL6 ....19 E6
Cookham Sta SL6 ......19 F7
Coolarne Rise GU15 ..152 A6
Coolgardie Rd TW15 ..98 C3
Coombe Cotts RG8 ....13 A6
Coombe Ct RG19 ....106 E3
Coombe Hill Cl SL4 ....66 D4
Coombe Hill Ct SL4 ....66 D4
Coombe Pine RG12 ..118 D3
Coombe Rd Compton RG20 ..31 F2
Yateley GU46 ....149 B7
Coombe Sq RG19 ....106 E3
Coombe The RG8 ......33 F6
Coombes Inch Sch RG2 ..114 E3
Coombes La RG41 ....115 C4
Coombesbury La RG20 ..76 D1
Cooper Ct RG2 ....113 C7
Cooper Rd
Henley-On-T RG9 ......15 D3
Windlesham GU20 ....146 D4
Cooper Way SL1 ......43 D4
Cooper's Hill La TW20 ..95 D4
Coopers Cl TW18 ......96 E3
Coopers Cres RG18 ..106 C4
Cope Ct SL6 ....39 C7
Cope Hall La RG14 ....130 C7
Copelands Cl SL1 ....152 D4
Copenhagen Cl RG42 ..91 B1
Copenhagen Wlk RG45 ..143 B4
Copped Hall Dr GU15 ..152 C6
Copped Hall Way GU15 ..152 C6
Copper Beech RG42 ..119 A8
Copper Beech Cl SL4 ..66 D6
Copperage Rd OX12 ....9 A2
Copperdale Cl RG6 ....86 F3
Copperfield Ave GU47 ..143 E2
Copperfield Terr SL2 ..43 B6
Copperfields RG4 ......58 F3
Coppermill Rd TW19 ..69 B2
Coppice Dr TW19 ......95 D8
Coppice Gdns
Crowthorne RG45 ....142 F5
Yateley GU46 ....149 C5
Coppice Gn RG42 ......90 F1
Coppice Rd RG5 ....88 A6
Coppice The TW15 ....98 B2
Coppins La SL0 ....44 F8
Copse Ave RG4 ....59 E3
Copse Cl
Camberley GU15 ....152 A6
Marlow SL7 ....1 C3
Purley On T RG31 ......57 D3
Slough SL1 ....43 B1
Copse Dr RG41 ....116 A7
Copse End GU15 ......152 A6
Copse Mead RG5 ......60 F2
Copse The RG10 ....36 E3
Copse View Cotts SL6 ..64 C4
Copse Way RG40 ....141 E7
Copthall Ho SL6 ....40 A7
Copthorn Cl SL6 ....40 A4
Copthorne Chase TW15 ..97 F4
Copthorne Cl TW17 ..125 C3
Copthorne Dr GU18 ..146 B1
Corbett Dr GU18 ......152 F7
Corbett Gdns RG5 ......87 F7
Corbridge Rd RG2 ......86 C4
Corby Cl
Englefield Green TW20 ..95 C2
Woodley RG5 ....61 A1
Corby Dr TW20 ....95 C2
Cordelia Croft RG42 ..118 C8
Cordelia Gdns TW19 ....97 E8
Cordelia Rd TW19 ......97 E8
Corderoy Cl RG19 ....106 F2
Corderoy Pl KT16 ....123 F3

Cordwalles Jun Sch
GU15 ....151 F8
Cordwalles Rd GU15 ..151 F8
Cordwallis Est 1 SL6 ..39 F8
Cordwallis Pk SL6 ......39 E8
Cordwallis Rd SL8 ......39 F8
Cordwallis St SL6 ......39 E8
Cores End Rd SL8 ......3 B3
Corfe Gdns Frimley GU16 ..151 F1
Slough SL1 ....42 A6
Corfe Mews RG4 ......59 E4
Corfe Pl SL6 ....39 C7
Corfield Ct RG40 ......141 E3
Corfield Gn RG41 ....115 F8
Coriander Ct SL5 ......120 E3
Coriander Way RG6 ....86 F1
Corinne Ct RG2 ....86 B1
Cormorant Pl GU47 ..150 E7
Corn Croft RG42 ......91 D1
Cornbunting Cl GU47 ..150 D8
Cornel Ho 1 SL4 ......67 D4
Cornerside TW15 ......98 C1
Cornerstones RG6 ......84 E8
Cornfield Rd RG5 ......88 A8
Cornfields GU46 ......149 C5
Cornflower Cl RG41 ..115 D7
Cornwall Ave SL2 ......22 C1
Cornwall Cl
Bracknell RG42 ....91 F2
Camberley GU15 ....151 F7
Eton SL4 ....41 E1
Maidenhead SL6 ......19 E2
Purley On T RG31 ......57 B4
Wokingham RG41 ....115 C6
Cornwall Lodge 11 SL6 ..39 F6
Cornwall Way TW18 ....96 E2
Cornwell Rd SL4 ....68 A1
Cornwood Gdns RG2 ..86 C3
Coronation Ave
Slough SL1 ....43 E7
Windsor SL4 ....67 F5
Coronation Cotts RG10 ..88 D4
Coronation Rd
Ascot SL5 ....120 A2
Littlewick Green SL6 ..38 B5
Yateley GU46 ....149 E7
Coronation Sq
Reading RG30 ....85 B4
Wokingham RG40 ....116 D4
Corporation Cotts 1
RG14 ....105 A4
Corrie Gdns GU25 ....122 C2
Corsair Cl TW19 ....97 E8
Corsair Rd TW19 ......97 E8
Corsham Rd RG41 ......84 F3
Corsham Way RG45 ..143 B5
Corwen Rd RG30 ......84 F7
Coster Cl RG14 ....104 D5
Costers Cotts SL8 ......3 A4
Cotswold Cl
Maidenhead SL6 ......40 B6
Slough SL1 ....42 B3
Staines TW18 ....97 A3
Cotswold Rd SL4 ......142 F1
Cotswold Way RG31 ..57 C2
Cottage Farm Way
TW20 ....123 C6
Cottage La RG30 ......85 C2
Cotterell Ct RG42 ......91 B1
Cotterell Gdns RG10 ..61 F3
Cottesbrooke Cl SL3 ..69 D6
Cottesloe Cl GU24 ..153 F3
Cottesmore RG12 ....118 A2
Cottesmore Rd RG5 ..87 D6
Cottrell Cl RG17 ......100 E6
Coulson Way SL1 ......41 B7
Council Cotts GU24 ..153 F7
Council Hos
Barkham RG41 ....115 B2
Farley Hill RG7 ......140 D5
Shiplake RG9 ....35 B2
Sindlesham RG41 ....115 A7
Winterbourne RG20 ..77 C5
Council Hos The
Inkpen RG17 ....127 F5
Tadley RG26 ....134 B1
Country Life Ho SL3 ..68 B7
County La RG42 ....91 E2
County Lane Rdbt RG42 ..91 E2
Courage Cl RG30 ......85 B5
Course Rd SL5 ....120 A6
Court Cl SL6 ....40 C2
Court Cres SL1 ....42 D7
Court Dr SL6 ....20 C3
Court Farm Ho SL1 ....42 B5
Court Farm Ind Est TW19 ..70 F1
Court Gdns
Camberley GU15 ....151 D5
Goring RG8 ....34 C7
Court Hill Rd OX12 ......7 C7
Court La Burnham SL1 ..21 D2
Dorney SL4 ....64 B3
Court One TW5 ....98 C5
Court Rd SL6 ....20 C3
Court The RG6 ....106 D4
Court Three TW15 ....98 C5
Court Two TW15 ......98 C5
Courtenay Dr RG4 ....59 B7
Courtfield Dr SL6 ......20 C4
Courtfield Rd TW15 ....98 B2
Courthouse Jun Sch SL6 ..39 B8
Courthouse Rd SL6 ....39 C8
Courtlands 14 SL6 ....39 F6
Courtlands Ave SL3 ..43 D2
Courtlands Hill RG8 ..56 C4
Courtlands Rd RG14 ..105 B1
Courtleigh Manor SL5 ..121 A2
Courtney Ho 4 GU15 ..151 B3

Courtney Pl RG42 ......90 C2
Courtney Rd TW6 ......71 A4
Courtney Way TW6 ....71 A5
Courts Rd RG14 ....87 B4
Courtyard The
12 Bourne End SL8 ......3 B3
7 Marlow SL7 ....1 D2
Marlow SL7 ....1 E2
Theale RG7 ....83 E3
Coventry Rd RG1 ......86 E8
Coverdale Way SL2 ....21 E1
Covert La RG12 ......118 C5
Covert The SL5 ......120 B2
Coves Farm Wood
RG42 ....117 D7
Cow La East Ilsley RG20 ..30 F7
Moulsford OX10 ......13 F3
Reading RG1,RG30 ....85 E8
Cowley Ave KT16 ....123 F2
Cowley La KT16 ......123 F2
Coworth Cl SL5 ....121 A4
Coworth Rd SL5 ......121 A4
Cowper Ct KT16 ......123 F3
Cowper Rd SL2 ....22 A1
Cowper Way RG30 ....85 D4
Cowslade RG14 ......104 D5
Cowslip Cl RG31 ......84 A6
Cowslip Cres RG18 ..106 E5
Cox Green La SL6 ......39 C3
Cox Green Rd SL6 ....39 D3
Cox Green Sch SL6 ....39 A4
Cox's La RG7 ....107 D3
Coxborrow Cl SL6 ......19 E7
Coxeter Rd RG14 ....104 E4
Coxgreen GU47 ......150 D6
Coxs Ave TW17 ......125 E6
Crabtree Cl
Chieveley RG18 ....72 E2
Hermitage RG18 ......78 F6
Crabtree Cnr TW20 ..123 B8
Crabtree La RG18 ......78 E6
Crabtree Office Village
TW20 ....123 C7
Crabtree Rd
Camberley GU15 ....151 B2
Thorpe TW20 ....123 C7
Cradock Rd RG2 ......86 D6
Crafnant Ct TW15 ......97 F3
Crafts End OX11 ......10 E8
Craig Ave RG30 ....85 B8
Craigwell Cl TW18 ..123 E8
Crail Cl RG41 ....116 A3
Crake Pl GU47 ....150 D8
Cranbourne Ct TW14 ..98 F7
Cranberry Wlk GU17 ..150 F3
Cranbourne Ave
Reading RG31 ....84 C4
Windsor SL4 ....66 F5
Cranbourne Cl SL1 ....42 C3
Cranbourne Cotts SL4 ..93 B5
Cranbourne Gdns RG30 ..58 A2
Cranbourne Hall Cvn Site
SL4 ....93 B7
Cranbourne Prim Sch
SL5 ....93 A4
Cranbourne Rd SL1 ....42 C3
Cranbrook Dr SL6 ......19 C1
Cranbury Rd RG30 ....85 D7
Crane Ct GU47 ......150 D8
Crane Wharf 8 RG1 ..86 B7
Craneswater UB3 ......71 F7
Cranford Ave TW19 ....97 E8
Cranford Ct TW19 ......97 E8
Cranford Dr RG10 ......88 F8
Cranford House Sch
OX10 ....13 A8
Cranford La
Harlington TW6 ....71 F6
Harlington UB3 ....71 E7
Hatton TW6 ....71 E1
Hatton TW6 ....71 F5
Cranford Mews 10 RG1 ..86 A6
Cranford Park Dr GU46 ..149 D6
Cranleigh Rd TW13 ....98 F4
Cranmer Cl RG41 ....115 F8
Cranmer Lodge GU15 ..151 E6
Cranwell Gr
Lightwater GU18 ....152 F8
Littleton TW17 ......124 F5
Cranwell Rd TW6 ......71 B5
Craufurd Ct SL6 ......39 E8
Craufurd Rise SL6 ....39 E8
Craven Cl RG17 ......102 B1
Craven Ct GU15 ......150 F4
Craven Dene RG14 ..105 B4
Craven Farm Cotts RG17 ..72 F2
Craven Rd Inkpen RG17 ..127 B6
Newbury RG14 ......104 F2
Reading RG1 ....86 D6
Craven Way RG17 ....102 B2
Crawford Cl RG6 ......87 B3
Crawford Gdns RG15 ..150 F4
Crawford Pl RG14 ....104 F3
Crawley Chase RG42 ..92 B2
Crawley Cl RG15 ......150 F4
Crawley Hill GU15 ....151 E6
Crawley Ridge GU15 ..151 F6
Crawley Ridge Inf Sch
GU15 ....151 F6
Crawley Rise GU15 ..152 A7
Crawley Wood Cl GU15 ..151 F5
Crawshay Dr RG4 ......59 B7
Crawshays SL6 ....2 A3
Crayle St SL2 ....22 B2
Crayonne Cl TW16 ..125 E8

Crazies Hill CE Prim Sch
RG10 ....36 F6
Crecy Cl RG41 ....115 E6
Creden Cl SL6 ....19 D1
Crediton Cl RG5 ....88 A6
Cree's Mdw GU20 ....146 D3
Creighton Ct RG2 ......86 D4
Cremyll Rd RG1 ....58 F1
Crendon Ct RG4 ......59 A2
Crescent 5 TW18 ......96 F3
Crescent Dale SL6 ....39 F6
Crescent Dr SL6 ......39 E7
Crescent Rd
Reading,Tilehurst RG31 ..57 D1
Reading,Whiteknights RG1 ..86 F6
Shepperton TW17 ..125 C4
Wokingham RG40 ....116 C5
Crescent The
Ashford TW15 ....97 F3
Bracknell RG12 ......118 C5
Chertsey KT16 ......124 A6
Egham TW20 ....95 F2
Harlington UB7 ....71 D7
Kintbury RG17 ......102 A1
Knowl Hill RG10 ......37 A6
Lower Halliford TW17 ..125 F2
Maidenhead SL6 ......39 E7
Mortimer RG7 ......137 A6
Sandhurst GU47 ....143 E3
Shiplake RG9 ....36 B4
Slough SL1 ....42 E4
Theale RG7 ....83 E4
Wentworth GU25 ....122 D3
Crescent Villas 4 SL4 ..67 C6
Cress Rd SL1 ....42 B4
Cressex Cl RG42 ......90 C2
Cressida Chase RG42 ..91 E1
Cressingham Rd RG2 ..86 D2
Cressington Ct 2 SL8 ..3 A4
Cressington Pl SL8 ......3 A4
Cresswell Rd RG14 ..105 D4
Cresswells Mead SL6 ..40 C1
Crest Rd RG10 ....61 E6
Crest The RG4 ....59 C5
Creswell Cl RG41 ....116 A3
Creswell Row SL7 ......1 D2
Cricket Field Gr RG45 ..143 D4
Cricket Hill RG40 ....141 E2
Cricket Hill La GU17,
GU46 ....149 E4
Cricketers RG20 ......103 E6
Cricketers La
Eversley Cross RG27 ..140 E1
Windlesham GU20 ..146 D4
Winkfield RG42 ....92 A3
Crimp Hill SL4,TW20 ..95 A6
Crisp Gdns RG42 ......90 E1
Crisp Rd RG9 ....15 C3
Crispin Cl RG4 ....58 D5
Crispin Way SL2 ....22 D8
Crocker Cl SL5 ....119 E7
Crockford Rd RG42 ....90 F1
Crockhamwell Rd RG5 ..87 E4
Crocus Mead RG18 ..106 E4
Crocus Way RG41 ....115 D7
Croft Cl Harlington UB7 ..71 C7
Wokingham RG41 ....116 A2
Croft Cnr SL4 ....68 A2
Croft La Newbury RG14 ..104 E4
Yateley GU46 ....149 D7
Croft Rd Goring RG8 ..34 C5
Hungerford RG17 ....100 D6
Mortimer RG7 ......136 F6
Newbury RG14 ......130 F8
Shinfield RG7 ....113 C2
Wokingham RG40 ....116 A2
Croft The Bracknell RG42 ..91 B1
Kintbury RG17 ......102 A2
Maidenhead SL6 ......39 C5
Marlow SL7 ....2 A3
Wokingham RG40 ....116 D5
Croft Way SL6 ....19 B8
Crofters Cl GU47 ....150 A8
Crofters SL4 ....68 A1
Crofters Cl Frimley GU16 ..152 D1
Stanwell TW19 ....97 E8
Crofthill Rd SL2 ....22 B1
Crofton Cl RG12 ......118 E4
Crofts The TW17 ....125 E5
Cromer Cl RG31 ....57 C1
Cromer Ct SL1 ....42 E7
Cromer Rd TW6 ....71 A5
Cromwell Cl RG9 ......35 E8
Cromwell Dr SL1 ......42 E8
Cromwell Gdns SL7 ....1 E2
Cromwell Lodge TW13 ..98 F5
Cromwell Pl 3 RG45 ..143 B4
Cromwell Rd Ascot SL5 ..120 B4
Camberley GU15 ....151 D7
Caversham RG4 ....59 B2
Henley-On-T RG9 ......35 E8
Maidenhead SL6 ......39 E8
Marlow SL7 ....1 E2
Newbury RG14 ......105 A3
Crondall Ct GU15 ....151 B3
Crondall End GU46 ..149 C7
Cropper Cl RG19 ....107 A3
Crosby Hill Dr GU15 ..151 F8
Crosby Way RG17 ..100 D5
Crosfields Cl RG2 ....113 D8
Crosfields Sch RG2 ..113 A6
Cross Fell RG12 ......118 A4
Cross Gates Cl RG12 ..118 F6
Cross Keys Rd RG8 ....54 B3
Cross La RG7 ....138 C7
Cross Oak SL4 ....67 A5

Cross Rd SL5 ....121 A1
Cross St Reading RG1 ..86 B8
Wokingham RG40 ....116 C6
Crossland Ho GU25 ..122 E5
Crossland Rd RG2 ......86 B7
Crossway RG12 ......118 C2
Crossways Ashford TW16 ..98 F1
Egham TW20 ....96 D2
Woodley RG5 ....87 E5
Crossways Ct 8 SL4 ..67 C5
Crossways Ct TW17 ..125 D3
Crosthwaite Way SL1 ..41 D8
Crouch La SL4 ....92 F7
Crow Piece La SL2 ....21 F4
Crowfield Dr RG19 ..106 C3
Crowle Rd RG17 ....25 A3
Crown Acre Cl RG19 ..106 C3
Crown Cl SL3 ....69 C7
Crown Colonnade 9
RG1 ....86 E7
Crown Cotts
Bracknell SL5 ....119 C4
Englefield Green TW20 ..95 A1
Windsor SL4 ....67 D3
Crown Ct RG19 ......106 C3
Crown Hill Ct SL5 ....120 B4
Crown La Burnham SL2 ..22 A4
Maidenhead SL6 ......39 F6
Marlow SL7 ....1 D2
Theale RG7 ....83 E3
Wentworth GU25 ....122 D3
Crown Mdw SL3 ......69 B7
Crown Mead RG18,RG19,106 C3
Crown Mews RG7 ....100 D5
Crown Pl 7 Reading RG1 ..86 C6
Sandhurst GU47 ....143 E1
Crown Rd Marlow SL7 ....1 D2
Wentworth GU25 ....122 C3
Crown Rise KT16 ....123 F1
Crown Row RG12 ....118 D3
Crown St Egham TW20 ..96 A4
Reading RG1 ....86 B6
Crown Wood Prim Sch
RG12 ....118 C3
Crowsley Rd RG9 ......36 A3
Croydon Rd TW6 ......71 B4
Cruikshank Lea GU47 ..150 E6
Crummock Cl SL1 ......41 C7
Crutchley Rd RG40 ..116 D7
Cuba Cotts SL6 ....20 B3
Cuckoo La GU24 ....153 D6
Cuckoo Vale GU24 ..153 D6
Culford Cl RG6 ....87 A3
Culham Dr SL6 ....19 E2
Culham Ho RG12 ....118 E5
Cullen Cl GU46 ......149 C5
Cullen's Pass SL6 ......39 F6
Culley Way SL6 ....39 A4
Culloden Way RG41 ..115 E6
Culver Croft RG42 ......90 E1
Culver La RG6 ....87 A7
Culver Rd Newbury RG14 ..130 F8
Reading RG6 ....86 F6
Sandhurst GU47 ....143 D1
Cumberland Ave Sl2 ..22 C1
Cumberland Ct TW15 ..97 D5
Cumberland Dr RG12 ..118 E8
Cumberland Rd SL4 ..94 D4
Cumberland Rd
Ashford TW15 ....97 D5
Frimley GU15 ....152 C4
Reading RG1 ....86 E7
Cumberland Way RG41 ..115 D6
Cumbernauld Gdns TW16 ..98 F3
Cumbrae Cl SL2 ....22 C1
Cumbria Cl SL6 ....39 C4
Cunworth Ct RG12 ..117 F3
Curfew Bell Rd KT16 ..123 F2
Curl Way RG41 ......116 A5
Curlew Dr RG31 ....84 C6
Curlew Hill Rd GU18 ..152 F7
Curling Way RG14 ..105 C4
Curls La SL6 ....39 E4
Curls Rd SL6 ....39 E4
Curly's Way RG40 ....139 D6
Curnock Ct RG14 ....104 E1
Curridge Gn RG18 ......78 A4
Curridge Piece RG18 ..78 D4
Curridge Prim Sch RG18 ..78 D4
Curridge Rd RG18 ....78 B5
Curriers La SL1 ....21 E5
Curtis Cl GU15 ....152 C7
Curtis Rd RG31 ....84 C4
Curzon Mall 7 SL1 ....42 F4
Curzon St RG30 ....85 E8
Cutbush Cl RG30 ....114 B8
Cutbush La Earley RG6 ..87 C1

Cutbush La continued
Lower Earley RG6 ....114 B8
Shinfield RG2 ....113 F6
Cutting Hill SN8,RG17 .126 A4
Cuttings The RG18 .....52 F5
Cwmcarn RG4 ....58 F6
Cygnet Cl RG19 ....106 B3
Cygnet Way RG17 ......100 D7
Cygnets The 14 TW18 ..96 F3
Cypress Cl RG40 ....142 A8
Cypress Ct GU25 ....122 F5
Cypress Hill Ct GU14 ..150 F1
Cypress Ho
  3 Newbury RG14 ......104 F2
  Slough SL3 ....44 B1
Cypress Rd RG5 ....88 A6
Cypress Way GU17 .....150 B5
Cypress Wlk TW20 .....95 B2
Cyril Vokins Rd RG14 ..105 E2

D

Daceberry Ct RG9 ......16 C1
Dacre Ave RG4 ....59 E4
Dagmar Rd SL4 ....67 D5
Dair House Sch SL2 ....22 C4
Dairy Ct SL6 ....65 A7
Dairy La RG9 ....16 B8
Daisy Mdw TW20 ......96 A3
Dalby Cl RG10 ....88 FB
Dalby Cres RG14 ......131 B8
Dalcross RG12 ....118 E3
Dale Cl SL5 ....121 A4
Dale Ct SL1 ....42 C4
Dale Gdns GU47 ....150 A8
Dale Lodge Rd SL5 ....121 A4
Dale Rd Ashford TW16 .98 F1
  Oatlands Park KT12 ..125 F2
  Reading RG2 ....86 B5
Daleham Ave TW20 ....96 A2
Dalley Ct GU47 ....150 D7
Dalston Cl GU15 ......152 D3
Dalton Cl RG30 ....84 E8
Damar Gdns RG9 ......35 E8
Damson Gr SL1 ....42 C4
Dandridge Cl SL3 .....43 D2
Dandridge Dr SL8 ......3 C3
Dane Rd TW15 ....98 D2
Danehill RG6 ....114 B8
Danehurst Ct TW20 ...95 E2
Danes Ct SL6 ....29 D7
Danes Gdns SL6 ......19 F6
Danesfield RG40 ......116 D6
Danesfield Sch SL7 ...17 E7
Danvers Cl RG19 .....106 D2
Danywern Dr RG41 ...88 C2
Darby Green La GU17 .150 B6
Darby Green Rd GU17 .150 B5
Darby La RG8 ....55 B5
Darby Vale RG42 .....91 B2
Darell Rd RG4 ....58 F3
Dark La Bradfield RG7 .82 C7
  Purley On T RG31 ....57 B2
  Wargrave RG10 ......36 D2
  Wickham RG17 ......101 A7
Darleydale Cl GU47 ..143 D2
Darling's La SL6 ......18 E1
Darracott Cl GU15 ...152 B8
Darrell Cl SL3 ....43 F2
Dart Cl Brands Hill SL3 .69 B8
  Thatcham RG18 .....106 B5
  Wokingham RG40 ...141 F6
Dartington Ave RG5 ..87 D4
Dartington Cl RG30 ..84 F8
Dartmouth Cl RG12 ..118 E6
Dartmouth Ct 2 SL1 ..42 F3
Dartmouth Terr 1 RG1 .86 D6
Darvill's La SL1 ......42 D4
Darvills La RG10 .....62 F1
Darwall Dr SL5 ......119 D7
Darwin Cl RG2 ....86 A1
Darwin Ct 2 GU15 ...151 B3
Darwin Rd SL3 ....43 F4
Dashwood Cl
  Bracknell RG12 .....118 D8
  Slough SL3 ....43 C2
Datchet Pl SL3 ......68 B6
Datchet Rd Horton SL3 .68 F4
  Old Windsor SL4 ....68 A3
  Slough SL3 ....43 A2
  Windsor SL4 ....67 D7
Datchet St Mary's CE Prim
  Sch SL3 ....68 B6
Datchet Sta SL3 ......68 B6
Dauntless Rd SL2 ....111 B3
Davenport Rd RG12 ..118 E8
Daventry Cl SL3 .....69 F6
Daventry Ct RG42 ...118 B8
David Cl UB3 ....71 E7
David Ct 3 TW18 ....97 A4
David Rd SL3 ....69 F5
David Smith Ct RG31 .84 F5
Davis Cl SL7 ....1 E1
Davis Gdns GU47 ....150 E7
Davis St RG10 ....88 D5
Davy Cl RG40 ....116 C5
Dawes East Rd SL1 ...23 C2
Dawes Moor Cl SL2 ..43 C7
Dawley Ride SL3 ....69 E6
Dawlish Rd RG2 .....86 C2
Dawn Cl GU15 ......151 F7
Dawn Redwood Cl SL3 .69 A4

Dawnay Cl SL5 ......119 F8
Dawnay Rd GU15 ...151 B7
Daws Cl SL0 ....44 F7
Dawsmere Cl GU15 ..152 C5
Dawson Cl SL4 ....67 A5
Daytona Dr RG19 ...107 B2
Dayworth Mews 2 RG30 .85 C7
De Beauvoir Rd RG1 ..86 E6
De Bohun Rd RG1 ....86 B8
De Havilland Way TW19 .70 E1
De Montfort Gr RG17 .100 D4
De Montfort Rd
  Newbury RG14 ......104 E5
  Reading RG1 ....59 A1
De Ros Pl TW20 ......96 A2
De-Vitre Gn RG40 ...116 F7
Deacon Cl RG40 .....116 C8
Deacon Ct SL4 ......66 D5
Deacon Way RG30 ...58 A2
Deaconfield RG8 .....14 C3
Deacons La RG18 ....79 C7
Deadman's La RG7 ...83 D3
Deadmans La RG14,
  RG19 ....131 B6
Deadmoor La RG20 ..130 E1
Deal Ave SL1 ....41 F7
Dean Cl KT16 ....124 A3
Dean Ct RG40 ......116 C7
Dean La SL6 ....18 C8
Dean Par RG45 .....151 F8
Dean St SL7 ....1 D2
Dean View SL6 ......19 E6
Dean's Cloisters SL4 .67 D7
Deanfield Ave RG9 ...15 D1
Deanfield Cl SL7 ......1 D3
Deanfield Rd RG9 ....15 D1
Deans Cl SL2 ....22 A4
Deans Ct GU20 .....146 D4
Deans Farm RG4 ....59 D1
Deansfield Cl SL6 ....19 D2
Deansgate RG12 ....118 B2
Deansgate Rd RG1 ...86 B6
Deanwood Ho RG20 ..104 B5
Decies Way SL2 ......23 A4
Dedmere Ct SL7 ......1 F2
Dedmere Rd SL7 .....1 F2
Dedmere Rise SL7 ....1 E2
Dedworth Dr SL4 ....66 F6
Dedworth Green Fst Sch
  SL4 ....66 E5
Dedworth Manor SL4 .66 F6
Dedworth Mid Sch SL4 .66 E6
Dedworth Rd SL4 ....66 D5
Dee Rd RG30 ....85 A6
Deena Cl SL3 ....41 E6
Deep Field SL3 ......68 B7
Deep Well Dr GU15 ..151 E5
Deepdale RG12 .....118 A5
Deepdene Cl RG1 ....85 E7
Deepfield Rd RG12 ..118 D7
Deer Leap GU18 ....153 A4
Deer Rock Hill RG12 ..118 C3
Deer Rock Rd GU15 ..151 F8
Deerhurst Ave RG41 ..88 C2
Deerhurst Cl RG31 ...84 E4
Deerswood SL6 ......20 A1
Defford Cl RG41 .....88 F1
Delafield Dr RG31 ...84 C4
Delaford Cl SL6 .....44 F7
Delamere Ho 5 RG1 .86 E5
Delamere Rd RG6 ...87 B8
Delane Dr RG41 .....88 B1
Delaney Cl RG30 ....84 F8
Delft Cl RG30 ....84 F8
Dell Cl SL2 ....22 C7
Dell Gr GU16 ....151 F2
Dell Rd
  Finchampstead RG40 .142 A3
  Purley On T RG31 ...57 C2
Dell The
  Englefield Green TW20 .95 A5
  Maidenhead SL6 ....38 F2
  10 Reading RG1 .....86 C7
  Yateley GU46 ......149 C5
Deller St RG42 ......90 F1
Dellwood Com Hospl
  RG30 ....85 C6
Dellwood Pk RG4 ....58 F4
Delph The RG6 .....87 D2
Delta Way TW20 ...123 C8
Dempsey Ho RG30 ..84 F7
Denbigh Pl RG1 .....58 F1
Denbury Gdns 1 RG2 .113 C8
Denby Way RG30 ...84 F7
Dencliffe 2 TW15 ...98 A3
Dene Cl RG6 ....87 A3
Dene Hollow OX11 ...10 E8
Dene Way RG14 ....105 A5
Denefield Sch SL3 ...57 B3
Denford La RG17 ....101 C8
Denham Cl SL6 .....39 C6
Denham Gr 1 GU46 .149 D5
Denham Gr RG12 ...118 C3
Denison Rd TW13 ...98 F4
Denly Way GU18 ...146 C1
Denman Dr TW15 ...98 B2
Denmark Ave RG5 ..61 A1
Denmark Rd
  Maidenhead SL6 ....39 E8
  Wokingham RG40 ..116 C5
Denmark St
  Wokingham RG40 ..116 C5
Denmead Ct RG12 ..118 E3
Dennis Cl TW15 ....98 D1
Dennis Way SL1 ....41 D6

Dennisford Rd RG20 ..31 A6
Dennistoun Cl GU15 .151 D5
Dennose Cl RG6 .....87 A1
Denny Rd SL3 ......43 F2
Denton Cl RG19 ....106 C2
Denton Ct SL7 ....1 F3
Denton Mews RG40 .116 C6
Denton Rd RG40 ...116 C6
Denton Way SL1 ...151 D2
Denvale Trade Pk RG14 .105 D2
Depot Rd SL6 ....40 A6
Derby Cl RG17 ......25 A2
Derby Rd Caversham RG4 .59 B3
  Newbury RG14 .....104 F1
  Sandhurst GU47 ...150 B4
Derby St RG1 ....85 FB
Derbyshire Grn RG42 .91 F1
Derek Horn Ct GU15 .151 B6
Derek Rd SL6 ......40 C8
Deridene Cl 2 TW19 .70 E1
Derrick Cl RG31 ....84 C4
Derwent Ave RG30 ..57 E2
Derwent Cl
  East Bedfont TW14 ..98 F7
  Wokingham RG41 ..115 E6
Derwent Dr Burnham SL1 .41 D3
  Maidenhead SL6 ....39 D8
Derwent Rd
  Lightwater GU18 ...153 B8
  Thatcham RG19 ....106 A3
  Thorpe Lea TW20 ...96 B1
Desborough Cl TW17 .125 A2
Desborough Cres SL6 .39 C5
Desborough Rd SL6 ..39 E5
Deseronto Wharf Ind Est
  SL3 ....43 E4
Desford Way TW15 ..97 F6
Devenish La GU20,SL5 .120 D1
Devenish Rd GU20,SL5 .120 D2
Devereux Rd SL4 ...67 D5
Dererills Way SL3 ...44 C2
Deveron Dr RG30 ...85 A8
Devil's Highway The
  RG45 ....142 F5
Devils La TW20 .....96 C2
Devitt Cl RG2 ....86 F1
Devon Ave SL1 .....42 C7
Devon Chase RG42 ..91 E2
Devon Cl Sandhurst GU47 .150 D7
  Wokingham RG41 ..115 E6
Devon Dr RG4 ......59 E4
Devonhurst Cl SL2 ..22 B3
Devonshire Dr GU15 .151 F7
Devonshire Gdns RG31 .57 B3
Devonshire Grn SL2 .22 B3
Devonshire Lodge 10 SL6 .39 F6
Devonshire Pk RG2 ..86 E2
Dewberry Down RG18 .106 F4
Dewe La RG30 .....84 E2
Dhoon Rise SL6 ....39 F6
Diamedes Ave TW19 .97 D7
Diamond Cotts RG10 .37 C6
Diamond Hill GU15 ..151 E7
Diamond Rd SL1 ...43 B4
Diamond Ridge GU15 .151 E7
Diamond Way RG41 ..115 E7
Diana Cl Slough SL3 ..43 E7
  Spencers Wood RG7 .113 A1
Dianthus Cl KT16 ...123 E2
Dianthus Pl RG42 ...92 B2
Dibleys OX11 ....12 A8
Dick Turpin Way TW14 .71 F3
Dickens Cl RG4 .....59 D2
Dickens Pl SL3 .....69 E6
Dickens Way GU46 ..149 C5
Dickens Wlk RG14 ..131 A8
Dickson Glade RG19 .106 C2
Diddenham Cotts RG7 .112 D2
Dido Rd OX11 ....9 FB
Dieppe Cl RG41 ....115 E6
Digby Rd RG14 .....104 E4
Digital Acad RG41 ..116 B4
Dines Way SL6 .....79 C7
Dingle Rd TW15 ....98 B3
Dittons The RG40 ..116 F1
Dobson's La RG9 ...15 C8
Dockett Eddy La TW17 .124 F1
Dockett Moorings KT16 .124 F1
Doctors La RG18 ...79 A6
Doddington Cl RG6 ..87 C1
Doddsfield Rd SL2 ..22 A2
Dodsells Well RG40 .141 F8
Dog La RG8 ....54 A6
Doghurst Ave UB7 ..71 B7
Doghurst Dr UB7 ...71 B7
Dogkennel La OX12 ..27 C4
Doles Hill RG41 ....115 E3
Doles La RG41 .....115 E3
Dolman Rd RG14 ...104 E3
Dolphin Cl Brimpton RG7 .134 F7

Dolphin Ho
  1 Camberley GU15 ..151 B3
  Wokingham RG40 ...116 B6
Dolphin Rd
  Charlton TW16 .....125 E8
  Slough SL1 ....43 B4
Dolphin Rd N TW16 ..125 E8
Dolphin Rd S TW16 ..125 E8
Dolphin Rd W TW16 .125 E8
Dolphin Sch 62 A2
Dolton Mews RG14 ..104 F3
Doman Rd GU15 ....151 A4
Domoney Cl RG19 ...106 E3
Don Cl RG30 ....85 A8
Donaldson Way RG5 .88 B8
Doncastle Rd RG12 ..117 E6
Donegal Cl RG4 ....59 C3
Donkey La SL8 ......3 A3
Donkin Hill RG4 ....59 C3
*Dominque Castle**
  RG14 ....104 E7
Donnington Cl
  Camberley GU15 ...151 B1
Donnington Gdns
  Maidenhead SL6 ....19 F1
  Reading RG1 ....86 B6
Donnington Hosp RG14 .104 F6
Donnington Lodge
  RG14 ....104 F7
Donnington Pk RG14 .104 F6
Donnington Pl RG41 ..88 D2
Donnington Rd RG1 ..86 D6
Donnington Sq RG14 .104 F5
Donnybrook RG12 ..118 A2
Dorcas Ct GU15 ....151 B3
Dorchester Cl SL6 ..19 B1
Dorchester Ct
  Reading RG30 ......85 C6
  8 Staines TW18 ....97 A4
Dorchester Dr TW14 .71 E1
Dorian Dr SL5 .....120 E8
Doris Rd TW15 .....98 D2
Dorking Way RG31 ..84 B4
Dorly Cl TW17 .....125 E4
Dormer Cl
  Crowthorne RG45 ..143 A5
  Newbury RG14 .....130 C7
Dormy Ho The GU25 .121 F3
Dorndon Ho RG10 ..88 FB
Dornels SL2 ....43 C7
Dorney Cl RG41 ....88 B1
Dorney Lake Pk* SL4 .66 B8
Dorney Lake Rowing Ctr*
  SL4 ....41 B1
Dorney Reach Rd SL6 .40 F3
Dorney Sch SL4 ....40 F3
Dorney Wood Rd SL1 .21 D6
Dorneywood Way RG14 .105 D4
Dorothy Ct RG14 ..105 D4
Dorothy St 7 RG1 ..86 C6
Dorset Cl GU15 ....151 FB
Dorset Lodge 9 SL6 .39 F6
Dorset Rd Ashford TW15 .97 D5
  Windsor SL4 ....67 C6
Dorset St SL6 ......85 C8
Dorset Vale RG42 ..91 E2
Dorset Way RG41 ..115 E5
Dorton Villas UB7 ..71 A6
Doublet Cl RG19 ...106 E3
Douglas Ct Earley RG6 .87 A3
  Marlow SL7 ....2 A3
Douglas Grange RG10 .88 D4
Douglas La TW19 ...68 F1
Douglas Rd
  Caversham RG4 .....59 D2
  Slough SL2 ....42 D8
  Stanwell TW19 .....70 D1
Douthes The TW18 ..97 A2
Douro Cl RG26 ....134 D1
Dove Cl RG6 ....113 F8
Dove Ct TW19 .....97 E8
Dove House Cres RG30 .21 E2
Dovecote Rd RG2 ..113 B7
Dovedale Cl
  Caversham RG4 .....58 F3
  Sandhurst GU47 ...143 D2
Dover Rd SL1 ......41 F7
Dover St RG1 ......86 A6
Doveton Way RG14 .105 B4
Dowding Cl RG5 ...88 A7
Dowding Ct RG45 ..143 C6
Dower Pk SL4 ......66 E3
Down Pl SL4 ....66 A8
Downe House RG18 ..79 A3
Downend La RG20 ..51 B2
Downfield La SL6 ...40 C6
Downfield Rd RG10 .63 A4
Downham Ct RG2 ...86 E2
Downing Rd RG31 ..84 D8
Downland Cl RG12 ..117 C6
Downlands Rd RG17 .47 C6
Downmill Rd RG12 ..117 F7
Downs Cl RG17 ....46 F7
Downs Rd Aldworth RG20 .32 A4
  Slough SL3 ....43 D4
Downs The SL6 ....20 D4
Downs View OX11 ..12 F8
Downs Way Chilton OX11 .9 FB
  Purley On T RG31 ...57 C2
Downshire Ct RG17 .46 B8
Downshire Sq RG1 ..85 E6
Downshire Way
  Bracknell RG12 ....118 B6
  Bracknell RG12,RG42 .118 A7
Downside OX11 .....10 C8
Downsway Prim Sch
  RG31 ....57 C3

Doyle Gdns GU46 ..149 C4
Doyle Ho RG45 ....143 B3
Drain Hill RG17 ....25 A4
Drake Ave Slough SL3 .43 D2
  Staines TW18 ......96 F3
Drake Cl Bracknell RG12 .118 B4
  Wokingham RG40 ..141 E7
Draper Cl RG19 ...106 D2
Draycott RG12 ....118 E4
Drayhorse Dr GU19 .145 E2
Draymans La 4 SL7 ..1 D1
Drayton Cl RG12 ..118 D7
Drayton Rd RG30 ..85 B8
Drayton Way RG19 .131 C7
Dresden Way RG30 .57 F1
Drew Mdw SL2 ....22 C8
Drewett Cl RG2 ...113 C6
Drey Ho RG41 .....115 F7
Drift Rd SL4,SL6 ...65 D3
Drift Way SL3 .....69 C7
Drifters Dr GU16 ..152 D1
Driftway Cl RG6 ...87 C1
Drill Hall Rd KT16 .124 A2
Drive The Ashford TW15 .98 D1
  Bourne End SL8 .....2 F4
  Datchet SL3 ....68 B6
  Earley RG6 ....87 A7
  Newbury RG14 .....130 E8
  Slough SL3 ....43 E4
  Thorpe GU25 ......122 F4
  Wraysbury TW19 ...68 D2
Droitwich Cl RG12 .118 E6
Drome Path RG41 ..88 A3
Dropmore Rd SL1 ..21 C5
Drove La RG18 ....79 C2
Drove The RG19 ..133 B1
Drovers Way
  Bracknell RG12 ....118 F6
  Woodley RG5 ....87 E5
Druce Way RG19 ..106 D3
Druce Wood SL5 ..119 E8
Drummond Cl RG12 .118 F8
Drummond Ho 4 SL4 .67 D4
Drury La RG7 .....137 A5
Dry Arch Rd SL5 ..120 F3
Dryden RG12 .....118 A2
Dryden Cl RG18 ...106 D5
Dryland Ho RG30 ..84 F7
Du Pre Wlk HP10 ...3 D4
Duchess Cl RG45 ..143 B7
Duchess St SL4 ....41 E5
Dudley Cl RG31 ...57 E1
Dudley Ct SL1 .....43 A3
Dudley Mews RG1 .118 C7
Dudley Rd Ashford TW15 .97 F4
  East Bedfont TW14 .98 D7
Duffield La SL2 ....22 F6
Duffield Pk SL2 ...23 A2
Duffield Rd RG5 ...60 F1
Dugdale Ho RG10 ..96 C3
Duke Of Cornwall Ave
  GU15 ....144 D1
Duke St Eton SL4 ..67 C7
  Henley-On-T RG9 ..15 E2
  Reading RG1 ....86 B7
Duke's Hill GU19 ..145 E5
Duke's La
  Old Windsor SL4,SL5 .94 B3
  Winkfield SL5 ....93 F1
Duke's Ride RG45 ..143 B5
Dukes Cl TW15 ....98 C4
Dukes Covert GU19 .145 E6
Dukes Dr SL1,SL2 ..22 A8
Dukes La Marlow SL7 .1 D2
  Slough SL1 ....42 F6
Dukes Ride RG7 ...136 B1
Dukes Wood RG45 .143 B5
Dukeshill Rd RG42 .118 B8
Dulnan Cl RG30 ...85 A8
Dulverton Gdns RG2 .86 C2
Dumas Cl GU46 ...149 C5
Dumbarton Way RG4 .59 E5
Dunally Pk TW17 ..125 D2
Dunaways Cl RG6 ..87 D3
Dunbar Cl SL2 .....43 A6
Dunbar Dr RG5 ....61 A4
Dunboe Pl TW17 ..125 C2
Duncan Dr RG40 ..116 E5
Duncan Gdns
  Purley On T RG8 ....57 C4
  Staines TW18 ......97 A2
Duncan Rd RG5 ...87 E6
Duncannon Cres SL4 .66 D4
Duncombe Ct TW18 .97 A1
Duncroft SL4 .....66 F4
Duncroft Manor TW17 .96 E4
Dundaff Cl GU15 ..152 A5
Dundas Cl RG12 ..118 B5
Dundee Rd SL1 ...42 A8
Dundela Cl RG5 ...87 E6
Dunedin Pl RG42 ..90 E1
Dungells Farm Cl GU46 .149 D4
Dungells La GU46 ..149 C4
Dungrovehill La SL6 .18 D3
Dunholme End SL6 ..39 D3
Dunkirk Cl RG41 ..115 E6
Dunleary Ct 12 RG30 .85 D6
Dunluce Gdns RG8 ..56 E5
Dunnock Way RG10 .36 E3
Dunoon Cl RG31 ...84 E4
Dunsfold Rd RG30 ..84 F7
Dunsmore Gdns GU46 .149 A5
Dunstable Ho 3 SL1 ..1 D2
Dunstall Cl RG31 ..84 D8
Dunstan Ct TW18 ..97 A4

Dunstan Park Inf Sch RG18 106 D4
Dunstan Rd RG18 106 E4
Dunstans Dr RG41 88 B2
Dunster Cl RG4 59 C6
Dunster Gdns SL1 42 A6
Dunt Ave RG10 88 F4
Dunt La RG10 88 E4
Dunwood Ct SL6 39 C5
Duppas Cl TW17 125 D4
Dupre Cl SL1 41 E4
Durand Rd RG6 87 A1
Durant Way RG31 57 D3
Durham Ave SL1 42 A7
Durham Cl Reading RG2 113 C8
Wokingham RG41 115 E6
Durham Dr GU16 152 D1
Durham Rd GU47 143 E2
Durley Mead RG12 118 F4
Durning Pl SL5 120 B6
Durrell Way TW17 125 D3
Dutch Barn Cl TW19 70 D1
Dutton Way SL0 44 E7
Duval Pl GU19 145 E3
Dwyer Rd RG30 85 A4
Dyer Rd RG40 116 E7
Dyer Straits OX12 9 F8
Dyers Ct RG5 87 D7
Dyson Cl SL4 67 B4
Dysons Cl RG14 104 E3
Dysonswood La RG4 58 E8

E

Eagle Cl
Crowthorne RG45 143 A7
Wokingham RG41 115 F5
Eagle House Sch GU47 143 B2
Eagle Rd Hatton TW6 71 F4
Newtown RG20 132 A2
Eaglehurst Cotts RG42 90 C3
Eagles Nest GU47 143 A1
Earle Croft RG42 91 C1
Earley Hill Rd RG6 87 A5
Earley Pl RG1 86 B7
Earley Sta RG6 87 C4
Earleydene SL5 120 B1
Earls Gr GU15 151 E6
Earls La SL1 41 F5
Earlsfield SL6 40 C2
Earlsfield Cl RG4 59 E4
Earlswood RG12 118 B2
Earlywood Pines SL5 120 A1
Easby Way RG6 87 D1
Easington Dr RG6 87 E2
East Berkshire Coll
Maidenhead SL6 39 D6
Slough SL3 44 A3
Windsor SL4 67 C5
East Burnham Cotts SL2 22 A4
East Burnham La SL2 22 A4
East Cres SL4 66 F6
East Dr Reading RG31 84 E5
Stoke Poges SL2 22 E2
Wentworth GU25 122 B3
East Gn GU17 150 C4
East La RG20 51 B1
East Paddock SL6 18 F6
East Park Farm Dr RG10 61 B4
East Ramp TW6 71 B6
East Rd East Bedfont TW14 98 D8
Maidenhead SL6 39 E7
East Ridge SL8 3 B4
East St RG1 86 B7
East Stratton Cl RG12 118 F4
East Terr SL4 67 E6
East View Cl RG10 36 E2
East View Rd RG10 36 E2
Eastbourne Rd SL1 42 A7
Eastbridge SL2 43 B5
Eastbury Ave RG31 84 B8
Eastbury Ct RG42 90 F1
Eastbury Pk RG41 88 D2
Eastbury Shute RG17 46 E2
Eastchurch Rd TW6 71 E4
Eastchurch Rd Rdbt TW6 71 E5
Eastcourt Ave RG6 87 A6
Eastcroft SL2 22 B1
Eastern Ave
Chertsey KT16 124 A6
Reading RG1 86 E6
Eastern Bsns Pk TW6 71 F5
Eastern Dr SL8 3 C4
Eastern Ind Area RG12 118 D7
Eastern La RG45 143 F4
Eastern Perimeter Rd TW14,TW6 71 F5
Eastern Rd RG12 118 D7
Eastfield OX11 12 A8
Eastfield Cl 4 SL1 43 A3
Eastfield La RG8 56 D7
Eastfield Rd SL1 41 A8
Easthampstead Mobile Home Pk RG40 143 C8
Easthampstead Park Sch RG12 117 D3
Easthampstead Rd
Bracknell RG12 118 A7
Wokingham RG40 116 E4
Eastheath Ave RG41 116 A4
Eastheath Gdns RG41 116 B3
Eastleigh Rd TW6 71 F4
Eastlyn Rd RG26 135 E1
Easton Hill RG20 76 A4
Eastwood Ct 1 SL7 1 F3
Eastwood Rd RG5 87 E4
Eastworth Rd KT15,KT16 124 A1
Eaton Ct GU15 151 B4
Eaton Pl RG1 85 F7
Eaton Rd GU15 151 B4
Ebborn Sq RG6 114 C8
Ebsworth Cl SL6 20 C3
Eccles Cl RG4 59 C2
Echelford Prim Sch The TW15 98 B3
Echelforde Dr TW15 98 A4
Eddington Hill RG17 100 F7
Eddington Rd RG12 117 E3
Eddystone Wlk TW19 97 E8
Eden Cl SL3 44 A1
Eden Way RG41 88 B1
Edenhall Cl RG31 57 D3
Edenham Cl RG6 87 E2
Edenham Cres RG1 85 E5
Edgar Milward Cl RG30 58 A1
Edgar Wallace Pl SL8 3 B5
Edgbarrow Rise GU47 143 A2
Edgbarrow Sch RG45 143 C3
Edgcumbe Park Dr RG45 143 A5
Edgecombe La RG14 105 C5
Edgedale Cl RG45 143 B4
Edgehill St RG1 86 B5
Edgell Cl GU25 122 F6
Edgell Rd TW18 96 F3
Edgemoor Rd GU16 152 C3
Edgewood Cl RG45 143 A7
Edinburgh Ave SL1 42 B7
Edinburgh Dr TW18 97 D2
Edinburgh Gdns SL4 67 D5
Edinburgh Rd
Maidenhead SL6 19 E2
Marlow SL7 1 E3
Reading RG30 85 E7
Edith Rd SL6 39 A7
Edmonds Ct RG12 118 C8
Edmunds Way SL2 43 B7
Edneys Hill RG41 115 D2
Edward Ave GU15 151 A5
Edward Ct TW18 97 C2
Edward Pauling Ho TW14 98 F8
Edward Pauling Prim Sch TW13 98 E6
Edward Pl 11 RG1 86 D7
Edward Rd Hatton TW14 71 E2
Twyford RG10 61 B5
Windlesham GU20 146 D4
Edward Way TW15 97 F6
Edwards Ct SL1 42 E4
Edwards Hill RG17 25 B2
Edwin Cl RG19 106 F3
Eeklo Pl RG14 105 A1
Egerton Rd Reading RG2 86 E1
Sandhurst GU15 150 F7
Sandhurst GU15 151 A7
Slough SL2 21 E1
Egham Bsns Village TW20 123 C7
Egham By-Pass TW20 96 A4
Egham Hill TW20 95 D2
Egham Hill Rdbt TW20 95 F3
Egham Mus* TW20 96 A3
Egham Sta TW20 96 A3
Eghams Ct 4 SL8 3 B3
Egremont Dr RG6 87 D3
Egremont Gdns SL1 42 A5
Egypt La SL2 22 B8
Eight Acres SL1 21 B1
Eight Bells 8 RG14 104 F2
Eighth Ave RG31 84 B6
Eisenhower Ave RG20 49 A4
Elan Cl RG30 84 F7
Elbow Mdw SL3 69 F6
Eldart Cl RG30 85 B7
Elder Cl RG31 57 C1
Elderberry Way RG6 87 D1
Elderfield Cres OX11 10 D8
Elderfield Rd SL2 22 F6
Eldon Pl RG1 86 C7
Eldon Rd RG1 86 C7
Eldon Sq RG1 86 D7
Eldon St RG1 86 D7
Eldon Terr RG1 86 D7
Eldrick Ct TW14 98 D7
Electra Ave TW6 71 F4
Elford Cl RG6 87 C1
Elgar Ave RG45 143 B7
Elgar Rd RG2 86 A5
Elgar Rd S RG2 86 B4
Elgarth Dr RG40 141 F8
Elgin Ave TW15 98 C2
Elgin Cres TW6 71 E5
Elgin Gate 5 RG1 85 F7
Elgin Ho SL3 69 E6
Elgin Rd GU17 149 E1
Eliot Cl Camberley GU15 152 B7
Caversham RG4 59 A4
Thatcham RG18 106 C5
Eliot Dr SL7 1 F4
Elizabeth Ave
Bagshot GU19 145 F2
Newbury RG14 130 D7
Staines TW18 97 C2
Elizabeth Cl
Bracknell RG12 118 C5
Cookham Rise SL6 19 F7
Henley-On-T RG9 35 B8
Elizabeth Ct
2 Reading RG31 84 D8
1 Slough SL1 43 A4
Theale RG7 83 F3
Wargrave RG10 36 E2
6 Windsor SL4 67 C5
Elizabeth Gdns
Ascot SL5 120 B4
Kintbury RG17 102 B2
Elizabeth Ho TW15 97 F4
Elizabeth Mews 5 RG1 86 B6
Elizabeth Par GU46 149 D4
Elizabeth Rd
Henley-On-T RG9 35 B8
Marlow SL7 1 E3
Wokingham RG40 116 D6
Elizabeth Rout Cl RG7 113 C2
Elizabeth Way SL2 22 F4
Elizabeth Wlk 4 RG1 86 B5
Elizabethan Cl TW19 97 D8
Elizabethan Way TW19 97 D8
Ellenborough Cl RG12 118 D8
Ellerton Cl RG7 83 E4
Ellesfield Ave RG12 117 E5
Ellesmere Cl RG4 59 B3
Ellies Mews TW15 97 E6
Elliman Ave SL2 42 F6
Ellington Ct SL6 40 C7
Ellington Gdns SL6 40 C7
Ellington Pk SL6 19 F1
Ellington Prim Sch SL6 19 F1
Ellington Rd
Feltham TW13 98 F4
Taplow SL6 40 C7
Elliots Way RG4 59 B2
Elliott Gdns TW17 125 A5
Elliott Rise SL5 119 D7
Ellis Ave SL1 42 E4
Ellis Rd RG45 143 B6
Ellis's Hill RG2 114 F4
Ellison Cl SL4 66 F4
Ellison Ho 17 SL4 67 D6
Ellison Way RG40 116 B6
Elm Bank GU46 149 C7
Elm Cl
Farnham Common SL2 22 C6
Stanwell TW19 97 D7
Elm Cotts Ball Hill RG20 129 F1
Holyport SL6 65 A8
Elm Croft SL3 68 C6
Elm Ct 5 Ashford TW16 98 F1
Henley-On-T RG9 35 D7
Sandhurst GU47 143 E2
Elm Dr
Burghfield Common RG30 111 B5
Winkfield SL4 93 B7
Elm Farm Cvn Pk KT16 123 C3
Elm Gr Maidenhead SL6 39 E7
Thatcham RG18 106 B5
Elm La Bourne End SL8 2 F5
Earley RG6 86 F2
Elm Lodge Ave RG30 85 D8
Elm Park Ct 5 RG30 85 C7
Elm Park Rd RG30 85 D7
Elm Pk Reading RG30 85 C7
Sunningdale SL5 120 E1
Elm Rd Earley RG2,RG6 86 F2
East Bedfont TW14 98 D8
Mapledurham RG4 58 D7
Windsor SL4 67 B4
Elm Tree Cl TW15 98 B3
Elmar Gn SL2 22 A2
Elmbank Ave TW20 95 B2
Elmcroft RG8 34 C5
Elmcroft Cl TW14 71 F1
Elmcroft Dr TW15 98 A3
Elmdon Rd TW6 71 F4
Elmfield Gdns RG14 104 E4
Elmhurst Ct SL3 44 A3
Elmhurst Rd Goring RG8 34 C7
Reading RG1 86 D5
Slough SL3 44 A3
Thatcham RG18 106 A5
Elmleigh Ct RG4 59 C3
Elmley Cl RG41 88 F1
Elms Ave RG19 106 E3
Elms Dr SL8 3 C3
Elms Rd RG40 116 B5
Elms The
5 Ashford TW15 98 A3
Blackwater GU17 150 D4
Newell Green RG42 92 A1
Elmshott La SL1 41 E6
Elmsleigh Ctr The TW18 96 F4
Elmsleigh Rd TW18 96 F3
Elmslie Ct SL6 39 E7
Elmstone Dr RG31 57 C1
Elmsway TW15 98 A3
Elmwood SL6 20 B4
Elmwood Cl RG5 87 D8
Elmwood Rd SL2 43 B6
Elsenwood Cres GU15 152 A6
Elsenwood Dr GU15 152 A7
Elsinore Ave TW19 97 E8
Elsley Rd RG31 57 E3
Elstow Ave RG4 59 C6
Elstree Cl RG31 57 D2
Elstree Sch RG7 108 D4
Elsworth Cl TW14 98 E7
Eltham Ave
Caversham RG4 59 E5
Slough SL1 41 E4
Elton Dr SL6 39 D8
Elvaston Way RG30 85 A7
Elveden Cl RG6 87 E2
Elvedon Rd TW13 98 F5
Elvendon Rd RG8 34 D7
Elwell Cl TW20 96 A2
Ely Ave SL1 42 C8
Ely Rd Hatton TW6 71 F5
Theale RG7 83 F3
Elyham RG8 57 B5
Embankment The TW19 95 C7
Ember Rd SL3 44 B3
Emblen Cres RG2 114 E2
Embrook Way RG31 84 A4
Emerald Ct RG41 115 E7
Emerald Ct SL1 42 E4
Emerson Ct
Crowthorne RG45 143 B5
Wooburn Green HP10 3 E6
Emery Acres RG8 55 A6
Emery Down Cl RG12 119 A6
Emilia Cl SL6 19 F1
Emlyns Bldgs SL4 67 D7
Emm Cl RG41 115 F8
Emma La RG10 36 E2
Emmbrook Ct RG2 86 E2
Emmbrook Gate RG41 115 F8
Emmbrook Inf Sch RG41 88 F1
Emmbrook Jun Sch RG41 88 F1
Emmbrook Rd RG41 115 F8
Emmbrook Sch The RG41 116 A8
Emmbrook Vale RG41 89 A1
Emmer Green Ct RG4 59 C5
Emmer Green Prim Sch RG4 59 B6
Emmets Nest RG42 90 C2
Emmets Pk RG42 90 D2
Emmview Cl RG41 115 F7
Empress Rd RG31 84 C5
Empstead Ct RG9 15 D2
Enborne CE Prim Sch RG20 129 E6
Enborne Cl RG31 84 C8
Enborne Gate RG14 104 D1
Enborne Gdns RG12 91 D1
Enborne Gr RG14 104 E2
Enborne Lodge La RG14 130 C6
Enborne Pl RG14 104 E2
Enborne Rd RG14 104 D1
Enborne St RG14 130 C6
Enborne Way RG7 133 F6
Enfield Rd TW6 71 E5
Enfield Road Rdbt TW6 71 E5
Engineer's Rd RG19 132 A5
Englefield CE Prim Sch RG7 83 B4
Englefield Cl TW20 95 C2
Englefield Green Inf Sch TW20 95 C3
Englefield Rd RG7 83 D4
Englehurst TW20 95 C2
Englemere Pk SL5 119 D5
Englemere Pond Nature Trail* SL5 119 C6
Englemere Rd RG42 90 F1
Englesfield GU15 152 D5
English Gdns TW19 68 D2
English Martyrs RC Prim Sch RG30 85 A7
Enid Wood Ho RG12 118 C7
Ennerdale RG12 118 A5
Ennerdale Cl TW14 98 F7
Ennerdale Cres SL1 41 C8
Ennerdale Rd RG2 86 D3
Ennerdale Way RG19 106 A3
Ensign Cl TW19 97 D7
Ensign Way TW19 97 D7
Enstone Rd RG5 88 A8
Enterprise Ct RG12 117 F7
Enterprise Way RG19 107 A2
EP Collier Prim Sch RG1 59 A1
Epping Cl RG1 85 F7
Epping Ho 3 RG1 85 E5
Epping Way RG12 118 F5
Epsom Cl GU15 151 C8
Epsom Cres RG14 105 B1
Epsom Ct RG1 85 F6
Epsom Sq TW6 71 F5
Equine Way RG14 131 B7
Eric Ave RG4 59 A6
Erica Cl Slough SL1 41 E6
West End GU24 153 E6
Erica Dr RG40 116 D5
Eriswell Cl RG6 87 E2
Erkenwald Cl KT16 123 E3
Erleigh Court Dr RG6 87 B7
Erleigh Court Gdns RG6 87 A7
Erleigh Dene RG14 104 F1
Erleigh Rd RG1 86 D6
Ermin St Lambourn RG17 46 D2
Stockcross RG20 103 D7
Ermin Wlk RG19 106 B3
Errington Dr SL4 67 A6
Erskine Cl RG26 135 F1
Escot Rd TW16 98 E1
Esher Cres TW6 71 F5
Esher Rd GU15 145 A1
Eskdale Gdns SL6 40 B2
Eskdale Rd RG41 88 B4
Eskdale Way GU15 152 D4
Eskin Cl RG30 85 A7
Essame Cl RG40 116 D6
Essex Ave SL2 42 C8
Essex Cotts RG7 111 B3
Essex Pl RG17 25 B3
Essex Rise RG42 91 F1
Essex St Newbury RG14 130 D7
Reading RG2 86 B5
Ethel Rd TW15 97 E3
Eton Cl SL3 68 A8
Eton Coll SL4 67 C8
Eton Coll Mus* SL4 67 C8
Eton Ct Eton SL4 67 D7
Staines TW18 96 F3
Eton End PNEU Sch SL3 68 A8
Eton Ho 6 TW20 96 A3
Eton Pl SL7 1 D2
Eton Porny CE Fst Sch SL4 67 D8
Eton Rd Datchet SL3 68 A8
Harlington UB3 71 F7
Eton Riverside SL4 67 D7
Eton Sq SL4 67 D7
Eton Wick CE Fst Sch SL4 42 A1
Eton Wick Rd SL4 42 B1
Eton Wlk 1 SL1 42 E3
European Weather Ctr RG2 113 D7
Eustace Cres RG40 116 D8
Evedon RG12 118 B2
Evelyn Cres TW16 125 F8
Evelyn Ct RG5 87 F5
Evelyn Way TW16 125 F8
Evendon's Cl RG41 116 A3
Evendon's La RG41 115 E2
Evenlode Rd SL8 3 B4
Evenlode Way GU47 150 D8
Everard Ave SL1 42 E4
Everest Rd
Camberley GU15 151 D8
Crowthorne RG45 143 B6
Stanwell TW19 97 E8
Evergreen Ct TW19 97 D8
Evergreen Dr RG31 84 F4
Evergreen Oak Ave SL4 68 A4
Evergreen Rd GU16 152 A3
Evergreen Way
Stanwell TW19 97 D8
Wokingham RG41 115 F5
Everington La RG18 53 C1
Everland Rd RG17 100 D6
Eversley Rd
Arborfield Cross RG2 114 E2
Barkham RG40 140 E6
Yateley GU46 149 A7
Eversley St RG27 141 A1
Eversley Way TW20 123 C7
Evesham Rd RG4 59 B5
Evesham Wlk GU47 143 D1
Evreham Rd SL0 44 E7
Evreux Cl RG19 106 F2
Ewing Way RG14 131 B8
Exbourne Rd RG2 113 C8
Exchange Rd SL5 120 C4
Exeforde Ave TW15 98 A4
Exeter Ct RG2 113 B8
Exeter Gdns GU46 149 B7
Exeter Rd TW6 71 E4
Exeter Way
Harlington TW6 71 E5
Theale RG7 83 F3
Exmoor Rd RG19 106 C3
Explorer Ave TW19 97 E7
Express Way RG14 105 E2
Exwick Sq RG2 113 D8
Eynsford Cl RG4 59 E5
Eynsham Cl RG5 87 E8
Eyre Ct RG40 116 B4
Eyre Gn SL2 22 A2

F

Faculty The 16 RG1 86 B6
Fagg's Rd TW14 71 F3
Fair Close Ho 1 RG14 105 A2
Fair Cross RG7 138 D2
Fair Lawn Gn RG2 86 F1
Fair Mile RG9 15 C4
Fair Mile Hospl OX10 14 B8
Fair View Cotts SL6 19 E7
Fairacre SL6 39 C6
Fairacres Ind Est SL4 66 D5
Faircroft SL2 22 B1
Faircross Bracknell RG12 118 B6
Hermitage RG18 78 F6
Faircross Rd RG30 85 C5
Fairfax RG42 118 A8
Fairfax Cl RG4 59 B3
Fairfax Pl RG14 105 E5
Fairfield RG20 31 D4
Fairfield App TW19 68 D1
Fairfield Ave Datchet SL3 68 D7
Staines TW18 96 F4
Fairfield Cl Bourne End SL8 3 A4
Datchet SL3 68 D7
Fairfield Dr GU16 151 E3
Fairfield La
Farnham Royal SL2 22 B3
West End GU24 153 F7
Fairfield Rd Burnham SL1 21 C2
Goring RG8 34 D7
Wraysbury TW19 68 D1
Fairfields Chertsey KT15 124 B1
Hungerford RG17 100 D5
Fairford Rd
Maidenhead SL6 39 F8
Purley On T RG31 57 C2
Fairhaven TW20 95 F3
Fairhaven Ct 1 TW20 95 F3
Fairholme TW14 98 E8
Fairholme Rd TW15 97 F3
Fairholme Sch TW14 98 D7
Fairlawn Pk SL4 66 E3
Fairlawns Cl TW18 97 B2
Fairlea SL6 39 B3
Fairlie Rd SL1 42 A8
Fairlight Ave SL4 67 D5
Fairlop Cl RG31 84 D4
Fairmead Cl GU47 150 E7
Fairmead Ct GU15 151 C4

Fairmead Rd RG2 ....113 E5
Fairmile Ct RG9 ....15 D3
Fairoak Way RG26 .....134 D1
Fairsted Cl RG30 ....85 A8
Fairview RG14 ....130 E8
Fairview Ave RG6 ......87 B6
Fairview Cotts GU25 ..122 D3
Fairview Ct Ashford TW15 .98 A3
Staines TW18 ....97 A2
Fairview Dr TW17 .....124 F4
Fairview Est RG9 ......35 F8
Fairview Rd Burnham SL6 .41 A7
Hungerford RG17 ......100 D5
Slough SL2 ....21 F1
Wokingham RG40 ......116 C5
Fairwater Dr RG5 ......87 D6
Fairway KT16 ....124 B1
Fairway Ave RG30 .....84 D6
Fairway Ct RG42 ......91 A1
Fairway Dr RG10 ......61 A5
Fairway Hts GU15 .....152 B6
Fairway The Burnham SL1 .21 C2
Flackwell Heath HP10 ....3 C7
Frimley GU15 ....152 A3
Maidenhead SL6 ......39 B3
Fairways TW15 ....98 B2
Faithfull Cl RG42 .....91 B2
Fakenham Cl RG6 .....114 A8
Fakenham Way GU47 ..143 D2
Falaise TW20 ....95 F3
Falcon Ave RG2 ....86 F1
Falcon Bsns Pk RG40 ..141 A6
Falcon Cl GU18 ....152 F8
Falcon Ct GU16 ....151 D1
Falcon Dr TW19 ....70 E1
Falcon Fields RG26 ...135 B2
Falcon House Gdns
RG20 ....129 F1
Falcon Way
Sunbury TW16 ....125 E7
Wokingham RG41 ......115 F6
Yateley GU46 ....149 B6
Falcons Croft HP10 ....3 E8
Falconwood TW20 .....95 E3
Falkland Dr RG14 .....130 F8
Falkland Garth RG14 ..130 D7
Falkland Ho SL6 ......39 F8
Falkland Prim Sch
RG14 ....130 D6
Falkland Rd
Caversham RG4 ....59 B2
Newbury RG14 ....130 D6
Fallowfield GU46 ......149 B7
Fallowfield Cl RG4 ....59 B4
Fallows The SL6 ......20 A1
Falmouth Cl GU15 ....152 A4
Falmouth Rd
Reading RG2 ....113 C7
Slough SL1 ....42 A7
Falmouth Way RG19 ..106 F3
Falstaff Ave RG6 .....86 F2
Fane Way SL6 ....39 C5
Fanes Cl RG42 ....117 F8
Fangrove Cvn Pk RG16 .123 B1
Fannys La RG7 ....80 C1
Faraday Cl
Arborfield RG2 ....140 E7
Slough SL2 ....42 B8
Faraday Rd
Newbury RG14 ....105 B3
Slough SL2 ....42 B8
Farccrosse Cl GU47 ..150 C8
Fareham Dr GU46 .....149 B7
Faringdon Cl GU47 ...143 C1
Faringdon Dr RG12 ..118 D4
Faringdon Wlk RG30 ..85 B4
Farleigh Mews RG4 ...59 E5
Farley Copse RG42 ...117 E8
Farley Ct RG7 ....140 C5
Farley Hill Prim Sch
RG7 ....140 D5
Farley Moor RG42 ...117 D8
Farm Cl Ascot SL5 ...120 C4
Bracknell RG42 ......117 F8
Crowthorne RG45 ....143 C7
Egham TW18 ....96 E3
Holyport SL6 ....40 C1
Lower Halliford TW17 .125 A2
Lyne KT16 ....123 A3
Maidenhead SL6 .....39 A7
Purley On T RG8 ....57 C5
Yateley GU46 ....149 D5
Farm Cotts RG17 ....100 A1
Farm Cres SL2 ......44 C8
Farm Ct GU16 ....151 F2
Farm Dr Old Windsor SL4 .68 B1
Reading RG31 ....84 B6
Farm Lea HP10 ......3 F7
Farm Rd Bourne End SL8 ..2 F4
Burnham SL6 ....41 A6
Frimley GU16 ....151 F2
Goring RG8 ....34 C6
Henley-On-T RG9 ....35 F8
Maidenhead SL6 .....39 A7
Staines TW18 ....97 B2
Farm View GU46 ....149 D5
Farm Way TW19 .....69 F1
Farm Yd SL4 ....67 D7
Farman Cl RG5 ......88 B8
Farmer's Rd TW18 ...96 E3
Farmers Cl
Maidenhead SL6 .....39 A4
Reading RG2 ....113 C6
Farmers End RG10 ...61 B4
Farmers Gate RG18 ..106 D5

Farmers Way SL6 ....39 A4
Farmiloe Cl RG8 .....57 C4
Farnburn Ave SL1 ...42 B8
Farnell Rd TW18 .....97 A5
Farnesdown Dr RG41 ..115 F8
Farnham Cl RG12 ....118 D7
Farnham Common Inf Sch
SL2 ....22 B8
Farnham Common Jun Sch
SL2 ....22 C8
Farnham Dr RG4 .....59 E4
Farnham La SL2 .....21 E2
Farnham Park La SL2 ..22 C4
Farnham Rd SL1, SL2 ..42 C7
Farnham Royal CE Comb Sch
SL2 ....22 C2
Farningham RG12 ....118 C6
Farnsfield Cl RG6 ...114 A8
Farrell Cl GU15 .....151 C3
Farrer Theatre SL4 ...42 D1
Farrier Cl 6 SL8 .....3 B3
Farrier Pl GU47 .....150 B7
Farriers Cl RG5 .....87 E7
Farriers La RG20 ....30 E7
Farringdon Ct RG1 ...86 F6
Farrowdene Rd RG2 ..113 C8
Farthing Ct 3 SL5 ...121 B2
Farthing Green La SL2 ..23 B4
Farthingales The SL6 ..40 B7
Fatherson Rd RG1 ...86 D7
Faulkner Pl GU19 ...145 F4
Faversham Rd GU47 ..143 D1
Fawcett Cres RG5 ...87 D6
Fawcett Rd SL4 .....67 B6
Fawler Mead RG12 ..118 F5
Fawley Bottom La RG9 .15 A8
Fawley Cl SL6 ....19 D2
Fawley Court House & Mus *
RG9 ....15 C5
Fawley Mews 2 RG1 ..85 F6
Fawley Rd RG30 ....85 B5
Fawns Manor Cl TW14 .98 C7
Fawns Manor Rd TW14 .98 D7
Fawsley Cl SL3 .....69 E7
Faygate Way RG40 ..87 B1
Feathers La TW19 ...96 A6
Felbridge Cl GU16 ..151 F1
Felbridge Ct UB3 ....71 D8
Felix La TW17 ....125 E8
Felixstowe Cl RG6 ...87 D2
Fellow Gn GU24 ....153 F6
Fellow Green Rd GU24 .153 F6
Fellowes Ct UB3 ....71 D8
Fells The RG31 ......84 A6
Fellstead Ct SL6 ....39 C6
Felstead Cl RG6 .....86 F3
Feltham Hill Inf Sch
TW13 ....98 F5
Feltham Hill Jun Sch
TW13 ....98 F5
Feltham Hill Rd TW15 .98 C2
Feltham Rd TW15 ...98 C4
Felthorpe Cl RG6 ...114 A8
Felton Way RG31 ....84 C8
Fenchurch Mews 8
RG41 ....88 A3
Fencote RG12 ......118 D3
Fennel Cl Ascot SL5 ..120 A5
Earley RG6 ....86 F1
Newbury RG14 ......105 D5
Fennel Ct RG18 .....106 D4
Fenns La GU24 .....153 E5
Fennscombe Ct GU24 .153 F6
Fenton Ave TW18 ...97 C3
Fenton Lodge GU15 ..151 E6
Fern Cl Crowthorne RG45 .143 A7
Frimley GU16 ....152 C3
Reading RG31 ....84 C5
Fern Cotts SL7 ......2 E5
Fern Dr SL6 ....41 B7
Fern Glen RG31 .....57 C1
Fern La SL7 ....2 E5
Fern Wlk Ashford TW15 .97 D3
Reading RG31 ....84 C5
Fernbank RG40 .....141 D6
Fernbank Cres SL5 ..119 D8
Fernbank Pl SL5 ....119 D7
Fernbank Rd SL5 ...119 D8
Fernbrook Rd RG4 ..58 E5
Ferndale Ave RG30 ..85 A4
Ferndale Cl RG31 ...57 E3
Ferndale Ct RG19 ...106 D3
Ferndale Pk Cvn Pk SL6 .65 E8
Ferndale Rd TW15 ..97 E3
Ferne Cl RG8 ....34 C7
Fernery The TW18 ...96 E3
Fernhill Cl Bracknell RG42 .90 F1
Farnborough GU17 ..150 F1
Fernhill La GU17 ....150 F1
Fernhill Prim Sch GU14 .150 F1
Fernhill Rd GU14,GU17 .150 E2
Fernhill Sch GU14 ...150 F1
Fernhill Wlk GU17 ...150 F1
Fernhurst Rd
Ashford TW15 ....98 C4
Reading RG31 ....84 C4
Fernihough Cl GU25 .151 F4
Fernley Ct SL6 ......19 D1
Ferrard Cl SL5 ......119 D8
Ferrers Cl SL1 ......41 E5
Ferriby Cl RG12 ....118 C7
Ferrier Gr RG14 ....131 B8
Ferry Ave TW18 ....96 E1
Ferry End SL6 ......40 C4
Ferry La Bourne End SL8 .3 B1
Chertsey KT16 ......124 A3
Cookham SL6 ....20 B7
Goring RG8 ....34 B6

Ferry La continued
Hambleden RG9 .....16 D6
Laleham TW18 ......124 C6
Lower Halliford TW17 ..125 A1
Medmenham SL7 ....17 B5
Moulsford OX10,RG8 ..14 A4
South Stoke RG8 ....14 A4
Wargrave RG10 ......36 C2
Wraysbury TW19 ....96 B5
Ferry Rd Maidenhead SL6 .40 C4
South Stoke RG8 ....14 C4
Ferry Wks TW17 ....125 A1
Festival Cotts SL3 ...69 C7
Fettiplace RG17 .....48 B3
Fetty Pl SL6 ....39 D4
Fidler's La RG20 ....30 E7
Fidlers Wlk RG10 ...56 B7
Field Cl
Burghfield Common RG7 .111 B2
Harlington UB7 ......71 C7
Field End Wargrave RG10 .36 F2
West End GU24 .....153 F6
Field House Cl SL5 ..120 A1
Field Hurst SL3 .....43 F1
Field La GU16 ....151 E1
Field Path GU14 ....150 F1
Field Rd RG12 ......118 D8
Field Rd
Farnborough GU14 ..150 F1
Peasemore RG20 ....50 D8
Reading RG1 ....86 A6
Field View Caversham RG4 .59 B3
Egham TW20 ....96 F2
Feltham TW13 ......98 D4
Fielden Pl RG12 ....118 D7
Fieldfare Ave GU46 ..149 B6
Fieldhead Gdns SL8 ..3 A3
Fieldhouse Ind Est SL7 .1 F2
Fieldhouse La SL7 ..1 F2
Fieldhouse Way SL7 ..1 F2
Fielding Gdns
Crowthorne RG45 ...143 B4
Slough SL3 ....43 C4
Fielding Rd
Maidenhead SL6 ....39 B8
Sandhurst GU47 ....150 E6
Fieldings The SL6 ...65 A7
Fieldridge RG14 ....105 D5
Fields The SL1 ......42 D4
Fieldview Ct TW18 ..97 A2
Fieldway RG41 .....88 D2
Fifehead Cl TW15 ..97 E2
Fifield Cotts SL6 ....65 D5
Fifield La SL4,SL6 ...65 D4
Fifield Rd SL6 ......65 D7
Fifield Way Cotts SL6 .65 D6
Fifth Ave RG31 .....84 B6
Fifth Rd RG14 ......104 E1
Fifth St RG19 ......131 F5
Filbert Dr RG31 ....84 C8
Filey Rd RG1 ....86 E7
Filey Spur SL1 .....42 B4
Filley Alley OX12 ....6 E7
Filmer Rd SL4 ......66 D5
Finbeck Way RG6 ..113 F8
Finch Cl SL6 ....39 D5
Finch Rd RG6 ......87 C4
Finch Way RG7 ....111 B3
Fincham End Dr RG45 .142 F4
Finchampstead CE Prim Sch
RG40 ....141 E3
Finchampstead Rd
Wokingham RG40 ...141 F6
Wokingham RG41,RG40 .116 B3
Findhorn Cl GU47 ..150 D7
Finlay Ho RG9 ......15 E3
Finmere RG12 ......118 A3
Finney Dr GU20 ....146 D4
Finstock Cl RG6 ....87 D1
Finstock Gn RG12 ..118 F5
Fir Cl RG19 ....133 B5
Fir Cottage Rd RG40 .141 E8
Fir Dr GU17 ....150 D3
Fir Tree Ave SL2 ...22 F1
Fir Tree Cl SL5 .....120 A2
Fir Tree Cnr RG26 ..134 E2
Fir Tree Cotts SL6 ..10 B2
Fir Tree La RG14 ...105 E4
Fir Tree Paddock SL6 .20 E7
Fir Tree Pl 7 TW15 ..98 A3
Fir Tree Prim Sch RG14 .105 E4
Fir's End RG7 ......111 A2
Firbank Pl TW20 ...95 B2
Fircroft Cl Reading RG31 .57 C1
Stoke Poges SL2 ...23 A6
Fircroft Ct SL2 .....23 A6
Fireball Hill SL5 ....120 D2
Firglen Dr GU46 ...149 D7
Firgrove Rd RG27,GU46 .149 C6
Firlands Bracknell RG12 .118 C4
North Ascot SL5 ....119 C8
Firlands Ave GU15 ..151 D5
Firs Ave SL4 ....66 F4
Firs Cl RG40 ....141 F7
Firs Dr SL3 ....43 F3
Firs End RG7 ....136 E6
Firs La Maidenhead SL6 .38 F4
Reading RG30 ......85 D5
Firs Rd RG31 ......84 C6
Firs The
8 Bracknell RG12 ...118 F5
Inkpen RG17 ....127 E6
Maidenhead SL6 ....39 E7
Reading RG18 ......106 B4
First Ave Marlow SL7 ..2 A2

First Ave continued
Reading RG31 ....84 B6
Tadley RG7 ....135 D2
First Cres SL1 ......42 C8
First St RG19 ....132 A5
Firtree Cl GU47 ....142 F1
Firview Cl SL7 ......1 F1
Firwood Cl GU15 ...151 C5
Firwood Dr GU15 ...151 C5
Firwood Rd GU25 ..121 E3
Fisher Gn RG42 ....90 B2
Fisher Ho 5 RG14 ..104 F2
Fisher's La RG18 ...79 A1
Fisherman's La RG7 .135 B8
Fisherman's Way SL3 .3 B4
Fisherman's Retreat SL7 .1 E1
Fishers Cotts RG4 ..59 C6
Fishers Ct RG4 .....59 C6
Fishers Wood SL5 ..121 C1
Fishery Rd SL6 .....40 C5
Fishguard Spur SL1 ..43 B4
Fishing Temple Park Homes
TW18 ....123 F8
Fishponds Cl RG41 ..116 A4
Fishponds Est RG41 ..116 A4
Fishponds Rd RG41 ..116 A4
Fiske Ct GU46 .....149 E6
Fitzgerald Ct RG14 ..104 F3
Fitzrobert Pl TW20 ..96 A2
Fitzroy Cl RG12 ....118 A3
Fitzroy Cres RG5 ...88 A6
Five Acre RG31 ....57 B1
Five Acres HP10 ....3 F7
Fiveways GU15 .....151 E5
Flagstaff Sq RG19 ..106 E2
Flambards RG4 .....59 C2
Flamborough Cl RG6 .87 E2
Flamborough Path 4
RG6 ....87 E2
Flamborough Spur SL1 .42 A4
Flamingo Cl RG41 ..115 E5
Flanders Ct TW20 ..96 C3
Flats The GU17 ....150 C4
Flaxman Cl RG6 ....86 F2
Flecker Cl RG18 ....106 C5
Fleet Cl RG41 ......115 F8
Fleet Hill RG40 .....141 C2
Fleet La RG40 ......141 B2
Fleetbrook Ho SL3 ..68 D6
Fleetham Gdns RG6 .87 C1
Fleetway TW20 ....123 C6
Fleetwood Cl RG14 ..105 D5
Fleetwood Ct 7 TW19 .70 E1
Fleetwood Rd SL2 ..42 F6
Fleming Cl RG2 ....140 E7
Fleming Rd RG18 ..106 C5
Flemish Fields KT16 .124 A2
Flemish Pl RG42 ...91 D1
Fletcher Gdns RG42 .117 D8
Flexford Gn RG12 ..117 E3
Flintgrove RG12 ....118 D8
Flintjack Pl RG17 ...25 A2
Flintlock Cl TW19 ..70 A3
Flodden Dr RG31 ...84 D4
Flood Alley RG40 ...62 A8
Floral Ho KT16 ....123 F1
Floral Way RG18 ...106 E5
Floreat Gdns RG14 ..104 F5
Florence Ave SL6 ...40 A8
Florence Cl GU46 ..149 C6
Florence Cotts SL4 ..92 C7
Florence Ct 10 RG30 .85 D6
Florence Gdns
Staines TW18 ....97 B1
Thatcham RG18 ....106 A5
Florence Rd GU47 ..150 E7
Florence Villas GU18 .146 B1
Florence Wlk RG1 ..86 D7
Florian Gdns RG30 ..85 B5
Florida Ct Reading RG1 .86 B6
Slough SL1 ....42 F4
Flower's Hill RG8 ...56 C4
Flowers Piece RG8 ..54 B6
Fobney St RG1 .....86 B7
Fokerham Rd RG19 ..106 F2
Folder's La RG42 ...91 C1
Foliejohn Way SL6 ..38 F1
Folly Cl Frimley GU16 .151 E1
Wokingham RG41 ...116 B5
Follett Cl SL4 ......68 B1
Folly La RG7,RG30 ..110 F5
Folly Rd Inkpen RG17 .127 E6
Lambourn RG17 ....25 A3
Folly The RG1 ......86 B8
Fontmell Cl TW15 ..98 A3
Fontmell Pk TW15 ..98 A3
Fontwell Cl SL6 ....39 A8
Fontwell Dr RG30 ..85 B6
Fontwell Rd RG14 ..105 B1
Forbes Chase GU47 ..150 D7
Forbury Ho 3 RG30 ..85 B7
Forbury La RG17,RG20 .128 C2
Forbury Rd RG1 ....86 C8
Forbury Ret Pk RG1 ..86 C8
Ford Cl Ashford TW15 .97 E2
Littleton TW17 ......125 A7
Ford La RG7 ....142 A7
Ford Rd Ashford TW15 .97 F4
Bisley GU24 ....153 B6
Chertsey KT16 ......124 B1
Fordbridge Cl KT16 ..124 B1
Fordbridge Ct
Ashford TW15 ....97 E2
Upper Halliford TW16,
TW17 ....125 A6
Fordham Way RG6 ..87 C1
Fordwater Rd KT15,KT16 .124 B1

Fordwater Trad Est
KT16 ....124 C1
Fordwells Dr RG12 ..118 F5
Forehead The RG7 ..137 F4
Forest Cl Bracknell SL5 .119 C6
Tadley RG26 ....134 E2
Forest Ct RG41 .....116 A4
Forest Dean RG2 ...113 C7
Forest Dr TW16 ....98 F1
Forest End GU47 ...143 A1
Forest End Rd GU47 .150 A8
Forest Gn Bracknell RG12 .118 D7
Holyport SL6 ....65 C5
Forest Green Rd SL6 .65 C5
Forest Hill RG30 ...57 F2
Forest Hills GU15 ...151 B4
Forest Rd Binfield RG42 .90 D3
Crowthorne RG45 ...143 C5
Windsor SL4 ....93 E7
Windsor,Dedworth SL4 .66 E5
Winkfield RG42,SL5 ..92 D2
Forest Sch The RG41 .88 C2
Forest View Cotts SL6 .65 C6
Forest Way RG42 ...92 A2
Foresters Way RG45 .143 F1
Forge Cl Caversham RG4 .59 C2
Kintbury RG17 ......102 A2
Forge Cotts SN8 ...99 B5
Forge Ct GU46 .....149 D7
Forge Dr SL2 ....22 C6
Forge Hill RG18 ....53 A5
Forge The Harlington UB3 .71 D8
Hungerford RG17 ...100 D6
Forlease Cl SL6 ....40 A6
Forlease Dr SL6 ....40 A6
Forlease Rd SL6 ...40 A6
Formby Cl Earley RG6 .87 E3
Slough SL3 ....44 C2
Forndon Cl RG6 ...87 E2
Forsters RG7 ....134 F7
Forsters Farm Ct RG7 .135 A6
Forsythia Gdns SL3 ..43 E3
Fort Narrien GU15 ..150 F7
Fortrose Cl GU47 ...150 D7
Fortrose Wlk RG31 ..84 E4
Fortuna Ct RG2 ....134 E2
Forty Green Dr SL7 ..1 B2
Forum The KT16 ....123 F1
Fosseway RG45 ....143 A5
Fossewood Dr GU15 .151 D7
Foster Ave SL4 ....66 E4
Fosters Gr GU20 ...146 B6
Fosters La RG5 ....87 E6
Fosters Path SL2 ...21 F1
Fotherby Ct SL6 ...40 A6
Fotheringay Gdns SL1 .42 A6
Foundation Pk SL6 ..38 F4
Foundry Ct KT16 ...124 A2
Foundry Ho RG17 ..100 F7
Foundry La SL3 ....63 F4
Foundry Mews KT16 ..124 A2
Foundry Pl 20 RG1 ..86 A6
Fountain Gdns SL4 ..67 D4
Fountain Garth RG12 .118 A6
Fourth Ave Marlow SL7 .2 A2
Reading RG31 ......84 B6
Fourth St RG19 ....131 F5
Fowler Cl RG6 .....87 A3
Fowlers La RG42 ...118 B8
Fox Cl RG7 ....111 A3
Fox Covert GU18 ...153 A8
Fox Covert Cl SL5 ..120 B4
Fox Cl GU47 ....150 C8
Fox Dr GU47 ....150 D7
Fox Hill Prim Sch RG12 .118 B4
Fox La RG21 ....149 A7
Fox La N KT16 .....123 F1
Fox La S KT16 .....123 F1
Fox Rd Bracknell RG12 .118 C5
Slough SL3 ....43 C3
Foxborough RG27 ..139 D6
Foxborough Cl SL3 ..44 A1
Foxborough Ct SL6 ..39 E4
Foxborough Prim Sch
SL3 ....44 A1
Foxbury RG17 ......25 B2
Foxcombe Dr RG31 ..84 C7
Foxcote RG40 ......142 A7
Foxdown Cl GU15 ..151 C5
Foxes Piece SL7 ....1 E3
Foxes Piece Sch SL7 .1 E3
Foxes Wlk RG10 ...61 A3
Foxglove Cl
Stanwell TW19 .....97 F8
Winkfield RG42 .....117 D7
Foxglove Gdns 2 RG6 .85 E7
Foxglove Way RG18 .106 D5
Foxhaven Ct SL5 ...120 C4
Foxhays Rd RG2 ...113 D8
Foxheath RG12 ....118 E4
Foxherne SL3 ......43 C4
Foxhill Cl RG4 .....60 A5
Foxhill Cres GU15 ..152 B8
Foxhill La RG4 .....60 A5
Foxhill Rd RG1 .....86 E6
Foxhollow Dr SL2 ..22 C7
Foxhunt Gr RG31 ...84 F4
Foxhunter Way RG19 .105 F3
Foxleigh Ct TW18 ..96 C3
Foxley Cl GU17 ....150 D1
Foxley La RG6 .....113 A8
Framewood Manor SL2 .23 C6
Framewood Rd SL2,SL3 .23 C6
Framlingham Dr RG4 .59 E5
Frampton Bridge Rdbt
RG42 ....90 F2

Frampton Cl RG5 ....60 E1
France Hill Dr GU15 ....151 C5
Frances Ave SL6 ....20 C1
Frances Ct SL5 ....120 D5
Frances Rd SL4 ....67 D5
Frances The RG18 ....106 D4
Francis Baily Prim Sch
RG19 ....106 F3
Francis Chichester Cl
SL5 ....120 B4
Francis Cl TW17 ....125 A5
Francis Gdns RG42 ....91 D1
Francis St RG1 ....86 B6
Francis Way Burnham SL1 .41 D6
Frimley GU15 ....152 C4
Francomes Field RG17 ...25 C1
Frank Lunnon Cl SL8 ......3 C3
Frank Sutton Way SL1 ...42 D6
Franklin Ave Slough SL2 ..42 B8
Tadley RG26 ....135 A1
Franklin Ct 8 RG1 ....85 F7
Franklin St RG1 ....85 F7
Franklyn Cres SL4 ....66 D4
Frantons The SL6 ....39 A7
Frascati Way SL6 ....39 F7
Fraser Ave RG4 ....59 C6
Fraser Mead GU47 ......150 E6
Fraser Rd RG42 ....118 B8
Fraunchies Ct SL1 ....42 E6
Frederick Ho TW15 ......97 E4
Frederick Pl RG41 ......116 A6
Free Prae Rd KT16 ......124 A1
Freeborn Way RG12 .....118 E7
Freeman Cl TW17 ....125 E5
Freeman Ct RG14 ....104 F3
Freemans Cl
Hungerford RG17 ....100 C5
Stoke Poges SL2 ....23 A6
Freemantle Rd GU19 ....145 F4
Freemantles Sch KT16 ..123 E2
Freesia Cl RG41 ....115 D7
French Gdns GU17 ......150 D4
Frenchum Gdns SL1 ......41 E6
Frensham RG12 ....118 D3
Frensham Cl GU46 ......149 B6
Frensham Gn RG2 ....86 F1
Frensham Rd RG45 ......143 B7
Frensham Wlk SL2 ....22 C7
Freshfield Cl RG6 ....87 E3
Freshfields La RG20 ......51 B2
Freshwater Rd RG1 ....86 E8
Freshwood Dr GU46 .....149 D4
Friar St RG1 ....86 A8
Friars Ct GU47 ....149 F8
Friars Keep RG12 ....118 B5
Friars Rd Newbury RG14 .131 A8
Virginia Water GU25 ....122 D5
Friars Way KT16 ....124 A3
Friars Wlk 4 RG1 ....86 A8
Friary Island TW19 ......95 C8
Friary Rd Ascot SL5 .....120 B3
Wraysbury TW19 ....68 C1
Friary The SL4 ....68 C1
Friday St RG9 ....15 E2
Friends Wlk 1 TW18 .....96 F3
Friendship Ho 4 TW18 ...97 A3
Friendship Way RG12 ...118 B6
Frieth Cl RG6 ....87 A1
Frieth Rd SL7 ....1 A3
Frilsham Rd RG30 ....85 B4
Frimley Cl RG5 ....87 D8
Frimley Green Rd GU16 .151 D1
Frimley Grove Gdns
GU16 ....151 E1
Frimley Hall Dr GU15 ....151 F6
Frimley High St GU16 ...151 D1
Frimley Park Hospl
GU16 ....151 D2
Frimley Rd GU15,GU16 ..151 B3
Frimley Sq GU16 ....151 E1
Fringford Cl RG6 ....87 C1
Frith Hill Rd GU16 ......152 B1
Frithe The SL2 ....43 B7
Frithwald Rd KT16 ......123 F2
Frobisher RG12 ....118 C2
Frobisher Cres TW19 .....97 E8
Frobisher Gdns TW19 ....97 E8
Frodsham Way GU47 ....143 E2
Frog Hall RG40 ....116 F5
Frog Hall Dr RG40 ......116 E5
Frog La RG12 ....118 A6
Frogmill SL6 ....17 C3
Frogmill Ct SL6 ....17 C3
Frogmore Cl SL1 ....42 A4
Frogmore Com Coll
GU46 ....149 F5
Frogmore Ct
Blackwater GU17 ....150 C4
11 Maidenhead SL6 ....39 F7
Frogmore Dr SL4 ....67 F5
Frogmore Flats SL4 ......67 F5
Frogmore Gr GU17 ......150 C4
Frogmore Inf Sch GU17 .150 B5
Frogmore Jun Sch
GU17 ....150 B5
Frogmore Park Dr
GU17 ....150 D4
Frogmore Rd GU17 ......150 C5
Frogmore Way RG30 .....85 B5
Fromer Rd HP10 ....3 D4
Fromont Dr RG19 ....106 D3
Fromow Gdns GU20 .....146 D4
Fronds Pk RG7 ....109 A2
Front St RG17 ....47 D6
Frouds Bridge Marina
RG7 ....108 F1
Frouds La RG7 ....109 A1
Froxfield Ave RG1 ....85 F5
Froxfield Down 6 RG12 .118 F4
Fruen Rd TW14 ....98 F8
Fry Ct RG4 ....59 B3
Fry La GU19 ....145 D2
Fry's La GU46 ....149 E7
Frymley View SL4 ....66 D6
Fuchsia Cl RG31 ....84 C5
Fuchsia Way GU24 ......153 E6
Fullbrook Cl
Maidenhead SL6 ....40 A8
Wokingham RG41 ....89 A1
Fullbrook Cres RG31 .....57 D3
Fuller Cl RG19 ....106 F2
Fuller's La RG7 ....112 B4
Fullers La RG20 ....129 D1
Fullers Yd SL6 ....20 B2
Fulmead Rd RG30 ....85 C8
Fulmer Chase SL3 ....23 C8
Fulmer Cl RG6 ....87 A2
Fulmer Common Rd SL3 .23 E6
Fulmer Inf Sch SL3 ....23 E8
Fulmer Rd SL3 ....23 E8
Fulwood Ct TW19 ....70 F1
Furlong Cl SL8 ....3 B3
Furlong Rd SL8 ....3 B3
Furness SL4 ....66 C5
Furness Pl 8 SL4 ....66 C5
Furness Row 9 SL4 ......66 C5
Furness Sq 6 SL4 ....66 C5
Furness Way SL4 ....66 C5
Furness Wlk 7 SL4 ....66 C5
Furnival Ave SL2 ....42 B8
Furnival Cl GU25 ....122 D3
Furrow Way SL6 ....39 A4
Furse Cl GU15 ....152 C4
Furze Hill Cres RG45 ....143 C4
Furze Platt Halt SL6 ......19 E1
Furze Platt Inf Sch SL6 ...19 C1
Furze Platt Jun Sch SL6 ..19 C1
Furze Platt Rd SL6 ....19 B1
Furze Platt Senior Sch
SL6 ....19 C2
Furze Rd Maidenhead SL6 ..19 D1
Tadley RG26 ....134 F2
Furzebank SL5 ....120 D5
Furzecroft 3 TW15 ....98 A3
Furzedown Cl TW20 .....95 E2
Furzemoors RG12 ....118 B4
Furzen Cl SL2 ....22 A2
Fuzzens Wlk SL4 ....66 E5
Fydlers Cl SL4 ....93 B2
Fyfield Cl GU17 ....150 D5
Fyfield Rd RG19 ....106 D2
Fylingdales RG19 ....106 C2

G

Gables Ave TW15 ....97 F3
Gables Cl Datchet SL3 ....68 A8
Maidenhead SL6 ....40 B8
Gables Way RG19 ....107 C2
Gabriel Dr GU15 ....152 B4
Gabriels The RG14 ......130 D5
Gadd Cl RG40 ....116 F7
Gage Cl SL6 ....39 E4
Gainsborough
Bracknell RG12 ....118 C3
Cookham Rise SL6 ....19 F5
Gainsborough Ave
RG17 ....102 B2
Gainsborough Cl
Camberley GU15 ....151 F7
Woodley RG5 ....88 A6
Gainsborough Cres RG9 ..35 C8
Gainsborough Dr
Maidenhead SL6 ....39 D3
North Ascot SL5 ....119 D7
Gainsborough Hill RG9 ...35 D8
Gainsborough Rd
Henley-On-T RG9 ....35 D8
Reading RG30 ....85 B5
Gairn Cl RG30 ....85 A7
Galahad Cl SL1 ....42 A4
Gale Dr GU18 ....146 A1
Galileo Ct RG12 ....118 E7
Galley La RG19 ....132 D1
Galleymead Rd SL3 ....69 F6
Gallop The GU46 ....149 D7
Gallops The RG20 ....30 E6
Galloway Chase SL2 ......43 A6
Galloway Ctr The RG14 ..105 E2
Galloway Ho 4 RG1 ......85 E5
Gallys Rd SL4 ....66 D6
Galsworthy Dr RG4 ....59 E5
Galsworthy Rd KT16 .....124 A2
Galton Rd SL5 ....120 F3
Galvin Rd SL1 ....42 C6
Galway Rd GU46 ....149 C4
Garde Rd RG4 ....60 E3
Garden Cl Ashford TW15 ..98 C2
Maidenhead SL6 ....39 A5
Garden Close La RG14 ..130 D4
Garden Cotts SL3 ....69 D7
Garden Mews
8 Reading RG30 ....85 D6
Slough SL1 ....42 F5
Gardeners La RG8 ....55 C4
Gardeners Rd RG42 ......92 A2
Gardenia Dr GU24 ......153 F6
Gardens The Hatton TW14 .71 D1
South Stoke RG8 ....14 C3
Gardner Ho SL6 ....19 E1
Gardner Rd SL6 ....19 D2
Garfield Pl 2 SL4 ....67 C5
Garfield Rd GU15 ....151 C5
Garford Cres RG14 ......130 D8
Garland Ho RG14 ....104 F2
Garland Jun Sch RG7 ...111 A3
Garlands Cl RG7 ....111 A2
Garnet Cl SL1 ....42 A4
Garnet Ct SL7 ....1 C1
Garnet Field GU46 ......149 A5
Garnet Hill 7 RG1 ....86 A6
Garnet St RG1 ....86 A6
Garrard Rd SL2 ....21 F1
Garrard St RG1 ....86 A8
Garrett Rd RG40 ....141 E8
Garrick Cl TW18 ....97 A1
Garson La TW19 ....95 D8
Garson's La SL4 ....92 A7
Garston Cl RG30 ....85 A4
Garston Cres RG31 ....84 B5
Garston Gr RG40 ....115 F1
Garston Park Home Village
RG31 ....84 B6
Garswood RG12 ....118 D3
Garth Cl RG41 ....88 C2
Garth Hill Coll RG12 ....118 C8
Garth Rd RG7 ....137 A5
Garth Sq RG42 ....91 B1
Garthlands SL6 ....19 D2
Gas House Hill RG17 ....25 C3
Gas La Maidenhead SL6 ...40 B3
Twyford RG10 ....61 D4
Gas Works Rd RG1 ....86 C7
Gascon's Gr SL2 ....22 A1
Gaskell Mews RG14 .....131 B8
Gaskells End RG4 ....58 D8
Gaston Bridge Rd
Shepperton TW17 ....125 D3
Upper Halliford TW17 ...125 E4
Gaston Way TW17 ....125 D4
Gatcombe Cl RG31 ....84 C4
Gatehampton Rd RG8 ....34 C5
Gatehouse Cl SL4 ....67 B4
Gatewick Cl SL1 ....42 E5
Gatward Ave SL6 ....39 A3
Gaveston Rd SL2 ....21 F2
Gayhurst Cl RG4 ....59 D6
Gays La SL6 ....65 B8
Gaywood Dr RG14 ......105 D4
Gazelle Cl RG41 ....88 A3
Geffers Ride SL5 ....119 E7
Gelder Cl RG6 ....87 D1
Genesis Cl TW19 ....97 F7
Geneva Cl TW17 ....125 E7
Geoffrey Ct TW18 ....97 A1
Geoffrey Field Jun & Inf Schs
RG2 ....113 C8
Geoffreyson Rd RG4 .....58 E5
George Cl SL7 ....1 F4
George Green Dr SL3 .....43 F8
George Green Rd SL3 ....43 E7
George Palmer Prim Sch
RG2 ....86 C4
George St Caversham RG4 .59 B1
Reading RG1 ....85 F8
Staines TW18 ....96 F4
George V Pl SL4 ....67 D7
Georgeham Rd GU47 ....143 D2
Georges Dr HP10 ....3 C7
Georgian Cl
Camberley GU15 ....151 E7
Staines TW18 ....97 B4
Georgian Hts SL8 ....3 B5
Geranium Cl RG45 ......143 B8
Gerrards Cross Rd SL2 ...23 A7
Gerring Rd RG2 ....140 F7
Gervaise Cl SL1 ....41 F5
Gibbet La GU15 ....152 A7
Gibbins La RG42 ....91 D3
Gibbons Cl GU47 ....150 C8
Gibbs Cl RG40 ....141 E6
Gibbs Way GU46 ....149 B4
Gibraltar La SL6 ....2 C1
Gibson Ct SL3 ....43 F1
Gibson Pl TW19 ....70 C1
Gidley La RG20 ....50 E2
Gifford Cl RG4 ....59 E5
Gifford Ho 2 RG4 ....59 C1
Gilbert Ct RG18 ....106 D3
Gilbert Rd GU15 ....151 C2
Gilbert Way RG40 ....115 E1
Gilbey Wlk HP10 ....3 D4
Gilchrist Way SL6 ....38 B5
Giles Cl RG14 ....104 F2
Giles Travers Cl TW20 ..123 C6
Gill Rise RG42 ....91 C2
Gillespie Ho GU25 ....122 E5
Gillette Way RG2 ....86 B2
Gilliat Rd SL1 ....42 E6
Gilliatt Cl SL0 ....44 E7
Gillott Ct SL6 ....39 F8
Gillott's Hill RG9 ....35 C7
Gillott's La RG9 ....35 B7
Gillotts Cl RG9 ....35 B8
Gillotts Sch RG9 ....35 B7
Gilman Cres SL4 ....66 D4
Gilmore Cl SL3 ....43 C4
Gilmore Cres TW15 ......98 A2
Gilpin Way UB3 ....71 D7
Gilroy Cl RG14 ....130 C6
Gilson Ct SL4 ....95 C8
Gingells Farm Rd RG10 ..61 B5
Gipsy La Bracknell RG12 .118 D7
Earley RG6 ....87 D1
Hungerford RG17 ....100 E8
Lower Earley RG6 ....87 D3
Reading RG30 ....57 E1
Sindlesham RG41 ....114 F7
Wokingham RG40 ....116 C4
Girton Cl GU47 ....143 E1
Glade Ho Ascot SL5 .....120 C4
3 Marlow SL7 ....1 E2
Glade Rd SL7 ....1 E2
Glade The Ascot SL5 .....120 C4
Newbury RG14 ....130 F7
Purley On T RG8 ....57 C4
Staines TW18 ....97 B2
Gladridge Cl RG6 ....87 C4
Gladstone Cl RG17 ......102 B2
Gladstone Ind Est SL6 ....39 E8
Gladstone La RG18 .....106 C8
Gladstone Way SL1 ......42 A5
Glaisdale RG19 ....106 C2
Glamis Way RG31 ....84 B4
Glanmor Rd SL2 ....43 B6
Glanty The TW20 ....96 B4
Glassonby Wlk GU15 ....152 C5
Glebe Cl Dorney SL6 ......40 F4
Lightwater GU18 ....146 C1
Moulsford OX10 ....13 F5
Glebe Cotts RG8 ....14 C3
Glebe Fields RG20 ....49 A7
Glebe Gdns RG4 ....60 E3
Glebe La Sonning RG4 ....60 E3
Stockcross RG20 ....103 E5
Glebe Pl RG17 ....73 A2
Glebe Rd Egham TW20 ....96 C2
Maidenhead SL6 ....40 B5
Old Windsor SL4 ....68 B2
Purley On T RG8 ....57 B5
Reading RG2 ....86 C5
Staines TW18 ....97 B3
Glebe Ride RG8 ....34 B6
Glebe The Aldworth RG8 ..32 F3
Blackwater GU17 ....150 E4
Glebefields RG14 ....105 B5
Glebeland Gdns TW17 ..125 C3
Glebeland Rd GU15 .....150 F4
Glebelands RG19 ....106 C3
Glebelands Rd RG40 ....116 C7
Glebewood RG12 ....118 C4
Glen Ave TW15 ....98 A4
Glen Cl TW17 ....125 A5
Glen Ct TW18 ....96 F1
Glen Innes GU47 ....143 E1
Glen The Ascot SL5 .....120 D5
Silchester RG26 ....135 E1
Slough SL3 ....43 C2
Glenalmond Ho TW15 ....97 E5
Glenapp Grange RG7 ....136 F6
Glenavon Gdns
Slough SL3 ....43 C3
Yateley GU46 ....149 D4
Glenbeigh Terr RG1 ......85 E6
Glendale Ave RG14 ......130 C5
Glendale Cl RG41 ....116 A3
Glendale Rd RG26 ....135 A1
Glendevon Rd RG5 ....87 F8
Gleneagles Cl TW19 ......70 D1
Gleneagles Ct 17 RG1 ....86 D7
Gleneagles Ho RG12 ....117 E3
Glenfield Cl SL2 ....22 F4
Glenfield Ho RG12 ......118 C5
Glenfield Rd TW15 ....98 C2
Glenhurst GU20 ....146 A6
Glenhurst Cl GU17 ......150 E4
Glenmore Cl RG19 ......106 D2
Glenn Miller Cl RG20 ....49 A5
Glennon Cl RG30 ....85 C4
Glenore SL6 ....20 A8
Glenrhondda RG4 ....58 F6
Glenridge Farm Cvn Site
GU25 ....122 B6
Glenrosa Rd RG30 ....85 A8
Glentworth Pl SL1 ....42 C5
Glenwood
Bracknell RG12 ....118 D5
Virginia Water GU25 ....122 C8
Glenwood Dr RG31 ....84 C7
Globe Farm La GU17 ....150 B5
Globeside Bsns Pk SL7 ....1 F2
Glory Cl HP10 ....3 F7
Glory Hill La HP9 ....3 F8
Glory Mill La HP10 ....3 E7
Gloucester Ave SL1 ....42 C8
Gloucester Cres TW18 ...97 D2
Gloucester Ct RG30 ......85 D7
Gloucester Dr TW18 .....96 D5
Gloucester Gdns GU19 ..145 E3
Gloucester Pl
Bracknell RG42 ....91 F1
Windsor SL4 ....67 D5
Gloucester Rd
Bagshot GU19 ....145 E3
Maidenhead SL6 ....19 E2
Newbury RG14 ....104 E2
Reading RG30 ....85 D7
Gloucestershire Lea
RG42 ....91 F1
Glyme Wlk RG31 ....84 F3
Glyncastle RG4 ....58 F5
Glynswood GU15 ....151 F3
Glynwood Ho SL6 ....40 A7
Goaters Rd SL5 ....119 C7
Goddard Cl
Littleton TW17 ....124 F6
Shinfield RG2 ....113 E5
Goddard Ct RG41 ....88 B1
Goddard Dr RG7 ....107 F3
Goddard Way RG42 ......91 D2
Goddards La GU15 ......151 B3
Goddinton Rd SL8 ....3 A5
Godfrey Cl GU47 ....150 D7
Godolphin Inf Sch SL1 ...42 C7
Godolphin Jun Sch SL1 ..42 D7
Godolphin Rd SL1 ....42 D6
Godstow Cl RG5 ....87 E8
Goffs Rd TW15 ....98 D2
Gogmore Farm Cl KT16 .123 F2
Gogmore La KT16 ....124 A2
Gold Cup La SL5 ....119 D8
Goldcrest Cl GU46 ......149 B6
Goldcrest Way RG31 .....84 B6
Golden Ball La SL6 ....19 A3
Golden Oak Cl SL2 ....22 C6
Golden Orb Wood RG42 .117 D8
Goldfinch La RG20 ......131 F3
Golding Cl RG19 ....106 F3
Goldney Rd GU15 ....152 C4
Goldsmid Rd RG1 ....85 F7
Goldsmith Cl
Thatcham RG18 ....106 C5
Wokingham RG40 ....115 E1
Goldsmith Way RG45 ....143 B4
Goldsworthy Way SL1 ....41 C7
Goldthorpe Gdns RG6 ...113 F8
Goldwell Dr RG14 ....104 F4
Golf Dr GU15 ....151 F4
Gooch Cl RG10 ....61 F3
Goodall Cl RG9 ....15 D1
Goodboy's La RG7 ......112 A1
Goodchild Rd RG40 .....116 D6
Goodings Gn RG40 ......116 F6
Goodings La RG17 ....47 B3
Goodliffe Gdns RG31 ....57 C4
Goodman Pk SL2 ....43 C5
Goodman Pl TW18 ....96 F4
Goodrich Cl RG4 ....59 E5
Goodways Dr RG12 .....118 D7
Goodwin Cl RG31 ....84 E4
Goodwin Mdws HP10 ......3 E6
Goodwin Rd SL2 ....21 F2
Goodwin Wlk RG14 .....130 C6
Goodwind Villas SL1 .....41 F5
Goodwood Cl
Burghfield Common RG7 .111 A2
Camberley GU15 ....151 C8
Goodwood Rise SL7 ....1 C7
Goodwood Way RG14 ..105 C1
Goose Cnr RG42 ....91 F3
Goose Gn
Farnham Royal SL2 ....22 B3
Lambourn RG17 ....25 B3
Goose Green Way RG19 .106 D3
Goose La RG20 ....49 E5
Goosecroft La RG8 ....57 B5
Gordon Ave GU15 ....151 C4
Gordon Cl TW18 ....97 B2
Gordon Cres
Camberley GU15 ....151 C4
Compton RG20 ....31 D4
Gordon Ct 1 RG14 ......105 B2
Gordon Dr TW17 ....125 D2
Gordon Palmer Cl RG7 ..137 D5
Gordon Palmer Ct RG30 ..85 C8
Gordon Pl RG30 ....85 C8
Gordon Rd Ashford TW15 ..97 E5
Camberley GU15 ....151 C5
Crowthorne RG45 ....143 D3
Egham TW18 ....96 C4
Maidenhead SL6 ....39 D7
Newbury RG14 ....105 B2
Shepperton TW17 ....125 D3
Thatcham RG18 ....106 A5
Windsor SL4 ....66 F5
Gordon Wlk GU46 ....149 F5
Gordon's Sch GU24 .....153 E7
Gore End Rd RG20 ......129 B3
Gore Rd SL1 ....21 B2
Gore The SL1 ....21 A2
Goring & Streatley Sta
RG8 ....34 C6
Goring CE Prim Sch RG8 .34 C7
Goring La RG7 ....111 A1
Goring Pl TW18 ....96 D3
Goring Rd TW18 ....96 E3
Goring's Sq TW18 ....96 E4
Gorrick Sq RG41 ....116 B3
Gorse Bank GU18 ....153 A8
Gorse Cottage Dr RG18 ..79 C1
Gorse Dr RG5 ....88 A8
Gorse Hill La GU25 ......122 D5
Gorse Hill Rd GU25 .....122 D5
Gorse Meade SL1 ....42 B5
Gorse Pl RG42 ....92 B1
Gorse Rd
Cookham Rise SL6 ....19 E6
Frimley GU16 ....151 E2
Gorse Ride Inf Sch
RG40 ....141 E7
Gorse Ride Jun Sch
RG40 ....141 E7
Gorse Ride N RG40 .....141 E7
Gorse Ride S RG40 .....141 E6
Gorselands
Caversham RG4 ....59 B6
Newbury RG14 ....130 D5
Gosbrook Ho 1 RG4 ......59 C1
Gosbrook Rd RG4 ....59 B2
Gosden Rd GU24 ....153 F6
Gosforth Cl RG6 ....87 D2
Goslar Way SL4 ....67 B5
Gosling Gn SL3 ....43 E3
Gosling Rd SL3 ....43 E3
Gosnell Cl GU16 ....152 D3
Gossmore Cl SL7 ....1 F1
Gossmore La SL7 ....1 F1
Gossmore Wlk SL7 ....1 F1
Goswell Hill SL4 ....67 D6
Goswell Rd SL4 ....67 D6
Gothic Ct Harlington UB3 .71 D8
Sandhurst GU47 ....150 B7
Gough's Barn La RG42 ...91 A8
Gough's La RG12 ....91 D1
Gough's Mdw GU47 .....150 B7
Gould Cl RG14 ....105 B3

Gould Rd TW14 . . . . .98 E8
Goulders Cotts RG10 . . . . .36 F7
Governor's Rd GU15 . . . .150 F6
Govett Ave TW17 . . . . . .125 C4
Govett Gr GU20 . . . . .146 D5
Gower Pk GU47 . . . . .150 D7
Gower St RG1 . . . . .85 E8
Gower The TW20 . . . . . .123 C6
Gowings Gn SL1 . . . . .41 E4
Grace Ct SL1 . . . . .42 E4
Grace Reynolds Wlk
  GU15 . . . . .151 C6
Graces La RG20 . . . . .78 B8
Graftham Cl RG6 . . . . . .114 B8
Grafton Cl Maidenhead SL6 .19 E2
  Slough SL3 . . . . .43 E7
Grafton Ct TW14 . . . . .98 D7
Grafton Rd RG30 . . . . .84 D7
Graham Cl Blewbury OX11 .12 A8
  Maidenhead SL6 . . . . . . .39 C5
  Reading RG31 . . . . .84 E4
Graham Rd
  Cookham Rise SL6 . . . . . .19 E6
  Windlesham GU20 . . . . .146 C4
Grahame Ave RG8 . . . . . . .56 D5
Grainford Ct RG40 . . . . .116 C5
Gramp's Hill OX12 . . . . .6 C5
Grampian Cl UB3 . . . . .71 D7
Grampian Rd GU47 . . . . .143 A2
Grampian Way SL3 . . . . . .44 A1
Granby Ct RG1 . . . . .86 E7
Granby End RG7 . . . . . . .111 B3
Granby Gdns RG1 . . . . . . .86 E7
Grand Ave SL1 . . . . .151 C6
Grand Regency Hts SL5 .119 E6
Grandison Ho RG9 . . . . . .15 E3
Grange Ave
  Crowthorne RG45 . . . . . .143 B6
  Reading RG6 . . . . .87 A6
Grange Cl Goring RG8 . . . . .34 B6
  Wraysbury TW19 . . . . . . .68 E1
Grange Ct Earley RG6 . . . . .87 B8
  Egham TW20 . . . . .95 F3
  Littleton TW17 . . . . .125 A5
  Newbury RG14 . . . . .105 B2
  ⁊ Staines TW18 . . . . .97 A3
Grange Dr HP10 . . . . .3 D3
Grange Gdns
  Farnham Common SL2 . . . .22 D7
  Newbury RG14 . . . . .130 C5
Grange La SL6 . . . . .19 F8
Grange Pl TW18 . . . . . . .124 C7
Grange Rd
  Bracknell RG12 . . . . .118 C8
  Camberley GU15 . . . . . .151 E5
  Cookham Rise SL6 . . . . . .19 F7
  Egham TW20 . . . . .95 F3
  Henley-On-T RG9 . . . . . . .15 E1
Grange The Burnham SL1 .21 C2
  Caversham RG4 . . . . .58 D6
  Newbury RG14 . . . . .130 C5
  Old Windsor SL4 . . . . . . .68 B2
  Thorpe GU25 . . . . .122 E5
Grange Way SL0 . . . . .44 F7
Grangely Cl RG31 . . . . .84 D4
Grangewood SL3 . . . . .43 C8
Grant Ave SL1 . . . . .42 E7
Grant Ct TW17 . . . . .125 B3
Grant Ho ⁊ SL8 . . . . .3 A4
Grant Rd RG45 . . . . .143 C3
Grant Wlk SL5 . . . . .120 E1
Grantham Cl GU47 . . . . .143 E1
Grantham Ho ⁊ TW16 . . . .98 E1
Grantham Rd RG30 . . . . . .84 F4
Granthams The RG17 . . . . .25 B3
Grantley Hts ⁊ RG1 . . . . . .86 C7
Granville Ave SL2 . . . . .42 D8
Granville Rd RG30 . . . . . . .85 B5
Grasholm Way SL3 . . . . . . .44 C2
Grasmere SL4 . . . . .66 E7
Grasmere Ave
  Reading RG30 . . . . .57 F2
  Slough SL2 . . . . .43 A6
Grasmere Cl
  East Bedfont TW14 . . . . . .98 F7
  Thorpe Lea TW20 . . . . . . .96 B1
  Winnersh RG41 . . . . .88 B1
Grasmere Par SL2 . . . . . . .43 B6
Grasmere Rd GU18 . . . . .146 B1
Grass Hill RG4 . . . . .58 E3
Grassington Pl RG19 . . . .106 D3
Grassmead RG19 . . . . . .106 F2
Grassy La SL6 . . . . .39 F7
Grattan Ct SL7 . . . . .2 A3
Gratton Dr SL4 . . . . .66 E3
Gratton Rd RG2 . . . . .113 C8
Gratwicke Rd RG30 . . . . . .85 B5
Gravel Hill Caversham RG4 .59 A6
  Henley-On-T RG9 . . . . . . .15 D2
  Stockcross RG20 . . . . . . .103 E5
Gravel Rd RG9 . . . . .35 A1
Gravelly Cl RG20 . . . . . . .129 A3
Graveney Dr RG4 . . . . .58 E3
Gravett Cl RG9 . . . . .35 C8
Gray Pl RG42 . . . . .117 E8
Gray's Mon⁊ SL2 . . . . . . .22 F2
Grayling Cl SL7 . . . . .18 C8
Grayling Ct ⁊ RG1 . . . . . . .59 A1
Grays Cres RG5 . . . . .87 C7
Grays La TW15 . . . . .98 B4
Grays Park Rd SL2 . . . . . . .23 A2
Grays Pl SL2 . . . . .42 F5
Grayshott Dr GU17 . . . . .150 C5

Grazeley Parochial CE Prim
  Sch RG7 . . . . .112 E2
Grazeley Rd RG7 . . . . . . .113 A4
Great Auclum Pl RG7 . . . .111 B2
Great Barn Ct RG19 . . . . .106 C3
Great Hill Cres SL6 . . . . . . .39 C6
Great Hollands Prim Sch
  RG12 . . . . .117 F4
Great Hollands Rd RG12 .117 F3
Great Hollands Sq RG12 .117 F3
Great Knollys St RG1 . . . . .85 F8
Great Lea RG7 . . . . .113 A5
Great Marlow Sch SL7 . . . .1 F4
Great Severals RG17 . . . . .102 A2
Great South-West Rd
  TW14,TW6,TW4,TW5 . . . .71 D2
Grebe Ct TW18 . . . . .97 B4
Green Acre Mount RG30 .38 D8
Green Bsns Ctr The
  TW18 . . . . .96 C4
Green Cl Burnham SL6 . . . .41 A7
  Maidenhead SL6 . . . . . . .19 F1
Green Cres HP10 . . . . .3 C7
Green Croft RG40 . . . . . .116 E8
Green Ct TW16 . . . . .98 F2
Green Dr RG40 . . . . .116 E4
Green Dragon La HP10 . . . .3 B7
Green End GU46 . . . . . . .149 D7
Green End Ct RG7 . . . . . .113 B2
Green Farm Rd GU19 . . . .145 F3
Green Farm Rise SN8 . . . . .99 B5
Green Hill Cl GU15 . . . . . .152 C6
Green Hill Rd GU15 . . . . .152 C6
Green La Ascot SL5 . . . . . .120 E8
  Ashford TW15 . . . . .98 F2
  Bagshot GU19 . . . . .145 F2
  Binfield RG40 . . . . .90 A3
  Blackwater GU17 . . . . . .150 B4
  Blackwater,Hawley GU17 .150 E4
  Burghfield Common RG30 . .85 A2
  Burnham SL1 . . . . .21 D4
  Caversham RG9 . . . . .35 A1
  Chieveley RG20 . . . . .78 B7
  Datchet SL3 . . . . .68 B6
  Egham TW20 . . . . .96 B3
  Farnham Common SL2 . . . .22 B6
  Henley-On-T RG9 . . . . . . .15 E3
  Holyport SL6 . . . . .64 A5
  Hurst RG10 . . . . .88 E3
  Littlewick Green SL6 . . . . .38 B5
  Maidenhead SL6 . . . . . . .40 A6
  Newbury RG14 . . . . .104 E2
  Pangbourne RG8 . . . . . . .56 C5
  Sandhurst GU47 . . . . . . .150 C7
  Shepperton TW17 . . . . . .125 C8
  Staines TW18 . . . . .123 E8
  Stanford Dingley RG7 . . . .81 F3
  Thatcham RG19 . . . . . . .106 C3
  Ufton Nervet RG7 . . . . . .110 C2
  Windsor SL4 . . . . .67 B5
  Wokingham RG41 . . . . . . .88 D1
  Yateley GU46 . . . . .149 B7
Green Lane Cl GU15 . . . . .151 D4
Green Lane Ct SL1 . . . . . . .21 C2
Green Leas TW16 . . . . .98 F2
Green Leas Cl TW16 . . . . . .98 F2
Green Leys RG19 . . . . .19 F2
Green Pk TW18 . . . . .96 E5
Green Rd Reading RG6 . . . .87 A5
  Virginia Water TW20 . . . .123 A5
Green The Ashford TW18 . . .97 D3
  Blackwater GU17 . . . . . .150 C5
  Bracknell RG12 . . . . .118 B5
  Burnham SL1 . . . . .21 B1
  Chieveley RG20 . . . . .51 B2
  Chilton OX11 . . . . .10 E8
  Datchet SL3 . . . . .68 B7
  Kintbury RG17 . . . . .102 B1
  Slough SL1 . . . . .42 D3
  Theale RG7 . . . . .83 C2
  Upper Halliford TW17 . . .125 E5
  Wokingham RG41 . . . . . .115 E7
  Wooburn Green HP10 . . . . .3 E5
  Wraysbury TW19 . . . . . . .68 E1
Green Verges SL7 . . . . .1 E3
Greenacre SL4 . . . . .66 E5
Greenacre Ct TW20 . . . . . .95 C2
Greenacres RG20 . . . . . . .129 E1
Greenacres Ave RG41 . . . .88 A3
Greenacres La RG41 . . . . .88 A3
Greenaway Terr TW19 . . . .97 E7
Greenbank Way GU15 . . .151 D2
Greencroft Gdns RG30 . . .84 F4
Greendale Mews SL2 . . . . .43 A6
Greene Fielde End TW18 . .97 F3
Greenfern Ave SL1 . . . . . .41 C7
Greenfield Way RG45 . . . .143 A7
Greenfields SL6 . . . . .40 A5
Greenfields Rd RG14 . . . .113 B8
Greenfinch Cl
  Crowthorne RG45 . . . . . .142 F6
  Reading RG31 . . . . .84 B6
  Sandhurst GU47 . . . . . . .150 D8
Greengates ⁊ RG30 . . . . . .85 C7
Greenham Cl
  Greenham RG19 . . . . . . .131 D8
  Woodley RG5 . . . . .88 A6
Greenham Court Prim Sch
  RG14 . . . . .131 B8
Greenham Mill RG14 . . . .105 B3
Greenham Rd RG14 . . . . .105 A3
Greenham Road Ret Pk
  RG14 . . . . .105 A2
Greenham Wood RG12 . . .118 C3
Greenhaven GU46 . . . . . .149 B5
Greenholme GU15 . . . . . .152 D5
Greenhow RG12 . . . . . . .118 A6
Greenidge ⁊ RG1 . . . . .85 E5

Greenlake Terr TW18 . . . . .97 A1
Greenlands
  Ball Hill RG20 . . . . .129 E1
  Flackwell Heath HP10 . . . . .3 B8
Greenlands Ct
  Maidenhead SL6 . . . . . . .39 B8
  ⁊ Staines TW18 . . . . .97 A4
Greenlands Rd
  Camberley GU15 . . . . . .151 B1
  Newbury RG14 . . . . .105 B1
  Staines TW18 . . . . .97 A4
Greenleaf Ct SL3 . . . . .68 A8
Greenleas GU16 . . . . .151 E2
Greenleas Ave RG4 . . . . . .59 B7
Greenleas Cl GU46 . . . . . .149 C7
Greeno Cres TW17 . . . . . .125 A4
Greenock Rd SL1 . . . . .42 A7
Greenside Bourne End SL8 . .3 A5
  Crowthorne RG45 . . . . . .142 F5
  Slough SL2 . . . . .42 A8
Greensward La RG22 . . . .114 C2
Greenway Ct TW15 . . . . . .97 F4
Greenway SL1 . . . . .21 B3
Greenway Dr TW18 . . . . .124 B8
Greenway The
  Fawley OX12 . . . . .27 C7
  Slough SL1 . . . . .41 D5
Greenways Ball Hill RG20 .129 E1
  Egham TW20 . . . . .95 E3
  Lambourn RG17 . . . . .25 B1
  Pangbourne RG8 . . . . . . .56 D5
  Sandhurst GU47 . . . . . . .143 B1
Greenways Dr
  Maidenhead SL6 . . . . . . .39 A8
  Sunningdale SL5 . . . . . . .120 E1
Greenways Ho RG14 . . . .104 E2
Greenwood
  ⁊ Bracknell RG12 . . . . . .118 F5
  North Ascot SL5 . . . . . . .119 C8
Greenwood Cotts SL5 . . .121 C3
Greenwood Gr RG41 . . . . .88 D3
Greenwood Rd
  Crowthorne RG45 . . . . . .143 B6
  Reading RG30 . . . . .84 F5
Gregory Cl RG6 . . . . .114 C8
Gregory Dr SL4 . . . . .68 B1
Grenfell Ave SL6 . . . . .39 F6
Grenfell Pl SL6 . . . . .39 F6
Grenfell Rd SL6 . . . . .39 E6
Grenville Cl SL1 . . . . .21 B3
Grenville Pl RG12 . . . . . . .118 C7
Gresham Ct ⁊ TW18 . . . . . .97 A3
Gresham Rd Slough SL1 . . .42 A7
  Staines TW18 . . . . .96 F2
Gresham Way RG30 . . . . . .58 A2
Greybery Copse Rd
  RG19 . . . . .131 D8
Greycoat Ct RG4 . . . . .59 B3
Greyfriars Dr SL5 . . . . . . .120 B3
Greyfriars Rd RG1 . . . . . . .86 A8
Greys Ct ⁊ RG1 . . . . .86 C7
Greys Hill RG9 . . . . .15 C8
Greystock Rd RG40 . . . . . .91 D2
Greystoke Ct RG45 . . . . . .143 A4
Greystoke Ho ⁊ RG1 . . . . .85 E5
Greystoke Rd
  Caversham RG4 . . . . .59 C4
  Slough SL2 . . . . .41 F8
Griffin Cl Maidenhead SL6 .39 F5
  Slough SL1 . . . . .42 C4
Griffiths Cl RG19 . . . . . . .106 F2
Grindle Cl RG18 . . . . .106 C5
Gringer Hill SL6 . . . . .39 E8
Groombridge Pl RG14 . . .104 E6
Grosvenor Ct
  Blackwater GU17 . . . . . .150 D3
  Slough SL1 . . . . .42 E7
Grosvenor Dr SL6 . . . . . . .40 C8
Grosvenor Ho ⁊ RG1 . . . . .85 F8
Grosvenor Lawn GU46 . . .104 E2
Grosvenor Rd
  Caversham RG4 . . . . .59 C4
  Staines TW18 . . . . .97 A1
Grove Cl Old Windsor SL4 . .95 B8
  ⁊ Slough SL1 . . . . .43 A3
  Wokingham RG40 . . . . . .142 E7
Grove Cotts
  Caversham RG4 . . . . .59 A5
  Wokingham RG40 . . . . . .142 E7
Grove Cross Rd GU16 . . . .151 D1
Grove Ct Egham TW20 . . . .96 A3
  Maidenhead SL6 . . . . . . .39 D7
  Newbury RG14 . . . . .131 A8
Grove End RG14 . . . . .105 B1
Grove Hill RG4 . . . . .59 A4
Grove Ho SL4 . . . . .95 C8
Grove La RG42 . . . . .92 B4
Grove Pk SL6 . . . . .63 E8
Grove Prim Sch The
  GU16 . . . . .151 E2
Grove Rd Burnham SL1 . . .21 E4
  Camberley GU15 . . . . . .151 F5
  Chertsey KT16 . . . . .123 F3
  Emmer Green RG4 . . . . . .59 B6
  Henley-On-T RG9 . . . . . . .15 E1
  Maidenhead SL6 . . . . . . .39 D7
  Newbury RG14 . . . . .104 E5
  Shepperton TW17 . . . . . .125 C3
  South Stoke RG8 . . . . . . .14 B7
  Windsor SL4 . . . . .67 D5
Grove The Egham TW20 . . .96 A3
  Frimley GU16 . . . . .151 D1
  Medmenham SL7 . . . . . . .17 E6
  North Ascot SL5 . . . . . . .119 C8
  Slough SL1 . . . . .43 A4
  Thatcham RG18 . . . . . . .106 D4

Grove The continued
  Twyford RG10 . . . . .61 D5
Grovebarns TW18 . . . . . . .97 A2
Grovefields Ave GU16 . . .151 D1
Groveland
  Workshops RG41 . . . . . . .88 D3
Groveland Pl RG30 . . . . . .85 B8
Groveland Rd RG14 . . . . .104 E5
Grovelands Ave RG41 . . . .88 D2
Grovelands Cl RG41 . . . . . .88 D3
Grovelands Rd
  Reading RG30 . . . . .85 B8
  Shinfield RG7 . . . . .113 C2
Groveley Rd TW16 . . . . . . .98 F3
Groves Cl SL8 . . . . .3 C3
Groves Lea RG7 . . . . .136 F6
Groves The RG17 . . . . .73 A2
Groves Way SL6 . . . . .19 E6
Grovestile Waye TW14 . . . .98 D8
Grubwood La SL6 . . . . .18 E5
Guards Club Rd SL6 . . . . . .40 C7
Guards Ct SL5 . . . . .121 B2
Guards Rd SL4 . . . . .66 C5
Guards Wlk ⁊ SL7 . . . . .1 E2
Guerdon Pl RG12 . . . . . . .118 D2
Guildford Ave TW13 . . . . . .98 F6
Guildford St
  Chertsey KT16 . . . . .124 A2
  Staines TW18 . . . . .97 A2
Gull Cl RG41 . . . . .115 E4
Gullane Ct ⁊ SL6 . . . . .86 D7
Gun St RG1 . . . . .86 A7
Gunthorpe Rd SL7 . . . . .2 A3
Gurney Cl RG4 . . . . .58 D5
Gurney Dr RG4 . . . . .58 D5
Gwendale SL6 . . . . .19 C1
Gwendolen Ho RG19 . . . . .97 E7
Gwendoline Ct TW15 . . . . .97 E4
Gweneth Ct SL7 . . . . .1 D3
Gwent Cl GU16 . . . . .152 A5
Gwyn Cl RG14 . . . . .130 E8
Gwynne Cl
  Purley On T RG31 . . . . . . .57 D3
  Windsor SL4 . . . . .66 E6
Gwyns Piece RG17 . . . . . . .25 B3
Gypsy La Marlow SL7 . . . . .1 E4
  Stoke Poges SL2 . . . . .22 E8

H

Habershon Dr GU16 . . . . .152 D2
Hackney Bottom RG18 . . . .53 A8
Haddenhurst Ct RG42 . . . .90 C2
Haddon Dr RG5 . . . . .87 E8
Haddon Rd SL6 . . . . .39 C5
Hadfield Rd TW19 . . . . . . .70 D1
Hadleigh Rise RG4 . . . . . . .59 E5
Hadley Ct SL3 . . . . .44 A2
Hadlow Ct SL1 . . . . .42 C5
Hadrian Cl TW19 . . . . .97 E8
Hadrian Way TW19 . . . . . .97 D8
Hadrian Wlk E RG2 . . . . . .86 C4
Hadrian Wlk W RG2 . . . . . .86 C3
Hafod RG4 . . . . .58 F6
Hag Hill La SL6 . . . . .41 A7
Hag Hill Rise SL6 . . . . .41 A7
Hagley Rd RG2 . . . . .86 B4
Haig Dr SL1 . . . . .42 B4
Haig Rd GU15 . . . . .150 F6
Hailey La RG20 . . . . .29 F1
Haileybury Cl SL4 . . . . .67 A4
Hailsham Cl GU47 . . . . . .143 D1
Halcyon Ct TW18 . . . . . . .124 B7
Halcyon Terr RG30 . . . . . . .84 F8
Haldane Rd RG4 . . . . .58 F5
Hale St SL4 . . . . .67 D6
Hale End RG12 . . . . .118 F5
Halewood RG12 . . . . .117 F3
Half Mile Rd RG17 . . . . . . .46 A1
Half Moon St GU19 . . . . .145 E3
Halfacre Cl RG7 . . . . .113 B3
Halfpenny Ct ⁊ SL5 . . . . .121 B2
Halfpenny La
  Cholsey OX10 . . . . .21 D5
  Sunningdale SL5 . . . . . . .121 A2
Halfway Farm Cotts
  RG20 . . . . .102 E5
Halfway Hos SL6 . . . . .41 A6
Halifax Cl SL6 . . . . .39 A8
Halifax Pl RG18 . . . . .106 C4
Halifax Rd SL6 . . . . .39 A8
Halifax Way SL6 . . . . .39 A8
Halkingcroft SL3 . . . . .43 C4
Hall Cl GU15 . . . . .151 E6
Hall Ct SL3 . . . . .68 B7
Hall Farm Cres GU46 . . . .149 D5
Hall Grove Farm Ind Est
  GU19 . . . . .145 E5
Hall Grove Sch GU19 . . . .146 A5
Hall La Harlington UB3 . . . .71 D7
  Yateley GU46 . . . . .149 C4
Hall Pl La SL6 . . . . .19 F5
Hall Place La KT16 . . . . . .123 F2
Hall Place SL6 . . . . .38 B7
Hallbrooke Gdns RG42 . . . .90 E1
Halldore Hill SL6 . . . . .19 D7
Halley Dr SL5 . . . . .119 D7
Hallgrove Bottom GU19 . .145 E5
Halliford Ct TW17 . . . . . .125 E6
Halliford Rd TW16,TW17 .125 F5

Halliford Sch TW17 . . . . .125 C2
Hallmark Cl GU47 . . . . . .150 E8
Halls La Earley RG7 . . . . . .86 E1
  Waltham St Lawrence RG10 .63 A7
Halls Rd RG30 . . . . .84 D6
Hallsmead Ct ⁊ RG1 . . . . .59 A1
Halpin Cl RG31 . . . . .84 B7
Halse Dr SL1,SL2 . . . . .21 F7
Halstead Cl RG5 . . . . .87 E7
Halters The RG14 . . . . . . .131 B7
Halt Island SL4 . . . . .68 C3
Ham La
  Englefield Green TW20 . . . .95 B4
  Old Windsor SL4 . . . . . . .68 C3
Ham Rd SN8 . . . . .126 A3
Hamble Ave GU17 . . . . . .150 D5
Hamble Ct ⁊ RG1 . . . . .86 B6
Hambleberry Ct RG31 . . . .84 C8
Hambleden Ct RG12 . . . . .118 E5
Hambleden Mill RG9 . . . . .16 C7
Hambleden Rise RG9 . . . . .16 D8
Hambleden Wlk SL6 . . . . . .19 C1
Hambledon Cl RG6 . . . . . . .87 E1
Hambleton Cl GU16 . . . . .152 B3
Hamblin Mdw RG17 . . . . .100 E7
Hambridge La RG14 . . . . .105 E2
Hambridge Rd RG14 . . . . .105 D3
Hamfield Cotts SL6 . . . . . .17 E8
Hamilton Ave RG9 . . . . . . .15 E1
Hamilton Cl Ashford TW13 .98 F3
  Bagshot GU19 . . . . .145 E3
  Chertsey KT16 . . . . .123 F1
Hamilton Ct
  Farnborough GU17 . . . . .150 E1
  Newbury RG14 . . . . .131 B8
Hamilton Dr SL5 . . . . .120 E2
Hamilton Gdns SL1 . . . . . .21 B2
Hamilton Pk SL6 . . . . .39 A6
Hamilton Rd
  Feltham TW13 . . . . .98 F4
  Reading RG1 . . . . .86 E6
  Slough SL1 . . . . .42 A7
  Wargrave RG10 . . . . .36 E2
Hamlet St RG42 . . . . .118 E8
Hammond Cl RG19 . . . . . .106 F2
Hammond Com Jun Sch
  GU18 . . . . .146 A1
Hammond End SL2 . . . . . . .91 A1
Hammond Rd SL2 . . . . .22 B8
Hammond Way GU18 . . . .146 B1
Hammonds Heath RG7 . . .136 D6
Hampden Cl SL2 . . . . .23 A2
Hampden Rd
  Caversham RG4 . . . . .59 B2
  Maidenhead SL6 . . . . . . .39 B8
  Slough SL3 . . . . .43 F3
Hampdens The RG14 . . . .130 C6
Hampshire Ave SL1 . . . . . .42 C6
Hampshire Lodge ⁊ SL6 . .39 F6
Hampshire Rd GU15 . . . . .151 F8
Hampshire Way RG41 . . . . .91 F2
Hampshire Wlk RG31 . . . . .84 A7
Hampstead Ct RG30 . . . . . .85 B7
Hampstead Hill RG9 . . . . .62 C8
Hampstead Norreys CE Prim
  Sch RG18 . . . . .52 F5
Hampstead Norreys Rd
  RG18 . . . . .69 D7
Hampton Ho SL3 . . . . .68 C8
Hampton Rd RG14 . . . . . .104 F1
Hampton Twrs ⁊ RG30 . . .85 D6
Hamstead Rd RG30 . . . . .103 C2
Hanbury Cl SL1 . . . . .41 A8
Hanbury Dr RG31 . . . . .84 D4
Hanbury Way GU15 . . . . .151 C3
Hancocks Mount SL5 . . . .120 D3
Hancombe Rd GU47 . . . . .143 A1
Handford La GU46 . . . . . .149 D5
Handpost Cnr RG40 . . . . .116 A1
Hanger Rd RG26 . . . . .134 F1
Hangerfield Cl GU46 . . . . .149 C5
Hangman's Stone La
  RG17 . . . . .49 A5
Hanley Cl SL4 . . . . .66 C6
Hannibal Rd TW19 . . . . . . .97 E8
Hanningtons Way RG7 . . .111 C3
Hanover Cl
  Englefield Green TW20 . . . .95 B2
  Frimley GU16 . . . . .151 E1
  Slough SL1 . . . . .43 A3
  Windsor SL4 . . . . .66 F6
Hanover Gdns
  Bracknell RG12 . . . . .117 F2
  Hanover Ho RG20 . . . . . .103 E6
Hanover Gate Mans
  RG30 . . . . .84 F6
Hanover Gdns
  Bracknell RG12 . . . . .117 F2
Hanover Ct
  Caversham RG4 . . . . .59 C6
  Reading RG30 . . . . .84 F6
Hanover Gdns . . . .
Hanover Mead
  Maidenhead SL6 . . . . . . .40 C3
  Newbury RG14 . . . . .130 D6
Hanover Way SL4 . . . . .66 F6
Hanson Cl GU15 . . . . .152 B7
Hanwood Cl RG5 . . . . .87 C8
Hanworth Cl RG12 . . . . . .118 C3
Hanworth La KT16 . . . . . .123 F1
Hanworth Rd RG12 . . . . . .118 A2
Hanworth Trad Est
  KT16 . . . . .123 F1
Haplin Ho RG7 . . . . .139 C3
Harborough Cl SL1 . . . . . . .41 D5
Harbury Ct RG14 . . . . . . .105 B2
Harcourt TW19 . . . . .68 E1

Harcourt Cl Dorney SL6 . . . .40 F3
Egham TW20 . . . . .96 C2
Henley-On-T RG9 . . . . .15 C1
Harcourt Dr RG6 . . . . .86 F3
Harcourt Rd
Bracknell RG12 . . . . .118 B4
Camberley GU15 . . . . .151 B5
Dorney SL6 . . . . .40 F3
Windsor SL4 . . . . .66 F6
Hardell Cl TW20 . . . . .96 A3
Harding Rd RG5 . . . . .87 C8
Hardwell Way RG12 . . . . . .118 E5
Hardwick Cl SL6 . . . . .39 A8
Hardwick La KT16 . . . . . . .123 D1
Hardwick Rd
Reading RG30 . . . . .84 F7
Whitchurch-on-T RG8 . . . . . .56 D7
Hardy Ave GU46 . . . . .149 C6
Hardy Cl Caversham RG4 . . .59 C2
Slough SL1 . . . . .42 A5
Thatcham RG18 . . . . .106 C5
Hardy Gn RG45 . . . . .143 B4
Hare Shoots SL6 . . . . .39 E5
Harebell Dr RG18 . . . . .106 E4
Harefield Cl RG41 . . . . .88 C2
Harefield Rd SL6 . . . . .39 A7
Harewood Dr RG18 . . . . . . .106 C4
Harewood Pl SL1 . . . . .43 A3
Hargrave Rd SL6 . . . . .39 D8
Hargreaves Way RG31 . . . .84 F4
Harkness Rd SL1 . . . . .41 B8
Harlech Ave RG4 . . . . .59 D6
Harlech Rd GU17 . . . . .150 D4
Harley Ct SL1 . . . . .42 C4
Harley Rd RG4 . . . . .59 B2
Harleyford La SL7 . . . . .18 B7
Harlington Cl UB7 . . . . .71 C7
Harlington Cnr UB3 . . . . . . .71 D6
Harlton Cl RG6 . . . . .114 C8
Harman Ct RG41 . . . . .88 B2
Harmans Water Prim Sch
RG12 . . . . .118 E4
Harmans Water Rd
RG12 . . . . .118 D4
Harmar Cl RG40 . . . . .116 E6
Harmondsworth La UB7 . . .70 E8
Harmondsworth Moor Ctry
Pk UB7 . . . . .70 B7
Harmondsworth Prim Sch
UB7 . . . . .70 D8
Harness Cl RG2 . . . . .113 B6
Harold Rd RG17 . . . . .102 B2
Harpdon Par RG46 . . . . . . .149 D7
Harpesford Ave GU25 . . . .122 C4
Harpsden Rd RG9 . . . . .35 E8
Harpsden Way RG9 . . . . . . .35 E7
Harpton Cl GU46 . . . . .149 D7
Harrier Cl RG5 . . . . .88 A6
Harrington Cl Earley RG6 . .87 C2
Newbury RG14 . . . . .105 E5
Windsor SL4 . . . . .66 F3
Harris Arc 5 RG1 . . . . .86 B8
Harris Cl Lambourn RG17 . . .25 B3
Woodley RG5 . . . . .88 B8
Harris Gdns SL1 . . . . .42 C4
Harris Way TW16 . . . . .125 E8
Harrison Cl RG10 . . . . .61 F3
Harrison Way
Burnham SL1 . . . . .41 D5
Shepperton TW17 . . . . .125 B4
Harrogate Ct SL3 . . . . .44 A1
Harrogate Rd RG4 . . . . .58 E4
Harrow Bottom Rd
GU25 . . . . .122 F3
Harrow Cl SL6 . . . . .19 E1
Harrow Ct RG1 . . . . .85 F6
Harrow La SL6 . . . . .19 E1
Harrow Mkt The SL3 . . . . . .44 A3
Harrow Rd Ashford TW15 . .98 A6
Slough SL3 . . . . .43 F3
Harrow Way
Charlton TW17 . . . . .125 C2
Sindlesham RG41 . . . . .115 A8
Harry Tee Ct 12 RG1 . . . . . .86 C7
Hart Dene Ct GU19 . . . . . .145 E3
Hart Dyke Cl RG41 . . . . . .116 B2
Hart St Henley-On-T RG9 . .15 E2
Reading RG1 . . . . .85 E8
Hart's La RG7 . . . . .110 C5
Hartford Rise GU15 . . . . . .151 D6
Hartigan Pl RG5 . . . . .88 A8
Hartland Cl SL1 . . . . .42 D5
Hartland Rd RG2 . . . . .86 C1
Hartley Cl
Blackwater GU17 . . . . .150 B5
Stoke Poges SL3 . . . . .23 C4
Hartley Copse SL4 . . . . .68 A1
Hartley Court Rd RG7 . . . .112 F6
Hartley Way RG18 . . . . . . .106 E4
Hartmead Rd RG19 . . . . . . .106 E3
Harts Cl RG2 . . . . .114 E2
Harts Hill Rd RG18 . . . . . . .106 F4
Harts Leap Cl GU47 . . . . . .143 B1
Harts Leap Rd GU47 . . . . .150 A8
Hartsbourne Rd RG6 . . . . . .87 A3
Hartshill Rd RG26 . . . . .134 E1
Hartslock Bridleway RG8 . .56 B8
Hartslock Ct RG8 . . . . .56 C6
Hartslock View RG8 . . . . . . .34 E2
Hartslock Way RG31 . . . . . .57 C2
Hartvale Ct 1 SL6 . . . . . . .152 A8
Harvard Cl RG5 . . . . .88 B8
Harvard Rd GU47 . . . . .143 E1
Harvaston Par RG30 . . . . . .85 B8
Harvest Cl Reading RG31 . . .84 B6
Yateley GU46 . . . . .149 B4
Harvest Cotts TW17 . . . . . .125 A5
Harvest Ct TW17 . . . . .125 A5

Harvest Dr RG41 . . . . .115 B7
Harvest Gn RG14 . . . . .104 E1
Harvest Hill SL8 . . . . .3 D2
Harvest Hill Rd SL6 . . . . . . .39 F3
Harvest Rd TW20 . . . . .95 D2
Harvest Ride
Bracknell RG42 . . . . .118 A7
Winkfield RG12,RG42,SL5 . .119 A8
Harvey Ho 11 RG30 . . . . . .85 D6
Harvey Rd
Oatlands Park KT12 . . . . . .125 F2
Slough SL3 . . . . .44 B4
Harveys Nurseries Pk Cvn
Site RG4 . . . . .59 C4
Harwell Int Bsns Ctr OX11 . .9 F8
Harwell International Bsns
Ctr OX11 . . . . .10 C8
Harwich Cl 4 RG6 . . . . .87 D1
Harwich Rd SL1 . . . . .42 A7
Harwood Gdns SL4 . . . . . . .95 B8
Harwood Rd SL7 . . . . .1 C1
Harwood Rise RG20 . . . . . .129 F2
Haslemere Cl GU16 . . . . . . .152 C3
Haslemere Rd SL4 . . . . .67 A6
Haslett Rd TW17 . . . . .125 E7
Hasting Cl SL6 . . . . .40 C2
Hastings Cl RG30 . . . . .85 A4
Hastings Mdw SL2 . . . . .23 A4
Hatch Cl RG7 . . . . .108 C7
Hatch End GU20 . . . . .146 C4
Hatch Gate Ct RG10 . . . . . .88 E6
Hatch Gate La RG10 . . . . . .37 A6
Hatch La Bucklebury RG7 . .108 C7
Burghfield Common RG30 . .111 D6
Harmondsworth UB7 . . . . . .70 D7
Windsor SL4 . . . . .67 A5
Hatch Ride
Crowthorne RG45 . . . . .143 B7
Wokingham RG40 . . . . .142 F8
Hatch Ride Prim Sch
RG45 . . . . .143 B7
Hatchet La SL4,SL5 . . . . . . .93 B5
Hatchets La RG18 . . . . .80 C7
Hatchett Rd TW14 . . . . .98 C7
Hatchgate Cl RG18 . . . . . . .106 C7
Hatchgate Copse RG12 . . .117 E3
Hatchgate Gdns SL1 . . . . . .21 D1
Hatchley RG2 . . . . .113 C7
Hatfield Cl SL6 . . . . .39 C6
Hatfield Ct
Camberley GU15 . . . . .151 B5
Reading RG31 . . . . .84 B4
Hatfield Rd SL1 . . . . .43 A4
Hatford Rd RG30 . . . . .85 B4
Hatherley Rd RG1 . . . . .86 E6
Hatherwood GU46 . . . . . . .149 F5
Hatton Ave SL2 . . . . .22 D1
Hatton Cross Rdbt TW6 . . .71 F4
Hatton Cross Sta TW6 . . . .71 F3
Hatton Ct SL4 . . . . .67 C5
Hatton Hill
Ashampstead RG8 . . . . .54 B7
Windlesham GU20 . . . . . . .146 C5
Hatton Rd
East Bedfont TW14 . . . . . . .98 D8
Hatton TW14,TW6 . . . . .71 E2
Hatton Rd N TW6 . . . . .71 F6
Haughurst Hill RG26 . . . . .134 C1
Havelock Bsns Pk SL6 . . . . .39 C7
Havelock Cres SL6 . . . . .39 B7
Havelock Rd
Maidenhead SL6 . . . . .39 B7
Wokingham RG41 . . . . .116 A6
Havelock St RG41 . . . . . . .116 A6
Haven Cl 8 RG1 . . . . .86 D7
Haven Of Rest SL6 . . . . . . .40 B7
Haven Rd TW15 . . . . .98 B5
Haven The RG17 . . . . .102 A1
Haversham Dr RG12 . . . . . .118 B3
Hawk La RG8,RG18 . . . . . . .53 E7
Hawk La RG12 . . . . .118 D5
Hawkchurch Rd RG2 . . . . .113 D8
Hawkedale Inf Sch
TW16 . . . . .125 F6
Hawkedon Prim Sch RG6 . .87 E2
Hawkedon Way RG6 . . . . . .87 E2
Hawker Ct SL3 . . . . .44 A3
Hawker Way RG5 . . . . .88 A7
Hawkes Cl RG41 . . . . .116 A7
Hawkes Leap GU20 . . . . . .146 B6
Hawkes Worth Dr GU19 . . .145 E1
Hawksworth Rd RG7 . . . . .111 B3
Hawley Cl RG31 . . . . .84 C4
Hawley Garden Cotts
GU17 . . . . .150 D4
Hawley Gn GU17 . . . . .150 E3
Hawley Gr GU17 . . . . .150 F2
Hawley Lodge GU17 . . . . .150 F2
Hawley Place Sch GU17 . .150 E1
Hawley Prim Sch GU17 . . .150 E3
Hawley Rd GU14,GU17 . . .150 F3
Hawley Way TW15 . . . . .98 B3
Hawthorn Cl RG42 . . . . . . .118 A8

Hawthorn Cotts RG7 . . . . . .112 C3
Hawthorn Gdns
Maidenhead SL6 . . . . .39 E5
Reading RG2 . . . . .86 E2
Hawthorn La Burnham SL2 . .22 A5
Newell Green SL4 . . . . .92 A7
Newell Green,Hawthorn Hill
RG42 . . . . .91 E8
Hawthorn Rd
Frimley GU16 . . . . .151 F2
Newbury RG14 . . . . .105 A4
Hawthorn Way
Sonning RG4 . . . . .60 E3
Upper Halliford TW17 . . . . .125 D5
Hawthorne Ave SL4 . . . . . . .93 B6
Hawthorne Cl Marlow SL7 . .1 E4
Thatcham RG18 . . . . .106 D4
Hawthorne Cres
Blackwater GU17 . . . . .150 E4
Slough SL1 . . . . .42 F7
Hawthorne Ct TW19 . . . . . .97 D8
Hawthorne Dr SL4 . . . . .93 D7
Hawthorne Rd
Caversham RG4 . . . . .59 E4
Egham TW18 . . . . .96 D3
Hawthorne Way
Great Shefford RG17 . . . . . .48 B4
Stanwell TW19 . . . . .97 D8
Winkfield SL4 . . . . .93 B7
Hawthornes RG31 . . . . .57 B3
Hawthorns The HP10 . . . . . .3 E6
Hawthorns Prim Sch The
RG41 . . . . .115 E7
Hawthorns The
Charvil RG10 . . . . .61 A3
Flackwell Heath HP10 . . . . . .3 B8
Poyle SL3 . . . . .69 F6
Wooburn Green HP10 . . . . . .3 E6
Hawtrey Cl SL1 . . . . .43 A4
Hawtrey Rd SL4 . . . . .67 C5
Hay La SL3 . . . . .23 D8
Hay Rd RG1 . . . . .85 F5
Haydon Ct
Maidenhead SL6 . . . . .39 D4
Twyford RG10 . . . . .61 E4
Haydon La RG20 . . . . .30 E7
Haydon Pl GU46 . . . . .149 E6
Hayes La RG41 . . . . .115 C4
Hayes Pl SL7 . . . . .1 D1
Hayfield Cl RG31 . . . . .84 C8
Hayfield Ct RG17 . . . . .46 F6
Hayley Gn RG42 . . . . .91 F3
Haymill Rd SL1,SL2 . . . . . . .21 F1
Haynes Cl SL3 . . . . .43 F1
Hayse Hill SL4 . . . . .66 D6
Haysoms Dr RG19 . . . . . . .131 B7
Hayward Pl SL8 . . . . .3 C2
Haywards Cl RG9 . . . . .15 C1
Haywards Mead SL4 . . . . . .41 F1
Haywards The RG18 . . . . . .106 D4
Haywood RG12 . . . . .118 C2
Haywood Ct RG1 . . . . .86 F7
Haywood Way RG30 . . . . . .84 F5
Hazel Cl
Burghfield Common RG30 . .111 B5
Englefield Green TW20 . . . . .95 B2
Marlow Bottom SL7 . . . . .1 C6
Wokingham RG41 . . . . .115 F5
Hazel Cres RG2 . . . . .86 E2
Hazel Dr RG5 . . . . .87 C5
Hazel Gn Staines TW18 . . . .97 C2
Thatcham RG18 . . . . .106 D5
Hazel Rd RG8 . . . . .57 C4
Hazelbank RG40 . . . . .141 E6
Hazelbank Ct KT16 . . . . . . .124 C1
Hazelbank Rd KT16 . . . . . . .124 C2
Hazeldene RG20 . . . . .51 B1
Hazelhurst Rd SL1 . . . . .21 D3
Hazell Hill RG12 . . . . .118 C6
Hazell Way SL2 . . . . .22 F6
Hazelmere Cl TW14 . . . . . . .71 F1
Hazels Paddock RG18 . . . .106 C8
Hazelwood Cl RG31 . . . . . . .57 C1
Hazelwood La RG42 . . . . . . .90 F4
Hazlemere Rd SL2 . . . . .43 B5
Heacham Cl RG6 . . . . .87 D3
Headington Cl
Maidenhead SL6 . . . . .39 A7
Wokingham RG40 . . . . .116 D8
Headington Rd SL6 . . . . . . .39 A7
Headlands Ct RG7 . . . . . . .110 F1
Headley Cl RG5 . . . . .88 A8
Headley Park Ind Est
RG5 . . . . .88 A6
Headley Rd RG5 . . . . .87 E7
Headley Rd E RG5 . . . . .88 A7
Heads La RG17 . . . . .128 A5
Heardman Cl RG19 . . . . . . .106 F2
Hearmon Cl GU46 . . . . .149 E6
Hearn Rd RG5 . . . . .87 E5
Hearn Wlk RG12 . . . . .118 D8
Hearne Dr SL6 . . . . .40 A1
Hearsey Gdns GU17 . . . . . .150 C4
Heath Cl Harlington UB3 . . .71 D7
Stanwell TW19 . . . . .70 C1
Virginia Water GU25 . . . . . .122 D5
Wokingham RG41 . . . . .116 B4
Heath Cnr GU15 . . . . .152 A3
Heath Ct RG26 . . . . .134 E2
Heath Dr RG9 . . . . .35 E1
Heath End Farm RG26 . . . .134 E1
Heath Flats GU15 . . . . .145 E3
Heath Gr TW16 . . . . .98 F1
Heath Hill Rd N RG45 . . . .143 B5
Heath Hill Rd S RG45 . . . .143 B4

Heath La RG18 . . . . .106 C5
Heath Rd Bagshot GU19 . . .145 E3
Bradfield RG7 . . . . .82 A2
Reading RG6 . . . . .87 A5
Silchester RG26 . . . . .135 E1
Wooburn Moor HP9 . . . . .3 F8
Heath Ride RG40,RG45 . . .142 C5
Heath Rise
Camberley GU15 . . . . .151 D5
Virginia Water GU25 . . . . . .122 D5
Heath Villa SL5 . . . . .120 A6
Heathacre SL3 . . . . .69 E6
Heathcote SL6 . . . . .40 B2
Heathcote Ct 2 SL4 . . . . . . .67 D4
Heathcote Rd GU15 . . . . . .151 D5
Heathcroft Ave TW16 . . . . . .98 F1
Heather Cl RG40 . . . . .141 E7
Heather Dr
Sunningdale SL5 . . . . .121 B2
Tadley RG26 . . . . .134 F2
Thatcham RG18 . . . . .106 D5
Heather Gdns RG14 . . . . . .130 F7
Heather Mead GU16 . . . . . .151 F2
Heather Mead Ct GU16 . . .151 F2
Heather Ridge Arc
GU15 . . . . .152 C4
Heather Ridge Inf Sch
GU15 . . . . .152 C4
Heatherdale Rd GU15 . . . .151 D4
Heatherden Cl RG2 . . . . . . .113 C7
Heatherdene Ave RG45 . . .142 E4
Heatherlands SL5 . . . . .120 C4
Heatherley Cl GU15 . . . . . .151 B5
Heatherley Rd GU15 . . . . . .151 B5
Heathermount RG12 . . . . . .118 E5
Heathermount Dr RG45 . . .143 A6
Heathermount Learning Ctr
The SL5 . . . . .120 D3
Heathers The TW19 . . . . . . .70 F8
Heatherside Cnr GU15 . . . .152 D6
Heatherside Dr GU25 . . . . .122 A3
Heatherway RG45 . . . . .143 A5
Heatherwood Hospl
SL5 . . . . .119 E6
Heathfield RG7 . . . . .137 A6
Heathfield Ave
Ascot SL5 . . . . .120 E4
Reading RG30 . . . . .84 D6
Shiplake RG9 . . . . .35 B2
Heathfield Cl RG9 . . . . .35 B2
Heathfield Cl TW15 . . . . . . .97 E5
Heathfield Rd SL1 . . . . .43 A5
Heathfield Sch SL5 . . . . . . .119 B7
Heathfields RG20 . . . . .78 A8
Heathlands RG26 . . . . .134 E1
Heathlands Ct
Wokingham RG40 . . . . .142 F8
Yateley GU46 . . . . .149 E4
Heathlands Dr SL6 . . . . .39 A6
Heathlands Rd RG40 . . . . .116 E2
Heathlea Ho RG31 . . . . .84 B7
Heathmoors RG12 . . . . . . .118 C4
Heathpark Dr GU20 . . . . . .146 E4
Heathrow Airport London
TW6 . . . . .71 A5
Heathrow Airport Visitor
Ctr* TW6 . . . . .71 A5
Heathrow Bvd UB7 . . . . . . .70 F7
Heathrow Cl TW6 . . . . .70 B8
Heathrow Copse RG26 . . . .134 D1
Heathrow Prim Sch UB7 . . .72 B8
Heathrow Terminal 4 Sta
TW6 . . . . .71 C1
Heathrow Terminals 1, 2, 3
TW6 . . . . .71 D4
Heathside Pk GU15 . . . . . .152 C7
Heathway
Camberley GU15 . . . . .151 D5
North Ascot SL5 . . . . .119 E8
Reading RG31 . . . . .84 C8
Heathway Cl GU15 . . . . . . .151 D5
Heathwood Cl GU46 . . . . . .149 D7
Heavens Lea SL8 . . . . .3 C2
Hebbecastle Down RG42 . . .91 C2
Hebden Cl RG10 . . . . .106 C2
Hedge Lea HP10 . . . . .3 A8
Hedgeway RG14 . . . . .105 C4
Hedingham Mews SL6 . . . . .39 D7
Hedley Rd RG17 . . . . .3 B8
Hedsor Hill SL8 . . . . .3 C1
Hedsor La HP10,SL1 . . . . . . .3 B7
Hedsor Rd SL8 . . . . .3 C2
Hedsor View Cotts SL8 . . . .19 F7
Heelas Rd RG41 . . . . .116 A5
Heights The
Camberley GU15 . . . . .151 E5
Marlow SL7 . . . . .18 B8
Helen Cotts SL4 . . . . .66 D5
Helena Cl RG30 . . . . .84 E8
Helgiford Gdns TW16 . . . . .98 E1
Helix Bsns Pk GU15 . . . . . .151 B3
Helksham Ct GU47 . . . . . . .143 D1
Hellyer Way SL8 . . . . .3 C2
Helmsdale RG12 . . . . .118 C4
Helmsdale Cl RG30 . . . . . . .85 B8
Helston Gdns RG2 . . . . .86 B1
Helston La SL4 . . . . .66 F6
Helvellyn Cl TW20 . . . . .96 C1
Hemdean Hill RG4 . . . . .59 A3
Hemdean House Sch
RG4 . . . . .59 A3
Hemdean Rd RG4 . . . . .59 A3
Hemmbrook Dr RG4 . . . . . .59 C6
Hemming Way SL2 . . . . .22 A1
Hemming Cnr RG12 . . . . . . .43 C3
Hempson Ave SL3 . . . . .43 C3
Hemsdale SL6 . . . . .19 B1
Hemwood Rd SL4 . . . . .66 D4

Hencroft St N SL1 . . . . .42 F4
Hencroft St S SL1 . . . . .42 F3
Hendon Terr TW15 . . . . .98 D2
Hendon Way TW19 . . . . . . .70 D1
Hendons Way SL6 . . . . .40 B1
Hengrave Cl RG6 . . . . .87 E2
Hengrove Cres TW15 . . . . . .97 D5
Henley Coll The (Deanfield
Bldgs) RG9 . . . . .15 D1
Henley Coll The (Rotherfield
Bldgs) RG9 . . . . .15 C1
Henley Gdns RG46 . . . . . . .149 D5
Henley Lodge 12 SL3 . . . . . .39 F6
Henley Rd Caversham RG9 . .59 D3
Hurley SL6 . . . . .17 D3
Maidenhead SL6 . . . . .38 E7
Marlow SL7 . . . . .18 B8
Shiplake RG9 . . . . .60 C8
Slough SL1 . . . . .41 F7
Henley Wood Rd RG6 . . . . .87 D4
Henley-on-Thames Sta
RG9 . . . . .15 E1
Henry Ct 13 RG1 . . . . .86 C7
Henry Randell's Almshouses
GU17 . . . . .150 E3
Henry Rd SL1 . . . . .42 D4
Henry St RG1 . . . . .86 B6
Henrys The RG18 . . . . .106 D4
Henshaw Cres RG14 . . . . . .130 D8
Hensworth Rd TW15 . . . . . .97 D3
Henwick Cl RG18 . . . . .106 B6
Henwick La RG18 . . . . .106 A4
Henwood Copse RG8 . . . . . .55 A6
Heppelwhite Cl RG26 . . . . .134 E1
Hepworth Croft GU47 . . . .150 E6
Hepworth Way KT12 . . . . . .125 F1
Herald Way RG5 . . . . .88 A6
Herbert Cl RG12 . . . . .118 B4
Hereford Cl TW18 . . . . .124 B8
Herewood Cl RG14 . . . . . . .104 F4
Heriot Ct GU15 . . . . .151 D3
Heriot Rd KT16 . . . . .124 A2
Heritage Ct
8 Egham TW20 . . . . .96 A3
13 Reading RG1 . . . . .85 F7
Hermes Cl RG41 . . . . .115 B7
Hermitage Cl
Frimley GU16 . . . . .151 F1
Littleton TW17 . . . . .125 A5
Slough SL3 . . . . .43 C3
Hermitage Ct TW18 . . . . . . .96 F3
Hermitage Cvn Pk The
RG42 . . . . .91 D3
Hermitage Dr
North Ascot SL5 . . . . .119 E7
Twyford RG10 . . . . .61 D5
Hermitage La SL4 . . . . .67 A4
Hermitage Par SL5 . . . . . . .120 A6
Hermitage Prim Sch
RG18 . . . . .79 B8
Hermitage Rd RG18 . . . . . . .79 B2
Hermitage The
Feltham TW13 . . . . .98 F5
Lambourn RG17 . . . . .46 F7
Hermits Cl RG7 . . . . .111 B8
Hermits Hill RG2,RG30 . . .111 D4
Herndon Cl TW20 . . . . .96 A4
Herne Pl SL5 . . . . .121 C4
Hernes Cl TW18 . . . . .124 B8
Heroes Wlk RG2 . . . . .113 B7
Heron Cl SL5 . . . . .119 D8
Heron Ct Staines TW18 . . . .97 B4
Stanwell TW19 . . . . .97 D8
Heron Dr Slough SL3 . . . . . .44 B2
Twyford RG10 . . . . .61 E6
Heron Ho RG14 . . . . .105 D3
Heron Ind Est RG7 . . . . . . .139 A8
Heron Island RG4 . . . . .59 C1
Heron Rd RG41 . . . . .115 E6
Heron Shaw RG8 . . . . .34 C7
Heron Way
Padworth RG7 . . . . .109 B3
Reading RG1 . . . . .85 E4
Thatcham RG19 . . . . .106 B3
Heron's Way RG40 . . . . . . .116 E7
Herondale RG12 . . . . .118 C2
Heronfield TW20 . . . . .95 C2
Herongate RG17 . . . . .100 D7
Herons Pl Maidenhead SL6 . .20 C3
Marlow SL7 . . . . .1 E2
Heronsbrook SL5 . . . . .120 E5
Heronscourt GU18 . . . . . . .153 C3
Herrick Cl GU16 . . . . .152 C3
Herries Sch SL6 . . . . .19 B8
Herrings La
Chertsey KT16 . . . . .124 A3
Windlesham GU20 . . . . . . .146 D4
Herriot Ct GU46 . . . . .149 C4
Herschel Gram Sch SL1 . . .42 C7
Herschel Grange RG42 . . . .91 D3
Herschel Park Dr SL1 . . . . . .42 F4
Herschel St SL1 . . . . .42 E4
Hertford Cl
Caversham RG4 . . . . .59 C6
Wokingham RG41 . . . . .115 E5
Hetherington Cl SL2 . . . . . .21 F2
Hetherington Rd TW17 . . . .125 C7
Hever Cl SL6 . . . . .39 C6
Hewett Ave RG4 . . . . .58 D4
Hewett Cl RG4 . . . . .58 D4
Hewgate Ct RG9 . . . . .15 E1
Hewlett Pl GU19 . . . . .145 F3
Hexham Rd RG2 . . . . .86 C3
Heynes Gn SL6 . . . . .39 B3

Heywood Dr GU19 . . . . .145 D3
Heywood Ave SL6 . . . . .39 A1
Heywood Court Cl SL6 . . . .39 A2
Heywood Gardens Cvn Site
SL6 .39 A1
Hibbert Rd SL6 . . . . .40 B4
Hibbert's Alley **15** SL4 . . . .67 D6
Hickox Ct HP10 . . . . .3 F7
Hicks La GU17 . . . . .150 B5
Higgs La GU19 . . . . .145 D3
High Beech RG12 . . . . .118 F5
High Beeches GU16 . . . . . .151 D2
High Beeches Cl SL7 . . . . . .1 C6
High Chys GU20 . . . . .146 E7
High Close Sch RG40 . . . . .116 C7
High Fields SL3 . . . . .120 F4
High Heavens Wood SL7 . .1 C8
High Mdw RG4 . . . . .58 D3
High Meadow PI KT16 . . . .123 F3
High Pines The RG42 . . . . .92 B5
High Rd SL6 . . . . .19 E6
High St Ascot SL5 . . . . .120 A6
Ascot,Sunninghill SL5 . . . . . .120 D4
Bagshot GU19 . . . . .145 E3
Boxford RG20 . . . . .76 B2
Bracknell RG12 . . . . .118 B7
Bray SL6 . . . . .40 C4
Burnham SL1 . . . . .21 C2
Camberley GU15 . . . . .151 D6
Chalvey SL1 . . . . .42 D3
Chieveley RG20 . . . . .51 B1
Colnbrook SL3 . . . . .69 C7
Compton RG20 . . . . .31 D4
Cookham SL6 . . . . .20 B7
Crowthorne RG45 . . . . .143 C4
Datchet SL3 . . . . .68 A6
East Ilsley RG20 . . . . .30 E7
Egham TW20 . . . . .96 A3
Eton SL4 . . . . .67 D8
Goring RG8 . . . . .34 C6
Harlington UB3 . . . . .71 D8
Harmondsworth UB7 . . . . . .70 D8
Hungerford RG17 . . . . .100 D5
Iver SL0 . . . . .44 F7
Kintbury RG17 . . . . .102 A2
Lambourn RG17 . . . . .25 B2
Lambourn, Upper Lambourn
RG17 .24 E6
Maidenhead SL6 . . . . .39 F7
Marlow SL7 . . . . .1 E1
4 Pangbourne RG8 . . . . .56 C6
Reading RG1 . . . . .86 B7
Sandhurst GU47 . . . . .149 D8
Sandhurst,Little Sandhurst
GU47 . . . . .143 A1
Shepperton TW17 . . . . .125 C3
Slough, Upton SL1 . . . . .42 F4
Slough,Langley SL3 . . . . . . .44 A2
Sonning RG4 . . . . .60 D4
Staines TW18 . . . . .96 F4
Stanwell TW19 . . . . .70 D1
Streatley RG8 . . . . .34 A6
Sunningdale SL5 . . . . .121 A4
Taplow SL6 . . . . .20 E1
Thatcham RG19 . . . . .106 D3
Theale RG7 . . . . .83 E3
Twyford RG10 . . . . .61 D5
Wargrave RG10 . . . . .36 D2
West End GU14 . . . . .153 F7
Whitchurch-on-T RG8 . . . . .56 C7
Windsor SL4 . . . . .67 D6
Wraysbury TW19 . . . . .68 F1
Feltham,Lower Feltham
TW13 . . . . .98 F5
High St Mall **1** SL6 . . . . .39 F7
High Street Harlington
TW6 .71 D7
High Town Rd SL6 . . . . .39 F7
High Tree Dr RG6 . . . . .87 B6
High View Cl SL7 . . . . .1 D8
High View Rd GU18 . . . . . .152 F8
Highbridge RG4 . . . . .59 E5
Highbridge Wharf **3**
RG1 . . . . .86 B7
Highbury Cres SL1 . . . . . . .152 A8
Highbury Rd RG31 . . . . .84 B7
Highclere SL5 . . . . .120 D4
Highclere Cl RG12 . . . . . . .118 E7
Highclere Dr GU15 . . . . . . .152 A7
Highcliffe Cl RG5 . . . . .60 F1
Highdown Ave RG4 . . . . . . .59 A6
Highdown Hill Rd RG4 . . . .59 A6
Highdown Sch RG4 . . . . . . .59 A5
Higher Alham RG12 . . . . . .118 E2
Highfield Bracknell RG12 . .117 F3
Earley RG6 . . . . .87 B2
Highfield Ave RG14 . . . . . .105 A2
Highfield Cl
Englefield Green TW20 . . . . .95 C2
Wokingham RG40 . . . . .116 B6
Highfield Ct
Burghfield Common RG7 . . .111 B3
Burnham SL2 . . . . .22 B4
Englefield Green TW20 . . . . .95 D2
Twyford RG10 . . . . .61 E4
Highfield La SL6 . . . . .39 A4
Highfield Pk
Arborfield RG2 . . . . .140 D8
Marlow SL7 . . . . .1 B1
Wargrave RG10 . . . . .36 D2
Highfield Rd
Bourne End SL8 . . . . .3 B4
Chertsey KT16 . . . . .124 A1
Flackwell Heath HP10 . . . . . .3 A8
Maidenhead SL6 . . . . .39 B8

Highfield Rd continued
Newbury RG14 . . . . .104 F1
Purley On T RG31 . . . . .57 B4
Upper Halliford TW16 . . . . .125 F4
Windsor SL4 . . . . .66 F4
Highfields Sch SL6 . . . . . . .39 C7
Highgate Rd RG5 . . . . .60 D5
Highgrove RG1 . . . . .88 C1
Highgrove Pk SL6 . . . . .39 E8
Highgrove PI RG10 . . . . . . .61 E5
Highgrove Rd RG1 . . . . .86 C5
Highgrove Terr RG1 . . . . . . .86 B6
Highland Pk TW13 . . . . .98 F4
Highland Rd GU15 . . . . . . .151 E8
Highlands
Flackwell Heath HP10 . . . . . .3 B7
Newbury RG14 . . . . .130 E7
Highlands Ave RG41 . . . . .115 C5
Highlands La RG9 . . . . .35 A8
Highlands Sch The RG31 . .57 D1
Highlands The SL2 . . . . .22 C7
Highlea Ave HP10 . . . . .3 A8
Highmead Cl RG2 . . . . .86 E2
Highmoor Rd RG4 . . . . .58 F3
Highview RG31 . . . . .84 B5
Highview Cres GU15 . . . . .144 F1
Highway Ave SL6 . . . . .39 A6
Highway Rd SL6 . . . . .39 B6
Highwayman's Ridge
GU20 . . . . .146 B6
Highwood Cl
Newbury RG14 . . . . .105 B6
Yateley GU46 . . . . .149 D5
Highwood Prim Sch RG5 .87 C6
Highwoods Cl SL7 . . . . .1 C7
Highwoods Dr SL7 . . . . .1 C7
Highworth Cotts RG26 . . .134 C1
Highworth Way RG31 . . . . .57 B2
Hilary Cl RG2 . . . . .113 D7
Hilary Ho **2** RG14 . . . . . .105 A1
Hilborn Way RG2 . . . . .115 A1
Hilbury Rd RG6 . . . . .87 A3
Hilcot Rd RG30 . . . . .85 D8
Hildens Dr RG42 . . . . .84 C7
Hildesley Ct RG20 . . . . .30 F7
Hilgrove Ho SL6 . . . . .19 D1
Hill Cl Newbury RG14 . . . . .130 D7
Wooburn Green HP10 . . . . . . .3 F7
Hill Copse View RG12 . . . .118 E8
Hill Cres RG7 . . . . .108 C3
Hill Farm App HP10 . . . . . . .3 F7
Hill Farm Rd
Marlow Bottom SL7 . . . . .1 E6
Taplow SL6 . . . . .20 E2
Hill Gdns RG8 . . . . .34 A6
Hill Lands RG10 . . . . .36 D2
Hill Piece OX11 . . . . .10 E7
Hill PI SL2 . . . . .22 B5
Hill Prim Sch The RG4 . . . .59 C5
Hill Rd
Arborfield Cross RG2 . . . . . .114 F1
Newbury RG14 . . . . .104 E4
Hill Side RG1 . . . . .86 C5
Hill St RG1 . . . . .86 B6
Hill Top Dr SL7 . . . . .1 B2
Hill View RG1 . . . . .113 A1
Hill View Mews RG30 . . . . .84 E8
Hill View Rd TW19 . . . . .68 D1
Hillary Ct TW19 . . . . .97 E7
Hillary Dr RG45 . . . . .143 B6
Hillary Rd SL3 . . . . .43 E4
Hillberry RG12 . . . . .118 C2
Hillbrow RG2 . . . . .86 E1
Hillbrow SL5 . . . . .121 A4
Hillcrest
Hampstead Norreys RG18 . . .52 F6
Tadley RG26 . . . . .135 B1
Hillcrest Ave SL6 . . . . .19 E6
Hillcrest Cotts RG14 . . . . .104 F7
Hillcrest Rd GU15 . . . . . . .152 B7
Hilldrop La RG17 . . . . .46 A3
Hillersdon SL2 . . . . .43 B8
Hillfoot RG7 . . . . .81 A1
Hillgreen La RG20 . . . . .50 C7
Hillhampton SL5 . . . . .120 F2
Hillhouse La RG19 . . . . . . .133 A1
Hillingdon Ave TW19 . . . . .97 E7
Hillmead Ct SL6 . . . . .40 F8
Hillrise Brands Hill SL3 . . . .69 A8
Oatlands Park KT12 . . . . . . .125 F2
Hills La SL6 . . . . .19 D7
Hillsborough Pk GU15 . . .152 C5
Hillside Ascot SL5 . . . . .120 D4
Burghfield Common RG7 . . .111 C3
East Garston RG17 . . . . .47 C6
Maidenhead SL6 . . . . .39 D5
Sandhurst GU15 . . . . .150 F7
Slough SL1 . . . . .42 E4
Wentworth GU25 . . . . .122 C3
Whitchurch-on-T RG8 . . . . . .56 D8
Hillside Dr RG42 . . . . .90 E1
Hillside Pk Earley RG2 . . . . .86 F1
Sunningdale SL5 . . . . .120 F1
Hillside Rd Earley RG6 . . . . .87 D3
Hungerford RG17 . . . . .100 D4
Marlow SL7 . . . . .1 E4
Hilltop Cl SL5 . . . . .120 E7
Hilltop Fst Sch SL4 . . . . . . .66 E4
Hilltop Rd Caversham RG4 .58 D5
Earley RG6 . . . . .87 B8
Twyford RG10 . . . . .61 E7
Hilltop View GU46 . . . . . . .149 B5
Hillview CI RG31 . . . . .57 B2
Hilmanton RG6 . . . . .113 F8
Hilperton Rd **3** SL1 . . . .42 E4
Hind's Head **7** RG17 . . . .25 B2

Hindhay La SL6 . . . . .19 C3
Hindhead Rd RG6 . . . . .87 A3
Hinksey Cl SL3 . . . . .44 B3
Hinton Cl SL3 . . . . .143 B7
Hinton Dr RG45 . . . . .143 B7
Hinton Rd Hurst RG10 . . . . .62 A1
Slough SL1 . . . . .41 E6
Hintonhatch Cnr RG10 . . .62 B2
Hirstwood RG30 . . . . .57 E1
Hirtes Ave RG2 . . . . .113 E5
Hitcham Ho SL1 . . . . .21 A1
Hitcham La SL1,SL6 . . . . . .20 F2
Hitcham Rd SL1,SL6 . . . . . .41 A8
Hitchcock Cl TW17 . . . . . .124 A5
Hitherhooks Hill RG42 . . . .90 E1
Hithermoor Rd TW19 . . . . .70 A2
Hobart Ct SL7 . . . . .2 A3
Hobbis Dr SL6 . . . . .39 A6
Hobbs End RG9 . . . . .35 B8
Hockett La SL6 . . . . .18 F5
Hockford La RG7 . . . . .134 A3
Hockham Rd RG20 . . . . .31 E5
Hockley La SL2 . . . . .23 B5
Hockwell By5 RG20 . . . . . . .30 B8
Hodge La SL5 . . . . .93 A3
Hodgedale La RG10 . . . . . . .37 D6
Hodges Cl RG12 . . . . .145 E1
Hodsoll Rd RG1 . . . . .85 F8
Hoe Benham La RG20 . . . .102 F7
Hoffman Cl RG42 . . . . .91 D2
Hogarth Ave
Ashford TW15 . . . . .98 C2
Reading RG8 . . . . .84 F5
Hogarth Cl
Sandhurst GU47 . . . . .150 E6
Slough SL1 . . . . .41 E6
Hogfair La SL1 . . . . .21 C1
Hogoak La SL4 . . . . .92 A8
Hogwood Ind Est RG40 . .141 A6
Hogwood La RG40 . . . . . . .141 A6
Holbeche Cl GU46 . . . . . . .149 A6
Holbeck RG12 . . . . .117 F3
Holberton Rd RG2 . . . . . . .113 D8
Holborn Hill OX12 . . . . .6 D7
Holborne Cl RG14 . . . . . . .130 C6
Holbrook Ct TW20 . . . . .96 C3
Holbrook Mdw TW20 . . . . .96 C2
Holder Cl RG2 . . . . .113 D5
Holford Cl RG31 . . . . .84 C8
Holkam Ct RG30 . . . . .84 F8
Holland Gdns TW20 . . . . .123 F7
Holland Pines RG12 . . . . . .117 F2
Holland Rd Marlow SL7 . . . .1 E3
Reading RG30 . . . . .84 D7
Hollands The RG10 . . . . . .106 E3
Hollerith Rise RG12 . . . . . .118 B3
Hollicombe Cl RG30 . . . . . .84 E7
Hollies The RG2 . . . . .108 D5
Hollington PI RG19 . . . . . .106 C3
Hollins Wlk RG30 . . . . .85 D6
Hollow Hill La SL0 . . . . .44 E6
Hollow La Shinfield RG2 . .113 E5
Virginia Water GU25 . . . . . .122 C6
Holloway Dr GU25 . . . . . . .122 E5
Holloway La UB7 . . . . .70 E8
Holly Acre **4** GU46 . . . . .149 D5
Holly Ave SL6 . . . . .41 D8
Holly Cl Brimpton RG19 . . .133 B6
Englefield Green TW20 . . . . .95 B2
Farnham Common SL2 . . . . .22 C8
Holly Cnr RG7 . . . . .140 B7
Holly Cotts GU47 . . . . .143 A1
Holly Cres SL4 . . . . .66 D5
Holly Ct RG45 . . . . .142 E4
Holly Dr Maidenhead SL6 . . .39 F8
Windsor SL4 . . . . .67 A6
Holly Hedge Cl GU16 . . . .151 E2
Holly Hedge Rd GU16 . . .151 E2
Holly Ho RG12 . . . . .118 B3
Holly La Ashampstead RG8 .54 B6
Bucklebury RG8 . . . . .80 B3
Holly Orch RG41 . . . . .115 F5
Holly Rd RG5 . . . . .88 A6
Holly Ridge GU24 . . . . . . .153 C6
Holly Spring Inf Sch
RG12 . . . . .118 E7
Holly Spring Jun Sch
RG12 . . . . .118 E7
Holly Spring La RG12 . . . .118 D8
Holly Way GU17 . . . . .150 D4
Holly Wlk SL4 . . . . .93 E4
Hollybank GU47 . . . . .153 F6
Hollybush Hill SL2 . . . . .23 B5
Hollybush La
Burghfield Common RG7 . . .110 E3
Cookham Dean SL6 . . . . .19 B6
Iver SL0 . . . . .44 B7
Hollybush Ride RG40,
RG45 . . . . .142 C6
Hollybush Tk GU19,GU20 .145 F6
Hollycombe TW20 . . . . .95 D7
Hollycroft RG19 . . . . .133 F1
Hollycroft Cl UB7 . . . . .71 A8
Hollycroft Gdns UB7 . . . . .71 A8
Holldale Ct RG2 . . . . .86 E1
Hollyfields Cl GU15 . . . . . .151 B5
Hollyhook Cl RG45 . . . . . . .143 A6
Hollym Cl RG6 . . . . .87 E2
Holmanleaze SL6 . . . . .40 A8
Holmbank Dr TW17 . . . . . .125 E5
Holmbury Ave RG45 . . . . .143 A7
Holmdale SL2 . . . . .43 C6
Holmdene RG7 . . . . .140 B5
Holme Cl RG45 . . . . .143 A7
Holme Grange Sch
RG40 . . . . .116 F3

Holme Park Farm La
RG4 .60 C2
Holmemoor Dr RG4 . . . . . .60 E2
Holmes Cl Ascot SL5 . . . . .120 C3
Wokingham RG41 . . . . .116 A4
Holmes Cres RG41 . . . . . . .116 A4
Holmes Rd RG6 . . . . .87 A5
Holmewood Cl RG41 . . . .116 A2
Holmlea Wlk SL3 . . . . .68 C6
Holmsdale Cl SL0 . . . . .44 F7
Holmwood Ave RG30 . . . . .84 F4
Holmwood Cl SL6 . . . . .39 B5
Holsworthy Cl RG6 . . . . . . .87 E3
Holt Rd RG17 . . . . .102 B2
Holt Sch The RG41 . . . . . . .116 B7
Holt The RG8 . . . . .57 D4
Holton Heath **9** RG12 . .118 F5
Holtspur La HP10 . . . . .3 F7
Holtspur Top La HP10 . . . . .3 F6
Holtwood Rd RG20 . . . . . . .51 D4
Holy Brook Sch The
RG30 .85 A4
Holy Family RC Sch SL3 . .43 F1
Holy Trinity CE Prim Sch
SL4 . . . . .67 D6
Holy Trinity CE Sch SL7 . . .1 D3
Holybrook Cres RG30 . . . . .85 A4
Holybrook Rd RG1 . . . . .85 F5
Holyport CE Prim Sch
SL6 . . . . .65 B8
Holyport Manor Sch SL6 .64 E8
Holyport Rd SL6 . . . . .40 B1
Holyport St SL6 . . . . .65 A8
Holyrood Cl RG4 . . . . .59 D6
Holywell Cl TW19 . . . . .97 E7
Holywell Ct RG19 . . . . .106 D3
Holywell Way TW19 . . . . . .97 E7
Hombrook Dr RG42 . . . . . .117 E8
Hombrook Ho RG42 . . . . . .117 E8
Home Cl GU25 . . . . .122 D3
Home Croft RG31 . . . . .57 B1
Home Farm RG20 . . . . .75 F6
Home Farm Cl
Reading RG2 . . . . .86 C4
Upper Halliford TW17 . . . . .125 F1
Home Farm Cotts RG41 . .115 B7
Home Farm La RG42 . . . . . .91 B1
Home Farm Way SL3 . . . . . .23 C4
Home Mead SL3 . . . . .22 C3
Home Mead Cl RG14 . . . . .130 E8
Home Meadow Dr HP10 . .3 B7
Home Park Rd GU46 . . . . .149 D6
Home Wood SL7 . . . . .17 F6
Homefield Way RG17 . . . . .100 D5
Homelands Way RG9 . . . . . .15 D1
Homer Fst Sch SL4 . . . . . . .66 B6
Homeside Cl SL6 . . . . .66 D6
Homestead Rd
Maidenhead SL6 . . . . .39 D4
Staines TW18 . . . . .97 A4
Homestead The RG9 . . . . . .35 B1
Homewaters Ave TW16 . .125 F8
Homewood SL3 . . . . .43 D7
Honesty Bottom RG20 . . . .28 D2
Honey End La RG30 . . . . . . .85 A6
Honey Hill Lambourn RG17 .25 B3
Wokingham RG40 . . . . .117 A1
Honey La SL6 . . . . .19 E2
Honey Meadow Cl RG4 . . .59 E2
Honeybottom Rd RG26 . .135 A1
Honeyfields RG17 . . . . .100 D5
Honeyhill Rd RG42 . . . . . . .118 A8
Honeysuckle Cl
Crowthorne RG45 . . . . .143 A7
Iver SL0 . . . . .44 F7
Yateley GU46 . . . . .149 A6
Honeysuckle Ct SL3 . . . . . .69 C7
Honister Wlk GU15 . . . . . .152 D4
Honnor Rd RG2 . . . . .86 C2
Honnor Rd TW18 . . . . .97 D1
Hook Cl RG19 . . . . .131 B7
Hook End La RG8 . . . . .34 B2
Hook La GU24 . . . . .153 C6
Hook Mill La GU18 . . . . . . .146 D2
Hookstone La GU24 . . . . . .153 F8
Hoops Way RG2 . . . . .112 F8
Hop Gdns RG9 . . . . .15 D2
Hope Ave RG12 . . . . .118 E2
Hope Cotts RG42 . . . . .92 A5
Hope Fountain GU15 . . . . .151 F4
Hopeman Cl GU47 . . . . . . .150 D7
Hopper Vale RG12 . . . . . . .118 A3
Hopwood Cl RG14 . . . . . . .105 A4
Horatio Ave RG42 . . . . .118 E8
Horewood Rd RG12 . . . . . .118 A3
Horizon West Ind Est
RG14 . . . . .105 D3
Hormer Cl GU47 . . . . .143 D1
Horn St RG20 . . . . .31 E5
Hornbeam Cl
Purley On T RG8 . . . . .57 C5
Sandhurst GU47 . . . . .143 A1
Wokingham RG41 . . . . .115 D3
Hornbeam Copse RG42 . .119 A8
Hornbeam Dr RG6 . . . . . . .113 D6
Hornbeam Gdns **7** SL1 . .43 A3
Hornbeam Pightle RG7 . . .111 B3
Hornbeams RG17 . . . . .139 C6
Hornby Ave RG12 . . . . .118 D3
Horncastle Dr RG30 . . . . . . .84 F5
Horndean Rd RG12 . . . . . . .118 F3

Horne Rd Littleton SL17 . .125 A5
Thatcham RG19 . . . . .106 E2
Hornsea Cl RG30 . . . . .57 E1
Horris Hill Sch RG20 . . . . .130 E3
Horse Cl The RG4 . . . . .59 C4
Horse Gate Ride SL5 . . . . .120 B3
Horsebrass Dr GU19 . . . . .145 E2
Horseguards Dr SL6 . . . . . .40 B7
Horsell Ct KT16 . . . . .124 B2
Horsemoor Cl SL3 . . . . .44 A2
Horseshoe Cl SL3 . . . . .81 E1
Horseshoe Cloisters **2**
SL4 . . . . .67 D6
Horseshoe Cres
Burghfield Common RG7 . . .111 B3
Camberley GU15 . . . . .151 F8
Horseshoe End RG14 . . . .131 B7
Horseshoe Hill SL1 . . . . . . .21 C8
Horseshoe Pk RG8 . . . . . . .56 D5
Horseshoe Rd RG8 . . . . . . .56 D5
Horsham Rd
East Bedfont TW14 . . . . .71 C1
Sandhurst GU47 . . . . .143 D1
Horsham Reach SL6 . . . . . .20 C2
Horsnape Gdns RG42 . . . . .90 B2
Horsneile La RG42 . . . . . . .118 B8
Horton Cl SL6 . . . . .20 C1
Horton Depot SL3 . . . . .69 C4
Horton Gdns SL3 . . . . .68 F4
Horton Grange SL6 . . . . . . .20 C1
Horton Rd Datchet SL3 . . . .68 D6
Horton SL3 . . . . .69 E4
Poyle SL3,TW19 . . . . .69 E4
Stanwell TW19 . . . . .70 A2
Horton Trad Est SL3 . . . . . .69 C4
Hose Hill RG7,RG30 . . . . . .111 A7
Hosier St RG1 . . . . .86 A7
Hoskins Place Ind Est
GU15 . . . . .151 B3
Houlton Ct GU19 . . . . .145 F2
Houston Ct **5** SL4 . . . . . . .67 C5
Houston Way RG45 . . . . . .142 D5
Howard Ave SL2 . . . . .42 E8
Howard Cl TW16 . . . . .98 F2
Howard Ct SL8 . . . . .3 A3
Howard Mews SL3 . . . . .69 B8
Howard Rd
Newbury RG14 . . . . .105 A1
Wokingham RG40 . . . . .116 C5
Howard St **17** RG1 . . . . . . .85 F7
Howards Gate SL2 . . . . .22 C2
Howarth Rd SL6 . . . . .40 A6
Howe La RG42 . . . . .63 F2
Howgate Dr RG8 . . . . .34 C7
Howth Dr RG5 . . . . .87 D7
Hoylake Cl SL1 . . . . .41 E4
Hubbard Cl RG10 . . . . .61 F2
Hubberholme RG12 . . . . . .118 A6
Hubert Rd SL3 . . . . .43 D3
Huckleberry Cl RG8 . . . . . . .57 C4
Huddington Glade
GU46 . . . . .149 A5
Hudson Rd Harlington UB7 .71 D8
Woodley RG5 . . . . .87 F6
Hugh Fraser Dr RG31 . . . . .84 C6
Hughenden Cl SL6 . . . . .39 C6
Hughenden Rd SL1 . . . . . . .42 D7
Hughes Rd Ashford TW15 . .98 D2
Wokingham RG40 . . . . .116 E7
Hull Cl SL1 . . . . .42 C4
Humber Cl
Thatcham RG18 . . . . .106 B5
Wokingham RG41 . . . . .115 C7
Humber Way
Sandhurst GU47 . . . . .150 D8
Slough SL3 . . . . .44 A2
Hummer Rd TW20 . . . . .96 A4
Humphrey's La RG17 . . . . .47 C6
Humphries Yd RG12 . . . . . .118 C5
Hungerford Ave SL2 . . . . . .42 E8
Hungerford Cl GU47 . . . . .150 C8
Hungerford Dr
Maidenhead SL6 . . . . .19 E3
Reading RG1 . . . . .85 E5
Hungerford Hill
East Garston RG17 . . . . .47 F1
Lambourn RG17 . . . . .25 A2
Hungerford La
Kintbury RG17 . . . . .101 E3
Stanford Dingley RG7 . . . . . .82 F1
Waltham St Lawrence RG10 .62 E2
Hungerford Newtown
RG17 .74 A3
Hungerford Prim Sch
RG17 . . . . .100 D5
Hungerford Sta RG17 . . . .100 E5
Hungerford Trad Est
RG17 . . . . .100 C5
Hunsford Lodge SL4 . . . . . .67 A4
Hunstanton Cl SL3 . . . . . . .69 C7
Hunt's La SL6 . . . . .20 E3
Hunter Cl SL1 . . . . .21 C1
Hunter's Ct RG5 . . . . .87 E6
Hunter's Hill RG7 . . . . .110 F3
Huntercombe Cl RG6 . . . . .41 C7
Huntercombe La N SL1,SL6 .41 C8
Huntercombe La S SL6 . . .41 C6
Huntercombe Manor Hospl
SL6 . . . . .41 C6
Huntercombe Spur SL1 . . .41 C6
Hunters Chase SL4 . . . . . . .58 F5
Hunters Mdw RG17 . . . . . . .48 A3
Hunters Mews SL4 . . . . .67 C6
Hunters Way
Shinfield RG7 . . . . .113 B1

Hunters Way *continued*
Slough SL1 41 E4
Hunters Wharf 19 RG1 86 A6
Huntingdon Cl RG6 87 E2
Huntingdonshire Cl
RG41 115 D6
Huntingfield Way TW20 96 D2
Huntington Pl SL3 44 B3
Huntley Ct RG1 86 E6
Huntley The RG30 85 D6
Hunts Cotts RG14 104 E6
Huntsgreen Ct RG12 118 C7
Huntsmans Mdw SL5 119 F8
Huntsmoor Rd RG26 135 A1
Huntswood La SL1,SL6 20 F4
Hurford Dr RG19 106 F3
Hurley Ct RG12 118 E5
Hurley High St SL6 17 F4
Hurley La SL6 18 B3
Hurricane Way
Slough SL3 44 B1
Woodley RG5 88 B8
Hursley Cl RG30 84 E7
Hurst Com Coll The
RG26 134 D1
Hurst Gr KT12 125 F1
Hurst La TW20 123 A7
Hurst Park Rd RG10 61 E2
Hurst Rd Slough SL1 41 D8
Twyford RG10 61 E3
Hurst Way RG2 112 F8
Hurstdene Ave TW18 97 B2
Hurstfield Dr SL6 41 B7
Hurstwood SL5 120 A3
Hurworth Ave SL3 43 C3
Huscarle Way RG31 57 C4
Huson Rd RG42 91 C2
Hutsons Cl RG40 116 D8
Hutton Cl Earley RG6 87 A2
Newbury RG14 105 B4
Windlesham GU20 146 D3
Hyde Cl TW15 98 E2
Hyde End La
Brimpton RG7 133 D5
Shinfield RG7 113 C3
Hyde End Rd RG7 113 D2
Hyde Gn SL7 1 F1
Hyde La RG20 132 A1
Hyde Terr TW15 98 E2
Hydes The RG31 57 C4
Hyland Ho 5 SL8 3 B3
Hylle Cl SL4 66 E6
Hyperion Way RG2 86 B3
Hythe Cl RG12 118 E4
Hythe End Rd TW19 96 A5
Hythe Field Ave TW20 96 D2
Hythe Park Rd TW20 96 D2
Hythe Prim Sch TW18 96 D3
Hythe Rd TW18 96 D3
Hythe The TW18 96 E3

I

Ian Mikardo Way RG4 59 D2
Iberian Way GU15 152 B6
Ibotson Ct SL3 69 E6
Ibstock Cl RG30 85 B7
Ibstone Ave RG4 59 E5
Icarus Ct 5 RG1 86 D7
Icknield Cotts RG8 34 A6
Icknield Pl RG8 34 D8
Icknield Rd RG8 34 D8
Iden Ct RG14 105 B4
Iffley Ct 11 TW18 96 F3
Ilbury Cl RG2 113 E5
Ilchester Cl SL6 39 C5
Ilchester Ct 7 RG14 105 A2
Ilchester Mews RG4 59 E6
Ilex Cl
Englefield Green TW20 95 B1
Silchester RG26 135 E1
Yateley GU46 149 B6
Ilfracombe Way RG6 87 E3
Ilkley Rd RG4 58 E3
Ilkley Way RG19 106 C2
Illingworth SL4 66 E4
Illingworth Ave RG4 59 E6
Illingworth Gr RG12 118 F8
Ilsley Rd RG20 31 D4
Ilsleys' Prim Sch The
RG20 30 E6
Imperial Ct
Henley-On-T RG9 15 E1
7 Newbury RG14 104 F2
Windsor SL4 67 A4
Imperial Ho GU25 122 E4
Imperial Rd
East Bedfont TW14 98 E8
Windsor SL4 67 A4
Imperial Way RG2 113 A7
Impstone Rd RG26 135 F1
In The Ray SL6 40 B8
Inchwood RG12 118 C1
India Rd SL1 43 B4
Ingle Dell GU15 151 D4
Ingle Glen RG40 142 A7
Ingleglen SL2 22 B7
Ingles Edge RG17 127 E4
Ingleside SL3 69 F6
Ingleton RG12 118 A6
Inglewood Ave GU15 152 D5
Inglewood Ct RG30 85 C6
Inglewood Rd RG17 101 E2
Ingoldsby Copse RG14 105 D5
Inhurst La RG26 134 C1
Inhurst Way RG26 134 F1
Inkerman Rd SL4 41 F2
Inkpen Cl RG30 85 A4
Inkpen Common Nature
Reserve* RG17 128 A5
Inkpen Prim Sch RG17 127 D6
Inkpen Rd
Hungerford RG17 100 F3
Kintbury RG17 102 A1
Inner Ring E TW6 71 B4
Inner Ring W TW6 71 A4
Innings La
White Waltham SL6 63 D7
Winkfield RG12 118 E8
Inniscrown Ho SL3 68 B7
Institute Rd Marlow SL7 1 E1
Taplow SL6 40 F7
Instow Rd RG6 87 B2
Invergordon Cl RG31 84 E4
Inverness Way GU47 150 D7
Invicta Cl TW14 98 F7
Inwood Cl SL6 19 B6
Iona Cres SL1 41 E7
Ipswich Rd SL1 42 A7
Iris Ct RG30 84 E7
Irish Hill Rd RG17 102 B2
Irvine Ho SL4 66 E5
Irvine Pl GU25 122 E4
Irvine Way RG6 114 C8
Isaac Newton Rd RG2 115 A1
Isis Cl RG41 88 B1
Isis Ct 1 RG1 59 A1
Isis Way Bourne End SL8 3 B4
Sandhurst GU47 150 D8
Island Cl TW18 96 E4
Island Farm Rd RG7 110 D2
Island Rd RG2 85 F2
Island The TW19 96 A5
Islandstone La RG10 89 A6
Islet Park Dr SL6 20 C3
Islet Park Ho SL6 20 C3
Islet Pk SL6 20 C3
Islet Rd SL6 20 C3
Ivanhoe Rd RG40 141 A6
Iveagh Ct RG12 118 C4
Iver La SL0 44 F7
Iver Lodge SL0 44 F8
Iver Sta SL0 44 F4
Iver Village Inf Sch SL0 44 F7
Iver Village Jun Sch The
SL0 44 E7
Iverdale Cl SL0 44 C6
Iverna Gdns TW14 71 D2
Ives Cl GU46 149 B7
Ives Rd SL3 44 A3
Ivy Cl SL6 65 A7
Ivy Cres SL1 41 F6
Ivy Dr GU18 153 A7
Ivybank RG31 57 C1
Ivydene Rd RG30 58 C1

J

Jack Price Ct 1 RG1 86 B5
Jack St RG14 105 A3
Jackson Cl RG12 118 B4
Jackson Ind Est SL8 3 B2
Jacksons La RG4 58 C5
Jacob Cl Bracknell RG42 117 D7
Windsor SL4 66 E6
Jacob Rd GU15 151 A7
Jakes Ho SL6 40 A8
James Butcher Dr RG7 83 F3
James Cl SL7 1 F4
James Ct RG30 85 D5
James Elliman Sch SL2 42 E6
James Rd GU15 151 B2
James St Reading RG1 85 F7
Windsor SL4 67 D6
James Watt Rd
Arborfield RG2 140 F7
Barkham RG2 141 A8
James Way GU15 151 B2
James's La RG7,RG30 111 E4
Jameston RG12 118 C1
Jamnagar Cl TW18 96 F2
Janson Ct RG1 85 F6
Japonica Cl RG41 115 D4
Jaques's La RG7 111 A6
Jardine Cotts SL2 23 A8
Jarratt Ho SL4 67 B4
Jarry Ct SL7 1 F3
Jarvis Dr RG10 61 D6
Jasmin Way RG19 133 B6
Jasmine Cl RG41 115 D7
Jay Cl RG6 87 B1
Jays Ct SL5 120 D5
Jays Nest Cl GU17 150 D4
Jayworth Ho RG1 86 E8
Jealott's Hill RG42 91 B7
Jedburgh Cl RG19 106 F3
Jefferson Cl
Caversham RG4 59 C7
Slough SL3 44 A2
Jeffries Ct SL8 3 B2
Jellicoe Cl SL1 42 B4
Jenkins Cl RG30 85 C6
Jenkins' Hill London Rd
GU19 145 D2
Jenner Wlk RG31 84 A7
Jennery La SL1 21 C2
Jennetts Cl RG7 81 E3
Jennings Field HP10 3 C7
Jennings Wharf SL4 67 D7
Jenny's Wlk GU46 149 E6
Jerome Cl SL7 1 F4
Jerome Cnr RG45 143 C3
Jerome Rd RG5 87 E6
Jerrymoor Hill RG40 141 F8
Jesmond Dene RG14 104 F4
Jesse Cl GU46 149 F5
Jesse Terr RG1 85 F7
Jessiman Terr TW17 125 A4
Jesus Hospl SL6 40 C3
Jevington RG12 118 C1
Jig's La N RG42 91 E2
Jig's La S Bracknell RG42 91 E1
Winkfield RG42 118 E8
Job's La SL6 19 B8
Jock's La RG42 90 F1
Joel Cl RG6 87 A3
Johannes Ct 5 RG30 85 D6
John Balliol Ct 14 RG1 86 D7
John Boys Ho RG14 130 C6
John Childs Cl RG14 105 A1
John F Kennedy Meml*
TW20 95 D6
John Hunt Cl RG19 106 E2
John Kaye Ct TW17 125 A4
John Kimber's Almshouses 1
RG14 104 F2
John Nike Way RG12 117 C7
John Norgate Ho RG14 105 E3
John O'Gaunt Com Tech Coll
RG17 100 D3
John Rankin Inf Sch
RG14 130 D8
John Rankin Jun Sch
RG14 130 D8
John Taylor Ct SL1 42 C5
Johns Cl TW15 98 C4
Johnson Dr RG40 142 B7
Johnsons La RG18 106 C8
Jonathan Ct SL6 39 E7
Jonathan Hill RG20 131 B3
Jones Cnr SL5 119 E7
Jordan Cl Caversham RG4 59 E5
Shinfield RG7 113 D1
Jordan's La RG7 110 F2
Jordans Cl TW19 97 C8
Joseph Ct RG42 91 E2
Josephine Ct RG30 85 E6
Jouldings La RG7 140 D4
Jourdelay's Pas SL4 67 D8
Journeys End SL2 42 E8
Joviel Ho TW18 97 A1
Jubilee Ave
North Ascot SL5 119 E8
Wokingham RG41 116 B7
Jubilee Cl
North Ascot SL5 119 E8
Silchester RG26 135 E1
Stanwell TW19 97 C8
Woodley RG5 87 E6
Jubilee Ct
Bracknell RG12 118 C6
9 Staines TW18 97 A4
Thatcham RG19 106 A3
Jubilee Rd
Finchampstead RG40 141 F3
Littlewick Green SL6 38 B5
Newbury RG14 105 B2
Reading RG6 87 A6
Jubilee Sq RG1 86 B6
Jubilee Way Datchet SL3 68 C7
East Bedfont TW14 98 F7
Juliet Gdns RG42 118 F8
Julius Hill RG42 118 F8
Julkes La RG2 114 E7
Junction Rd
Ashford TW15 98 D3
Lightwater GU18 146 B1
Reading RG1 86 E6
Junction Terr RG14 105 C2
Juniper RG12 118 C1
Juniper Ct SL1 43 A4
Juniper Dr SL6 40 B8
Juniper Gdns TW16 98 F2
Juniper Hill Sch HP10 3 B7
Juniper La HP10 3 D7
Juniper Pl RG19 133 B6
Juniper Rd SL7 1 D5
Juniper Way RG31 57 D2
Junipers The RG41 115 D4
Jupiter Ho RG7 134 E2
Jupiter Way RG41 115 F6
Justice Cl RG19 106 F2
Jutland Cl RG41 115 E6
Jutland Ho SL4 66 F5
Jutland Pl TW20 96 C3

K

Katesgrove La RG1 86 A6
Katesgrove Prim Sch
RG1 86 A6
Katherine Ct 2 GU15 151 D5
Kathleen Sanders Ct RG7 83 E4
Kaynes Pk SL5 119 E8
Kaywood Cl SL3 43 C3
Keane Cl RG5 87 E8
Kearsley Rd RG30 85 C6
Keates Gn RG42 118 B8
Keats Cl RG5 87 E4
Keats La SL4 67 C8
Keats Rd RG5 87 E4
Keats Way
Crowthorne RG45 143 B6
Yateley GU46 149 B4
Keble Rd SL6 39 E8
Keble Way GU47 143 E2
Keeble Ho RG41 116 A6
Keel Dr SL1 42 C4
Keeler Cl SL4 66 E4
Keep Hatch Prim Sch
RG40 116 D7
Keepers Combe RG12 118 D3
Keepers Farm Cl SL4 66 E5
Keepers Terr GU25 122 B4
Keepers Wlk GU25 122 D4
Keephatch Ho RG40 116 F7
Keephatch Rd RG40 116 E7
Keighley Cl RG19 106 C2
Kelburne Cl RG41 88 C3
Keldholme RG12 118 A6
Kelly Cl TW17 125 E7
Kelmscott Cl RG4 58 F3
Kelpatrick Rd SL1 41 D7
Kelsall Pl SL5 120 B2
Kelsey Ave RG40 141 E6
Kelsey Cl SL6 39 D3
Kelsey Gr GU46 149 E5
Kelso Mews RG4 59 E6
Kelton Cl RG6 87 E2
Kelvedon Way RG4 58 E5
Kelvin Cl RG2 140 E7
Kelvin Rd RG14 105 B4
Kemble Ct RG31 84 D4
Kemerton Cl RG31 84 D4
Kemp Ct GU19 145 F2
Kempe Cl SL3 44 C2
Kempton Cl RG14 105 C1
Kemsley Chase SL2 22 C4
Kenavon Dr RG1 86 C8
Kendal Ave
Caversham RG4 59 E5
Shinfield RG2 113 E6
Kendal Cl
East Bedfont TW14 98 F7
Slough SL2 43 A6
Thatcham RG18 106 C4
Kendal Dr SL2 43 A6
Kendal Gr GU15 152 D4
Kendall Ct Bsns Pk
GU15 150 F4
Kendrick Cl RG40 116 C5
Kendrick Ct 5 RG1 86 C6
Kendrick Girls' Gram Sch
RG1 86 C7
Kendrick Rd
Newbury RG14 130 D5
Reading RG1 86 C6
Slough SL3 43 B3
Kenilworth Ave
Bracknell RG12 118 D8
Reading RG30 85 D5
Kenilworth Cl SL1 42 F3
Kenilworth Gdns TW18 97 C3
Kenilworth Rd TW15 97 D5
Kenneally SL4 66 C5
Kenneally Cl 11 SL4 66 C5
Kenneally Pl 12 SL4 66 C5
Kenneally Row 13 SL4 66 C5
Kenneally Wlk 10 SL4 66 C5
Kennedy Cl
Farnham Common SL2 22 C6
Maidenhead SL6 39 C6
Marlow SL7 1 E3
Newbury RG14 130 D6
Kennedy Ct TW15 98 C3
Kennedy Dr RG8 56 E5
Kennedy Gdns RG6 87 B3
Kennedy Ho SL1 41 D5
Kennedy Mdw RG17 100 C4
Kennel Ave SL5 119 F8
Kennel Cl SL5 92 F2
Kennel Gn SL5 119 E8
Kennel La Bracknell RG42 91 B1
Cookham Dean SL6 19 C7
Windlesham GU20 146 C5
Kennel Lane Sch RG42 91 B2
Kennel Ride SL5 92 F1
Kennel Wood SL5 119 F8
Kennet & Avon Canal Visitor
Ctr* RG7 109 C3
Kennet Cl RG19 106 E3
Kennet Cotts RG30 85 A1
Kennet Ct
Hungerford RG17 100 E7
1 Newbury RG14 105 A1
Wokingham RG41 115 F6
Kennet Ctr The RG14 105 A2
Kennet Ent Ctr RG17 100 D7
Kennet Pl
Burghfield Common RG7 111 B3
Chilton Foliat RG17 73 A1
10 Newbury RG14 105 B4
Kennet Rd Bourne End SL8 3 B4
Kintbury RG17 102 B2
Maidenhead SL6 39 F8
Newbury RG14 104 F2
Kennet Sch RG19 106 E3
Kennet Side
Newbury RG14 105 C3
13 Reading RG1 86 C7
Kennet St RG1 86 C7
Kennet Valley Prim Sch
RG31 84 F4
Kennet Way RG17 100 D7
Kennet Weir Bsns Pk
RG7 83 F2
Kennet Wlk RG1 86 D8
Kennett Rd SL3 44 B3
Kensington Cl RG6 87 B1
Kensington Rd RG30 85 D7
Kent Ave SL1 42 C8
Kent Cl Staines TW18 97 D2
Wokingham RG41 115 D5
Kent Cotts RG7 139 C3
Kent Folly RG42 91 F2
Kent Lodge 6 SL6 39 F6
Kent Rd Reading RG30 85 D7
Windlesham GU20 146 D5
Kent Way SL6 19 E1
Kentigern Dr RG45 143 E5
Kenton Cl
Bracknell RG12 118 D7
Frimley GU16 151 F1
Marlow SL7 1 E2
Kenton Rd RG6 87 C4
Kenton's La RG10 36 D7
Kentons La SL4 66 F5
Kentwood Cl RG30 57 E1
Kentwood Farm RG40 116 D8
Kentwood Hill RG31 57 E1
Kenwood Cl
Harmondsworth UB7 71 A8
Maidenhead SL6 39 A7
Kenworth Gr GU18 146 A1
Keppel Spur SL4 95 B8
Keppel St SL4 67 D5
Kepple Pl GU19 145 F3
Kernham Dr RG31 57 C4
Kerria Way GU24 153 F6
Kerris Way RG6 87 B1
Kersey Cres RG14 104 E5
Kesteven Way RG41 115 E6
Keston Cl RG4 59 C2
Kestrel Ave TW18 96 F5
Kestrel Cl RG19 106 B3
Kestrel Path SL2 21 E1
Kestrel Way
Burghfield Common RG7 111 B3
Reading RG30 85 A4
Wokingham RG41 115 F5
Keswick Ave TW17 125 E6
Keswick Cl Frimley GU15 152 D4
Reading RG30 84 D7
Keswick Ct SL2 42 F6
Keswick Dr GU18 153 B8
Keswick Gdns RG5 87 E5
Keswick Rd TW20 96 B1
Ketcher Gn RG42 90 C4
Kettering Cl RG31 84 E4
Kevins Dr GU46 149 E7
Kew Cotts RG14 104 E1
Kew Gdns SN8 126 A3
Keynsham Way GU47 143 D2
Keys Pl SL6 39 F6
Kibble Gn RG12 118 C3
Kibblewhite Cres RG10 61 D6
Kidderminster Rd SL2 22 A2
Kidmore End Rd RG4 59 B7
Kidmore Rd RG4 58 F5
Kidwells Cl SL6 39 F8
Kidwells Park Dr SL6 39 F7
Kielder Wlk GU15 152 C4
Kier Pk SL5 120 C6
Kilburn Cl RG31 84 D4
Kildare Gdns RG4 59 C3
Killarney Dr SL6 39 E7
Killigrew Ho 4 TW16 98 E1
Kilmartin Gdns GU16 151 F1
Kilmington Cl RG12 118 E2
Kilmiston Ave TW17 125 C3
Kilmiston Ho TW17 125 C3
Kilmore Dr GU15 152 B4
Kilmuir Cl GU47 150 D7
Kiln Cl Harlington UB3 71 D8
Hermitage RG18 79 C7
Kiln Croft Cl SL7 2 A3
Kiln Dr RG18 78 E5
Kiln Hill RG7 140 B7
Kiln La Bracknell RG12 118 A7
Mortimer RG7 137 C5
Reading RG31 84 B8
Shiplake RG9 35 C2
Sunningdale SL5 121 A4
Winkfield SL4 93 B2
Wooburn SL8,HP10 3 D3
Kiln Pl SL6 19 A3
Kiln Rd Caversham RG4 59 D8
Newbury RG14 105 C5
Kiln Ride
Upper Basildon RG8 54 F5
Wokingham RG40 142 A8
Kiln Ride Extension
RG40 142 A6
Kiln Terr RG18 78 E5
Kiln View Rd RG2 86 D2
Kilnsea Dr RG6 87 D1
Kilnside RG12 91 D1
Kilowna Cl RG10 61 A4
Kilross Rd TW14 98 E7
Kimber Cl SL4 67 A4
Kimber's Cl RG14 104 F3
Kimber's La SL6 39 E3
Kimberley RG12 118 C1
Kimberley Cl
1 Reading RG1 85 E5
Slough SL3 43 F2
Kimbers Dr Burnham SL1 21 D2
Newbury RG14 104 C5
Kimmeridge RG12 118 E3
Kimpton Cl RG6 113 E8
Kinburn Dr TW20 95 E3
King Acre Ct TW18 96 E5
King Edward Ct 4 SL4 67 D6
King Edward St SL1 42 D4
King Edward VII Ave SL4,
SL3 67 E8
King Edward VII Hospl
SL4 67 C4
King Edwards Cl SL5 119 E8
King Edwards Rd SL5 119 E8
King Edwards Rise SL5 119 E8
King George Cl TW16 98 E3
King James Way RG9 35 C8
King John's Cl TW19 68 C1

King John's Pal SL3 ....69 D6
King St Chertsey KT16 ...124 A1
Maidenhead SL6 ....39 F6
Mortimer RG7 ....137 A6
Reading RG1 ....86 B7
King Stable St SL4 .....67 D7
King Street La RG14 ...88 C1
King's Ave TW16 ....98 F2
King's Cl TW18 ....97 D1
King's Court Fst Sch
SL4 ....95 B8
King's Keep GU47 .....143 B1
King's Meadow Rd RG1 .86 B8
King's Oak Ct **5** RG1 ...86 C7
King's Rd Ascot SL5 ...120 D4
Caversham RG4 ....59 C2
Crowthorne RG45 .....143 C5
Egham TW20 ....96 A4
Henley-On-T RG9 ......15 D2
Reading RG1 ....86 D7
Slough SL1 ....42 E3
King's Ride Bracknell SL5 119 D5
Camberley GU15 ....151 D7
King's Ride Ho SL5 ....119 E5
King's Road Ho **2** SL4 ..67 D5
King's Terr SL3 ....69 B8
King's Wlk GU15 ......150 F6
King's Yd SL5 ....119 E5
Kingfisher Cl RG7 .....109 B3
Kingfisher Court Ind Est
RG14 ....105 D3
Kingfisher Ct Slough SL2 .22 B1
Twyford RG10 ....61 E3
Kingfisher Dr
Staines TW18 ....96 F4
Woodley RG5 ....87 C6
Yateley GU46 ....149 B6
Kingfisher Gr RG7 ....113 A3
Kingfisher Ho SL7 .....1 F2
Kingfisher Par GU17 ..150 B5
Kingfisher Pl RG1 .....86 B8
Kinghorn La SL6 ....19 D3
Kinghorn Pk SL6 ......19 D3
Kings Apartments GU15 .151 C4
Kings Cl RG9 ....15 D2
Kings Common Cl RG9 ..35 B1
Kings Cres GU15 ......151 C8
Kings Gr SL6 ....39 E6
Kings Grove Ind Est SL6 .39 E6
Kings International Coll for
Bsns & Fine Arts GU15 .151 C2
Kings La
Cookham Dean SL6 ....19 B8
Englefield Green TW20 ..95 A2
Windlesham GU20 .....146 E5
Kings Mead RG14 .....130 C5
Kings Rd Newbury RG14 .105 B2
Silchester RG7 ....136 B2
West End GU24 ....153 F5
Windsor SL4 ....67 D5
Kings Rd W RG14 .....105 A2
Kings Reach Ct **7** RG1 .86 B7
Kings Ride Pk SL5 .....119 C4
Kings Wlk
Henley-On-T RG9 ......15 D2
4 Maidenhead SL6 ....39 F7
Reading RG1 ....86 B7
Kings Wood SL7 ....17 D7
Kingsbridge Cotts RG40 142 E7
Kingsbridge Hill RG7 ..139 A6
Kingsbridge Rd
Newbury RG14 ....104 E1
Reading RG2 ....86 C2
Kingsbury Cres TW18 ..96 D4
Kingsbury Dr SL4 ......95 A8
Kingsclear Pk GU15 ...151 D4
Kingsley Ave
Camberley GU15 ......151 D3
Englefield Green TW20 ..95 B2
Kingsley Cl Charvil RG10 ..61 A5
Crowthorne RG45 .....143 B3
Newbury RG14 ....105 B5
Reading RG2 ....113 B7
Kingsley Dr SL7 ....1 C6
Kingsley Path SL2 .....21 D1
Kingsmead Ho SL1 ....42 C5
Kingsmere Rd RG42 ...117 F8
Kingston Ave TW14 ....71 F1
Kingston Cres TW15 ...97 D2
Kingston Gdns RG2 ....86 C2
Kingston La RG7 ......110 D6
Kingston Rd Ashford TW15 .97 F2
Camberley GU15 ......145 A1
Staines TW15,TW18 ....97 B2
Kingsway
Blackwater GU17 .....150 E5
Caversham RG4 ....59 E6
Farnham Common SL2 ..22 C6
Stanwell TW19 ....97 E7
Kingswick Cl SL5 .....120 D5
Kingswick Dr SL5 .....120 D5
Kingswood Cl TW20 ...95 D4
Kingswood Creek TW19 .68 D2
Kingswood Ct
Maidenhead SL6 ......39 F5

Kingswood Ct continued
17 Reading RG30 ....85 D6
Kingswood Hall of Residence
TW20 ....95 D4
Kingswood Ho SL1 ....42 C8
Kingswood Par SL7 ....1 D5
Kingswood Rise TW20 ..95 D4
Kinnaird Cl SL1 ....41 C7
Kinross Ave SL5 ......119 F4
Kinross Cl TW16 ......98 F3
Kinross Ct SL5 ....119 F4
Kinross Dr TW16 .....98 F3
Kinson Rd RG30 ......58 A1
Kintbury Mill RG17 ...102 B3
Kintbury Rd RG17 ....127 F6
Kintbury Sq RG17 ....102 A2
Kintbury Sta RG17 ...102 B3
Kinver Wlk **6** RG1 ....86 B5
Kipling Cl
Thatcham RG18 ....106 C5
Woodley RG5 ....87 E4
Yateley GU46 ....149 C4
Kipling Ct SL4 ....67 B5
Kirkby Ct GU16 ......151 E1
Kirkfell Cl RG31 ......57 C2
Kirkham Cl
Caversham RG4 ....59 E6
Sandhurst GU47 .....143 D2
Kirkstall Ct RG31 ....84 D4
Kirkstone Cl GU15 ...152 D4
Kirkwall Spur SL1 ....42 E8
Kirkwood Cres RG7 ..110 F3
Kirton Cl RG30 ....85 D1
Kirtons Farm Rd RG30 .85 C1
Kittiwake Cl RG5 .....88 B7
Kitwood Dr RG6 ......87 E1
Klondyke SL7 ....1 D2
Knapp Rd TW15 ....97 F4
Knapp The RG6 ....87 B4
Knappe Cl RG9 ....35 C8
Knight's Pl **9** SL4 ....67 C5
Knighton Cl RG4 .....59 A3
Knights Cl Egham TW20 .96 D2
Windsor SL4 ....66 D6
Knights La RG20 .....129 C3
Knights Lea RG20 ...129 B3
Knights Way
Caversham RG4 ....59 B5
Frimley GU15 ....152 C4
Knightsbridge Cres
TW18 ....97 B2
Knightsbridge Ct **7** SL3 .44 A2
Knightsbridge Dr RG12 .132 B3
Knightsbridge Rd GU15 .151 E7
Knightswood RG12 ...118 B1
Knock The GU47 .....150 D7
Knole Wood SL5 .....120 C1
Knoll Cl OX12 ....6 E7
Knoll Park Rd KT16 ..123 F1
Knoll Rd GU15 ....151 D6
Knoll The RG31 ....57 B2
Knollmead RG31 .....84 D4
Knollys Rd RG26 ....135 F1
Knolton Way SL2 .....43 C7
Knossington Cl RG6 ..87 C2
Knott La RG7 ....109 B4
Knowl Hill CE Prim Sch
RG10 ....37 F4
Knowl Hill Comm RG10 .37 E3
Knowl Hill Terr RG10 .37 E4
Knowle Cl RG4 ....58 D4
Knowle Gn TW18 .....97 A3
Knowle Gr GU25 .....122 C2
Knowle Grove Cl GU25 .122 C2
Knowle Hill GU25 ....122 C2
Knowle Park Ave TW18 ..97 B3
Knowle Park Inf Sch
TW18 ....97 A3
Knowle Rd RG5 ....87 E4
Knowles Ave RG45 ..142 F5
Knowsley Cl SL6 .....39 A4
Knowsley Rd RG31 ...57 C3
Knox Gn RG42 ....90 C3
Kola Ho SL2 ....43 B6
Korda Cl TW17 ......124 F6
Krooner Rd GU15 ....151 B3
Kybes La RG7 ....112 D5
Kyftle Court Flat **11**
RG14 ....104 F2
Kyle Cl RG12 ....118 B6

L

La Roche Cl SL3 .....43 C3
Laburnham Rd SL6 ...39 E6
Laburnum Cl SL7 ....1 C4
Laburnum Ct KT16 ..124 A1
Laburnum Gdns RG2 ..86 E1
Laburnum Gr
Brands Hill SL3 ......69 B8
Newbury RG14 ....105 A4
Laburnum Pl TW20 ..95 B2
Laburnum Rd
Chertsey KT16 ....124 A1
Winnersh RG41 ....88 C1
Laburnum Rise RG19 .133 B5
Laburnum Way TW19 .97 F7
Laburnums The GU17 ..150 B5
Lacewood Gdns RG2 ..86 E1
Lacey Cl TW20 ....96 D1
Ladbroke Cl RG5 ....87 F6
Ladbroke Rd SL1 ....42 B4
Ladwell Cl RG14 ...130 D5
Lady Jane Ct RG4 ...59 C3
Lady Margaret Rd SL5 .120 F2
Ladybank RG12 .....118 B1
Ladyday Pl SL1 ......42 C5

Ladymask Cl RG31 .....84 F4
Laffords The RG7 ......82 A2
Laggan Rd SL6 ....19 F1
Laggan Sq SL6 ....19 F1
Laird Ct GU19 ....145 E1
Lake Ave SL1 ....42 D6
Lake End Ct SL6 ......41 A7
Lake End Rd SL4,SL6 ..41 B5
Lake Rd GU25 ....122 B5
Lake Side The GU17 ..150 D4
Lake View SL6 ....20 A1
Lakeland Dr GU16 ...151 A1
Lakes The SL7 ....18 A6
Lakeside Earley RG6 ..87 B3
Maidenhead SL6 ......20 B1
Lakeside Bsns Pk GU47 .150 F4
Lakeside Dr SL2 ......22 F4
Lakeside Est SL3 .....70 A8
Lakeside Pk KT16 ....124 C1
Lakeside Prim Sch
GU16 ....151 F1
Lakeside Rd SL3 ......69 F7
Lakeview SL5 ....119 D6
Lalande Cl RG41 ....115 E6
Laleham Abbey TW18 .124 C5
Laleham CE Prim Sch
TW18 ....124 C7
Laleham Ho TW18 ...124 C5
Laleham Rd
Littleton TW17 ....125 A4
Staines TW18 ....96 F2
Laleham Reach KT16 .124 A6
Lamb Cl RG16 ....106 D5
Lambdens Hill RG7 ..109 D7
Lambert Ave SL3 ....43 E3
Lambert Cres GU17 .150 C4
Lambeth Ct RG30 ....84 F7
Lambfields RG7 ......83 D3
Lambly Hill GU25 ...122 E6
Lamborne Cl GU47 ..143 A1
Lambourn CE Prim Sch
RG17 ....25 B1
Lambourn Ct RG14 ..105 B4
Lambourn Pl RG17 ...25 B3
Lambourn Rd RG20 .104 C6
Lambourne Cl RG31 ..84 D4
Lambourne Ct Cvn Site
RG17 ....25 B2
Lambourne Dr
Bagshot GU19 ....145 D2
Maidenhead SL6 ......39 C3
Lambourne Gdns RG6 .87 D4
Lambourne Gr RG12 .118 E2
Lambridge La RG9 ...15 C3
Lambridge Wood Rd RG9 .15 B4
Lambrook Haileybury Sch
RG42 ....92 A3
Lambs Farm Bsns Pk
RG7 ....139 B8
Lambs La RG7 ....139 A7
Lambs Lane Prim Sch
RG7 ....139 A8
Lambton Ho SL4 .....67 A6
Lambwood Hill RG7 ..112 D2
Lamden Way RG7 ...111 B3
Lamerton Rd RG2 ...113 B6
Lamesley Ho SL6 ....39 E6
Lammas Ave **4** SL4 ..67 D5
Lammas Ct TW18 ...97 A3
Lammas Ct Staines TW19 .96 D5
Windsor SL4 ....67 C5
Lammas Dr TW18 ...96 D4
Lammas Mead RG42 .90 E1
Lammas Rd SL1 ......41 D8
Lamorna Cres RG31 ..57 C1
Lamp Acres RG14 ...105 B5
Lamplighters Wlk RG31 ..84 F4
Lanark Cl Frimley GU16 .151 E2
Woodley RG5 ....88 A6
Lancashire Hill RG42 .91 F2
Lancaster Ave SL2 ...22 C1
Lancaster Cl
Ashford TW15 ....97 E4
Englefield Green TW20 .95 D3
Hungerford RG17 ....100 C4
2 Reading RG1 ......86 C5
Stanwell TW19 ....70 E1
Thatcham RG18 ......106 C4
Lancaster Ct Reading RG2 .86 E1
Stanwell TW17 ......97 E7
Lancaster Dr GU15 ..151 D6
Lancaster Gdns RG6 ..87 B3
Lancaster Ho RG12 ..118 B4
Lancaster Rd SL6 ....39 B8
Lancaster Sq RG17 ..100 D4
Lancastria Mews SL6 ..39 D7
Lancelot Cl SL1 ......42 A4
Lanchester Dr RG45 .143 C7
Lancing Cl RG30 .....85 D7
Lancing Rd TW13 ....98 F6
Landen Cl RG5 ....88 A7
Landon Way TW15 ...98 B2
Landrake Cres RG2 ..86 E1
Landseer Cl GU47 ...150 E6
Landsend La RG10 ...61 B2
Lane End Cl RG2 ....113 A6
Lane The Chertsey KT16 .124 A6
Chilton OX11 ....10 E8
Thorpe GU25 ....122 C5
Laneswood RG7 .....136 E5
Lang Ho TW15 ....97 E7
Langborough Rd RG40 .116 C5
Langdale Cl SL6 .....20 A6
Langdale Dr SL5 .....119 E7

Langdale Gdns RG6 ...86 F2
Langdon Cl GU15 ....152 C4
Langford Cl RG4 .....59 C5
Langham Pl TW20 ....95 F3
Langhams Way RG10 ..36 E2
Langley Broom SL3 ..43 F1
Langley Bsns Ctr RG20 .51 C5
Langley Bsns Ctr SL3 ..44 A4
Langley Cmn Rd SL3 ..44 A4
Langley Common Rd
RG2,RG40 ....114 F1
Langley Cres UB3 ....71 F7
Langley Dr GU15 ....151 D6
Langley Farm Cotts RG20 .51 E6
Langley Green Sch SL3 ..43 F2
Langley Hill RG31 ....84 D2
Langley Hill Cl RG31 ..84 D6
Langley Manor Sch SL3 ..43 E5
Langley Park Rd SL0 ..44 A6
Lansdowne Ave SL1 ..42 E5
Lansdowne Gdns RG7 .113 C1
Lansdowne Rd
Reading RG30 ....84 C7
Staines TW18 ....97 B1
Lanterns Wlk SL6 ....40 B7
Lapwing Cl RG31 ....84 C6
Larbert Cotts SL6 ....38 B5
Larch Ave Ascot SL5 .120 E4
Wokingham RG41 ....116 A7
Larch Cl
Burghfield Common RG30 .111 B4
Camberley GU15 ....151 E8
Newbury RG14 ....104 D5
Slough SL2 ....42 B8
Larch Ct RG4 ....59 B3
Larch Dr Brimpton RG19 .133 B6
Woodley RG5 ....87 E5
Larches The RG42 ...92 A1
Larches Way GU17 ..150 C4
Larchfield Prim Sch SL6 ..39 E4
Larchfield Rd SL6 ...39 E5
Larchmoor Pk SL2 ...23 A7
Larchside Cl RG7 ....113 B2
Larchwood **6** RG12 .118 F5
Larchwood Dr TW20 ..95 B2
Larchwood Glade GU15 .152 A7
Lardon Cotts RG8 ...34 A6
Larges Bridge Dr RG12 .118 D6
Larges La RG12 .....118 C7
Larissa Cl RG31 .....57 E1
Lark Ave TW18 ......96 F5
Larken Cl RG5 ....87 A1
Larkfield SL6 ....40 B1
Larkham Cl TW13 ...98 E5
Larkings La SL2 .....23 B4
Larksfield TW20 .....95 C1
Larkspur Cl RG41 ..115 D7
Larkspur Gdns RG18 .106 F4
Larkswood Cl
Sandhurst GU47 ....143 A1
Larkwood Dr RG45 ..143 A4
Lascelles Ho **3** SL1 ..43 A4
Lascelles Rd SL3 ....43 A4
Lashbrook Mead RG9 .36 B3
Lashbrook Rd RG9 ...36 B4
Lassell Gdns SL6 ....40 B7
Lasswade Ct KT16 ..123 F2
Lasswade Rd KT16 ..123 F2
Lastingham Ct TW18 .97 A2
Latham Ave GU16 ...151 E2
Latimer RG12 ....118 B1
Latimer Dr RG31 ....84 C4
Latimer Rd RG41 ...116 B5
Latton Cl OX11 ......10 E8
Laud Cl Newbury RG14 .105 D5
Reading RG2 ....86 A6
Laud Way RG40 .....116 E6
Laud's Cl RG9 ....15 C1
Lauder Cl GU16 .....151 A1
Lauderdale Ho **12** TW18 .96 F3
Launceston Ave RG4 ..59 E6
Launcestone Cl RG6 ..87 D2
Laundry La GU47 ...150 D7
Laundry La GU47 ...150 B3
Lauradale RG12 .....118 A5
Laurel Ave
Brimpton RG19 ....133 A5
Englefield Green TW20 ..95 B3
Slough SL3 ....43 E4
Laurel Cl
Camberley GU15 ....151 D4
Poyle SL3 ....69 E7
Wokingham RG41 ...116 A7
Laurel Ct **7** RG12 ...118 F5
Laurel Dr RG31 .....84 C4
Laurel Terr GU47 ...142 F1
Laurels The
Hungerford RG17 ....100 E7
Pangbourne RG8 .....56 C5
Laurence Allison Mews
RG4 ....58 E2
Laurence Ct **1** SL7 ..1 D6
Lauser Rd TW19 ....97 C8
Lautree Gdns SL6 ...19 E6

Lavender Pk SL5 ....119 C6
Lavender Row SL5 ...92 E1
Lavenham Dr RG5 ...87 F8
Lawford Cres GU46 .149 D6
Lawkland SL2 ....22 C2
Lawn Cl SL3 ....68 C7
Lawn The SL3 ....68 C6
Lawns The
North Ascot SL5 ....119 D6
Reading RG2 ....86 D3
Lawrence Cl RG40 ..116 D6
Lawrence Cres GU20 .146 D4
Lawrence Ct SL4 ....67 C5
Lawrence Ctr RG41 .116 A4
Lawrence Ct RG42 ..117 D8
Lawrence Lodge GU15 .151 D7
Lawrence Mead RG17 .102 B2
Lawrence Pl RG14 ..105 C5
Lawrence Rd RG30 ..85 A8
Lawrence Way
Camberley GU15 ....150 F4
Slough SL1 ....41 D8
Lawrences La RG18 .106 C6
Lawrences Way RG18 .106 C5
Lawson La OX11 .....10 E8
Lawson Rd RG9 .....35 F7
Lawson Way SL5 ...121 B3
Laxton Gn SL6 ......39 C3
Layburn Cres SL3 ...69 B8
Layland's Gn RG17 ..102 B1
Laylands Gn RG17 ..102 B1
Layleys Gn RG18 ....78 F4
Laytom Rise RG31 ...57 C3
Layton's La TW16 ...125 F7
Lazare Ct **7** RG6 .....96 F3
Le Marchant Rd GU15,
RG6 ....151 F3
Lea Cl Marlow Bottom SL7 .1 D6
Reading RG30 ....85 A3
Lea Croft RG45 .....143 B6
Lea Inf Sch SL2 ......43 B6
Lea Jun Sch SL2 ....43 B6
Lea Rd GU15 ....151 B2
Lea The Thorpe Lea TW20 .96 C1
Wokingham RG40 ...141 F8
Leacroft Staines TW18 ..97 B4
Sunningdale SL5 ....121 A4
Leacroft Cl TW18 ...97 B4
Leacroft Rd SL0 ....44 E7
Leafield Copse RG12 .118 F5
Leaholme Sch SL1 ..41 D8
Leander Pl RG31 ....84 D4
Leas Dr SL0 ....44 E7
Leaver Rd RG9 ......15 C1
Leaves Gn RG12 ...118 D3
Ledbury Cl RG30 ...85 D1
Ledbury Dr RG31 ...84 D4
Ledgar La SL6 ....65 D5
Ledger's Rd SL1 ....42 D4
Ledran Cl Earley RG6 ..87 C1
Lower Earley RG6 ...114 C8
Lee Ct RG5 ....87 E7
Lee La SL6 ....18 E2
Lees Cl SL6 ....39 B5
Lees Gdns SL6 .....39 B5
Leeson Gdns SL4 ...41 E6
Legoland Windsor* SL4 .66 D2
Leicester RG12 .....118 E2
Leicester Cl RG9 ...15 D3
Leigh Field RG7 ....136 F6
Leigh Pk SL3 ....68 C6
Leigh Rd GU15 .....151 B6
Leigh Sq SL4 ....66 D5
Leighton Cr RG2 ...86 E3
Leighton Gdns SL6 .20 B1
Leighton Ho **5** SL7 ..1 E2
Leighton Park Sch RG2 .86 F4
Leiston Cl **2** RG6 ....87 D1
Leiston Spur SL1 ....42 E7
Leith Cl Crowthorne RG45 .143 A7
Slough SL1 ....43 A5
Lemart Cl RG30 ....84 D8
Lemington Gr RG12 .118 B3
Leney Cl RG40 ......116 D8
Lenham Cl RG41 ...88 E1
Lennox Cl RG21 ....84 A6
Lennox Rd RG6 .....87 A5
Lent Green La SL1 ..21 B1
Lent Green La SL1 ..21 B1
Lent Rise Comb Sch SL1 .41 B8
Lent Rise Rd SL1 ...21 B1
Leonard Ct RG7 .....83 E3
Leonardslee Cres RG14 .105 C4
Leopold Mall **3** SL1 ..42 F4
Leopold Wlk RG1 ...86 D7
Leppington RG12 ...118 B2
Lerwick Dr SL1 .....42 E7
Lesford Rd RG1 .....85 E5
Lesley Ct **10** RG30 ..85 D6
Leslie Southern Ct
RG14 ....105 B4
Lesters Rd SL6 ......19 D6
Letchworth Ave TW14 .98 F8
Letcombe Cl **4** RG1 ..86 B6
Letcombe Ct RG12 .118 F5
Letcombe St RG1 ...86 B6
Leverkusen Rd RG12 .118 B6
Leverton La RG17 ...73 B1
Levendon Rd RG14 .104 E5
Lewes Ct SL1 ....42 C5
Lewes Ho RG12 ....118 F4
Lewins Way SL1 ....42 A5
Lewins Farm Ct SL1 ..41 F6
Lewis Cl SL6 ....40 D4
Lewis Wlk RG14 ....130 C6
Lewisham Way GU47 .143 D2

Lexington Ave SL6 ....39 D5
Lexington Gr RG2 ....113 C6
Leyburn Cl RG5 ....88 A8
Leycester Cl GU20 ......146 B6
Leyland Gdns RG2 ....113 E6
Leylands La TW19 ....70 A2
Leys Gdns RG14 ....104 F4
Leyside RG45 ....143 A5
Libra Ho HP10 ....3 A8
Library Par RG5 ....87 E7
Licensed Victuallers Sch
SL5 ....119 C7
Lichfield Cl 1 RG6 ....87 C1
Lichfields RG12 ....118 E7
Liddel Way SL5 ....119 F5
Liddell SL4 ....66 C4
Liddell Cl RG40 ....141 E3
Liddell Pl SL4 ....66 C4
Liddell Sq 14 SL4 ....66 C5
Liddell Way SL4 ....66 C4
Lido Rd OX11 ....9 F8
Lidstone Cl RG6 ....114 D8
Liebenrood Rd RG30 .....85 C6
Lightlands La SL6 ....19 F5
Lightwater Ctry Pk
GU18 ....145 F1
Lightwater Mdw GU18 ..153 B8
Lightwater Rd GU18 ....153 C8
Lightwater Village Sch
GU18 ....146 A1
Lightwood RG12 ....118 D3
Liguel Cl RG17 ....100 D4
Lilac Cl RG8 ....57 C5
Lilac Ct SL2 ....21 F2
Lilac Wlk Brimpton RG19 .133 B5
Reading RG31 ....84 C5
Lilacs The RG41 ....115 C4
Lilley Way SL1 ....41 E5
Lillibrooke Cres SL6 .....39 A3
Lily Ct RG41 ....116 A6
Lily Hill Dr RG12 ....118 F7
Lily Hill Rd RG12 ....118 F7
Lima Ct RG1 ....85 F6
Lime Ave
Camberley GU15 ....152 A6
Windsor SL4 ....67 F7
Winkfield SL4 ....93 F5
Lime Cl Brimpton RG19 ...133 A5
Newbury RG14 ....105 D4
Wokingham RG41 ....115 F5
Lime Lodge 3 TW16 .....98 F1
Lime Mews TW20 ....95 F3
Lime Tree Copse RG42 ....92 A1
Lime Tree Ct SL4 ....95 C8
Lime Tree Rd RG8 ....34 B6
Lime Wlk Bracknell RG12 .118 C5
Maidenhead SL6 ....39 A8
Limecroft GU46 ....149 C5
Limefield Ct RG6 ....87 E3
Limerick Cl RG42 ....118 A8
Limes Cl TW15 ....98 A3
Limes Rd TW20 ....95 F3
Limes The SL4 ....66 C6
Limetree Wlk GU25 .....122 E5
Limmer Cl RG41 ....115 C4
Limmerhill Rd RG41 .....115 E5
Linchfield Rd SL3 ....68 C6
Lincoln Cl Frimley GU15 ..152 B4
Winnersh RG41 ....88 A3
Lincoln Ct Newbury RG14 .104 F2
3 Slough SL1 ....42 E3
Lincoln Gdns RG10 ....61 D5
Lincoln Hatch La SL1 .....21 C1
Lincoln Ho HP10 ....3 D3
Lincoln Rd
Maidenhead SL6 ....39 B8
Reading RG2 ....86 C4
Lincoln Way
Charlton TW16 ....125 E8
Slough SL1 ....41 D6
Lincolnshire Gdns RG42 ..91 E1
Lind Cl RG6 ....87 B2
Lindale Cl GU25 ....121 F5
Lindberg Way RG5 ....61 B1
Linden 3 Bracknell RG12 .118 F4
Slough SL3 ....44 B1
Linden Ave SL6 ....19 D1
Linden Cl Newbury RG14 ..104 F4
Wokingham RG41 ....115 F4
Linden Ct
Camberley GU15 ....151 F7
Englefield Green TW20 ....95 B2
North Ascot SL5 ....119 E6
Linden Dr SL2 ....22 C4
Linden Hill La RG10 .....37 C2
Linden Pl TW18 ....97 A4
Linden Rd Reading RG2 ...86 E2
Woodley RG5 ....87 D4
Linden Way TW17 ....125 C4
Lindenhill Rd RG42 .....117 F8
Lindenmuth Way RG19 ..131 F5
Lindores Ho SL6 ....65 B8
Lindores Rd SL6 ....65 B8
Lindsay Cl TW19 ....70 D2
Lindsay Dr TW17 ....125 D3
Lindsey Cl RG41 ....115 E6
Lindsey Gdns TW14 ......98 D8
Lines Rd RG10 ....88 F5
Ling Dr GU18 ....152 F7
Lingholm Cl
Maidenhead SL6 ....39 C6
Reading RG30 ....84 F5
Lingwood RG12 ....118 C3
Link Ho 2 RG14 ....105 A2
Link Rd Datchet SL3 ......68 C6
East Bedfont TW14 ....98 F8
Newbury RG14 ....105 A2
Link The Slough SL2 ......43 B7
Link The *continued*
Yateley GU46 ....149 C7
Link View RG14 ....104 F7
Link Way
Arborfield Cross RG2 .....114 E2
Staines TW18 ....97 B2
Thatcham RG18 ....106 B4
Links App HP10 ....3 B8
Links Dr RG30 ....85 A8
Links Rd Ashford TW15 ....97 E3
Flackwell Heath HP10 ......3 C8
Links The SL5 ....119 E7
Links Wy HP10 ....3 B8
Linkscroft Ave TW15 ......98 B2
Linkswood Rd SL1 ....21 C3
Linkway Camberley GU15 .151 C4
Crowthorne RG45 ....142 F5
Linnet Cl RG31 ....84 B6
Linnet La RG20 ....131 F3
Linnet Wlk RG41 ....115 F6
Lintott Ct TW19 ....70 D1
Lion Cl TW17 ....124 E6
Lion Mews 3 RG17 ....25 B2
Lionel Ct RG10 ....61 D5
Lip La Wickham RG20 .....75 E2
Wickham,Elcot RG20 ....102 D8
Lippincote Ct RG31 ....57 E3
Lipscomb Cl RG18 ....79 B6
Lipscombe Cl RG14 .....104 E2
Liscombe RG12 ....118 B2
Liscombe Ho RG12 ......118 B2
Lisle Cl RG14 ....104 F5
Lismore Cl RG5 ....87 E4
Lismore Ct TW18 ....97 B3
Lismore Pk SL2 ....42 F7
Lisset Rd SL6 ....40 A6
Lister Cl RG8 ....57 C5
Liston Ct 5 SL7 ....1 D2
Liston Rd SL7 ....1 D2
Litcham Spur SL1 ....42 D7
Lithgow's Rd TW14,TW6 ..71 F3
Littington Cl RG6 ....114 C8
Little Aldershot La
RG26 ....134 B2
Little Boltons 7 SL7 ......1 E2
Little Bowden La RG8 ....55 F4
Little Buntings SL4 ....66 F4
Little Cl HP10 ....3 B6
Little Copse GU46 ......149 D7
Little Croft GU46 ....149 D4
Little Croft Rd RG8 ......34 C5
Little Elms UB3 ....71 D7
Little Foxes RG40 ......142 A7
Little Fryth RG40 ....142 D6
Little Glebe RG4 ....60 E3
Little Heath Rd RG31 ....84 A7
Little Heath Sch RG31 ...84 B7
Little Hill Rd RG10 ......88 D4
Little John's La RG30 ....85 C8
Little La RG7 ....107 C6
Little London Rd RG7 ...136 B1
Little Marlow CE Fst Sch
SL7 ....2 C5
Little Marlow Rd SL7 ......1 E3
Little Moor GU47 ....143 C1
Little Oak Cl TW17 .....124 F5
Little Oaks Dr RG31 .....84 C8
Little Paddock GU15 ....152 A8
Little Ringdale RG12 ...118 E5
Little Saffron RG18 ......79 B6
Little St RG1 ....85 E8
Little Sutton La SL3 .....44 C1
Little Vigo GU46 ....149 B4
Little Woodlands SL4 .....66 F4
Littlebrook Ave SL2 ......41 E8
Littlecote Dr RG1 ....85 E6
Littlecote Rd SN8 ....99 B5
Littlecroft Rd 2 TW20 ....95 F3
Littledale Cl RG12 .....118 E6
Littledown Cotts SL1 ....42 F5
Littledown Rd SL1 ....42 E5
Littledown Sch SL1 ......42 F6
Littlefield Ct UB7 ....70 D7
Littlefield Gn SL6 ....63 F6
Littlejohn's La RG30 .....58 C1
Littleport Spur SL1 ......42 E7
Littlestead Cl RG4 ....59 E5
Littleton CE Inf Sch
TW17 ....125 A6
Littleton La TW17,TW18 .124 E4
Littleton Rd TW15 ....98 C1
Littlewick Green Montessori
Sch SL6 ....38 C4
Litton Rd RG2 ....86 D2
Liverpool Rd Reading RG1 .86 E8
Slough SL1 ....42 B7
Livery Cl RG1 ....86 B7
Living Rainforest The*
RG18 ....53 C5
Livingstone Ct TW19 .....97 E7
Livingstone Gdns RG5 ....87 E5
Livingstone Rd RG14 ....105 B2
Llangar Gr RG45 ....143 A5
Llanvair Cl SL5 ....120 A3
Llanvair Dr SL5 ....119 F3
Llewellyn Pk RG10 ....61 D6
Lochinvar Cl SL1 ....42 B4
Lochinver RG12 ....118 B2
Lock Ave SL6 ....20 C2
Lock Bridge Rd SL8 ......3 A3
Lock La SL6 ....39 C4
Lock Mead SL6 ....20 C2
Lock Path SL4 ....66 D8
Lock Pl RG1 ....86 D7
Lock Rd SL7 ....1 F1
Lockbridge Ct SL6 ....40 C8
Locke Gdns SL3 ....43 C4
Lockets Cl SL4 ....66 D6
Lockram La RG7 ....111 C1
Locks Ride SL5 ....92 C2
Lockside Ct RG7 ....109 C3
Locksley Ct 4 SL1 ....42 E3
Lockstile Mead RG8 ......34 C7
Lockstile Way RG8 ....34 C6
Lockton Chase SL5 .....119 D6
Lockton Ho RG40 ....116 C6
Lockyer Cl RG41 ....88 A2
Lodden View RG10 ....61 E3
Loddon Bridge Rd RG5 ...87 F6
Loddon Cl GU15 ....152 A6
Loddon Court Farm Park
Homes RG7 ....138 F7
Loddon Dr Charvil RG10 ...61 A8
Maidenhead SL6 ....39 D8
Loddon Hall Rd RG10 ....61 E5
Loddon Inf Sch The RG6 ..87 D3
Loddon Jun Sch RG6 .....87 D3
Loddon Rd SL8 ....3 A4
Loddon Spur SL1 ....42 E7
Loddon Vale Ctr RG5 ....88 A7
Lodge Cl
Englefield Green TW20 ....95 D3
Marlow SL7 ....1 E1
Slough SL1 ....42 C4
Lodge Gr GU46 ....149 F6
Lodge Rd RG10 ....88 E7
Lodge The
Newbury RG14 ....105 A4
Slough SL2 ....43 B8
Lodge Way
Charlton TW17 ....125 C7
Stanwell TW15 ....97 E6
Windsor SL4 ....66 E4
Lodgings of the Military
Knights 3 SL4 ....67 D6
Logan Cl RG30 ....84 F7
Lois Dr TW17 ....125 B4
Lomond Ave RG4 ....59 E5
London Ct RG14 ....105 C3
London Rd Ascot SL5 ...120 D5
Ashford TW15,TW18,TW19 ..97 D5
Bagshot GU15,GU19 .....145 D2
Blackwater GU15,GU17 ...150 E4
Blewbury OX11 ....11 E8
Bracknell RG12,SL5 .....119 C6
Brands Hill SL3 ....69 B8
Camberley GU15 ....151 C6
Datchet SL3 ....68 C7
Egham TW18 ....96 F4
Englefield Green TW20 ....95 C1
Newbury RG14 ....105 C3
Reading RG1 ....86 D7
Slough SL3 ....43 D2
Sunningdale,Blacknest SL5 .121 B6
Sunningdale,Shrubs Hill
SL5,GU25 ....121 C4
Thatcham RG18,RG19 ....106 F3
Twyford RG10 ....61 E6
Virginia Water GU25,
TW20 ....122 B7
Windlesham GU19,GU20,
SL5 ....146 C7
Wokingham RG40 ....116 E6
Woodley RG6 ....87 B8
London Road Bsns Pk
RG14 ....105 C4
London Road Ind Est
RG14 ....105 B3
London St Chertsey KT16 .124 A2
Reading RG1 ....86 B7
Loneacre GU20 ....146 E4
Long Barn La RG2 ....86 C3
Long Cl
Farnham Common SL2 .....22 B5
Kintbury RG17 ....102 B2
Long Close Sch SL3 ......43 A3
Long Dr SL1 ....21 C2
Long Furlong Dr SL2 .....21 E1
Long Gr Tadley RG26 ....134 D2
Upper Bucklebury RG7 ...107 C5
Long Half Acre SL6 ......38 B4
Long Hedge RG17 ....25 D2
Long Hill Rd RG12,SL5 ..119 A7
Long La Brightwalton RG20 .28 E3
Cookham Rise SL6 ....19 D5
Hermitage RG14,RG18 ....78 F2
Holyport,Braywoodside SL6 .64 D4
Holyport,Touchen-end SL6 ..64 E6
Newbury RG18 ....105 D7
Purley On T RG31 ....57 B4
Stanwell TW19 ....97 F7
Long Lane Prim Sch
RG31 ....57 B4
Long Mdw RG8 ....34 B5
Long Mickle GU47 ......143 B1
Long Readings La SL2 ....22 B2
Long Row RG20 ....49 A7
Long Wlk The
Old Windsor SL4 ....94 D7
* Windsor SL4 ....67 D4
Long's Way RG40 ....116 E7
Longacre RG14 ....130 D8
Longbourn SL4 ....67 A4
Longbourne Way KT16 ..123 F3
Longbridge Rd RG19 ....106 F2
Longcroft Rd RG19 .....106 E2
Longcross Sta KT16 ....121 F1
Longdon Rd RG41 ....88 C1
Longdown Lodge GU47 ..150 B8
Longdown Rd GU47 .....143 B1
Longfield Rd RG10 ......61 D6
Longford Ave
Feltham TW14 ....71 F1
Stanwell TW19 ....97 E7
Longford Cl GU15 ....151 D4
Longford Com Sch TW14 ..98 F8
Longford Rdbt UB7 ......70 B6
Longford Way TW19 ......97 E7
Longhurst Cl RG4 ....59 C3
Longlands Way GU15 ...152 D5
Longleat Dr RG31 ....57 B3
Longleat Gdns SL6 ......39 D6
Longleat Way TW14 .....98 D8
Longmead Ball Hill RG20 ..129 F1
Windsor SL4 ....66 E6
Longmead La SL1 ....21 D5
Longmeadow GU15,
GU16 ....151 F3
Longmoor Cl RG40 .....141 E6
Longmoor La RG7 ......137 A7
Longmoors RG42 ....117 E8
Longmore Rd RG2 ......113 D6
Longridge Cl RG30 ......85 B7
Longshot Ind Est RG12 ..117 E7
Longshot La RG12 ......117 E7
Longside Cl TW20 ......123 C8
Longview HP9 ....3 F8
Longwater Ave RG2,
RG30 ....112 D8
Longwater La RG40 ....141 E2
Longwater Rd
Bracknell RG12 ....118 C3
Finchampstead RG40 ....141 E2
Longworth Ave RG31 .....84 B7
Longworth Dr SL6 ....20 C1
Lonsdale Cl SL6 ....20 A1
Lonsdale Way SL6 ....40 C1
Look Ahead SL1 ....42 E4
Look Out Discovery Ctr The*
RG12 ....118 D1
Loosen Dr SL6 ....39 A3
Lord Knyvett Cl TW19 ....70 D1
Lord Knyvetts Ct 12
TW19 ....70 E1
Lord Mayors Dr SL2 .....22 A7
Lord Raglan Ho SL4 .....67 C4
Loring Rd SL4 ....66 F6
Lorne Cl SL1 ....42 B3
Lorne Pl 4 RG1 ....85 E7
Lorne St RG1 ....85 E7
Lorraine Rd GU15 ......151 F8
Lorraine Sch GU15 .....151 E8
Lory Ridge GU19 ....145 E4
Losfield Rd SL4 ....66 E6
Lossie Dr SL0 ....44 B6
Loughborough RG12 ....118 E3
Loundyes Cl RG18 .....106 B4
Lovatt Cl RG31 ....84 B7
Love Green La SL0 ......44 E8
Love Hill La SL3 ....44 A6
Love La Iver SL0 ....44 D7
Newbury RG14 ....105 A6
Love's Cl RG7 ....111 A3
Lovedean Ct RG12 .....118 E3
Lovegrove Dr SL2 ....21 F1
Lovejoy La SL4 ....66 D5
Lovel La SL4 ....93 B3
Lovel Rd SL4 ....93 A4
Lovelace Cl SL6 ....17 F4
Lovelace Rd RG12 ......117 E5
Lovell Cl RG9 ....35 C8
Lovells Cl GU18 ....146 B1
Loverock Rd RG30 ....58 D1
Loves Wood RG7 ....136 F5
Lovett Gdns SL6 ....20 C3
Lovett Rd TW18 ....96 C4
Lowbrook Dr SL6 ....39 A3
Lowbrook Prim Sch SL6 ..39 A3
Lowbury RG12 ....118 E5
Lower Armour Rd RG31 ...57 D1
Lower Boyndon Rd SL6 ...39 E6
Lower Britwell Rd SL2 ...21 D1
Lower Broadmoor Rd
RG45 ....143 D4
Lower Brook St 18 RG1 ...86 A6
Lower Canes GU46 .....149 A6
Lower Charles St GU15 .151 C6
Lower Church Rd GU47 .149 E8
Lower Cippenham La
SL1 ....41 F6
Lower Comm RG27 ......140 F1
Lower Cookham Rd SL6 ..20 C2
Lower Earley Way RG6 ..114 C8
Lower Earley Way (W)
RG6 ....113 F7
Lower Earley Way N RG6 .87 F2
Lower Earley Way W
RG6 ....114 A8
Lower Elmstone Dr RG31 .57 C1
Lower Farm Ct RG19 ....105 F1
Lower Field Rd RG1 .....86 A6
Lower Henley Rd RG4 ....59 D3
Lower Lees Rd SL2 ......22 B2
Lower Meadow Rd RG2 ...86 D2
Lower Mill Field GU19 ..145 D2
Lower Moor 2 GU46 ....149 D5
Lower Mount RG1 ....86 D5
Lower Nursery SL5 .....121 A4
Lower Pound La SL7 .....18 D8
Lower Raymond Almshouses
18 RG14 ....104 F2
Lower Rd Chilton OX11 ....10 D8
Cookham Rise SL6 ....19 E7
Lower Ridge SL8 ....3 B4
Lower Sandhurst Rd
RG40,GU47 ....142 C2
Lower Ventnor Cotts SL6 .19 C8
Lower Village Rd SL5 ...120 C4
Lower Way RG19 ....106 B3
Lower Wokingham Rd
RG40,RG45 ....142 D5
Lowes Cl RG9 ....36 B4
Lowestoft Cl RG6 ....87 D2
Lowestoft Dr SL1 ....41 D7
Loweswater Wlk GU15 ..152 D4
Lowfield Cl GU18 ......153 A8
Lowfield Ct RG4 ....59 C5
Lowfield Gn RG4 ....59 E4
Lowfield Rd RG4 ....59 D5
Lowlands Dr TW19 ......70 D2
Lowlands Rd GU17 .....150 C4
Lowry Cl GU47 ....150 D6
Lowther Cl RG41 ....115 F8
Lowther Rd RG41 ......115 F8
Loxwood RG6 ....87 C2
Loxwood Cl
East Bedfont TW14 ......98 D7
Three Mile Cross RG7 ...113 A4
Lucan Dr TW18 ....97 D1
Lucas Cl GU46 ....149 D5
Lucas Gn GU24 ....153 D4
Lucas Green Rd GU24 ..153 E5
Lucey Cl RG31 ....57 B3
Lucie Ave TW15 ....98 B2
Luckley Path RG40 .....116 C6
Luckley Rd RG41 ......116 B3
Luckley Wood RG41 ....116 B3
Luckley-Oakfield Sch
RG40 ....116 B3
Luckmore Dr RG6 ....87 A3
Lud Lodge TW15 ....97 E6
Luddington Ave GU25 ..122 F7
Ludgrove Sch RG40 ....116 D3
Ludlow RG12 ....118 B2
Ludlow Cl RG14 ....105 E4
Ludlow Ho SL6 ....39 E6
Ludlow Rd Feltham TW13 ..98 F5
Maidenhead SL6 ....39 E6
Luff Cl SL4 ....66 E4
Luker Ave RG9 ....15 D3
Lulworth Rd RG2 ......113 C8
Lunds Farm Rd RG5 ....88 A8
Lundy Ct SL1 ....41 E6
Lundy La RG30 ....85 C7
Lupin Cl GU19 ....145 C1
Lupin Ride RG45 ......143 B7
Luscombe Cl RG4 ......59 D2
Lutman La SL6 ....19 F2
Lutman's Haven RG10 ...37 E5
Lutter Worth Cl RG42 ...91 C1
Lutton Cl RG6 ....113 F8
Lych Gate Cl GU47 ....149 F8
Lycroft Cl RG8 ....34 C7
Lydbury RG12 ....118 F6
Lydford Ave SL2 ....42 D8
Lydford Rd RG1 ....86 E6
Lydiaville Mobile Home Pk
RG41 ....88 A2
Lydney RG12 ....118 B2
Lydsey Cl SL2 ....22 A2
Lyefield Ct RG4 ....59 B6
Lyell Place E SL4 ......66 C4
Lyell Place W SL4 .....66 C4
Lyell Rd SL4 ....66 C4
Lyell Walk E SL4 ....66 C4
Lyell Walk W SL4 ......66 C4
Lyme Gr RG31 ....57 D1
Lymington Ave GU46 ...149 C5
Lymington Gate RG4 ....58 E5
Lynch Hill La SL1 ......21 E2
Lynch Hill Prim Sch SL2 ..21 F2
Lynch La RG17 ....25 B3
Lynchets View RG17 ....24 E5
Lynden Cl SL6 ....65 B8
Lynden Mews RG2 ......86 B5
Lyndhurst Ave
Blackwater GU17 ......150 C6
Cookham Rise SL6 ......19 E6
Lyndhurst Cl RG12 ....119 A6
Lyndhurst Rd Ascot SL5 ..120 A5
Goring RG8 ....34 C7
Reading RG30 ....58 A1
Lyndhurst Sch GU15 ...151 B5
Lyndwood Dr SL4 ......68 A1
Lyndwood Par SL4 .....68 A1
Lyne Cl GU25 ....122 F3
Lyne Crossing Rd KT16,
GU25 ....123 B3
Lyne Ct KT16 ....122 F2
Lyne La Lyne KT16 .....123 A2
Virginia Water KT16,TW20,
GU25 ....123 A3
Lyne Place Manor GU25 .122 F2
Lyne Rd GU25 ....122 E3
Lynegrove Ave TW15 ....98 C3
Lyneham Gdns SL6 ......19 B1
Lyneham Rd RG45 .....143 B5
Lyngfield Pk SL6 ....65 D8
Lynmouth Ct RG1 ......59 B1
Lynmouth Rd RG1 ......59 A1
Lynn Cl TW15 ....98 D3
Lynton Cl RG5 ....87 C5
Lynton Ct
4 Newbury RG14 ......105 A4
4 Reading RG1 ....59 A1
Lynton Gn SL6 ....39 E7
Lynwood Ave
Egham TW20 ....95 E2
Slough SL3 ....43 D3
Lynwood Cres SL5 ....120 E3
Lynwood Ct TW15 ......97 F3
Lynwood Flats SL5 ....120 E4
Lyon Cl RG19 ....106 F2
Lyon Oaks RG42 ....91 B2
Lyon Rd RG45 ....143 C6
Lyon Sq RG30 ....85 A8
Lyon Way GU16 ......151 C1
Lyon Way Ind Est GU16 .151 C1
Lysander Cl RG5 ....88 A8

Lysander Mead SL6 . . . . .40 C8
Lytchet Minster Cl **4**
  RG12 . . . . .118 F4
Lytham RG12 . . . . .117 E3
Lytham Cl RG30 . . . . .85 C4
Lytham Ct SL5 . . . . .120 C4
Lytham End RG31 . . . . .57 B3
Lytham Rd RG5 . . . . .87 E7

M

Mabett Cl RG2 . . . . .140 E8
Mabley Ct RG12 . . . . .118 A3
Macadam Ave RG45 . . . . . . .143 C7
Macbeth Ct RG42 . . . . .118 E8
Macdonald Rd GU18 . . . . . . .153 C8
Mace Cl RG6 . . . . .87 A1
Mackay Cl RG31 . . . . .84 E3
Mackenzie Mall **8** SL1 . . .42 F4
Mackenzie St **2** SL1 . . . . .42 F4
Macklin Cl RG17 . . . . .100 D5
Maclaren Dr RG42 . . . . .119 A8
Macnaghten Woods
  GU15 . . . . .151 E6
Macphail Cl RG40 . . . . .116 E8
Macrae Rd GU46 . . . . .149 C6
Maddle Rd RG17 . . . . .24 D7
Madeira Pl **8** RG14 . . . . .105 A2
Madejski Stad (Reading FC)
  RG2 . . . . .112 F8
Madingley RG12 . . . . .118 B1
Madox Brown End
  GU47 . . . . .150 C6
Mafeking Rd TW19 . . . . .96 B6
Magdalene Rd
  Littleton TW17 . . . . .124 F6
  Sandhurst GU47 . . . . .143 F2
Magill Cl RG7 . . . . .113 B2
Magna Carta La TW19 . . . . .95 E7
Magna Carta Sch The
  TW18 . . . . .96 D2
Magna Rd TW20 . . . . .95 B2
Magnolia Cl
  Sandhurst GU47 . . . . .143 D1
  Winkfield RG42 . . . . .119 A8
Magnolia Ct
  Brimpton RG19 . . . . .133 B6
  Woodley RG5 . . . . .88 A7
Magnolia Gdns SL3 . . . . . . .143 C3
Magnolia Way
  Wokingham RG41 . . . . .115 F5
  Wooburn Green HP10 . . . . . .3 E7
Magpie Cl RG19 . . . . .106 B3
Magpie Way
  Reading RG31 . . . . .84 B6
  Slough SL2 . . . . .21 F1
Maguire Dr GU16 . . . . .152 C3
Mahonia Cl GU24 . . . . .153 F6
Maiden Erlegh Dr RG6 . . . . .87 B4
Maiden Erlegh Sch RG6 . . .87 B4
Maiden Lane Ctr **1** RG6 . .87 D1
Maiden Pl RG6 . . . . .87 D2
Maiden's Gn SL4 . . . . .92 B5
Maidenhead Bsns Campus
  The SL6 . . . . .38 E3
Maidenhead Court Pk
  SL6 . . . . .20 B3
Maidenhead Office Pk
  SL6 . . . . .38 E2
Maidenhead Rd
  Binfield RG40 . . . . .89 E3
  Cookham Rise SL6 . . . . .19 F6
  Newell Green RG42 . . . . . . .91 B6
  Windsor SL4 . . . . .66 E7
Maidenhead Sta SL6 . . . . . .39 F6
Maidensfield RG41 . . . . .88 D2
Main Ave RG31 . . . . .84 B6
Main Dr Bracknell RG42 . . . .91 F1
  Iver SL0 . . . . .44 E3
  Winkfield RG42,SL5 . . . . . .119 B8
  Winkfield,Newell Green
  RG42 . . . . .92 A1
Main Gate Lodges SL4 . . . . .94 F5
Main St
  Chaddleworth RG20 . . . . . .49 A7
  Chilton OX11 . . . . .10 D8
  Greenham RG19 . . . . .131 F5
  Newtown RG19 . . . . .132 A5
Mainprice Rd RG12 . . . . . . .118 E7
Mainstone Rd GU24 . . . . . .153 F3
Maise Webster Cl TW19 . . . .73 D2
Maisonettes The RG8 . . . . . .34 D8
Maitland Rd RG1 . . . . .85 E7
Maiwand Gdns RG30 . . . . . .84 D7
Maize La RG42 . . . . .91 E2
Majendie Cl RG14 . . . . .104 D5
Major's Farm Rd SL3 . . . . . .68 D7
Makepiece Rd RG42 . . . . . . .91 B1
Maker Cl RG30 . . . . .85 B5
Makins Rd RG9 . . . . .35 B7
Malders La SL6 . . . . .19 C3
Maldon Cl RG30 . . . . .85 D6
Malet Cl TW20 . . . . .96 D2
Malham Fell RG12 . . . . .118 A5
Malham Rd RG19 . . . . .106 C3
Mallard Cl Earley RG6 . . . . . .87 A3
  Twyford RG10 . . . . .61 E3
Mallard Ct RG14 . . . . .104 F3
Mallard Dr SL1 . . . . .41 F6
Mallard Row RG1 . . . . .86 A7
Mallard Way
  Padworth RG7 . . . . .109 B3
  Yateley GU46 . . . . .149 B6

Mallards The
  Frimley GU16 . . . . .151 F2
  Great Shefford RG17 . . . . . .48 A3
  Laleham TW18 . . . . .124 B7
Mallards Way GU18 . . . . . . .153 A8
Mallory Ave RG14 . . . . .59 D6
Mallow Gdns RG18 . . . . . . .106 D5
Mallow Pk SL6 . . . . .19 C1
Mallowdale Rd RG12 . . . . . .118 E2
Malone Rd RG5 . . . . .87 D6
Malpas Rd SL2 . . . . .43 B6
Malt Hill Egham TW20 . . . . . .95 F2
  Newell Green RG42 . . . . . . .91 E5
Malt Ho SL4 . . . . .95 B8
Malt House Cl SL4 . . . . .95 B8
Malt Shovel La RG17 . . . . . .24 F4
Maltby Way RG6 . . . . .113 F8
Malthouse Ct RG19 . . . . . . .106 F2
Malthouse Flats RG9 . . . . . .16 D6
Malthouse La
  4 Reading RG1 . . . . .85 F8
  West End GU24 . . . . .153 F7
Malthouse Way **2** SL7 . . . .1 D1
Maltings Pl **3** RG1 . . . . . .86 A7
Maltings The
  Staines TW18 . . . . .96 E4
  Thatcham RG18 . . . . .106 F2
  West Ilsley RG20 . . . . .10 B1
Malton Ave SL1 . . . . .42 B6
Malvern Cl RG5 . . . . .87 F6
Malvern Ct Brands Hill SL3 . . .69 A8
  Newbury RG14 . . . . .104 F1
  Reading RG1 . . . . .86 D6
Malvern Rd
  Harlington UB3 . . . . .71 E7
  Maidenhead SL6 . . . . .19 D1
  Yateley GU17 . . . . .149 F1
Malvern Way RG10 . . . . .61 D7
Malyons The TW17 . . . . . . .125 D3
Man's Hill RG7 . . . . .111 C2
Managua Rd RG4 . . . . .59 E2
Manchester Rd RG1 . . . . . . .86 E7
Mandarin Ct RG14 . . . . .105 C2
Mandela Ct **2** RG1 . . . . . . .86 D7
Mandeville Cl RG30 . . . . . . .84 F6
Mandeville Ct TW20 . . . . . . .96 A4
Mandeville Rd TW17 . . . . . .125 A4
Manea Cl RG6 . . . . .114 C8
Manfield Cl SL2 . . . . .22 A2
Manners Rd RG5 . . . . .87 D7
Mannock Ave RG4 . . . . .59 C7
Manor Bglws RG20 . . . . .31 D4
Manor Cl RG42 . . . . .91 A1
Manor Cres RG20 . . . . .31 D4
Manor Ct Marlow SL7 . . . . . . .1 C3
  Slough, Cippenham SL1 . . . .41 F5
  4 Slough, Upton Park SL1 . .42 F3
Manor Farm Ave TW17 . . . .125 B3
Manor Farm Cl SL4 . . . . .66 F4
Manor Farm Ct SL4 . . . . .66 F4
Manor Farm Ct TW20 . . . . . .96 A3
Manor Farm Ho SL4 . . . . . . .66 F4
Manor Farm La
  Egham TW20 . . . . .96 A3
  Tidmarsh RG8 . . . . .56 C2
Manor Farm Rd RG2 . . . . . . .86 B2
Manor Gdns HP10 . . . . .3 F5
Manor Gr SL6 . . . . .65 D6
Manor Ho The GU15 . . . . . .151 D6
Manor House Ct
  Lower Halliford TW17 . . . . .125 B2
  Reading RG6 . . . . .87 A5
Manor House Dr SL5 . . . . . . .93 A1
Manor House La SL3 . . . . . . .68 B6
Manor La Brimpton RG7 . . . .133 C6
  Chieveley RG20 . . . . .51 F4
  Harlington UB3 . . . . .71 D8
  Hermitage RG18 . . . . .79 B8
  Leckhampstead RG20 . . . . . .49 F4
  Maidenhead SL6 . . . . .39 E4
  Newbury RG14 . . . . .105 E5
Manor Leaze TW20 . . . . .96 B3
Manor Mead SL6 TW17 . . . .125 B4
Manor Park Cl RG30 . . . . . . .84 C6
Manor Park Dr
  Wokingham RG40 . . . . . . .141 E6
  Yateley GU46 . . . . .149 E6
Manor Pk Froxfield SN8 . . . . .99 B4
  Staines TW18 . . . . .96 D5
Manor Pl Newbury RG14 . . . .104 D5
  Wokingham RG41 . . . . .116 B4
Manor Prim Sch RG30 . . . . . .85 A4
Manor Rd Ashford TW15 . . . .98 A3
  Goring RG8 . . . . .34 B5
  Henley-On-T RG9 . . . . .35 D8
  Letcombe Bassett OX12 . . . . .7 C5
  Maidenhead SL6 . . . . .39 E4
  Oatlands Park KT12 . . . . . .125 F2
  Whitchurch-on-T RG8 . . . . . .56 C7
  Windsor SL4 . . . . .66 E5
  Wokingham RG41 . . . . .116 A2
Manor The RG12 . . . . .113 E5
Manor Way
  Bagshot GU19 . . . . .145 F3
  Egham TW20 . . . . .95 F2
  Holyport SL6 . . . . .65 C4
Manor Wood Gate RG9 . . . . .36 A4
Manorcroft Prim Sch
  TW20 . . . . .96 A2
Manorcrofts Rd TW20 . . . . . .96 A2
Manse Cl UB3 . . . . .71 D8
Mansel Cl SL2 . . . . .43 B8
Mansell Cl SL4 . . . . .66 E5
Mansell Ct RG2 . . . . .113 B6
Mansfield Cl SL5 . . . . .119 D7
Mansfield Cres RG12 . . . . . .118 B3
Mansfield Ho **4** TW18 . . . .96 F3

Mansfield Pl SL5 . . . . .119 D8
Mansfield Rd Reading RG1 . . .85 F6
  Wokingham RG41 . . . . .116 A5
Mansion House St **7**
  RG14 . . . . .105 A3
Mansion La SL0 . . . . .44 C6
Manston Dr RG12 . . . . .118 C3
Mant Cl RG20 . . . . .75 D5
Manygate La TW17 . . . . . . .125 C3
Maple Bank RG10 . . . . .61 E6
Maple Cl
  Blackwater GU17 . . . . .150 C5
  Maidenhead SL6 . . . . .39 C5
  Sandhurst GU47 . . . . .142 F1
  Winnersh RG41 . . . . .88 D3
Maple Cres
  Newbury RG14 . . . . .105 A4
  Slough SL2 . . . . .43 B6
Maple Ct Ashford TW15 . . . .98 D1
  3 Bracknell RG12 . . . . . .118 F5
  Englefield Green TW20 . . . . .95 B2
  Goring RG8 . . . . .34 B6
  Marlow SL7 . . . . .1 E3
  Windsor SL4 . . . . .67 C4
Maple Dr
  Crowthorne RG45 . . . . .143 C7
  Lightwater GU18 . . . . .152 F8
  Reading RG30 . . . . .84 D6
Maple Gdns Reading RG2 . . . .86 E2
  Stanwell TW19 . . . . .97 E6
  Yateley GU46 . . . . .149 D5
Maple Gr RG4 . . . . .60 E1
Maple La RG8 . . . . .55 B5
Maple Rise SL7 . . . . .1 E3
Mapledean RG4 . . . . .58 E3
Mapledurham Dr RG8 . . . . . .57 C5
Mapledurham Ho* RG31 57 E6
Mapledurham View
  RG31 . . . . .57 D2
Mapledurham Watermill* . . .
  RG31 . . . . .57 D6
Mapledurham Wlk SL6 . . . . .19 E3
Maples The **13** SL8 . . . . . . .3 C3
Maplin Pk SL3 . . . . .44 B4
Marathon Cl RG6 . . . . .88 B8
Marbeck Cl SL4 . . . . .66 D6
Marbull Way RG42 . . . . .91 B2
Marchant Cl RG19 . . . . .131 D7
Marchant Ct SL7 . . . . .2 A3
Marcheria Cl RG12 . . . . .118 A3
Marchwood Ave RG4 . . . . . . .59 C7
Marcia Ct SL1 . . . . .41 F5
Marconi Rd RG14 . . . . .105 B4
Marcus Cl RG30 . . . . .85 B7
Mardale RG12 . . . . .152 C4
Mardy Rd4 . . . . .58 E5
Mare La RG10 . . . . .63 E3
Marefield RG6 . . . . .87 C2
Marefield Rd SL7 . . . . .1 C2
Marescroft Rd SL2 . . . . .21 E1
Mareshall Ave RG42 . . . . . . .91 B2
Marfleet Cl **1** RG6 . . . . . . .87 C2
Margaret Cl
  Reading RG2 . . . . .113 C7
  Staines TW18 . . . . .97 D2
Maria Ct **13** RG30 . . . . . . .85 C6
Marie Davis Ct **11** RG1 . . .86 B7
Marigold Cl RG45 . . . . .142 F6
Marina Cl KT16 . . . . .124 C1
Marina Way Burnham SL1 . . .41 D6
  Iver SL0 . . . . .44 F6
Mariners La RG7 . . . . .82 B3
Marino Way RG40 . . . . .141 A6
Marion Ave TW17 . . . . .125 B4
Marish Ct SL3 . . . . .44 A3
Marish Jun Sch SL3 . . . . .44 A3
Marish Wharf Ind Est
  SL3 . . . . .43 E4
Marjory Kinnon Sch
  TW14 . . . . .71 E2
Markby Way RG6 . . . . .87 E2
Market La SL3 . . . . .44 A2
Market Pl Bracknell RG12 . . .118 B7
  Colnbrook SL3 . . . . .69 C7
  Henley-On-T RG9 . . . . .15 D2
  Lambourn RG17 . . . . .25 B2
  8 Newbury RG14 . . . . . .105 A3
  Reading RG1 . . . . .86 B7
  Wargrave RG10 . . . . .36 D3
  Wokingham RG40 . . . . .116 B7
Market Place Mews RG9 . . . .15 D2
Market Sq **8** Marlow SL7 . . .1 D2
  Staines TW18 . . . . .96 E4
Market St Bracknell RG12 . . .118 B7
  Maidenhead SL6 . . . . .39 F7
  Newbury RG14 . . . . .105 A2
  6 Windsor SL4 . . . . .67 D6
Market Way **11** RG1 . . . . . .86 B7
Markham Centre Trad Est
  The RG7 . . . . .83 F2
Markham Ct GU15 . . . . .151 D6
Markham Mews RG40 . . . . . .116 C6
Marks Rd RG41 . . . . .116 A8
Marlborough Ave RG1 . . . . . .86 D5
Marlborough Cl SL6 . . . . .39 A6
Marlborough Cres UB3 . . . . . .71 D7
Marlborough Ct
  Hungerford RG17 . . . . .100 D5
  Reading RG1 . . . . .85 F6
  Slough SL1 . . . . .41 E7
  Wokingham RG40 . . . . .116 D7
Marlborough Ho
  8 Maidenhead SL6 . . . . . .39 F6
  Marlow SL7 . . . . .1 D2
Marlborough Rd
  Ashford TW15 . . . . .97 E3
  Maidenhead SL6 . . . . .39 A6

Marlborough Rd *continued*
  Slough SL3 . . . . .43 D2
Marlborough Rise GU15 . . . .151 E6
Marlborough Way RG31 . . . . .84 B4
Marley Croft TW18 . . . . .96 E5
Marlin Cl TW16 . . . . .98 E2
Marlin Ct SL7 . . . . .1 D1
Marling Cl RG31 . . . . .57 C2
Marlow Bridge La SL7 . . . . . .18 E8
Marlow CE Inf Sch SL7 . . . . .1 D3
Marlow Com Hospl SL7 . . . . . .1 C2
Marlow Lodge **13** SL6 . . . .39 F6
Marlow Mill SL7 . . . . .1 E1
Marlow Rd Bisham SL6 . . . . . .18 E4
  Bisham SL7 . . . . .18 E4
  Henley-On-T RG9 . . . . .15 E3
  Little Marlow SL7,SL8 . . . . . .2 D5
  Maidenhead SL6 . . . . .39 F7
  Marlow Bottom SL7 . . . . .1 B7
  Marlow Bottom SL7 . . . . . . .84 E6
  Marlow Sta SL7 . . . . .1 E1
Marlowes The RG14 . . . . . . .130 F8
Marlston Cotts RG18 . . . . . . .79 F5
Marlston Rd RG18 . . . . .79 D5
Marmion Rd RG9 . . . . .35 D8
Marquis Ct TW19 . . . . .97 E7
Marquis Pl **4** RG1 . . . . .86 E7
Marriott Cl TW14 . . . . .71 D1
Mars Cl RG41 . . . . .115 F6
Mars Ho RG7 . . . . .134 E2
Marsack St RG4 . . . . .59 C2
Marsh Ct RG30 . . . . .85 D8
Marsh La Curridge RG18 . . . . .78 D4
  Hungerford RG17 . . . . .100 B5
  Newbury RG14 . . . . .105 A3
  Taplow SL6 . . . . .40 E5
Marsh Mills RG9 . . . . .16 A4
Marsh Rd RG18 . . . . .106 E4
Marshall Cl
  Frimley GU16 . . . . .152 D2
  Purley On T RG8 . . . . .57 D4
Marshall Ho **1** RG30 . . . . .85 B7
Marshall Rd GU47 . . . . .150 D6
Marshalls Ct RG14 . . . . .104 D5
Marsham Ho RG42 . . . . .91 B1
Marshaw Ct RG2 . . . . .86 C3
Marshfield SL3 . . . . .68 C6
Marshgate Trad Est SL4 . . . . .41 A7
Marshland Sq RG4 . . . . .59 B5
Marston Way SL5 . . . . .119 E7
Martel Cl GU15 . . . . .152 C7
Marten Pl RG31 . . . . .57 B3
Martin Cl Windsor SL4 . . . . . .66 D6
  Woodley RG5 . . . . .87 E6
Martin Rd Maidenhead SL6 . . .39 F8
  Slough SL1 . . . . .42 E3
Martin Way GU16 . . . . .151 E2
Martin's Heron Sta
  RG12 . . . . .118 F5
Martin's Plain SL2 . . . . .22 F3
Martindale Ave GU15 . . . . . .152 C4
Martineau La RG10 . . . . .88 E7
Martins Cl GU17 . . . . .150 D4
Martins Dr RG41 . . . . .116 C6
Martins The RG19 . . . . .106 F2
Marunden Gn SL2 . . . . .21 C2
Marvyn Cotts RG7 . . . . .110 C3
Mary Drew Almshouses The
  TW20 . . . . .95 D2
Mary Hare Gram Sch
  RG14 . . . . .77 F3
Mary Lyne Almshouses
  RG30 . . . . .84 F5
Mary Mead RG42 . . . . .91 D2
Mary Morgan Ct SL2 . . . . . . .42 D8
Maryland RG40 . . . . .141 E8
Maryside SL3 . . . . .43 E4
Mascoll Path SL2 . . . . .21 F2
Masdar Gdns RG40 . . . . . . .141 E6
Masefield Gdns RG45 . . . . . .143 E3
Masefield Rd RG18 . . . . .106 D4
Masefield Way TW19 . . . . . . .97 F7
Mason Cl GU46 . . . . .149 E5
Mason Ct Ball Hill RG20 . . . .129 F1
  3 Reading RG1 . . . . .85 F8
Mason Pl GU47 . . . . .149 F8
Mason St RG1 . . . . .85 E8
Masonic Hall Rd KT16 . . . . . .123 F3
Masons Rd SL1 . . . . .41 E6
Master Cl RG5 . . . . .88 B8
Mathisen Way SL3 . . . . .69 E6
Matlock Rd RG4 . . . . .58 E4
Matson Dr RG9 . . . . .15 F2
Matthew Arnold Cl TW18 . . . .97 C2
Matthew Arnold Sch The
  TW18 . . . . .97 C2
Matthew Ct TW15 . . . . .97 E5
Matthews Chase RG42 . . . . . .90 F1
Matthews Ct RG19 . . . . .106 B4
Matthews La TW18 . . . . .96 F4
Matthews Rd GU15 . . . . .151 B7
Matthewsgreen Rd
  RG41 . . . . .116 A8
Maudsley Ho SL6 . . . . .40 B7
Maultway Cl GU15 . . . . .152 B8
Maultway Cres GU15 . . . . . .152 B8
Maultway N GU15 . . . . .145 B1
Maultway The GU15,
  GU16 . . . . .152 D6
Maureen Campbell Ct
  RG14 . . . . .125 B4
Mawbray Cl RG6 . . . . .87 E2
Maxdata Ctr The RG12 . . . . .118 A7
Maxine Cl GU47 . . . . .143 B1
Maxwell Cl RG5 . . . . .87 E8

Maxwell Ct SL1 . . . . .21 C1
Maxwell Rd TW15 . . . . .98 C2
May Cl **2** GU47 . . . . .150 D8
May Fields
  Sindlesham RG41 . . . . .115 A8
  Winnersh RG41 . . . . .88 A1
May Pk RG31 . . . . .84 E4
May Tree Cl SL7 . . . . .1 C6
May's La RG7 . . . . .136 A7
Maybrick Cl GU47 . . . . .142 F1
Maybury Cl SL1 . . . . .41 D7
Mayfair RG30 . . . . .84 D7
Mayfair Dr RG14 . . . . .104 E1
Mayfield Ave RG31 . . . . .84 B4
Mayfield Cl TW15 . . . . .98 B2
Mayfield Cotts RG20 . . . . . . .31 C4
Mayfield Dr
  Caversham RG4 . . . . .59 D3
  Windsor SL4 . . . . .67 A4
Mayfield Gdns TW18 . . . . . . .96 F2
Mayfield Light Ind Est
  SL4 . . . . .93 B5
Mayfield Rd
  Camberley GU15 . . . . .151 B1
  Wooburn Green HP10 . . . . . .3 E6
Mayflower Ct **8** RG1 . . . . . .86 B7
Mayflower Dr GU46 . . . . . . .149 A6
Mayflower Way SL2 . . . . .22 C8
Maying The RG2 . . . . .113 B6
Maynard Ct RG18 . . . . .106 D5
Maynard Ct
  6 Staines TW18 . . . . .97 A4
  Windsor SL4 . . . . .67 A6
Mayo Rd RG17 . . . . .125 F2
Mayors La RG14 . . . . .105 A2
Mayow Cl RG19 . . . . .106 F2
Maypole Rd SL6 . . . . .41 A8
Mays Cl RG6 . . . . .87 B5
Mays La RG6 . . . . .87 B5
Mays Rd RG40 . . . . .116 E6
Maywood Dr GU15 . . . . .152 A7
Mc Carthy Way RG40 . . . . . .141 F8
McAuliffe Dr SL1,SL2 . . . . . . .21 F8
McCrae's Wlk RG10 . . . . .36 D2
McKay Trad Est SL3 . . . . .69 E5
McKernan Ct GU47 . . . . .149 F8
McNair Cl RG6 . . . . .87 A1
Meachen Ct RG40 . . . . .116 C6
Mead Ave SL3 . . . . .44 B4
Mead Cl Egham TW20 . . . . . .96 B2
  2 Marlow SL7 . . . . .1 F3
  Reading RG31 . . . . .84 B4
  Slough SL3 . . . . .44 B4
Mead Ct TW20 . . . . .96 C2
Mead Haze SL6 . . . . .20 C2
Mead La Chertsey KT16 . . . .124 C1
  Upper Basildon RG8 . . . . . . .55 D8
Mead Ho The RG17 . . . . .48 B2
Mead Way SL1 . . . . .41 D8
Mead Wlk SL3 . . . . .44 B4
Meade Ct GU19 . . . . .145 F3
Meadfield Ave SL3 . . . . .44 A3
Meadfield Rd SL3 . . . . .44 A3
Meadhurst Pk TW16 . . . . . . .98 E2
Meadhurst Rd KT16 . . . . . . .124 B1
Meadow Bank
  Blackwater GU17 . . . . .150 D4
  Compton RG20 . . . . .31 E5
  Goring RG8 . . . . .34 C6
  Marlow SL7 . . . . .1 F1
  Moulsford OX10 . . . . .13 F4
  Old Windsor SL4 . . . . .68 B2
Meadow Cotts
  Shepperton TW17 . . . . .125 B3
  West End GU24 . . . . .153 F7
Meadow Croft RG17 . . . . .73 A1
Meadow Ct TW18 . . . . .96 E5
Meadow Gdns TW18 . . . . . . .96 D3
Meadow La Eton SL4 . . . . . . .67 C7
  Pangbourne RG8 . . . . .56 D5
Meadow Rd Ashford TW15 . . .98 D3
  Earley RG6 . . . . .87 D3
  Henley-On-T RG9 . . . . .15 E1
  Newbury RG14 . . . . .130 F8
  Reading RG1 . . . . .58 F1
  Slough SL3 . . . . .43 E3
  Wentworth GU25 . . . . .121 E4
  Wokingham RG41 . . . . .116 A5
Meadow Vale Prim Sch
  RG42 . . . . .117 D8
Meadow View
  Chertsey KT16 . . . . .124 C1
  Marlow Bottom SL7 . . . . .1 E6
  Winnersh RG41 . . . . .88 D3
Meadow View La SL6 . . . . . . .64 E8
Meadow Way
  Blackwater GU17 . . . . .150 C5
  Bracknell RG42 . . . . .91 A1
  Dorney SL6 . . . . .65 C6
  Fifield SL6 . . . . .65 D6
  Old Windsor SL4 . . . . .68 B2
  Theale RG7 . . . . .83 D3
  West Ilsley RG20 . . . . .10 A5
  Wokingham RG40 . . . . .116 A5
Meadow Wlk
  Bourne End SL8 . . . . .3 A5
  Wokingham RG40 . . . . .116 A6
Meadowbank RG20 . . . . .29 B8
Meadowbank Rd GU18 . . . . .146 C1
Meadowbrook Cl SL3 . . . . . . .69 F6
Meadowbrook Montessori
  Sch RG42 . . . . .91 F4
Meadowcroft Rd RG2 . . . . . .113 C8
Meadowlea Cl UB7 . . . . .70 D8

Meadows (Superstores) The GU47 ....150 E5
Meadows Bsns Pk The GU17 ....150 A2
Meadows Sch The HP10 ...3 E7
Meadows The HP10 ....3 B8
Meadowside RG31 ......57 B1
Meadowside Rd RG8 ....56 D5
Meadowsweet Cl RG18 .106 E4
Meadowview TW19 ......69 F2
Meads Cl RG20 ....50 D7
Meads The
  Stoke Poges SL2 ....23 A2
  4 Windsor SL4 ....67 A5
Meadway Ashford TW15 ..98 A4
  Frimley GU16 ....151 F2
  Staines TW18 ....97 A1
Meadway SL1 ....21 C2
Meadway Prec RG40 ....85 A6
Meadway The RG30 .....84 E7
Meare Est HP10 ....3 E8
Mearings The RG30 ....111 F5
Measham Way RG6 ....87 C2
Meashill Way OX11 ....9 F8
Meavy Gdns RG2 ....86 B2
Medallion Pl SL6 ......40 B7
Mede Cl TW19 ....95 D7
Mede Ct TW18 ....96 E5
Medina Cl RG41 ....115 E7
Medlake Rd TW20 ......96 C2
Medlar Dr GU17 ....150 F3
Medway Cl
  Thatcham RG18 ....106 B5
  Wokingham RG41 ....115 F7
Medway Ct RG30 ......85 D6
Melbourne Ave
  Slough SL1 ....42 C7
  Winnersh RG41 ....88 C1
Melbury Cl KT16 ......124 A2
Meldreth Way Earley RG6 .87 C1
  Shinfield RG6 ....114 D8
Melford Gn RG14 ......130 C6
Melford Gn RG4 ....59 C6
Melksham Cl RG6 ......113 E8
Melling Cl RG6 ....87 E3
Mellor Wlk
  3 Reading RG1 ....86 B5
  12 Windsor SL4 ....67 D6
Melody Cl RG41 ....88 C3
Melrose RG12 ....118 B1
Melrose Ave RG6 .....87 A5
Melrose Gdns RG14 ...114 E2
Melton Ct SL16 ....39 F6
Melville Ave GU16 ....151 F1
Membury Wlk RG12 ..118 F5
Memorial Ave RG9 ....35 E2
Mendip Cl Charvil RG10 ..61 B4
  Harlington UB3 ....71 D7
  Slough SL3 ....44 A1
Mendip Dr RG31 ....84 A6
Mendip Rd RG12 ......118 E4
Menpes Rd RG31 .....57 C4
Mentone Cotts RG10 ..62 F5
Meon Cl RG26 ....135 A1
Merchants Pl 5 RG1 ...86 A8
Mercia Rd SL6 ....39 C4
Mercian Way SL1 ....41 D5
Mercury Ave RG41 ...115 E6
Mercury Ho RG7 .....134 E2
Mere Cl SL7 ....1 F2
Mere Rd
  Shepperton TW17 .....125 B3
  Slough SL1 ....42 F3
Mereoak La
  Grazeley RG7 ....112 F4
  Three Mile Cross RG7 .113 A5
Mereoak Pk RG7 .....113 A5
Mereside Pk TW15 ...98 C4
Meridian Ct SL5 .....120 D5
Merlewood RG12 .....118 D4
Merley Ct SL4 ....69 B8
Merlin Clove RG42 ...92 B2
Merlin Ct Frimley GU16 .151 D1
  Maidenhead SL6 ......39 B8
Mermaid Cl RG41 ....88 B2
Merrifield Cl RG6 ....114 D8
Merrivale Gdns RG2 ..86 B1
Merron Cl GU46 .....149 C5
Merryhill Green La RG41 .88 D3
Merryhill Rd RG42 ...118 B8
Merryman Dr RG45 ..143 A7
Merryweather Cl RG40 .115 F1
Merrywood Pk GU15 .151 F4
Mersey Way RG18 ...106 B5
Merthyr Vale RG4 ...59 A6
Merton Cl Maidenhead SL6 .39 C3
  Sandhurst GU47 ......143 E2
Merton Rd SL1 ......43 A3
Merton Rd N RG2 ...86 B1
Merton Rd S RG2 ...86 B1
Mertonford RG40 ...116 D5
Mervyn Rd TW17 ...125 C2
Merwin Way SL4 ...64 D4
Meryton Ho SL4 ...67 A8
Metcalf Rd TW15 ...98 B3
Meteor Cl RG5 .....88 A7
Metro Ctr The RG41 .89 A2
Mews The Newbury RG14 .104 E2
  Sonning RG4 ....60 E6
  Swallowfield RG7 .....140 C7
Mey Cl RG41 ....84 C5
Meyrick Dr RG14 ...105 D4
Mezel Hill Cotts SL4 .94 C3
Michael Cl SL6 .....39 C5
Michaelmas Cl GU46 .149 D4
Micheldever Way RG12 .118 F4

Michelet Cl GU18 .....146 B1
Micklands Prim Sch RG4 .59 D4
Micklands Rd RG4 ....59 E3
Mickle Hill GU47 .....143 A1
Micro Ctr The RG2 ...86 B2
Midas Ho RG7 ......134 E2
Midcroft SL2 ....22 B1
Middle Cl Frimley GU15 .152 C6
  Newbury RG14 ....130 D7
Middle Farm Cl RG20 .51 B2
Middle Gn Slough SL3 .43 E6
  Staines TW18 ....97 D1
Middle Gordon Rd
  GU15 ....151 D5
Middle Hill TW20 ....95 D3
Middle Springs RG8 ..34 C8
Middle Wlk SL1 ......21 C2
Middlefields RG10 ...61 E6
Middlefields GU10 ...61 E6
Middlegreen Rd SL3 ..43 F5
Middlegreen Trad Est
  SL3 ....43 D4
Middleton Cl RG14 ...105 E5
Middleton Rd GU15 ..151 F7
Middletons Cl RG17 ..100 E7
Midgham Halt RG7 ...108 C2
Midsummer Mdw RG4 .58 F6
Midway Ave
  Chertsey KT16 ....124 A6
  Thorpe TW20 ....123 B6
Midway Cl TW19 ....97 B5
Midwinter Cl RG30 ..84 E8
Milam Cl RG2 ....140 E8
Milbanke Ct RG12 ...117 F7
Milbanke Way RG12 .117 F7
Mildenhall Cl RG6 ...87 D2
Mildenhall Rd SL1 ...42 E7
Mile Elm SL7 ....2 A3
Miles Pl GU18 ......152 F7
Miles Way RG5 ......88 A7
Milestone Ave RG10 .61 A5
Milestone Cres RG10 .61 A4
Milestone View Ct RG4 .59 E4
Milestone Way RG4 ..59 D6
Milford Ct SL1 ....43 A4
Milkhouse Rd RG20 ..103 D4
Mill Bank RG17 .....102 A3
Mill Cl Bagshot GU19 .145 D3
  Wokingham RG41 ...115 F7
Mill Cotts HP10 .....3 D5
Mill Ct SL3 ....69 C4
Mill Farm Ave TW16 .98 E1
Mill Field GU19 ....145 D3
Mill Gn Bracknell RG42 .90 E1
  Caversham RG4 ......59 A1
Mill Hall Sch RG20 ..131 D8
Mill House La RG10 ..123 B5
Mill La Ascot SL5 ...121 A7
  Bracknell RG12 ......117 F5
  Colthrop RG19 ......107 B2
  Cookham SL6 ....20 C7
  Earley RG6 ....87 E3
  Henley-On-T RG9 ....35 F8
  Horton SL3 ....69 C4
  Hurley SL6 ....17 F4
  Lamborn RG17 ....25 C2
  Newbury RG14 ......105 B3
  Padworth RG7 ......109 C2
  Reading RG1 ....86 B7
  Shiplake RG9 ....36 A2
  Sindlesham RG41 ...115 A8
  Taplow SL6 ....40 C8
  Thorpe TW20 ....123 C5
  Windsor SL4 ....67 A7
  Winnersh RG41 .....87 F1
  Yateley GU46 ....149 D8
Mill Mead TW18 ...96 F4
Mill Pl SL3 ....68 D5
Mill Place Cott SL3 ..68 D5
Mill Pond Rd GU20 ..146 B6
Mill Rd
  Burghfield Common RG30 ..84 F2
  Caversham RG4 .....59 C1
  Goring RG8 ....34 C8
  Marlow SL7 ....1 E1
  Shiplake RG9 ....36 B3
Mill Reef Cl RG19 ..105 F3
Mill Ride SL5 ......119 D8
Mill St Colnbrook SL3 .69 D7
  Slough SL2 ....42 F5
Mill W SL2 ....42 F5
Millars Bsns Ctr RG41 .116 A4
Millbank SL7 ....1 F2
Millbank Cres RG5 ..87 F6
Millboard Rd SL8 ..3 B3
Millbridge Rd GU46 .149 B8
Millbrook Way SL3 ..69 E5
Milldown Ave RG8 ..34 C7
Milldown Rd RG8 ...34 C7
Millennium Ct RG2 ..86 D4
Millennium Way RG12 .118 C8
Miller Dr RG41 .....88 A2
Miller's Ct TW20 ..96 D2
Miller's Field RG17 .75 F1
Miller's La SL4 ....68 A1
Millers Cl Goring RG8 .34 B7
  Staines TW18 ......97 B3
Millers Ct SL4 .....59 C1
Millers Gr RG31 ...84 E4
Milley Rd RG10 ...62 B8
Milley Rd RG10 ...62 B8
Millfield Charlton TW16 .125 D8
  Lambourn RG17 ....25 C2
Milford Rd RG1 ...86 D7
Millgreen La RG19 .132 F3
Millholme Wlk GU15 .152 C6
Millington Cl RG2 ..86 D3

Millins Cl GU47 .....143 E1
Millmead RG41 .....116 A7
Millmere GU46 .....149 D7
Mills Spur SL4 .....95 B8
Millside SL3 ....3 C3
Millstream Cl RG14 .105 D3
Millstream La SL1 ..41 E5
Millstream Way HP10 .3 E8
Millworth La RG2 ...113 E4
Milman Cl RG12 ....119 A7
Milman Rd RG2 ....86 B5
Milner Rd SL1 .....41 A8
Milsom Ct RG2 ....113 E5
Milton Cl Bracknell RG12 .118 B3
  Henley-On-T RG9 ...15 D2
  Horton SL3 ....69 A4
Milton Ct RG40 ....116 B7
  Lower Littleton TW17 .124 E5
  Wokingham RG40 ...116 B6
Milton Gdns
  Stanwell TW19 ......97 F7
  Wokingham RG40 ...116 B6
Milton Rd Earley RG6 ..87 A7
  Egham TW20 ....95 F3
  Slough SL2 ....22 D1
  Wokingham RG40,RG41 .116 B6
Milton Way SL6 ....61 F5
Milverton Cl SL6 ...39 E3
Milward Gdns RG12 .117 C7
Mina Ave SL3 ......43 D4
Minchin Gn RG42 ...90 C3
Minden Cl RG41 ....115 E6
Minerva Cl TW19 ...70 A2
Minerva Ho RG7 ...134 E2
Ministry Rd RG19 ..132 A5
Minley Rd RG17 ...149 E1
Minniecroft Rd SL1 .21 B2
Minorca Ave GU16 .152 E2
Minorca Rd GU16 ..152 E1
Minoru Pl RG42 ....90 D3
Minstead Cl RG12 ..118 F6
Minstead Dr GU46 .149 C5
Minster Ct
  Camberley GU15 ...151 D7
  Camberley,York Town
  GU15 ....150 F4
Minster St RG1 ....86 B7
Minster Way SL3 ..44 C2
Minsterley Ave TW16, TW17 ....125 C5
Mint Cl RG6 ......86 F1
Minter Ct RG40 ...134 F1
Minton Cl RG30 ...84 F8
Minton Rise SL6 ..41 B7
Mirador Cres SL2 ..43 B6
Mire La RG10 .....62 D4
Misbourne Ct SL3 .44 A2
Missenden Ct TW14 .98 F7
Missenden Gdns SL1 .42 B3
Mistletoe Rd GU46 .149 D4
Mitcham Cl RG2 ...86 B5
Mitcham Rd GU15 .145 A1
Mitchell Bldgs GU46 .149 B5
Mitchell Cl SL1 ...42 A4
Mitchell Way RG5 .88 B7
Mitford Cl RG2 ....113 D8
Mitre Cl TW17 ....125 D5
Mitre Pl RG42 ....91 B2
Mixnams La KT16 .124 A6
Moat Dr SL2 ....43 C8
Modbury Gdns RG2 .86 C2
Moffats Cl GU47 ...150 A8
Moffy Hill SL6 ....19 E2
Mohawk Way RG5 .88 B7
Mole Rd RG2,RG41 .114 F5
Moles Cl RG40 ....116 B5
Mollison Cl RG5 ...88 B8
Molly Millar Bridge RG41 ....116 B4
Molly Millar's La RG41 .116 A4
Molyneux Rd GU20 .146 D4
Molyns Ho RG9 ...15 E3
Molyns Mews SL1 .41 A5
Monarch Cl TW14 .98 E8
Monastry The 22 RG30 .85 D6
Monck Ct 7 RG30 .85 D6
Mondial Way UB7 ..71 C7
Moneyrow Gn SL6 .65 A7
Monkey Island Ct SL6 .65 E8
Monkey Island La SL6 .65 E8
Monkley Ct 6 RG4 .59 C1
Monks Cl SL5 .....120 B3
Monks Dr SL5 ....120 B3
Monks Hollow SL7 .1 C5
Monks La RG14 ...130 F7
Monks Rd
  Virginia Water GU25 .122 D5
  Windsor SL4 ......66 D7
Monks Way
  Harmondsworth UB7 .70 E8
  Reading RG30 .....85 D1
  Staines TW18 .....97 D1
Monks Wlk SL5 ...120 B3
Monksbarn RG2 ...86 D2
Monksfield Way SL2 .22 A2
Monkshood Cl RG40 .116 E7
Monkswood Cl RG14 .130 E7
Monkswood Ct 8 SL7 .1 F2
Monktons La RG7 .137 C5
Monmouth Ct 5 RG1 .59 E1
Mons Cl RG41 ....115 E6
Mons Wlk TW20 ...96 C3
Monsell Gdns TW18 .96 E3
Montacute Dr RG19 .106 F3
Montagu Rd SL3 ..68 E6
Montague Cl
  Camberley GU15 ...151 B1
  Lightwater GU18 ...146 A1

Montague Cl *continued*
  Wokingham RG40 ...116 C7
Montague Rd SL1 ..42 F6
Montague St
  Caversham RG4 ....59 C2
  Reading RG1 ....86 D7
Monteagle La
  Yateley GU46 ......149 A6
  Yateley GU46 ......149 B5
Montem La SL1 ....42 D4
Montem Prim Sch SL1 .42 D4
Montgomery Cl GU47 .150 B8
Montgomery Dr RG7 .113 B2
Montgomery Pl SL2 .43 C7
Montgomery Rd RG14 .130 E8
Montpelier Dr RG4 .59 D5
Montpellier Cl SL4 .67 C5
Montreal Terr RG10 .61 E6
Montrose Ave Datchet SL3 .68 C7
  Slough SL1 ....42 B7
Montrose Cl
  Ashford TW15 .....98 C3
  Frimley GU16 ......151 E2
Montrose Dr SL6 ..39 A6
Montrose Ho 3 RG1 .86 A8
Montrose Rd TW14 .71 D1
Montrose Way SL3 .68 D7
Montrose Wlk RG31 .84 C6
Monument Cl RG14 .130 D7
Monycrower Dr SL6 .39 F7
Moor Cl Sandhurst GU47 .143 E1
Moor Copse Cl RG6 .87 B3
Moor End SL6 .....40 C1
Moor Furlong SL1 ..41 A6
Moor La Bracknell RG12 .117 C6
  Harmondsworth UB7 .70 C8
  Maidenhead SL6 ...19 F1
  Newbury RG14 .....104 E3
  Staines TW19 ......96 B6
Moor Park Ho RG12 .117 E3
Moor Pl GU20 .....146 B5
Moor The SL7 .....2 C4
Moorbridge Rd SL6 .40 A7
Moordale Ave RG42 .90 F1
Moore Cl SL1 .....41 C8
Moore Grove Cres TW20 .95 F1
Moore's Pl RG17 ..100 C5
Moores Gn RG40 ..116 E8
Moores La SL4 ....41 F2
Moorfield Terr SL6 .40 A8
Moorfields Cl TW18 .123 E8
Moorhayes Dr TW18 .124 C6
Moorhen Dr RG6 ..87 B1
Moorings The
  Old Windsor SL4 ...95 C8
  Windsor SL4 ......67 A7
Moorland Rd UB7 ..70 C8
Moorlands Dr SL6 .38 F8
Moorlands Pl GU15 .151 B5
Moorlands Prim Sch
  RG30 ....84 F7
Moorlands Rd GU15 .151 B4
Moormede Cres TW18 .96 F4
Moors Cl RG40 ....141 E8
Moors The
  Pangbourne RG8 ...56 D5
  Thatcham RG19 ...106 D2
Moorside Cl
  Farnborough GU14 .151 A1
  Maidenhead SL6 ...19 F1
Moorstown Ct 7 SL1 .42 E4
Moray Ave GU47 ..150 D7
Moray Dr SL2 .....22 A1
Mordaunt Dr RG45 .143 B3
Morden Cl RG12 ...118 F5
Moreau Wlk SL3 ..43 E7
Morecambe Ave RG4 .58 E5
Moreland Ave SL3 .69 C7
Moreleigh Cl RG2 ..113 B8
Moreleton Cl SL4 ..66 D7
Morello Dr SL3 ...43 F5
Moretaine Rd TW15 .97 D5
Moreton Ct RG1 ...86 C5
Moreton Way SL1 ..41 D5
Morgan Ct 2 TW15 .98 B3
Morgan Rd RG1 ...86 C6
Moriston Cl RG30 ..85 B8
Morlais SL4 ....66 C6
Morlands Ave RG30 .85 A5
Morley Cl Slough SL3 .43 F4
  Yateley GU46 .....149 B5
Morley Ct SL5 ....120 F3
Morley Pl RG17 ..100 C5
Mornington Ave RG40 .141 F8
Mornington Cl RG26 .134 E1
Mornington Rd TW15 .98 C3
Morpeth Ct RG2 ..86 C3
Morrice Cl SL3 ...68 F6
Morris Ct 14 RG1 .86 C7
Mortimer Cl RG2 .113 C7
Mortimer Hall RG7 .137 C5
Mortimer La
  Silchester RG7 ...137 D7
Mortimer Rd
  Grazeley RG7 .....112 D2
  Slough SL3 ....43 F4
Mortimer St John's CE Sch
  RG7 ....137 C5
Mortimer St Mary's CE Jun
  Sch RG7 ....137 D5
Mortimer Sta RG7 .137 E5
Morton Dr SL1 ...21 F8

Morton Pl SL1 ....83 E4
Morval Rd GU17 ..149 F1
Moss Cl RG4 ......59 C3
Mossy Vale SL6 ..19 D1
Mostyn Ho RG42 .91 B1
Moulsford Prep Sch
  GU46 ....149 B7
Moulsham Copse La
  GU46 ....149 B7
Moulsham La GU46 .149 B7
Moundsfield Way SL1 .41 E4
Mount Cl
  Farnham Common SL2 .22 C8
  Newbury RG14 ....105 A1
Mount Cl The GU25 .122 D3
Mount Felix KT12 .125 F2
Mount La Bracknell RG12 .118 C7
  Chaddleworth RG20 .49 A8
Mount Lee TW20 ..95 F3
Mount Pleasant
  Beenham RG7 .....108 F5
  Bracknell RG12 ....118 C6
  Reading RG1 ......86 B6
  Tadley RG26 ......135 B1
  Wokingham RG41 ..116 A6
Mount Pleasant Cl
  GU18 ....146 A1
Mount Pleasant Cotts
  7 Bourne End SL8 .3 B3
  Englefield Green TW20 .95 D2
Mount Pleasant Gr RG1 .86 B6
Mount Rd RG18 ...106 D4
Mount St SL6 .....86 B5
Mount The Caversham RG4 .58 F3
  Reading RG1 ......86 D5
  Wentworth GU25 ..122 D3
Mount View RG1 ..15 D2
Mount View Ct RG9 .15 D2
Mountain Ash SL7 .1 D6
Mountbatten Cl
  Newbury RG14 ....105 C5
  6 Slough SL1 .....43 A3
Mountbatten Rise GU47 .142 F1
Mountbatten Sq 7 SL4 .67 C6
Mountfield RG8 ...34 C7
Mounts Hill SL4 ..93 C3
Mountsfield Cl TW19 .70 A2
Mowbray Cres TW20 .96 A3
Mowbray Dr RG30 .85 A8
Mower Cl RG40 ...116 F7
Moyleen Rise SL7 .1 C1
Mrs Bland's Inf Sch
  RG7 ....110 F2
Muckhatch La TW20 .123 B7
Mud La
  Finchampstead RG27 .140 F1
  Peasemore RG20 ..50 D6
Mud La Cotts RG27 .140 F1
Muirfield Cl RG1 ..86 D7
Muirfield Ho
  Bracknell RG12 ....117 E3
  Sunningdale SL5 ..121 A1
Mulberry Ave
  Stanwell TW19 ....97 E7
  Windsor SL4 ......67 F5
Mulberry Bsns Pk RG41 .116 A4
Mulberry Cl
  Crowthorne RG45 .143 C4
  1 Sandhurst GU47 .150 D8
  Woodley RG5 ......87 E6
Mulberry Ct
  1 Bracknell RG12 .118 F4
  2 Newbury RG14 ...104 F2
  Wokingham RG40 ..116 C6
Mulberry Dr SL3 ..43 E1
Mulberry Ho RG42 .91 B1
Mulberry Trees TW17 .125 D2
Mulberry Way SL7 .83 E3
Mulberry Wlk SL6 ..39 A8
Mulfords Hill RG26 .135 B1
Mulgrave Rd GU16 .151 F2
Mullens Rd TW20 .96 C3
Mullens Terr RG4 .58 D8
Mullion Cl 10 RG1 .85 F7
Mulroy Dr GU15 ..152 A6
Mumbery Hill RG10 .36 E1
Muncaster Cl TW15 .98 A4
Muncaster Rd TW15 .98 B3
Muncies Rd SL7 ..1 D6
Munday Ct RG42 ..90 E1
Mundaydean La SL7 .1 B4
Mundesley Spur SL1 .42 E7
Mundesley St RG1 .86 B6
Munkle Marsh RG19 .107 A3
Munnings Dr GU47 .150 E6
Munro Ave RG5 ...88 A6
Murdoch Cl TW18 .97 A3
Murdoch Rd RG40 .116 D5
Murdoch Rd RG40 .116 D5
Murray Ct SL5 ...120 C3
Murray Rd RG14 ..116 A6
Murray Rd RG41 ..116 A6
Murrellhill La
  Binfield RG42 .....90 C1
  Bracknell RG42 ...117 C8
Murrells La GU15 .151 B3
Murrin Rd SL6 ...39 C8
Mus of Berkshire Aviation
  The* RG5 ....88 B6
Mus of English Rural Life*
  RG6 ....86 D6
Mus of Reading* RG1 .86 B8
Mushroom Castle RG42 .92 B2
Mustard La RG4 ...60 E2

Mustard Mill Rd TW18 .....96 F4
Muswell Cl RG7 ....83 E3
Mutton Oaks RG12 ....117 D8
Myers Way GU16 ....152 D2
Mylne Sq RG40 ....116 D6
Mylum Cl RG2 ....113 C6
Myrke The SL3 ....42 F2
Myrtle Ave TW14 ....71 E2
Myrtle Cl
  Burghfield Common RG7 ..111 B3
  Lightwater GU18 ....153 B8
  Poyle SL3 ....69 E6
  Tadley RG7 ....57 C3
Myrtle Cres SL2 ....42 F6
Myrtle Dr GU17 ....150 D5
Myton Wlk RG7 ....83 E3

N

Nabbs Hill Cl RG31 ....84 C5
Nairn Cl GU16 ....151 E2
Nalderhill Rd RG20 ......103 B6
Napier Cl RG45 ....143 D5
Napier Dr GU15 ....152 A8
Napier Lodge TW15 ....98 D2
Napier Rd Ashford TW15 ..98 D1
  Crowthorne RG45 ....143 C4
  Harmondsworth TW6 .....70 D6
  Maidenhead SL6 ....39 B6
  Reading RG1 ....86 C8
Napier Wlk TW15 ....98 D1
Napper Cl SL5 ....119 D7
Narromine Dr RG31 ....84 F4
Naseby RG12 ....118 B1
Naseby Rise RG14 ....105 D5
Nash Cl RG6 ....87 A3
Nash Gdns SL5 ....119 E7
Nash Grove La RG40 .....115 E1
Nash Pk RG42 ....90 B2
Nash Rd SL3 ....44 A2
Nashdom SL1 ....20 F5
Nashdom La SL1 ....21 A6
Natalie Cl TW14 ....98 D8
Nathan Cl 2 RG1 ....85 F7
Naylors The RG7 ....139 D6
Neath Gdns RG30 ....84 F7
Needham Cl SL4 ....66 E6
Neil Cl TW15 ....98 E7
Nell Gwynn Ave TW17 ...125 D3
Nell Gwynne Ave SL5 ...120 D5
Nell Gwynne Cl GU15 ...120 D5
Nelson Cl Bracknell RG12 ..118 E7
  East Bedfont TW14 ......98 F7
  Slough SL3 ....43 D2
Nelson Ct KT16 ....124 A1
Nelson Rd Ashford TW15 ..97 E3
  Caversham RG4 ....59 C2
  Harmondsworth TW6 .....70 F6
  Windsor SL4 ....64 F4
Nelson Terr 3 RG1 ....86 B6
Nelson Way GU15 ....150 F4
Nelson's La RG10 ....89 B6
Nene Rd TW6,UB7 ....71 B6
Nene Rd Rdbt TW6 ....71 B6
Neptune Cl RG41 ....115 E6
Neptune Rd TW6 ....71 C6
Neptune Way SL1 ....41 E4
Netherton RG12 ....118 A5
Netley Cl RG4 ....59 E6
Netley Rd (W) TW6 ......71 D6
Nettlecombe RG12 ....118 D3
Nettleton Rd TW6 ....71 B6
Neuman Cres RG12 ......118 A3
Neve Ho SL6 ....39 F8
Nevelle Cl RG42 ....117 D8
Neville Cl Stoke Poggs SL2 ..22 F6
  Waltham St Lawrence RG10 ..62 F6
Neville Ct SL1 ....21 C2
Neville Dr RG19 ....106 E3
Nevis Rd RG31 ....57 D3
New Bath Rd RG10 ....61 C6
New Bldgs RG7 ....81 D4
New Bright St 6 RG1 .....86 A6
New Church Street Cofm Prim
  Sch RG1 ....86 B5
New Cl RG9 ....16 A8
New Ct SL7 ....1 D2
New Forest Ride RG12 ...118 F4
New Greenham Pk
  RG19 ....131 F5
New Hill RG9 ....57 C5
New Hope Terr RG1 ....59 A1
New Lane Hill RG30 ....84 E6
New Mdw SL5 ....119 D8
New Mile Rd SL5 ....120 C7
New Mill La RG27 ....140 E2
New Mill Rd RG40 ......140 E3
New Par TW15 ....97 F4
New Park Rd TW15 ....98 C3
New Rd Bagshot GU19 ...145 F3
  Blackwater GU17 ....150 E4
  Bourne End SL8 ....3 B4
  Bracknell RG12 ....118 E7
  Burghfield Common RG7 ..111 E1
  Cookham Rise SL6 ....19 E7
  Crowthorne RG45 ....143 C5
  Datchet SL3 ....68 D6
  East Bedfont TW14 ......71 D1
  Egham TW18 ....96 C4
  Harlington TW6,UB7 .....71 C7
  Holyport SL6 ....65 B8
  Hurley SL6 ....17 F2
  Littleton TW17 ....125 B6
  Marlow Bottom SL7 ....1 D6

New Rd *continued*
  Newbury RG14 ....105 C1
  North Ascot SL5 ....92 F1
  Reading RG1 ....86 D5
  Sandhurst GU47 ....150 A8
  Shiplake RG9 ....36 A3
  Sindlesham RG41 ....115 B8
  Slough SL3 ....44 A3
  Twyford RG10 ....61 D7
  Twyford,Ruscombe RG10 ..61 F6
  Windlesham GU19,GU20 ..146 A4
New Road Hill RG7 ......108 B3
New Scotland Hill Prim Sch
  GU47 ....143 A2
New Sq East Bedfont TW14 ..98 C7
  Slough SL1 ....42 F4
New St Beech Hill RG7 ...138 B1
  Henley-On-T RG9 ....15 E2
  Staines TW18 ....97 A4
New Town Prim Sch RG1 ..86 D8
New Villas RG20 ....129 B3
New Way RG7 ....82 A2
New Wickham La TW20 ...96 B1
New Wokingham Rd
  RG45 ....143 A6
New Zealand Ave KT12 ..125 F1
Newall Rd TW6 ....71 C6
Newalls Rise RG10 ....36 E2
Newark Rd
  Windlesham GU20 ......146 B6
  Windlesham GU20 ....149 E2
Newark St RG1 ....86 B6
Newberry Cres SL4 ....66 D5
Newbery Cl RG31 ....57 D1
Newbery Way SL1 ....42 D4
Newbold Coll RG42 ....90 D1
Newbold Rd RG14 ......104 D5
Newbold Sch RG42 ....90 D1
Newbolt Cl RG18 ....106 C5
Newbury Cl RG10 ....61 D7
Newbury Coll RG14 .....131 A7
Newbury Dr SL6 ....40 B6
Newbury Hill RG18 ....52 F5
Newbury La RG20 ....31 D4
Newbury Racecourse Sta
  RG14 ....105 C2
Newbury Ret Pk RG14 ...131 B7
Newbury St
  Kintbury RG17 ....102 B2
  Lambourn RG17 ....25 B2
Newbury Way SL1 ....105 A2
Newcastle Rd RG2 ....86 E1
Newchurch Rd Slough SL2 ..41 F8
  Tadley RG26 ....135 A1
Newell Gn RG42 ....91 C3
Newell Hall RG42 ....91 C3
Newfield Gdns SL7 ....1 F3
Newfield Rd SL7 ....1 F3
Newfield Way SL7 ....1 F2
Newhaven Cres TW15 ....98 D3
Newhurst Spur SL2 ....22 B1
Newhurst Gdns RG42 .....91 D3
Newlands Ave SL4 ....59 B3
Newlands Cl GU46 ......149 D5
Newlands Cotts RG41 ...114 F7
Newlands Dr
  Maidenhead SL6 ....39 A7
  Poyle SL3 ....69 E4
Newlands Girls' Sch SL4 ..39 A7
Newlands Prim Sch
  GU46 ....149 C5
Newlands Rd GU15 ......151 B1
Newlyn Gdns RG2 ....86 B1
Newmans Pl SL5 ....121 B2
Newmarket Cl RG6 ....87 D2
Newport Cl 11 RG14 ....105 B4
Newport Dr RG42 ....91 B2
Newport Rd
  Harmondsworth TW6 .....71 A6
  Newbury RG14 ....105 B4
  Reading RG1 ....59 A1
  Slough SL2 ....21 E1
Newquay Dr RG6 ....87 D2
Newstead Rise RG2 ......86 E1
Newton Ave RG4 ....59 D5
Newton Cl SL3 ....43 F4
Newton Ct SL4 ....68 A1
Newton La SL4 ....68 B1
Newton Mews RG17 ....100 D6
Newton Side Orch SL4 ...68 A1
Newtonside SL4 ....68 A1
Newtown RG26 ....135 A1
Newtown Gdns RG9 ......35 E8
Newtown Rd
  Henley-On-T RG9 ....35 F8
  Marlow SL7 ....1 F3
  Newbury RG14,RG19,
  RG20 ....131 A7
  Sandhurst GU47 ....150 B8
Niagara Rd RG9 ....35 E8
Nicholas Cl 11 RG1 ....85 F7
Nicholas Gdns SL1 ....41 C5
Nicholas Rd RG10 ....88 B8
Nicholls SL4 ....66 D4
Nicholls Wlk SL4 ....66 C4
Nicholsons Ctr 8 SL6 ....39 F7
Nicholsons La 2 TW20 ..96 A3
Nicholsons Ctr 6 SL6 ....39 F7
Nideggan Cl RG19 ......106 D3
Night Owls RG19 ....131 C7
Nightingale Cres RG12 ..118 D4
Nightingale Ct 9 Slough SL1 ..43 A3

Nightingale Gdns GU47 ..150 B8
Nightingale Ho 11 RG1 ...85 F5
Nightingale La
  Maidenhead SL6 ....19 D3
  Mortimer RG7 ....137 D6
Nightingale Pk SL2 ....21 F5
Nightingale Pl SL4 ....19 F7
Nightingale Rd RG5 ......87 D4
Nightingale Shott TW20 ..95 F2
Nightingale Wlk SL4 .....67 C4
Nightingales The
  Newbury RG14 ....131 B8
  Stanwell TW19 ....97 F7
Nimrod Cl RG5 ....88 B7
Nimrod Way RG2 ....86 B5
Nine Acres SL1 ....41 F5
Nine Elms Cl 11 TW14 ....98 F7
Nine Mile Ride
  Bracknell RG12,RG40 ...118 C1
  Crowthorne RG40 ......142 D7
  Wokingham RG40 ....141 D6
Nine Mile Ride Ind
  RG40 ....141 D5
Nine Mile Ride Prim Sch
  RG40 ....141 F6
Ninth Ave RG31 ....84 B6
Niplands Cotts HP10 ......3 D2
Nire Rd RG14 ....59 E2
Nixey Cl SL1 ....43 A4
No 4 RG30 ....85 C6
Noakes Hill RG8 ....54 B7
Nobel Dr TW6 ....71 E7
Noble Ct SL2 ....42 F5
Noble Rd RG9 ....35 F7
Nobles Way TW20 ....95 E2
Nodmore RG20 ....49 B7
Norcot Rd RG30 ....84 F8
Norden Cl SL6 ....39 C5
Norden Mdws SL6 ....39 C5
Norden Rd SL6 ....39 C5
Norelands Dr SL1 ....21 C3
Nores Rd RG2 ....113 D7
Norfolk Ave SL1 ....42 C8
Norfolk Chase RG42 .....91 F1
Norfolk Rd Maidenhead SL6 ..39 F8
Norfolk Park Cotts SL6 ...39 F8
Norfolk Rd
  Maidenhead SL6 ....39 F8
  Reading RG30 ....85 D7
Norland Dr HP10 ....3 C8
Norland Nursery Training
  Coll RG17 ....101 C7
Norlands RG18 ....106 C5
Norman Ave RG9 ....15 E1
Norman Ct 4 TW18 ......97 A4
Norman Ho TW17 ......125 A2
Norman Keep RG42 .....118 F8
Norman Pl RG1 ....59 B1
Norman Rd Ashford TW15 ..98 D2
  Caversham RG4 ....59 C4
Normandy Wlk TW20 ....96 F3
Normanhurst TW15 ......98 A3
Normans The SL2 ....43 B7
Normanstead Rd RG31 ...84 C8
Normay Rise RG14 .....130 C5
Normoor Rd RG7 ....110 F1
Norreys Ave RG40 ......116 D7
Norreys Dr SL6 ....39 D4
Norris Field RG20 ....49 B8
Norris Gn RG5 ....61 A1
Norris Ho SL6 ....39 E7
Norris La RG20 ....49 B8
Norris Rd Reading RG6 ...87 A6
  Staines TW18 ....96 F4
North Burnham Cl SL1 ...21 B3
North Cl
  East Bedfont TW14 ......71 D1
  Maidenhead SL7 ....17 D7
  Windsor SL4 ....66 F6
North Cotts SL2 ....22 C2
North Dr
  Sulhamstead RG7 ......110 D7
  Wentworth GU25 ....121 E4
North End La SL5 ....121 B2
North Farm Cl RG17 ....123 E7
North Fryerne GU46 ....149 D8
North Gn Bracknell RG12 ..118 D8
  3 Maidenhead SL6 ......19 F1
  Slough SL1 ....42 E6
North Gr KT16 ....123 F3
North Links Rd HP10 .....3 B8
North Lodge Dr SL5 ....119 C7
North Lodge Mews RG30 ..85 D5
North Pk SL0 ....44 D3
North Rd
  East Bedfont TW14 ......71 D1
  Maidenhead SL6 ....39 E7
  Moulsford OX10 ....13 F4
  Winkfield SL5 ....119 B8
North Row SL3 ....23 E8
North St Caversham RG4 ..59 B2
  Egham TW20 ....95 F2
  Reading RG1 ....85 F8
  Winkfield SL4 ....94 E1
North Standen Rd RG17 ..100 A4
North Star La SL6 ....39 C6
North Terr SL4 ....67 E7
North Town Cl 1 SL6 .....19 F1
North Town Mead 4 SL6 ..19 F1
North Town Moor SL6 ....19 F1
North Town Rd SL6 ....19 F1
North View RG12 ....117 C6
North View Gdns
  RG14 ....105 B4
North Wlk RG7 ....83 E4
Northam Cl RG6 ....87 B3
Northampton Ave SL1 ...42 C7

Northampton Cl RG12 ...118 E6
Northborough Rd SL2 ....22 B1
Northbourne Cl RG6 .....87 B2
Northbrook Copse
  RG12 ....118 F3
Northbrook Pl SL2 .....105 C4
Northbrook Rd RG4 ......59 D6
Northbrook St RG14 ....105 A3
Northbury Ave RG10 .....61 E5
Northbury La RG10 ......61 E6
Northcott Cl RG12 .....118 A1
Northcourt Ave RG2 .....86 D4
Northcroft Slough SL2 ....22 B1
  Wooburn Green HP10 .....6 F4
Northcroft Cl TW20 ....95 B3
Northcroft Gdns TW20 ...95 B3
Northcroft La RG14 .....104 F3
Northcroft Rd TW20 .....95 B3
Northcroft Terr RG14 ...104 F3
Northcroft Villas TW20 ...95 B3
Northdean 8 SL6 ....19 F1
Northdown Rd HP10 ......3 C7
Northern Ave RG14 .....105 A6
Northern Hts SL8 ....3 B5
Northern Perimeter Rd
  TW6 ....71 E6
Northern Perimeter Road
  (W) TW6 ....70 D6
Northern Rd SL2 ....22 D1
Northern Way RG1 ....85 F1
Northern Woods HP10 ....3 C7
Northfield GU18 ....153 B8
Northfield Ave RG9 ......36 A4
Northfield Cl
  Henley-On-T RG9 ....15 D3
  Staines TW18 ....124 B8
Northfield End RG9 ......15 D3
Northfield Rd Eton SL4 ...41 F2
  Maidenhead SL6 ....19 F1
  Reading RG1 ....59 A1
  Shiplake RG9 ....36 B4
  Staines TW18 ....124 B8
  Thatcham RG18 ....84 B4
Northfields
  Chievely RG20 ....51 B4
  Lambourn RG17 ....25 B3
Northfields Terr RG17 ...25 C3
Northgate Dr GU15 .....152 A7
Northington Cl RG12 ...118 F3
Northmead Rd SL2 ......41 F8
Northolt Rd TW6 ....70 E6
Northrop Rd TW6 ....71 E6
Northumberland Ave
  RG2 ....86 C3
Northumberland Cl
  Bracknell RG42 ....91 F1
  Stanwell TW19 ....70 E1
Northumberland Cres
  TW14 ....71 E1
Northumbria Rd SL6 ......39 B4
Northview RG42 ....100 D5
Northview Hts RG17 ....100 D5
Northway Newbury RG14 ..105 B2
  Thatcham RG18 ....84 C4
  Wokingham RG41 ......115 E7
Northwood Dr RG40 ....105 C4
Northwood Rd TW6 ......70 D6
Norton Cl RG14 ....130 C6
Norton Pk SL5 ....120 C4
Norton Rd Frimley GU15 ..152 C4
  Reading RG1 ....86 F7
  Riseley RG7 ....139 C3
  Wokingham RG40 ......116 C5
  Woodley RG5 ....87 F5
Norway Dr SL2 ....43 B8
Norwich Ave RG14 .....151 E3
Norwich Dr RG5 ....87 C8
Norwich Rd SL6 ....39 E8
Norwood Cres TW6 ......71 C6
Norwood Rd RG1 ....86 E7
Notley End TW20 ....95 C1
Notton Way RG6 ....113 F8
Nuffield Dr GU47 ......143 F1
Nuffield Rd
  Barkham,Arborfield Garrison
  RG2 ....140 F2
  Barkham,Langley Common
  RG2 ....141 A8
Nugee Ct RG45 ....143 B5
Nugent Ct SL7 ....1 F3
Nun's Acre RG8 ....34 B7
Nuneaton RG12 ....118 E3
Nunhide La RG8,RG31 ....83 F6
Nuns Wlk GU25 ....122 D4
Nuptown La
  Newell Green SL4 ....92 A8
  Winkfield RG42 ....91 F7
Nursery Cl Hurst RG10 ...88 A6
  Shiplake RG9 ....36 A4
Nursery Gdns
  Purley On T RG8 ....57 B5
  Staines TW18 ....97 B1
  Sunbury TW16 ....125 F7
Nursery La
  North Ascot SL5 ....119 A8
  Slough SL3 ....43 D5
Nursery Pl SL4 ....68 B1
Nursery Rd Burnham SL6 ..41 B7
  Sunbury TW16 ....125 F7
Nursery Way TW19 ......68 D1
Nursery Wlk SL7 ....1 B1
Nut La RG10 ....88 B8
Nutbean La RG7 ....139 F5
Nutbourne Ct TW18 .....96 F1
Nutfield Cl GU15 ....151 D7
Nuthatch Cl TW19 .....108 C7
Nuthatch Dr RG6 ....87 B4
Nuthurst RG12 ....118 E4

Nutley RG12 ....118 A1
Nutley Cl GU46 ....149 D5
Nutmeg Cl RG6 ....86 F1
Nutter's La RG2 ....140 A8
Nuttingtons RG20 ....49 F6
Nutty La TW17 ....125 C6

O

O'Bee Gdns RG26 ......134 F1
Oak Ave Egham TW20 ....96 D1
  Sandhurst GU47 ....143 D1
Oak Dr
  Burghfield Common RG7 ..110 F2
  Newbury RG14 ....104 F2
  Woodley RG5 ....88 A6
Oak End Way RG7 ....109 C4
Oak Farm Cl GU17 .....150 C5
Oak Gn RG2 ....113 D8
Oak Grove Cres GU15 ..150 F6
Oak Hill SN8 ....99 C3
Oak La
  Englefield Green TW20 ..95 C5
  Windsor SL4 ....67 A6
Oak Leaf Ct SL5 ....119 D8
Oak Lodge
  11 Ashford TW16 ....98 F1
  Crowthorne RG45 ......143 C5
Oak Ridge Cl RG14 ....130 E8
Oak Stubbs La SL6 ......40 F4
Oak The OX10 ....14 C6
Oak Tree Ave SL7 ....1 D3
Oak Tree Cl Tadley RG26 ..135 B1
  Wentworth GU25 ....122 D3
Oak Tree Copse RG31 ...57 E3
Oak Tree Dr TW20 ......95 D1
Oak Tree Rd Marlow SL7 ..1 E4
  Reading RG31 ....57 E2
  Thatcham RG19 ....106 E2
Oak Tree Wlk RG8 ....57 D5
Oak View RG31 ....84 C8
Oak Way
  East Bedfont TW14 ......98 E7
  Woodley RG5 ....87 D4
Oakdale RG12 ....118 D3
Oakdale Cl RG31 ....84 C8
Oakdale Wlk RG5 ....88 A8
Oakdene
  Burghfield Common RG7 ..111 A2
  Sunningdale SL5 ......120 F3
Oaken Copse GU15 .....152 D7
Oaken Gr Maidenhead SL6 ..19 C1
  Maidenhead SL6 ......130 D8
Oakengates RG12 ......118 A1
Oakes Ct RG17 ....100 D5
Oakey Dr RG40 ....86 B5
Oakfield Ave SL1 ....42 B5
Oakfield Ct RG41 ......116 A5
Oakfield Fst Sch SL4 ....67 B5
Oakfield Rd Ashford TW15 ..98 F3
  Bourne End SL8 ....3 A4
  Silchester RG26 ....135 E1
Oakfields
  Oakhall Ct TW16 ....98 F1
  Oakhall Dr TW16 ....98 F3
Oakham Cl RG31 ....57 D2
Oakhurst SL6 ....20 B4
Oaklands Curridge RG18 ..78 C3
  Reading RG1 ....86 F6
  Yateley GU46 ....149 D6
Oaklands Bsns Ctr
  RG41 ....116 A4
Oaklands Cl SL5 ....92 F1
Oaklands Cvn Pk RG41 ..114 F1
Oaklands Dr
  North Ascot SL5 ....92 F1
  Wokingham RG41 ......116 A5
Oaklands Inf & Jun Schs
  RG45 ....143 A6
Oaklands La RG45 .....143 B7
Oaklands Pk RG41 .....116 A4
Oaklea Dr RG27 ....140 E2
Oakleigh GU18 ....153 C8
Oakley HP10 ....3 F7
Oakley Cres SL1 ....42 A8
Oakley Green Rd
  Fifield SL4 ....65 E5
  Oakley Green SL4 ....65 A7
  Oakley Green SL4 ....66 B7
Oakley Rd
  Camberley GU15 ....151 B4
  Caversham RG4 ....58 F4
  Newbury RG14 ....105 D4
Oakmede Pl RG42 ....90 C2
Oakridge GU24 ....153 F6
Oakridge Pl SL2 ....22 C8
Oaks Rd Shiplake RG9 ....36 A4
  Stanwell TW19 ....70 D1
Oaks The
  Blackwater GU17 ......150 E3
  Bracknell RG12 ....118 D7
  Newbury RG14 ....131 A7
  Staines TW18 ....96 F4
  Yateley GU46 ....149 D5
Oakside Way RG6 ......113 E8
Oaktree Ave RG19 .....133 B5
Oaktree Cl SL7 ....1 D3
Oaktree Way GU47 .....143 A1
Oakview RG40 ....116 C6
Oakway Dr GU16 ......151 E1
Oakwood Rd
  Bracknell RG12 ....118 E7
  Virginia Water GU25 ..122 C4
  Windlesham GU20 .....146 E4
Oareborough RG12 ....118 E4

Oareborough La RG18 ....52 A1
Oast Ct TW18 ....96 F4
Oast House Cl TW19 ....95 E8
Oatlands Dr SL1 ....42 D7
Oatlands Rd RG2 ....113 F5
Oban Ct SL1 ....42 D4
Oban Gdns RG5 ....87 E4
Obelisk Way GU15 ....151 C6
Oberon Way TW17 ....124 E6
Observatory The 6 RG30 .85 E7
Ockwells Rd SL6 ....39 C2
Octavia RG12 ....118 A1
Octavia Way TW18 ....97 A2
Oddfellows Rd RG14 ....104 F2
Odell Cl RG6 ....114 B8
Odencroft Rd SL2 ....22 A2
Odette Gdns RG26 ....135 C1
Odiham Ave RG4 ....59 E5
Odiham Rd RG7 ....139 D1
Odney La SL6 ....20 B7
Ogden Pk RG12 ....118 E6
Ogmore Cl RG30 ....84 E7
Okingham Cl GU47 ....143 D1
Old Acre La RG10 ....61 B5
Old Apple Yd The RG41 ..88 A3
Old Bakehouse Ct RG45 .143 B4
Old Bakery Ct SL0 ....44 F7
Old Barn Cl RG4 ....59 A6
Old Bath Rd Charvil RG10 ..61 B5
Newbury RG14 ....104 F4
Sonning RG4 ....60 D1
Old Bisley Rd GU16 ....152 C3
Old Bix Rd RG9 ....15 A6
Old Bothampstead Rd
RG20 ....51 D6
Old Bracknell Cl RG12 ..118 B6
Old Bracknell La E
RG12 ....118 B6
Old Bracknell La W
RG12 ....118 B6
Old Chapel Cotts RG18 ..53 E1
Old Chapel The RG7 ....113 A2
Old Charlton Rd TW17 ..125 C4
Old Coalyard The TW20 ...95 F2
Old College Rd RG14 ...104 F4
Old Court Cl SL6 ....39 B3
Old Dean Rd GU15 ....151 D7
Old Elm Dr RG30 ....84 D7
Old Farm Cres RG31 ....57 C2
Old Farm Dr RG12 ....91 C1
Old Ferry Dr TW19 ....68 D1
Old Fives Ct SL1 ....21 B2
Old Forest Rd RG41 ....88 F1
Old Forge Cl SL6 ....40 A3
Old Forge Cres TW17 ..125 B3
Old Forge End GU47 ...150 B7
Old Forge The
Streatley RG8 ....34 A6
Tadley RG26 ....134 E1
Old Green La GU15 ....151 C7
Old Hayward La RG17 ...73 D2
Old House Ct SL3 ....43 D7
Old Kennels Ct RG30 ....85 A5
Old Kiln Ind Est SL6 ....19 A3
Old Kiln Rd HP10 ....3 A8
Old La
Hamstead Marshall RG20 ..102 E1
Headley RG19 ....133 F1
Old La The RG1 ....85 F5
Old Lands Hill RG12 ...118 D8
Old Marsh La SL6 ....40 F4
Old Mill Ct RG10 ....61 D5
Old Mill La SL6 ....40 D4
Old Mill Pl TW19 ....69 B1
Old Mill The RG8 ....56 D6
Old Monteagle La GU46 .149 B5
Old Moor La HP10 ....3 E8
Old Newtown Rd RG14 ..104 F1
Old Nursery Pl TW15 ....98 B3
Old Orch The RG31 ....84 E4
Old Palace Ct SL3 ....69 D6
Old Papermill Cl HP10 ....3 E8
Old Pasture Rd GU16,
GU15 ....151 F3
Old Pharmacy Ct RG45 .143 C4
Old Pond Cl GU15 ....151 C1
Old Portsmouth Rd
GU15 ....152 A5
Old Post Office La 10 SL6 .39 F7
Old Priory La RG42 ....91 D2
Old Riseley Stores The
RG7 ....139 C3
Old Row Ct RG40 ....116 C6
Old Sawmill La RG45 ...143 C6
Old Sawmills The RG17 ..127 E6
Old School Ct TW19 ....95 E8
Old School La GU46 ....149 C6
Old School Mews TW20 ..96 D3
Old School The
Hampstead Norreys RG18 ..52 F5
Wooburn HP10 ....3 D4
Old School Yd The 4
RG17 ....25 B2
Old Silk Mill The RG10 ..61 D5
Old Slade La SL0 ....44 F2
Old St Chieveley RG18 ....51 F1
Chieveley,Beedon Common
RG20 ....51 C5
Hermitage RG18 ....78 F8
Old Stanmore Rd RG20 ...30 E6
Old Station Bsns Pk
RG20 ....31 E4
Old Station Way HP10 ....3 E5
Old Station Yd The RG17 ..25 B2
Old Stocks Ct RG8 ....54 F5
Old Vicarage Way HP10 ...3 D4
Old Watery La HP10 ....3 E8
Old Welmore GU46 ....149 E5
Old Whitley Wood La
RG2 ....113 C6
Old Wokingham Rd
RG45 ....143 C7
Old Woosehill La RG41 ..115 F7
Oldacre GU24 ....153 F7
Oldacres SL6 ....40 B7
Oldbury RG12 ....117 F6
Oldbury Rd KT16 ....123 E2
Oldcorne Hollow GU46 ..149 A5
Olde Farm Dr GU17 ....150 B5
Oldean Cl RG31 ....57 C1
Oldershaw Mews SL6 ....39 B8
Oldfield Cl RG6 ....87 B7
Oldfield Prim Sch SL6 ....40 B6
Oldfield Rd SL6 ....40 B7
Oldfield Rd Ind Est SL6 ...40 B7
Oldhouse La GU18 ....146 C2
Oldstead RG12 ....118 D4
Oldway La SL1 ....41 D5
Oleander Cl RG45 ....143 A7
Oliver Dr RG31 ....84 C5
Oliver Rd SL5 ....120 B5
Oliver's Paddock SL7 ....1 D5
Ollerton RG12 ....118 A1
Omega Way TW20 ....123 C8
Omer's Rise RG7 ....110 F3
One Pin La SL2 ....22 C8
Onslow Dr SL5 ....93 A1
Onslow Gdns RG4 ....59 C3
Onslow Lodge TW18 ....96 F1
Onslow Mews KT16 ....124 A3
Onslow Rd SL5 ....121 B2
Onyz The RG12 ....118 E6
Opal Ct SL3 ....23 C1
Opal Way RG41 ....115 E7
Opendale Rd SL1 ....41 B8
Opladen Way RG12 ....118 E4
Oracle Ctr The RG1 ....86 B7
Oracle Parkway RG6 ....60 A1
Oram Ct 2 SL7 ....1 D2
Orbit Cl RG40 ....141 E6
Orchard Ave
Ashford TW15 ....98 C2
Hatton TW14 ....71 D2
Slough SL1 ....41 D8
Windsor SL4 ....67 A6
Orchard Bglws Mobile Home
Pk SL2 ....21 F5
Orchard Chase RG10 ....88 F7
Orchard Cl Ashford TW15 ..98 C2
Egham TW20 ....96 B3
Farnborough GU17 ....150 F1
Henley-On-T RG9 ....15 E1
Hermitage RG18 ....79 C8
Maidenhead SL6 ....40 A3
Newbury RG14 ....105 C5
Purley On T RG31 ....57 B4
Shinfield RG7 ....113 B2
Shiplake RG9 ....35 E2
West End GU24 ....153 D6
Wokingham RG40 ....116 D6
Woolhampton RG7 ....108 C2
Orchard Cotts RG10 ....62 F6
Orchard Ct
Bracknell RG12 ....118 C7
Camberley GU15 ....151 B2
Harmondsworth UB7 ....70 C7
Oatlands Park KT12 ....125 F1
Reading RG2 ....113 C7
Thatcham RG19 ....106 E3
Orchard Dene Dr RG7 ...109 C2
Orchard Dr
Sunbury TW17 ....125 E6
Wooburn HP10 ....3 D4
Orchard Est RG10 ....61 E5
Orchard Gate
Farnham Common SL2 ....22 C7
Sandhurst GU47 ....150 B8
Orchard Gdns SL6 ....20 B7
Orchard Gn RG17 ....73 A1
Orchard Gr
Caversham RG4 ....59 E4
Flackwell Heath HP10 ....3 B7
Maidenhead SL6 ....39 C7
Orchard Hill GU20 ....146 D3
Orchard Ho 8 SL8 ....3 A4
Orchard Lea RG20 ....30 E7
Orchard Lodge SL1 ....41 E5
Orchard Mill SL8 ....3 B1
Orchard Park Cl RG17 ...100 D4
Orchard Pl RG40 ....116 C6
Orchard Rd Hurst RG10 ....88 F7
Mortimer RG7 ....137 B5
Old Windsor SL4 ....68 B1
Orchard St RG1 ....86 B6
Orchard The
Flackwell Heath HP10 ....3 B7
Lightwater GU18 ....153 B8
Marlow SL7 ....1 E3
Theale RG7 ....83 E4
Thorpe GU25 ....122 E4
Orchard Way
Ashford TW15 ....97 F6
Camberley GU15 ....151 B2
Slough SL3 ....43 E5
Orchardene RG14 ....105 B4
Orchardville SL1 ....21 B1
Orchardwood SL5 ....119 E7
Orchids The OX11 ....10 D7
Oregon Ave RG31 ....57 D3
Oregon Wlk RG40 ....141 E7
Oriel Hill GU15 ....151 D4
Oriental Rd SL5 ....120 D5
Orion RG12 ....118 A1
Orkney Cl RG31 ....84 E4
Orkney Ct SL6 ....20 E5
Ormathwaites Cnr RG42 ..91 E1
Ormonde Rd RG41 ....116 A5
Ormsby St RG1 ....85 E7
Orpheus Ho RG7 ....134 E2
Orpington Cl RG10 ....61 E4
Orrin Cl RG30 ....85 A8
Orts Rd Newbury RG14 ...105 B2
Reading RG1 ....86 D7
Orville Cl RG5 ....88 A7
Orwell Cl Caversham RG4 ..58 F4
Windsor SL4 ....67 D4
Osborne Ave TW19 ....97 F7
Osborne Ct SL4 ....67 C5
Osborne Dr GU18 ....153 A8
Osborne La RG42 ....91 C4
Osborne Mews SL4 ....67 C5
Osborne Rd Egham TW20 ..95 F2
Reading RG30 ....85 B8
Windsor SL4 ....67 D4
Wokingham RG40 ....116 C6
Osborne St SL1 ....42 F4
Osier Pl TW20 ....96 C2
Osman's Cl RG42 ....92 B1
Osnaburgh Hill GU15 ....151 B5
Osney Rd SL6 ....19 E2
Osprey Ct 4 RG1 ....86 C7
Osterley Cl RG40 ....116 F5
Osterley Dr RG4 ....59 E6
Ostler Gate SL6 ....19 C1
Ostlers Dr TW15 ....98 C3
Oswald Cl RG42 ....91 D2
Othello Gr RG42 ....118 E8
Otter Cl RG45 ....143 A7
Otter Ct RG2 ....113 C7
Our Lady of Peace RC Inf Sch
SL1 ....41 C8
Our Lady of Peace RC Jun
Sch SL1 ....41 C8
Our Lady of the Rosary RC
Sch TW18 ....97 A2
Our Lady's Prep Sch
RG45 ....143 B5
Our Ladys RC First Sch
KT16 ....124 A1
Ouseley Lodge SL4 ....95 C8
Ouseley Rd TW19 ....95 D8
Overbecks RG14 ....105 D4
Overbridge Sq RG14 ....105 E3
Overbury Ave RG41 ....88 F1
Overdale Rise GU16 ....151 E3
Overdown Rd RG31 ....57 D3
Overlanders End RG31 ....57 E3
Overlord Cl GU15 ....151 C8
Owen Cl SL3 ....43 F1
Owen Rd Newbury RG14 ..105 B6
Windlesham GU20 ....146 D5
Owl Cl RG41 ....115 E5
Owletts Gr RG14 ....105 D4
Owlsmoor Prim Sch
GU47 ....143 E1
Owlsmoor Rd GU47 ....143 D1
Owston RG6 ....87 C2
Oxenhope RG12 ....118 A5
Oxford Ave Burnham SL1 ...21 B3
Harlington TW6 ....71 F7
Slough SL1 ....41 F8
Oxford Cl TW15 ....98 C1
Oxford Ho RG41 ....116 A6
Oxford Rd Chieveley RG20 ..51 C1
Marlow SL7 ....1 D2
Newbury RG14 ....104 F5
Reading RG30,RG1 ....85 D8
Reading,Purley on T RG8,
RG30 ....57 D4
Sandhurst GU47 ....143 E2
Windsor SL4 ....67 C6
Wokingham RG41 ....116 A6
Oxford Rd E SL4 ....67 C6
Oxford Road Com Sch
RG1 ....85 F7
Oxford St Caversham RG4 ..59 A2
Hungerford RG17 ....100 E7
Lambourn RG17 ....25 B3
Newbury RG14 ....104 F4
Oxfordshire Pl RG42 ....91 F1

P

Pacific Cl TW14 ....98 F7
Pack & Prime La RG9 ....15 C2
Packman Dr RG10 ....61 D6
Padbury Cl TW14 ....98 D7
Padbury Oaks UB7 ....70 B6
Paddick Cl RG4 ....60 E3
Paddick Dr Earley RG6 ....87 D1
Lower Earley RG6 ....114 D8
Paddison Ct RG19 ....106 E2
Paddock Cl
Camberley GU15 ....152 A6
Maidenhead SL6 ....39 A2
Paddock Cotts SL6 ....39 A2
Paddock Hts RG10 ....61 E4
Paddock Rd RG4 ....59 D1
Paddock The
Bracknell RG12 ....118 C6
Chilton OX11 ....10 D8
Crowthorne RG45 ....143 A6
Datchet SL3 ....68 B6
Maidenhead SL6 ....19 C2
Newbury RG14 ....105 C2
Paddocks Cvn Site The
GU25 ....122 E3
Paddocks The HP10 ....3 B8
Paddocks Way KT16 ....124 B1
Padley Ct 8 RG1 ....86 C7
Padstow Cl SL3 ....43 E3
Padstow Gdns RG2 ....86 B1
Padstow Wlk TW14 ....98 F7
Padworth Coll RG7 ....109 E1
Padworth La RG7 ....109 E3
Padworth Rd RG7 ....136 C7
Page Rd TW14 ....71 D1
Page's Croft RG40 ....116 D5
Pages Wharf SL6 ....40 C8
Paget Cl Camberley GU15 .152 B7
Marlow SL7 ....1 F4
Paget Dr SL6 ....39 A4
Paget Rd SL3 ....43 F2
Pagoda The SL6 ....20 B1
Paice Gn RG40 ....116 D7
Paices Hill RG7 ....135 A5
Pakenham Rd RG12 ....118 D2
Palace Cl SL1 ....41 F5
Paley St SL6 ....64 B6
Palgrave Ho RG45 ....143 C4
Palmer CE Jun Sch The
RG40 ....116 D7
Palmer Cl
Crowthorne RG40 ....143 A8
Peasemore RG20 ....50 D7
Palmer Park Ave RG6 ....87 A6
Palmer School Rd RG40 .116 C6
Palmer The 23 RG30 ....85 D6
Palmer's Hill RG8 ....54 C5
Palmer's La
Burghfield Common RG7 ..111 A2
Burghfield Common,Poundgreen
RG7 ....112 A3
Palmera Ave RG31 ....84 C4
Palmers Cl SL6 ....39 A3
Palmerston Ave SL3 ....43 B3
Palmerstone Ct GU25 ...122 E4
Palmerstone Rd RG6 ....87 B6
Pamber Heath Rd RG26 .135 E1
Pamber Rd RG7 ....136 B1
Pamela Row SL6 ....65 A8
Pan's Gdns GU15 ....151 F4
Pangbourne Coll RG8 ....56 A4
Pangbourne Hill RG8 ....56 C5
Pangbourne Mews RG8 ..56 D6
Pangbourne Pl RG8 ....56 D6
Pangbourne Prim Sch
RG8 ....56 E5
Pangbourne Rd RG8 ....55 C4
Pangbourne St 2 RG30 ..85 B8
Pangbourne Sta RG8 ....56 C6
Pankhurst Dr RG12 ....118 D4
Pannells Cl KT16 ....123 F1
Pantile Row SL3 ....44 A2
Papist Way OX10 ....14 A8
Papplewick Sch SL5 ....120 A8
Paprika Cl RG6 ....86 F1
Parade Ct 7 SL8 ....3 A4
Parade The Ashford TW16 ..98 F1
Bourne End SL8 ....3 A3
Earley RG6 ....87 B3
Egham TW18 ....96 D3
Farnham Common SL2 ....22 C6
Reading RG30 ....85 D5
Tadley RG26 ....135 B1
Wentworth GU25 ....122 D3
Windsor SL4 ....66 D6
Woodley RG5 ....87 E4
Woodley RG5 ....87 F8
Paradise La RG7 ....108 C7
Paradise Mews RG9 ....15 D2
Paradise Rd RG9 ....15 D1
Paradise Way RG7 ....108 C7
Park Ave
Camberley GU15 ....151 D4
Staines TW18 ....97 A2
Thatcham RG18 ....106 D4
Thorpe Lea TW20 ....96 C1
Upper Halliford TW17 ....125 E6
Wokingham RG40 ....116 B6
Wraysbury TW19 ....68 D3
Park Cl SL4 ....67 D5
Park Close Cotts TW20 ....94 F3
Park Cnr SL4 ....66 E4
Park Cotts
3 Camberley GU15 ....151 B3
Kintbury RG17 ....101 B3
Park Cres Reading RG30 ..85 B6
Sunningdale SL5 ....120 F3
Park Dr SL5 ....120 F3
Park End RG14 ....105 A4
Park Farm Ind Est GU15 .151 C1
Park Gr RG30 ....85 B6
Park Ho
Englefield Green TW20 ....95 C2
Maidenhead SL6 ....39 E6
Park House Sch & Sports Coll
RG14 ....130 E6
Park La Barkham RG40 ....141 B5
Beech Hill RG7 ....138 C2
Bracknell RG42 ....90 E1
Burnham SL1 ....21 E7
Camberley GU15 ....151 C5
Charvil RG10 ....61 B3
Horton SL3 ....69 A4
Newbury RG14 ....105 A4
Reading RG31 ....84 C7
Silchester RG7 ....137 C2
Slough SL3 ....43 B3
Stockcross RG20 ....103 B2
Thatcham RG18 ....106 D4
Winkfield SL4 ....93 B7
Park Lane Prim Sch
RG31 ....84 D8
Park Lane Prim Sch Annexe
RG31 ....84 D8
Park Lawn SL2 ....22 C2
Park Mews TW19 ....97 F8
Park Pl GU17 ....150 F3
Park Rd Ashford TW15 ....98 B3
Bracknell RG12 ....118 D8
Park Rd *continued*
Camberley GU15 ....151 C4
Egham TW20 ....96 A4
Henley-On-T RG9 ....15 E1
Lower Halliford TW17 ....125 A1
Sandhurst GU47 ....150 C8
Stanwell TW19 ....70 C1
Stoke Poges SL2 ....22 E3
Wokingham RG40 ....116 B6
Park St Bagshot GU19 ....145 E3
Camberley GU15 ....151 C5
Hungerford RG17 ....100 D5
Maidenhead SL6 ....39 F7
Newbury RG14 ....105 A4
Poyle SL3 ....69 D6
Slough SL1 ....42 F4
Windsor SL4 ....67 D6
Park Terr RG14 ....105 A3
Park The RG17 ....25 A3
Park View Ascot SL5 ....120 E8
Bagshot GU19 ....145 D3
Burghfield Common RG7 ..111 A2
Reading RG1 ....86 A5
Beech Hill RG7 ....138 D5
Park View Dr N RG10 ....61 A5
Park View Dr S RG10 ....61 A4
Park Wall La RG8 ....34 C1
Park Way
Hungerford RG17 ....100 E4
Newbury RG14 ....105 A3
Park Wlk RG8 ....57 D5
Parkcorner La RG2,RG41 .114 F6
Parker's Cnr RG7 ....83 A3
Parker's La RG42 ....92 B5
Parkers Ct GU19 ....145 E3
Parkfields GU46 ....149 D6
Parkgate SL1 ....21 C1
Parkhill Cl GU17 ....150 D4
Parkhill Dr RG31 ....57 D2
Parkhill Rd GU17 ....150 D4
Parkhouse Ct 9 RG30 ....85 D6
Parkhouse La RG30 ....85 D6
Parkhurst 20 RG30 ....85 D6
Parkland Ave SL3 ....43 D2
Parkland Dr RG12 ....118 E8
Parkland Gr TW15 ....98 A4
Parkland Rd TW15 ....98 A4
Parkside Henley-On-T RG9 .15 C2
Maidenhead SL6 ....19 D1
Woolhampton RG7 ....108 D4
Parkside Lo 11 SL3 ....43 A3
Parkside Pl TW18 ....97 A2
Parkside Rd Reading RG30 .85 D6
Sunningdale SL5 ....121 A4
Thatcham RG18 ....106 D5
Parkside Wlk SL1 ....43 A3
Parkstone Dr GU15 ....151 C4
Parkview
Flackwell Heath HP10 ....3 B7
Maidenhead SL6 ....39 F7
Parkview Chase SL1 ....41 E7
Parkway Camberley GU15 .151 C3
Crowthorne RG45 ....143 A5
Marlow SL7 ....2 A3
Parkway Dr RG4 ....60 E3
Parlaunt Park Prim Sch
SL3 ....44 B3
Parlaunt Rd SL3 ....44 B2
Parliament La SL1,SL6 ....20 F5
Parnham Ave GU18 ....153 D8
Parry Gn N SL3 ....43 F2
Parry Green S SL3 ....44 A2
Parsley Cl RG6 ....86 F1
Parson's Wood La SL2 ..22 D5
Parsonage Gdns SL7 ....1 E1
Parsonage La
Farnham Common SL2 ....22 D4
Hungerford RG17 ....100 D6
Lambourn RG17 ....25 A3
Windsor SL4 ....67 A6
Parsonage Pl RG17 ....25 A3
Parsonage Rd TW20 ....95 D3
Parsonage Way GU16 ...151 E1
Parsons Cl Barkham RG2 .141 A8
Newbury RG14 ....104 E2
Parsons Down Jun & Inf Schs
RG19 ....106 A3
Parsons Field GU47 ....150 B8
Parsons Rd SL3 ....43 F1
Part La RG7 ....139 E4
Parthia Cl RG1 ....86 A6
Partridge Ave GU46 ....149 B6
Partridge Cl GU16 ....151 E1
Partridge Dr RG31 ....84 C6
Partridge Mead SL6 ....19 F2
Paschal Rd GU15 ....151 F8
Pasture Cl RG6 ....114 B8
Patches Field SL7 ....1 E5
Paterson Cl GU16 ....152 C3
Pates Manor Dr TW14 ....98 D8
Pathway The RG42 ....90 C3
Patricia Cl SL1 ....41 E6
Patrick Gdns RG42 ....91 E1
Patrick Rd RG4 ....59 B2
Patriot Pl RG1 ....86 C7
Patten Ash Dr RG40 ....116 E7
Patten Ave GU46 ....149 C5
Patterson Ct HP10 ....3 E7
Pattinson Rd RG2 ....113 D6
Pavenham Cl RG6 ....114 B8
Pavilion Gdns TW18 ....97 B1
Pavilions End The GU15 .151 D3
Pavy Cl RG19 ....106 F2
Paxton Ave SL1 ....42 C3
Payley Dr RG40 ....116 E8

Paynesdown Rd RG19 ....106 B4
Peace La SL6 ....19 F6
Peach St RG40 ....116 C6
Peachey Dr RG19 ....106 F2
Peacock Ave TW14 ....98 D7
Peacock Cotts RG40 .....117 C5
Peacock La RG12 ....117 D6
Peacock Rd SL7 ....2 A3
Peacock Wlk RG41 ....115 E5
Pear Ave TW17 ....125 E6
Pear Tree Ct GU15 ....152 B8
Pear Tree La RG14 ....105 C5
Pear Tree Rd TW15 ....98 C3
Pearce Cl SL6 ....19 F1
Pearce Dr SL6 ....19 F7
Pearce Rd SL6 ....19 F1
Pearce's Orch RG9 ....15 D3
Pearl Gdns SL3 ....42 B5
Pearmain Cl TW17 ......125 B4
Pearmans Glade RG2 ....113 E8
Pearson Rd RG4 ....60 D3
Pearson Way RG5 ....87 E5
Peartree Cl SL1 ....41 F5
Peascod Pl **11** SL4 ......67 D6
Peascod St SL4 ....67 D6
Pease Hill RG7 ....107 F7
Peasemore Hill RG20 ....50 B8
Pebble Hill RG17 ....128 B6
Peckmoor Dr RG19 ....131 C7
Peddlars Gr GU46 ....149 E6
Peel Cl Caversham RG4 ....59 D2
   Windsor SL4 ....67 B4
   Woodley RG5 ....88 B8
Peel Ct SL1 ....42 B8
Peel Ctr The RG12 ....118 B7
Peel Ho TW20 ....95 F2
Peg's Green Cl RG30 .....85 B6
Pegasus Cl RG19 ....106 A4
Pegasus Ct
   2 Lambourn RG17 ....25 B2
   Reading RG31 ....84 C7
Peggotty Pl GU47 ....143 E2
Peket Cl TW18 ....123 E8
Pelham Ct
   Maidenhead SL6 ....39 E7
   11 Reading RG30 ....85 D6
   Staines TW18 ....97 B3
Pelican La RG14 ....105 A4
Pelican Rd RG26 ....135 E2
Pell St RG1 ....86 B6
Pelling Hill SL4 ....95 B7
Pemberley Lodge SL4 ....67 A4
Pemberton Gdns RG31 ....84 D4
Pemberton Rd SL2 ....21 E1
Pembroke RG12 ....118 A1
Pembroke Broadway
   GU15 ....151 C5
Pembroke Cl Ascot SL5 ..120 D4
   Burghfield Common RG7 ..111 C3
Pembroke Ho **3** RG4 ....59 C1
Pembroke Mews SL5 ....120 D4
Pembroke Pl RG4 ....59 C3
Pembroke Rd **3** RG14 ..105 A3
Pembury Ct UB3 ....71 D8
Pendals Cl RG18 ....52 F5
Pendeen Ct SL1 ....42 A5
Pendell Ave UB3 ....71 F7
Pendennis Ave RG4 ......59 E6
Pendine Pl RG12 ....118 B4
Pendlebury RG12 ....118 A2
Pendragon Ct RG30 ......85 D5
Pendragon Way GU15 ...152 D3
Pendred Rd RG2 ....113 D6
Penfurzen La RG42 ....91 D8
Peninsula Cl GU15 ......152 B7
Peninsular Cl TW14 ......71 E1
Penling Cl SL6 ....19 E6
Penn Cl RG4 ....59 C4
Penn Ct **8** SL7 ....1 E2
Penn Mdw SL2 ....22 F4
Penn Rd Datchet SL3 ....68 D6
   Newbury RG14 ....104 D5
   Slough SL2 ....22 D1
Pennfields RG10 ....61 E6
Pennine Cl RG31 ....84 B6
Pennine Rd SL2 ....22 C8
Pennine Way Charvil RG10 ..61 B4
   Harlington UB7 ....71 D7
Penny Hill Cvn Site
   GU17 ....149 C2
Penny La TW17 ....125 E2
Pennylets Gn SL2 ....23 A5
Pennypiece RG8 ....34 C7
Pennyroyal Ct RG1 ....86 A6
Penroath Ave RG30 ......85 C6
Penrose Ave RG5 ....87 E6
Penrose Cl RG14 ....104 F5
Penrose Ct TW20 ....95 C2
Pensford Cl RG45 ....143 B7
Penshurst Rd SL6 ....39 D5
Pentangle The **12** RG14 ..105 A4
Pentland Ave TW17 ....125 D3
Pentland Cl RG30 ....84 F5
Pentland Pl RG19 ....106 C2
Pentland Rd SL2 ....42 A8
Pentlands The RG17 ....102 C2
Penton Ave TW18 ......123 F8
Penton Cl TW18 ....96 F2
Penton Hall TW18 ......124 A8
Penton Rd TW18 ....124 A8
Penton Hook Marina
   KT16 ....124 A6
Penton Hook Rd TW18 ..124 A4
Penton Rd TW18 ....96 F1
Pentridge Ho **2** RG22 ..113 C8

Penwood Ct SL6 ....39 B7
Penwood Gdns RG12 ...117 D3
Penwood La SL7 ....1 C1
Penwood Rd RG20 ......130 C3
Penyston Rd SL6 ....39 C7
Penzance Spur SL2 ......22 B1
Pepler Way SL1 ....21 B2
Peppard La RG9 ....35 E7
Peppard Rd
   Caversham RG4 ....59 B3
   Emmer Green RG4 ......59 C6
Pepper La RG2 ....86 E3
Pepys Cl SL3 ....69 B8
Perch Cl SL7 ....18 C8
Percival Rd TW13 ....98 F6
Percy Ave TW15 ....98 A3
Percy Bryant Rd TW16 ..98 E1
Percy Pl SL3 ....68 B6
Peregrine Cl
   Bracknell RG12 ....118 B4
   Wokingham RG41 ......115 F5
Peregrine Rd TW16 .....125 F7
Periam Cl RG9 ....35 C8
Perkins Ct TW15 ....97 F3
Perkins Way RG41 ......116 A5
Perpetual Park Dr RG9 ..35 F8
Perrin Cl TW15 ....97 F3
Perrin Ct TW15 ....98 A4
Perry Ho SL1 ....21 B1
Perry Oaks RG12 ....118 E7
Perry Oaks Dr TW6,UB7 ..70 C5
Perry Way
   Bracknell RG12 ....118 E7
   Lightwater GU18 ......152 F7
Perrycroft SL4 ....66 F4
Perryfields Way SL1 .....21 B1
Perryhill Dr GU47 ......142 F1
Perryman Way SL2 ......21 F2
Perseverance Hill RG9 ..35 A5
Perth Ave SL1 ....42 B7
Perth Cl RG5 ....61 A1
Perth Trad Est SL1 ....42 B8
Peterhead Mews SL3 ....44 A1
Peterhouse Cl GU47 ...143 F2
Peters La SL6 ....65 B8
Petersfield Ave
   Slough SL2 ....43 A5
   Staines TW15,TW18 .....97 C2
Petersfield Rd TW18 ....97 C3
Petrel Cl RG41 ....115 E5
Petts La TW17 ....125 A5
Petty Cl SL1 ....41 E7
Petty Cross SL1 ....41 E7
Petworth Ave RG30 ......84 F3
Petworth Ct
   Frimley GU15 ....151 F4
   Reading RG31 ....85 E6
   Windsor SL4 ....67 A6
Pevensey Ave RG4 ....59 E5
Pevensey Ct RG12 ....86 E1
Pevensey Rd SL2 ....42 A8
Pewsey Vale RG12 ......118 F4
Pheasant Cl RG41 ....88 C2
Pheasant La RG10 ......131 F3
Pheasants Croft SL6 ....39 A4
Pheasants Ridge SL7 .....1 C7
Philbye Mews SL1 ....41 F4
Philip Cotts SL8 ....3 C3
Philip Dr HP10 ....3 C7
Philip Rd TW18 ....97 D2
Phillimore Rd RG4 ....59 C8
Phillip Copse RG12 .....118 D2
Phillips Cl RG5 ....61 B1
Phipps Cl SL6 ....39 A2
Phipps Rd SL1 ....41 E8
Phoebe Ct **16** RG1 .....86 A6
Phoenix Bsns Pk RG12 .117 C7
Phoenix Cl RG41 ....115 E6
Phoenix Ct SL6 ....39 D4
Phoenix Pl **3** TW18 ....97 A3
Phoenix Wlk RG14 ......130 C6
Phyllis Court Dr RG9 ....15 E3
Pickering RG12 ....118 A5
Pickets Cl GU47 ....143 E1
Picketts La RG8 ....55 E4
Pickford Dr SL3 ....43 F5
Pickfords Gdns SL1 ......42 E5
Pickins Piece SL3 ....69 A6
Pickwell Cl RG6 ....87 C1
Pickwick Gdns GU15 ...152 B4
Pickwick Terr SL2 ....43 B6
Picton Cl GU15 ....152 B7
Picton Way RG4 ....59 B4
Pierce's Hill RG31 ....57 C1
Piercefield Rd SL1 ....84 C4
Pierson Rd SL4 ....66 D6
Pigeonhouse La SL5 .....92 E4
Pigeons Farm Rd RG19 ..131 D8
Piggott Sch The RG10 ...61 C7
Piggott's Rd **2** RG4 ....59 C1
Pightle The RG7 ....111 F3
Pigott Cl RG40 ....116 D6
Pigott Rd RG40 ....116 D6
Pike Cl SL7 ....18 C8
Pike St RG14 ....105 B4
Pikeshaw Way RG31 .....57 C2
Pimento Dr RG6 ....86 F1
Pimpernel Pl RG18 .....106 F4
Pincents Kiln Ind Est
   RG31 ....84 A4
Pincents La RG31 ....84 A4
Pinchcut RG7 ....111 A3
Pinchington La
   RG19 ....131 B7
Pindar Pl RG14 ....105 E5
Pine Ave GU15 ....151 D3
Pine Cl Maidenhead SL6 ..39 B7
   Sandhurst GU15 ....150 E7

Pine Croft Rd RG41 ....116 A2
Pine Ct RG12 ....118 C5
Pine Dr Blackwater GU17 ..150 E3
   Mortimer RG7 ....136 F6
   Wokingham RG40 ......142 A7
Pine Gr Twyford RG10 ....61 D5
   Windlesham GU20 .....146 D4
Pine Mount Rd GU15 ...151 D4
Pine Ridge RG14 ....105 C5
Pine Ridge Inf Sch
   GU15 ....145 A1
Pine Ridge Rd RG7 .....111 A3
Pine Trees Bsns Pk
   TW18 ....96 E3
Pine Way TW20 ....95 B2
Pinecote Dr SL5 ....120 F2
Pinecroft SL7 ....1 D4
Pinefields SL5 ....143 B4
Pinehill Rd RG45 ....143 C5
Pinehill Rise GU47 .....150 E8
Pinehurst SL5 ....120 D4
Pinel Cl GU25 ....122 E5
Pinelands Cvn Pk RG7 ..135 F4
Piner Cotts SL4 ....66 E4
Pineridge Gdns RG30 ....85 D6
Pines Inf Sch The RG12 .118 A2
Pines Jun Sch The
   RG12 ....118 A2
Pines The
   Camberley GU15 ....151 F7
   Twyford RG10 ....61 E7
Pinetree Cl RG4 ....59 A5
Pinewood Ave RG45 ....143 C6
Pinewood Cl
   Sandhurst GU47 ....149 F8
   Tadley RG26 ....134 D1
Pinewood Cotts RG45 ...143 A8
Pinewood Dr
   Caversham RG4 ....58 E5
   Newtown RG20 ....131 A2
   Staines TW18 ....97 A3
Pinewood Gdns GU19 ..145 C3
Pinewood Mews TW19 ...70 D1
Pinewood Pk RG40 ......143 C8
Pinewood Rd GU25 .....122 A5
Pingewood Cl RG30 .....85 A2
Pingewood Rd N RG30 ..85 A1
Pingewood Rd S RG7,
   RG30 ....112 C7
Pinglestone Cl UB7 ......70 E7
Pink La SL1 ....21 B3
Pinkneys Dr SL6 ....38 F8
Pinkneys Rd SL6 ....39 A8
Pinks La RG26 ....134 E1
Pinnacle The RG1 ....86 D7
Piper's End GU25 ......122 D6
Pipers Cl SL1 ....21 C2
Pipers Ct Burnham SL1 ..21 C1
   Thatcham RG19 ....107 A2
Pipers La RG19 ....106 F1
Pipers Way RG19 ....106 F2
Pipit Ct RG19 ....106 B3
Pippins Ct TW15 ....98 B2
Pippins Sch SL3 ....69 F6
Pippins The SL3 ....43 F5
Pipsons Cl GU46 ....149 D6
Pitch Pl RG42 ....90 D3
Pitcroft Ave RG6 ....87 B3
Pitfield La RG7 ....137 C4
Pitford Rd RG5 ....88 A8
Pitt's La RG6 ....87 B8
Pitts Cl RG42 ....90 C2
Pitts Rd SL1 ....42 C5
Plackett Way SL1 ....41 D5
Plaines Cl SL1 ....41 F5
Planes The KT16 ....124 C2
Plantagenet Pk RG42 ..118 F8
Plantation Cl RG18 ......78 F5
Plantation Rd Chilton OX12 ..9 F8
   Tadley RG26 ....134 F2
Plantation Row GU15 ..151 B5
Plantinum Apartments **14**
   RG1 ....86 B6
Plateau The RG42 ....92 A1
Platt Ct RG17 ....100 E3
Platt La RG17 ....45 C6
Play Platt RG7 ....83 D4
Playhatch Rd RG4 ....87 E5
Playhatch Rd RG4 ....60 B5
Plough La Shiplake RG9 ..35 E1
   Stoke Poges SL2 ......23 B4
   Wokingham RG40 ......116 F6
Plough Rd GU46 ....149 B6
Ploughlands RG42 .....117 F8
Ploughlees La SL1 ....42 E6
Plover Cl Staines TW18 ..96 F5
   Wokingham RG41 ......115 F5
Plover La RG20 ....140 E1
Plowden Way RG9 ....35 E1
Plummery The **1** RG1 ..86 C7
Plumpton Rd RG14 .....105 C1
Plumtrees RG6 ....87 B2
Pluto Cl SL1 ....41 F4
Pluto Rd OX11 ....9 F8
Plymouth Ave RG6 ....87 C5
Plymouth Rd SL1 ....41 E8
Plympton Cl RG6 ....87 C3
Pocket Cl Bracknell RG42 ..117 D7
   Earley RG6 ....87 B4
Pocketts Yd SL6 ....20 B7
Pococks La SL4 ....67 F5
Poffley Pl RG17 ....107 A3
Point Royal RG12 ....118 B4
Pointers Cl RG20 ....51 B2
Points The SL6 ....39 B3
Polehampton CE Inf Sch
   RG10 ....61 D5
Polehampton Cl RG10 ...61 D4

Polehampton Ct RG10 ...61 D4
Polehampton Jun Sch
   RG10 ....61 D5
Pollard Cl SL4 ....68 B2
Pollardrow Ave RG42 ..117 F8
Pollards Way RG31 ......84 D4
Polo Ctr The SL5 ....121 C6
Polsted Rd RG31 ....84 F5
Polyanthus Way RG45 ..143 B8
Polygon Bsns Ctr SL3 ...69 F5
Pond Cl
   Farnborough (Berks) OX12 ..8 E1
   Newbury RG14 ....130 D7
Pond Head La RG4 .....149 C6
Pond Head La RG4 ......87 D4
Pond Ho KT16 ....124 B2
Pond La Hermitage RG18 ..79 C2
   Mapledurham RG4 ......58 A6
Pond Rd TW20 ....96 C2
Pondmoor Rd RG12 ....118 B4
Pondside Cl UB3 ....71 D7
Pool End Cl TW17 .....125 A4
Pool La Slough SL1 ......42 E6
   Waltham St Lawrence RG10 ..63 A5
Poole Cl RG30 ....85 A7
Pooley Ave TW20 ....96 B3
Pooley Green Cl TW20 ..96 C3
Pooley Green Rd TW20 ..96 C3
Poolmans Rd SL4 ....66 D4
Pope Cl TW14 ....98 F7
Popes Cl SL3 ....69 C7
Popes La SL6 ....39 C7
Popeswood Rd RG42 ...117 D8
Popeswood Rdbt RG42 ..117 D7
Popham Ct RG12 ....118 F4
Poplar Ave Reading RG30 ..84 F5
   Windlesham GU20 .....146 C4
Poplar Cl Bracknell RG12 ..118 D6
   Brimpton RG19 ....133 A6
   Poyle SL3 ....69 E6
Poplar Gdns RG2 ....86 E1
Poplar Ho SL3 ....43 F1
Poplar La Hurst RG10 ...62 A2
   Winnersh RG41 ....88 D3
Poplar Rd Ashford TW15 ..98 C3
   Wooburn Green HP10 ....3 E7
Poplars Gr SL6 ....3 E7
Poplars The SL5 ....120 A4
Poppy Dr RG18 ....106 F4
Poppy Way RG31 ....84 C5
Poppyhills Rd GU15 ....151 F8
Porchester SL5 ....120 A5
Porchester Rd RG14 ...105 A1
Porchfield Cl RG6 ....87 A1
Porlock Cl RG10 ....106 D2
Porlock Pl RG31 ....84 C4
Port Down RG17 ....100 E5
Porter Cl RG6 ....114 C8
Porter End RG14 ....131 B8
Portesbery Hill Dr GU15 ..151 E6
Portesbery Rd GU15 ...151 D6
Portia Gr RG42 ....118 C8
Portland Bsns Ctr SL3 ..68 B6
Portland Cl SL1 ....21 D1
Portland Cres TW13 .....98 D4
Portland Gdns Marlow SL7 ..2 A1
   Reading RG30 ....84 D7
Portland Rd TW15 ....97 E5
Portlock Rd SL6 ....39 C7
Portman Cl **5** RG42 ....117 E8
Portman Ctr The RG30 ..58 D1
Portman Rd RG30 ....58 D1
Portmeirion Gdns RG30 ..57 F1
Portnall Cl GU25 ....121 F4
Portnall Dr GU25 ....121 F4
Portnall Rise GU25 .....121 F3
Portrush Cl RG5 ....87 D6
Portsmouth Cl RG30 .....42 E6
Portsmouth Rd GU15 ..152 A7
Portway Riseley RG2 ...139 C2
   Tadley RG26 ....134 C1
Portway Cl RG1 ....85 E6
Post Horn Pl RG12 ......84 B4
Post Office Cotts SL2 ....23 A5
Post Office La
   Burghfield Common RG30 ..111 D5
   Slough SL3 ....43 D7
Post Office Rd RG17 ...127 E5
Posting House Mews
   RG14 ....104 E4
Potkiln La RG8 ....56 A1
Potbury Cl SL4 ....93 B2
Potley Hill Prim Sch
   GU46 ....150 A5
Potley Hill Rd GU46 ...149 F5
Pottery La RG17 ....127 E5
Pottery Rd RG30 ....57 F1
Potts Pl **5** SL7 ....1 F2
Poulcott TW19 ....68 E1
Pound Cotts RG8 ....34 A6
Pound Cres SL7 ....1 C1
Pound La Hurst RG10 .....88 F6
   Little Marlow SL7 ....2 C1
   Marlow SL7 ....1 C1
   Newbury RG20 ....130 F5
   Sonning RG4 ....60 F5
   Thatcham RG18,RG19 ..106 A3
   Windlesham GU20 .....146 D4
Pound Piece RG17 .....100 C5
Pound Rd KT16 ....124 B2
Pound St RG14 ....104 F2
Pound The SL3 ....43 E3
Poundfield La SL6 ....19 F7
Poundfield Way RG10 ...61 F3

Powis Cl SL6 ....39 B4
Powney Rd SL6 ....39 B6
Poyle 14 Trad Est SL3 ...69 E4
Poyle Gdns RG12 ......118 D8
Poyle La SL1 ....21 B3
Poyle New Cotts SL3 ....69 F5
Poyle Rd SL3 ....69 E5
Poyle Tech Ctr The SL3 ..69 E5
Poynings The SL0 ....44 F2
Prancing Horse Cl
   RG19 ....106 E3
Precinct The TW20 ......96 A3
Precincts The SL1 ....21 C1
Prescott RG12 ....117 F2
Prescott Rd SL3 ....69 E5
Presentation Coll RG30 ..85 D5
Preston Rd
   Littleton TW17 ....125 A4
   Reading RG2 ....86 B5
   Slough SL2 ....43 C6
Prestwick Ct **21** RG1 ..86 D7
Prestwood SL2 ....43 B7
Pretoria Rd KT16 ......123 F1
Price Gdns RG42 ....91 B2
Prides Crossing SL5 .....93 A1
Priest Ave RG40 ....116 F5
Priest Hill Caversham RG4 ..59 A3
   Englefield Green SL4,TW20 ..95 C1
Priest La GU24 ....153 C5
Priestwood Ave RG42 ..117 F8
Priestwood Court Rd
   RG42 ....118 A8
Priestwood Sq **7** RG42 ..118 A8
Primrose Cl RG8 ....57 C5
Primrose La RG41 ....88 C3
Primrose Way GU47 ...143 B1
Primrose Wlk
   Bracknell RG12 ....118 C4
   Yateley GU46 ....149 B6
Prince Albert Ct **6** TW16 ..98 E1
Prince Albert Dr SL5 ...119 D4
Prince Albert's Wlk SL3,
   SL4 ....68 B6
Prince Andrew Cl SL6 ...20 B1
Prince Andrew Rd SL6 ...20 B1
Prince Andrew Way
   SL5 ....119 D7
Prince Consort Cotts
   SL4 ....67 D5
Prince Consort Dr SL5 ..119 C6
Prince Consort's Dr
   Old Windsor SL4 ....94 A6
   Windsor SL4 ....67 A1
Prince Dr GU47 ....143 A1
Prince Hold Rd RG19 ..106 A3
Prince Of Wales Ave
   RG30 ....85 D7
Prince of Wales Wlk
   GU15 ....151 C6
Prince William Ct TW15 ..97 F3
Prince William Dr RG31 ..57 C1
Prince's Rd SL0 ....50 D6
Prince's St RG1 ....86 C7
Princes Cl Bagshot GU19 ..145 E1
   Eton SL4 ....41 F1
Princes Ct Bourne End SL8 ..3 C4
   Englefield Green TW20 ..95 C3
Princes Rd Ashford TW15 ..97 E3
   Bourne End SL8 ....3 C3
Princess Gdns SL5 ......95 F2
Felham TW13 ....98 F5
Princess St SL1 ....43 B4
Princess Terr SL8 ....3 C3
Princess Ave SL4 ....67 B4
Princess Christians Hospl
   SL4 ....67 D7
Princess Margaret Hospl The
   SL4 ....67 D5
Princess Marina Dr
   Barkham, Arborfield Garrison
   RG2 ....140 F7
   Barkham,Langley Common
   RG2 ....115 A1
Princess Sq RG12 ......118 B7
Princess St SL6 ....39 F6
Princess Way GU15 ....151 C5
Prior Croft Cl GU15 ....152 A4
Prior End GU15 ....152 A5
Prior Heath Com Inf Sch
   GU15 ....152 A5
Prior Place Cross Roads
   GU15 ....152 B4
Prior Rd GU15 ....152 A4
Prior's La GU17 ....150 A5
Priors Cl Maidenhead SL6 ..40 B2
   3 Slough SL1 ....43 A3
Priors Court Cotts
   Chieveley RG18 ....78 A5
   Hermitage RG18 ....78 F7
Priors Court Rd RG18 ...78 E7
Priors Court Sch RG18 ..78 D8
Priors Ct **8** RG1 ....86 B6
Priors Rd Tadley RG26 ..135 A1
   Windsor SL4 ....66 D4
Priors Way SL6 ....40 B2
Priors Way Ind Est SL6 ..40 B2
Priors Wood RG45 .....142 D4
Priory Ave Caversham RG4 ..59 C2
   Hungerford RG17 ......100 D4
Priory Ct
   Camberley GU15 ....150 F5
   Caversham RG4 ....59 A2
   Egham TW20 ....96 C2
   Winnersh RG41 ....88 C3

Priory Gdns TW15 ......98 D3
Priory Gn TW18 ......97 B3
Priory La RG42 ......91 C2
Priory Mews TW18 ......97 B3
Priory Pl
  Hungerford RG17 ......100 D4
  Newbury RG19 ......131 B6
Priory Rd Burnham SL1 ......41 C8
  Hungerford RG17 ......100 D4
  Newbury RG14 ......105 A1
  Sunningdale SL5 ......121 A2
  Winkfield SL5 ......119 B7
Priory Sch SL1 ......41 D8
Priory The RG41 ......88 C3
Priory Way Datchet SL3 ......68 B7
  Harmondsworth UB7 ......70 E8
Priory Wlk RG12 ......118 F5
Priscilla Ho 8 TW16 ......98 F1
Pritchard Cl RG19 ......131 D7
Privet Cl RG6 ......87 B1
Proctors Rd RG42 ......116 F6
Progress Bsns Ctr SL1 ......41 D7
Promenade SL4 ......67 C7
Promenade Rd RG4 ......59 A2
Prospect Coll RG30 ......85 A5
Prospect Cotts RG42 ......117 D8
Prospect La TW20 ......95 A3
Prospect Mews 4 RG1 ......85 F7
Prospect Park Hospl
  RG30 ......85 B6
Prospect Pl 5 SL1 ......17 F3
  Newbury RG14 ......105 A1
  Staines TW18 ......96 F3
  3 Windsor SL4 ......67 D4
Prospect Rd
  Hungerford RG17 ......100 D5
  Marlow SL7 ......1 D2
Prospect St
  Caversham RG4 ......59 B2
  Reading RG1 ......85 F7
Providence Ho GU19 ......145 E3
Providence La UB3 ......71 D7
Providence Pl SL6 ......39 A7
Prudential Bldgs 1 SL1 ......42 F4
Prune Hill TW20 ......95 E1
Prunus Cl GU24 ......153 E6
Pudding Hill RG10 ......37 D6
Pudding La RG20 ......28 E1
Pudseys Cl SL6 ......19 B6
Puffers Way RG14 ......104 E2
Pullmans Pl 6 TW18 ......97 A3
Pump La Ascot SL5 ......120 E8
  Grazeley RG7 ......112 C2
Pump La N SL7 ......1 F6
Pump La S SL7 ......2 A4
Pumpkin Hill SL1 ......21 E6
Pundles La SL6 ......63 C6
Purbeck Ho 3 RG2 ......113 C8
Purbrook Ct RG12 ......118 E3
Purcell Rd RG45 ......143 B7
Purfield Dr RG10 ......36 E2
Purley CE Inf Sch RG8 ......57 C5
Purley La RG8 ......57 C5
Purley Rise RG8 ......57 A5
Purley Village RG8 ......56 E5
Purley Way RG8 ......56 E5
Pursers Ct SL2 ......42 E6
Pursers Farm RG7 ......113 B3
Purslane RG40 ......116 D6
Purssell Cl SL6 ......39 A3
Purton Ct SL2 ......22 C5
Purton La SL2 ......22 C5
Putman Pl RG9 ......15 E1
Pyegrove Chase RG12 ......118 E2
Pyke Cl RG40 ......116 D6
Pykes Hill RG8 ......54 D4
Pyle Hill RG14 ......105 B1
Pyrcroft Ct KT16 ......123 F2
Pyrcroft Grange Prim Sch
  KT16 ......123 E3
Pyrcroft Rd KT16 ......123 E2

Q

Quadrant Ct
  Bracknell RG12 ......118 E6
  12 Reading RG1 ......86 B6
Quadrant The SL6 ......40 A6
Qualitas RG12 ......117 F1
Quantock Ave RG4 ......59 D5
Quantock Cl Charvil RG10 ......61 B4
  Harlington UB3 ......71 F7
  Slough SL3 ......44 A1
Quantocks The RG19 ......106 D2
Quarrington Cl RG19 ......106 E2
Quarry Bank GU18 ......153 A8
Quarry La Shiplake RG9 ......36 A4
  Yateley GU46 ......149 E5
Quarry Wood Rd SL6,SL7 ......19 A8
Quarrydale Dr SL6 ......19 E5
Quartz Cl RG41 ......115 D7
Quaves Rd SL3 ......43 C3
Quebec Gdns GU17 ......150 D4
Quebec Rd RG9 ......35 E8
Queen Anne Royal Free CE
  Fst Sch The SL4 ......67 D4
Queen Anne's Cl SL4 ......94 B5
Queen Anne's Ct 5 SL4 ......67 D6
Queen Anne's Rd SL4 ......67 C3
Queen Anne's Sch RG4 ......59 B3
Queen Annes Gate RG4 ......59 C3
Queen Charlotte St 8
  SL4 ......67 D6
Queen Cl RG9 ......15 E1
Queen Elizabeth Rd
  GU15 ......144 D1

Queen Elizabeth's Wlk
  SL4 ......67 F5
Queen Mary Ave GU15 ......151 A5
Queen Mary Ct TW19 ......97 E7
Queen Mary Rd TW17 ......125 C7
Queen St Caversham RG4 ......59 A3
  Chertsey KT16 ......124 A1
  Henley-On-T RG9 ......15 E1
  Maidenhead SL6 ......39 F7
Queen Victoria Cross Roads
  GU15 ......151 A6
Queen Victoria Ho
  RG40 ......116 D6
Queen Victoria St RG1 ......86 B8
Queen Victoria's Wlk SL4 ......67 F6
Queen's Cl
  North Ascot SL5 ......119 E8
  Old Windsor SL4 ......68 A2
Queen's Cotts
  Reading RG1 ......86 B7
  Wargrave RG10 ......36 D2
Queen's Dr TW18 ......97 D2
Queen's Dr SL3 ......23 F4
Queen's Dr The RG2,RG6 ......86 E4
Queen's La 8 SL6 ......39 F7
Queen's Pl SL4 ......120 A6
Queen's Rd Ascot SL5 ......120 D4
  Caversham RG4 ......59 C1
  Datchet SL3 ......68 B7
  Egham TW20 ......95 F2
  Marlow SL7 ......1 D2
  Newbury RG14 ......105 B2
  Reading RG1 ......86 C7
Queen's Terr 5 SL4 ......67 D4
Queen's Wharf RG1 ......86 C7
Queens Acre SL4 ......67 D3
Queens Acre Ho 6 SL4 ......67 D4
Queens Ct
  9 Newbury RG14 ......105 A1
  Slough SL1 ......42 F6
Queens Gate SL4 ......67 D3
Queens Hill Rise SL4 ......120 C6
Queens Keep GU15 ......151 D5
Queens Lawns RG1 ......86 D6
Queens Park Gdns TW13 ......98 F5
Queens Pine RG12 ......118 E3
Queens Rd Bisley GU24 ......153 F1
  Camberley GU15 ......151 B4
  Eton SL4 ......41 F1
  Slough SL1 ......42 F6
  Windsor SL4 ......67 C5
Queens Ride RG45 ......143 B7
Queens Way RG17 ......102 C1
Queens Wlk TW19 ......97 D4
Queens Wlk Mall 3 SL6 ......39 F7
Queensborough Dr RG4 ......58 E5
Queensbury Pl GU17 ......150 C3
Queenshill Lodge SL5 ......120 B6
Queensmead
  Ashford TW15 ......97 F3
  Datchet SL3 ......68 B6
Queensmere 8 SL1 ......43 A4
Queensmere Sh Ctr SL1 ......42 F4
Queensway
  Caversham RG4 ......59 D6
  Maidenhead SL6 ......19 E2
Quelm Park Rdbt RG42 ......91 B2
Quentin Rd RG5 ......87 D6
Quentin Way GU25 ......122 B5
Quinbrookes SL2 ......43 E7
Quince Cl SL5 ......120 D5
Quincy Rd TW20 ......96 A3
Quinn Ct 4 RG30 ......85 C7
Quintilis RG12 ......117 F1
Quoiting Sq SL7 ......1 D2
Quoitings Dr SL7 ......1 C2
Quoitings Gdns SL7 ......1 C2

R

Race Course Rd RG14 ......105 B1
Raceview Bsns Ctr
  RG14 ......105 B2
Rachaels Lake View
  RG42 ......91 E1
Rackstraw Rd GU47 ......143 D2
Radbourne Rd RG31 ......84 D4
Radcliffe Way RG42 ......117 E8
Radcot Ave SL3 ......44 B3
Radcot Cl Maidenhead SL6 ......19 E3
  Woodley RG5 ......60 E1
Radical Ride RG40 ......141 F7
Radius Pk TW14 ......71 F3
Radley Bottom
  Hungerford RG17 ......101 E7
  Hungerford Newtown RG17 ......74 B3
Radley Cl TW14 ......98 F7
Radnor Cl RG9 ......15 E2
Radnor Ho 10 RG1 ......85 E5
Radnor Rd
  Bracknell RG12 ......118 F6
  Earley RG6 ......87 C3
Radstock La SL3 ......43 A2
Radstock Prim Sch RG6 ......87 B2
Radstock Rd RG6 ......86 E7
Raeburn Way GU47 ......150 D6
RAF Staff Coll RG12 ......118 B5
Ragdale RG7 ......111 A3
Raggleswood Cl RG6 ......87 C3
Raghill RG7 ......135 D6
Raglan Ct RG2 ......86 D1
Raglan Gdns RG4 ......59 C4
Ragley Mews RG4 ......59 D6
Ragmans Cl SL7 ......1 D8
Ragstone Rd SL1 ......42 E3
Railside RG7 ......108 F2

Railton Cl RG2 ......113 D7
Railway App KT16 ......123 F1
Railway Cotts RG8 ......34 C6
Railway Rd RG14 ......105 B2
Railway Terr Egham TW18 ......96 D3
  Mortimer RG7 ......137 E5
  Slough SL2 ......42 F5
Rainbow Pk RG41 ......88 B2
Rainsborough Chase SL6 ......39 B3
Rainworth Cl RG6 ......114 A8
Raleigh Cl Slough SL1 ......42 A5
  Woodley RG5 ......87 E5
Raleigh Ct TW18 ......97 A4
Raleigh Rd TW13 ......98 F6
Raleigh Way GU16 ......151 F3
Ralphs Ride RG12 ......118 E6
Ralston Ct 10 SL4 ......67 D6
Ram Alley RG19 ......133 D1
Rambler Cl SL6 ......41 B7
Rambler La SL3 ......43 C3
Ramptons La RG7 ......136 B6
Ramsay Cl GU15 ......152 B8
Ramsay Rd GU20 ......146 E5
Ramsbury Cl RG12 ......117 E3
Ramsbury Dr Earley RG6 ......87 B4
  Hungerford RG17 ......100 E5
Ramsbury Terr RG17 ......100 E5
Ramsey Cl RG6 ......87 E2
Ramsey Ct SL2 ......21 D1
Ramsdale Cotts RG12 ......118 C6
Ramslade Rd RG12 ......118 D5
Rances La RG40 ......116 E5
Randall Cl SL3 ......43 F1
Randall Ct SL4 ......67 D6
Randall Mead RG42 ......90 B2
Randell Cl GU17 ......150 E1
Randolph Rd Reading RG1 ......59 A1
  Slough SL3 ......43 E3
Ranelagh CE Sch RG12 ......118 C6
Ranelagh Cres SL5 ......119 D8
Ranelagh Dr RG12 ......118 C6
Range Rd RG40 ......142 B7
Range Rde GU15 ......150 F7
Range View GU47 ......150 E8
Range Villas TW17 ......124 E2
Range Way TW17 ......125 A2
Rangewood Ave RG30 ......84 F3
Rankhert Prim Sch RG30 ......85 A8
Rapley Cl GU15 ......151 F8
Rapley Gn RG12 ......118 C3
Ratby Cl RG6 ......87 C2
Raven Cl GU46 ......149 B6
Ravendale Rd TW16 ......125 F7
Ravenglass Cl RG6 ......87 C3
Ravens Field SL3 ......43 D4
Ravensbourne Ave TW19 ......97 E7
Ravensbourne Dr RG5 ......87 E8
Ravenscote Com Jun Sch
  GU16 ......152 A3
Ravenscourt Marlow SL7 ......2 A3
  Sunbury TW16 ......125 F6
Ravenscroft Rd RG9 ......15 D2
Ravensdale Mews TW19 ......97 B2
Ravensdale Rd SL5 ......120 A4
Ravensfield TW20 ......95 C2
Ravenshoe Cl SL8 ......3 A3
Ravenstone Rd GU15 ......152 D5
Ravenswing Mobile Home Pk
  RG7 ......135 D2
Ravenswood Ave RG45 ......142 E5
Ravenswood Dr GU15 ......152 A5
Ravenswood Village
  Settlement RG45 ......142 E6
Ravensworth Rd
  Mortimer RG7 ......136 E5
  Slough SL2 ......22 A2
Rawcliffe Ho SL6 ......40 A6
Rawlinson Rd GU15 ......150 F6
Ray Dr SL6 ......40 B7
Ray Ho 5 SL6 ......3 A4
Ray Lea Cl SL6 ......40 B8
Ray Lea Rd SL6 ......40 B8
Ray Lodge SL6 ......40 A8
Ray Lodge Mews SL6 ......20 A1
Ray Mdw SL6 ......20 A1
Ray Mead Ct SL6 ......20 C1
Ray Mead Rd SL6 ......40 C8
Ray Mill Rd E SL6 ......20 B1
Ray Mill Rd W SL6 ......40 A8
Ray Park Ave SL6 ......40 B8
Ray Park La SL6 ......40 B8
Ray Park Rd SL6 ......40 B8
Ray St SL6 ......40 B8
Rayfield SL6 ......40 B8
Raymond Cl SL3 ......69 E7
Raymond Rd
  Maidenhead SL6 ......39 D7
  Slough SL3 ......44 A3
Rayner Dr RG2 ......140 E8
Rayners Cl SL3 ......44 C8
Rays Ave SL4 ......66 F7
Raywood Cl UB7 ......71 C7
Reade Ct SL2 ......22 C6
Reading Alternative Sch
  RG1 ......86 C5
Reading Blue Coat Sch
  RG4 ......60 C3
Reading Bridge RG1 ......86 B8
Reading Coll & School of
  Arts & Design
  Reading RG1 ......86 D7
  Reading RG1 ......86 F6
Reading Gate Ret Pk
  RG2 ......85 F1
Reading Girls Sch RG2 ......86 C3
Reading International Bsns
  Pk RG2 ......113 A6
Reading Link Ret Pk RG2 ......86 A5

Reading Rd
  Aldermaston RG7 ......135 F5
  Aldworth RG8 ......33 A2
  Arborfield RG2 ......114 C3
  Blackwater GU17 ......150 B4
  Burghfield Common RG7 ......111 B2
  Finchampstead RG27 ......140 D8
  Goring RG8 ......34 E6
  Henley-On-T RG9 ......15 E1
  Moulsford OX10 ......14 A7
  Pangbourne RG8 ......56 D5
  Streatley RG8 ......34 A6
  Winnersh RG41 ......88 C2
  Wokingham RG41 ......115 E8
  Woodley RG5 ......87 D8
  Yateley GU46 ......149 D6
Reading Sch RG1 ......86 D6
Reading Sta RG1 ......86 B8
Reading Stadium (Speedway)
  RG2 ......85 F1
Reading West Sta RG30 ......85 E7
Recreation Cl GU14 ......150 F1
Recreation La RG7 ......113 B2
Recreation Rd
  Bourne End SL8 ......3 B3
  Burghfield Common RG7 ......111 A2
  Reading RG30 ......84 E8
  Wargrave RG10 ......36 E2
Rectory Cl
  Bracknell RG12 ......118 C5
  Farnham Royal SL2 ......22 C2
  Littleton TW17 ......125 A6
  Newbury RG14 ......104 F1
  Sandhurst GU47 ......149 F8
  Windsor SL4 ......67 A6
  Wokingham RG40 ......116 C6
Rectory La
  Aston Tirrold OX11 ......12 F8
  Bracknell RG12 ......118 B5
  Letcombe Bassett OX12 ......6 F7
  Windlesham GU20 ......146 C4
Rectory Rd
  Caversham RG4 ......59 A2
  Padworth RG7 ......135 F7
  Streatley RG8 ......33 C7
  Taplow SL6 ......20 E1
  Wokingham RG40 ......116 C6
Rectory Row RG12 ......118 B5
Rectory Terr SL4 ......22 C3
Red Cottage Dr RG31 ......84 C4
Red Cottage Mews SL3 ......43 C3
Red Cross Rd RG8 ......34 C6
Red Ct SL1 ......42 E5
Red Hill RG9 ......35 A5
Red House Ct RG6 ......114 B8
Red La RG45 ......143 D5
Red Leaf Cl SL3 ......43 F5
Red Lion Cotts SL2 ......23 B1
Red Lion Way HP10 ......3 F6
Red Rd GU18,GU24,GU15 ......153 C7
Red Rose RG42 ......90 C3
Red Shute Hill RG18 ......79 A4
Red Shute Ind Est RG18 ......79 A4
Redberry Cl RG4 ......59 D5
Redcrest Gdns GU15 ......151 F5
Reddington Dr SL3 ......43 E2
Redditch RG12 ......118 D2
Redfield Ct RG14 ......105 D4
Redford Rd SL4 ......66 D6
Redgauntlet RG40 ......141 D6
Redgrave Pk SL7 ......1 F3
Redhatch Dr RG6 ......87 A2
Redlake La RG40 ......116 F2
Redlands Pl RG40 ......116 E5
Redlands Prim Sch RG1 ......86 E5
Redlands Rd RG1 ......86 D6
Redlane Cl RG1 ......86 D5
Redleaves Ave TW15 ......98 B2
Redmayne GU15 ......152 C4
Redpitch Pk HP10 ......3 F6
Redruth Gdns RG6 ......86 B1
Redshank Ct RG19 ......106 A3
Redshots Cl SL7 ......1 E4
Redvers Rd RG12 ......118 B4
Redwood Burnham SL1 ......21 B1
  Staines TW20 ......123 E7
Redwood Ave RG5 ......88 A6
Redwood Dr
  Frimley GU15 ......152 D4
  Sunningdale SL5 ......121 B3
Redwood Gdns SL1 ......42 D6
Redwood Mews TW15 ......98 D1
Redwood Way RG31 ......57 D3
Redwoods The SL4 ......67 D4
Reed Cl SL4 ......44 F7
Reed's Hill RG12 ......118 A4
Reeds Ave
  Lower Earley RG6 ......87 A3
  Reading RG6 ......86 F3
Reedsfield Cl TW15 ......98 B5
Reedsfield Rd TW15 ......98 B4
Reeve Rd SL6 ......19 E8
Reeves Way RG41 ......116 A4
Reform Rd SL6 ......40 B7
Regal Ct SL6 ......40 B2
Regal Ho 8 TW18 ......96 F3
Regency Hts RG4 ......58 E4
Regent Cl Earley RG6 ......87 C1
  Hungerford RG17 ......100 D5
  9 Maidenhead SL6 ......39 F7
  Reading RG1 ......86 A8
  Slough SL1 ......42 E7

Regent Ct continued
  Windsor SL4 ......67 D5
Regent St RG1 ......86 E7
Regent Way GU16 ......152 A1
Regents Ct
  Newbury RG14 ......104 F3
  Staines TW18 ......97 B2
Regents Ho 8 TW20 ......96 A3
Regents Pl GU47 ......150 C8
Regents Riverside RG1 ......59 A1
Regents Wlk SL5 ......120 C2
Regis Cl RG2 ......113 D7
Regis Ct TW14 ......71 D1
Regnum Dr RG14 ......105 B4
Reid Ave SL6 ......39 E5
Rembrandt Cl RG41 ......115 D6
Rembrandt Way RG1 ......85 E5
REME Mus of Technology*
  RG2 ......141 A8
Remembrance Rd RG14 ......104 E2
Remenham Church La
  RG9 ......16 A4
Remenham La RG9 ......15 F3
Remenham Row RG9 ......15 F2
Remenham Terr RG9 ......16 C2
Renault Rd RG5 ......88 A6
Renfree Way TW17 ......125 A4
Rennie Cl TW15 ......97 D5
Rennie Ct RG14 ......104 F4
Repton Cl SL6 ......39 C2
Repton Rd RG6 ......87 C3
Restwold Cl RG30 ......85 C4
Retford Cl RG5 ......60 F1
Retreat The
  Englefield Green TW20 ......95 E3
  Fifield SL6 ......65 D7
Revel Rd HP10 ......3 D8
Revesby Cl
  Maidenhead SL6 ......39 D3
  West End GU24 ......153 D6
Rex Ave TW15 ......98 A3
Reynards Ct RG41 ......88 C2
Reynolds Ct RG18 ......106 D3
Reynolds Gn GU47 ......150 D6
Rhema Ct 9 RG1 ......85 F7
Rhigos RG4 ......58 F6
Rhine Cl RG4 ......59 D2
Rhodes Cl Earley RG6 ......87 E3
  Egham TW20 ......96 B3
Rhodes Cl TW20 ......96 C3
Rhododendron Cl SL5 ......92 E1
Rhododendron Cnr
  RG40 ......142 B4
Rhododendron Rd
  GU16 ......152 B1
Rhododendron Ride SL4,
  TW20 ......94 F3
Rhododendron Wlk
  Brimpton RG19 ......133 B5
  North Ascot SL5 ......92 E1
Ribbleton Cl RG6 ......87 C3
Ribstone Rd SL6 ......39 B3
Ricardo Rd SL4 ......68 B1
Richard Ct TW15 ......97 F3
Richard Nevill Ct 1 RG4 ......59 C2
Richards Way SL1 ......42 A8
Richardson's Lawn Cotts
  SL4 ......94 B5
Richborough Cl RG6 ......87 B2
Richfield Ave RG1 ......58 F1
Richings Way SL0 ......44 F3
Richmond Ave
  Feltham TW14 ......71 E1
  Thatcham RG19 ......106 A3
Richmond Cl GU16 ......151 F1
Richmond Cres
  Slough SL1 ......43 A5
  Staines TW18 ......96 F3
Richmond Dr TW17 ......125 D3
Richmond Ho GU47 ......150 E7
Richmond Rd
  Caversham RG4 ......58 A4
  Sandhurst GU47 ......150 D8
  Staines TW18 ......96 F3
Richmond Rise RG41 ......115 C7
Richmond Wood SL5 ......121 B1
Rickman Cl
  Arborfield Cross RG2 ......114 C1
  Bracknell RG12 ......118 C3
  Woodley RG5 ......87 D5
Rickman's La SL2 ......22 E6
Riddings La RG19 ......131 C2
Rider's La RG7 ......112 A4
Rideway Cl GU15 ......151 B4
Ridge Ct SL4 ......67 C4
Ridge Hall Cl RG4 ......58 E3
Ridge Mount Rd SL5 ......121 A1
Ridge The Cold Ash RG18 ......106 D8
  Sunningdale SL5 ......121 B3
  Upper Basildon RG8 ......55 F8
Ridge Way Iver SL0 ......44 F6
  Thorpe GU25 ......122 E4
Ridgebank SL1 ......41 F6
Ridgemead Rd TW20 ......95 B5
Ridgemount Cl RG31 ......57 B2
Ridgeway
  Hermitage RG18 ......79 B7
  Lightwater GU18 ......153 A8
  Marlow SL7 ......1 E4

Ridgeway Prim Sch The
  RG2 . . . . .86 D1
Ridgeway Sch SL6 . . . . . . .38 E5
Ridgeway The
  Bracknell RG12 . . . . .118 C6
  Caversham RG4 . . . . .59 B3
  Letcombe Bassett OX12 . . . .7 D5
  Lightwater GU18 . . . . .146 B1
  Marlow SL7 . . . . .1 E4
  Woodley RG5 . . . . .87 F5
Ridgeway Trad Est The
  SL0 .44 A2
Ridgewood Ctr (Hospl)
  GU16 . . . . .152 C3
Ridgewood Dr GU16 . . . .152 D3
Riding Court Rd SL3 . . . . .68 D7
Riding Ct SL3 . . . . .68 C8
Riding Way RG41 . . . . . . .115 E6
Ridings The
  Caversham RG4 . . . . .59 C8
  Frimley GU16 . . . . .152 B3
  Iver SL0 . . . . .44 F2
  Maidenhead SL6 . . . . .39 A7
Ridlington Cl RG6 . . . . . . .87 E2
Rigby Lodge SL1 . . . . .42 E7
Righton Cl RG10 . . . . .41 E5
Riley Rd Marlow SL7 . . . . . .1 D2
  Reading RG30 . . . . .84 F8
Ring The RG12 . . . . .118 C7
Ringmead
  Bracknell, Great Hollands
  RG12 . . . . .117 E4
  Bracknell,Hanworth RG12 .118 B2
Ringwood RG12 . . . . .117 F2
Ringwood Cl SL5 . . . . . . .120 B5
Ringwood Rd
  Blackwater GU17 . . . . . . .150 C6
  Reading RG30 . . . . .58 A1
Ripley Ave TW20 . . . . .95 E2
Ripley Cl SL3 . . . . .43 E2
Ripley Rd RG30 . . . . .58 A1
Ripon Cl GU15 . . . . .152 D3
Ripon Rd RG41 . . . . .149 F1
Ripplesmere RG12 . . . . . .118 C4
Ripplesmere Cl GU47 . . . .150 B8
Ripston Rd TW15 . . . . .98 D3
Risborough Rd SL6 . . . . . . .39 E8
Rise Rd SL5 . . . . .120 F3
Rise The Caversham RG4 . . .59 B4
  Cold Ash RG18 . . . . .106 C7
  Crowthorne RG45 . . . . . . .142 F5
  Finchampstead RG40 . . . . .141 A2
  Winkfield RG42 . . . . .119 A8
  Wokingham RG41 . . . . . . .116 A7
Riseley Bsns Pk RG7 . . . . .139 C3
Riseley Rd SL6 . . . . .39 D7
Rissington Cl RG31 . . . . . .57 E8
River & Rowing Mus*
  RG9 . . . . .15 F1
River Ct Taplow SL6 . . . . . . .40 C7
  Twyford RG10 . . . . .61 B5
River Gdns
  Maidenhead SL6 . . . . .40 D4
  Purley On T RG8 . . . . .57 D5
River Mount KT12 . . . . . . .125 F2
River Park Ave TW18 . . . . .96 D4
River Rd Caversham RG4 . . .58 D3
  Maidenhead SL6 . . . . .40 C6
15 Reading RG1 . . . . .86 A6
  Staines TW18 . . . . .123 F8
  Yateley GU46 . . . . .149 B8
River Side Cotts HP10 . . . . .3 E8
River St SL4 . . . . .67 D7
River View
  Flackwell Heath HP10 . . . . .3 B7
  Froxfield SN8 . . . . .99 C5
River Wlk RG14 . . . . .105 C4
Riverbank TW18 . . . . .96 F2
Riverbank The SL4 . . . . . . .67 B7
Riverdale Ct RG14 . . . . . . .105 C5
Riverdene Dr **4** RG41 . . . .88 A3
Riverfield Rd SL4 . . . . .96 F2
Rivermead Ct SL7 . . . . .18 E8
Rivermead Ind Est RG19 .106 F1
Rivermead Prim Sch RG5 .87 F6
Rivermead Rd
  Camberley GU15 . . . . . . .151 B2
  Woodley RG5 . . . . .87 F5
Riverpark Dr SL7 . . . . .1 F1
Riverpark Ind Est RG14 .105 B3
Riversdale SL8 . . . . .3 B1
Riversdale Cotts SL8 . . . . .3 B1
Riversdale Ct
  Bourne End SL8 . . . . .3 B1
  Reading RG1 . . . . .86 E8
Riversdell Cl KT16 . . . . . .123 F2
Riverside Bradfield RG7 . . . .82 C6
  Chilton Foliat RG17 . . . . . . .72 F1
  Egham TW20 . . . . .96 A5
  Marlow SL7 . . . . .1 E1
  Oatlands Park TW17 . . . . . .125 E2
  Wraysbury TW19 . . . . .95 C8
Riverside Ave GU18 . . . . .153 C8
Riverside Cl TW18 . . . . . .123 F8
Riverside Ct **1** RG4 . . . . . . .59 A2
Riverside Dr Egham TW18 .96 E3
  Staines TW18 . . . . .123 F8
Riverside Ho RG41 . . . . . . .88 C8
Riverside Mus* RG1 . . . . .86 C8
Riverside Pk SL3 . . . . .69 E5
Riverside Pl TW19 . . . . .70 D1
Riverside Rd Staines TW18 .96 F1
  Stanwell TW19 . . . . .70 E1
Riverside Way GU15 . . . .151 A3
Riverside Wlk SL4 . . . . . . .67 D7

Riverview TW17 . . . . .125 D2
Riverview Rd RG8 . . . . .56 C5
Riverway
  Great Shefford RG17 . . . . . .48 A3
  Staines TW18 . . . . .124 B8
Riverwood Ave SL7 . . . . . . .2 A1
Riverwoods Dr SL7 . . . . . . .2 A1
Rixman Cl SL6 . . . . .39 D5
Rixon Cl SL3 . . . . .43 E7
Robert Palmer Cotts The
  RG4 . . . . .60 D3
Robert Piggott CE Inf Sch
  RG10 . . . . .36 E1
Robert Piggott CE Jun Sch
  RG10 . . . . .36 D1
Robert Sandilands Prim Sch
  RG14 . . . . .104 E4
Roberts Cl TW19 . . . . .70 C1
Roberts Gr RG41 . . . . .115 F4
Roberts Rd GU15 . . . . .151 A6
Roberts Way TW20 . . . . . . .95 C1
Robertsfield RG19 . . . . . . .105 F3
Robertson Cl RG14 . . . . . .131 B8
Robin Cl RG7 . . . . .111 B3
Robin Hill Dr GU15 . . . . . .152 A3
Robin Hood Cl SL1 . . . . . . .41 F5
Robin Hood Way RG41 . . . .88 C3
Robin La
  Bishops Green RG20 . . . . . .131 F3
  Sandhurst GU47 . . . . .143 C1
Robin Par SL2 . . . . .22 C7
Robin Way Reading RG1 . . .84 B6
  Staines TW18 . . . . .96 F5
Robin Willis Way SL4 . . . . .68 A1
Robin's Bow GU15 . . . . . . .151 B4
Robina Ho RG42 . . . . .117 F8
Robindale Ave RG6 . . . . . . .87 D3
Robinhood La RG41 . . . . . .88 C3
Robins Cl RG14 . . . . .130 F7
Robins Grove Cres
  GU46 . . . . .149 B6
Robins Hill RG17 . . . . .127 E6
Robinson Cl OX11 . . . . .12 A8
Robinson Crusoe Pk
  RG40 . . . . .141 B6
Robinson Ct RG6 . . . . .87 A1
Roby Dr RG12 . . . . .118 D2
Rochester Ave
  Feltham TW13 . . . . .98 F6
  Woodley RG5 . . . . .60 E1
Rochester Rd TW20 . . . . . . .96 D2
Rochford Way SL6 . . . . .41 A7
Rochfords Gdns SL2 . . . . . .43 C5
Rockall Ct SL3 . . . . .44 B3
Rockbourne Gdns RG30 . . .58 A1
Rockfel Rd RG17 . . . . .25 A2
Rockfield Way **7** RG47 . . .150 D8
Rockingham Rd RG14 . . . .104 F2
Rockley Ct RG7 . . . . .83 D2
Rockmoor La SP11 . . . . . . .147 A1
Rodd Est TW17 . . . . .125 D4
Rodney Ct **11** RG1 . . . . . . .86 A6
Rodney Way SL3 . . . . .69 E6
Rodway Rd RG30 . . . . .57 F1
Roebuck Est RG42 . . . . .90 C1
Roebuck Gn SL1 . . . . .41 A5
Roebuck Rise RG31 . . . . . . .57 D3
Roebuts Cl RG14 . . . . .130 F8
Rogers La SL2 . . . . .22 F4
Rogers's La RG17 . . . . .47 C6
Rokeby Cl
  Bracknell RG12 . . . . .118 D8
  Newbury RG14 . . . . .131 A7
Rokeby Dr RG4 . . . . .58 D8
Rokes Pl GU46 . . . . .149 B6
Rokesby Rd SL2 . . . . .21 F2
Roland's Copse RG7 . . . . .108 C2
Rolls La SL6 . . . . .64 E8
Roman La SL6 . . . . .19 F7
Roman Pl SL6 . . . . .39 C6
Roman Ride RG45 . . . . . . .142 D5
Roman Way Bourne End SL8 .3 B4
  Earley RG6 . . . . .87 D3
  Thatcham RG18 . . . . .106 B4
  Winkfield RG42 . . . . .118 F8
Romana Ct TW18 . . . . .97 A4
Romano Ct **2** RG14 . . . . .105 B2
Romans Field RG7 . . . . . . .136 B1
Romans Gate RG26 . . . . . .135 F1
Romany Cl RG30 . . . . .58 A1
Romany La RG30 . . . . .58 A1
Romeo Hill RG42 . . . . .118 F8
Romney Cl TW15 . . . . .98 C3
Romney Ct **11** SL7 . . . . . . .1 F3
Romney Ho RG12 . . . . . . .118 A5
Romney Lock Rd SL4 . . . . .67 D7
Romsey Cl
  Blackwater GU17 . . . . . . .150 C6
  Slough SL3 . . . . .43 F3
Romsey Rd RG30 . . . . .58 A1
Rona Ct RG30 . . . . .85 B8
Ronaldsay Spur SL1 . . . . . .42 E8
Ronita Ct RG1 . . . . .86 F6
Rood Hill RG20 . . . . .76 B4
Rook Cl RG41 . . . . .115 E5
Rook Rd HP10 . . . . .3 D4
Rookery Ct
  Barkham RG40 . . . . .141 A6
  Marlow SL7 . . . . .1 D2
Rookery Rd TW18 . . . . .97 B3
Rookery The RG20 . . . . .50 D7
Rooksfield RG20 . . . . .132 A2
Rooksmead Rd TW16 . . . .125 F7
Rooksnest La RG17 . . . . . .128 A5
Rookwood
  Bracknell RG42 . . . . .91 B1
  Stockcross RG20 . . . . .103 F6
Rookwood Ave GU47 . . . .143 E2

Rope Wlk RG19 . . . . .106 C3
Rosa Ave TW15 . . . . .98 A4
Rosary Gdns
  Ashford TW15 . . . . .98 B4
  Yateley GU46 . . . . .149 D6
Rose Bsns Est SL7 . . . . .1 D5
Rose Cl RG5 . . . . .88 B7
Rose Cotts
  Maidenhead SL6 . . . . .39 C3
  Sandhurst GU47 . . . . .143 A1
Rose Ct RG40 . . . . .116 C6
Rose Gdns Stanwell TW19 .97 D8
  Wokingham RG40 . . . . . . .116 C6
Rose Hill Binfield RG42 . . . .90 C3
  Burnham SL1 . . . . .21 A5
Rose Kiln La RG1,RG2 . . . .86 A4
Rose La RG10,RG9 . . . . .37 A8
Rose St RG40 . . . . .116 C6
Rose Wlk Reading RG1 . . . .86 A7
  Slough SL2 . . . . .42 B8
Roseacre Cl TW17 . . . . . . .125 A4
Rosebank Cl SL6 . . . . .19 E7
Rosebay RG40 . . . . .116 E8
Rosebery Rd RG4 . . . . .58 D7
Rosecourt Way RG2 . . . . .113 E5
Rosedale RG42 . . . . .90 C3
Rosedale Cres RG6 . . . . . . .87 A8
Rosedale Gdns
  Bracknell RG12 . . . . .118 A4
  Thatcham RG19 . . . . .106 C2
Rosedene La GU47 . . . . . .150 D7
Rosefield Rd TW18 . . . . . . .97 A4
Rosehill Ct SL1 . . . . .43 A3
Rosehill Ho RG4 . . . . .59 C7
Rosehill Pk RG4 . . . . .59 C7
Roselawn Park Cvn Site
  RG30 . . . . .111 D5
Roseleigh Cl SL6 . . . . .39 A7
Rosemary Ave RG6 . . . . . . .86 F1
Rosemary Gdns GU17 . . . .150 D5
Rosemary La
  Blackwater GU17 . . . . . . .150 D5
  Thorpe TW20 . . . . .123 B6
Rosemary Terr RG14 . . . . .104 E2
Rosemead KT16 . . . . .124 B2
Rosemead Ave
  Feltham TW13 . . . . .98 F6
  Purley On T RG31 . . . . .57 B3
Rosemoor Gdns RG14 . . . .105 D4
Rosen Ct RG19 . . . . .113 C6
Rosery The SL8 . . . . .3 A3
Roses La SL4 . . . . .66 D5
Rosewood RG5 . . . . .87 D4
Rosewood Dr TW17 . . . . . .124 F4
Rosewood Way
  Farnham Common SL2 . . . . .22 C7
  West End GU24 . . . . .153 E6
Rosier Cl RG19 . . . . .106 E2
Rosken Gr SL2 . . . . .22 B3
Roslyn Rd RG5 . . . . .87 D6
Ross Ho **2** RG30 . . . . .85 D6
Ross Rd Maidenhead SL6 . . .39 E4
  Reading RG1 . . . . .59 A1
Rossendale Rd RG4 . . . . . . .59 D3
Rosset Cl RG12 . . . . .118 B5
Rossington Pl **5** RG2 . . . .113 C6
Rossiter Cl SL3 . . . . .43 E2
Rossobe GU20 . . . . .146 A6
Rosslyn Cl TW16 . . . . .98 E2
Rothbury Wlk GU15 . . . . .152 C4
Rother Cl GU47 . . . . .150 C8
Rother Field Cl RG7 . . . . . . .83 F4
Rotherfield Ave RG41 . . . .116 A7
Rotherfield Rd RG4 . . . . . . .59 B4
Rotherfield Way RG4 . . . . . .59 B4
Rothwell Gdns RG5 . . . . . . .61 A1
Rothwell Ho RG45 . . . . . . .143 C4
Rothwell Wlk RG4 . . . . . . .59 D2
Rotten Row Hill RG7 . . . . . .81 F3
Roughgrove Copse RG42 . .90 B2
Round Cl GU46 . . . . .149 D5
Round Oak Rd GU20 . . . . .146 A6
Roundabout La RG41 . . . .115 D8
Roundfield RG7 . . . . .107 B6
Roundhead Rd RG7 . . . . . . .83 D3
Roundway Egham TW20 . . .96 C3
  Frimley GU15 . . . . .152 C6
Roundway Cl GU15 . . . . . .152 C6
Rounton Rd KT4 . . . . .98 D6
Routh La RG30 . . . . .84 E6
Row La RG4 . . . . .59 E7
Rowallan Cl RG4 . . . . .59 D6
Rowan **2** RG12 . . . . .118 F4
Rowan Ave TW20 . . . . .96 C3
Rowan Cl
  Camberley GU15 . . . . . . .151 F8
  Wokingham RG41 . . . . . . .115 F5
Rowan Ct RG6 . . . . .87 B1
Rowan Dr
  Crowthorne RG45 . . . . . . .143 C6
  Newbury RG14 . . . . .105 A5
  Woodley RG5 . . . . .87 F8
Rowan Ho
1 Bourne End SL8 . . . . . . .3 A4
  East Bedfont TW14 . . . . . . .71 D1
Rowan Way
  Burghfield Common RG30 .111 B5
  Slough SL2 . . . . .42 B8
Rowanhurst Dr SL2 . . . . . . .22 C7
Rowans Cl GU14 . . . . .150 E1
Rowans The TW16 . . . . . . .98 F3
Rowanwood RG40 . . . . . . .142 A4
Rowcroft Rd RG2 . . . . .140 F7
Rowdell Dr RG2 . . . . .86 D1
Rowdown RG7 . . . . .24 E5
Rowe Ct RG30 . . . . .85 B8
Rowland Cl SL4 . . . . .66 D4

Rowland Hill Almshouses **7**
  TW15 . . . . .98 A3
Rowland Way Earley RG6 . .86 F2
  Littleton TW15 . . . . .98 D1
Rowland's Cl RG7 . . . . . . .136 C5
Rowles Paddock RG20 . . . .10 A2
Rowley Cl RG12 . . . . .118 E6
Rowley La SL3 . . . . .23 D4
Rowley Rd RG2 . . . . .86 B4
Roxborough Way SL6 . . . . .38 F4
Roxburgh Cl GU15 . . . . . .152 C4
Roxeth Ct **6** TW15 . . . . . . .98 A3
Roxford Cl TW17 . . . . .125 E4
Roxwell Cl SL1 . . . . .41 E5
Roy Cl RG18 . . . . .78 F6
Royal Ave RG31 . . . . .84 C5
Royal Berkshire Hospl The
  RG1 . . . . .86 E7
Royal Cotts SL6 . . . . .19 C7
Royal Ct **1** RG1 . . . . .86 C7
Royal Free Ct **13** SL4 . . . .67 D6
Royal Fst Sch The SL4 . . . .94 C4
Royal Holloway Univ of
  London TW20 . . . . .95 D2
Royal Hunt Ho SL5 . . . . . .119 D8
Royal Mans RG9 . . . . .15 E1
Royal Military Acad
  GU15 . . . . .150 F6
Royal Oak Cl GU46 . . . . . .149 A6
Royal Oak Dr RG45 . . . . . .143 B8
Royal Station Ct RG10 . . . .61 E7
Royal Victoria Gdns
  SL5 . . . . .120 A4
Royal Way RG2 . . . . .112 F8
Roycroft La RG40 . . . . .141 E8
Roydon Ct TW20 . . . . .96 D2
Royston Ct RG30 . . . . .84 F7
Royston Way SL1 . . . . .41 D8
Rubus Cl GU24 . . . . .153 E6
Ruby Cl Slough SL1 . . . . . . .42 A4
  Wokingham RG41 . . . . . . .115 E7
Rudd Hall Rise GU15 . . . .151 E4
Ruddlesway SL4 . . . . .66 D6
Rudland Cl RG19 . . . . .106 D2
Rudsworth Cl SL3 . . . . .69 D7
Rufus Isaacs Rd RG4 . . . . .59 B2
Rugby Cl GU47 . . . . .143 E1
Ruggles-Brise Rd TW15 . . .97 D3
Rugosa Rd GU24 . . . . .153 E6
Rumsey's La OX11 . . . . .12 A8
Runnemede Rd TW20 . . . . .96 A4
Runnymede* TW20 . . . . . . .95 F5
Runnymede Cotts TW19 . .96 D7
Runnymede Ct TW20 . . . . .96 A4
Runnymede Rdbt TW20 . . .96 B4
Rupert Cl RG9 . . . . .15 E3
Rupert House Sch RG9 . . . .15 E2
Rupert Rd RG14 . . . . .130 F7
Rupert Sq **3** RG1 . . . . .86 D7
Rupert St RG1 . . . . .86 D7
Rupert Wlk **4** RG1 . . . . . . .86 D7
Rupert's Ave RG14 . . . . . . .115 E3
Ruscombe Bsns Pk RG10 . .61 E5
Ruscombe Gdns SL3 . . . . . .68 A7
Ruscombe La RG10 . . . . . . .61 E5
Ruscombe Pk RG10 . . . . . . .61 E5
Ruscombe Rd RG10 . . . . . .61 E5
Ruscombe Turn RG10 . . . . .61 F4
Ruscombe Way TW14 . . . . .98 F8
Rushall Cl RG6 . . . . .113 E7
Rusham Park Ave TW20 . . .96 A2
Rusham Rd TW20 . . . . .95 F2
Rushbrook Rd RG5 . . . . . . .87 C7
Rushburn HP10 . . . . .3 E6
Rushden Dr RG2 . . . . .86 E1
Rushes The
  Maidenhead SL6 . . . . .40 C6
  Marlow SL7 . . . . .18 C8
Rushey Ho RG12 . . . . .118 E5
Rushey Way Earley RG6 . . .87 C2
  Lower Earley RG6 . . . . .114 A8
Rushington Ave SL6 . . . . . .39 F5
Rushmere Cotts RG5 . . . . .88 A5
Rushmere Pl TW20 . . . . . . .95 E3
Rushmon Ct KT16 . . . . . . .123 F2
Rushmoor Gdns RG31 . . . .84 B4
Ruskin Ave TW14 . . . . .71 F1
Ruskin Ct RG45 . . . . .142 F4
Ruskin Rd TW18 . . . . .96 F2
Ruskin Way RG41 . . . . . . .115 D6
Russel Ct RG12 . . . . .118 D2
Russell Ct
  Blackwater GU17 . . . . . . .150 D5
  Maidenhead SL6 . . . . .39 F7
Russell Dr TW19 . . . . .70 D1
Russell Gdns UB7 . . . . .71 A8
Russell Ho **4** SL6 . . . . .3 A4
Russell Ct TW19 . . . . .69 F1
Russell St RG1 . . . . .151 D3
Russet Cl TW19 . . . . .97 F8
Russet Gate RG4 . . . . .59 C3
Russet Glade
  Caversham RG4 . . . . .59 C7
  Cold Ash RG18 . . . . .106 C4
Russet Way RG20 . . . . .51 C5
Russington Rd TW17 . . . . .125 D3
Russley Gn RG40 . . . . .116 A1
Rustington Cl **1** RG6 . . . . .87 B1
Ruston Way SL5 . . . . .119 E7
Rutherford Cl SL4 . . . . .66 F6

Rutherford Wlk RG31 . . . . .84 A7
Rutherwyk Rd KT16 . . . . .123 E2
Rutland Ave SL1 . . . . .42 C8
Rutland Gate SL6 . . . . .39 C6
Rutland Pl SL6 . . . . .39 C6
Rutland Rd
  Maidenhead SL6 . . . . .39 D6
  Reading RG30 . . . . .85 D7
Ruxbury Ct TW15 . . . . .97 E5
Ruxbury Rd KT16 . . . . . . .123 D3
Ruxley Gdns TW17 . . . . . .125 C4
Ryan Mount GU47 . . . . . . .150 A8
Ryans Mount SL7 . . . . .1 C2
Rycroft SL4 . . . . .66 F4
Rydal Ave RG30 . . . . .57 F2
Rydal Cl GU15 . . . . .152 D5
Rydal Dr RG9 . . . . .106 A3
Rydal Pl GU18 . . . . .153 B8
Rydal Way TW20 . . . . .96 B1
Ryde Gdns GU46 . . . . .149 B6
Ryde The TW18 . . . . .124 B8
Rydings SL4 . . . . .66 F4
Rye Cl Bracknell RG12 . . . . .91 D1
  Maidenhead SL6 . . . . .39 A4
  Winkfield RG12 . . . . .118 D8
Rye Ct SL1 . . . . .43 A3
Rye Gr GU20,GU18 . . . . . .146 F2
Ryecroft Cl
  Wargrave RG10 . . . . .36 E2
  Woodley RG5 . . . . .60 E1
Ryecroft Gdns GU17 . . . . .150 E4
Ryefield Terr SL3 . . . . .69 D7
Ryehurst La RG42 . . . . .90 F5
Ryeish Green Sch RG7 . . .113 C3
Ryeish La RG7 . . . . .113 C3
Ryemead La SL4 . . . . .92 C5
Ryhill Way RG6 . . . . .113 F8
Ryland Cl TW13 . . . . .98 F4
Rylstone Cl SL6 . . . . .39 C3
Rylstone Rd RG30 . . . . .85 D8
Ryvers End SL3 . . . . .43 F3
Ryvers Prim Sch SL3 . . . . .43 D3
Ryvers Rd SL3 . . . . .43 F3
Ryves Ave GU46 . . . . .149 A5

S

Sabah Ct TW15 . . . . .98 A4
Sabin Gates RG12 . . . . . . .118 B6
Sackville St RG1 . . . . .86 A8
Sacred Heart RC Prim Sch
  The RG9 . . . . .15 D1
Saddleback Rd GU15 . . . .151 E8
Saddlebrook Pk TW16 . . . .98 E1
Saddler Cnr GU47 . . . . . . .150 B7
Saddlers Ct GU47 . . . . . . .151 C4
Sadlers Cl RG41 . . . . .88 D1
Sadlers End RG41 . . . . . . .115 C7
Sadlers La RG41 . . . . .115 D8
Sadlers Mews SL7 . . . . .1 F3
Sadlers Rd RG17 . . . . .127 A6
Sadlers The RG31 . . . . .57 B1
Saffron Cl Datchet SL3 . . . .68 C6
Saffron Ct
  Newbury RG14 . . . . .104 F3
Saffron Ct TW14 . . . . .98 C8
Saffron Rd RG12 . . . . .118 B5
Sage Cl RG6 . . . . .87 A1
Sage Ct SL4 . . . . .95 A8
Sage Rd RG31 . . . . .57 C3
Sage Wlk RG42 . . . . .91 D1
Sagecroft Rd RG18 . . . . . .106 C5
Sailing Club Rd SL3 . . . . . . .3 A3
Sainsbury Ctr The KT16 . .124 C4
Saint Sebastian's CE Prim
  Sch RG40 . . . . .142 A6
St Adrian's Cl SL6 . . . . .39 B4
St Agnes Mews RG2 . . . . . .86 C2
St Agnes Terr RG17 . . . . . . .25 B2
St Alban's St SL4 . . . . .67 D6
St Albans Cl **10** SL6 . . . . . .67 D6
St Andrew's Ave SL4 . . . . .66 F5
St Andrew's Cl
  Old Windsor SL4 . . . . .95 A7
  Upper Halliford TW17 . . . . .125 D5
  Wraysbury TW19 . . . . .68 E1
St Andrew's Cres SL4 . . . . .66 F5
St Andrew's Rd
  Caversham RG4 . . . . .58 F4
  Henley-On-T RG9 . . . . .35 D8
St Andrew's Sch RG8 . . . . .55 C1
St Andrew's Way SL1 . . . . .41 D6
St Andrews RG17 . . . . .117 E3
St Andrews Cl
  Bradfield RG7 . . . . .82 C6
  Crowthorne RG45 . . . . . . .143 B8
St Andrews Cotts **1** SL4 .67 A5
St Andrews Ct Ascot SL5 .120 C4
  Colnbrook SL3 . . . . .69 D7
20 Reading RG1 . . . . .86 B5
2 Slough SL1 . . . . .42 E3
St Ann's Cl RG17 . . . . .117 E3
St Ann's Heath Jun Sch
  GU25 . . . . .122 E4
St Ann's Hill Rd KT16 . . . .123 D3
St Anne's Ct TW19 . . . . . . .70 D8
St Anne's Cl RG9 . . . . .15 D1
St Anne's Prim Sch TW19 .97 B2
St Anne's Rd RG4 . . . . .59 A2
St Annes Dr RG40 . . . . . . .142 A4
St Annes Glade GU19 . . . .145 D3

St Anthony's RC Prim Sch
SL2 .22 C1
St Anthony's Way TW14 . .71 F3
St Anthonys Cl RG42 . . . .118 A8
St Augustine's RC Prim Sch
GU16 . . . . .151 F2
St Barnabas Rd
Caversham RG4 . . . . .59 A6
Earley RG2 . . . . .86 F1
St Bartholomew's Sch
RG14 . . . . .104 E1
St Bartholomews Rd RG1 .86 F7
St Bernard's Convent Sch
SL3 .43 C4
St Bernard's Prep Sch
SL1 .43 B4
St Bernards Rd SL3 . . . . . .43 C3
St Birinus Rd RG31 . . . . . .84 C5
St Catherine's Cl RG41 . . .88 B1
St Catherine's Hill RG7 . .136 E6
St Catherine's Sch
SL5 .21 A8
St Catherines Cl
2 Staines TW18 . . . . .97 A4
3 Windsor SL4 . . . . .67 A5
St Catherines Pl 1
TW20 . . . . .96 A3
St Cecelia Ct RG2 . . . . . . .86 C2
St Chad's Rd SL6 . . . . .39 B4
St Christophers Gdns
SL5 . . . . .119 D8
St Clements Cl RG6 . . . . . .87 C1
St Columba's Cl SL6 . . . . .39 B4
St Crispin's Sch RG40 . . .116 E6
St Cuthbert's Cl SL6 . . . . .95 D2
St Cuthbert's RC Prim Sch
TW20 . . . . .95 C1
St David's Cl
Caversham RG4 . . . . .58 F5
Maidenhead SL6 . . . . .39 A4
St David's Rd RG14 . . . . .104 F2
St Davids Dr TW15 . . . . . .97 F5
St Davids Rd SL6 . . . . .39 A4
St Dominic Savio RC Prim
Sch RG5 . . . . .87 D8
St Donats Pl RG14 . . . . . .105 A2
St Dunstan's Rd TW13 . . .98 F5
St Edmund Campion RC Prim
Sch SL6 . . . . .39 B6
St Edward's RC Fst Sch
SL4 .67 A6
St Edward's Rd RG6 . . . . . .87 A6
St Edward's Royal Free
Ecumenical Mid Sch
RG30 . . . . .85 D7
Windsor SL4 . . . . .67 A6
St Edward's Sch RG2 . . . . .85 D7
St Elizabeth Cl RG2 . . . . .113 B7
St Elmo Cl SL2 . . . . .22 D1
St Elmo Cres SL2 . . . . .22 D1
St Ethelbert's RC Prim Sch
SL2 .43 A7
St Finian's RC Prim Sch
RG18 . . . . .106 D8
St Francis RC Sch SL5 . . .120 A3
St Gabriel's Sch RG20 . . .131 B5
St Gabriels Ct GU15 . . . .151 D5
St George's Ave RG14 . . .104 E2
St George's Cl SL4 . . . . . . .66 E6
St George's Cres SL1 . . . . .41 D6
St George's Ct GU47 . . . .143 E2
St George's La SL5 . . . . . .120 B5
St George's Rd
Camberley GU15 . . . . .151 B3
Reading RG30 . . . . .85 C8
St George's Sch
Ascot SL5 . . . . .120 B6
Windsor SL4 . . . . .67 D7
St Georges Terr RG30 . . . .85 C8
St Georges Ind Est
GU15 . . . . .151 B3
St Giles Cl RG1 . . . . .86 B6
St Giles Ct 1 RG1 . . . . . . .86 B6
St Helens Cres GU47 . . . .150 B8
St Helier Cl RG41 . . . . . . .116 B3
St Hilda's Ave TW15 . . . . .97 E3
St Ives Cl RG7 . . . . .83 D2
St Ives Rd SL6 . . . . .40 A7
St James Cl
Pangbourne RG8 . . . . .56 C6
Twyford RG10 . . . . .61 E5
St James Ctyd 4 SL7 . . . . .1 E2
St James Pl SL1 . . . . .41 C7
St James Rd RG40 . . . . . .141 E8
St James Wlk SL0 . . . . . . .44 E4
St John the Evangelist CE
Sch RG14 . . . . .104 F1
St John's Beaumont Sch
TW19 . . . . .95 B6
St John's CE Prim Sch
RG1 .86 D7
St John's Gdns RG14 . . . .104 F1
St John's Hill RG1 . . . . . . .86 C7
St John's Rd
Caversham RG4 . . . . .59 A3
Mortimer RG7 . . . . .137 A5
Newbury RG14 . . . . .105 A1
North Ascot SL5 . . . . .92 F1
Reading RG1 . . . . .86 D7
Sandhurst GU47 . . . . .150 C7
Thatcham RG19 . . . . .106 C3
St Johns Ct SL6 . . . . .86 C7
St Johns Dr SL4 . . . . .67 A5
St Johns Rd Slough SL2 . . .43 A6
Windsor SL4 . . . . .67 A5
St Johns St RG45 . . . . . . .143 B4

St Johns Way KT16 . . . . . .124 A1
St Joseph's Convent Sch
RG1 .86 E5
St Joseph's RC High Sch
SL2 .43 A7
St Joseph's RC Prim Sch
Bracknell RG12 . . . . .118 D7
Newbury RG14 . . . . .105 B4
St Josephs Ct 7 RG14 . . . .105 B4
St Jude's CE Sch TW20 . . .95 C2
St Jude's Cl TW20 . . . . . . .95 C3
St Jude's Cotts TW20 . . . .95 C3
St Jude's Rd TW20 . . . . . . .95 C3
St Katherine's Rd RG9 . . . .35 D7
St Laurence Way SL1 . . . . .43 A3
St Lawrence Sq RG17 . . .100 C6
St Leger Ct RG14 . . . . . . .104 E4
St Leonard's Ave SL4 . . . . .67 C5
St Leonard's Rd
Windsor SL4 . . . . .67 C4
Windsor,Clewer Green SL4 .66 D1
St Leonards Hill SL4 . . . . .66 E4
St Leonards Wlk SL0 . . . . .44 F3
St Luke's CE Prim Sch
SL6 .39 F8
St Luke's Rd
Maidenhead SL6 . . . . .39 F8
Old Windsor SL4 . . . . .68 A1
St Lukes Ct RG4 . . . . .59 B4
St Lukes Way RG4 . . . . . . .59 B5
St Margaret Clitherow RC
Prim Sch RG12 . . . . .117 F2
St Margaret's Rd SL4 . . . . .39 A7
St Margarets Ave TW15 . . .98 B3
St Mark's Cl RG7 . . . . .83 B5
St Mark's Cres SL6 . . . . . . .39 B7
St Mark's Hospl SL6 . . . . .39 C7
St Mark's Pl SL4 . . . . .67 C5
St Mark's Rd
Bracknell RG42 . . . . .117 C8
Henley-On-T RG9 . . . . .35 D8
Maidenhead SL6 . . . . .39 D7
Windsor SL4 . . . . .67 C5
St Marks Cl RG19 . . . . . . .106 C3
St Martin's Ct TW15 . . . . .97 C3
St Martin's RC Prim Sch
RG4 .59 C6
St Martins Cl 3 RG8 . . . . .87 C1
St Mary's All Saints CE Prim
Sch RG1 . . . . .85 E5
St Mary's Ave
Purley On T RG8 . . . . .57 D5
Stanwell TW19 . . . . .97 D8
St Mary's Butts RG1 . . . . . .86 A7
St Mary's CE Jun Sch
Stanwell TW19 . . . . .97 E8
Thatcham RG18 . . . . .106 D4
St Mary's CE Prim Sch
Kintbury RG17 . . . . .102 B2
Slough SL1 . . . . .43 A3
St Mary's Ct
Henley-On-T RG9 . . . . .35 A8
Maidenhead SL6 . . . . .40 A7
Stanwell TW19 . . . . .97 D8
St Mary's Cres TW19 . . . . .97 D8
St Mary's Ct 6 RG14 . . . . .105 A4
St Mary's Dr TW14 . . . . . . .98 C8
St Mary's Gdns GU19 . . . .145 E3
St Mary's Gr RG1 . . . . .86 A7
St Mary's Hill SL5 . . . . . . .120 C4
St Mary's Ho RG18 . . . . . . .79 C1
St Mary's Pl 8 RG14 . . . . .105 A4
St Mary's RC Prim Sch
SL6 .19 F2
St Mary's Rd Ascot SL5 . .120 B3
Camberley GU15 . . . . .151 C6
Mortimer RG7 . . . . .137 A5
Newbury RG14 . . . . .105 B8
Sindlesham RG41 . . . . . . .115 B8
Slough SL3 . . . . .43 E3
Winnersh RG41 . . . . .88 B1
St Mary's Sch SL5 . . . . . .120 B2
St Mary's Way RG41 . . . .111 B3
St Mary's Wlk SL6 . . . . . . .39 F7
St Marys Cl GU47 . . . . . . .150 C8
St Marys La SL4 . . . . .92 D5
St Matthew's Ct 8
RG30 . . . . .85 A7
St Michael Prim Sch
SL2 .21 D1
St Michael's Easthampstead
CE Prim Sch RG12 . . . . . .118 A4
St Michael's Pl GU15 . . . .151 B5
St Michael's RC Prim Sch
TW15 . . . . .98 A3
St Michael's Rd
Newbury RG14 . . . . .104 F2
Reading RG30 . . . . .84 D7
Sandhurst GU47 . . . . .149 F8
St Michaels CE Prim Sch
GU47 . . . . .149 F8
St Michaels Cl SL5 . . . . . . .92 C2
St Michaels Cotts RG40 . .143 C8
St Michaels Ct RG10 . . . . .61 E6
St Michaels La RG10 . . . .110 D5
St Michaels Rd
Ashford TW15 . . . . .98 A3
Camberley GU15 . . . . .98 A3
St Micheal's CE Prim Sch
SL5 . . . . .120 D4
St Nazaire Cl TW20 . . . . . .96 C3
St Nicholas CE Comb Sch
SL6 .20 E1
St Nicholas CE Prim Sch
Hurst RG10 . . . . .88 F7
Shepperton TW17 . . . . . .125 B3
St Nicholas Dr TW17 . . . .125 A2

St Nicholas' Rd RG14 . . . .104 F2
St Nicolas CE Jun Sch
RG14 . . . . .105 A2
St Olave's Cl TW18 . . . . . .96 F1
St Patrick's Ave RG10 . . . .61 A5
St Patrick's Cl SL6 . . . . . . .39 B4
St Paul's CE Comb Sch,
Wooburn HP10 . . . . .3 D4
St Paul's CE Jun Sch
RG41 . . . . .116 A6
St Paul's Ct TW15 . . . . . . .98 C3
St Paul's Ct
Maidenhead SL6 . . . . .39 F6
Reading RG1 . . . . .86 A6
St Paul's Gate RG41 . . . .116 A6
St Paul's Mews RG2 . . . . .113 B7
St Paul's RC Prim Sch
RG31 . . . . .84 C7
St Paul's Rd TW18 . . . . . . .96 D2
St Pauls Ave SL2 . . . . .43 A5
St Peter Sl SL7 . . . . .1 E1
St Peter's Ave RG4 . . . . . . .58 E3
St Peter's CE Comb Sch
SL1 .21 B2
St Peter's CE Jun Sch
GU46 . . . . .149 E6
St Peter's CE Mid Sch
SL4 .67 F1
St Peter's CE Prim Sch
RG6 .87 B5
St Peter's Cl Burnham SL1 .21 B1
Old Windsor SL4 . . . . .68 A2
Staines TW18 . . . . .96 F2
St Peter's Gdns GU46 . . .149 D6
St Peter's Hill RG4 . . . . . . .58 F3
St Peter's RC Prim Sch
SL7 . . . . .1 D3
St Peter's Rd
Maidenhead SL6 . . . . .19 D2
Reading RG6 . . . . .87 A5
St Peters Cl RG19 . . . . . . .132 D2
St Peters Rd RG6 . . . . .87 A5
St Peters Way UB3 . . . . . . .71 D8
St Pinnock Ave TW18 . . . .124 A8
St Pirans Sch SL6 . . . . .19 E1
St Richards Rd RG14 . . . .105 B4
St Ronans Rd RG30 . . . . . .85 B8
St Saviour's Rd RG1 . . . . . .85 F5
St Saviour's Terr 9 RG1 . . .86 A6
St Sebastian's Cl RG40 . .142 E7
St Stephens Cl RG4 . . . . . .59 A2
St Swithins Cl RG20 . . . . . .75 D4
St Swithuns Ct RG10 . . . . .61 D4
St Teresa's RC Prim Sch
RG40 . . . . .116 D5
St Theresa's Rd TW14 . . . .71 F3
St Thomas Ct RG18 . . . . .106 E3
St Thomas Wlk SL3 . . . . . .69 D7
Salamanca RG45 . . . . .142 E5
Salcombe Dr RG6 . . . . .87 B4
Salcombe Rd
Ashford TW15 . . . . .97 E5
Newbury RG14 . . . . .104 E1
Reading RG2 . . . . .86 D5
Sale Garden Cotts RG40 .116 C5
Saleby Cl RG6 . . . . .87 E2
Salesian Gdns KT16 . . . . .124 A1
Salesian Sch KT16 . . . . . .124 A1
Salford Cl RG2 . . . . .113 C7
Salisbury Cl RG41 . . . . . . .116 A2
Salisbury Ct RG41 . . . . . .116 A2
Salisbury Ct SL6 . . . . .19 E1
Salisbury Mews SL2 . . . . . .22 C1
Salisbury Rd
Blackwater GU17 . . . . .150 C5
Harlington TW6 . . . . .71 C1
Hungerford RG17 . . . . . . .100 C3
Reading RG30 . . . . .85 B8
Salisbury Row RG17 . . . .100 D5
Salmon Cl RG2 . . . . .113 B2
Salmond Rd RG2 . . . . .113 C6
Salt Hill Ave SL1 . . . . .42 C5
Salt Hill Dr SL1 . . . . .42 C5
Salt Hill Mans SL1 . . . . . . .42 C5
Salt Hill Way SL1 . . . . .42 D5
Salters Cl SL6 . . . . .40 A7
Salters Rd SL6 . . . . .40 A7
Saltersgate Cl RG6 . . . . . . .87 D2
Saltire Gdns 2 RG42 . . . . .118 A8
Salwey Cl RG12 . . . . .118 B3
Samarkand Cl GU15 . . . . .152 B4
Samian Pl RG42 . . . . .90 E1
Sampage Cl RG2 . . . . .113 C6
Sampson Bsns Pk GU15 .151 B3
Sampson Ct TW17 . . . . . .125 D4
Sampson Rd RG42 . . . . . .117 D8
Sampsons Gn SL2 . . . . . . .21 F2
Sanctuary Cl RG30 . . . . . . .84 F8
Sanctuary Rd TW19,TW6 . .71 A1
Sandbrooke Wlk RG7 . . . .111 A3
Sandcroft Rd RG4 . . . . .58 E6
Sandells Ave TW15 . . . . . .98 C4
Sanden Ct RG17 . . . . .100 C5
Sandford Ct RG41 . . . . .88 D1
Sandford Down RG12 . . . .118 F4
Sandford Dr RG5 . . . . .60 F1
Sandford La RG5,RG10 . . .88 D6
Sandgate Ave RG30 . . . . . .57 F2
Sandgates KT16 . . . . .123 E1
Sandhills Cl GU25 . . . . . . .37 D3
Sandhills La GU25 . . . . . . .122 F4
Sandhills Mdw TW17 . . . .125 D3
Sandhills Way RG31 . . . . . .84 F4
Sandhurst La GU17 . . . . . .150 B6
Sandhurst Lodge RG45 . .142 E1
Sandhurst Rd
Crowthorne RG45 . . . . .143 B3

Sandhurst Rd continued
Wokingham RG40 . . . . . . .142 B8
Yateley GU46 . . . . .149 F7
Sandhurst Royal Military
Acad Hospl GU15 . . . . . . .151 A8
Sandhurst Sch GU47 . . . .150 E8
Sandhurst Sta GU47 . . . .150 A7
Sandisplatt Rd SL6 . . . . . . .39 A6
Sandleford Ct RG2 . . . . . .113 C6
Sandleford Lodge Pk
RG19 . . . . .131 B6
Sandlers End SL2 . . . . .22 B1
Sandown Ave RG31 . . . . . .84 B4
Sandown Cl GU17 . . . . . . .150 D5
Sandown Dr GU16 . . . . . .151 E2
Sandown Rd SL2 . . . . .41 F8
Sandown Way RG14 . . . . .105 C1
Sandpit La RG14,RG20 . . .130 C4
Sandpit La Caversham RG4 .59 F8
Swallowfield RG7 . . . . .140 B5
Sandringham Ct SL1 . . . . . .41 D7
Sandringham Dr TW15 . . . .97 D4
Sandringham Rd
Maidenhead SL6 . . . . .19 E2
Stanwell TW6 . . . . .70 D2
Sandringham Way RG31 . .84 B4
Sands Farm Dr SL1 . . . . . . .21 C1
Sandstone Cl RG41 . . . . . . .88 C1
Sandy Cl RG18 . . . . .79 A4
Sandy Dr TW14 . . . . .98 E7
Sandy La Bracknell RG12 .118 C8
Camberley GU15 . . . . .151 E6
Hermitage RG18 . . . . .78 F4
North Ascot SL5 . . . . .119 C8
Sandhurst GU47 . . . . .143 A2
Sunningdale SL5 . . . . .121 A4
Thorpe GU25 . . . . .122 E5
Wokingham RG41 . . . . . . .115 D4
Sandy Lane Prim Sch
RG42 . . . . .91 C1
Sandy Mead SL6 . . . . .40 C1
Sandy Ride SL5 . . . . .120 E5
Sandy Way KT12 . . . . .125 F1
Sandygate Cl SL7 . . . . .1 D3
Sandygate Rd SL7 . . . . .1 D3
Sapphire Cl RG41 . . . . . . .115 E7
Sargood Cl RG19 . . . . .106 E2
Sarsby Dr TW19 . . . . .96 A6
Sarum RG12 . . . . .117 F1
Sarum Cres RG40 . . . . . . .116 D7
Sarum Ct 1 RG30 . . . . .85 D6
Sarum Rd RG26 . . . . .135 A1
Sarum Way RG17 . . . . . . .100 D4
Satis Ho SL3 . . . . .68 C7
Saturn Cl RG6 . . . . .87 C1
Saturn Croft RG42 . . . . . . .92 B2
Saturn Ho RG2 . . . . .134 E2
Saunders Cl RG10 . . . . . . .61 F3
Saunders Ct RG8 . . . . .57 B5
Saunton Ave UB3 . . . . .71 F7
Savernake Cl RG30 . . . . . . .84 F7
Savernake Way RG12 . . . .118 F4

Savill Gardens The*
TW20 . . . . .94 C2
Savill Mews SL6 . . . . .95 D2
Savill Way SL7 . . . . .1 F2
Saville Cres TW15 . . . . . . .98 D2
Saville Gdns GU15 . . . . . .152 B5
Saville Ho 5 TW20 . . . . . . .96 A3
Savory Rd RG42 . . . . .90 C2
Savoy Cl SL6 . . . . .19 F1
Savoy Gr GU17 . . . . .150 D5
Sawmill Cotts SL3 . . . . . . .23 F2
Sawmill Rd RG18 . . . . .79 A4
Sawpit Rd RG10 . . . . .88 E7
Sawtry Cl RG6 . . . . .87 E2
Sawyer's Cl SL4 . . . . .66 E7
Sawyers Cl SL6 . . . . .39 A2
Sawyers Cres SL6 . . . . .39 A2
Sawyers Ley RG7 . . . . .137 D8
Saxby Cl RG7 . . . . .111 B3
Saxham Lodge RG40 . . . .116 C5
Saxon Cl SL3 . . . . .43 F4
Saxon Ct 9 Reading RG1 . .86 D7
Stanwell TW19 . . . . .70 A2
Thatcham RG19 . . . . .106 A3
Saxon Dr RG42 . . . . .118 E8
Saxon Gdns SL6 . . . . .20 D1
Saxon Lodge SL1 . . . . .41 F5
Saxon Prim Sch TW17 . . .125 A4
Saxon Rd TW15 . . . . .98 D2
Saxon Way
Harmondsworth UB7 . . . . . .70 C8
Old Windsor SL4 . . . . .68 B1
Saxons Acre RG20 . . . . . . .28 D3
Saxony Way GU46 . . . . . . .149 C4
Sayers Cl RG41 . . . . .131 B8
Scafell Cl RG31 . . . . .57 B2
Scafell Rd SL2 . . . . .41 F8
Scania Wlk RG42 . . . . .92 B2
Scarborough Rd TW6 . . . . .71 C1
Scarborough Way SL1 . . . .42 B4
Scarlet Oaks GU15 . . . . . .151 E3
Scarletts La RG10 . . . . .37 C1
Sch of Electronic
Engineering RG2 . . . . . . .114 F1
Scholars Ct
Caversham RG4 . . . . .58 F3
Great Shefford RG17 . . . . .48 A3
Scholars Wlk SL3 . . . . .44 A4
School Cl GU20 . . . . .153 F4
School Gn RG2 . . . . .113 E4
School Hill
Crowthorne RG45 . . . . . . .143 D4
Sandhurst GU47 . . . . .143 A1
Wargrave RG10 . . . . .36 D1
Woolhampton RG7 . . . . . .107 F3
School Ho TW19 . . . . .70 C1

School La Bagshot GU19 . .145 C2
Boxford RG20 . . . . .76 E4
Burghfield Common RG7 . .110 F2
Caversham RG4 . . . . .59 A2
Cookham SL6 . . . . .20 B7
Cookham Dean SL6 . . . . . .19 B7
East Garston RG17 . . . . . . .47 D6
Egham TW20 . . . . .96 A3
Emmer Green RG4 . . . . . . .59 B6
Froxfield SN8 . . . . .99 A1
Little Marlow SL7 . . . . .2 C5
Littlewick Green SL6 . . . . . .38 B4
Lower Halliford TW17 . . . .125 B2
Maidenhead SL6 . . . . .19 E1
Medmenham SL7 . . . . .17 B6
North Ascot SL5 . . . . .119 D8
Riseley RG7 . . . . .139 E3
Slough SL2 . . . . .42 F6
Stoke Poges SL2 . . . . .23 B5
Wargrave RG10 . . . . .36 D2
Windlesham GU20 . . . . . . .146 D4
Yateley GU46 . . . . .149 B6
School of Military Survey
RG18 . . . . .78 F7
School Rd
Arborfield Cross RG2,
RG41 . . . . .114 F2
Ascot SL5 . . . . .120 D4
Ashford TW15 . . . . .98 B2
Burghfield Common RG30 .111 C6
Chieveley RG20 . . . . .77 F8
Compton RG20 . . . . .31 E4
Harmondsworth UB7 . . . . . .70 D8
Hurst RG10 . . . . .88 F8
Padworth RG7 . . . . .109 F1
Reading RG3 . . . . .84 D8
Riseley RG7 . . . . .139 E3
Waltham St Lawrence RG10 .62 F3
Windlesham GU20 . . . . . . .146 B5
Wooburn Green HP10 . . . . .3 E6
School Terr RG1 . . . . .86 E8
Schroder Ct TW20 . . . . . .106 F3
Scobell Cl RG2 . . . . .113 D5
Scotland Hill GU47 . . . . . .150 A8
Scotlands Dr SL2 . . . . .22 B6
Scots Cl TW19 . . . . .97 D7
Scots Dr RG41 . . . . .115 E7
Scott Cl Caversham RG4 . . .59 A5
Farnham Common SL2 . . . .22 C7
Woodley RG5 . . . . .88 A7
Scott Terr RG12 . . . . .118 E8
Scott's Ave TW16 . . . . .98 E1
Scott's Way TW16 . . . . .98 E1
Scottalls La RG18 . . . . .52 F5
Scotts Mews SL5 . . . . .119 B8
Scours La RG30 . . . . .58 B1
Scratchface La RG7 . . . . . .81 E7
Scrivens Mead RG19 . . . .106 F3
Scylla Cres TW6,TW14 . . . .98 B8
Scylla Rd TW14,TW6 . . . . .71 B1
Seacourt Rd SL3 . . . . .44 B2
Seafield Cl SL2 . . . . .85 F7
Seaford Gdns RG5 . . . . . . .87 E6
Seaford Rd Stanwell TW6 . .70 D2
Wokingham RG40 . . . . . . .116 D6
Sealand Rd TW6 . . . . .70 C3
Searing Way RG26 . . . . . .135 A1
Searles Farm La RG30 . . . .85 B1
Searlwood Ct GU24 . . . . . .153 F5
Seaton Dr TW15 . . . . .97 E6
Seaton Gdns RG2 . . . . .86 C2
Seaton Rd GU15 . . . . .151 B5
Second Ave Reading RG31 .84 B6
Tadley RG7 . . . . .135 C2
Second Cres SL1 . . . . .42 C8
Second St E RG19 . . . . . . .132 A5
Seddon Hill RG42 . . . . .91 B2
Sedge Gr RG18 . . . . .106 E4
Sedgefield Rd RG14 . . . . .131 C8
Sedgmoor Cl HP10 . . . . . . .3 A7
Sedgmoor Gdns HP10 . . . .3 A8
Sedgmoor La HP10 . . . . . . .3 A7
Sedgmoor Rd HP10 . . . . . . .3 A8
Seebys Oak GU47 . . . . . . .150 E6
Sefton Cl Stoke Poges SL2 .22 F4
West End GU24 . . . . .153 F6
Sefton Paddock SL2 . . . . . .23 A5
Sefton Park Cotts SL2 . . . .23 A4
Segrave Cl RG4 . . . . .60 E2
Segsbury Gr RG12 . . . . . . .118 E5
Selborne RG12 . . . . .118 B6
Selborne Cl GU17 . . . . . . .150 C6
Selborne Ct 2 RG1 . . . . . . .86 C7
Selborne Gdns RG30 . . . . .58 A1
Selby Rd TW15 . . . . .98 C2
Selcourt Cl RG5 . . . . .87 D8
Selim Ct 3 SL1 . . . . .43 A4
Sellafield Way RG6 . . . . . . .87 E3
Selsdon Ave RG5 . . . . .87 F8
Selsey Way RG6 . . . . .114 B8
Selva Ct 6 RG1 . . . . .86 C6
Selwood Cl TW19 . . . . .70 C1
Selwood Gdns TW19 . . . . .70 C1
Selwyn Cl SL4 . . . . .66 E5
Selwyn Dr GU46 . . . . .149 B6
Selwyn Pl SL1 . . . . .41 F6
Sen Cl RG42 . . . . .91 C2
Send Rd RG4 . . . . .59 C1
Sermed Ct SL2 . . . . .43 C5
Servite Ho SL6 . . . . .40 B8
Setley Way RG12 . . . . .118 F6
Seton Dr RG31 . . . . .84 F5
Sett The GU46 . . . . .149 B5

Setter Cl RG42 .....91 D2
Settrington Cl 2 RG6 ...87 E2
Sevenoaks Dr RG7 ...113 B3
Sevenoaks Rd RG6 ...87 B3
Seventh Ave RG31 ...84 B6
Seventh St RG19 ...131 F5
Severalls The SN8 ...126 D3
Severn Cl
  Sandhurst GU47 ...150 C8
  Thatcham RG18 ...106 B5
Severn Cres SL3 ...69 B8
Severn Way RG30 ...84 F6
Sewell Ave RG41 ...116 A8
Sewell Cl RG18 ...79 B1
Seymour Ave RG2 ...113 E5
Seymour Cl SL6 ...39 B3
Seymour Court La SL7 ...1 B5
Seymour Court Rd SL7 ...1 C4
Seymour Ct RG45 ...142 E4
Seymour Dr GU15 ...152 B7
Seymour Ho SL3 ...43 E4
Seymour Park Rd SL7 ...1 D3
Seymour Plain SL7 ...1 C5
Seymour Rd SL1 ...42 D3
Seymour Way TW16 ...98 E1
Shackleton Ct 8 TW19 ...70 E1
Shackleton Rd SL1 ...42 F6
Shackleton Way RG5 ...88 A7
Shafer Ct RG14 ...105 A1
Shaftesbury Cl RG12 ...118 D4
Shaftesbury Cres TW18 ...97 D1
Shaftesbury Ct
  Maidenhead SL6 ...39 E5
  8 Slough SL1 ...42 E4
  Wokingham RG40 ...116 D7
Shaftesbury Mount
  GU17 ...150 D3
Shaftesbury Rd
  Bisley GU24 ...153 F3
  Reading RG30 ...85 B8
Shaggy Calf La SL2 ...43 A6
Shakespeare Cl RG42 ...59 D5
Shakespeare Lodge SL1 ...41 F5
Shakespeare Rd RG18 ...106 C4
Shakespeare Way RG42 ...118 E8
Shalbourne Cl RG17 ...100 B5
Shalbourne Rise GU15 ...151 D5
Sharney Ave SL3 ...44 B3
Sharnwood Dr RG31 ...84 F5
Sharonelle Ct RG40 ...116 B6
Sharpthorpe Cl 2 RG6 ...87 B1
Shaw Cl SL4 ...68 A2
Shaw Farm Rd RG14 ...105 B6
Shaw Hill RG14 ...105 B5
Shaw Mill RG14 ...105 B5
Shaw Pk RG45 ...143 B3
Shaw Rd Newbury RG14 ...105 B4
  Reading RG1 ...85 F5
Shaw The SL6 ...19 E6
Shaw-Cum-Donnington
  Parochial Prim Sch
  RG14 ...105 A6
Shears Ct TW16 ...98 E1
Sheehy Way SL2 ...43 B8
Sheep Fair Way RG17 ...25 B2
Sheep Leaze La RG20 ...29 D2
Sheep Wlk Caversham RG4 ...59 B4
  Littleton TW17 ...125 A4
Sheepcote La
  Holyport SL6 ...64 C4
  Wooburn SL1 ...3 F1
Sheepcote Rd Eton SL4 ...42 A1
  Windsor SL4 ...66 E5
Sheepdown RG20 ...30 E7
Sheepdrove Rd RG17 ...25 C3
Sheephouse Rd SL6 ...20 B2
Sheephouse Way RG20 ...49 A6
Sheepridge La SL7,HP10 ...2 E7
Sheeps Ditch Cl TW18 ...97 A1
Sheepwalk TW17 ...124 F5
Sheepwash RG20 ...131 A2
Sheepways La RG4 ...58 B8
Sheerlands Rd RG2 ...140 F7
Sheet La SL4 ...67 C6
Sheet Street Rd SL4 ...94 A7
Sheffield Rd
  Harlington TW14,TW6 ...71 C2
  Slough SL1 ...42 C7
Sheffield Way TW14,TW6 ...71 D2
Shefford CE Prim Sch
  RG17 ...48 B4
Shefford Cres RG40 ...116 D8
Shefford Lodge 8
  RG14 ...105 A2
Sheldon Gdns RG2 ...86 C1
Shelgate Wlk RG5 ...87 C7
Shelley Ave RG12 ...118 E7
Shelley Cl
  Medmenham SL7 ...17 D7
  Slough SL3 ...43 F1
  Wooburn Green HP10 ...3 E8
  Woodley RG5 ...87 E4
Shelley Ct
  Camberley GU15 ...151 C5
  Reading RG1 ...86 Rd
Shelley Rd 2 Marlow SL7 ...1 F3
  Thatcham RG18 ...106 C4
Shelley Wlk GU46 ...149 B5
Shellfield Cl TW19 ...70 A2
Shelson Ave TW13 ...98 F4
Shelton Ct SL3 ...43 C3
Shenstone Cl SL4 ...66 D7
Shenstone Ct RG40 ...142 A8
Shenstone Dr SL1 ...21 D1
Shenstone Pk SL5 ...120 E5

Shenstone Rd RG2 ...86 B4
Shepherd's Hill RG20 ...76 E4
Shepherd's House La
  RG6 ...87 A8
Shepherds Ave RG6 ...87 B8
Shepherds Chase GU19 ...145 E2
Shepherds Cl Hurley SL6 ...17 F3
  Shepperton TW17 ...125 B3
Shepherds Ct SL4 ...66 E5
Shepherds Hill
  Bracknell RG12 ...118 C8
  Compton RG20 ...31 E3
  Earley RG6 ...87 C8
Shepherds La
  Bracknell RG42 ...91 B1
  Caversham RG4 ...58 D6
  Hurley SL6 ...17 E4
Shepherds Mount RG20 ...31 E3
Shepherds Rise RG20 ...31 E4
Shepherds Way RG45 ...142 E4
Shepherds Wlk RG6 ...87 C8
Shepley Dr Reading RG30 ...85 C4
  Wentworth SL5 ...121 D3
Shepley End SL5 ...121 D4
Sheppee Rdbt RG42 ...91 E1
Shepperton Bsns Pk
  TW17 ...125 C4
Shepperton Court Dr
  TW17 ...125 B4
Shepperton Ct TW17 ...125 B3
Shepperton Rd TW17,
  TW18 ...124 D5
Shepperton Sta TW17 ...125 C4
Shepperton Studios
  TW17 ...124 F6
Sheraton Cl GU17 ...150 E4
Sheraton Dr RG31 ...57 B1
Sherborne Cl SL3 ...69 E6
Sherborne Cl SL6 ...39 E6
Sherborne Rd TW14 ...98 D7
Sherbourne Dr
  Maidenhead SL6 ...39 C3
  Wentworth SL5 ...121 D4
  Windsor SL4 ...66 F3
  Woodley RG5 ...87 F8
Sherbourne Gdns TW17 ...125 E2
Sherbourne Wlk SL2 ...22 C8
Sherfield Cl RG2 ...86 D4
Sherfield Dr RG2 ...86 D4
Shergold Way SL6 ...40 B5
Sheridan Ave RG4 ...59 A4
Sheridan Cres RG26 ...134 E1
Sheridan Ct
  Maidenhead SL6 ...40 B8
  Newbury RG14 ...105 C3
  Slough SL1 ...41 E6
Sheridan Grange SL5 ...121 A3
Sheridan Way RG41 ...115 C5
Sheringham Ct 8 RG41 ...86 C5
Sherman Rd Reading RG1 ...86 B6
  Slough SL1 ...42 E8
Sherrard Mead RG14 ...105 B5
Sherring Cl RG41 ...91 C1
Sherwood Cl
  Bracknell RG12 ...119 A7
  Slough SL3 ...43 E3
Sherwood Ct
  Colnbrook SL3 ...69 D7
  Slough SL1 ...43 F1
Sherwood Dr SL6 ...39 A6
Sherwood Gdns RG9 ...35 C8
Sherwood Ho 8 RG1 ...85 E5
Sherwood Pl RG8 ...57 B4
Sherwood Rd RG41 ...88 C2
Sherwood Rise RG8 ...57 B5
Sherwood St RG30 ...85 C8
Shetland Rd TW6 ...71 C1
Shield Rd TW15 ...98 C4
Shifford Cres SL6 ...19 E3
Shildon Cl GU15 ...152 D3
Shilling Cl RG30 ...85 B6
Shinfield Inf Sch RG2 ...113 E4
Shinfield Rd Earley RG2 ...113 E8
  Reading RG2 ...86 E3
Shinfield Rise RG2 ...86 E1
Shinfield St Mary's CE Jun
  Sch ...113 F4
Shiplake CE Sch RG9 ...35 E2
Shiplake Coll RG9 ...35 F1
Shiplake Ho Bourne End SL8 ...3 B4
  Bracknell RG12 ...118 F5
Shiplake Sta RG9 ...36 B4
Shipton Cl RG31 ...57 C2
Shire Cl GU19 ...145 E2
Shire Cotts RG7 ...108 F6
Shire's Head Cl RG30 ...85 D6
Shires The RG41 ...115 D6
Shires Way RG41 ...149 D7
Shirley Ave Reading RG1 ...113 C7
  Windsor SL4 ...66 F6
Shirley Rd SL6 ...39 C5
Shoesmiths Ct 8 RG1 ...86 A8
Sholto Rd TW6 ...71 A2
Shooter's Hill RG8 ...56 B7
Shooters Way RG2 ...112 F8
Shop La
  Leckhampstead RG20 ...49 F5
  Newbury RG14 ...104 E6
Shoppenhanger's Rd SL6 ...39 E4
Shoppenhangers Rd SL6 ...39 C2
Shoreham Rd (E) TW6 ...70 E2
Shoreham Rd (W) TW6 ...70 E2
Shoreham Rise SL2 ...21 D1
Shorland Oaks RG42 ...91 C2
Short Cl TW15,TW19 ...97 F7
Short Rd TW19 ...70 E1
Short St Caversham RG4 ...59 B2

Short St continued
  Pangbourne RG8 ...56 D5
  Reading RG1 ...86 B6
Short The RG8 ...57 D5
Shortfern SL2 ...43 C7
Shortheath La RG42 ...110 E3
Shortlands UB3 ...71 D8
Shortlands Hill OX10 ...13 D4
Shortwood Ave TW18 ...97 B5
Shortwood Inf Sch TW18 ...97 B5
Shrewsbury Rd TW14,
  TW6 ...71 D1
Shrewsbury Terr RG14 ...104 E1
Shrivenham Cl 8 GU47 ...150 D8
Shropshire Gdns RG42 ...91 F1
Shrubbs Hill La SL5 ...121 C3
Shrubland Dr RG30 ...85 A4
Shrublands Dr GU18 ...153 B8
Shute End RG40,RG41 ...116 B6
Shyshack La RG26 ...134 F1
Sibley Park Rd RG6 ...87 A2
Sibson RG6 ...87 C2
Sidbury Cl SL5 ...121 A4
Sidestrand Rd RG14 ...130 E8
Sidings The TW18 ...97 B4
Sidmouth Grange Cl RG6 ...87 B7
Sidmouth Grange Rd
  RG6 ...87 B7
Sidmouth St RG1 ...86 B7
Sidney Rd Staines TW18 ...97 A4
  Windsor SL4 ...66 C4
Silbury Cl RG31 ...84 D4
Silchester CE Prim Sch
  RG7 ...136 B1
Silchester Ct TW15 ...97 E6
Silchester Ho SL6 ...40 B8
Silchester House Sch
  SL6 ...40 D7
Silchester Rd
  Reading RG30 ...85 C4
  Tadley RG26 ...135 D1
Silco Dr SL6 ...39 E6
Silver Birches RG41 ...115 D3
Silver Cl SL6 ...39 A5
Silver Dr GU16 ...152 C3
Silver Fox Cres RG5 ...87 D6
Silver Hill GU47 ...150 E8
Silver La RG7 ...136 B8
Silver St RG1 ...86 B6
Silver Street Flats 10
  RG1 ...86 B6
Silverbeck Way TW19 ...70 A2
Silverdale Rd Earley RG6 ...87 C3
  Tadley RG26 ...135 B1
  Wargrave RG10 ...36 E1
Silverglades GU46 ...149 C4
Silverthorne Dr RG4 ...58 D5
Silvertrees Dr SL6 ...39 A5
Silverwood Dr GU15 ...152 A7
Silwood RG12 ...117 E1
Silwood Cl SL5 ...120 D7
Silwood Park (Imperial Coll)
  SL5 ...120 F6
Silwood Rd SL5 ...120 F5
Simkins Cl RG42 ...92 B2
Simmonds Cl RG42 ...117 E8
Simmonds Malthouse 8
  RG1 ...86 A6
Simmonds St RG1 ...86 A7
Simmons Cl 8 SL3 ...44 A2
Simmons Field RG18 ...106 F4
Simmons Fields RG10 ...16 E3
Simmons Rd RG9 ...15 D3
Simms Farm La RG7 ...136 F4
Simod Ct 8 RG30 ...85 C7
Simons Cl RG31 ...57 C4
Simons La RG41 ...115 D6
Simons Wlk TW20 ...95 C1
Simpson Cl SL6 ...39 B6
Simpsons Way SL1 ...42 E5
Sinclair Rd SL4 ...67 C4
Sindle Cl RG41 ...88 B7
Sindlesham Rd RG2 ...114 E3
Singer La RG9 ...15 E1
Singers Cl RG9 ...35 E8
Singers La RG9 ...35 E8
Sinhurst Rd GU15 ...151 B4
Sipson Cl UB7 ...71 A8
Sipson La UB3,UB7 ...71 B8
Sipson Rd UB7 ...71 A7
Sipson Way UB7 ...71 A7
Sir Henry Peeks Dr SL2 ...22 A6
Sir Sydney Camm Ho
  SL4 ...67 B6
Sir William Borlase's Gram
  Sch SL7 ...1 C1
Sir William Perkin's Sch
  KT16 ...123 F1
Sirius Cl RG42 ...91 F2
Sirl Cotts SL5 ...120 C5
Six Acre La RG17 ...126 A5
Sixth Ave RG31 ...84 B6
Sixth St RG19 ...131 F5
Skarries View RG4 ...58 D8
Skeffling Cl RG42 ...87 E2
Skelmersdale Way RG6 ...87 E3
Skelton Fields RG42 ...91 C1
Skerries Ct 8 SL3 ...44 A2
Skerritt Way RG8 ...57 D4
Skillman Dr RG19 ...106 F3
Skilton Rd RG31 ...57 C3
Skimpedhill La RG12 ...118 B7
Skinners Green La
  RG14 ...129 F3
Skippons Cl RG14 ...130 C6
Sky Bsns Pk TW20 ...123 C7

Skydmore Path SL2 ...21 F2
Skye Cl RG31 ...84 E4
Skylings RG14 ...105 C4
Skyport Dr UB7 ...70 D7
Skyway 14 Trad Est SL3 ...69 F4
Slade Hill Gdns RG20 ...129 F2
Slaidburn Gn RG12 ...118 E2
Slanting Hill RG18 ...79 B4
Sledmere Ct TW14 ...98 F7
Slim Rd GU15 ...151 C2
Sloane Cl RG8 ...34 C6
Slopes The RG4 ...59 D2
Slough & Eton CE Sch
  SL1 ...42 D3
Slough Gram Sch SL3 ...43 B3
Slough Mus* SL1 ...43 A4
Slough Rd Datchet SL3 ...68 C8
  Eton SL4 ...42 C2
Slough Sta SL1 ...42 F5
Slough Trad Est SL1 ...42 B7
Smalley Cl RG41 ...115 E4
Smallholdings TW15 ...98 B4
Smallmead Rd
  Burghfield Common RG7 ...85 D1
  Reading RG2 ...86 C1
Smallridge RG14 ...130 C4
Smallwood Dr RG26 ...135 B1
Smeaton Ct RG14 ...104 F4
Smewins Rd RG10,SL6 ...63 D5
Smith Sq RG12 ...118 D7
Smith's Hill OX12 ...6 F5
Smitham Bridge Rd
  RG17 ...100 C5
Smithfield Cl SL6 ...38 F3
Smithfield Rd SL6 ...39 A3
Smiths La SL4 ...66 E6
Smithy's Gn GU20 ...146 D4
Snake La RG20 ...104 A7
Snape Spur SL1 ...42 E7
Snelsmore Common Cntry
  Pk* RG14 ...77 D2
Snipe La RG20 ...131 F2
Snowball Hill
  Maidenhead SL6 ...39 A1
  White Waltham SL6 ...64 B8
Snowberry Cl RG41 ...115 F5
Snowden Cl SL4 ...66 D3
Snowden Dr RG31 ...84 A6
Snowdon Ct RG45 ...143 A5
Snowdon Rd TW6 ...71 C1
Snowdrop Copse RG14 ...106 F4
Snowdrop Gr RG41 ...88 C2
Snows Paddock GU20 ...146 B2
Snows Rdbt GU20 ...146 B6
Soane End RG4 ...59 A7
Soham Cl RG6 ...114 C8
Soho Cres HP10 ...3 D4
Soke Rd RG7 ...135 C8
Soldiers Rise RG40 ...142 D7
Solent Ct 2 RG1 ...86 B6
Somerford Cl SL6 ...40 B8
Somersby Cres SL6 ...39 E3
Somerset Cl
  Hungerford RG17 ...100 C5
  Wokingham RG41 ...116 A8
Somerset Gr RG42 ...91 F1
Somerset Hospl SN8 ...99 B5
Somerset Lodge 8 SL6 ...39 F3
Somerset Way SL0 ...44 F4
Somerstown Ct RG1 ...86 A7
Somerton Gdns RG6 ...87 A2
Somerton Gr RG19 ...106 C2
Somerville Cl RG41 ...115 D4
Somerville Cres GU46 ...149 E6
Somerville Rd SL4 ...42 C1
Songbird Cl RG2 ...113 E5
Sonning CE Prim Sch
  RG4 ...60 D3
Sonning Gate RG4 ...60 E2
Sonning La RG4 ...60 C2
Sonning Mdws RG4 ...60 C1
Sonninge Cl GU47 ...150 D8
Sopwith Cl RG5 ...88 A7
Sorrel Cl
  Burghfield Common RG7 ...111 B3
  Newbury RG14 ...105 D5
  Wokingham RG40 ...116 D4
Sospel Ct SL2 ...22 C3
South Ave Egham TW20 ...96 C2
  Henley-On-T RG9 ...15 E1
South Bank RG8 ...14 C3
South Cl Burnham SL1 ...41 D6
  Medmenham SL7 ...17 D7
  Wokingham RG40 ...116 C6
South Dr Reading RG2 ...86 F2
  Sonning RG4 ...60 C1
  Sulhamstead RG7 ...109 F2
  Wentworth GU25 ...122 A2
  Wokingham RG40 ...116 A8
South End Rd RG7 ...82 B2
South Farm La GU46 ...149 A2
South Field Cl SL4 ...43 C3
South Gr KT16 ...123 F3
South Gn SL1 ...123 E8
South Groves RG17 ...25 D4
South Hill Rd RG12 ...118 B3
South Lake Cres RG5 ...87 E5
South Lake Inf Sch RG5 ...87 E5
South Lake Prim Sch
  RG5 ...87 E5
South Lynn Cres RG12 ...118 B4
South Mdw RG45 ...143 D4
South Meadow La SL4 ...67 C8
South Oak Way RG6 ...112 F7

South Path SL4 ...67 C6
South Pl Marlow SL7 ...1 E1
  Wokingham RG40 ...116 C6
South Rd Bisley GU24 ...153 F3
  Bracknell RG40,RG12 ...117 E1
  Crowthorne RG45 ...143 E3
  Englefield Green TW20 ...95 D2
  Maidenhead SL6 ...39 E6
South Row Chilton OX11 ...10 D7
  Fulmer SL3 ...23 E8
South St Blewbury OX11 ...12 A8
  Caversham RG4 ...59 B2
  Reading RG1 ...86 C7
  Staines TW18 ...96 F3
South Stoke Prim Sch
  RG8 ...14 B4
South Terr SL4 ...67 E6
Southview
  Bracknell RG12 ...117 D6
  Cookham Rise SL6 ...19 E7
South View Ave RG4 ...59 C2
South View Gdns 9
  RG18 ...105 B4
South View Pk RG4 ...59 C2
Southampton Cl GU17 ...150 C6
Southampton Rd TW6 ...70 F1
Southampton St RG1 ...86 B6
Southbank Gdns RG17 ...25 C2
Southbury Dr SL8 ...3 A3
Southbury La RG10 ...61 F5
Southcote Ave TW13 ...98 F6
Southcote La RG30 ...85 A4
Southcote La RG30 ...85 C4
Southcote Lodge RG30 ...85 A4
Southcote Prim Sch
  RG30 ...85 C4
Southcote Rd RG30 ...85 B6
Southcroft
  Englefield Green TW20 ...95 B3
  Slough SL2 ...22 B1
Southdown Rd
  Caversham RG4 ...59 B5
  Tadley RG26 ...135 A1
  Thatcham RG19 ...105 F4
Southend RG18 ...106 D6
Southern Cotts TW19 ...70 A2
Southern Ct 8 RG1 ...86 B7
Southern Gate Pk RG2 ...113 A8
Southern Hill RG1 ...86 D5
Southern Ind Area
  RG12 ...117 F6
Southern Perimeter Rd
  East Bedfont TW6 ...71 B1
  Harlington TW14,TW6 ...71 D2
  Stanwell TW19,TW6 ...70 D2
Southern Rd GU15 ...151 C6
Southerndene Cl RG31 ...57 C2
Southfield Gdns SL1 ...41 B8
Southfield Rd RG40 ...116 D5
Southfields Boxford RG20 ...76 E3
  Chieveley RG20 ...78 B8
Southfields Ave TW15 ...98 B2
Southgate Ho SL6 ...39 F7
Southglade RG12 ...118 B2
Southlake Ct RG5 ...87 D5
Southlands Cl RG40 ...116 C6
Southlands Rd RG40 ...116 D4
Southlea Rd SL3 ...68 B5
Southside KT16 ...124 A6
Southview Ct RG10 ...61 E6
Southview Rd SL7 ...1 E4
Southville Cl TW14 ...98 E7
Southville Cres TW14 ...98 E7
Southville Jun & Inf Schs
  TW14 ...98 F7
Southville Rd TW14 ...98 E8
Southwark Cl GU46 ...149 C4
Southway RG45 ...151 B4
Southwell Park Rd
  GU15 ...151 C5
Southwick GU19 ...145 E1
Southwick Ct RG12 ...118 E3
Southwold Cl RG6 ...87 D1
Southwold Spur SL3 ...44 C4
Southwood RG40 ...116 D4
Southwood Gdns
  Burghfield Common RG7 ...111 A3
  Cookham Rise SL6 ...19 E5
Southwood Rd
  Cookham Rise SL6 ...19 E5
  Yateley GU17 ...149 E2
Sovereign Beeches SL2 ...22 B8
Sovereign Ct 4 SL5 ...121 B2
Sovereign Dr GU15 ...152 B7
Sovereign Ho TW15 ...97 E4
Sovereign Pk 8 RG31 ...84 D8
Sovereign Way RG31 ...84 C5
Sovoy Ct GU15 ...151 C5
Sowbury Pk RG20 ...78 A3
Spa Meadow Cl RG10 ...131 C8
Spackman Ct RG19 ...106 D2
Spackmans Way SL1 ...42 D3
Spade Oak Farm SL8 ...2 E3
Spade Oak Mdw SL8 ...2 F4
Span Hill RG4 ...60 A4
Sparrow Cl RG41 ...115 E5
Sparrowbill RG20 ...22 D4
Sparvell Way GU15 ...151 C6
Speedbird Way UB7 ...70 C7
Speedwell Way RG18 ...106 F4
Speen La RG14 ...104 E4
Speen Lodge Ct RG14 ...104 E4
Speenhamland Ct 8
  RG14 ...105 A4

Speenhamland Prim Sch
RG14 . . . . .104 F4
Spelthorne Coll TW15 . . . .97 F4
Spelthorne Gr TW16 . . . . .98 F1
Spelthorne Inf Sch TW15 .98 E2
Spelthorne Jun Sch
TW15 . . . . .98 D2
Spelthorne La TW15,
TW17 . . . . .125 C8
Spelthorne Mus* TW18 96 E3
Spencer Cl
Silchester RG26 . . . . .135 E1
Wokingham RG41 . . . . . .115 D6
Spencer Gdns TW20 . . . . .95 D3
Spencer Rd
Bracknell RG42 . . . . .117 F8
Newbury RG14 . . . . .130 D6
Reading RG2 . . . . .113 B7
Slough SL3 . . . . .43 F3
Spencers Cl SL6 . . . . .39 D8
Spencers La SL4 . . . . .113 A3
Spencers La SL6 . . . . .19 E7
Spencers Rd SL6 . . . . .39 D8
Spenwood Cl RG21 . . . . . .113 B2
Sperling Rd SL6 . . . . .19 F1
Spey Rd RG30 . . . . .85 A7
Spinfield La SL7 . . . . .1 B2
Spinfield La W SL7 . . . . .1 C1
Spinfield Mount SL7 . . . . . . .1 B1
Spinfield Pk SL7 . . . . .1 C1
Spinfield Sch SL7 . . . . .1 B2
Spinis RG12 . . . . .117 F1
Spinner Gn RG12 . . . . . . .118 B4
Spinners Wlk Marlow SL7 . .1 C1
Windsor SL4 . . . . .67 C6
Spinney SL1 . . . . .42 B5
Spinney Cl RG4 . . . . .59 B7
Spinney Dr TW14 . . . . .98 C8
Spinney La SL4 . . . . .93 B7
Spinney The Ascot SL5 . . .120 E4
Frimley GU15 . . . . .152 C6
Wokingham RG40 . . . . . .141 F8
Yateley GU46 . . . . .149 C7
Spinningwheel La RG42 . .90 C8
Spires Ct KT16 . . . . .124 A3
Spitfire Cl SL1 . . . . .44 J2
Spitfire Way RG5 . . . . .88 A7
Spittal St SL7 . . . . .1 D2
Splash The RG42 . . . . .91 B2
Spode Cl RG30 . . . . .84 E8
Spout La TW19 . . . . .70 A3
Spout La N TW19 . . . . .70 B3
Spray La RG20 . . . . .28 C1
Spray Rd SN8,RG17 . . . . .126 E3
Spriggs Cl RG19 . . . . .106 D2
Spring Ave TW20 . . . . .95 F2
Spring Cl Maidenhead SL6 .19 F2
Pangbourne RG8 . . . . .55 D5
Spring Cnr TW13 . . . . .98 F5
Spring Farm Mews RG8 . .14 C1
Spring Gdns Ascot SL5 . . .120 B5
Bourne End SL8 . . . . .3 A4
Frimley GU15 . . . . .152 A5
Marlow SL7 . . . . .1 E3
Newbury RG20 . . . . .130 B3
Shinfield RG7 . . . . .113 B2
Theale RG7 . . . . .83 D3
Wooburn Green HP10 . . . . .3 E6
Spring Gr RG1 . . . . .86 B6
Spring Hill SL6 . . . . .39 E3
Spring La
Aldermaston RG7 . . . . . .135 C6
Aston Tirrold OX11 . . . . . . .12 E8
Caversham RG4 . . . . .60 B5
Cold Ash RG18 . . . . .106 C8
Cookham Dean SL6 . . . . . .19 C5
Farnham Common SL2 . . . .22 C5
Mortimer RG7 . . . . .137 A4
Riseley RG7 . . . . .139 A4
Slough SL1 . . . . .41 F5
Spring Mdw RG12 . . . . . .118 D8
Spring Mdws RG17 . . . . . .48 B4
Spring Meadows Bsns Ctr
RG10 . . . . .36 F5
Spring Rd TW13 . . . . .98 F5
Spring Rise TW20 . . . . .95 E2
Spring Terr ⑤ RG1 . . . . . . .86 B5
Spring Wlk RG10 . . . . .36 D1
Spring Wood La RG7 . . . . .111 A2
Spring Woods
Sandhurst GU47 . . . . .143 C1
Virginia Water GU25 . . . . .122 B5
Springate Field SL3 . . . . . .43 E4
Springcross Ave GU17 . . .150 D4
Springdale Earley RG6 . . . .87 B2
Wokingham RG40 . . . . . .141 E8
Springfield
Lightwater GU18 . . . . . . .153 D8
Slough SL1 . . . . .43 A3
Springfield Cl SL4 . . . . .67 B5
Springfield Ct
Maidenhead SL6 . . . . .40 B7
Twyford RG10 . . . . .61 E5
Springfield End RG8 . . . . . .34 C8
Springfield Gr TW16 . . . . .125 F8
Springfield La RG14 . . . . .131 B8
Springfield Mews RG4 . . .59 B4
Springfield Pk
Maidenhead SL6 . . . . .40 C1
Twyford RG10 . . . . .61 E5
Springfield Prim Sch
Reading RG31 . . . . .84 B7
Sunbury TW16 . . . . .125 F7
Springfield Rd
Ashford TW15 . . . . .97 F3
Bracknell RG12 . . . . .117 C8
Brands Hill SL3 . . . . .69 B7

Springfield Rd continued
Frimley GU15 . . . . .152 B5
Silchester RG26 . . . . .135 E1
Windsor SL4 . . . . .67 B5
Springfields Cl KT16 . . . . .124 B1
Springhill Ct RG12 . . . . . .118 B5
Springhill Rd RG8 . . . . .34 C8
Springmead Cl GU47 . . . .143 E1
Spruce Ct ① SL1 . . . . .42 F3
Spruce Dr GU18 . . . . .153 A7
Spruce Rd RG5 . . . . .88 A6
Spur The Slough SL1 . . . . . .41 D8
Wargrave RG10 . . . . .36 E3
Spurcroft Prim Sch
RG19 . . . . .106 D2
Spurcroft Rd RG19 . . . . . .106 D2
Square The
Bagshot GU19 . . . . .145 E3
Bracknell RG12 . . . . .118 E5
Earley RG6 . . . . .114 A8
Harmondsworth TW6 . . . . .70 B6
Lightwater GU18 . . . . . . .146 C1
Newtown RG19 . . . . .132 A4
Pangbourne RG8 . . . . .56 D6
Shinfield RG7 . . . . .113 B2
Yattendon RG18 . . . . .53 E1
Squire's Bridge Rd
TW17 . . . . .125 A6
Squire's Rd TW17 . . . . . . .125 A5
Squires Bridge Rd KT17 .124 F5
Squires Ct
Camberley GU15 . . . . . . .151 C3
Chertsey KT16 . . . . .124 B1
Squires Wlk TW15 . . . . . . .98 D1
Squirrel Cl GU47 . . . . .150 B8
Squirrel Dr SL4 . . . . .93 B7
Squirrel Rise SL7 . . . . .1 D6
Squirrel Wlk RG41 . . . . . .115 F7
Squirrels Drey RG45 . . . . .142 F5
Squirrels Way RG6 . . . . . . .87 B2
Stable Cl RG7 . . . . .111 A3
Stable Cotts SL7 . . . . .18 C5
Stable Croft GU19 . . . . . . .145 D2
Stable Ct RG14 . . . . .105 B6
Stable View GU46 . . . . . . .149 D7
Stables Ct SL7 . . . . .1 D2
Stables The SL5 . . . . .121 B1
Stacey's Ind Est RG26 . . .135 C1
Staddlestone Cl RG31 . . . .57 C2
Stadium Way RG30 . . . . . .58 B1
Stafferton Way SL6 . . . . . . .40 A6
Stafford Ave SL2 . . . . .22 C1
Stafford Cl Burnham SL6 . .41 B7
Woodley RG5 . . . . .87 F7
Stafford Lake GU21,
GU24 . . . . .153 F1
Staffordshire Cl RG30 . . . .84 F8
Staffordshire Croft RG42 .91 F2
Stag Hill RG17 . . . . .73 A2
Stainash Cres TW18 . . . . . .97 B3
Stainash Par TW18 . . . . . . .97 B3
Staines By-Pass TW15,
TW18 . . . . .97 C3
Staines La KT16 . . . . .124 A3
Staines Lane Cl KT16 . . . .123 F4
Staines Prep Sch TW18 . . .97 A3
Staines Rd
Chertsey KT16 . . . . .124 A5
East Bedfont TW14 . . . . . . .98 D8
Laleham TW18 . . . . .124 B5
Wraysbury TW19 . . . . .95 F7
Staines Rd W TW15 . . . . . .98 D1
Staines Sta TW18 . . . . .97 A3
Stainford Cl TW15 . . . . .98 D3
Stamford Ave GU16 . . . . .151 F1
Stamford Rd SL6 . . . . .39 C6
Stanbrook Cl RG7 . . . . .82 A2
Stanbury Gate RG7 . . . . . .113 A3
Stanfield RG26 . . . . .135 B1
Stanford Dingley Circular
Wlks* RG18 . . . . .80 E7
Stanham Rd RG30 . . . . . . .84 F8
Stanhope Heath TW19 . . . .70 C1
Stanhope Rd
Camberley GU15 . . . . . . .150 F4
Reading RG2 . . . . .86 D3
Slough SL1 . . . . .41 D7
Stanhope Way TW19 . . . . .70 C1
Stanlake La RG10 . . . . .61 F4
Stanley Cl SL7 . . . . .1 F3
Stanley Cotts SL2 . . . . .42 F5
Stanley Gn E SL3 . . . . .43 F2
Stanley Gn W SL3 . . . . .43 F2
Stanley Gr ① RG1 . . . . .85 F7
Stanley Ho SL4 . . . . .68 A2
Stanley Rd Ashford TW15 . .97 E3
Newbury RG14 . . . . .105 B2
Wokingham RG40 . . . . . .116 E6
Stanley Spencer Art Gal*
SL6 . . . . .20 B7
Stanley St RG1 . . . . .85 F8
Stanmore Cl SL5 . . . . .119 F6
Stanmore Gdns RG2 . . . .136 F5
Stanmore Rd RG20 . . . . . . .30 C2
Stanshawe Rd RG1 . . . . . . .86 A8
Stansted Rd TW6 . . . . .70 F1
Stanton Cl RG6 . . . . .87 C4
Stanton Way SL3 . . . . .43 E2
Stanway Cotts RG1 . . . . . . .86 F6
Stanwell Cl TW19 . . . . .70 D1
Stanwell Fields CE Prim Sch
TW19 . . . . .70 D1
Stanwell Moor Rd
Harmondsworth TW19,TW6,
UB7 . . . . .70 B4
Stanwell TW19 . . . . .70 B4
Stanwell New Rd TW18 . .97 B5
Stanwell Rd Ashford TW15 .97 E3

Stanwell Rd continued
East Bedfont TW14,TW19,
TW6 . . . . .98 B8
Horton SL3 . . . . .69 C4
Stapleford Rd RG30 . . . . . .85 C4
Staplehurst RG12 . . . . .117 E2
Stapleton Cl Marlow SL7 . . .1 F2
Newbury RG14 . . . . .130 C6
Star La Knowl Hill RG10 . . .37 E4
Reading RG1 . . . . .86 B7
Star Post Rd GU15 . . . . . .151 F8
Star Rd RG4 . . . . .59 C2
Starling Cl RG41 . . . . .115 F5
Starlings Dr RG31 . . . . .84 B6
Starmead Dr RG40 . . . . . .116 E5
Starting Gates RG14 . . . . .105 C1
Startins La SL6 . . . . .19 C8
Starwood Ct SL3 . . . . .43 C3
Statham Ct RG42 . . . . .117 E8
Station App Ashford TW15 .97 F4
Blackwater GU17 . . . . .150 E4
Maidenhead SL6 . . . . .39 F6
Marlow SL7 . . . . .1 E1
Reading RG1 . . . . .86 A8
Shepperton TW17 . . . . . . .125 C4
Staines TW18 . . . . .97 A3
Virginia Water GU25 . . . . .122 D5
Station Cres TW15 . . . . . . .97 F8
Station Hill Ascot SL5 . . . .120 A5
Cookham Rise SL6 . . . . . . .19 F7
Reading RG1 . . . . .86 B7
Station Ind Est RG40 . . . .116 B6
Station Par Ashford TW15 . .97 F4
Cookham Rise SL6 . . . . . . .19 F6
Sunningdale SL5 . . . . .121 A2
Thorpe GU25 . . . . .122 E4
Station Path TW18 . . . . . . .96 F4
Station Rd Ashford TW15 . .97 F4
Bagshot GU19 . . . . .145 E4
Ball Hill RG20 . . . . .130 A3
Bourne End SL8 . . . . .3 A3
Bracknell RG12 . . . . .118 E7
Chertsey KT16 . . . . .124 A1
Cookham Rise SL6 . . . . . . .19 F7
Earley RG6 . . . . .87 C4
East Garston RG17 . . . . . . .47 C6
Egham TW20 . . . . .96 A3
Frimley GU16 . . . . .151 C1
Goring RG8 . . . . .34 C6
Great Shefford RG17 . . . . . .48 A3
Henley-On-T RG9 . . . . .15 E1
Hungerford RG17 . . . . . . .100 D6
Kintbury RG17 . . . . .102 B2
Lambourn RG17 . . . . .25 B2
Marlow SL7 . . . . .1 E1
Mortimer RG7 . . . . .137 C5
Newbury RG14 . . . . .105 A2
Newbury,Speen RG14 . . .104 E2
① Pangbourne RG8 . . . . . .56 C6
Reading RG1 . . . . .86 B8
Shepperton TW17 . . . . . . .125 C4
Slough SL1 . . . . .41 E7
Slough,Langley SL3 . . . . . .44 A4
Sunningdale SL5 . . . . .121 A2
Taplow SL6 . . . . .40 F7
Thatcham RG19 . . . . .106 C2
Theale RG7 . . . . .83 E3
Twyford RG10 . . . . .61 D4
Wargrave RG10 . . . . .36 C1
Wokingham RG40 . . . . . .116 B6
Woolhampton RG7 . . . . . . .107 E5
Wraysbury TW19 . . . . .69 A1
Station Rd N ⑤ TW20 . . . .95 F3
Station Rise SL1 . . . . .1 E2
Station Road Ind Est
RG19 . . . . .106 F1
Station Terr RG10 . . . . .61 D4
Station Way RG12 . . . . . . .118 C7
Station Yard Ind Est
RG17 . . . . .100 D5
Staunton Rd SL2 . . . . .22 D5
Staveley Rd TW15 . . . . .98 D2
Staverton Cl
Bracknell RG42 . . . . .91 B1
Wokingham RG40 . . . . . .116 F6
Staverton Rd RG2 . . . . .86 D3
Stayne End GU25 . . . . . . .122 A5
Steam Farm La TW14 . . . . .71 F3
Steeple Point SL5 . . . . . . .120 B6
Steeple Wlk RG6 . . . . .113 F8
Steerforth Copse GU47 . .143 E2
Steggles Ct RG7 . . . . .87 D8
Stephanie Chase Ct
RG40 . . . . .116 D6
Stephen Cl Egham TW20 . .96 C2
Twyford RG10 . . . . .61 F3
Stephens Cl RG27 . . . . . . .136 F6
Stephens Firs RG7 . . . . . .136 F6
Stephens Rd RG7 . . . . .136 F6
Stephenson Cl RG18 . . . .106 D4
Stephenson Ct
Newbury RG14 . . . . .104 F4
⑩ Slough SL1 . . . . .42 F4
Stephenson Dr SL4 . . . . . .67 B7
Stephenson Way RG7 . . .136 F4
Sterling Ave TW17 . . . . . .125 A4
Sterling Ctr The RG12 . . .118 D6
Sterling Gdns GU47 . . . . .150 E8
Sterling Ind Est RG14 . . .105 B2
Sterling Way RG30 . . . . . . .58 B8
Stern Ct KT16 . . . . .124 C1
Stevens Hill GU46 . . . . . . .149 E5

Stevenson Dr RG42 . . . . . . .90 C3
Stewart Ave
Littleton TW17 . . . . .125 A5
Slough SL1 . . . . .42 F8
Stewart Cl SL6 . . . . .65 D6
Stewarts Dr SL2 . . . . .22 B8
Stewarts Way SL7 . . . . .1 D7
Stile Rd SL3 . . . . .43 D3
Stilton Cl RG6 . . . . .87 E2
Stilwell Cl GU46 . . . . .149 E6
Stirling Cl Caversham RG4 .59 D6
Frimley GU16 . . . . .151 E2
Windsor SL4 . . . . .66 D5
Stirling Gr SL6 . . . . .39 B8
Stirling Ho ⑨ RG1 . . . . .86 B5
Stirling Rd Slough SL1 . . . .42 B8
Stanwell TW6 . . . . .70 F1
Stirling Way RG18 . . . . . .106 C4
Stirrup Cl RG14 . . . . .131 B7
Stockbridge Way GU46 . .149 D4
Stockbury Cl RG6 . . . . .87 B1
Stockcross CE Sch
RG20 . . . . .103 E6
Stockdales Rd SL4 . . . . . . .41 F2
Stockton Rd RG2 . . . . .86 C1
Stockwells SL6 . . . . .20 D1
Stockwood Rise GU15 . . . .23 B8
Stoke Common Rd SL3 . . .23 B8
Stoke Court Dr SL2 . . . . . . .22 F4
Stoke Gdns SL1 . . . . .42 F5
Stoke Gn SL2 . . . . .23 A1
Stoke Park Ave SL2 . . . . . . .22 C2
Stoke Poges La SL1,SL2 . .42 E7
Stoke Poges Sch
SL2 . . . . .22 F5
Stoke Poges SL2 . . . . .23 B5
Stoke Rd SL2 . . . . .42 F7
Stoke View SL1 . . . . .42 F5
Stoke Wood SL2 . . . . .22 F8
Stokeford Cl ⑤ RG12 . . . .118 F4
Stokes Farm RG40 . . . . . .116 F8
Stokes La RG26 . . . . .134 C1
Stokes View RG8 . . . . .56 C5
Stokesay RG8 . . . . .42 F6
Stokesley Rise HP10 . . . . . . .3 E8
Stomp Rd SL1 . . . . .41 C8
Stompits Rd SL6 . . . . .65 C8
Stone Copse GU14 . . . . . .105 E7
Stone Cres TW14 . . . . .98 F8
Stone House La SL6 . . . . . . .2 C1
Stone St RG30 . . . . .58 B1
Stone's Wlk RG7 . . . . .111 A3
Stonebridge Field SL4 . . . .42 B1
Stonecroft Ave SL0 . . . . . . .44 E7
Stonefield Pk SL6 . . . . .39 C6
Stonegate GU15 . . . . .152 C6
Stoneham Cl RG30 . . . . . . .85 A6
Stonehaven Dr RG5 . . . . . .88 A6
Stonehill Rd GU16 . . . . . . .120 D3
Stonehouse Rise GU16 . .151 E1
Stoneleigh Ct
Frimley GU16 . . . . .151 F1
Theale RG7 . . . . .83 D2
Stoney Cl GU46 . . . . .149 D4
Stoney La Burnham SL2 . . .22 A4
Newbury RG4,RG18 . . . . .105 D6
Thatcham RG19 . . . . .106 E3
Stoney Meade SL1 . . . . . . .42 B5
Stoney Rd RG42 . . . . .118 A8
Stoney Ware SL7 . . . . .18 C4
Stoney Ware Cl SL7 . . . . . . .18 C4
Stoneyfield RG7 . . . . .109 A6
Stoneylands Ct ⑤ TW20 . .95 F3
Stoneylands Rd TW20 . . . .95 F3
Stony La RG17 . . . . .46 D3
Stookes Way GU46 . . . . . .149 B4
Storronaway Rd SL3 . . . . . .44 C2
Stour Cl Reading RG30 . . . .85 A8
Slough SL1 . . . . .42 B3
Stovell Rd SL1 . . . . .66 F6
Stowe Rd SL1 . . . . .41 E6
Strachey Cl RG8 . . . . .56 C2
Straight Bit HP10 . . . . .3 B8
Straight Mile The
Hurst RG10,RG40 . . . . .89 D6
Waltham St Lawrence RG10 .62 A4
Straight Rd SL4 . . . . .68 B1
Strand Way RG6 . . . . .87 C1
Strande La SL6 . . . . .19 F5
Strande Pk SL6 . . . . .19 F5
Strande View Wlk SL6 . . . .19 F5
Stranraer Gdns SL1 . . . . . .42 A5
Stranraer Way ⑪ TW6 . . . .70 E1
Stratfield RG42 . . . . .117 E1
Stratfield Ct SL6 . . . . .39 A2
Stratfield Rd SL1 . . . . .43 A4
Stratford Cl SL2 . . . . .21 D1
Stratford Dr HP10 . . . . .3 D7
Stratford Gdns SL6 . . . . . . .39 C4
Stratford Rd TW6 . . . . .71 C2
Stratford Way RG31 . . . . . .84 A6
Strathcona Cl HP10 . . . . . . .3 C7
Strathcona Way HP10 . . . . .3 C7
Strathearn Ave SL3 . . . . . . .22 E1
Stratheden Pl ⑥ RG1 . . . . .85 F8
Strathmore Ct ⑧ GU15 . . .151 D5
Strathmore Dr SL6 . . . . . . .10 B3
Strathy Cl RG30 . . . . .85 B8
Straton Gdns RG2 . . . . . . .113 D8
Stratton Rd TW16 . . . . . . .125 F7
Strawberry Hill
Newbury RG14 . . . . .104 F4
Newell Green RG42 . . . . . . .91 E5
Streamside SL1 . . . . .41 F5

Streatley & Goring Bridge
RG8 . . . . .34 B6
Streatley CE Sch RG8 . . . .33 F6
Streatley Farm Cotts
RG8 . . . . .34 A8
Streatley Hill RG8 . . . . . . .33 F6
Street The
Aldermaston RG7 . . . . . . .135 A7
Englefield RG7 . . . . .83 B5
Mortimer RG7 . . . . .137 D5
Moulsford OX10 . . . . .14 A6
Swallowfield RG7 . . . . . . .139 C6
Tidmarsh RG8 . . . . .56 D2
Waltham St Lawrence RG10 .63 A6
Streets Heath GU24 . . . . .153 F7
Stretton RG7 . . . . .82 A1
Stretton Cl RG7 . . . . .82 A1
Strode St TW20 . . . . .96 A4
Strode's Coll TW20 . . . . . .95 F3
Strode's Cres TW18 . . . . . .97 C3
Strodes College La TW20 .95 F3
Stroller Cl RG19 . . . . .105 F4
Stroma Ct SL1 . . . . .41 D6
Strongrove Hill RG17 . . . .100 C6
Strood La SL5 . . . . .93 C2
Stroud Cl
Aldermaston RG26 . . . . . .135 C1
Windsor SL4 . . . . .66 D4
Stroud Farm Rd SL6 . . . . .65 B8
Stroud La GU17 . . . . .150 A4
Stroud Way TW15 . . . . .98 B2
Stroude Rd Egham TW20 . .96 A1
Stroude TW20 . . . . .122 E6
Strouds Mdw RG18 . . . . . .106 C7
Strouds The RG7 . . . . .108 F6
Stuart Cl Caversham RG4 . .59 B3
Windsor SL4 . . . . .66 F5
Stuart Ho RG42 . . . . .117 F8
Stuart Rd RG14 . . . . .130 D6
Stuart Way Staines TW18 . .97 B2
Virginia Water GU25 . . . . .122 A5
Windsor SL4 . . . . .66 F5
Stubbles La SL6 . . . . .1 B6
Stubbles La SL6 . . . . .19 B6
Stubbs Folly GU47 . . . . . .150 D7
Studios Rd TW17 . . . . .124 F6
Studland Cl RG2 . . . . .113 C7
Studland Ind Est RG20 . .129 B3
Sturbridge Cl RG6 . . . . .87 C1
Sturdee Cl GU16 . . . . .151 E1
Sturges Rd RG40 . . . . .116 D5
Sturt Gn SL6 . . . . .64 E8
Styventon Pl KT16 . . . . . .123 F2
Suck's La RG8 . . . . .54 D3
Suffolk Cl Bagshot GU19 . .145 E2
Slough SL1 . . . . .41 E7
Wokingham RG41 . . . . . .115 D6
Suffolk Combe RG42 . . . . .91 F1
Suffolk Ct ⑧ SL6 . . . . .39 F8
Suffolk Rd
Maidenhead SL6 . . . . .39 D4
Reading RG30 . . . . .85 D3
Sulham La RG8 . . . . .56 E3
Sulham Wlk RG30 . . . . . . .85 B4
Sulhamstead & Ufton Nervet
CE Prim Sch RG7 . . . . . . .110 C4
Sulhamstead Rd
Burghfield Common RG7,
RG30 . . . . .111 B5
Ufton Nervet RG7 . . . . . . .110 B6
Sullivan Rd GU15 . . . . . . .151 A5
Sullivans Reach KT12 . . . .125 F2
Sumburgh Way SL1 . . . . . .42 B8
Summer Gdns GU15 . . . . .152 C5
Summerfield Cl RG41 . . . . .88 F1
Summerfield Rise RG8 . . . .34 B8
Summerhouse La UB7 . . . .70 D8
Summerlea SL1 . . . . .41 F6
Summerleaze Rd SL6 . . . . .20 B1
Summers Rd SL1 . . . . .21 C2
Summit Cl RG40 . . . . .141 F7
Summit Ctr UB7 . . . . .70 F8
Sumner Cl SL4 . . . . .67 D8
Sun Gdns RG7 . . . . .111 A1
Sun Hill RG7 . . . . .108 F2
Sun La Maidenhead SL6 . . .39 F7
Riseley RG7 . . . . .139 B2
Sun Pas ⑭ SL6 . . . . .67 D6
Sun Ray Est GU47 . . . . . . .150 A8
Sun St RG1 . . . . .86 C7
Sunbury Cres TW13 . . . . . .98 F4
Sunbury Cross Ctr ⑨
TW16 . . . . .98 F1
Sunbury Ct SL4 . . . . .66 F5
Sunbury Int Bsns Ctr
TW16 . . . . .125 E8
Sunbury Manor Sch
TW16 . . . . .125 E8
Sunbury Rd Eton SL4 . . . . .67 A8
Feltham TW13 . . . . .98 F4
Sunderland Cl RG5 . . . . . . .88 B8
Sunderland Ct ⑪ TW19 . . .70 E1
Sunderland Pl RG18 . . . . .106 C4
Sunderland Rd SL6 . . . . . . .39 B8
Sunderland Rd RG30 . . . . .85 A6
Sundew Cl
Lightwater GU18 . . . . . . .153 D8
Wokingham RG40 . . . . . .116 E7
Sundial Ct RG30 . . . . .85 A6
Sundon Cres GU25 . . . . . .122 C4
Sundown Rd TW15 . . . . . . .98 C3
Sunley Cl RG14 . . . . .130 C6
Sunmead Rd TW16 . . . . . .125 F6

Sunning Ave SL5 ....120 E2
Sunning Ho Ascot SL5 ....120 C5
 Windlesham GU20 ....146 F8
Sunningdale Park (Civil
 Service Coll) SL5 ....120 F4
Sunningdale Sch SL5 .....120 D5
Sunningdale Sta SL5 .....121 A2
Sunninghill Cl SL5 ......120 D5
Sunninghill Ct SL5 ......120 D5
Sunninghill Lodge
 Ascot SL5 ....120 C7
 Ascot SL5 ....120 D5
Sunninghill Rd
 Ascot SL5 ....120 D5
 Windlesham GU20 ......146 A7
 Winkfield SL4,SL5 .....93 E2
Sunnybank Ascot SL5 ....120 A5
 Marlow SL1 ....1 D4
Sunnymeads Sta TW19 ...68 E4
Sunnyside RG14 ....104 E6
Sunrise Hill RG20 ......30 F7
Superity Cotts RG20 ....31 D6
Surbiton Rd GU15 ......143 A1
Surley Row RG4 ....59 A5
Surly Hall Wlk SL4 .....66 F6
Surrey Ave
 Camberley GU15 ....151 A4
 Slough SL2 ....22 C1
Surrey Ct RG42 ....91 F1
Surrey Heath Mus*
 GU15 ....151 D6
Surrey Rd RG2 ....86 B4
Surridge Ct GU19 ......145 E2
Sussex Cl SL1 ....43 B4
Sussex Gdns RG5 ......87 E2
Sussex Ho SL2 ....22 C6
Sussex Keep SL1 ....43 B4
Sussex La RG7 ....113 C1
Sussex Lodge **7** SL6 ..39 F6
Sussex Pl SL1,SL3 .....43 B3
Sutcliffe Ave RG6 .....87 D3
Sutherland Ave TW16 ..125 F7
Sutherland Chase SL5 ..119 E7
Sutherland Gdns TW16 .125 F7
Sutherland Gr RG1 .....84 A4
Sutherland Grange SL4 .66 D7
Sutherlands RG14 .....130 E7
Sutherlands Ave RG1 ..86 C5
Sutton Ave SL3 ....43 C4
Sutton Cl Cookham SL6 ..20 B7
 Maidenhead SL6 ......39 C5
Sutton La Brands Hill SL3 .69 B8
 Slough SL3 ....44 C1
Sutton Pl SL3 ....69 B8
Sutton Rd
 Camberley GU15 ......145 A1
 Cookham SL6 ....20 B6
 Newbury RG14 ....104 D5
Sutton Wlk RG1 ......86 C5
Suttons Park Ave RG6 ..86 E8
Swabey Rd SL3 ....44 A2
Swainstone Rd RG2 ...86 B5
Swaledale RG12 ......118 A4
Swallow Cl Reading RG31 .84 C6
 Staines TW18 ....96 F4
 Yateley GU46 ....149 B6
Swallow Field Gdns RG7 .83 E4
Swallow Ho SL7 ......2 A2
Swallow St SL0 ....44 D8
Swallow Way RG41 ...115 E5
Swallowfield TW20 ...95 B2
Swallowfield Dr RG2 ..113 C6
Swallowfield Pk* RG7 139 E7
Swallowfield Rd
 Arborfield RG2 ....114 D2
 Swallowfield RG7 .....139 F6
Swallowfield St RG7 ..139 C7
Swallows Croft RG1 ...85 E5
Swan Ct RG14 ....104 F3
Swan Dr RG7 ....109 C3
Swan Ho GU47 ....150 B7
Swan La GU47,GU47 ..150 B7
Swan Pl **5** RG1 ......86 A7
Swan Rd SL0 ....44 F7
Swan Ter SL4 ....67 B7
Swan Wlk TW17 ......125 E2
Swanbrook Ct SL6 ....40 A7
Swancote Gn RG12 ...118 B4
Swandrift TW18 ......96 F1
Swangate RG17 ......100 D7
Swanholm Gdns RG31 .84 F4
Swanmore Cl RG6 ....87 E1
Swanmore Rd GU10 ..61 E3
Swansdown Wlk RG19 .106 B3
Swansea Rd
 Harlington TW14,TW6 .71 D1
 Reading RG1 ....59 A1
Swansea Terr RG31 ...57 D1
Swanston Field RG8 ..56 D7
Sweeps La TW20 .....95 F3
Sweet Briar Dr RG31 ..84 D4
Sweetbriar RG45 .....143 A7
Sweeter's Piece RG7 ..136 E6
Swepstone Cl RG6 ....87 C2
Swift Cl RG41 ....115 E5
Swift Ho SL7 ....2 A2
Swift La GU19 ....145 F3
Swinbrook Cl RG31 ...57 D3
Swindon Ct RG6 .....82 B8
Swinley Prim Sch SL5 .120 A4
Swinley Rd SL5 ......119 C4
Swinnerton Ho RG9 ..15 E3
Swiss Cottage Cl RG31 .84 C8
Swiss Ct GU17 ....150 C4

Switchback Cl SL6 .....19 D2
Switchback Rd N SL6 ..19 E3
Switchback Rd S SL6 ..19 D2
Switchback The SL6 ...19 D2
Swithin Chase RG42 ..91 E1
Sycamore Cl
 8 Bourne End SL8 ...3 B3
 Burghfield Common RG30 .111 B4
 Frimley GU16 ....151 E1
 Maidenhead SL6 ......39 C3
 Sandhurst GU47 ......150 B8
 Woodley RG5 ....87 C5
Sycamore Ct
 Pangbourne RG8 ......56 C6
 Windsor SL4 ....67 C4
Sycamore Dr
 Frimley GU16 ....151 A1
 Marlow Bottom SL7 ...1 D5
 Twyford RG10 ....61 E5
Sycamore Lodge **7**
 TW16 ....98 F1
Sycamore Rd RG2 ....86 B4
Sycamore Rise
 Bracknell RG12 ....118 D6
 Newbury RG14 ....105 C5
Sycamore Wlk
 Englefield Green TW20 .95 B2
 Slough SL3 ....43 E7
Sycamores The GU17 ..150 B5
Sydings The RG14 ....104 D5
Sydney Cl
 Crowthorne RG45 .....143 C7
 Reading RG19 ....106 E3
Sydney Cres TW15 ...98 B2
Sydney Gr SL1 ....42 C7
Sydney Loader Pl GU17 .150 A5
Sydney Lodge RG19 ..106 E3
Syke Cluan SL0 ......44 E4
Syke Ings SL0 ....44 F4
Sykes Dr TW18 ......97 B3
Sykes Rd SL1 ....42 B7
Sylvan Ridge GU47 ..143 A1
Sylvan Wlk RG30 ....57 B6
Sylvanus RG12 ......117 F2
Sylverns Ct RG42 ....91 D1
Sylvester Cl
 Newbury RG14 ....104 E5
 Winnersh RG41 ......88 D3
Sylvester Rd SL6 ....19 E2
Symondson Mews RG42 .90 C4
Sympson Rd RG26 ...135 D1

T

Tachbrook Rd TW14 ...98 F8
Tadcroft Wlk RG31 ...84 E3
Tadham Pl RG19 .....106 C2
Tadley Common Rd
 RG26 ....135 C1
Tadmor Cl TW16 .....125 F5
Taff Way RG30 ......85 A7
Tag La RG10 ....37 A1
Talbot Ave SL3 ......43 F4
Talbot Cl Caversham RG4 .59 D2
 Newbury RG14 ....104 E5
Talbot Ct **2** Reading RG1 .86 A7
 Windsor SL4 ....67 B4
Talbot Pl Bagshot GU19 .145 E4
 Datchet SL3 ....68 C6
Talbot Rd TW15 .....97 E3
Talbot Way RG31 ....57 C3
Talbots Dr SL6 ......39 B6
Talfourd Ave RG6 ...87 A5
Talisman Cl RG45 ...142 D5
Tall Trees SL3 ....69 E6
Tallis La RG30 ....85 D4
Tamar Ct RG30 .....85 D6
Tamar Gdns RG2 ....86 C3
Tamar Way Slough SL3 .44 B2
 Wokingham RG41 ....115 A3
Tamarind Ct **3** TW20 .95 F3
Tamarind Way RG6 ..86 F1
Tamarisk Ave RG2 ...86 E1
Tamarisk Ct RG18 ...106 F4
Tamarisk Rise RG40 .116 C7
Tamarisk Way SL1 ...42 A5
Tamesa Ho TW17 ...125 A2
Tamesis Pl RG4 .....59 A5
Tamworth RG12 ....118 D2
Tamworth Cl **2** RG6 .87 C1
Tangier Ct SL4 ......67 D8
Tangier La SL4 ......67 D8
Tanglewood RG40 ...142 A7
Tanglewood Ride GU24 .153 D7
Tangley Dr RG41 ....116 B4
Tanglyn Ave TW17 ..125 B4
Tanhouse La RG41 ..116 A5
Tank Rd GU15 ......150 F5
Tanner Ct RG14 .....105 A4
Tanners Cl RG10 ....110 F1
Tanners La RG4 .....58 F8
Tanners Yd GU19 ...145 E3
Tape La RG10 ....88 F8
Tapestries The SL4 ..68 A2
Taplow Common Rd SL1 .21 A3
Taplow Rd SL6 ......41 A7
Taplow Sta SL6 .....40 F7
Tarbat Ct **6** GU47 ..150 D8
Tarbay La SL4 ......66 B5
Target Cl TW14 .....71 E1
Target Hill RG42 ....91 E1
Targold Ct RG42 ....88 B2
Tarleton Ct RG30 ...84 F6
Tarmac Way UB7 ...70 B7
Tarn Howes Cl RG19 .106 A3
Tarn La RG17 ......130 F8
Tarnbrook Way RG12 .118 D2

Tarragon Cl
 Bracknell RG42 ....91 D1
 Earley RG6 ....86 F1
Tarragon Way RG7 ..111 B3
Tarrant Gn RG42 ....91 C1
Tarrant's Hill RG17 .100 D5
TASIS-The American Sch in
 England TW20 ....123 C6
Tasker Cl UB7 ....71 C7
Tasman Ct TW16 ...98 E1
Tatchbrook Cl SL6 ..40 A8
Tattersall Cl RG40 ..116 E5
Tavistock Cl
 Maidenhead SL6 .....39 A8
 Staines TW18 ....97 D1
Tavistock Ind Est RG10 .61 F5
Tavistock Rd RG2 ...86 B3
Tawfield RG12 ......90 E2
Tay Rd RG30 ....85 A7
Taylor Cl **2** RG42 ..91 A1
Taylor's Cl SL7 .....1 F2
Taylors Ct SL6 .....39 B8
Taynton Wlk **8** RG6 .86 B5
Tazewell Ct RG1 ....85 F6
Teagle Rd RG17 ....100 D7
Tebbit Cl RG12 .....118 D3
Teesdale Rd SL1 ...41 F8
Teikyo Sch (UK) SL3 .23 D5
Tekels Ave GU15 ...151 D4
Tekels Ct GU15 ....151 E4
Tekels Way GU15 ..151 F3
Telford Ave RG45 ..143 C8
Telford Cres RG5 ...60 F1
Telford Ct SL4 .....104 F5
Telford Dr SL1 .....42 A4
Telston Cl SL8 .....3 A5
Tempest Rd TW20 ..96 C2
Templar Cl GU47 ..150 A8
Templars Pl **1** SL7 ..1 E1
Temple Gdns TW18 .123 F8
Temple Ho RG6 .....15 E3
Temple La SL7 .....18 D6
Temple Mews RG6 ..87 F7
Temple Mill Cotts SL7 .18 C5
Temple Mill Island SL7 .18 C5
Temple Park Rdbt RG42 .90 F2
Temple Pk SL6 .....17 F3
Temple Pl **7** RG1 ..86 A6
Temple Way
 Bracknell RG42 ......90 E1
 Farnham Common SL2 .22 C7
Templecroft TW15 ..98 D2
Templedene Ave TW18 .97 C1
Templeton Gdns RG2 .86 C1
Templeton Ho RG9 ..35 F8
Templewood Gate SL2 .22 C7
Templewood La SL2 .22 D8
Ten Acre La TW20 ..123 F7
Tenaplas Dr RG8 ...54 F5
Tenby Ave RG4 ....59 D5
Tenby Dr SL5 ......120 D4
Tennyson Rd
 Ashford TW15 ....97 E3
 Thatcham RG18 .....106 C4
 Woodley RG5 ....87 E4
Tennyson Way SL2 ..21 E1
Tensing Ct TW19 ...97 E7
Tenth Ave RG31 ...84 B6
Teresa Vale RG42 ..91 C2
Tern Cl RG30 ......85 A6
Terrace Rd N RG42 ..90 C4
Terrace Rd S RG42 ..90 C2
Terrace The Ascot SL5 .120 D4
 Camberley GU15 ....151 A5
 Crowthorne RG45 ...143 D5
 Maidenhead SL6 ....40 C3
 Wokingham RG40 ...116 B6
Terrent Ct SL4 .....67 A5
Terrington Hill SL7 .1 C2
Terry's La SL6 .....19 F8
Tesimond Dr GU46 .149 A6
Tessa Rd RG1 .....58 F1
Test Cl RG30 ......85 A7
Testwood Rd SL4 ..66 D6
Tetbury Ct **8** RG1 ..85 F8
Teviot Rd RG30 ...84 E7
Thackery Lodge TW14 .71 D1
Thakerays The RG19 .106 D2
Thames Ave
 Chertsey KT16 ......124 A6
 Pangbourne RG8 ....56 C6
 Reading RG1 ....59 A1
 Windsor SL4 ....67 D7
Thames Bank SL4 ..28 B7
Thames Cl Bourne End SL8 .3 B4
Thames Cres SL6 ..20 E2
Thames Ct Goring RG8 .34 B6
 Reading RG1 ....59 B1
Thames Edge Ct TW18 .96 E4
Thames Ho RG9 ...15 E3
Thames Ind Est SL7 .18 E2
Thames Mdw KT12,
 TW17 ....125 C1
Thames Mead SL4 .66 E6
Thames Mead RG Goring RG8 .34 B6
 Slough SL3 ....44 D3
 Thatcham RG18 ....106 C4
Thames Reach
 Medmenham SL7 ...17 D6
 Reading RG1 ....59 A1
Thames Side
 Henley-On-T RG9 ...15 E2
 Laleham KT16,TW18 .124 D4
 Reading RG1 ....59 A1
 Staines TW18 ......96 F2

Thames Side continued
 Windsor SL4 ....67 D7
Thames Side Prom RG1 .59 A2
Thames St
 Oatlands Park KT12 .125 F2
 Sonning RG4 ....60 D4
 Staines TW18 ......96 F3
 Windsor SL4 ....67 D7
Thames Valley Bsns Pk
 RG6 ....60 B1
Thames Valley Com Inf Sch
 SL1 ....42 D4
Thames Valley Nuffield Hospl
 The SL3 ....23 C4
Thames Valley Univ SL1 .42 D3
Thamesbourne Mews SL8 .3 A3
Thamesfield Ct TW17 .125 C2
Thamesfield Gdns SL7 .1 E1
Thamesgate TW18 ..124 B8
Thameside Prim Sch
 RG4 ....59 B2
Thameside Reach RG8 .14 A4
Thamesmead Sch
 TW17 ....125 D3
Thamington Way RG6 .87 B2
Thatcham Nature Discovery
 Ctr* RG19 ....106 A2
Thatcham Sta RG19 .106 F1
Thatchers Dr SL6 ..39 A5
Theal Cl GU47 .....150 D8
Theale CE Prim Sch RG7 .83 D3
Theale Green Com Sch
 RG7 ....83 D3
Theale Rd RG30 ...111 C6
Theobald Dr RG31 .57 D4
Theobalds Way GU16 .152 C3
Thetford Ho **7** RG1 .85 E5
Thetford Mews RG4 .59 D6
Thetford Rd TW15 .97 E5
Thibet Rd GU47 ...150 C8
Thicket Gr SL6 ....38 F7
Thicket Rd RG30 ..84 E8
Thickthorne La TW18 .97 C1
Third Ave Marlow SL7 .1 C2
 Reading RG31 ......84 B6
 Tadley RG7 ....135 C2
Third Cres SL1 ....42 C8
Third St E RG19 ...132 A5
Thirkleby Cl SL1 ..42 C5
Thirlmere Ave
 Burnham SL1 ......41 C8
 Reading RG30 .....57 F1
Thirlmere Cl TW20 .96 B1
Thirlmere Wlk GU15 .152 D4
Thirtover Cl GU19 .79 B1
Thistledown RG31 .57 C1
Thistleton Way RG6 .87 E2
Thomas Cl SL6 ....39 A2
Thomas Dr RG42 ..91 E1
Thomas La RG40 ..141 E8
Thomas Merriman Ct
 RG14 ....105 A2
Thomas Rd HP10 ..3 D4
Thompkins La SL2 .22 A5
Thompson Cl
 Hermitage RG18 ...78 F6
 Slough SL3 ....44 A2
Thompson Dr RG19 .106 E2
Thompsons Yd **13** RG1 .86 B6
Thomson Wlk RG14 .84 E4
Thorburn Chase GU47 .150 E6
Thorn Cl RG45 ....143 A7
Thorn Dr SL3 .....43 E7
Thorn La **2** RG1 ..86 A7
Thorn St RG1 .....86 A7
Thornaby Pl HP10 .3 D4
Thornbank Cl TW19 .70 A2
Thornbers Way RG10 .61 A5
Thornbridge Rd RG2 .113 B8
Thornbury Cl RG45 .143 B5
Thornbury Gn RG10 .61 D5
Thorncroft TW20 ..95 C1
Thorndike SL2 ....22 A5
Thorndown La GU20 .146 D3
Thorne Cl
 Crowthorne RG45 ..143 A7
 Henley-On-T RG9 ..35 B8
 Littleton TW15 ....98 C1
Thorney Cl RG6 ...87 E2
Thorney La N SL0 ..44 E5
Thorney La S SL0 ..44 F5
Thornfield RG10 ..132 D3
Thornfield Gn GU17 .150 F3
Thornford Rd RG19 .132 E3
Thornhill RG12 ...118 E5
Thornhill Way TW17 .125 A4
Thorningdown OX11 .10 D8
Thornton Mews
 Crowthorne RG45 ..143 C4
 Reading RG30 .....85 C8
Thornton Rd RG30 .85 C8
Thorp Cl RG42 ....90 C3
Thorpe By-Pass TW20 .123 A5
Thorpe CE Inf Sch
 TW20 ....123 B6
Thorpe Cl RG41 ...116 A3
Thorpe Ho **4** RG30 .85 B7
Thorpe Ind Est TW20 .123 C4
Thorpe Ind Pk TW20 .123 C4
Thorpe Lea Prim Sch
 TW20 ....96 C2
Thorpe Lea Rd TW20 .96 C2
Thorpe Rd
 Chertsey KT16 .....123 D4
 Egham TW18,TW20 .96 D3

Thorpeside Cl TW18,
 TW20 ....123 E7
Thrale Mews RG30 .85 B8
Three Acre Rd RG14 .130 F8
Three Firs Way RG7 .110 F1
Three Gables La RG8 .34 A7
Three Post La **1** RG17 .25 B2
Threshfield RG12 ..118 A3
Thrift La SL6 ......39 D1
Throgmorton Rd GU46 .149 A5
Thrush Cl RG42 ...111 B3
Thurlby Way SL6 ..39 D3
Thurlestone Cl TW17 .125 C3
Thurlestone Gdns RG2 .86 C2
Thurlestone Par RG17 .125 B5
Thurley Bsns Units RG7 .112 A5
Thurley Cotts SL3 .23 B3
Thurnscoe Cl RG6 .113 F8
Thurso Cl RG30 ...85 A8
Thurston Rd SL1 ..42 E7
Thyme Cl RG6 ....87 A1
Tichborne Cl GU17 .150 D5
Tichbourne Cl GU16 .151 F3
Tickenor Dr RG40 .141 F7
Tickhill Cl RG6 ...113 F7
Tickleback Row RG42 .91 B6
Tides End Ct GU15 .151 F4
Tidmarsh Cl RG8 ..56 C1
Tidmarsh La RG8 ..56 B2
Tidmarsh Rd RG8 .56 C4
Tidmarsh St **1** RG30 .85 B8
Tidwells Lea RG12 .118 E8
Tierney Ct **2** SL7 ..1 E1
Tiffany Cl RG41 ...115 D6
Tiger Cl RG5 .....88 B7
Tigerseye Cl RG41 .115 D7
Tiggell Cl RG42 ..87 D4
Tilbury Cl RG4 ...59 C3
Tilbury Wlk SL3 ..44 B3
Tile Barn Row RG20 .129 E1
Tilebarn Cl RG9 ..15 C1
Tilecotes Cl SL7 ..1 D2
Tilehurst La RG42 .90 D3
Tilehurst Rd RG1,RG30 .85 D7
Tilehurst Sta RG31 .57 E3
Tilling Ct RG1 ....57 B2
Tilly's La TW18 ...96 F4
Tilney Way Earley RG6 .113 F8
 Lower Earley RG6 ..114 A8
Tilstone Ave SL4 ..41 E2
Tilstone Cl SL4 ...41 E1
Timberley Pl RG45 .142 E4
Timbers Wlk SL6 ..39 B5
Timline Gn RG12 ..118 F7
Timson Ct RG14 ..105 B3
Timsway TW18 ...96 F3
Tindal Cl GU46 ...149 D6
Tinkers La SL4 ...66 D5
Tinsey Cl TW20 ..96 B3
Tinsley Cl RG6 ...113 F8
Tintagel Dr **1** GU16 .151 F1
Tintagel Rd RG40 .142 A8
Tintern Cl SL1 ...42 C5
Tintern Cres RG1 .85 F5
Tinwell Cl RG6 ...87 E2
Tippett Rise RG2 .86 B5
Tippings La RG5 ..88 A8
Tippits Mead RG42 .117 D8
Tiptree Cl RG6 ...113 F8
Tiree Ho SL2 ....42 B8
Tirwell Cl RG42 ..91 F1
Titcombe Way RG17 .102 A2
Tite Hill TW20 ...95 D3
Tithe Barn Dr SL6 .40 C1
Tithe Cl Maidenhead SL6 .40 C1
 Wentworth GU25 ..122 D3
Tithe Ct Slough SL3 .44 A2
 Wokingham RG40 ..116 C7
Tithe La TW19 ...69 A1
Tithe Mdws GU25 .122 D3
Tithebarn Gr RG31 .84 F4
Titlarks Hill Rd SL5 .121 B1
Tiverton Cl RG5 ..60 E1
Tiverton Way GU16 .151 F1
Toad La GU17 ...150 E4
Tocker Gdns RG42 .91 B2
Tockington Ct GU46 .129 D6
Tockley Rd SL1 ..21 B2
Tofrek Terr RG30 .85 C7
Tokers Green La RG4 .58 D7
Toll Gdns RG12 ..118 F6
Tollgate SL5 .....39 A6
Tolpuddle Way GU46 .149 F5
Tomlin Cl RG19 ..106 E2
Tomlin Rd SL2 ...21 C1
Tomlins Ave GU16 .151 F2
Tomlinscote Sch & Sixth
 Form Coll GU16 ...152 A2
Tomlinscote Way GU16 .152 A2
Tomlinson Dr RG40 .142 A2
Tonkins Dr RG19 .106 E2
Toogood Pl RG42 .91 D3
Top Comm RG42 .91 D1
Topaz Cl Slough SL1 .42 B5
 Wokingham RG41 ..115 E7
Tope Cres RG2 ...140 F7
Tope Rd RG2 ....140 F8
Torcross Gr RG31 .84 B4
Torin Ct TW20 ...95 C3
Torquay Spur SL2 .22 B2
Torridge Rd SL3 .69 B8
Torrington Rd RG2 .86 C2
Toseland Way RG6 .87 C3
Totale Rise RG42 .91 B2
Totnes Rd RG2 ..86 C2
Tottenham Wlk GU47 .143 D1
Totterdown RG7 .110 F1

Toulouse Cl GU15 . . . . .152 B7
Toutley Cl RG41 . . . . .88 F1
Toutley Rd RG41 . . . . .89 A1
Toutley Works RG41 . . . . .89 A2
Tower Cl Caversham RG4 . . . .59 C8
Flackwell Heath HP10 . . . . . .3 C7
Tower Hill RG20 . . . . .49 A8
Tower Ho Iver SL0 . . . . .44 E7
Marlow SL7 . . . . .1 E2
Slough SL1 . . . . .42 E4
Towers Dr RG45 . . . . .143 B4
Town Farm Prim Sch
TW19 . . . . .97 D8
Town Farm Way TW19 . . . .97 D8
Town Hall (Mus)*
KT15 . . . . .124 A2
Town La Stanwell TW19 . . . . .97 D7
Wooburn HP10 . . . . .3 D4
Town Mills 6 RG14 . . . . .105 A3
Town Quay TW18 . . . . .124 C6
Townsend Rd RG1 . . . . .118 E4
Townsend
Aldworth RG8 . . . . .32 E3
Ashford TW15 . . . . .98 E3
Streatley RG8 . . . . .34 A7
Townside Pl GU15 . . . . .151 D6
Tozer Wlk SL4 . . . . .66 D4
Trafalgar Cl RG41 . . . . .115 E6
Trafalgar Ct RG1 . . . . .85 E6
Trafalgar Way GU15 . . . . . . .150 F4
Trafford Rd RG1 . . . . .86 E6
Transcend Osbourne Mews
7 SL4 . . . . .67 C5
Trash Gn RG30 . . . . .111 B7
Travis Cl SL2 . . . . .21 F2
Travic Ct SL2 . . . . .22 B2
Travis La GU47 . . . . .150 C7
Treacher Ct RG10 . . . . .61 E5
Tredegar Rd RG4 . . . . .59 A6
Tree Cl RG30 . . . . .84 D8
Tree Tops Ave GU15 . . . . . .152 B8
Trees Rd SL8 . . . . .3 A3
Treesmill Dr SL6 . . . . .39 C3
Treeton Cl RG6 . . . . .113 F8
Trefoil Cl RG40 . . . . .116 E7
Trefoil Dro RG18 . . . . .106 F4
Treforgan RG4 . . . . .58 F5
Trelawney Ave SL3 . . . . .43 F3
Trelawney Dr RG31 . . . . .57 B1
Trelleck Rd RG1 . . . . .86 E6
Tremayne Wlk GU15 . . . . . .152 C4
Trenchard Rd SL6 . . . . .65 B8
Trenches La SL0,SL3 . . . . . . .44 A6
Trent Cl RG41 . . . . .115 E7
Trent Cres RG18 . . . . .106 B5
Trent Rd SL3 . . . . .69 B8
Trent Villas Est SL3 . . . . .68 B6
Trenthams Ct RG40 . . . . . . .116 C8
Trenton Cl GU16 . . . . .152 A1
Tresham Cres GU46 . . . . . . .149 A6
Tressell The SL6 . . . . .39 D6
Trevelyan RG12 . . . . .117 E2
Trevelyan Mid Sch SL4 . . . .67 C3
Trevithick Cl TW14 . . . . .98 F7
Trevor Ct TW19 . . . . .70 A2
Trevor Ho 2 RG30 . . . . .85 B7
Trevose Ho SL2 . . . . .22 B1
Triangle The
Newbury RG14 . . . . .131 B7
Reading RG30 . . . . .84 D8
Trident Ho TW19 . . . . .97 E8
Trident Ind Est SL3 . . . . .69 E4
Trilakes Ctry Pk* GU46,
GU47 . . . . .149 E8
Trindledown RG42 . . . . .91 A2
Tring Rd RG31 . . . . .57 C2
Tringham Cotts GU24 . . . . .153 F7
Trinity GU47 . . . . .143 E2
Trinity Ave SL7 . . . . .1 D3
Trinity CE Prim Sch RG9 . . .15 D1
Trinity Cl TW19 . . . . .70 C1
Trinity Cres SL5 . . . . .121 A4
Trinity Ct Bracknell RG12 . .117 F7
Theale RG7 . . . . .83 D3
Trinity Ho SL6 . . . . .19 F6
Trinity Pl Reading RG1 . . . . . .85 F7
Windsor SL4 . . . . .67 C5
Trinity Rd SL7 . . . . .1 D2
Trinity Sch SL4 . . . . .105 B5
Trinity St Stephens CE Fst
Sch SL4 . . . . .67 B6
Triumph Cl Harlington UB7 . .71 C6
Woodley RG5 . . . . .87 F5
Troon Ct Ascot SL5 . . . . . . .120 C4
18 Reading RG1 . . . . .86 D7
Troston Ct TW19 . . . . .96 F3
Trotsford Mdw GU17 . . . . . .150 C4
Trotsworth Ave GU25 . . . . .122 D5
Trotsworth Ct GU25 . . . . . . .122 D5
Trotwood Cl GU47 . . . . .143 E2
Trout Cl Earley RG6 . . . . .87 A8
Marlow SL7 . . . . .18 C8
Trout Wlk RG14 . . . . .105 C4
Troutbeck Cl Slough SL2 . . .43 A6
Twyford RG10 . . . . .61 D6
Troutbeck Wlk GU15 . . . . . .152 D3
Trows La
Beech Hill RG7 . . . . .138 D4
Swallowfield RG7 . . . . .139 D5
Trumbull Rd RG42 . . . . .91 A1
Trumper Way SL1 . . . . .41 F5

Trumps Green Ave
GU25 . . . . .122 D3
Trumps Green Cl GU25 . . . .122 E4
Trumps Green Inf Sch
GU25 . . . . .122 D3
Trumps Mill La GU25 . . . . .122 F4
Trumpsgreen Rd GU25 . . . .122 D3
Truro Cl SL6 . . . . .39 A7
Truss Hill Rd SL5 . . . . .120 C4
Trust Cnr RG7 . . . . .35 E8
Trusthorpe Cl RG6 . . . . .87 E2
Tubbs Farm Cl RG17 . . . . . . .25 B2
Tubwell Rd SL2 . . . . .23 B4
Tudor Ave RG20 . . . . .51 C4
Tudor Cl Ashford TW15 . . . . .97 E4
Wokingham RG40 . . . . .116 F5
Tudor Ct Maidenhead SL6 . . .20 F2
3 Stanwell TW19 . . . . .70 E1
Thatcham RG18 . . . . .106 C4
Tudor Dr
Wooburn Green HP10 . . . . . .3 D7
Yateley GU46 . . . . .149 D4
Tudor Gdns SL1 . . . . .41 C8
Tudor Hall GU15 . . . . .151 F6
Tudor Ho RG12 . . . . .118 B4
Tudor La SL4 . . . . .95 C8
Tudor Rd Ashford TW15 . . . . .98 D2
Newbury RG14 . . . . .105 A1
Reading RG1 . . . . .86 A8
Tudor Way SL4 . . . . .66 E6
Tull Way RG19 . . . . .131 A6
Tunnel Link Rd TW6 . . . . . . .71 A2
Tunnel Rd E TW6 . . . . .71 B6
Tunnel Rd W TW6 . . . . .71 B6
Tuns Hill Cotts RG6 . . . . .87 A5
Tuns La Henley-On-T RG9 . . .15 E2
Slough SL1 . . . . .42 C4
Tupsley Rd SL1 . . . . .85 F5
Turbary Gdns RG26 . . . . . . .135 B1
Turf Hill Rd GU15 . . . . .151 F8
Turing Dr RG12 . . . . .118 A4
Turk's La RG7 . . . . .137 A4
Turmeric Cl RG6 . . . . .86 F1
Turnberry RG12 . . . . .117 E2
Turnberry Ct 18 RG1 . . . . . .86 D7
Turnberry Ho SL5 . . . . .121 A1
Turnbridge Cl RG6 . . . . .114 B8
Turner Pl GU47 . . . . .150 D6
Turner Rd SL3 . . . . .43 C4
Turners Cl TW18 . . . . .97 B3
Turners Dr RG19 . . . . .106 C2
Turnery The RG10 . . . . .106 C3
Turnfields RG19 . . . . .106 D3
Turnoak Pk SL4 . . . . .66 B5
Turnpike Ind Est RG14 . . . .105 D5
Turnpike Rd
Bracknell RG42 . . . . .117 D7
Newbury RG14,RG18 . . . . .105 E4
Turnstone Cl RG41 . . . . .88 B3
Turnstone End GU46 . . . . . .149 B6
Turnville Cl GU18 . . . . .146 A1
Turpin Rd TW14 . . . . .71 F1
Turpins Gn SL6 . . . . .39 A5
Turpins Rise GU20 . . . . .146 B6
Turton Way SL1 . . . . .42 D3
Tuscam Way GU15 . . . . .150 F4
Tuscan Cl RG30 . . . . .57 E1
Tuscany Villas GU18 . . . . . .146 B1
Tuscany Way GU46 . . . . . . .149 B4
Tuxford Mews RG30 . . . . . . .85 B7
Tweed Cl RG30 . . . . .85 B7
Tweed Rd SL3 . . . . .69 B8
Twin Oaks RG4 . . . . .59 B6
Twinches La SL1 . . . . .42 B5
Twinwoods RG20 . . . . .31 A4
Two Mile Dr SL1 . . . . .41 E4
Two Rivers Way RG14 . . . . .105 D3
Two Rivers Way RG14 . . . . .105 D3
Two Tree Hill RG9 . . . . .35 B8
Twycross Rd RG40 . . . . .84 F6
Twyford Orchards Cvn Pk
RG10 . . . . .61 F7
Twyford Rd
Binfield RG10,RG42 . . . . . . .90 C7
Waltham St Lawrence RG10 .62 E6
Wokingham RG40 . . . . .88 B7
Twyford Sta RG10 . . . . .61 E4
Twynersh Ave KT16 . . . . . . .123 F3
Twynham Rd SL1 . . . . .39 B7
Tyberton Pl RG1 . . . . .85 F5
Tydehams RG14 . . . . .130 F7
Tyle Pl SL4 . . . . .68 A2
Tyle Rd RG30 . . . . .85 B6
Tyler Cl RG4 . . . . .58 E5
Tyler Dr RG2 . . . . .140 E7
Tyler Wlk SL3 . . . . .43 F1
Tyler's La RG7 . . . . .80 B1
Tylorstown RG4 . . . . .58 F5
Tymawr RG4 . . . . .58 F5
Tyne Way RG18 . . . . .106 B5
Tyrell Gdns SL4 . . . . .94 B4
Tyrrel Ct 9 RG1 . . . . .86 C7
Tytherton RG12 . . . . .118 C7

U

Uffcott Cl RG6 . . . . .113 F7
Uffington Cl RG31 . . . . .84 C8
Uffington Dr RG12 . . . . .118 E5
Ufton Court Yd SL8 . . . . .3 B4
Ufton Ct SL4 . . . . .3 B4
Ullswater Cl RG30 . . . . .85 B6
Ullswater Dr Burnham SL1 . .41 C8
Lightwater GU18 . . . . .146 B1

Ullswater Cl continued
Thatcham RG19 . . . . .106 A3
Ullswater Dr RG31 . . . . .57 D3
Ullswater Rd GU18 . . . . .146 B1
Ulster Cl RG4 . . . . .59 D5
Umberville Way SL2 . . . . .21 F2
Underhill OX10 . . . . .14 A4
Underhill Cl SL6 . . . . .39 E6
Underwood RG12 . . . . .117 E3
Underwood Cotts RG8 . . . . . .33 F6
Underwood Ct RG42 . . . . .90 C1
Underwood Rd RG30 . . . . . . .85 A4
Union Cl GU47 . . . . .143 E2
Union Rd RG7 . . . . .82 D4
Union St RG1 . . . . .86 A8
Unity Cl RG4 . . . . .59 B6
Unity Ct RG4 . . . . .59 B6
Univ of Reading
Earley RG6 . . . . .87 B6
Reading RG1 . . . . .86 C6
Reading,Whiteknights RG6 . .86 F4
Unwin Ave TW14 . . . . .71 D2
Upavon Dr RG1 . . . . .85 F6
Upavon Gdns RG12 . . . . . . .118 F4
Upcroft SL4 . . . . .67 B4
Upcroft Prim Sch SL4 . . . . . .84 F8
Updown Hill GU20 . . . . .146 D4
Upland Rd GU15 . . . . .151 D7
Uplands Hungerford RG17 .100 C5
Marlow Bottom SL7 . . . . .1 D6
Uplands Cl GU47 . . . . .150 B8
Uplands Prim Sch GU47 . . .150 B8
Uplands Rd RG4 . . . . .58 E5
Upper Bray Rd SL6 . . . . .40 C3
Upper Broadmoor Rd
RG45 . . . . .143 D5
Upper Charles St SL5 . . . . . .151 C6
Upper Chobham Rd
GU15 . . . . .152 B4
Upper College Ride
GU15 . . . . .151 E8
Upper Crown St RG1 . . . . . . .86 B6
Upper Eddington RG17 . . . .100 E7
Upper End RG20 . . . . .49 A8
Upper Gordon Rd GU15 . . . .151 D5
Upper Halliford Rd
TW17 . . . . .125 E5
Upper Halliford Sta
TW17 . . . . .125 E7
Upper Lambourn Rd
RG17 . . . . .25 A3
Upper Lees Rd SL2 . . . . .22 B2
Upper Meadow Rd RG2 . . . .86 D2
Upper Nursery SL5 . . . . .121 A4
Upper Park Rd GU15 . . . . . .151 E6
Upper Raymond Almshouses
14 RG14 . . . . .104 F2
Upper Red Cross Rd RG8 . .34 C7
Upper Redlands Rd RG1 . . . .86 E5
Upper Terr RG41 . . . . .115 B8
Upper Ventnor Cotts SL6 . . .19 D8
Upper Verran Rd GU15 . . . .151 D3
Upper Village Rd SL5 . . . . . .121 A4
Upper Warren Ave RG4 . . . . .58 D3
Upper Wlk GU25 . . . . .122 E5
Upper Woodcote Rd RG4 . . .58 D5
Uppingham Dr RG5 . . . . .60 F1
Uppingham Gdns RG4 . . . . . .59 D6
Upshire Gdns RG12 . . . . . . .118 F5
Upton Cl Henley-On-T RG9 . .15 F1
Slough SL1 . . . . .42 F3
Upton Court Rd SL3 . . . . . . .43 B2
Upton Hospl SL1 . . . . .42 F3
Upton House Sch SL1 . . . . . .67 C5
Upton Lea Par SL2 . . . . .42 F3
Upton Pk SL1 . . . . .42 F3
Upton Rd Reading RG30 . . . .85 B7
Slough SL1,SL3 . . . . .43 A3
Urquhart Rd RG19 . . . . .106 E2
Usk Rd RG30 . . . . .84 F6
Uxbridge Rd SL1,SL2,SL3 . .43 C6

V

Vachel Rd RG1 . . . . .86 A8
Vale Cres RG30 . . . . .57 E1
Vale Gr SL1 . . . . .42 E3
Vale Rd Camberley GU15 . . .151 A4
Windsor SL4 . . . . .66 F6
Vale View RG10 . . . . .61 B4
Vale View Dr RG7 . . . . .138 D5
Valentia Cl RG30 . . . . .85 D8
Valentia Rd RG30 . . . . .85 D8
Valentine Cres RG4 . . . . .59 C1
Valley Cl Caversham RG4 . . .59 A4
Goring RG8 . . . . .34 C6
Valley Cres RG41 . . . . .116 A8
Valley End C of E Fst Sch
GU24 . . . . .153 C1
Valley Gdns* TW20 . . . . . .121 E7
Valley Rd
Burghfield Common RG7 . .111 A3
Henley-On-T RG9 . . . . .35 A8
Newbury RG14 . . . . .130 E8
Frimley GU16 . . . . .152 C1
Valley Road Sch RG30 . . . . .85 A4
Valley View GU47 . . . . .150 A7
Valley Vineyards* RG10 .62 A3
Valley Way RG41 . . . . .135 C1
Valon Rd RG2 . . . . .113 D8
Valpy St RG1 . . . . .86 B8
Valroy Cl GU15 . . . . .151 D6
Vandyke RG12 . . . . .117 E3
Vanguard Ho 5 TW9 . . . . . .71 E5
Vanguard Way TW6 . . . . .71 E5
Vanlore Way RG31 . . . . .84 C5

Vanners La RG20 . . . . .129 D5
Vansittart Est SL4 . . . . .67 C6
Vansittart Rd Bisham SL7 . . .18 E7
Windsor SL4 . . . . .67 B6
Vantage Rd SL1 . . . . .42 B5
Vanwall Bsns Pk SL6 . . . . . . .39 C5
Vanwall Rd SL6 . . . . .39 C5
Vastern Rd RG1 . . . . .59 B1
Vaughan Almshouses 1
TW15 . . . . .98 B3
Vaughan Copse SL4 . . . . .42 D2
Vaughan Gdns SL4 . . . . .41 F2
Vaughan Way SL2 . . . . .21 E1
Vauxhall Dr RG5 . . . . .88 A6
Vegal Cres TW20 . . . . .95 C2
Veitch Cl TW14 . . . . .98 F8
Venetia Cl RG4 . . . . .59 C7
Venning Rd RG2 . . . . .140 F8
Ventnor Rd RG31 . . . . .57 D1
Venture Ho TW18 . . . . .97 A4
Venus Cl RG41 . . . . .115 F6
Verbena Cl RG41 . . . . .88 B3
Verdon Ct SL2 . . . . .22 B2
Verey Cl RG10 . . . . .61 F3
Verica Gdns RG26 . . . . .135 E2
Vermont Rd SL2 . . . . .21 F1
Vermont Woods RG40 . . . . .141 E7
Verney Cl SL7 . . . . .1 D2
Verney Mews RG30 . . . . .85 C7
Verney Rd SL3 . . . . .43 A3
Vernon Cl TW19 . . . . .97 E7
Vernon Cres RG12 . . . . .113 B7
Vernon Dr SL5 . . . . .119 E7
Vernon Rd TW13 . . . . .98 F6
Verran Rd GU15 . . . . .151 D3
Vibia Cl TW19 . . . . .97 D8
Viburnum Cl GU24 . . . . .153 E6
Vicarage Ave TW20 . . . . .96 B3
Vicarage Cl Cookham SL6 . . .20 B7
Wokingham RG40 . . . . .141 F6
Vicarage Cres TW20 . . . . . . .96 B3
Vicarage Ct
East Bedfont TW14 . . . . .98 C8
Egham TW20 . . . . .96 B2
Shinfield RG2 . . . . .113 D5
Vicarage Dr SL6 . . . . .40 C4
Vicarage Flats SL4 . . . . .67 D8
Vicarage Gdns
Ascot SL5 . . . . .120 A4
White Waltham SL6 . . . . .63 F8
Vicarage La
Cold Ash RG18 . . . . .106 C8
Laleham TW18 . . . . .96 C1
Wraysbury TW19 . . . . .69 A1
Yateley GU46 . . . . .149 C7
Vicarage Rd Ashford TW16 .98 F2
Bagshot GU19 . . . . .145 C3
Blackwater GU17 . . . . .150 E4
Egham TW20 . . . . .96 B3
Henley-On-T RG9 . . . . .35 E8
Maidenhead SL6 . . . . .39 F8
Reading RG2 . . . . .86 C5
Staines TW18 . . . . .96 B3
Yateley GU46 . . . . .149 C7
Vicarage Way SL3 . . . . .69 D7
Vicarage Wd GU15 . . . . .40 C4
Vicarage Wood Way
RG31 . . . . .57 B1
Vickers Cl Shinfield RG2 . . .113 F4
Woodley RG5 . . . . .88 B7
Vickers Ct 3 TW19 . . . . .70 E1
Victor Cl SL6 . . . . .21 F6
Victor Rd Thatcham RG18 . .106 E3
Windsor SL4 . . . . .67 C4
Victor Way RG5 . . . . .88 A7
Victoria Ave GU15 . . . . .151 A5
Victoria Cres SL0 . . . . .44 F6
Camberley GU15 . . . . .151 A5
Henley-On-T RG9 . . . . .15 E1
2 Marlow SL7 . . . . .1 E2
Slough SL1 . . . . .42 E5
Victoria Dr
Blackwater GU17 . . . . .150 C4
Burnham SL1,SL2 . . . . .22 F6
Victoria Gdns Marlow SL7 . . . .1 E2
Newbury RG14 . . . . .105 A4
Victoria Ho SL4 . . . . .68 A2
Victoria La UB7 . . . . .71 D8
Victoria Mews RG30 . . . . . . .85 C7
Victoria Rd Ascot SL5 . . . . . .120 A4
Caversham RG4 . . . . .59 A3
Eton SL4 . . . . .41 F1
Farnham Common SL2 . . . . .22 C6
Marlow SL7 . . . . .1 E2
Mortimer RG7 . . . . .136 F6
Reading RG31 . . . . .84 D8
Sandhurst GU47 . . . . .143 E1
Slough SL2 . . . . .42 E8
Staines TW18 . . . . .96 E5
Wargrave RG10 . . . . .61 E5
Victoria St
Englefield Green TW20 . . . . .95 C2
Reading RG1 . . . . .85 F8
10 Slough SL1 . . . . .42 F4
Windsor SL4 . . . . .67 D6
Victoria Way 3 RG1 . . . . . . .86 D7
Victory Ct TW15,TW19 . . . . .97 E7
Victory Rd KT16 . . . . .124 A1
Victory Way RG7 . . . . .83 E4
Villa Mews 2 RG1 . . . . .86 E7
Villa Pl RG2 . . . . .139 C6
Village Cl SL5 . . . . .120 C4
Village Gate SL7 . . . . .125 B4
Village Mews SL5 . . . . .120 C5

Village Rd Dorney SL4 . . . . . .41 B3
Thorpe TW20 . . . . .123 C6
Village Sh Ctr The 5
SL1 .42 F4
Village The
Finchampstead RG40 . . . . .141 E3
Old Windsor SL4 . . . . .94 B5
Village Way Ashford TW15 . .98 A3
Yateley GU46 . . . . .149 D7
Villiers Cl SL4 . . . . .67 B7
Villiers Mead RG41 . . . . . . .116 A6
Villiers Rd SL2 . . . . .42 D8
Villiers Way RG14 . . . . .130 C6
Villiers Wlk RG14 . . . . .130 C6
Vincent Cl Chertsey KT16 . .123 E2
Harmondsworth UB7 . . . . . .71 A8
Woodley RG5 . . . . .87 F6
Vincent Dr TW17 . . . . .125 E6
Vincent Ho 8 RG1 . . . . .85 F8
Vincent Rd
Chertsey KT16 . . . . .123 E2
Thatcham RG18 . . . . .106 E4
Vincent Rise RG12 . . . . .118 E6
Vine Cl TW19 . . . . .70 A2
Vine Cotts Newbury RG14 . .105 B8
Stoke Poges SL2 . . . . .23 A6
Vine Rd SL2 . . . . .22 F6
Vineries Cl UB7 . . . . .71 A8
Vinery The RG10 . . . . .36 D2
Vines The RG41 . . . . .115 C3
Vineyard Dr SL8 . . . . .3 A5
Vinter Ct TW17 . . . . .125 A4
Vinters Ho RG31 . . . . .57 D1
Viola Ave TW19 . . . . .97 E7
Viola Croft RG42 . . . . .118 F8
Violet Gr RG18 . . . . .106 E5
Virginia Ave GU25 . . . . .122 C4
Virginia Cl TW18 . . . . .124 C6
Virginia Beeches GU25 . . . .122 C6
Virginia Ct Ashford TW15 . . .97 E4
Virginia Water GU25 . . . . . .122 D5
Virginia Dr GU25 . . . . .122 C5
Virginia Water* SL5 . . . .121 E6
Virginia Water Sta
GU25 . . . . .122 E4
Virginia Way RG30 . . . . .85 B5
Viscount Cl SL4 . . . . .67 C6
Viscount Ind Est SL3 . . . . . . .69 E4
Viscount Rd TW19 . . . . .97 E7
Viscount Way Hatton TW6 . .71 F5
Woodley RG5 . . . . .88 A7
Vivien Cl SL6 . . . . .19 F6
Vivienne Ho TW18 . . . . .97 A3
Vo-Tec Ctr RG14 . . . . .105 E2
Voller Dr RG31 . . . . .84 C6
Volunteer Rd RG7 . . . . .83 D2
Vulcan Cl
Sandhurst GU47 . . . . .150 A7
Woodley RG5 . . . . .61 B1
Vulcan Ct GU47 . . . . .150 A7
Vulcan Ho RG7 . . . . .134 E2
Vulcan Way GU47 . . . . .150 B7

W

Waborne Rd SL8 . . . . .3 B4
Wade Dr SL1 . . . . .42 A5
Wadham GU47 . . . . .143 F1
Wadham Cl TW17 . . . . .125 C2
Wagbullock Rise RG12 . . . .118 C3
Waggoners Hollow
GU19 . . . . .145 E2
Wagner Cl SL6 . . . . .38 F3
Wagtail Cl RG10 . . . . .61 E4
Waingel's Copse Sch
RG5 .61 A2
Waingels Rd RG5,RG10 . . . .61 A2
Wainscott SL5 . . . . .120 F3
Wainwright Cl RG40 . . . . . . .117 A6
Wakefield Cres SL2 . . . . .22 F6
Wakeford Cl RG26 . . . . .135 E2
Wakeford Ct RG26 . . . . .135 E2
Wakelins End SL6 . . . . .19 E7
Wakeman Rd SL8 . . . . .3 A3
Wakemans RG8 . . . . .55 D4
Walbury RG12 . . . . .118 E5
Waldeck Rd SL6 . . . . .40 A7
Waldeck St RG1 . . . . .86 B5
Waldegrave Pl RG14 . . . . . .105 A2
Walden Ave RG2 . . . . .114 C3
Waldens Cl SL8 . . . . .3 A3
Waldorf Hts GU17 . . . . .150 D3
Waldron Ho RG10 . . . . .118 F8
Waldrons The RG17 . . . . .47 C6
Waleys Pl 2 RG4 . . . . .59 C2
Walgrove Gdns SL6 . . . . .63 E7
Walk The Ashford TW16 . . . . .98 F1
Walker Cl TW14 . . . . .98 F8
Walker Gdns SL6 . . . . .39 D7
Walker Rd SL6 . . . . .40 A4
Walker's La RG17 . . . . .25 B3
Walker's Ridge GU15 . . . . . .151 E5
Walkers Pl RG30 . . . . .85 C7
Wall La RG7 . . . . .136 D2
Wallace Cl Marlow SL7 . . . . . .1 E4
Upper Halliford TW17 . . . . .125 D5
Woodley RG5 . . . . .87 D5
Wallace Gr RG7 . . . . .113 A4
Wallace Wlk SL4 . . . . .42 F1
Wallcroft Cl RG42 . . . . .90 E1
Walled Gdn The RG10 . . . . .36 D2
Waller Ct RG4 . . . . .59 B2

Waller Dr RG14 105 E5
Wallingford Cl RG12 118 E5
Wallingford Rd
Compton RG20 31 E5
Moulsford RG8,OX10 14 A1
South Stoke RG8,OX10 14 C5
Streatley RG8 34 A7
Wallington Rd GU15 145 A1
Wallingtons Rd RG17 101 F1
Wallis Ct SL1 43 A4
Wallner Way RG40 116 E5
Walmer Cl
Crowthorne RG45 143 C5
Reading RG30 85 A6
Walmer Rd RG5 60 F1
Walnut Cl
Thatcham RG18 106 C4
Wokingham RG41 115 F5
Yateley GU46 149 D4
Walnut Ct RG40 116 C6
Walnut Gr HP10 3 E6
Walnut Lo SL1 42 D3
Walnut Mews RG42 117 F8
Walnut Tree Cl
Bourne End SL8 3 B2
Twyford RG10 61 F6
Walnut Tree Cotts RG20 75 D8
Walnut Tree Ct RG8 34 C6
Walnut Tree Rd TW17 125 C7
Walnut Way Bourne End SL8 3 B2
Reading RG30 84 D8
Walpole Rd
Old Windsor SL4 95 B8
Slough SL1 41 D7
Walrus Cl RG5 88 B7
Walsh Ave RG42 91 E1
Walter Inf Sch RG41 116 A6
Walter Rd RG41 115 E7
Walters Cl RG18 106 C8
Waltham Cl
Maidenhead SL6 38 F2
Sandhurst GU47 143 D1
Waltham Ct RG8 34 C8
Waltham Rd
Maidenhead SL6 38 F1
Twyford RG10 61 E4
Twyford,Ruscombe RG10 62 B5
Waltham St Lawrence Prim Sch RG10 62 F3
Walton Ave RG9 35 E8
Walton Bridge Rd KT12, TW17 125 E2
Walton Cl RG5 87 C7
Walton Dr SL5 119 F8
Walton Gdns TW13 98 F4
Walton La Burnham SL2 21 F3
Lower Halliford TW17 125 D2
Oatlands Park KT12 125 E1
Walton Lodge KT12 125 F1
Walton Manor KT12 125 F2
Walton Way RG14 105 C4
Wandhope Way RG31 57 C2
Wansey Gdns RG14 105 D5
Wanstraw Gr RG12 118 E2
Wantage Cl RG12 118 E4
Wantage Rd
Great Shefford RG17 48 C5
Lambourn RG17 25 C5
Reading RG30 85 C7
Sandhurst GU47 150 D8
Streatley RG8 33 F8
Wapshott Rd TW18 96 E3
War Meml Pl RG9 35 E7
Waram Cl RG17 100 E7
Warbler Cl RG31 84 B6
Warbler Dr RG6 87 B1
Warborough Ave RG31 84 B8
Warborough Rd OX12 7 A7
Warbreck Dr RG31 57 B3
Warbrook La RG27 141 A1
Ward Cl Iver SL0 44 F7
Wokingham RG40 116 D8
Ward Gdns SL1 41 E6
Ward Royal 5 SL4 67 C6
Ward Royal Par 2 SL4 67 C6
Wardle Ave RG31 57 D1
Wardle Cl GU19 145 E3
Wards Cotts TW19 97 F8
Wards Pl TW20 96 C2
Wards Stone Pk RG12 118 E2
Wareham Rd RG12 118 F4
Warehouse Rd RG19 131 F5
Warfield CE Prim Sch RG42 91 E1
Warfield Rd
Bracknell RG12,RG42 91 C1
East Bedfont TW14 98 E8
Warfield Rdbt RG42 91 C2
Warfield St RG42 91 D3
Wargrave Hill RG10 36 D2
Wargrave Rd
Henley-On-T RG9,RG10 36 B8
Twyford RG10 61 D5
Wargrave Sta RG10 36 C1
Wargrove Dr GU47 150 D8
Waring Cl RG6 114 C8
Warings The RG7 109 A7
Warley Rise RG31 57 C3
Warner Cl Harlington UB3 71 D7
Slough SL1 41 E5
Warner Ct GU47 150 E7
Warners Hill SL6 19 C8
Warnford Rd RG30 84 F7
Warnham La RG20 31 B2
Warnsham Cl 1 RG6 87 B1
Warren Cl
Burghfield Common RG7 111 A3
Sandhurst GU47 150 A8
Slough SL3 43 E3
Wokingham RG40 141 F6
Warren Ct Caversham RG4 58 F2
Farnham Common SL2 22 C7
Warren Down RG42 117 E8
Warren Farm RG17 26 B8
Warren Ho RG4 58 F2
Warren House Ct RG4 58 F2
Warren House Rd RG40 116 D8
Warren La RG40 141 E5
Warren Rd Ashford TW15 98 E1
Newbury RG14 130 D6
Woodley RG4,RG5 60 D1
Warren Rise GU16 151 F3
Warren Row SL5 119 D7
Warren Row Rd
Knowl Hill RG10 37 C6
Wargrave RG10 36 F7
Warren The RG4 58 D3
Warrington Ave SL1 42 C7
Warrington Spur SL4 95 B8
Warwick RG12 118 E3
Warwick Ave Slough SL2 22 C1
Staines TW18 97 C2
Thorpe TW20 123 C8
Warwick Cl Frimley GU15 152 B3
Maidenhead SL6 39 B4
Warwick Ct 3 SL4 67 C5
Warwick Dr RG14 105 B1
Warwick Ho RG2 86 C4
Warwick Rd Ashford TW15 97 E3
Reading RG2 86 C4
Warwick Villas TW20 123 C8
Wasdale Cl GU47 143 D2
Wash Hill HP10 3 E3
Wash Hill Lea HP10 3 E4
Wash Hill Mobile Home Pk HP10 3 E3
Wash Water RG20 130 B3
Washbury Ho RG14 130 C8
Washington Ct Marlow SL7 2 A2
Thatcham RG19 106 A3
Washington Dr
Slough SL1 41 D6
Windsor SL4 66 E4
Washington Gdns RG40 142 A8
Washington Rd RG4 59 B2
Wasing La RG7 134 D6
Watchetts Dr GU15 151 C2
Watchetts Jun Sch GU15 151 B2
Watchetts Lake Cl GU15 151 D3
Watchetts Rd GU15 151 B4
Watchmoor Pk GU15 151 B4
Watchmoor Rd GU15 151 A4
Watchmoor Trade Ctr GU15 151 A3
Water La RG19 131 C7
Water Oakley Cotts SL4 65 F8
Water Oakley Farm Cotts SL4 65 F8
Water Rd RG30 85 B7
Water St RG18 52 F6
Waterbeach Cl SL1 42 D7
Waterbeach Rd SL1 42 D7
Waterfall Cl GU25 122 A6
Waterford Way RG40 116 C6
Waterham Rd RG12 118 B3
Waterhouse Mead GU47 150 D7
Waterloo Cl
Camberley GU15 152 B7
East Bedfont TW14 98 F7
Moulsford OX10 14 A7
Waterloo Cres RG40 116 E4
Waterloo Rd
Crowthorne RG45 143 B4
Reading RG2 86 B5
Wokingham RG40 116 F5
Waterloo Rise RG2 86 B4
Waterman Ct SL1 41 E5
Waterman Pl RG1 59 A1
Waterman's Rd RG9 35 E8
Watermans Way RG10 36 C1
Watermead TW14 98 E7
Watermeadows The RG14 105 B4
Watermill Ct RG7 108 C2
Waters Dr TW18 96 F4
Watersfield Cl 4 RG6 87 B1
Waterside HP10 3 E7
Waterside Cotts RG4 60 B4
Waterside Ct
Newbury RG14 105 B3
Twyford RG10 61 C5
Waterside Dr Langley SL3 43 F4
Purley On T RG8 57 D5
Theale RG7 83 F3
Waterside Gdns 4 RG1 86 A7
Waterside Lodge SL6 40 C8
Watersplash La
Ascot SL5 120 E8
Newell Green RG42 91 B2
Watersplash Rd TW17 125 A5
Watery La Chertsey KT16 123 D2
Kintbury RG20 128 F5
Wooburn Green HP10 3 E8
Watkins Cl RG40 141 E7
Watlington St RG1 86 C7
Watmore La RG41 88 D2
Watson Cl RG40 115 F1
Watt's La OX11 12 A8
Wavell Cl RG2 86 F1
Wavell Gdns SL2 21 F2
Wavell Rd SL6 39 B6
Wavendene Ave TW20 96 C1
Waverley RG12 117 E4
Waverley Cl GU15 151 F4
Waverley Ct 18 RG30 85 D6
Waverley Dr
Camberley GU15 151 F5
Virginia Water GU25 122 A5
Waverley Rd
Bagshot GU19 145 E3
Reading RG30 85 C7
Slough SL1 42 C8
Waverley Sch RG40 115 E1
Waverley Way RG40 115 F1
Waverleys The RG18 106 D4
Wawcott Farm Cotts RG20 102 C4
Waybrook Cres RG1 86 F6
Wayewood GU15 151 E6
Wayland Cl RG12 118 F5
Waylands TW19 68 E1
Waylands Cl RG7 82 D4
Waylen St RG1 85 F7
Ways End GU15 151 E4
Waysend Ho GU15 151 E4
Wayside Cotts GU20 146 F6
Wayside Mews SL6 39 F8
WC Lee's Resthouses GU20 146 D4
Weald Rise RG30 57 F2
Wealden Way RG30 84 F8
Weardale Cl RG2 86 D4
Weather Way RG12 118 C7
Weathervane Cotts RG17 100 C5
Weaver Moss GU47 150 B7
Weavers Ct
22 Reading RG1 86 D7
Wokingham RG40 116 C6
Weavers La RG17 127 C6
Weavers Way RG10 61 D4
Weavers Wlk 2 RG14 105 A3
Webb Cl Bagshot GU19 145 E1
Bracknell RG42 90 E1
Slough SL3 43 D2
Webb Ct RG40 116 E8
Webb's Cl RG1 85 F6
Webbs Acre RG19 106 F2
Webbs La RG7 109 B7
Webster Cl SL6 39 A5
Wedderburn Cl RG41 88 D2
Wedgewood Way RG30 57 F1
Weedon Cl OX10 14 A8
Weekes Dr SL1 42 B4
Weighbridge Row RG1 58 F1
Weir Cl RG31 84 F4
Weir Pl TW18 123 E8
Weir Pool Ct RG10 61 C4
Weir Rd KT16 124 B2
Weirside Ct 1 RG1 86 D7
Welbeck RG12 117 E4
Welbeck Rd SL6 39 D5
Welby Cl SL6 39 A4
Welby Cres RG41 88 B1
Weldale St RG1 85 F8
Welden SL2 43 C7
Welford & Wickham CE Prim Sch RG20 75 D4
Welford Pk RG20 75 E7
Welford Rd
Wickham RG20 75 D4
Woodley RG5 88 A8
Well Cl GU15 151 B4
Well End Cotts SL8 2 F5
Well House La RG27 140 B3
Well Mdw RG14 105 B5
Welland Cl Brands Hill SL3 69 B8
Reading RG31 57 C1
Wellbank SL6 20 E1
Wellburn Cl GU47 150 B7
Wellcroft Rd SL1 42 B5
Weller Dr Barkham RG40 141 A6
Camberley GU15 151 C3
Weller's La RG42 91 C7
Wellesley Ave SL0 44 F4
Wellesley Cl GU19 145 C3
Wellesley Ct SL0 44 F4
Wellesley Dr RG45 142 E5
Wellesley Ho SL4 67 B6
Wellesley Path SL1 43 A4
Wellesley Rd SL1 43 A4
Welley Ave TW19 68 E3
Welley Rd TW19 68 E3
Wellfield Cl RG31 84 C7
Wellhill Rd OX12 27 C6
Wellhouse La RG18 79 E6
Wellhouse Rd SL6 19 E2
Wellington Ave
Reading RG2 86 D4
Virginia Water GU25 122 B4
Wellington Bsns Pk RG45 142 F4
Wellington Cl
Maidenhead SL6 39 B8
Newbury RG14 105 C5
Oatlands Park KT12 125 F1
Sandhurst GU47 150 C8
Wellington Coll RG45 143 A3
Wellington Cotts
Ball Hill RG20 129 B2
Knowl Hill RG10 37 C6
Wellington Cres RG26 134 D1
Wellington Ct
Ashford TW15 97 E3
Shinfield RG7 113 A3
Stanwell TW19 97 E8
Wellington Ctry Pk* RG7 139 D1
Wellington Dr RG12 118 E4
Wellington Gdns RG7 82 A1
Wellington Ind Est RG7 113 A1
Wellington Lodge SL4 93 B6
Wellington Rd
Ashford TW15 97 E3
Crowthorne RG45 143 C4
Hatton TW14 71 E2
Maidenhead SL6 39 D7
Sandhurst GU47 150 C8
Wokingham RG40 116 B5
Wellington St SL1 43 A4
Wellington Terr GU47 150 D8
Wellingtonia Ave RG45, RG40 142 C3
Wellingtonia Rdbt RG45 142 E4
Wellingtonias RG42 92 A1
Wells Cl SL4 67 A7
Wells La SL5 120 B5
Welsh La RG7,RG7 139 A2
Welshman's Rd RG7 136 A5
Welwick Cl RG6 87 E2
Welwyn Ave TW14 71 F1
Wendan Rd RG14 130 F8
Wendover Ct TW18 96 C3
Wendover Dr GU16 152 C3
Wendover Pl TW18 96 D3
Wendover Rd
Bourne End SL8 3 A5
Burnham SL1 41 B8
Egham TW18,TW20 96 D3
Wendover Way RG30 84 D7
Wenlock Edge RG10 61 B4
Wenlock Way RG19 106 D2
Wensley Cl RG10 61 D5
Wensley Rd RG1 85 E5
Wensleydale Dr GU15 152 D5
Wentworth Ave
North Ascot SL5 119 C7
Reading RG2 113 D8
Slough SL2 22 A2
Wentworth Cl
Ashford TW15 98 B4
Crowthorne RG45 142 F6
Yateley GU46 149 D5
Wentworth Cres SL6 39 C6
Wentworth Ct RG14 105 B1
Wentworth Dr GU25 121 F5
Wentworth Golf Club GU25 122 A4
Wentworth Lodge RG14 104 E2
Wentworth Way SL5 119 C7
Wescott Inf Sch RG40 116 D6
Wescott Rd RG40 116 D6
Wesley Dr TW20 96 A2
Wesley Pl SL4 93 B6
Wessex Cl RG17 100 C5
Wessex Ct 4 TW19 70 E1
Wessex Gdns RG10 61 E3
Wessex Inf Sch SL6 39 B4
Wessex Jun Sch SL6 39 B4
Wessex Rd Bourne End SL8 3 B2
Harmondsworth TW19,TW6 70 E4
Wessex Road Ind Est SL8 3 B2
Wessex Way SL6 39 B4
Wessons Hill SL6 19 C7
West Berkshire Community Hospl RG14 105 E4
West Berkshire Mus* RG14 105 A3
West Cl Ashford TW15 97 E4
Medmenham SL7 17 D7
West Cres SL4 66 F6
West Ct Maidenhead SL6 40 C4
Sonning RG4 60 E2
West Dean SL6 39 F8
West Dr Reading RG31 84 E5
Sonning RG4 60 D1
Wentworth GU25,SL5 121 E2
West End Ct SL2 22 F4
West End Ho RG14 105 B5
West End La
Harlington UB7 71 C7
Newell Green RG42 91 B3
Stoke Poges SL2 22 E4
West End Rd RG7 136 F5
West Fryerne GU46 149 D8
West Gn GU46 149 B7
West Green Ct RG1 85 F5
West Hill RG1 86 B6
West Ilsley Ho RG20 10 A1
West La RG9 15 D2
West Lawn RG41 115 A7
West Mead SL6 19 F2
West Mead Sch RG40 116 E6
West Mills RG14 104 F3
West Mills Yd RG14 104 F3
West Point SL1 41 D5
West Ramp TW6 71 A6
West Rd Bracknell RG40 117 D2
Camberley GU15 151 D5
East Bedfont TW14 98 D8
Maidenhead SL6 39 E7
West Ridge SL8 3 B4
West Sq SL0 44 F7
West St Henley-On-T RG9 15 D2
Maidenhead SL6 39 F7
Marlow SL7 1 D1
Newbury RG14 104 F3
Reading RG1 86 A7
West Surrey Estates TW15 125 C8
West View
East Bedfont TW14 98 C8
Peasemore RG20 50 C7
West View Cotts RG18 52 F6
West Way TW17 125 D3
Westacott Bsns Ctr SL6 38 E2
Westacott Way SL6 38 D4
Westborough Ct SL6 39 C6
Westborough Rd SL6 39 C6
Westbourne Rd
Feltham TW13 98 F5
Sandhurst GU47 150 E7
Staines TW18 97 B1
Westbourne Terr
3 Newbury RG14 105 A4
Reading RG30 85 C7
Westbrook SL6 40 E1
Westbrook Cl RG17 100 C5
Westbrook Gdns RG12 118 D8
Westbrook Gn OX11 11 F8
Westbrook Rd
Reading RG30 58 C1
2 Staines TW18 96 F3
Westbrook St OX11 11 F8
Westbury Cl
Crowthorne RG45 143 B6
Shepperton TW17 125 B3
Westbury La RG8 57 A6
Westcoign Ho SL6 40 B8
Westcombe Cl RG12 118 E2
Westcote Rd RG30 85 D6
Westcotts Gn RG42 91 D1
Westcroft SL2 22 B1
Westdene Cres RG4 58 E4
Westende RG40 116 D6
Westende Jun Sch RG40 116 D6
Westerdale RG19 106 D3
Westerdale Dr GU16 152 B3
Westerham Wlk 9 RG1 86 B5
Western Ave
Chertsey KT16 124 A6
Henley-On-T RG9 35 E8
Newbury RG14 104 E4
Thorpe TW20 123 B6
Woodley RG5 60 E1
Western Cl
Chertsey KT16 124 A6
Henley-On-T RG9 35 E8
Western Ctr The RG12 117 F7
Western Dr
Shepperton TW17 125 D3
Wooburn Green HP10 3 E5
Western Elms Ave RG30 85 E7
Western End RG14 104 E2
Western House Inf Sch SL1 41 F6
Western Ind Area RG12 117 F7
Western Oaks RG31 57 E2
Western Perimeter Rd TW19,TW6,UB7 70 B5
Western Perimeter Rd Rdbt TW19 70 C2
Western Rd
Bracknell RG12 117 F7
Henley-On-T RG9 35 E8
Reading RG1 85 E6
Westfield Bglws SL7 16 F6
Westfield Cotts SL7 16 F6
Westfield Cres
Shiplake RG9 36 B3
Thatcham RG18 106 B4
Westfield Rd
Camberley GU15 151 B2
Caversham RG4 59 B2
Cholsey OX10 13 D6
Maidenhead SL6 39 B7
Slough SL2 22 B1
Thatcham RG18 106 B5
Winnersh RG41 88 B2
Westfield Sch SL8 3 B4
Westfield Way RG14 104 E2
Westfields Compton RG20 31 D4
Kintbury RG20 128 A3
Westfields Jun & Inf Sch GU46 149 B5
Westgate Cres SL1 41 F6
Westgate Ct RG14 104 E1
Westgate Rd RG14 104 E2
Westgate Sch The SL1 42 A5
Westhatch Cnr RG42 91 C5
Westhatch La RG42 91 C5
Westhead Dr RG14 131 A8
Westhorpe Park Cvn Site SL7 2 B3
Westhorpe Rd SL7 1 F3
Westland RG18 106 B4
Westland Cl TW19 70 E1
Westlands Ave Earley RG2 86 E1
Slough SL1 41 C7
Westlands Cl SL1 41 C7
Westleigh Ho RG31 84 B7
Westley Mill Binfield RG42 90 E8
Holyport RG42 63 F1
Westlyn Rd RG26 135 E1
Westmacott Dr TW14 98 F7
Westmead SL4 67 B4
Westminster Way RG6 87 C1
Westmorland Cl RG41 115 D6
Westmorland Dr
Bracknell RG42 91 F1
Frimley GU15 152 B3
Westmorland Rd SL6 39 D6
Weston Gr GU19 145 F2
Weston Rd SL1 41 F8
Weston's RG20 51 D8
Westonbirt Dr RG4 58 E3
Westridge Ave RG8 57 C5
Westside Ct GU24 153 E6
Westview Dr RG10 61 E6
Westward Rd RG41 115 F7
Westwates Cl RG12 118 D8
Westway RG8 34 C8

Westwood Farm Jun & Inf Schs RG31 .....57 C3
Westwood Glen RG31 ...57 C1
Westwood Gn SL6 ....19 F6
Westwood Rd Marlow SL7 ..1 C1
Newbury RG14 ....105 B1
Reading RG31 ....57 D1
Windlesham GU20 ....146 E6
Westwood Row RG31 ...57 C2
Wetherby Cl RG4 ......59 C6
Wetherby Ho GU15 ...151 D7
Wethered Pk SL7 ......1 D1
Wethered Rd Marlow SL7 ..1 D2
Slough SL1 ....41 B8
Wetton Pl TW20 ....95 F3
Wexford Ct SL6 ....90 B7
Wexham Park Hospl SL3 .23 C1
Wexham Park La SL3 ...23 C1
Wexham Pl SL2 ....23 D6
Wexham Prim Sch SL2 ..43 C7
Wexham Rd SL1,SL2 ...43 B6
Wexham Sch SL2 ......43 C8
Wexham St SL3 ....23 B3
Wexham Woods SL3 ...43 C8
Wey Ave KT16 ....124 A6
Wey Cl GU15 ....151 B5
Weybridge Mead GU46 .149 E7
Weycrofts RG42 ....90 F1
Weymead Cl KT16 ....124 C1
Whaley Rd RG40 .....116 D8
Wharf La SL8 ....3 A3
Wharf Rd Newbury RG14 .105 A3
Wraysbury TW19 ......95 D8
Wharf St RG14 ....105 A3
Wharfe La RG9 ....15 E2
Wharfedale Rd RG41 ...88 A3
Wharfside RG7 ....109 C3
Whatley Gn RG12 ....118 B3
Whatmore Cl TW19 ...70 A1
Wheat Ho TW19 ......97 E7
Wheatbutts The SL4 ..41 F2
Wheatfield Cl SL6 .....39 A4
Wheatfields Rd RG2 ..113 E5
Wheatlands Cl RG31 ..84 E4
Wheatlands La RG14 .130 B6
Wheatlands Rd SL3 ...43 C3
Wheatley RG12 ......117 E4
Wheatley Cl RG2 .....86 E1
Wheatsheaf La
Newbury RG14 ....105 B4
Staines TW18 ....96 F1
Wheatsheaf Par SL4 ..68 A2
Wheatstone Cl [10] SL3 .43 A3
Wheble Dr RG5 ....87 D8
Wheeler Cl
Burghfield Common RG7 .111 B3
Wokingham RG41 ....115 F5
Wheeler Ct RG31 .....57 E1
Wheelers Green Way
RG19 ....106 F2
Wheelton Cl RG6 .....87 E3
Wheelwrights Pl SL3 ..69 C7
Whins Cl GU15 ......151 B4
Whins Dr GU15 .....151 B4
Whinshill Ct SL5 ....121 A1
Whistler Gr GU47 ...150 D6
Whistlers La RG7 ....136 B1
Whistley Cl RG12 ...118 E6
Whistley Court Farm
RG10 ....61 E1
Whitakers Cl RG18 ..106 B4
Whitamore Row RG9 ..35 E8
Whitby Ct RG4 ....59 D6
Whitby Dr [1] RG1 ...86 C5
Whitby Rd SL6 ....59 D6
Whitby Rd SL1 ......42 C6
Whitchurch Cl SL6 ...19 E3
Whitchurch Prim Sch
RG8 ....56 E7
Whitchurch Rd RG8 ..56 D6
White Bridge Cl TW14 .71 F1
White City RG45 ....143 D5
White Cl Hermitage RG18 .78 F6
Slough SL1 ....42 D5
White Gates RG20 ...75 D5
White Hart Ind Est
GU17 ....150 E4
White Hart Rd
[2] Maidenhead SL6 ..39 F7
Slough SL1 ....42 D3
White Hart Row KT16 .124 A2
White Hermitage SL4 ..68 C2
White Hill
Ashampstead RG8 ....54 D6
Remenham Hill RG9 ..16 A2
Shiplake RG9 ....35 A5
Windlesham GU20 ..146 B6
Wooburn Moor HP9 ...3 F8
White Horse Rd RG40 .141 D5
White Horse Rd SL4 ..66 D5
White House Gdns
GU46 ....149 C7
White House La
Beech Hill RG7 .....138 F8
Swallowfield RG7 ...139 A8
White House Prep Sch
RG41 ....116 A3
White House Rd OX10 .14 F8
White Lilies Island SL4 .67 B7
White Lion Way GU46 .149 D7
White Lodge Cl
Marlow Bottom SL7 ...1 C6
Purley On T RG31 ....57 B3
White Paddock SL6 ...39 A2
White Rd Chilton OX11 .10 D8
Sandhurst GU15 ....150 F6
White Rock SL6 .....20 B1

White Shoot OX11 ....12 A5
White Waltham CE Prim Sch
SL6 ....63 D7
White's Hill RG7 ....110 D5
Whiteacres Dr SL6 ...40 C1
Whitebeam Cl RG41 .115 D3
Whitefields Cotts RG14 .104 F7
Whiteford Rd SL2 ...42 E8
Whitegates La RG6 ...87 A7
Whitegrove Prim Sch
RG42 ....91 F1
Whitegrove Rdbt RG42 .91 D2
Whitehall SL6 ....20 B1
Whitehall Dr RG2 ...140 E8
Whitehall Farm La
GU25 ....122 E6
Whitehall La Egham TW20 .95 F1
Wraysbury TW19 .....69 A1
Whitehart Cl RG7 ....83 E4
Whitehaven SL1 .....42 F6
Whitehill Cl
Camberley GU15 ....151 D7
Marlow SL7 ....1 C6
Whitehill Pl GU25 ..122 E4
Whitehills Gn RG8 ...34 C6
Whitehouse Way SL3 ..43 D3
Whiteknights Prim Sch
RG6 ....86 F1
Whiteknights Rd RG6 ..86 F5
Whitelands Dr SL5 ..119 D8
Whitelands Park Prim Sch
RG18 ....106 C4
Whitelands Rd RG18 .106 D4
Whiteley SL4 ....66 E7
Whitelocke Ho RG9 ...15 E3
Whitelocke Inf Sch
RG40 ....116 D7
Whitelocks Piece RG17 .73 A2
Whitemoor La
Lower Basildon RG8 ..34 C1
Upper Basildon RG8 ..54 E5
Whitepit La HP10 .....3 D7
Whites La Beenham RG7 .109 B7
Datchet SL3 ....68 B8
Whitestone Cl RG6 ...87 E3
Whitewalls Cl RG20 ..31 E5
Whiteways Ct TW18 ..97 B1
Whitewell Cl RG2 ...114 E2
Whitley Cl TW19 .....70 E1
Whitley Park Inf Sch
RG2 ....86 B2
Whitley Park Jun Sch
RG2 ....86 B2
Whitley Park La RG2 ..86 D4
Whitley Rd GU46 ...149 D4
Whitley St RG2 ......86 B5
Whitley Wood La RG2 .113 C7
Whitley Wood Rd RG2 .113 C7
Whitmoor Rd GU19 .145 F2
Whitmore Cl GU47 ..143 D1
Whitmore La SL5 ...121 A5
Whitstone Gdns RG2 ..86 C1
Whittaker Rd SL2 ....21 E1
Whittenham Cl SL2 ..43 A5
Whittle Cl
Sandhurst GU47 ....143 A1
Wokingham RG40 ...141 E7
Whittle Parkway SL1 ..41 D7
Whitton Cl [2] RG6 ..87 D1
Whitton Rd RG12 ...118 B6
Whitworth Rd RG12 .141 A7
Whurley Way SL6 ....38 C8
Whybrow Ct RG18 ..106 D3
Whynstones Rd SL5 .120 A4
Whyteladyes La SL6 ..19 E6
Wick Hill Ho RG12 ..118 C8
Wick Hill La RG40 ..142 A5
Wick La TW20 ....94 F3
Wick Rd TW20 ....95 B1
Wickens Cnr RG7 ...109 A6
Wickets The
Ashford TW15 ....97 F5
Maidenhead SL6 .....39 C7
Wickford Way RG6 ..113 F8
Wickham La TW20 ...96 A1
Wickham Rd
Camberley GU15 ....151 E8
Earley RG6 ....87 E1
Wickham Vale RG12 .117 E3
Wickhurst Cotts SL6 ..38 B5
Wicks Gn RG42 ......90 B3
Wicks La RG10 ....62 E2
Widbrook Rd SL6 ....20 B3
Widecroft Rd SL0 ....44 E7
Widmere La SL7 ......1 A6
Wield Ct RG6 ....87 E1
Wiggett Gr RG42 .....90 C2
Wiggington Ho SL4 ..67 D7
Wigmore La Reading RG30 .58 B1
Theale RG7 ....83 C1
Wigmore Rd RG26 ..134 F1
Wilberforce Mews SL6 .39 F7
Wilberforce Way RG12 .118 E4
Wilcox Gdns TW17 ..124 F6
Wild Briar RG40 ....141 F7
Wild Cl RG6 ....114 C8
Wildcroft Rd RG40 ..116 A1
Wilde Theatre RG12 .118 C2
Wilder Ave RG8 ......56 E5
Wilderness Ct RG6 ...87 A4
Wilderness Rd Earley RG6 .87 A4
Frimley GU15 ....151 E2
Wilders Cl Bracknell RG12 .91 A1
Frimley GU15 ......151 E2
Wildgreen N [1] SL3 ..44 A2
Wildgreen S [2] SL3 ..44 A2
Wildoaks TW18 ......97 B3

Wildridings Prim Sch
RG12 ....118 A5
Wildridings Rd RG12 .118 A5
Wildridings Sq RG12 .118 A5
Wildwood Dr RG26 ..134 D1
Wildwood Gdns GU46 .149 C4
Wilford Rd SL3 ....43 F2
Wilfred Way RG19 ..107 A3
Wilfrids Wood Cl HP10 ..3 B6
Willant Cl SL4 ....38 F2
Willats Cl KT16 ....124 A3
William Byrd Sch UB7 ..71 D8
William Cl RG19 ...106 D2
William Ellis Cl SL4 ..68 A1
William Hartley Yd SL3 .23 B1
William Penn Sch The
SL2 ....22 D1
William Sim Wood RG42 .92 B2
William St Reading RG1 ..85 F8
Slough SL1 ....42 F5
Windsor SL4 ....67 D6
Williams Ct RG17 ..100 D5
Williamson Cl RG41 ..88 B3
Willington Cl GU15 .151 B6
Willink Sch The RG7 .110 F2
Willis Cl RG18 ....79 B3
Willoners SL2 ....42 A7
Willoughby Rd
Bracknell RG12 ....117 F6
Slough SL1 ....44 A3
Wokingham RG40 ...116 B6
Willow Bank SL7 ......1 D5
Willow Bank Jun & Inf Schs
RG5 ....60 F1
Willow Cl
Burghfield Common RG30 .111 B5
Colnbrook SL3 ......69 C7
Flackwell Heath HP10 ..3 C6
Newbury RG14 ....104 F1
Willow Cotts OX10 ...13 F5
Willow Court La OX10 .13 F5
Willow Dr
Bracknell RG12 ....118 C8
Maidenhead SL6 ....40 D1
Twyford RG10 ....61 D6
Willow Gdns
Purley On T RG31 ...57 B2
Reading RG2 ....86 E1
Willow Gn GU24 ...153 F6
Willow La
Blackwater GU17 ...150 D4
Wargrave RG10 ....36 C4
Willow Lodge [6] TW16 .98 F1
Willow Par SL1 ......44 A3
Willow Pk SL2 ....23 A5
Willow Pl [1] SL4 ...67 C8
Willow Rd
Bishops Green RG20 .131 F2
Poyle SL3 ....69 E5
Willow St [3] RG1 ...86 A6
Willow Tree Glade RG31 .84 C7
Willow Way GU47 ..142 F1
Willow Wlk
Chertsey KT16 .....124 B2
Englefield Green TW20 .95 C3
Willow Wood Cl SL1 ..21 D3
Willowbrook SL4 ....41 F8
Willowbrook RG40 ..141 F8
Willowdale RG40 ...149 D6
Willowford Cl SL7 ...116 C7
Willowherb Cl RG40 .124 D1
Willowmead TW18 ..124 B8
Willowmead Cl
[10] Marlow SL7 .....1 F3
Newbury RG14 ....130 C5
Willowmead Gdns SL7 ..1 F3
Willowmead Rd [8] SL7 ..1 F3
Willowmead Sq [9] SL7 ..1 F3
Willows Ct [2] RG8 ..56 C6
Willows End GU47 ..150 B8
Willows Rd SL8 ....3 B4
Willows Riverside Pk The
SL4 ....66 C7
Willows The
[1] Bourne End SL8 ..3 B3
[3] Bracknell RG12 ..118 F5
Caversham RG4 ......59 A2
Lightwater GU18 ...146 C1
Windsor SL4 ....66 D7
Willowside SL5 ......60 F1
Willson Rd TW20 ....95 B3
Wilmington Cl RG5 ..87 F8
Wilmot Cl RG42 .....90 C2
Wilmot Rd SL1 ......21 B2
Wilmot Way GU15 ..151 F3
Wilmot Wlk RG14 ..130 C5
Wilsford Cl RG40 ...116 B6
Wilson Ave RG9 .....35 E8
Wilson Cl RG20 .....31 E4
Wilson Prim Sch RG40 .88 B1
Wilson Rd RG30 .....85 C7
Wilson Valkenburg Ct
RG14 ....104 E4
Wilstrode Ave RG42 ..90 F1
Wilton Cl UB7 ....70 D8
Wilton Cres SL6 .....40 C4
Wilton Rd
Camberley GU15 ...151 B3
Reading RG30 ......85 D8
Wiltshire Ave
Crowthorne RG45 ..143 B5
Slough SL1 ....42 C7
Wiltshire Cl RG17 ..100 C5
Wiltshire Dr RG40 ..116 D7

Wiltshire Gr RG42 ....91 F2
Wiltshire Lodge [2] SL6 ..39 F6
Wiltshire Rd Marlow SL7 ..1 F4
Wokingham RG40 ...116 C7
Wiltshire Wlk RG31 ..84 B6
Wilwood Rd RG42 ..117 E8
Wilwyne Cl RG4 .....59 C4
Wimbledon Cl GU15 .144 F1
Wimbledon Rd GU15 .144 F1
Wimblington Dr RG6 .114 C8
Wimbushes RG40 ..141 D6
Winbury Ct SL6 ......39 E7
Winbury Sch SL6 ....40 B4
Wincanton Rd RG2 ..113 C7
Winch Cl RG42 ....90 C3
Winch Terr SL4 ......66 D5
Winchbottom La SL2 .12 B6
Winchcombe Jun & Inf Schs
RG14 ....105 A4
Winchcombe Rd
Newbury RG14 ....105 A2
Twyford RG10 ....61 D8
Winchester Cl SL3 ...69 E6
Winchester Dr SL6 ..40 A4
Winchester Ho [5] RG14 .105 A2
Winchester Rd
Harlington UB3 .....71 E7
Reading RG2 ....86 B4
Winchester Way GU17 .150 C6
Winchgrove Rd RG42 ..91 A1
Winchstone Cl TW17 .124 F5
Wincroft Rd RG4 ....58 E5
Windermere Cl
East Bedfont TW14 ..98 F7
Stanwell TW19 ......97 D6
Thorpe Lea TW20 ...96 B1
Winnersh RG41 .....88 C3
Windermere Rd
Lightwater GU18 ..146 B1
Reading RG2 ....86 D3
Windermere Way
Slough SL1 ....41 C7
Thatcham RG19 ...106 A3
Windermere Wlk GU15 .152 D5
Winding Wood Dr GU15 .152 B3
Windle Cl GU20 ....146 D4
Windlebrook Gn [3]
RG42 ....118 A8
Windlesham Ct GU20 .146 C6
Windlesham Rd
Bracknell RG42 ....117 F6
West End GU24 ....153 F7
Windlesham Village Inf Sch
GU20 ....146 B6
Windmill Ave RG41 .116 A6
Windmill Bsns Village
TW16 ....125 E8
Windmill Cl
Charlton TW16 ......98 E1
Windsor SL4 ....67 B5
Wokingham RG41 ..115 E8
Windmill Cnr RG7 ..137 A6
Windmill Cl RG7 ...137 A6
Windmill Field RG20 .146 D4
Windmill La RG7 ...108 C8
Windmill Lodge TW16 .125 E8
Windmill Rd
Bracknell RG42 ....118 A8
Charlton TW16 .....19 E6
Cookham Rise SL6 ..19 E6
Fulmer SL3 ....23 D7
Mortimer RG7 .....137 A6
Slough SL1 ....42 D5
Windmill Rd W TW16 .125 E8
Windmill Shott TW16 .95 F2
Windmill Terr TW17 .125 E6
Windrush Ave SL3 ...44 B3
Windrush Hts GU47 .150 B8
Windrush Way
Maidenhead SL6 ....39 F8
Reading RG30 ......85 A8
Windsor & Eton Central Sta
SL4 ....67 D6
Windsor & Eton Riverside Sta
SL4 ....67 E7
Windsor Boys' Sch The
SL4 ....67 B6
Windsor Bsns Ctr The
SL4 ....67 C7
Windsor Castle* SL4 ..67 E7
Windsor Cl
Camberley GU15 ...151 C3
Newbury RG14 ....105 B2
[9] Reading RG1 ....85 E7
Windsor Dr TW15 ....97 D4
Windsor Forest Ct SL5 .119 D8
Windsor Girls' Sch SL4 .67 A4
Windsor Great Pk* SL4 .94 D4
Windsor Ho
[4] Slough SL2 .....96 A3
Henley-On-T RG9 ...35 E8
Windsor La SL1 ......44 A3
Windsor Park Rd UB3 ..71 F7
Windsor Pl TW20 ...124 A3
Windsor Rd Datchet SL3 .68 A7
Englefield Green SL4,TW19,
TW20 ....95 B4
Fulmer SL2 ....23 A8
Maidenhead SL6 ....40 C1
North Ascot SL5 ...120 A8
Oakley Green SL4 ..66 C5
Slough SL1 ....42 E4
Wraysbury TW19 ....68 E1

Windsor Ride
Bracknell SL5 ......119 C4
Sandhurst GU15 ...151 A8
Wokingham RG40 ..142 A7
Windsor Rise RG14 .131 C8
Windsor Sq [1] RG1 ..86 B6
Windsor St KT16 ...124 A3
Windsor Way RG31 ..84 B4
Wing Cl SL7 ....1 C1
Wingate Rd RG5 .....87 E6
Wingfield Gdns GU16 .152 D3
Wingrove Rd RG30 ..85 C6
Winkfield Cl RG41 ..116 B3
Winkfield La SL4 ....92 D7
Winkfield Rd Ascot SL5 .120 B7
Windsor SL4 ....66 E2
Winkfield Row RG42 .92 B3
Winkfield St Mary's CE Prim
Sch SL4 ....92 B3
Winkfield La RG7,RG26 .135 C2
Winnersh Gate RG41 .88 D2
Winnersh Gr RG41 ..88 C1
Winnersh Prim Sch
RG41 ....88 D3
Winnersh Sta RG41 ..88 C1
Winnersh Triangle Ind Est
RG41 ....88 B3
Winnersh Triangle Sta
RG41 ....88 A3
Winscombe RG12 ..117 E4
Winser Dr RG30 .....85 D5
Winslett Pl RG30 ....58 B1
Winston Cl RG7 ....113 D2
Winston Way
Purley On T RG8 ....57 B5
Thatcham RG19 ...105 F4
Winston Wlk
Winter Hill SL6 ......2 C1
Winter Hill Rd SL6 ..19 A4
Winterberry Way RG4 .58 E6
Winterbourne Ct RG12 .118 D7
Winterbourne Rd RG6 .76 E4
Winterton Dr RG14 .104 D5
Winton Cres GU46 .149 D5
Winton Rd RG2 ....113 D8
Wintoun Path SL2 ...21 E1
Wintringham Way RG8 .57 D5
Winvale SL1 ....42 E3
Winwood Slough SL2 .43 C7
Windsor SL4 ....66 F7
Wisdom Ct [3] RG30 .85 D6
Wise's Firs RG7 ....110 D3
Wishmoor Cl GU15 .151 E8
Wishmoor Rd GU15 .151 E8
Wispington Cl RG6 ..87 D2
Wistaria La GU46 ..149 C5
Wisteria Cl RG41 ..115 F5
Wiston Terr RG1 ....86 A4
Witcham Cl RG6 ...114 D8
Witham Cl SL4 ......66 E6
Witheygate Ave TW18 .97 B2
Withy Cl Lightwater GU18 .146 C1
Reading RG30 ......84 C5
Withybed Way RG17 .101 E3
Withybed Way RG18 .106 E5
Withycroft SL3 ......43 E7
Withys The RG18 ....53 E1
Wittenham Ave RG31 .84 B8
Wittenham Rd RG12 .118 F8
Wittington Cotts SL7 .17 D6
Woburn Cl Caversham RG4 .58 F2
Frimley GU16 ....152 A1
Woburn Ho SL5 ....121 A1
Wokefield Row RG7 .137 D8
Wokingham Hospl
RG41 ....116 A6
Wokingham Rd
Bracknell RG42 ....117 F8
Earley RG6 ....87 C4
Hurst RG10 ....88 F8
Sandhurst RG45,GU47 .142 E2
Wokingham Sta RG40 .116 B6
Wolf La SL4 ....66 E4
Wolseley St RG1 ....86 A6
Wolsey Rd Ashford TW15 .97 F4
Ashford,Felthamhill TW14 .98 F1
Caversham RG4 ....59 C2
Wolsingham Way RG19 .106 D2
Wondesford Dale RG42 .90 F1
Wooburn Grange HP10 .3 D3
Wooburn Manor Pk HP10 .3 E5
Wooburn Mead HP10 .3 E6
Wooburn Mews HP10 .3 E6
Wooburn Town HP10 ..3 E5
Wood Cl SL4 ....67 C3
Wood End RG45 ...142 F4
Wood Gn RG2 ......86 E1
Wood Green Cl RG30 .85 E7
Wood La Arborfield RG41 .114 F3
Beech Hill RG7 ....138 E5
Binfield RG42 ....90 D1
Bracknell RG42 ...117 E8
Iver SL0 ....44 C8
Slough SL1 ....42 A4
Wood Rd
Camberley GU15 ...151 B1
Littleton TW17 ....125 A5
Wood Ridge RG14 .130 C2
Woodberry Cl RG14 ..90 C1
Woodborough Rd RG9 ..35 E7
Sandhurst GU47 ...150 C7
Woodbine Cl Earley RG6 .87 C1
Woodbine Cotts TW20 .95 F2
Woodbine La RG20 .130 F1

Woodbourne Cl GU46 . . .149 D6
Woodbridge Dr GU15 . . .151 D7
Woodbridge Manor
GU15 . . . . .151 D7
Woodbridge Rd
Blackwater GU17 . . . . . .150 B5
Reading RG31 . . . . .84 B6
Woodbury RG17 . . . . .25 C1
Woodbury Cl SL8 . . . . .3 C4
Woodbury Ct RG7 . . . . . .140 D4
Woodby Dr SL5 . . . . .120 F2
Woodcock Ct RG7 . . . . . .113 A4
Woodcote SL6 . . . . .39 D6
Woodcote House Sch
GU20 . . . . .146 B5
Woodcote Pl SL5 . . . . . . .119 F8
Woodcote Rd
Caversham RG4 . . . . .58 E4
South Stoke RG8 . . . . . . .14 E4
Woodcote Way RG4 . . . . .58 D5
Woodcott Ho RG26 . . . . .135 A1
Wooden Hill Prim Sch
RG12 . . . . .117 E2
Woodend GU15 . . . . .152 A7
Woodend Cl SL5 . . . . . . .119 E8
Woodend Dr SL5 . . . . . . .120 B4
Woodenhill RG12 . . . . . .117 E1
Woodfield Cotts RG8 . . . .34 A6
Woodfield Dr SL6 . . . . . . .39 A6
Woodfield Way RG7 . . . . .83 E4
Woodford Cl RG4 . . . . . . .58 E4
Woodford Gn RG12 . . . . .118 F5
Woodford Way SL2 . . . . . .22 A2
Woodhall La SL5 . . . . . . .146 E8
Woodhaw TW20 . . . . .96 B4
Woodhouse La RG19 . . . .133 E2
Woodhouse St RG42 . . . . .90 E1
Woodhurst La RG41 . . . . .115 F8
Woodhurst Rd SL6 . . . . . .20 B1
Woodhurst S SL6 . . . . . . .20 C1
Woodies Cl RG42 . . . . . . .90 C1
Woodland Ave Slough SL1 . .42 D6
Windsor SL4 . . . . .66 F3
Woodland Cl SL7 . . . . .1 E4
Woodland Cres RG42 . . . .91 C1
Woodland Dr RG30 . . . . . .84 D7
Woodland Way SL7 . . . . . . .1 E4
Woodlands GU46 . . . . . . .149 D4
Woodlands Ave
Burghfield Common RG7 . . .111 A3
Wokingham RG41 . . . . . .115 E8
Woodley RG5 . . . . .87 C7
Woodlands Cl Ascot SL5 . .119 F3
Curridge RG18 . . . . .78 D5
Farnborough GU17 . . . . .150 E1
Woodlands Cotts SL2 . . . .22 C7
Woodlands Ct GU47 . . . . .143 F1
Woodlands Gr RG4 . . . . . .59 D4
Woodlands La GU20,
GU24 . . . . .146 E3
Woodlands Par TW15 . . . .98 C2
Woodlands Park Ave SL6 . .39 A2
Woodlands Park Prim Sch
SL6 . . . . .39 A1
Woodlands Park Rd SL6 . .39 A2

Woodlands Rd
Camberley GU15 . . . . . . .151 B5
Harpsden RG9 . . . . .35 E4
Tadley RG26 . . . . .134 D1
Virginia Water GU25 . . . .122 C5
Woodlands Rd E GU25 . . .122 C5
Woodlands Rd W GU25 . . .122 C5
Woodlands Ride SL5 . . . .120 A3
Woodlands The RG41 . . . .115 D4
Woodlands Wlk GU17 . . . .150 E1
Woodlark Glade GU15 . . .151 D7
Woodlee Cl GU25 . . . . . .122 C7
Woodleigh Mans SL5 . . . .120 E4
Woodley CE Prim Sch
RG5 . . . . .88 B8
Woodley Gn RG5 . . . . . . .87 F8
Woodley Park Est RG5 . . .87 D8
Woodman's La RG7 . . . . .110 F3
Woodmancott Cl RG12 . . .118 F3
Woodmere RG12 . . . . . . .118 E5
Woodmere Cl RG6 . . . . . .87 B2
Woodmoor Ct SL5 . . . . . .119 D6
Woodmoor RG40 . . . . . . .141 F2
Woodmoor End SL6 . . . . . .20 B7
Woodpecker Cl RG10 . . . . .61 E3
Woodpecker Wlk RG41 . . .115 F5
Woodpeckers RG12 . . . . .118 B5
Woodridge Cl RG12 . . . . .118 C6
Woodridge Ho
Bracknell RG12 . . . . .118 C6
Newbury RG14 . . . . .130 E7
Woodrow Ct RG4 . . . . .58 F2
Woodrow Dr RG40 . . . . . .116 F6
Woods Rd RG4 . . . . .59 E4
Woodsend Cl RG6 . . . . . .113 E8
Woodshore Cl GU25 . . . .122 B3
Woodside
Blackwater GU17 . . . . . .150 C3
Cold Ash RG18 . . . . .79 C1
Flackwell Heath HP10 . . . .3 E4
Newbury RG14 . . . . .130 D7
Sandhurst GU15 . . . . . . .150 F7
Woodside Ave HP10 . . . . . .3 C7
Woodside Bsns Pk RG2 . .113 B7
Woodside Cl
Bucklebury RG7 . . . . . . .107 C5
Mortimer RG7 . . . . .137 A6
Wokingham RG40 . . . . . .141 E8
Woodside Dr RG18 . . . . . .79 B6
Woodside La SL4 . . . . . . .93 C3
Woodside Rd SL4 . . . . . . .93 B2
Woodside Way
Reading RG2 . . . . .113 D7
Virginia Water GU25 . . . .122 B6
Woodstock RG40 . . . . . . .116 C6
Woodstock Ave SL3 . . . . .43 D2
Woodstock Cl SL6 . . . . . . .19 F1
Woodstock St RG1 . . . . . .86 E7
Woodthorpe Rd TW15 . . . .97 D4
Woodview Rd RG8 . . . . . . .56 D5
Woodville Cl GU17 . . . . . .150 B5
Woodward Cl RG41 . . . . . .88 D1
Woodway GU15 . . . . .151 B5
Woodway Rd OX11 . . . . . .12 A7
Woodways RG5 . . . . .87 D7
Woodyer Cl RG5 . . . . .87 E5
Woolacombe Dr RG6 . . . . .86 F2
Woolf Dr RG40 . . . . .116 C7

Woolf Meml Cotts RG40 .116 C7
Woolford Cl RG42 . . . . . . .92 C1
Woolhampton CE Prim Sch
RG7 . . . . .108 D4
Woolhampton Hill RG7 . .108 C3
Woolhampton Way
RG12 . . . . .118 D4
Woolley Firs SL6 . . . . .38 E5
Woolton Lodge Gdns
RG20 . . . . .129 F2
Woosehill RG41 . . . . .115 E6
Woosehill Ct RG41 . . . . . .115 F7
Woosehill La RG41 . . . . . .115 E6
Wootton Cl RG31 . . . . .84 C8
Wootton Dr HP10 . . . . .3 E8
Wootton Rd RG9 . . . . .35 C8
Wootton Way SL6 . . . . . . .39 C6
Worcester Cl
Maidenhead SL6 . . . . .39 D3
Reading RG30 . . . . .85 A5
Worcester Ct ⁴ TW15 . . . .98 B3
Worcester Dr TW15 . . . . . .98 B3
Worcester Gdns SL1 . . . . .42 D4
Worcestershire Lea RG42 .91 F1
Wordsworth RG12 . . . . . .117 F4
Wordsworth Ave GU46 . . .149 B4
Wordsworth Ct RG4 . . . . . .59 C7
Wordsworth Rd
Slough SL2 . . . . .21 D1
Thatcham RG18 . . . . . . .106 C4
World Bsns Ctr TW6 . . . . .71 C6
Worlds End Hill RG12 . . .118 F3
Wormersley Rd RG19 . . . .131 D7
Worple Ave TW18 . . . . . . .97 B2
Worple Rd TW18 . . . . .97 B1
Worple The TW19 . . . . . . .68 F1
Worrall Way RG6 . . . . . . .113 F8
Worsley Pl RG7 . . . . .83 E4
Worster Rd SL6 . . . . .19 E6
Worton Dr RG2 . . . . .113 A8
Worton Grange Ind Est
RG2 . . . . .113 A8
Wrabness Way TW18 . . . .124 B8
Wraysbury Gdns TW18 . . .96 E4
Wraysbury Prim Sch
TW19 . . . . .68 E1
Wraysbury Rd TW18,
TW19 . . . . .96 C5
Wraysbury Sta TW19 . . . . .69 A1
Wren Cl
Burghfield Common RG7 . .111 B3
Wokingham RG41 . . . . . .115 E5
Yateley GU46 . . . . .149 B6
Wren Ct Egham TW20 . . . .96 A3
Wrenfield Dr RG4 . . . . . . .58 F5
Wrens Ave TW15 . . . . .98 C4
Wrensfield SL7 . . . . .1 C2
Wrenswood Cl RG2 . . . . .113 B7
Wright SL4 . . . . .66 C4
Wright Cl RG5 . . . . .88 A7
Wright Gdns TW17 . . . . . .125 A4
Wright Sq SL4 . . . . .66 C4
Wright Way SL4 . . . . .66 C4
Wroxham RG12 . . . . .117 F4
Wroxham Rd RG30 . . . . . .87 D8
Wulwyn Ct RG45 . . . . . . .142 F5
Wyatt Rd Staines TW18 . . .97 A3
Windsor SL4 . . . . .66 D4

Wychcotes RG4 . . . . .58 F3
Wychelm Rd
Lightwater GU18 . . . . . .153 C8
Shinfield RG2 . . . . .113 E5
Wychwood Ave RG12 . . . .118 F5
Wychwood Cl RG6 . . . . . . .86 F2
Wychwood Cres RG6 . . . . .86 F2
Wychwood Pl GU15 . . . . .152 B8
Wycombe La HP10 . . . . . . .3 E7
Wycombe Rd Marlow SL7 . . .1 E4
Marlow Bottom SL7 . . . . . .1 E6
Wye Cl Ashford TW15 . . . .98 B4
Reading RG30 . . . . .84 F6
Wye Ct SL8 . . . . .3 A3
Wye Rd HP10 . . . . .3 D8
Wye Valley Sch The SL8 . . .3 B4
Wykeham Cl UB7 . . . . .71 A8
Wykeham Rd RG6 . . . . . . .87 A6
Wylam RG12 . . . . .117 F4
Wylands Rd SL3 . . . . .44 A2
Wyld Court Hill RG18 . . . .53 B5
Wyldewood SL5 . . . . .120 D3
Wymers Cl SL1 . . . . .21 B3
Wymers Wood Rd SL1 . . . .21 A3
Wyncote Cl RG2 . . . . .86 F1
Wyndale Cl RG9 . . . . .15 E1
Wyndham Cl GU46 . . . . .149 D7
Wyndham Cres
Burnham SL1 . . . . .21 B3
Woodley RG5 . . . . .60 D1
Wyndham Rd RG14 . . . . .105 D5
Wynford Cl RG30 . . . . . . .85 C4
Wynnstay Gdns SL7 . . . . . .1 E5
Wynsham Way GU20 . . . .146 B6
Wyre Ct RG31 . . . . .57 C3
Wyresdale RG12 . . . . . . .118 F2
Wythegate TW18 . . . . .96 F1
Wythemede RG42 . . . . . . .90 B2
Wyvern Cl RG12 . . . . .118 A5
Wyvern Ct SL7 TW15 . . . . .97 E5

Y

Yale Cl GU47 . . . . .143 F2
Yard Mead TW20 . . . . . . .96 A5
Yardley RG12 . . . . .117 F4
Yarmouth Rd SL1 . . . . . . .42 C6
Yarnold Cl RG40 . . . . . . .116 F7
Yarnton Cl RG4 . . . . .59 C6
Yarrow Cl RG18 . . . . .106 D5
Yateley Common Cntry Pk*
GU17,GU46 . . . . .149 F3
Yateley Inf Sch GU46 . . . .149 D6
Yateley Manor Sch
GU46 . . . . .149 D6
Yateley Rd GU47 . . . . . . .149 F8
Yateley Sch GU46 . . . . . .149 C5
Yates Copse RG14 . . . . . .105 E5
Yattendon CE Prim Sch
RG18 . . . . .53 F2
Yattendon Ct RG18 . . . . . .53 F2
Yattendon La RG8,RG18 . .54 D2
Yattendon Rd RG18 . . . . . .79 C7
Yaverland Dr GU19 . . . . .145 D2
Ye Meads SL6 . . . . .40 F5
Ye Meads Cotts SL6 . . . . .40 F5
Yelverton Rd RG2 . . . . . . .86 C3
Yeoman Dr TW15 . . . . . . .97 E7

Yeoman Pl RG5 . . . . .87 C7
Yeomans La RG20 . . . . . .131 A1
Yeomans Way GU15 . . . . .151 E5
Yeosfield RG7 . . . . .139 C3
Yeoveney Cl TW19 . . . . . . .96 D6
Yeovil Ent Ctr SL1 . . . . . . .41 F8
Yeovil Rd
Sandhurst GU47 . . . . . . .143 E1
Slough SL1 . . . . .41 E8
Yew Cl Newell Green RG42 . .92 A1
Wokingham RG41 . . . . . .115 F5
Yew Cnr RG12 . . . . .118 C6
Yew Gate RG14 . . . . .104 F6
Yew La RG1 . . . . .85 F5
Yew Tree Cl SL6 . . . . .39 E8
Yew Tree Ct RG8 . . . . .34 C6
Yew Tree Mews RG20 . . . .31 E4
Yew Tree Rd SL1 . . . . .43 A3
Yew Tree Rise RG31 . . . . . .84 C5
Yew Tree Stables RG20 . . .31 E4
Yew Tree Wlk GU16 . . . . .151 F1
Yew Trees TW17 . . . . .124 F5
Yewhurst Cl RG10 . . . . . . .61 D6
Yews The TW15 . . . . .98 B4
Yewtrees TW20 . . . . .123 C6
Yield Hall La ⁴ RG1 . . . . . .86 B7
Yield Hall Pl RG1 . . . . .86 B7
Yockley Cl GU15 . . . . . . .152 D3
Yoreham Cl RG6 . . . . .87 E1
York Ave Slough SL1 . . . . .42 D7
Windsor SL4 . . . . .67 B5
York Cl RG14 . . . . .105 B2
York Ho Bracknell RG12 . .117 F8
Reading RG31 . . . . .84 B4
York Pl GU15 . . . . .151 D7
York Rd Binfield RG42 . . . .90 D3
Camberley GU15 . . . . . . .151 D7
Henley-On-T RG9 . . . . . . .15 D2
Hungerford RG17 . . . . . .100 D4
Maidenhead SL6 . . . . .40 A7
Marlow SL7 . . . . .1 D2
Newbury RG14 . . . . .105 B2
Reading RG1 . . . . .59 A1
Windsor SL4 . . . . .67 B5
York Terrace La GU15 . . .151 A5
York Town Ind Est
GU15 . . . . .151 A5
Yorke Way SL3 . . . . .150 B8
Yorkshire Pl RG42 . . . . . . .91 F2
Yorktown Rd
Sandhurst GU47 . . . . . . .150 D5
Sandhurst GU47 . . . . . . .150 E7
Youlden Cl GU15 . . . . . . .152 A5
Youlden Dr GU15 . . . . . . .152 B6
Young Cres RG19 . . . . . . .131 D8
Young's Ind Est RG7 . . . .134 F4

Z

Zealand Ave UB7 . . . . .70 C7
Zenith Ct GU47 . . . . .143 E1
Zephyr Ho RG7 . . . . .134 E2
Zetland Ct SL6 . . . . .40 B8
Zinnia Cl RG41 . . . . .115 D7
Zinzan St RG1 . . . . .85 F7
Zodiac Ho RG7 . . . . .134 E2

Addresses

Name and Address	Telephone	Page	Grid reference

NG NH NJ NK
NM NN NO NP
NR NS NT NU
NX NY NZ
SC SD SE TA
SH SJ SK TF TG
SM SN SO SP TL TM
SR SS ST SU TQ TR
SW SX SY SZ TV

Any feature in this atlas can be given a unique reference to help you find the same feature on other Ordnance Survey maps of the area, or to help someone else locate you if they do not have a Street Atlas.

The grid squares in this atlas match the Ordnance Survey National Grid and are at 500 metre intervals. The small figures at the bottom and sides of every other grid line are the National Grid kilometre values (**00** to **99** km) and are repeated across the country every 100 km (see left).

To give a unique National Grid reference you need to locate where in the country you are. The country is divided into 100 km squares with each square given a unique two-letter reference. Use the administrative map to determine in which 100 km square a particular page of this atlas falls.

The bold letters and numbers between each grid line (**A** to **F**, **1** to **8**) are for use within a specific Street Atlas only, and when used with the page number, are a convenient way of referencing these grid squares.

Example   The railway bridge over DARLEY GREEN RD in grid square B1

Step 1: Identify the two-letter reference, in this example the page is in **SP**

Step 2: Identify the 1 km square in which the railway bridge falls. Use the figures in the southwest corner of this square: Eastings **17**, Northings **74**. This gives a unique reference: **SP 17 74**, accurate to 1 km.

Step 3: To give a more precise reference accurate to 100 m you need to estimate how many tenths along and how many tenths up this 1 km square the feature is (to help with this the 1 km square is divided into four 500 m squares). This makes the bridge about **8** tenths along and about **1** tenth up from the southwest corner.

This gives a unique reference: **SP 178 741**, accurate to 100 m.

Eastings (read from left to right along the bottom) come before Northings (read from bottom to top). If you have trouble remembering say to yourself "Along the hall, THEN up the stairs"!

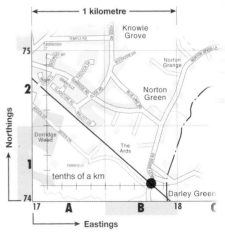

PHILIP'S MAPS
the Gold Standard for serious driving

◆ Philip's street atlases cover every county in England and Wales, plus much of Scotland

◆ All our atlases use the same style of mapping, with the same colours and symbols, so you can move with confidence from one atlas to the next

◆ Widely used by the emergency services, transport companies and local authorities

◆ Created from the most up-to-date and detailed information available from Ordnance Survey

◆ Based on the National Grid

For national mapping, choose
Philip's Navigator Britain –
the most detailed road atlas available of England, Wales and Scotland. Hailed by Auto Express as 'the ultimate road atlas', this is the only one-volume atlas to show every road and lane in Britain.